Encyclopedia of the Great Depression and the New Deal

Volume One

James Ciment, Editor

SHARPE REFERENCE

An imprint of M.E. Sharpe, INC.

SHARPE REFERENCE

Sharpe Reference is an imprint of M.E.Sharpe INC.

M.E.Sharpe INC.
80 Business Park Drive
Armonk, NY 10504

Library of Congress Cataloging-in-Publication Data

Ciment, James.
Encyclopedia of the Great Depression and the New Deal / James Ciment
p. cm.
Includes bibliographical references and index.
ISBN 0-7656-8033-5 (set; alk. paper)
1. United States–History–1933-1945–Encyclopedias. 2. Depressions–1929–United States–Encyclopedias. 3. New Deal, 1933-1939–Encyclopedias. I. Title.
E806.C543 2000
973.917′03–dc21   00-056285
CIP

Printed and bound in the United States of America

The paper used in this publication meets the minimum requirements of American National Standard for Information Sciences—Permanence of Paper for Printed Library Materials,
ANSI Z 39.48.1984.

(BM) 10 9 8 7 6 5 4 3 2 1

In Memory
of
Stan Davis

CONTENTS

Contributors xi
Acknowledgments xiii
Introduction xv

VOLUME ONE

PART I. THEMATIC ESSAYS

Government and Politics 3
Business and Economy 10
Labor and Unions 20
Daily Life 28
International Affairs 35

PART II. GENERAL ENTRIES

Introduction to Part II 45
Advertising and Consumption 47
African Americans 50
Agriculture 57
Alcoholics Anonymous 62
American Federation of Labor 62
American Guide Series 64
American Labor Party 65
American Newspaper Guild 65
Amos 'n' Andy 66
Arts, fine 67
Asian Americans 71
Automobile Industry 73
Banking 76
Black Legion 80
Bonus Army 80
Brotherhood of Sleeping Car Porters 82
Charity and Philanthropy 83
Christian Front 86
Citizen Kane 87
Commonwealth Club Speech 87
Communist Party 88
Congress of Industrial Organizations 92
Court-Packing Plan 95
Crime 96
Dams 99

Delta Council 99
Democratic Party 100
Dionne Quintuplets 106
Dust Bowl 107
Education 111
Elderly, The 116
Election of 1930 118
Election of 1932 118
Election of 1934 122
Election of 1936 123
Election of 1938 126
Election of 1940 127
Empire State Building 130
End Poverty in California 131
Esquire 133
Family Circle 133
Fantasia 134
Farmer-Labor Party 134
Farm Holiday Association 135
Fascism, domestic 136
Films, documentary and newsreel 137
Films, feature 140
Fireside Chats 144
Flash Gordon 145
Footlight Parade 146
Ford Motor Company 146
"Forgotten Man" Radio Address 148
42nd Street 148
General Motors 149
German-American Bund 150
Gold Diggers of 1933 151
Gone with the Wind 151
Good Earth, The 153
Grapes of Wrath, The 153
Group Theatre 154
Harlem Riot (1935) 155
Hindenburg Disaster 155
Hispanic Americans 156
Hoboes and Transients 160
How to Win Friends and Influence People 162
Hunger Marches 153
I Am a Fugitive from a Chain Gang 164

Insurance Industry 164
International Ladies' Garment Workers' Union 166
It Happened One Night 167
Jackson Day Speech 168
Keynesian Economics 168
King Kong 170
Legion of Decency 171
Let Us Now Praise Famous Men 171
Liberty League 172
Life 172
Li'l Abner 173
Lindbergh Kidnapping 173
Literature 175
Little Caesar 179
"Little Steel" 179
Lone Ranger, The 180
Lynching 180
March on Washington Movement 182
Memorial Day Massacre 183
Mercury Theatre 183
Metro-Goldwyn-Mayer 184
Mining 184
Motion Picture Production Code/Production
    Code Administration 186
Mr. Smith Goes to Washington 186
Music 187
Nation, The 190
National Association for the Advancement of
    Colored People 190
National Union for Social Justice 191
National Urban League 191
Native Americans 192
New Deal, second 193
New Masses 197
New Republic, The 198
Newspapers and Magazines 198
Okies 201
Photography 203
Popular Front 206
Porgy and Bess 207
Prohibition 208
Public Enemy 210
Radio 211
Railroads 216
Republican Party 219
Saturday Evening Post 222
Scarface: The Shame of a Nation 223
Scottsboro Case 223
Sergeant York 225
Service Sector 225
Share Our Wealth Society 229
Silver Shirts 231
Socialist Party 231
Southern Tenant Farmers Union 235
Sports 237
Stagecoach 241
Steel Industry 242

Steel Workers Organizing Committee 245
Stock Market 247
Strikes, general 251
Strikes, sit-down 255
Superman 260
Time 261
Tobacco Road 261
Townsend Plan 262
Trade Union Unity League 264
Unemployed Councils 265
Union Party 266
Unions and Union Organizing 267
United Automobile Workers 271
United Mine Workers 275
United States Steel Corporation 276
Utilities Industry 277
War of the Worlds, The 280
Wisconsin Progressive Party 280
Wizard of Oz, The 281
Women 282
World's Fairs 287
Youth 289

PART III. GOVERNMENT

Introduction to Part III 295
Agricultural Adjustment Act (1933) 297
Aid to Dependent Children 299
Banking Holidays 300
"Black Cabinet" 301
Bonus Bill 302
Brain Trust 303
Budget, federal 304
Civil Rights Section (Department of Justice) 307
Civil Works Administration 307
Civilian Conservation Corps 308
Commodity Credit Corporation 311
Economy Act 312
Emergency Banking Act (1933) 312
Emergency Educational Program 313
Emergency Relief and Construction Act 313
Emergency Relief Appropriations Act (1935) 314
Fair Employment Practices Committee 314
Fair Labor Standards Act 315
Farm Security Administration 318
Federal Art Project 319
Federal Bureau of Investigation 320
Federal Communications Commission 323
Federal Deposit Insurance Corporation 324
Federal Emergency Relief Administration 326
Federal Housing Administration 328
Federal Music Project 330
Federal Reserve System 331
Federal Securities Act 332
Federal Surplus Relief Corporation/
    Federal Surplus Commodities Corporation 333
Federal Theater Project 333

Federal Writers' Project 336
Glass-Steagall Act 338
Gold Standard 339
Hatch Act 340
Home Owners Loan Corporation 341
House Un-American Activities Committee
    (Dies Committee) 342
Indian Reorganization Act 344
Jones-Connally Farm Relief Act 346
National Credit Corporation 346
National Industrial Recovery Act 347
National Labor Relations Act (Wagner Act) 351
National Youth Administration 354
NLRB v. Jones & Laughlin 356
New Deal, first 356
Norris-La Guardia Anti-Injunction Act 363
Office of Production Management 364
Pecora Investigation 364
President's Organization of Unemployment Relief 365
Public Utility Holding Company Act 365
Public Works Administration 367
Public Works 368
Public Works of Art Project 373
Reconstruction Finance Corporation 373
Resettlement Administration 375
Revenue Act 376
Rural Electrification Administration 377
Schechter Poultry Corporation v. United States 380
Section 7 (National Industrial Recovery Act) 380
Securities and Exchange Commission 381
Silver Purchase Act 384
Smith Act 384
Social Security Act 386
Soil Conservation and Domestic Allotment Act 390
Soil Erosion Service/Soil Conservation Service 390
Supreme Court 391
Taxation 396
Temporary Emergency Relief Administration 398
Tennessee Valley Authority 398
United States v. Butler et al. 402
Wagner-Steagall Housing Act 402
Wealth Tax Act 403
West Coast Hotel v. Parrish 403
Wheeler-Rayburn Act 404
Works Progress Administration 405

PART IV. INTERNATIONAL AFFAIRS

Introduction to Part IV 413
Abraham Lincoln Brigade 415
America First Committee 415
Atlantic Charter 416
Canada 417
Cash-and-Carry Policy 419
China 420
Ethiopian War 421
Fascism, Italy 422
France 425

Good Neighbor Policy 426
Great Britain 428
Japan 430
Johnson Act 434
League of Nations 434
Lend-Lease Act 435
London Economic Conference 436
Manchuria, Invasion of 436
Mexico 437
Munich Conference 438
Nazi Germany 438
Nazi-Soviet Nonaggression Pact 444
Neautrality Acts 444
Nye Committee 445
Olympic Games (Berlin 1936) 446
Refugees 447
Rhineland, Reoccupation of 449
Smoot-Hawley Tariff 449
Soviet Union 450
Spanish Civil War 452
World War II, Early History of 455

VOLUME TWO

PART V. BIOGRAPHIES

Introduction to Part V 463
Abbott (Bud) and Costello (Lou) 465
Ace, Goodman and Jane 465
Acuff, Roy 466
Adamic, Louis 466
Agee, James 467
Alexander, Will 467
Anderson, Marian 468
Armstrong, Louis 469
Arnold, Thurman 470
Astaire, Fred and Rogers, Ginger 471
Autry, Gene 471
Bailey, Josiah 472
Baldwin, Stanley 473
Barkley, Alben 473
Baruch, Bernard M. 474
Basie, William "Count" 474
Bennett, Harry 475
Bennett, Richard Bedford 476
Benton, Thomas Hart 476
Bergen, Edgar 477
Berkeley, William "Busby" 477
Berle, Adolph A., Jr. 478
Berlin, Irving 478
Bethune, Mary McLeod 479
Bilbo, Theodore 480
Black, Hugo 481
Blitzstein, Marc 482
Blum, Léon 482
Bogart, Humphrey 483
Bonnie (Parker) and Clyde (Barrow) 483

Bourke-White, Margaret, ... 484
Brandeis, Louis 485
Bridges, Harry 486
Broun, Heywood 487
Browder, Earl 487
Brundage, Avery 488
Buck, Pearl 489
Burns (George) and Allen (Gracie) 489
Butler, Pierce 490
Byrnes, James F. 491
Cagney, James 492
Cain, James M. 493
Caldwell, Erskine 493
Calloway, Cab 494
Capone, Al 495
Capra, Frank 496
Cárdenas, Lázaro 496
Cardozo, Benjamin 497
Carnegie, Dale 498
Chamberlain, (Arthur) Neville 498
Chandler, Raymond 499
Chiang Kai-Shek 500
Churchill, Winston 501
Cohen, Benjamin V. 502
Cooper, Gary 503
Copland, Aaron 503
Corcoran, Thomas G. 504
Coughlin, Father Charles 505
Cowley, Malcolm 507
Daladier, Édouard 507
Dawes, Charles G. 508
Dewey, Thomas E. 508
Didrikson, Mildred "Babe" 509
Dies, Martin, Jr. 510
Dietrich, Marlene 511
Dillinger, John 512
DiMaggio, Joe 513
Disney, Walt 514
Divine, Father (George Baker) 515
Dos Passos, John 516
Douglas, William O. 516
Dubinsky, David 517
Earhart, Amelia 518
Eccles, Marriner 519
Einstein, Albert 520
Ellington, Edward Kennedy "Duke" 521
Evans, Walker 521
Farley, James 522
Faulkner, William 523
Fields, W.C. 524
Floyd, Charles Arthur "Pretty Boy" 525
Flynn, Errol 526
Ford, Henry 526
Ford, John 527
Foster, William Z. 528
Franco, Francisco 529
Frankfurter, Felix 530

Gable, Clark 531
Garbo, Greta 531
Garner, John Nance 532
Gehrig, Lou 533
Gershwin, George and Ira 534
Glass, Carter 534
Goldwyn, Samuel 535
Goodman, Benjamin David "Benny" 536
Grant, Cary 536
Green, William 537
Greenberg, Hank 538
Guthrie, Woodrow Wilson "Woody" 539
Hammett, Dashiell 540
Hastie, William 541
Hawks, Howard 541
Hays, Will H. 542
Hearst, William Randolph 542
Henie, Sonja 543
Hemingway, Ernest 544
Hepburn, Katharine 545
Hickok, Lorena 545
Hicks, Granville 546
Hillman, Sidney 547
Hitler, Adolf 548
Holiday, Billie 550
Hook, Sidney 550
Hoover, Herbert 551
Hoover, J. Edgar 554
Hopkins, Harry 555
Hopper, Hedda 557
Howe, Louis M. 557
Hughes, Charles Evans 558
Hughes, Howard 559
Hughes, Langston 559
Hull, Cordell 560
Hurston, Zora Neale 561
Ickes, Harold L. 562
Insull, Samuel 563
Johnson, Hiram 564
Johnson, Hugh 564
Kennedy, Joseph P. 565
King, William Lyon Mackenzie 566
Knox, Frank 567
La Follette Brothers 567
La Guardia, Fiorello H. 568
Landon, Alfred "Alf" 570
Lange, Dorothea 571
Ledbetter, Hudson William "Leadbelly" 572
Lemke, William 573
Lewis, John L. 574
Lewis, Sinclair 575
Lindbergh, Charles A. 576
Lippmann, Walter 577
Lombard, Carole 578
Lombardo, Guy 578
Long, Huey P. 579
Louis, Joe 581

Luce, Henry R. 582
MacArthur, Douglas 582
MacDonald, Ramsay 584
MacLeish, Archibald 585
Mao Zedong 585
Marcantonio, Vito 586
Marshall, George C. 587
Marx Brothers 588
Mayer, Louis B. 589
McCormick, Robert R. 590
Mellon, Andrew W. 590
Mitchell, Charles E. 591
Moley, Raymond 592
Morgenthau, Henry Jr. 593
Muni, Paul 594
Murphy, Frank 594
Murray, Philip 595
Murrow, Edward R. 596
Mussolini, Benito 596
Nelson, George "Baby Face" 598
Niebuhr, Reinhold 598
Norris, George W. 599
Odets, Clifford 600
Olson, Floyd 600
Owens, Jesse 601
Paige, Leroy Robert "Satchel" 602
Parsons, Louella 603
Peek, George 603
Pepper, Claude 604
Perkins, Frances 605
Porter, Cole 606
Powell, William 607
Randolph, A. Phillip 607
Rankin, John 608
Raskob, John J. 609
Rayburn, Sam 610
Reed, Stanley F. 610
Reuther, Walter 611
Rivera, Diego 612
Robeson, Paul 613
Roberts, Owen J. 614
Robinson, Edward G. 615
Robinson, Joseph T. 616
Rockwell, Norman 616
Rodgers (Richard) and Hart (Lorenz) 617
Rogers, Will 617
Roosevelt, Eleanor 619
Roosevelt, Franklin Delano 622
Ruth, George Herman "Babe" 632
Shahn, Ben 632
Sinclair, Upton 633
Sloan, Alfred P., Jr. 634
Smith, Alfred E. 635
Smith, Ellison D. 636
Smith, Gerald L.K. 636
Smith, Kate 637
Stalin, Joseph 638

Steinbeck, John 639
Stimson, Henry L. 640
Stone, Harlan Fiske 641
Stryker, Roy E. 641
Sutherland, George 642
Temple, Shirley 643
Thomas, Norman 644
Three Stooges, The 645
Townsend, Francis 646
Tracy, Spencer 647
Tugwell, Rexford G. 648
Valleé, Rudy 649
Van Devanter, Willis 649
Vidor, King 650
Wagner, Robert F. 650
Wallace, Henry A. 651
Warren, Robert Penn 652
Weaver, Robert C. 653
Weismuller, Johnny 654
Welles, Orson 655
Welles, Sumner 656
West, Mae 657
Wheeler, Burton K. 657
White, Walter Francis 658
Whitney, Richard 659
Williams, Aubrey 659
Willkie, Wendell L. 660
Wilson, Edmund 661
Winchell, Walter 661
Wood, Grant 662
Wright, Richard 663

PART VI. DOCUMENTS

Introduction to Part VI 667

Section 1. Government: Domestic Bills, Acts, Veto Statements, Official Letters, Executive Orders, and Committee Reports

Section 1. Government: Domestic Bills, Acts, Veto
Statements, Official Letters, Executive Orders,
and Committee Reports 669
Hoover's Appeal to Governors for Stimulation of
    State Public Works, November 23, 1929 671
Veto of Amendment to World War Veterans'
    Bonus Act, June 26, 1930 671
Hoover's Veto of Muscle Shoals Bill,
    March 3, 1931 674
Hoover's Outline of Program to Secure Cooperation
    of Bankers to Relieve Financial Difficulties,
    October 6, 1931 675
Norris-La Guardia Anti-Injunction Bill,
    March 20, 1932 677
Agricultural Adjustment Act, May 12, 1933 679
Tennessee Valley Act, May 18, 1933 681
Abandonment of the Gold Standard, June 5, 1933 683
National Industrial Recovery Act, June 16, 1933 684
National Labor Relations Act, July 5, 1935 689
Social Security Acts, August 14, 1935 693
Reform of the Federal Judiciary, 1937 701

Wagner-Steagall National Housing Act,
September 1, 1937 710
Hatch Act, August 2, 1939 713

**Section 2. Domestic Politics: Platforms, Speeches, and
Press Conferences** 715
Hoover's "Rugged Individualism" Speech,
October 22,1928 717
Hoover's Press Conference Warning Against Deficit
Spending, February 25, 1930 719
Hoover's Lincoln Birthday Address,
February 12, 1931 720
Democratic Party Platform, 1932 723
Roosevelt's New Deal Speech to Democratic
Convention, July 2, 1932 725
Republican Party Platform, 1932 730
Hoover Campaign Speech, October 31, 1932 742
Roosevelt's First Inaugural Address, March 4, 1933 752
Fireside Chat on the Banking Crisis, March 12, 1933 ... 754
Speech on the National Recovery Administration,
July 24, 1933 756
Huey P. Long's "Every Man a King" Speech,
February 23, 1934 760
Roosevelt's Fireside Address on Social Security Acts,
January 17, 1935 763
Roosevelt's Fireside Chat on Work Relief Programs,
April 28, 1935 765
Democratic Party Platform, 1936 769
Republican Party Platform, 1936 772
Roosevelt Campaign Speech, October 14, 1936 777
Roosevelt's Second Inaugural Address,
January 20, 1937 781
Eleanor Roosevelt's Press Conference Discussion
on Married Women in the Labor Force,
June 16, 1938 784
Eleanor Roosevelt's Press Conference Discussion
on Crossing Picket Lines, January 17, 1939 785
Eleanor Roosevelt's Press Conference Discussion
on Cuts in Works Progress Administration Jobs,
January 31, 1939 786
Democratic Party Platform, 1940 788
Republican Party Platform, 1940 795
Roosevelt's Third Inaugural Address,
January 20, 1941 800

Section 3. Court Cases 803
United States v. One Book Called "Ulysses," 1933 805
*Schechter Poultry Corporation v. United States,
1935* 807
United States v. Butler et al., 1936 812
Ashwander v. Tennessee Valley Authority, 1936 817
*National Labor Relations Board v. Jones &
Laughlin Steel Corporation, 1937* 821
West Coast Hotel Company v. Parrish, 1937 827
Chief Justice Charles Evans Hughes's Opinion
on Admission of a Negro Student to the
University of Missouri Law School, 1938 831

Section 4. International Affairs 835
Hoover's Proposal for One-Year Moratorium
on Intergovernmental Debts,
June 20, 1931 837
Roosevelt's Letter to Soviet Diplomat
Maksim Litvinov on U.S. Recognition
of the Soviet Union, November 16, 1933 838
State Department Report on Nazi Germany,
April 17, 1934 839
State Department Report on Imperial Japan,
December 27, 1934 841
Roosevelt on the Good Neighbor Policy,
December 1, 1936 843
Roosevelt's "Quarantine" of Aggressor Nations
Speech, October 5, 1937 846
Roosevelt's Fireside Chat on the European War,
September 3, 1939 849
Act of Havana on Hemispheric Defense,
July 29, 1940 850
Roosevelt's "Four Freedoms" Speech,
January 6, 1941 852
Lend-Lease Act, March 11, 1941 857
Atlantic Charter, August 14, 1941 858
Roosevelt's War Message to Congress,
December 8, 1941 859

Glossary and Acronyms 861

Bibliography 871

Subject Index 893
Biographical Index 907
Legal Index 915

CONTRIBUTORS

Robert Asher
University of Connecticut

Erin Ausk
Purdue University

William D. Baker
Arkansas School for Math and Sciences

Todd Bennett
University of Georgia

Allida Black
George Washington University

Michael Bonislawski
Boston College

Jeremy Bonner
Catholic University of America

Charlotte Brooks
Northwestern University

Vincent T. Brooks
Library of Virginia

Ron Capshaw
Graduate Center of the City University of New York

Jeffrey Cole
King College

Erik Blaine Coleman
University of North Carolina

Jane Collings
University of California at Los Angeles

Jeff Crane
Washington State University

Jennifer Delton
Skidmore College

Pattie Dillon
Mississippi State University

Catherine Whittenburg Dolinski
University of Virginia

Christine Erickson
Indiana University-Purdue University at Fort Wayne

Duncan Fisher
University of Edinburgh

Richard Flanagan
College of Staten Island (City University of New York)

Brett Flehinger
Harvard University

Jennifer Forbes
Purdue University

Bonnie Ford
Sacramento City College

Richard Greenwald
U.S. Merchant Marine Academy

James R. Hackney Jr.
Northeastern University School of Law

Shannon Harris
Purdue University

A. Scott Henderson
Furman University

Justin Hoffman
Georgetown University

Stephen Hoogenraad
Carleton University

Richard Hughes
University of Kansas

Patrick Jones
University of Wisconsin-Milwaukee

Elizabeth Keane
New York University

Andrew Kersten
University of Wisconsin-Green Bay

Henry E. Kilpatrick
George Mason University

Tamara King
University of Findlay

Steven Kite
Oklahoma State University

Karen Lewis
Graduate Center of the City University of New York

Stan Luger
University of Northern Colorado

Nicholas Maher
Oglethorpe University

Michael McAllister

ACKNOWLEDGMENTS

Many people contributed their time and efforts to the *Encyclopedia of the Great Depression and the New Deal*. First, there are the contributors whose fine entries are the heart and soul of these volumes. The editing and production staff at M.E. Sharpe was also critical in making sure that this project met the high standards associated with this publishing house.

I would like to thank Evelyn Fazio for coming up with the idea for this encyclopedia; editors Andrew Gyory and Henrietta Toth for their skills in turning raw manuscript into finished galleys; Aud Thiessen, who kept track of the myriad elements of the encyclopedia; cartographers Alice and Will Thiede for the fine maps; photo researcher Anne Burns for the captivating illustrations; Gina Misiroglu, Anne Newman, and Kenneth Wenzer for the factchecking; and Laurie Lieb for the copyediting.

Whatever merits this *Encyclopedia of the Great Depression and the New Deal* possess are due to the efforts of this extraordinary team; whatever defects are my responsibility.

JAMES CIMENT

INTRODUCTION

Few eras in American history are as clearly delineated in time as the Great Depression. Its commencement and conclusion can be marked almost to the hour: when stock prices first went into free fall on "black Thursday," October 24, 1929, and when Japanese bombs began falling on the fleet at Pearl Harbor in the early morning hours of December 7, 1941.

Of course, this is a bit of an oversimplification. The stock market had been slipping for weeks before that frantic Thursday in October, and key economic indicators, such as new car sales and housing construction, had peaked two years earlier. And, at the other end of the era, American naval vessels had been engaged in shooting incidents with German submarines in the Atlantic two months before Pearl Harbor.

Still, the Great Depression remains a most well-defined moment in time. What caused it, however, is not as easy to identify. Clearly, the stock market crash—although the Depression's precipitating event—was not its cause. True, in a matter of days, stock values fell from $87 to $55 billion, wiping out vast fortunes, even if those fortunes were largely paper ones. But, despite the myth of a stock-market obsessed country in the late 1920s, the vast majority of Americans had no money invested on Wall Street. Indeed, the crash merely brought overvalued securities closer to the underlying worth of the companies that issued the shares.

Instead, economic historians cite several deeper, underlying causes of the Great Depression. First, there were fundamental structural weaknesses in the American economy. Several key sectors—most notably agriculture, but also coal, timber, and textiles—remained depressed throughout the so-called Roaring Twenties. Having vastly expanded to meet the demands of the "Great War" (World War I, 1914–18 in Europe), they were burdened with too much capacity for the domestic market when the conflict ended. Prices collapsed and incomes with them. In 1929, farmers earned roughly one-third ($273) of their urban fellow citizens ($750). And with about one-third of the country in-

volved directly or indirectly in agriculture, this disparity was a serious problem.

This gap between rural and urban America was only a part of a bigger problem of wealth and income distribution in the 1920s. Income was more poorly distributed in the year 1929 than in any other year in American history. The top 5 percent of the population received 30 percent of the income; the bottom 40 percent got just 12.5 percent. This situation was exacerbated by falling income tax rates for the wealthy. To put things simply, a large portion of Americans could not afford to buy the things they were making. Finally, there was the matter of debt—and lots of it. Many individuals, enticed by the first great expansion of consumer credit in American history, had borrowed heavily during the 1920s, as had businesses bent on expansion and consolidation. When the crash came—and general panic set in—debt was called in, mortgages were foreclosed, liquidity disappeared.

The word "great" is not attached to the economic crisis of the 1930s lightly. America, of course, had been through several severe economic downturns in its post–Civil War history, most notably the depressions of the 1870s and the 1890s. But no previous downturn had been as deep or long lasting. The statistics are staggering: between 1929 and 1933, America's gross national product fell from $103.1 to $58 billion; private investment fell by nearly 90 percent; the consumer price index dropped 25 percent; over 9,000 banks and 100,000 businesses closed their doors; and the official unemployment rate soared from 3.2 to 24.9 percent. And it would take years to recover. Virtually none of these statistics would be fully reversed until well into World War II. Unemployment, for example, remained in double digits until 1941 and would not fall to 1929 levels until 1943, when some 16 million Americans were in uniform.

While the economy can be measured in statistics, the decade's despair cannot. People were desperate and they were scared and they were looking for leadership. In President Herbert Hoover, they had a strong leader but the wrong one for the moment. Hoover, in the public imagination, still retains his reputation as a gloomy, unsympathetic, do-nothing president, especially when compared to his successor, Franklin Delano Roosevelt. But while Hoover was not particularly adept at assuaging people's fears, he did take action. Indeed, New Dealers themselves—in their more honest moments—credited his administration with laying the groundwork for their own efforts to overcome the Depression. And, as the statistics noted earlier indicate, the Roosevelt administration and its plethora of New Deal programs were only modestly more successful in fighting the Depression than the Hoover administration had been.

But what Roosevelt offered the American people was hope. A master of the new media of radio and newsreel, the polio-stricken aristocrat from Hyde Park, New York was able to convey a sense that he cared about ordinary people and that he was taking action—any action—to alleviate their distress. Of course, Roosevelt's New Deal did much more than merely fight the Depression: it created America's modern federal government, with its vast array of regulatory agencies, subsidies, entitlement programs, and its deep, direct, day-to-day connection to—conservatives would say intrusiveness into—the lives of ordinary citizens. In creating this connection, the Roosevelt administration also created a new political order—a New Deal coalition that united the white, urban, and working-class ethnics (and later blacks) into a dominant Democratic Party for half a century. More immediately, during the Depression itself, the Democrats channeled the growing frustration and anger of the American people. The fears of old-age penury that fueled the supporters of the Townsend plan and the Share-Our-Wealth Society (see entries on these subjects) were pacified with Social Security; the anticapitalist agitation of Communists and other working-class leftists was undermined by the National Labor Relations Act (see entry).

Economically stagnant but politically dynamic, the Great Depression era was culturally exciting. Part of this excitement was due to new or newly accessible technology. Both radio and talking movies—although invented before the Depression began, the latter just barely—truly came into their own between 1929 and 1941. (Television was also perfected during the decade but had to await the post–World War II era to become widely available.) But another element in the cultural flowering of the Depression era was its contradictions. The 1930s was a time of clever escapist entertainment— ritzy musicals and screwball comedies—and the great era of social realism in theater, the fine arts, and lit-

erature. Moreover, never before and never since has the federal government been more involved in the arts, through programs for writers, musicians, theatrical people, and, with the great public works projects, visual artists as well.

In foreign affairs, the 1930s is the decade of transition. When the Great Depression began, most Americans—and, to a lesser degree, the American government—were recovering from the disappointment of World War I. High hopes for the spread of democracy and self-determination had been killed, not on the battlefields of Flanders but in the mirrored halls of Versailles in 1919, where victorious Allies chose a vindictive peace and continued imperialism. As the rise of Fascists in Italy, militarists in Japan, and Nazis in Germany illustrated the flaws of the post–World War I global order, America retreated further into an ocean-protected isolationism that was not easy to get out of. For all of Roosevelt's persuasive powers, for all the heroic fortitude of the British people, for all the brutality of Adolf Hitler and Benito Mussolini, it still took a surprise attack against American soil to bring the country into World War II.

The Great Depression and the New Deal, then, forever shaped America at home and abroad. They created new regulatory structures to rein in the excesses of laissez-faire capitalism; they established a new and more intimate relationship between the American people and their federal government; they erected a political coalition that has endured through much of the twentieth century; they left behind an extraordinary cultural legacy; and they laid the foundation for America's permanent reentry into world affairs.

At the dawn of the twenty-first century, it is not too much to say that the impact of the most traumatic peacetime event of the twentieth can still be felt.

HOW TO USE THIS ENCYCLOPEDIA

The *Encyclopedia of the Great Depression and the New Deal* is divided into six separate parts: Part I, thematic essays; Part II, general entries; Part III, government; Part IV, international affairs; Part V, biographies; and Part VI, historical documents. Except for Parts I and IV, all entries are listed in alphabetical order within each part of the encyclopedia.

Thematic essays cover government and politics, business and economy, labor and unions, daily life, and international affairs. These essays provide overviews of these topics and are useful in establishing the general historical context for the entries and documents in the rest of the encyclopedia.

The general entries cover a host of topics. There are entries on population sectors, such as ethnic, gender, and age groups; politics, including parties, events, advocacy groups, and federal elections; labor, including unions and strikes; business, including companies, economic sectors, and trade associations and groupings; sociological, political, and economic phenomena; and culture, including the various branches of the arts, different types of media, and specific cultural and media production.

The section on government includes entries on domestic legislation, agencies, congressional committees, and court decisions. The section on international affairs has articles on key foreign countries; international events that precipitated World War II; domestic events, organizations, and legislation that affected U.S. foreign policy; and a few miscellaneous entries that fit into none of these categories, but are nevertheless of critical importance to the period. The biography section includes over 230 biographies of important (largely American) figures from the period.

The section on historical documents includes subsections on legislation, politics, court cases, and international affairs. Within each subsection, documents are listed chronologically. Among the documents are bills and acts of Congresss, executive orders and statements, State Department reports, congressional committee reports, press conferences, speeches, and court cases. Shorter documents are reprinted in full; some longer documents are excerpted. In addition, the encyclopedia includes a glossary of terms, acronyms, and definitions of less important events and legislation.

All entries—except for those in Part I—are cross-referenced to other appropriate entries and documents. And all entries include bibliographical references for further research. Both the cross-references and the bibliographical information can be found at the end of each entry.

PART I
THEMATIC ESSAYS

GOVERNMENT AND POLITICS

The New Deal created new governmental structures and agencies that changed the relationship between the president and Congress, redefined political discourse, transformed the party system, and won new voters to the Democratic Party.

GOVERNMENT

The Administrative State

The proliferation of governmental agencies to administer New Deal programs and enforce new laws expanded the reach and responsibility of the federal government in ways unprecedented in American history. The programs that became known as the New Deal initially had little ideological or philosophical coherence. New Dealers held a wide variety of opinions as to what they were up to and what government should do, and, indeed, the aims of the programs they cobbled together were often at odds with each other. By the late 1930s, however, a concept of the state had emerged that lent some coherence to the new programs. In this conception, the new role of the modern state, or national government, was to balance, or integrate, all of the diverse interests and groups in society, thereby maintaining social order. By addressing the needs of certain groups and restraining the excesses of others, the state could theoretically integrate all interests into a harmonious whole. It did this through legislation, such as the Wagner Act (1935), which protected labor's right to organize, and also through agencies like the Agricultural Adjustment Administration (AAA, 1933), which insured farmers' economic security through a system of price supports and subsidies. The state could most efficiently perform its integrative function if the offices and agencies that administered its programs were removed from politics, staffed by professionals, and coordinated through the executive branch of government.

The Reorganization of Government

Franklin D. Roosevelt's efforts to make the national state into an authoritative balancing force in American society involved reorganizing and strengthening the executive branch of government. Roosevelt had been able to secure New Deal reforms through his own charm and political popularity, and because of the crisis of the Depression, but he wanted to make the programs a permanent part of government, to protect them from the whims of a partisan Congress or a hostile court. He thought that America would have been better prepared to deal with the Depression had it had a modern bureaucratic state in place, and he wanted to build such a state so that America would be prepared for the next crisis. His efforts, however, were hampered by Congress, the Supreme Court, and Americans' fears of both centralized government and increased executive power.

Arguing against those who feared the loss of rights under an enlarged state, Roosevelt asserted that a beneficent administrative state in fact better insured the democratic rights of ordinary Americans by providing for their material and social needs. He believed that modern society had outgrown the concept of rights as individual liberties protected from state power. He offered a more expansive concept of rights based on the premise that economic and social oppression deprived individuals of their liberty more often than an oppressive state did. By alleviating oppressive economic and social conditions, a strong state could actually protect individual liberty. His reorganization of the executive office was aimed at creating a more responsive, "positive" government that could identify social and economic problems that impinged on ordinary people's liberties, and develop and implement programs to solve them. Far from subverting democracy, an empowered executive branch could work directly for the people. A permanent New Deal state would unite New Deal beneficiaries (the people) and state power against the capitalist powers in the marketplace.

In 1937, Roosevelt introduced two bills to reorganize government and create a stronger administrative state. The Judicial Reorganization bill allowed the president to appoint a new justice, not exceeding six, to the Supreme Court for any justice who did not retire at the age of seventy. With its implication that Roosevelt was "packing" the court in his favor, the bill set off a furor, and Roosevelt was forced to withdraw it. More successful, although just as controversial, was the Executive Reorganization bill of 1937, which was eventually passed in more moderate form as the Executive Reorganization Act of 1939.

Drawing on the recommendations of the President's Committee on Administrative Management, the Executive Reorganization bill proposed a series of measures intended to centralize government machinery and expedite government action. The bill would have empowered the executive office to create and coordinate across-the-board government policy. It would have insured that New Dealers staffed agencies and programs, even if a conservative executive was elected. It would have moved all of the independent and semi-autonomous commissions, boards, authorities, and agencies, into one or the other of the twelve major executive departments (State, Treasury, Justice, etc.). It would have placed the regulation of executive expenditures under executive, rather than congressional control. These measures were intended to provide the institutional foundation for a modern social welfare state that responded promptly and effectively to its citizens' needs.

Congress defeated the bill in April 1938. Opponents argued that the bill transferred control of administrative organization to the executive branch at a time when government was becoming more administrative, and thus violated the Constitution's separation of powers. The system of checks and balances had been set up precisely to impede this sort of consolidation of executive power. Critics accused Roosevelt of trampling the Constitution and attempting to set up a dictatorship.

The Reorganization Act of 1939 was not as bold as the original plan, but it became law and its impact on American government was great. It allowed Roosevelt to establish the Executive Office of the President. Staffed by six administrative assistants, the office was intended to develop and enhance the President's management of budget, planning, and personnel. Roosevelt was able to transfer the Bureau of the Budget out of the Treasury and into the executive office, where it became the major agent in the development and implementation of his Keynesian economic policies. He was able to establish the National Resources Planning Board, which researched and proposed policy for an activist government. The bill also made possible legislation that extended merit protection to New Dealers in the civil service (otherwise those civil service jobs were part of the spoils system, and the New Dealers were at risk of being replaced by the next administration).

The Reorganization Act of 1939 institutionalized the shift in authority and power from Congress and the courts to the office of the presidency. The popularity of New Deal programs and new interpretations of constitutional principles had legitimated this shift among the people. The reorganization of the executive office established the institutional structures that made it operational within the government.

Executive Power and the Parties

Prior to the New Deal much of the government's activity had been conducted with regard to party. Through the spoils system, the president, as party leader, distributed cabinet appointments, administrative positions, and the vast network of civil service jobs according to party loyalty, rather than ideological commitment or administrative ability. As party leader, the president was beholden to carry out a party platform that had been hammered out at the party convention, rather than formulating his own policies and agendas. Ideally, the parties were supposed to be the link between citizens and their government, between Congress and the president. In practice, they tended to be dominated by bosses who placed partisan concern for power ahead of citizens' needs. Nonetheless, parties were associated with democratic principles because they impeded the centralization of presidential power. They were themselves decentralized and local, which, prior to the New Deal, was an indication that they were somehow closer to the pulse of the people. They could constrain a president's ability to lead or initiate any kind of program. They required a president to fill patronage posts according to partisan loyalty, and they could withhold support for presidential initiatives in Congress and at the polls. It is thus no surprise that reformers and progressive presidents saw the parties as one of the main impediments to establishing a modern, enlightened administrative state.

As a consequence of the New Deal, and particularly Roosevelt's successful attempt to consolidate power in the executive office, the role of parties declined in American politics and government. Roosevelt changed the business of politics from furthering partisan ends to strengthening programmatic liberalism (i.e., using the state to develop and implement programs that addressed the needs of various groups in society). When Roosevelt argued that an enlightened administrative state, efficiently controlled from the executive office, could best address the needs of individual American citizens, he changed the focus and identification of the American voter from party to the president. According to political historian Sidney Milkis, the president displaced parties as the key agent of democracy after the New Deal.

The New Deal and the States

The New Deal changed the balance of power between the states and the federal government, thereby impairing traditional federalism. State and local governments were unable to deal with the crisis of the Depression. The national scope of the Depression necessarily precluded the possibility that state governments could formulate or carry out a recovery plan. The interdependent character of the economy thwarted those state-level economic reform efforts which were attempted, although most states did not try. Nor were states even able to offer relief to their citizens. The states necessarily turned to the federal government for help.

The clashes between state-level politicians and New Dealers over the distribution of relief funds affirmed liberal arguments that the United States needed a modern, nonpolitical, centrally controlled, bureaucratic state. New Dealers were dismayed at the misuse of Federal Emergency Relief Act funds that were channeled through state governments for distribution. Politicians in charge of disbursing funds too often saw it as an opportunity to strengthen their own power. In the South, African Americans failed to receive relief funds distributed by state governments. New Dealers thus sought to lessen state-level involvement in relief, and the popular works programs—Civil Works Administration, Civilian Conservation Corps (CCC), and the Works Progress Administration—were placed under federal control and administration.

New Dealers bypassed state governments altogether by using private organizations to administer federal programs in local areas. For instance, the AAA used the Farm Bureau Federation to enlist farmers in the AAA program, monitor acreage, and disburse checks to participating farmers. The use of such private associations, or interest groups, was consistent with New Dealers' group-based definition of society, but it blurred the line between public and private and contributed to the growth of interest-group politics.

One of the consequences of the New Deal's diminishment of states' power was that ordinary Americans felt more removed from the processes of government that most affected their lives. Traditional American definitions of democracy held that local, decentralized government was necessary for real participatory democracy. The fact that so much of government was being moved to Washington and at the same time being placed outside traditional party politics seemed antithetical to notions of participatory democracy. Even as citizens came to identify the president as the defender of their interests, the local avenues by which they could participate in shaping politics and policy had disappeared.

A less recognized consequence of the transfer of policy and government from the states to Washington meant that individual states were less likely to experiment with social and economic reforms. During the Progressive Era, states like Wisconsin and Minnesota had served as laboratories in developing solutions to the problems of modern society. Indeed, many New Deal programs were themselves based on programs developed by the Farmer-Labor Party in Minnesota and the La Follettes, an influential political family, in Wisconsin. With the New Deal, however, political reformers would look to Washington to find their ideas.

The growing power of the federal government at the expense of state sovereignty alarmed conservatives and white southerners. Conservatives feared the overwhelming and, they felt, unconstitutional concentration of power in the federal government. They feared its power to tax Americans, to redistribute wealth through a graduated tax system, to dictate socialistic economic doctrines that diminished the autonomy and profits of individual business owners. For white southerners, the increased power of the federal government potentially threatened the state laws on which the jim crow system of white supremacy and segregation rested. The political rhetoric of the New Deal, with its emphasis on national economies and centralized administration, had already diminished the potency of states' rights ideology, which was the constitutional justification for jim crow and restrictive suffrage laws. White southern fears were not unfounded. One of the most important long-term implications of the growth of federal power and corresponding decline in states' autonomy was the eventual success of the civil rights movement and the demise of jim crow segregation.

POLITICS

The New Deal Realignment

The New Deal marked a major political realignment that ended the persistent sectionalism of the nineteenth-century party system, brought voters back to the polls, and made the Democrats a national party. Sectionalism refers to the entrenched political pattern that came out of the Civil War and Reconstruction, wherein the South was Democratic and the more populated North and West were largely Republican, with a few big-city Democratic machines of little national importance. This basic pattern was maintained into the 1920s because voters continued to vote according to regional loyalties, ethnicity, and tradition. An increasingly national economy and Progressive Era reforms contributed to the decline of these factors, but it was not until the New Deal's recognition of the interests of labor unions and its response to the needs of citizens that sectional politics gave way to what was called "class" politics—the idea that people voted according to their economic interests, as opposed to section, ethnicity, or tradition.

The New Deal's appeal to ordinary people's economic interests transformed the Democratic Party. Before 1932, the Democratic Party consisted of rural southerners and northern urban machine bosses with their ethnic voting pools. These two parochial groups had nothing in common; each had ended up in the Democratic Party for historical reasons peculiar to itself. In addressing voters' economic concerns, the New Deal pulled previously Republican voters, as well as millions of people who had never bothered to vote before, into the Democratic Party on the basis of their economic plight. The New Deal's programmatic approach (i.e., its creation of national programs that addressed the needs of different economic groups in society) anticipated a new party system organized around economic interests, "issues," and the competition of interest groups.

The Roosevelt Coalition

The Roosevelt coalition, known also as the New Deal coalition, first emerged in the 1936 election and would keep the Democrats in power until 1952. The coalition was the result of the New Deal's popularity among emerging new groups of voters. In addition to southern Democrats and urban ethnic machines already in the Democratic Party, the coalition consisted of workers, small farmers, black Americans (with some caveats), and educated progressive liberals.

Southern Democrats were key to the electoral success of the Roosevelt coalition. Despite their adherence to states' rights ideology, southern Democrats generally supported Roosevelt's expansive federal programs. Their states benefited from the agricultural relief offered by the AAA and development projects like the Tennessee Valley Authority, a controversial government-operated dam and power plant that brought electricity to thousands of poor southerners for the first time. Moreover, the New Deal had strengthened the Democratic Party in Congress, and this in turn meant more power for senior southern Democratic leaders. There were clashes over programs that would have altered the racial caste system in southern states, but Roosevelt compromised with white southerners on the issue of white supremacy. Segregation was allowed in the CCC in the South, for instance, and domestics and farm workers (overwhelmingly black) were initially excluded from Social Security coverage. The contradiction between the expansive federal state of the New Deal and the states' rights ideology of the white South would eventually prove irreconcilable. During the '30s however, both white southerners and Roosevelt benefited from the alliance.

The urban, largely ethnic, masses were among Roosevelt's most loyal voters. Their allegiance to the Democratic Party predated the Depression. Big-city Democratic bosses had incorporated immigrants into well-oiled political machines in the late nineteenth century. The power of these votes was not felt nationally, however, until 1928, when New York governor Alfred E. Smith, a Catholic, became the Democratic candidate for president. Al Smith was a champion of the immigrant masses in northern cities, and it is an indication of their political strength that he was chosen to head the Democratic ticket in 1928. His candidacy alienated the Protestant South and the rural West, but the gains he made in cities across the North foretold the importance of these voters for the Democratic Party. Roosevelt's relief programs, his support of unions (discussed below), and the Social Security Act (1935), which signified the government's responsibility to care for the vulnerable and weak, solidified the support of these first- and second-generation immigrant voters in the major cities.

Workers and their unions were the most significant group of the Roosevelt coalition in terms of the numbers of new voters flocking to the Democratic party. Before the Depression, workers had not been a political group that politicians paid particular attention to. For

"THAT'S MORE LIKE IT!"

In 1933, a main objective of the National Recovery Administration (NRA) was to bring wages and prices into better alignment to prevent destructive business competition and plummeting wages. The NRA also established a new role for the government, that of regulating the economy. *(Brown Brothers)*

one thing, most did not identify themselves as workers, but rather as Italian, southern, Protestant, or as a member of some other ethnic/regional/religious group. For another, it was difficult if not impossible to form industrial unions, a necessary prerequisite before management or politicians would take workers seriously as workers. Factory owners and management fought the formation of unions by harassing organizers and firing workers who dared to join them. Skilled trade unionists in the American Federation of Labor (AFL) had worked out arrangements with business owners, but held themselves aloof from politics and tended to see themselves not so much as "workers," but rather as craftsmen or carpenters. Seeking to bring order and stability to the economy, Roosevelt upheld industrial workers' right to organize, first in Section 7 of the National Industrial Recovery Act (1933), and, after that act was declared unconstitutional in May 1935, with the Wagner Act (July 1935). In 1935, the Committee for Industrial Organization (CIO), a splinter group within the AFL, began a series of organizing campaigns

in the steel and auto industries. The promise of economic security backed by the new legislation helped industrial workers overcome ethnic and religious divisions to unite as workers in new unions. The momentum of these campaigns carried into the political arena. The CIO mobilized voters, provided campaign workers, and donated $700,000 to Roosevelt's 1936 campaign. Of that sum, the United Mine Workers gave $469,000, the largest single contribution made to the party that year, which transformed the financial base of the party. In 1932, bankers had contributed a quarter of the funds to the Democratic Party; in 1936 only 3 percent of contributions came from bankers, about a third of the amount contributed by the CIO. As the number of people in unions rose, so too did the number of new voters in the Democratic Party. In 1932, only 2.8 million workers were in unions; by 1942, there were 10.5 million union members in the United States, all loyal to the party that represented their interests.

Small farmers, especially in the Midwest, benefited from Roosevelt's agricultural and relief programs. The AAA gave farmers the price supports they had been demanding since the 1920s and paid subsidies for reducing acreage in order to raise prices. The Farm Credit Act (1933) refinanced farm mortgages and thus prevented thousands of foreclosures. Farmers benefited from drought relief and rural electrification programs. The prominence of Secretary of Agriculture Henry A. Wallace in the New Deal also attracted farmers to the Democratic Party. A former progressive Republican from Iowa, Wallace spoke eloquently of the farmers' role in American society and of the government's responsibility to uphold that role. Conservative and traditionally Republican (outside the South), farmers never became as uniformly Democratic as workers did. But there were enough grateful farmers in rural midwestern states to swing some of those states into the Democratic column.

African-American voters had a more complicated, contingent relationship to the Roosevelt coalition and the Democratic Party. On the one hand, the New Deal's emphasis on federal legislation and its empowerment of the executive office were good for blacks who had been, historically, oppressed by the state laws and states' rights ideology of the white supremacist South. Moreover, the New Deal's alliance with the interracial CIO, Roosevelt's consultation with black advisers (the "black cabinet"), New Deal relief and jobs programs, and Eleanor Roosevelt's civil rights activism all made Roosevelt attractive to black voters. Indeed, beginning in 1936, many left the "party of Lincoln" to vote for Roosevelt. However, to the extent that the Democratic

Party was still dominated by southerners who vigorously opposed any legislation that would alter the southern racial hierarchy, black voters remained wary of the party. Black leaders maintained that black voters supported the New Deal and Roosevelt, but not the Democratic Party. It should be noted that in the 1930s most blacks still lived in the South, where they could not vote. Not until after the war would there be enough black voters in a few key northern cities to swing the vote.

Crucial to the political success of the Roosevelt coalition was a group of educated liberals, who formulated, justified, and fought for the beneficent, responsive administrative state embodied in the New Deal. A smallish elite, it was not their numbers that mattered, but their intellectual expertise and ability to articulate the ways in which a strong responsive state was consistent with democracy. Based in universities, these liberals formulated policies, wrote legislation, influenced public opinion, and provided political leadership for enacting the policies that brought the new voters into the Democratic Party. They included people in Roosevelt's Brain Trust, like Harry Hopkins, Harold Ickes, Frances Perkins, and Adolph Berle, but there were similar sorts of intellectual liberals in capitals and state agencies across the nation. One of the reasons they were so successful in implementing their ideas of how government should operate was that they had no counterparts in the Republican Party.

The Fate of Political Alternatives

The New Deal programs deflated the need for, and stole supporters from, more radical political solutions to the economic crisis. Between 1930 and 1935, political movements and ideologies of all sorts flourished. Calling for the nationalization of private enterprise, the Communists made themselves a part of union organizing drives and protest organizations of all sorts. The Communist Party never had a large membership—just 15,000 in 1932—but Communists were effective and disciplined organizers, and their ideology appealed to many activists during these years. Working in the electoral system, Socialists likewise saw a surge in their popularity in the '30s. The Minnesota Farmer-Labor party called for the "abolition of capitalism" in its 1934 platform. In California, Socialist Upton Sinclair launched EPIC (End Poverty in California) and ran for governor on a platform promising a $50 pension to Californians over sixty and government-run factories for the unemployed. Louisiana governor Huey P. Long promised to break up the fortunes of the rich and "share the wealth" with all Americans. A series of violent strikes in 1934 roused labor militants to envision change far more substantial than the right to organize. The swift implementation and relative relief brought by the New Deal, however, rechanneled this radical energy into the confines of the two-party system.

The Conservative Coalition

The New Deal brought forth angry reaction on the part of businessmen and conservatives of both parties. In Congress, this took the form of the Conservative Coalition, an alliance of conservative Democrats and Republicans that effectively thwarted Roosevelt's efforts to expand and solidify reforms after 1937. These conservatives opposed social welfare programs, organized labor, and government spending. They believed Roosevelt's reforms fostered class conflict. They defended states' rights and limited government. Some of them, including Vice President John Nance Garner of Texas and Republican senator Charles McNary of Oregon, had initially supported at least some of Roosevelt's program. The recession of 1937–38, Roosevelt's attempt to pack the Supreme Court (1937), and Roosevelt's attempt to purge conservatives from the Democratic Party, however, led them to oppose his plans after 1937. Others, like Democratic senators Josiah Bailey of North Carolina and Harry Byrd of Virginia had decried the New Deal as "socialistic" right from the start, and Roosevelt's later "excesses" merely confirmed their position. Alarmed businessmen formed the American Liberty League to lobby against the New Deal and publicize its subversion of the American concept of freedom.

JENNIFER DELTON

Bibliography

Braeman, John, Robert Bremner, and David Brody. "Introduction." In *The New Deal: The State and Local Levels*, Vol. 2, ed. Braeman et al., Columbus: Ohio State University Press, 1975.

Brinkley, Alan. *The End of Reform: New Deal Liberalism in Recession and War.* New York: Random House, 1995.

Cohen, Lizabeth. *Making a New Deal: Industrial Workers in Chicago.* New York: Cambridge University Press, 1990.

Fraser, Steve, and Gary Gerstle, eds. *The Rise and Fall of the New Deal Order, 1930–80.* Princeton: Princeton University Press, 1989.

Leuchtenberg, William. *Franklin Delano Roosevelt and the New Deal.* New York: Harper & Row, 1963.

Lubell, Samuel. "The Roosevelt Coalition." In Alonzo Hamby, ed. *The New Deal: Analysis and Interpretation.* New York: Weybright and Talley, 1969.

Milkis, Sidney. *The President and the Parties: The Transformation of the American Party System Since the New Deal.* New York: Oxford, 1993.

Nash, Gerald. *The Great Depression and World War II: Organizing America, 1933–1945.* New York: St. Martin's, 1979.

Patterson. James. *The New Deal and the States: Federalism in Transition.* Princeton: Princeton University Press, 1969.

Plotke, David. *Building a Democratic Order: Reshaping American Liberalism in the 1930s and 1940s.* Princeton: Princeton University Press, 1996.

Valelly, Richard. *Radicalism in the States: The Minnesota Farmer-Labor Party and the American Political Economy.* Chicago: University of Chicago Press, 1989.

BUSINESS AND ECONOMY

The Great Depression, and the political response it provoked, proved a watershed for the modern American political economy. The Depression spelled the end of relatively uncontrolled industrial and financial business power in the United States, and it led to a fundamental reorganization of intrabusiness, business/labor, and business/government relations. Governmental regulatory initiatives had proceeded apace since the 1870s, and World War I had itself spurred important new experiments in the use of national authority. But the Depression represented a significant turning point in the establishment of new national institutions with expansive authority over the national economy and market relations. Economic devastation dramatically ended the public faith in limited government, and both business and public pressures spurred the growth of national responsibility for economic stability.

As the Depression deepened, many business interests clamored for the lifeline of governmental intervention to stabilize the economy and revive profits; at the same time, business grew fearful and alarmed at the scope of growing governmental authority. Hoping, in the face of the Depression, to build on the World War I promise of a business-dominated corporatism, prominent business forces gained much of what they desired. Yet they also found the new political environment much less hospitable to business influence. In fact, the political pressures unleashed by the Depression and the 1932 election of Franklin D. Roosevelt expanded the political influence and leverage of forces seeking a more inclusive and accountable political economy (including here industrial workers, the unemployed, the elderly, and smaller farmers). Despite their limited challenge to business power, Roosevelt's New Deal programs established greater political accountability within the national economy as they broadly expanded both the national government's role in the economy and the variety of social and economic forces benefiting from national action. Business fear and distrust of Roosevelt thus grew during the 1930s,

keeping pace with increasing national authority and with the growing influence of organized labor.

CAUSES OF THE GREAT DEPRESSION

The Depression itself was instigated by the crash of the stock market in October 1929. And the crash was caused by an unsustainable massive inflation of market values through questionable new sales methods involving broker loans (using stocks as collateral), pyramid schemes, and investment trusts that encouraged freewheeling speculation and heavy indebtedness. The market value of all shares listed on the New York Stock Exchange rose from $27 billion in 1925 to $67 billion in January 1929 and then to $87 billion in October—by March 1933 their value had dropped to $19 billion.

That a depression followed on the heels of the market crash was due, according to economist John Kenneth Galbraith, to the fact that "the economy was fundamentally unsound." While business opinion simplistically blamed accumulating government regulations and government debts for the worsening economic crisis, Galbraith identifies five factors that explain why the crash led to the Great Depression: 1) a highly unequal income distribution that depressed mass consumption; 2) a corporate business structure that maximized greed when times were good and fearfulness at the sight of any economic difficulties; 3) inherent weaknesses in the banking structure that maximized and spread bank failures; 4) international financial troubles, including the debt load of our trading partners and high domestic tariffs that both slowly squeezed international trade; 5) what Galbraith calls the "uniquely perverse" advice offered by the nation's economists, who promoted the traditional remedies of balanced budgets and adherence to the gold standard that together made a bad situation worse.

More recently, economist Michael Bernstein has shown that the crash enormously disrupted the nation's financial system during a crucial period of transition from an economy based on infrastructural and primary goods industries to newer mass-consumption industries—from production of heavy steel for railroads and construction, for example, to lighter steels for use in appliances, canning, and auto bodies. With the crash, "certain major industries such as textiles, iron and steel, and lumber saw their markets weaken; others, notably appliances, chemicals, and processed foods, faced a new set of opportunities, but were not yet sufficiently strong to ensure recovery." It was difficult for the newer industries to achieve that strength since, as Bernstein notes, it was "precisely those sectors that . . . relied most heavily on the securities market for their growth." Investments that could have spurred the newer and more dynamic sectors of the economy—and so spur economic recovery—did not materialize because of the impact of the Wall Street crash on the availability of investment funds and because of investor fears about the worthiness of risky new ventures. Those firms that could still attract investor interest—because of their past records of profitability—were those heavily invested in the declining "mature" sectors of the economy. The main ingredient for recovery, however, remained sufficient consumer demand, since growing purchases would drive the development of the new economic sectors that could then, in turn, begin to absorb the millions of the unemployed. But this was just the problem. As the mature industries stagnated, they laid off workers in droves, negating any chance for a consumer-driven recovery.

Thus, the Depression spread and continued for so long because of the misery at the bottom of American society. Little in the way of mass consumption could be generated to drive development of the emerging consumer-oriented economic sectors. The vast majority of Americans saw their income fall even during the later boom years of the 1920s as most industries used their economic and political clout to weaken organized labor and cut wages. The low levels of mass purchasing power or aggregate demand inherited from the 1920s worsened as unemployment rose to unimagined heights by the early 1930s. By 1933, unemployment rose to a high of 13 million workers, representing 25 percent of the civilian labor force. During the 1930s, between 1 and 2 million Americans simply hit the road in a restless and fruitless search for work. Even in 1938, one in five workers remained out of work, and, by 1940, unemployment had only dropped to 14 percent.

The extent of economic devastation is captured by any number of indicators. For example, between 1930 and 1932, 5,000 banks and 85,000 businesses shut their doors. The national income fell from $87.8 billion in 1929 to $75.7 billion in 1930, before dropping to just $42.5 billion in 1932. Housing starts dropped from 937,000 in 1925 to 509,000 in 1929 and then to 134,000 in 1932 and 93,000 in 1933. The sales of automobiles dropped from 2,790,000 in 1929 to 617,000 in 1932. It was not until 1941, when massive military expenditures and armed forces buildup forcefully pulled the economy into recovery, that the dollar value of industrial production exceeded that of 1929. The farm sector suffered likewise, as agricultural income dropped from $8.3 billion in 1929 to $3.3 billion in 1932.

THE EARLY DEPRESSION YEARS

American business executives were unprepared for the experience of the Great Depression given their faith in the resiliency of free markets. And so, disoriented and discredited, many U.S. business leaders turned to politics for solutions to their economic woes. But President Herbert Hoover, afraid of disrupting the balance of governmental and business power, proved unwilling to truly test the national government's capacity to meet the economic crisis. He resisted radical business proposals calling for suspension of the antitrust laws on matters like prices and wages. Instead, Hoover relied upon exhortation and voluntarism until very late in his administration, utilizing national power primarily to sponsor conferences of private associations and state and city governments to focus on what could be done through existing public and private agencies. Yet private associations of business leaders, and the nation's cities and states, proved incapable of doing much to meet the crisis. In the face of the enormous economic disaster, the failure of voluntary business action and ostensibly free markets became apparent to all observers.

As the deepening economic crisis took its toll on the nation's banks, Hoover was finally forced to intervene using national authority. The highlight of his new activism was the Reconstruction Finance Corporation (RFC). Convinced that the continuing Depression was being fed by tight money markets, but unable to rouse the private banking community to action, Hoover agreed to an RFC modeled on World War I's War Finance Corporation. The RFC attempted unsuccessfully to restart the economy by furnishing credit to tottering large banking institutions and railroads. (Small amounts found their way into the hands of the unemployed in the form of relief.) Despite the early failures of the RFC, Hoover's move represented a dramatic

Like these drought-stricken farmers in Oklahoma, many Americans faced hard times in the 1930s. *(Library of Congress)*

shift in both the use of peacetime governmental power and in business/government relations. The RFC pointed to the end of an era when it was assumed that the economy could regulate itself naturally and also to the beginning of overt governmental responsibility for economic stability. The RFC proved significant also since it was to be, for the next fifteen years, the largest single lending agency in the United States.

Hoover had to act because of the bankruptcy of business voluntarism; since corporate leaders could not save their own system, national intervention became the basis for ensuring economic stability. Business leaders, incapable of coherent unified action in the best of times, remained for the most part fearful and befuddled by the continuing Depression. At first, business leaders and organizations like the National Association of Manufacturers—the association of the nation's largest manufacturers—treated the crash and the ensuing Depression as simply another cyclical downturn that would actually strengthen the economy. Then, as the downturn worsened, many business leaders turned to tariffs and protectionism to stabilize domestic industry. The Smoot-Hawley Act of 1930 raised duties on imports 40 percent and set off a chain of retaliatory measures among America's international trading partners that dropped U.S. exports from a level of $9.5 billion in 1929 to $2.9 billion in 1932. (It was not until 1942, with the United States involved in the World War II, that trade would reach $10.7 billion.)

As protectionism further fueled the economic disaster, business leaders turned to both the business/government cooperation of World War I and to postwar efforts to build business cooperation through governmental sponsorship of trade and industry associations as models for utilizing national authority on behalf of industrial recovery and economic stability. Plans were developed and expounded by Gerard Swope of General Electric. Henry Harriman of the U.S. Chamber of Commerce also advocated plans that emphasized the suspension of the antitrust laws and government-supervised industry-wide planning through trade associations. Their plans, historian William Leuchtenburg reports, "drew on the experience of [World War I's] War Industries Board because it offered an analogue which provided a maximum of government direction with a minimum of challenge to the institutions of a profit economy." The call for cartelization thus appealed to many industrialists, though many also shied from Swope's call for a "federal supervisory body" and for governmental enforcement of unemployment, retirement, insurance, and disability standards. Business plans therefore remained tentative since business support for relief of competitive pressures was matched by fears that such plans could mean granting peacetime government unprecedented regulatory authority over business activities. As historian Robert Himmelberg has recognized, U.S. businessmen were driven by the "fundamental attitude . . . that economic power and the determination of economic policy were as much as possible to be reserved to the business community; responsibility and accountability to political agencies were to be avoided at all cost."

ROOSEVELT AND THE BUSINESS COMMUNITY

Business attitudes about government intervention shifted as the Depression worsened throughout 1932, and many in the business community endorsed the Democratic candidate, Franklin D. Roosevelt, in that year's presidential contest. Hoover's reluctance to consider the Swope and Harriman plans (he referred to the former as "the most gigantic proposal for monopoly ever made in history" and the latter as "sheer fascism") and his commitment to the deflationary gold standard drove many businesspeople out of the GOP and into the Democratic camp. Of course, the 1932

election also provoked deep concern among many other business leaders over the landslide electoral victory of Roosevelt, a relative unknown, with his ominous rhetorical appeals to the "forgotten man at the bottom of the economic pyramid."

Roosevelt's first moves as president, however, seemed designed to convince conservative financial and industry leaders that he planned no radical spending initiatives to jump-start the economy. By signing onto a conservative bankers bill (the Emergency Banking Act) designed to arrest the sudden and alarming collapse of the banking system (by Roosevelt's inauguration, thirty state governors had halted or restricted bank withdrawals and the banks in thirty-eight states had been closed, as were the New York Stock Exchange and the Chicago Board of Trade), and by committing himself to cuts in federal wages and veterans' benefits, Roosevelt restored confidence in the nation's banking system and calmed business fears about his intentions. But his next moves forcefully broke with the past. While Hoover was reluctant to preempt local responsibility, Roosevelt proved willing to initiate a national program for the unemployed. Creation of the Civilian Conservation Corps was soon followed by the Federal Emergency Relief Act (both in 1933), which provided, through state and local administration, direct relief payments to the unemployed.

After Roosevelt dealt with the farm crisis through the first Agricultural Adjustment Act (1933), industrial recovery and financial reform—both of key interest to business leaders—took center stage. Alongside the Emergency Banking Act noted above, Congress passed the Securities Act of 1933 and the Securities Exchange Act of 1934. The latter created the Securities Exchange Commission, and both laid the foundation for a mixture of self-regulation and national oversight of the nation's stock market. Congress also passed the Glass-Steagal Act in 1933, which established the Federal Deposit Insurance Corporation to insure bank deposits while also mandating the separation of commercial banking from investment banking. Roosevelt's plan for industrial recovery and the centerpiece of his administration's recovery efforts emerged in the National Industrial Recovery Act (NIRA) of June 16, 1933.

The act promoted the often contradictory goals of freely flowing commerce, industry collusion, labor/management cooperation, full utilization of industrial capacity, increased purchasing power, relieving unemployment, and improving working conditions. Yet the core of the NIRA suspended antitrust enforcement and empowered trade associations to formulate "codes of fair competition." Under the loose direction of a

National Recovery Administration (NRA), each industry would design codes regulating prices and limiting production. The aim, of course, was to stabilize prices and profits. NRA codes were most often designed by trade associations and their officials, which were themselves dominated by an industry's largest firms. Trade associations also remained the only organizational means readily available for implementing industry codes, while many NRA officials themselves came from industry. Thus we find that the NRA reproduced the industry men-in-government oversight of industry actions that marked the economic mobilization experience of World War I. Reliance on trade associations and industry officials led to patterns of industrial self-government the implications of which were clear. Himmelberg sums up most scholarship by concluding that the NRA "established cartelist patterns which survived

WHAT'S THE NEXT PLAY GOING TO BE?

As this 1933 cartoon illustrates, the National Recovery Administration (NRA), an anti-depression program designed to regulate competition, was vigorously opposed by many business leaders. (*Brown Brothers*)

the demise of the agency itself" and also displayed "a disturbing tendency on the part of businessmen to seize state power and use it to defend their position and improve their wealth."

Big business did particularly well under the NRA. The largest corporations (those with assets over $10 million) had suffered a loss of $163 million in 1932 (the only year that these corporations lost money), but rebounded by 1935 to realize profits of $4.3 billion. By contrast, small firms (assets under $1 million) lost $2.2 billion in 1932, $908 million in 1933, and $249 million in 1934, before recovering to earn $189 million in 1935 (only 4.4 percent of the profit gained by the largest corporations).

NATIONAL INDUSTRIAL RECOVERY ACT

Although big business made gains under the NRA, the act also spelled trouble for employers. First off, the NIRA was notable for legitimizing the rights of organized labor. Section 7 of the act, which outlawed yellow-dog contracts (contracts requiring employees to agree not to join a union) and declared labor's right to organize and to bargain collectively, was thought to be a bone thrown to labor to solidify support for the bill. Yet its existence also testified to the increasing electoral significance of labor, the rising agitation of the employed and unemployed, and the growing congressional support for labor concerns, especially among urban liberals like Senator Robert Wagner (D-NY). Labor's actual participation in the fashioning of NRA codes was minimal due to business dominance within the NRA, yet inclusion of section 7 alongside the introduction of large-scale national unemployment relief indicated a substantive break with the business/government relations of the recent past.

Section 7 revived moribund labor unions and spurred labor struggles as labor gained the legitimacy of national law and apparent presidential endorsement. Although neither Roosevelt nor the authors of section 7 intended nor envisioned the labor insurgency that ensued, Roosevelt's election, his activist initiatives, and his on-again, off-again populist rhetoric combined with 7 to spur rising labor agitation. Labor militancy in the face of determined employer resistance to unionization quickly burst the bounds of the traditionally conservative American Federation of Labor's (AFL) craft unions, threatening major mass production industries and so economic and political stability. Unlike government leaders in the 1920s, however, Roosevelt and many Democrats, reliant upon working-class electoral support, declined to actively side with business against labor. Without the threat of government force to break strikes, labor could finally gain some leverage in its search for formal recognition and collective bargaining.

Besides granting government legitimacy to organized labor, the NIRA also expanded government authority over business for two interrelated reasons. First, government regulatory capacities grew to compel adherence to and oversee compliance with NRA codes. Second, discomfort with big-business dominance of the codes resulted in pressure for greater independent government oversight of code authorities. Initially, NRA administrator Hugh Johnson relied primarily upon the discretionary and informal code-making process that evolved under trade association dominance. But popular patience with codes fashioned by industry leaders eroded quickly as prices rose while wages fell and competition atrophied. As consumers and many small businesses paid the price for stabilizing profits in bigger firms and powerful industries, their complaints about Johnson and his informal system flooded Congress, inevitably weakening the NRA. Likewise, labor leaders increasingly protested the failure to deliver on the promise of section 7, nicknaming it the "national runaround."

As the NRA moved slowly to increase independent government oversight over the business forces dominating the NRA and its codes, the business community came to regard the NRA with increasing suspicion and hostility. Already many smaller firms distrusted the NRA because of both growing government intrusion and the willingness to sacrifice marginal firms that had resulted in greater economic concentration. Once forced to share power within the NRA and faced with growing governmental authority, many large firms had reason to turn against the NRA as well. In turn, many firms, blaming section 7 for the sudden escalation of labor strife and seeing labor influence increase within the national government, increased their opposition to unionization by relying upon well-worn techniques of violence and intimidation and by expanding the use of company unions.

Increasing numbers of businesspeople also jettisoned their support for Roosevelt and the New Deal. Most businesspeople had sought political intervention because of their failure to discover and implement their own voluntary collective solutions. And yet, while believing they could contain and control government initiatives, they found two aspects of the new political shift troubling. First, Roosevelt's election initiated an expanding scope of government intervention that over time pushed many economic problems into the political sphere, where business was forced to share power with other competing interests (e.g., workers, consumers, government officials, competitors). Rising popular expectations, increasing popular political agitation, and the growing relations between the Democratic Party and an urban and working-class mass base eroded pre-existing business dominance within national politics. Second, U.S. business leaders worried that increasing government authority might lead to government attacks on private business prerogatives. National authority greatly increased during the 1930s, and in the process national officials imposed a greater degree of public accountability upon most corporations. Only the most prescient and politically astute of businesspeople were not frightened into some form of opposition.

By mid-1934, government authority had expanded into previously sacrosanct realms of business privilege and prerogative by establishing programs in support of workers and the unemployed, programs regulating Wall Street, and increasing authority under the NRA to regulate the behavior of corporations. Disgruntlement over the NRA, the labor insurgency, the controversial Securities Exchange Act, and a proposed social welfare program drove many businesspeople into opposition. As historian Robert Collins has written, by the summer of 1934, "a generalized fear that the New Deal threatened business autonomy developed among businessmen of all sorts" because of increasing government authority and the government/labor accommodation manifested in section 7.

The National Association of Manufacturers (NAM) reinvented itself during the early Roosevelt years and became a key source of anti–New Deal pressure. As the Depression deeply hurt the small and medium-sized firms that represented its traditional constituents, the NAM parlayed a vigorous anti–New Deal stance into greater support from big business. The U.S. Chamber of Commerce, representing a broad-based business membership (although its core supporters were capital-intensive industries alongside elite commercial and banking interests), split with Roosevelt in 1934 after having cooperated with his administration the year before. Last, a group of conservative Democrats (including 1928 Democratic presidential candidate Al Smith) and protectionist and labor-intensive industries (lead by the DuPonts) formed the Liberty League. The League intended to rouse and lead the business community against Roosevelt's New Deal, against any pro-labor reforms, and against the New Dealers in Congress during the 1934 midterm elections.

Roosevelt, meanwhile, hedged on pursuing further reforms, fearful of 1934 midterm congressional losses and still wanting to placate most interests, including most importantly the U.S. business community. Thus, he deferred action on key parts of the progressive agenda for reform, including public works, old-age pensions, unemployment insurance, and Senator Wagner's labor reform bill.

But while a business offensive proved generally successful in resisting unionization after labor's initial surge in 1933, mounting labor militancy heralded huge victories for the Democrats in the 1934 midterm elections. (The party that controls the presidency usually loses seats in midterm elections; in 1934, however, Democrats gained fourteen seats in the House and ten in the Senate.) Up to this point of the New Deal, Roosevelt had remained especially attuned to the hopes and fears of U.S. firms and industries, considering their demands central to recovery. However, as business forces increasingly strayed into formal opposition to the New Deal, increasing pressure from the Left—including the labor insurgency, the general expansion of popular radicalism and unrest, and the overwhelming progressive makeup of Congress—prodded Roosevelt to contemplate a less business-friendly approach to recovery.

BUSINESS TURNS ON ROOSEVELT

Although the 1934 election forced Roosevelt to recognize the shift in the balance of class and political forces, his conversion to an activist and reformist agenda was neither simple nor quick. Yet, refusing to lead, Roosevelt was prodded by an increasingly activist popular base and especially by the building momentum for a labor rights act. Orchestrated and tirelessly promoted by Senator Wagner, the National Labor Relations Act, also known as the Wagner Act, threatened to become law without Roosevelt's blessing. As continued labor strife threatened economic and political stability and as conservatives and businesspeople continued to turn against the New Deal, Roosevelt slowly drifted from ambivalence to tepid support of a labor measure. Only when the Supreme Court struck down the NIRA in *Schechter Poultry Corp. v. United States* (1935), did Roosevelt finally turn to full-hearted support of the Wagner bill. Roosevelt's conversion was certainly helpful, but less decisive than Wagner's own persistent efforts, and both were less significant in their impact than the growing popular insurgency of workers. The law itself made history by dramatically changing the relations between employees and employers. As Leuchten-

burg notes, "The Wagner Act was one of the most drastic legislative innovations of the decade. It threw the weight of the government behind the right of labor to bargain collectively, and compelled employers to accede peacefully to the unionization of their plants."

Roosevelt's belated progressive shift seemed to boost his confidence in the face of business opposition and the 1935 Schechter decision. Passage of the Wagner Act rescued and strengthened the part of the NRA concerned with collective bargaining, and it represented an important step toward asserting an independent government program, less reliant on particular business support and oriented toward building recovery through the Keynesian principle of increased mass purchasing power. The act also augured the beginning of a series of legislative enactments often cited as the Second Hundred Days. A seeming decisive break, it was also a pragmatic recognition of great human suffering, overwhelming public and congressional sentiment, and disruptive social movements. The reform initiatives of the so-called Second New Deal, however, did not receive a strong endorsement from Roosevelt, who continued to hedge in his support for reform.

Reflecting Roosevelt's practical orientation and the continuing divisions within his administration, many of these measures embodied the ambivalence that characterized much of the New Deal; even as they intensified the national government's responsibilities to greater numbers of persons, they incarnated and represented a conservative compromise. For example, the Social Security Act of 1935, notwithstanding its essentially regressive (in terms of taxation) and conservative (in terms of whom it excluded) elements, permanently extended national responsibility to ordinary citizens and redistributed income. Leuchtenburg thus deems this legislation "inept and conservative," while also recognizing that "it reversed historic assumptions about the nature of social responsibility, and it established the proposition that the individual has clear-cut social rights." Accordingly, although key business leaders had themselves worked on the Social Security Act, most of them perceived a clear antibusiness threat in the New Deal's new direction and in the disturbing emerging alliance between the Roosevelt administration and the avowedly militant new labor organization, the Congress of Industrial Organizations (CIO). The Second New Deal thus generated a growing storm of business complaints.

Still, while it's generally true that many businesspeople began to treat Roosevelt and the New Deal as an abomination, not all business interests turned against the administration. While traditional business organizations such as the Chamber of Commerce and the NAM tended to reject government intervention altogether, other businessmen recognized the importance of a certain measure of national responsibility for economic stability. According to Francis X. Sutton et al., the Chamber of Commerce and the NAM embodied traditional beliefs in "decentralized, private, competitive capitalism" free of the obstructive influences of "Big Labor and Big Government," and during the New Deal, Robert Collins adds, engaged in "negativistic opposition" to expanding government activities. Yet other elements within the American business community, resisting knee-jerk antagonism to expanding government authority, worked hard to remain close to the Roosevelt administration. The Business Advisory Council (BAC), for example, had been created in 1933 by Roosevelt's first secretary of commerce, Daniel Roper, as a semi-public organization linking the most influential members of the business community to the new Roosevelt administration. Members of the BAC, who represented some of the largest U.S. corporations, understood the benefits to be derived from a strong and activist national government, but they wished to limit that activism in order to limit the threat of independent or democratic government intervention.

To ensure that government would not grow too obtrusive, these business leaders wanted to cooperate with the administration as it developed new policies. Cooperation provided influence over what these business leaders saw as the inevitable increase in government authority. Besides allowing business leaders privileged access to the highest levels of government, the BAC provided a mechanism for major corporations to transcend narrow parochial and competitive concerns in order to consider both long-range plans for economic stability and the national state's part in these plans. As Collins observes, "Throughout the 1930s, the BAC remained a bastion of those who dreamed of a business commonwealth—a system involving national planning and regulation of industry, with government cooperation but without government control." Although a minority within the business community as a whole, this group proved very influential because it offered crucial support for a particular type of limited government interventionism.

Roosevelt's New Deal did not so much turn government and business against one another as it created a whole new system of business/government cooperation. The previous business/government alignment included national Republicans closely allied with protectionist, labor-intensive industries (e.g., steel, textiles, coal) concerned about foreign competition, along-

side the investment and commercial bankers who had helped to build these industries. This alignment began to break up as economic changes brought on by World War I drove a wedge between industry and finance, and even between different types of industries. On the one hand, as World War I spurred international trade and investments and as the United States became a net creditor nation, investment banks broke with protectionist industries to encourage European exports into the United States in order to recoup their wartime loans. On the other hand, a breach grew within American industry between labor-intensive firms terribly anxious about growing labor power during World War I and those capital-intensive firms that, because they were less threatened by an assertive labor force, sought accommodation with labor. Thus, questions of both labor and foreign policy began to erode the previously close-knit relations within the U.S. business community. Roosevelt tried to sustain a shaky alliance with protectionist industries during the early New Deal, but as the NRA failed he shifted to a strong free trade position (one of the reasons why many firms joined the Liberty League in opposing Roosevelt).

With lines of support and hostility growing clearer after the 1934 election, Roosevelt constructed a new and lasting business/government alignment by seeking common cause with capital-intensive firms and industries, investment banks, and internationally oriented commercial banks. Firms from these industries were less fearful of the New Deal's strengthening of organized labor (since they were reliant on large potentially organizable work forces and interested in reviving world trade in order to increase exports. Historian Thomas Ferguson reports that, during the 1936 presidential race, Roosevelt gained the backing of top executives in the oil industry, Reynolds Tobacco, American Tobacco, General Electric, Coca-Cola, International Harvester, Johnson & Johnson, Zenith, IBM, Sears Roebuck, ITT, United Fruit, and Pan Am, and broad support from banking and finance. These firms, from the emerging, dynamic, mass-consumption industries, supported Roosevelt's turn to reform because these policies encouraged the mass consumption crucial to their success and because of the strong stand on free trade.

THE SECOND NEW DEAL

By 1936, Roosevelt's New Deal had stabilized the economy. Six million jobs had been created, industrial output had doubled in the three years since Roosevelt took office, and in that year U.S. corporations earned $5 billion in profits. By early 1937, the economy finally outdid 1929 pre-Depression levels of output. And so, by mid-1937, Roosevelt, overconfident about the ability of the economy to stand on its own and pressed by conservatives, instigated a recession-within-a-depression through cutbacks in work relief and public works programs. The so-called Roosevelt depression dramatically exposed the continuing dependence of the national economy on government spending as businessmen proved reluctant to initiate new investments on their own.

The economic downturn of the late 1930s discredited the balanced budget approach of Treasury Secretary Henry Morgenthau Jr. and instigated a broad debate over alternative positive measures associated with deficit spending within the Roosevelt administration. In fact, the recession of 1937–38 convinced many of Roosevelt's economic advisors that the Depression was not just another business downturn, but rather a permanent condition reflecting the "secular stagnation" of a "mature economy" and the dominance of huge corporations capable of "administered" or controlled prices. (These concepts are developed in Alvin Hansen's 1938 Keynesian analysis of the Great Depression, *Full Recovery or Stagnation?*) Since recovery could not therefore be expected simply by boosting business confidence, more permanent and formalized government involvement would be necessary. Most New Dealers distinguished between earlier attempts at temporary "pump priming" and the now-accepted need for a permanent public investment program. A national spending program would necessarily be more interventionist than the monetary and security regulation implemented earlier in the New Deal. A national investment program would necessitate a presidential-level capability to plan and implement public spending policies, to regulate destructive monopolistic or competitive business tendencies, and to redistribute income.

The spending alternative was immediately implemented as Roosevelt easily convinced a Congress anxious over 1938 midterm elections to authorize new spending for public works and work relief. Though many thought the program too tame, economist Robert Lekachman reports that, due to deficit spending of $2.9 billion, "a grateful economy responded appropriately: GNP [gross national product] in 1939 returned to its 1937 level." Meanwhile, other changes in government policy toward business proceeded. On the one hand, we find Thurman Arnold's antitrust offensive, which began with his appointment in 1938 as head of the Justice Department's Antitrust Division and finally ran out of steam by 1942, when the wartime emergency encouraged the very industry collusion Arnold fought against. Until then, Arnold not only tried to reinvent antitrust enforcement (prosecuting "bad" firms who controlled prices and hampered consumption rather than "big" firms per se), but he also tried to expand the Justice Department's administrative ability to regulate monopoly power. On the other hand, New Dealers led by Leon Henderson orchestrated a massive joint congressional/executive investigation into the workings and structure of the U.S. economy. Henderson and others intended that this Temporary National Economic Committee (TNEC) investigation would guide and inform the national interventions that would complement a public investment program. The hopes of those who spearheaded the TNEC hearings were dashed as the war in Europe dramatically altered the political equation at home and shifted attention from the potential abuse of business power to the need for business cooperation with wartime preparations.

EPILOGUE: THE COMING OF WORLD WAR II

Depression conditions had reduced corporate political leverage while the hopeful rhetoric of Roosevelt roused popular pressure; both conditions granted national politicians greater freedom of action from business power. Yet the Depression-era relationship between assertive national officials and vulnerable business forces began to turn as the onset of the war in Europe revived the U.S. economy and as the need to produce war matériel increased governmental dependence on the nation's dominant firms and industries. In this new environment, business executives rushed to reclaim their "privileged position" within the U.S. political system, using their power and influence to discourage political departures that might threaten their ownership or managerial prerogatives. Business executives thoroughly dominated wartime mobilization as their concerns about profits, market share, and expanding New Dealer authority spurred actions designed to limit the political control of the U.S. economy.

BRIAN WADDELL

Bibliography

Bernstein, Michael. *The Great Depression*. New York: Cambridge University Press, 1987.

Cochran, Thomas. *The American Business System*. Cambridge: Harvard University Press, 1957.

Collins, Robert. *The Business Response to Keynes, 1929–1964.* New York: Columbia University Press, 1981.

Eisner, Marc Allen. *From Warfare State to Welfare State.* University Park: The Pennsylvania State University Press, 2000.

Galbraith, John Kenneth. *The Great Crash.* Boston: Houghton-Mifflin, 1954.

Gordon, Colin. *New Deals.* New York: Cambridge University Press, 1994.

Hacker, Louis. *The Course of American Economic Growth and Development.* New York: John Wiley, 1970.

Hansen, Alvin. Full Recovery or Stagnation? New York: W. W. Norton, 1938.

Hawley, Ellis. *The New Deal and the Problem of Monopoly.* Princeton: Princeton University Press, 1966.

Himmelberg, Robert. *The Origins of the National Recovery Administration.* New York: Fordham University Press, 1976.

Lekachman, Robert. *The Age of Keynes.* New York: Vintage, 1968.

Leuchtenburg, William E. *Franklin D. Roosevelt and the New Deal.* New York: Harper & Row, 1963.

Levine, Rhonda. *Class Struggle and the New Deal.* Lawrence: University Press of Kansas, 1988.

Lindblom, Charles. *Politics and Markets.* New York: Basic Books, 1977.

McQuaid, Kim. *Big Business and Presidential Power.* New York: William Morrow, 1982.

Sobel, Robert. *The Age of Giant Corporations.* Westport, CT: Greenwood Press, 1972.

Sutton, Francis X., Seymour E. Harris, Carl Kaysen, and James Tobin. *The American Business Creed.* Cambridge: Harvard University Press, 1956.

David Vogel. "Why Businessmen Distrust Their State: The Political Consciousness of American Corporate Executives." *British Journal of Political Science* 8 (1978).

LABOR AND UNIONS

The Great Depression and the New Deal transformed the lives of ordinary working Americans. Changes in the structure of American industry, both cause and effect of the Great Depression, altered employment patterns and industrial workers' everyday experience. The massive unemployment of the Great Depression disrupted their plans, dreams, and expectations. The rise of the active state under the New Deal provided sustenance and power for industrial workers and represented a fundamental shift in the government's role in workers' lives. Finally, industrial workers themselves experienced a sea change: an increased militance and unity best illustrated by the creation of the first mass-production industrial labor organization, the Congress of Industrial Organizations (CIO).

Agricultural labor likewise suffered from the collapse of the economy, yet benefited less from New Deal legislation. Migrant agricultural laborers received sustenance and shelter from the state, but empowering legislation excluded them. Furthermore, small landowners, tenant farmers, and sharecroppers actually suffered from New Deal efforts to bolster farm prices.

INDUSTRIAL WORKERS IN THE 1920s

In the 1920s, American industrial workers experienced significant shifts in the patterns and nature of employment. Many of these changes stifled labor organization and left workers unprepared to deal with a crisis the magnitude of the Great Depression.

Patterns of employment changed during the 1920s as one set of industries declined while another prospered. Heavy industry, and the skills associated with it, declined. Mass-production industries increased. This change, as discussed below, deepened the cyclical collapse of the economy in 1929 and frustrated efforts to spark a recovery. It also marked the everyday experience of millions of workers. "Speed" was the new maxim. Machines increasingly set the pace for unskilled

and semiskilled men and women. Most of these workers had never before been organized in labor unions.

Changes in the workforce complemented changed employment patterns. From 1920 to 1930, women's participation in the work-for-wages labor force increased by 27 percent, from 8.3 million to 10.6 million. In 1930, women made up approximately 25 percent of the work-for-wages labor force. Legislation passed in the early 1920s slowed immigration, but new movements of workers supplied industry and agriculture. African-American internal migration to northern industrial centers continued after the surge of World War I. More than 2 million African Americans migrated north between 1910 and 1930. Mexican migration also increased. More than 1.5 million Mexicans crossed into the United States between 1900 and 1930. These "new" workers were outside the traditional realm of organized labor.

Steadier employment and improved wages and conditions impeded labor organizing. Though unemployment soared to 12 percent during the immediate postwar recession of 1921–22, by 1923 it was down to 3.2 percent, and, according to government figures, it hovered around 2 to 3 percent for the rest of the decade. Many historians discount the overly optimistic official figures and estimate that unemployment was between 7 and 10 percent throughout the 1920s. Regional conditions varied widely. Detroit, for example, the center of automobile production, prospered; whereas Lowell, Massachusetts, an old northern textile town, did not. For workers in dynamic industries, however, employment remained steady and well paid throughout the 1920s. From 1914 to 1926, average annual earnings increased 40 percent from $682 to $1,473, even as average hours of employment declined from 59 to 50 (1900 to 1926). Ford's mass-production auto workers earned on average $1,700 a year, and many took advantage of new credit mechanisms to extend their consumption power. Almost half owned their own car; many owned washing machines, radios, and other products new to the period. They enjoyed more leisure and privacy. They ate better than ever before.

High profits engendered a more generous form of employer hegemony. Employer-sponsored welfare capitalism and "industrial democracy"—employee representation plans—sought to usurp the role of organized labor. Overall, although employee representation plans largely failed, the paternalistic benevolence of welfare capitalism, coupled with increased wages and consumption, stifled labor organization and militance. Though union membership reached a high of almost 5 million workers in 1920–21, by 1929 it declined to 3.6 million workers. In 1928, there were fewer strikes than in any other year since 1884.

It was thus a hobbled labor movement that faced the hardships of the Great Depression. The rise of mass-production industries, increased consumption and leisure, and employer paternalism worked against labor organization and militance. Consequently, organized labor did not have a powerful voice in society. President Herbert Hoover agreed with industrialists that the "American Way" was the open shop, "freedom of choice," voluntarism, and individualism. Organized labor too was voluntaristic. It was not until the bitter winter of 1932 that the American Federation of Labor (AFL), the nation's largest labor organization, renounced its long-standing position against unemployment insurance.

STRUCTURAL UNEMPLOYMENT

Numerous cyclical factors initiated the crash of 1929. Inventory buildup (as production outpaced consumption), diminished international trade, and stock market speculation initiated a massive cyclical collapse of the economy. Structural problems also plagued the economy and had disastrous effects for American workers. Put simply, older industries that dominated the demand for labor declined faster than newer industries grew. In 1935, primary metals, textile mills, and lumber ranked first, second, and third respectively in shares of national employment. As noted above, these industries declined through the 1920s. The 1929 crash, with its spectacular fall in demand, only exacerbated their condition. Newer industries—electronics (radio and home appliances), aircraft production, and others—simply could not absorb labor demand in significant numbers. Other dynamic industries, such as food products, chemicals, tobacco, and petroleum, maintained their position throughout the Depression, but did not increase their share of national employment. These

industries, like the newer industries, were capital-intensive: machines, not workers, increased in importance.

For many older male workers in heavy industry, this was a permanent shift that terminated their working lives. "It is apparent that many of our unemployed," claimed then Secretary of Agriculture Henry C. Wallace (father of President Franklin D. Roosevelt's second vice president, Henry A. Wallace), "may never get jobs again. Machines and younger people have taken their places." Women, on the other hand, suffered less in this respect from the Depression. Segregated into lower income jobs in mass-production industries, women experienced less unemployment and wage decline. Many married women whose husbands maintained their jobs did suffer job discrimination. Section 213 of the Federal Economy Act (1932), for example, discriminated against employees whose spouse also held a job with the federal government. Private industry often followed the spirit of this measure and fired women workers whose husbands held good jobs. Nevertheless, women's proportion of the workforce and participation rate increased during the Depression.

Unemployment persisted despite efforts to accelerate the economy. Although Hoover responded to the Depression with public works (the Hoover Dam, for example) and financial regulation and support (the Reconstruction Finance Corporation), it was too little, too late. Aggregate demand did not respond. A strong believer that America was a nation of individuals and that government charity corrupted American values, Hoover refused to initiate direct relief programs. During a drought in Kansas, for example, he offered relief for cattle but not for farmers. Although he accumulated an unprecedented peacetime deficit, the recession instigated by the collapse of the stock market did not slacken and was soon a full depression. By 1931, 8 million men and women—18 percent of the nation's workforce—were unemployed. In the terrible "winter of despair" of 1933, the unemployed totaled 13 million, or 25 percent of the nation's workforce.

THE NEW DEAL

During the 1932 election campaign, Democrat Franklin D. Roosevelt criticized Hoover as a spendthrift and promised to balance the budget. Once in office, however, President Roosevelt relied on deficit spending to finance public works programs and direct relief in an effort to ameliorate the worst conditions and increase aggregate demand. During the First Hundred Days of his administration, Roosevelt initiated many programs that greatly improved the lives of working people. The Civilian Conservation Corps (CCC) employed more than 3 million men over approximately a decade in environmental projects all over the nation. The Federal Emergency Relief Act (FERA) doled out more than $500 million to the neediest Americans. The Tennessee Valley Authority provided immediate construction jobs as well as long-term electrical power and other benefits to some of the nation's most impoverished citizens. The National Industrial Recovery Act's (NIRA) Public Works Administration (PWA) promised $3.3 billion in road building and other public construction projects. It was, however, in the field of labor organization where the most significant long-term shift in emphasis took place.

The NIRA created the National Recovery Administration (NRA). Section 7 of the NRA charter empowered workers to organize into unions and enter into collective bargaining agreements with their employers. Section 7 was not without precedent. The Clayton Act of 1914 had promised to tilt the balance of power in the direction of workers. It forbade the use of injunctions against labor unions, except in cases of injury to property rights. The Railway Labor Act of 1926 also facilitated union organization, at least in the railroads. Even before Roosevelt's election, Congress responded to the crisis and passed the Norris–La Guardia Act (1932). The Norris–La Guardia Act outlawed so-called yellow-dog contracts (such contracts allowed employers to discriminate against union members) guaranteed freedom of association, reaffirmed the Clayton Act, and severely impaired the use of injunctions against unions.

Thus, Section 7 was not so new or unprecedented. It did, however, supersede these previous efforts and placed the power of the state firmly behind workers at a time of national crisis. Three important measures in Section 7 greatly increased labor's power: workers were free to organize and collectively bargain with employers (employers could not in any way interfere with this process); workers were free to join any union of their own choosing (and not necessarily a company union); and employers had to recognize and maintain minimum wage and maximum hours standards set by the NRA. Section 7 of the NRA charter empowered American workers and set off a blitz of union organization.

UNION RESURGENCE

"The President wants you to join the union," placards announced to coal miners as they entered the pits in the summer of 1933. John L. Lewis, the president of the United Mine Workers (UMW), was, however, preaching to the converted. Many workers had long wanted to join the unions, and often did not wait for official union representatives to begin organizing drives; rather, they organized themselves and handed startled union organizers full union locals.

The most significant increase came in those unions organized along industrial lines. The UMW recouped 300,000 members and made new ground in previously unorganized territory. The International Ladies' Garment Workers Union and the Amalgamated Clothing Workers also added 100,000 and 50,000 members respectively to their organizations. In October 1933, the president of the AFL, William Green, announced that the AFL had close to 4 million members—up 1.5 million new recruits since the passage of the NIRA and Section 7. A new AFL drive also promised significant change. For the first time, the AFL promised to organize unskilled and semiskilled workers in the mass-production industries.

The organization of mass-production workers suggested a massive philosophical shift within the AFL. The AFL was a craft organization founded in 1886. Individual unions within the federation were, for the most part, not based along industry lines, but rather across industries on a craft or skill basis. Thus, for example, carpenters in different industries belonged to the carpenters' AFL affiliate, the United Brotherhood of Carpenters and Joiners. Workers in the rising mass-production industries did not, however, lend themselves to this type of organization. Workers in these industries were often unskilled or semiskilled machine operators traditionally spurned by the AFL as unorganizable. Following the passage of Section 7, however, the AFL promised to "Organize the Unorganized in Mass-production Industries." Under this slogan, the AFL began an unprecedented drive to reach workers never before in a labor union.

This effort was flawed from the start. Years of entrenched power and AFL leaders' ideas about whose interests the federation represented undermined this new initiative. The AFL did not organize mass-production workers permanently along industrial lines. Instead, organizers herded workers into temporary "federal" unions. Under this system, the AFL chartered almost 1,500 "federal" unions between 1932 and 1934.

In theory, the permanent craft unions would then divide the workers up depending upon their actual role in the work process. In practice, mass-production workers did not identify along craft lines. They were, for example, steelworkers, autoworkers, and rubber workers, not carpenters or machinists. Old bottles could not hold the new wine. The craft unions also expressed a continued reluctance to wager their all in organizing workers they had no truck with: Were they not successful enough in representing their skilled craftsmen? Why should they gamble with their members' money to organize the unskilled? Conservative labor leaders entrenched in powerful positions felt no obligation to reach out to workers traditionally isolated from union activity.

The NRA also proved less than satisfactory. Workers widely derided it as the "National Run Around." Workers received increased wages and benefits under the industry codes. The NRA codes established the hours of labor at forty, maintained average wages at $12 to $15 a week, and outlawed child labor. Employers, however, soon found ways to usurp collective bargaining and unions. Company unions, for example, almost doubled to represent 2.5 million workers during the NRA's existence. In theory, employers could not coerce employees to join company unions. In practice, many employers did their best to promote their organizations over independent labor unions. The NRA for its part retreated from the spirit of the law and sanctioned any type of labor organization. Other exceptions to NRA rules allowed employers to differentiate between workers, thus discriminating against union members. Once again, employers' efforts frustrated labor's organization.

WORKERS' INCREASED MILITANCE

Labor's frustration engendered strikes and violence in 1933 and 1934. In Toledo, labor disputes culminated in violence when non-AFL labor radicals organized the city's workers—employed and unemployed—and battled the National Guard in the streets. In San Francisco, labor radical Harry Bridges organized the International Longshoremen's and Warehousemen's Union and stopped work up and down the Pacific Coast. In Minnesota, self-described Trotskyites led a violent strike of the Twin Cities' (St. Paul and Minneapolis) teamsters. Labor radicalism and violence marked all of these strikes, and they were all successful; workers in Toledo, San Francisco, and the Twin Cities benefited greatly from labor militance. These victories contrasted sharply

with the AFL's utter failure. During the largest strike in American history up to that time—the Great Textile Strike of 1934, which involved up to 500,000 men and women from Maine to northern Alabama—the AFL balked when Roosevelt intervened. Leaders accepted the administration's appointment of a new Textile Labor Relations Board and called off the strike. Employers, however, felt no compulsion to rehire union members. The AFL's defeat dampened labor militance. Some 1,856 labor strikes involving almost 1.5 million workers—7 percent of the workforce—marked 1934. Yet by 1935 labor had lost its edge. AFL membership declined well below the 4 million mark of 1933, 600 of the federal unions disbanded, and the significant gains made by unions in steel, automobiles, and textiles disappeared. The effort to organize workers seemed lost, but passage of the Wagner Act in July 1935 would resuscitate the labor movement.

THE WAGNER ACT

The Wagner Act replaced a much beleaguered and increasingly unsatisfactory NRA. Employers' hostility to the labor provisions of the NRA stifled organized labor's efforts. Labor grew frustrated with the NRA's diminished power. Popular opinion also turned against the elaborate price and wage controls that marked the NRA's efforts to bolster demand and production. The Supreme Court agreed, and in *Schechter Poultry Corporation v. United States* (1935) it struck down the NIRA as unconstitutional. The Supreme Court decision destroyed the NRA. Prior to the decision, however, labor's advocates in Congress worked to strengthen provisions to support union organization. Eleven days before the Supreme Court's decision struck down the NIRA, the Senate passed New York Senator Robert F. Wagner's National Labor Relations Act, commonly known as the Wagner Act.

This law greatly increased labor's power. Created with an eye to Section 7 of the NRA, it lacked Section 7's shortcomings. The spirit and letter of the act tipped the scales in favor of workers. The Wagner Act placed numerous restraints on employers' efforts to impede union organization. Most importantly, it banned company unions. "By preventing practices which tend to destroy the independence of labor," Roosevelt proclaimed, "[the Wagner Act] seeks, for every worker within its scope, that freedom of choice and action which is justly his."

The National Labor Relations Act resurrected the NRA's industrial dispute administrative body, the

During the Great Depression, as this photo of a march in New York City in 1936 illustrates, labor unions and working people exercised a militancy and power rarely seen in American political history. The American labor movement made more gains in the 1930s than in any other decade of the century. *(Brown Brothers)*

National Labor Relations Board (NLRB). The new NLRB was a quasi-judicial administrative organization that handled all disputes arising from the implementation of the Wagner Act. It did not act as an arbitration board, but over a ten-year period, from 1935 to 1945, it handled 36,000 unfair labor practice complaints and 38,000 cases dealing with employee representation. Almost 85 percent of these cases did not reach the final semijudicial stage. As an administrative arm of the NRA, the old NLRB had no power to back its decisions. Under the Wagner Act, the new NLRB had the bite to back its bark. Over ten years, it reinstated more than 300,000 workers improperly dismissed for union membership with more than $9 million in back pay, and it disestablished 2,000 com-

pany unions. It also supervised more than 24,000 union elections involving more than 6 million workers. As late as 1937, however, employers continued to resist labor's right to organize.

LABOR'S CONTINUED STRUGGLE

Continued employer hostility to labor organization ranged from outright gangsterism to courtroom battles. Labor struck back, and in 1937 more than 2 million workers participated in thousands of strikes. Labor faced recalcitrant employers in these struggles. In 1937, Senator Robert La Follette's Civil Liberties Committee revealed that more than 2,500 corporations utilized labor spies and stockpiled weapons as part of their industrial relations strategies. The Republic Steel Corporation and the Youngstown Sheet and Tube Company prepared for the "little steel" strike of 1937 with dozens of machine guns, hundreds of rifles and shotguns, and tear gas. Employers also implemented a less violent, yet no less sinister form of resistance in the Mohawk Valley Formula. Promoted by the National Association of Manufacturers, this blueprint of union resistance advised employers to smear union organizers as radicals, organize local committees to intimidate strikers, threaten the community's vitality by threatening to leave, and use other effective, if insidious, tactics.

Behind this employer resistance lay the confidence of corporation lawyers that the Supreme Court was sure to strike down the Wagner Act. The Court, however, also experienced a sea change during this period, and in 1937, in *National Labor Relations Board v. Jones & Laughlin Steel Corporation*, it upheld the Wagner Act. Armed with the Supreme Court's ruling, the NLRB defined unfair labor practices broadly and moved against employers' efforts to hobble union organization. With the judicial sanction of the Wagner Act, unions reached a milestone. After repeated halting and frustrating efforts to organize freely, unions finally gained the power they needed. The Wagner Act recognized that the balance of power in labor relations lay with employers so it gave employers compensatory rights. It institutionalized the role of the federal government in employee–employer relations.

The New Deal did much for working people. The Wagner Act empowered millions of workers, but it was not the only New Deal measure that affected working Americans during the Great Depression. In the First Hundred Days, Roosevelt created the previously mentioned FERA, CCC, and PWA programs to bolster employment and distribute relief. In the so-called Second New Deal of 1935, Roosevelt continued his public works efforts with the Works Progress Administration (WPA). He also initiated a much more significant measure in the Social Security Act. The Social Security Act established unemployment insurance, old-age pensions, and financial assistance to the needy, including dependent children and the disabled. In 1938 the president engineered the passage of the Fair Labor Standards Act. This measure established minimum wages and maximum hours in industry. It also abolished child labor for all industries in interstate commerce. The Supreme Court upheld all of these measures. In sum, these changes represented a fundamental shift in the role the federal government played in people's lives: voluntarism died and a new era marked by an active

federal government began. The state was not, however, the only factor that changed. Workers too changed, grew more militant, more sure of their rights, more united in their struggles. The growth of the Congress of Industrial Organizations (CIO) best represents this shift.

THE CONGRESS OF INDUSTRIAL ORGANIZATIONS

In part, the creation of the CIO and the massive surge in organization that followed was the result of John L. Lewis's will to act. In part, it was the result of the Wagner Act. Lewis predicted a wave of rank-and-file union militancy following the passage of the Wagner Act and sought to harness it. More importantly, workers themselves changed during this period. Disappointed by the failure of welfare capitalism and united by hardship across ethnic and racial lines for the first time, workers expressed an increased enthusiasm, militancy, and unity.

The CIO grew directly out of a schism within the AFL. As noted above, the AFL was, in large part, a craft union. The schism that rent it was not, however, between craft and industrial organization. After all, the UMW was an AFL-affiliated industrial union. The schism between Lewis and the conservative AFL leadership derived from the need to organize the semiskilled and unskilled machine operators in mass-production industries. UMW president John L. Lewis saw this need as the greatest opportunity for labor. Mass production represented the future of the economy and thus the future of union organization. Lewis had what other AFL labor leaders did not: the will to organize and lead millions of previously unorganized working Americans.

The conflict between Lewis, his allies, and their more conservative colleagues in the AFL dragged on through 1934. At the AFL's San Francisco convention of 1934, the advocates of industrial unionism and the craft union stalwarts reached a compromise of sorts. Lewis was hopeful and quickly promoted a plan to organize the autoworkers. However, continued jurisdictional disputes, a lack of financial commitment, and an underlying hostility to mass-production workers by AFL labor leaders all stifled Lewis's efforts. In 1935, at the AFL's Atlantic City convention, he attempted one last time to convince the old guard that new workers required new methods and organizations. The old guard voted down his efforts and stifled debate on points of order. Never at a loss for a dramatic gesture,

Lewis coolly socked Big Bill Hutcheson, leader of the conservative Brotherhood of Carpenters and Joiners of America, in the jaw. With his fist, Lewis symbolically ended the effort at compromise and launched a new era in labor organization.

In the wake of the failed Atlantic City effort to organize industrial unions within the AFL, Lewis and a number of trusted allies—Philip Murray, also of the United Mine Workers, Sidney Hillman of the Amalgamated Clothing Workers of America, David Dubinsky of the International Ladies' Garment Workers' Union, and others—created a Committee for Industrial Organization (changed to Congress of Industrial Organizations in 1938). The CIO immediately made important gains in the steel, automobile, rubber, and radio industries. By the end of 1937, the CIO surpassed the AFL in membership, 3.7 million to 3.4 million, and total union membership far exceeded the 1920–21 high of 5 million.

Labor organizations could not have reached this point had not workers also changed. Out of the "furnace" of repeated struggle and disappointment came newly tempered workers demanding their rights: "All I know is there's certain things I've got to have or I don't want to go on living," the character Dobie claims in *Out of This Furnace*, Thomas Bell's fictional account of steelworkers in Braddock, Pennsylvania. "I want certain things bad enough to fight for them, bad enough to die for them. Patrick Henry Junior—that's me. Give me liberty or give me death. But he meant every word of it and by God I think I do too."

In 1937, workers forcefully demonstrated this new spirit in Flint, Michigan. The United Auto Workers had begun as an AFL affiliate but joined the CIO in 1936. That year the UAW sought a place at the bargaining table with General Motors (GM), Chrysler, and Ford. When General Motors flippantly dismissed union efforts to bargain collectively, militant workers occupied the Chevrolet No. 1 factory in Flint. "The Great Sit-Down Strike" of 1937 paralyzed production at GM. General Motors called upon the state of Michigan to protect its property rights. The governor of Michigan, Frank Murphy, was, however, sympathetic to labor and refused to intervene. National Guardsmen were on hand, but he would not order them out against workers. President Roosevelt too demanded compromise and negotiations. Lewis praised the workers and negotiated a settlement that recognized the union's power to enter into collective bargaining agreements with GM.

The victory was important for the UAW. Prior to the agreement, perhaps only 14,000 auto workers be-

longed to the union. By October 1937, six months after the settlement, the UAW represented close to half a million autoworkers. Overall, labor organization and militance greatly increased as a result of the strike. More than half of the 477 strikes of 1937 occurred during January, February, and March, during or immediately following the Flint sit-down strike (December 30 to February 11). Many employers yielded to increased labor power. Myron C. Taylor of U.S. Steel, for example, recognized that, given the increased militancy of workers and the power of their alliance with the state, unionization was inevitable. U.S. Steel succumbed to the CIO's Steel Workers Organizing Committee (SWOC) several weeks after the Flint sit-down strike without a strike of any kind. Shortly thereafter, SWOC boasted 300,000 members.

The CIO faltered during the recession of 1937–38, but with the advent of war in Europe it quickly regained its strength. More importantly, workers entered the war period sure of their rights and empowered to secure them. In the postwar period, workers and their unions secured for themselves a quality of life never before imagined by working people.

AGRICULTURAL WORKERS IN THE GREAT DEPRESSION AND THE NEW DEAL

Overall, the New Deal was less kind to agricultural laborers. Landowners forced tenants and sharecroppers off the land to cash in on the Agricultural Adjustment Administration's (AAA) price maintenance programs. In addition, legislation that empowered industrial labor for the most part excluded agricultural workers. The New Deal did, however, improve the lives of thousands of migrant farm families through the creation of extensive housing facilities.

The AAA price maintenance programs paid farmers not to farm. Landowners thus found it profitable to evict tenants and sharecroppers, pocket the payments, and invest in laborsaving equipment such as tractors. Large farms actually increased in size and benefited most from the AAA programs. Small farmers often lost their land and joined an increased stream of migrant, landless, agricultural laborers. Drought, the numerous vagaries of farming, and AAA policies pushed hundreds of thousands of farmers and farm workers from the South and Southwest to California. These men and women often displaced Mexican and Mexican-American farm workers. By 1936, these Anglo migrants held 90 percent of the cotton jobs in California.

Migrant laborers did not enjoy the fruits of labor's increased power. Although the CIO included some 100,000 agricultural workers and numerous other agricultural workers' unions affiliated with the AFL, most of these were packinghouse workers. The Wagner Act protected packinghouse workers but not field workers. Both the NIRA and the Wagner Act did, however, inspire workers to organize, and a rash of agricultural strikes marked the "turbulent years" of 1933 and 1934. In October 1933, for example, 18,000 cotton workers inflamed by Section 7 of the NRA charter struck in California. These largely Mexican workers revitalized the moribund Cannery and Agricultural Workers Industrial Union. State intervention settled the strike with mixed results for workers. They received higher wages but no union recognition. Furthermore, the tepid role of the state in this strike marked a high point for government intervention in agricultural labor disputes. In 1938 and 1939, the newly formed United Cannery, Agricultural, Packing and Allied Workers of America failed in its strike efforts. Without state power, short-lived agricultural labor organizations had little long-term impact on wages and conditions.

The New Deal did, however, improve the material conditions of thousands of migrant workers. First the Resettlement Administration and, later, the Farm Security Administration (FSA) housed tens of thousands of families. This program operated twenty-six permanent camps by 1936 and ninety-five camps by 1942. In the latter year, the FSA housed more than 19,000 families and 75,000 persons. These camps exceeded their mandate to house and feed workers. They became centers of reform and provided poor migrant workers with education, health services, and the organizational structure and knowledge to create voluntary associations. They could not, and did not, however, encourage labor organization. In the long run, they also served the needs of farmers rather than those of native-born farm workers. With the coming of the war and labor shortages, the camps subsidized the migration and settlement of foreign-born temporary farm workers.

In short, agricultural labor suffered under New Deal legislation. Although day-to-day living conditions improved for many migrant workers, these were short-term gains lost as the nation entered World War II. Overall, New Deal legislation institutionalized large farmers' power and stifled rank-and-file agricultural labor's militancy.

JOE TORRE

Bibliography

Bell, Thomas. *Out of This Furnace.* Pittsburgh: University of Pittsburgh Press, 1976.

Bernstein, Michael A. *The Great Depression: Delayed Recovery and Economic Change in America, 1929–1939.* New York: Cambridge University Press, 1987.

Brody, David. *Workers in Industrial America: Essays on the Twentieth Century Struggle.* New York: Oxford University Press, 1980.

Cohen, Lizabeth. *Making a New Deal: Industrial Workers in Chicago, 1919–1939.* New York: Cambridge University Press, 1990.

Dubofsky, Melvyn. *The State and Labor in Modern America.* Chapel Hill: University of North Carolina Press, 1994.

Dubofsky, Melvyn, ed. *The New Deal: Conflicting Interpretations and Shifting Perspectives.* New York: Garland, 1992.

Dubofsky, Melvyn, and Foster Rhea Dulles. *Labor in America: A History.* Wheeling, IL: Harlan Davidson, 1999.

Dubofsky, Melvyn, and Warren Van Tine. *John L. Lewis: A Biography.* Urbana and Chicago: University of Illinois Press, 1986.

Hahamovitch, Cindy. *The Fruits of Their Labor: Atlantic Coast Farmworkers and the Making of Atlantic Poverty, 1870–1945.* Chapel Hill: University of North Carolina Press, 1997.

Hofstadter, Richard. *The American Political Tradition.* New York: Vintage, 1948.

Kessler-Harris, Alice. *Out to Work: A History of Wage-Earning Women in the United States.* New York: Oxford University Press, 1983.

Leuchtenburg, William E. *Franklin D. Roosevelt and the New Deal, 1932–1940.* New York: Harper & Row, 1963.

Weber, Devra. *Dark Sweat, White Gold: California Farm Workers, Cotton and the New Deal.* Berkeley: University of California Press, 1994.

Zieger, Robert H. *American Workers, American Unions, 1920–1985.* Baltimore: Johns Hopkins University Press, 1986.

DAILY LIFE

The Great Depression (1929–41) posed daily challenges of subsistence, emotional insecurity, and technological change to millions of Americans in both city and countryside. Throughout the 1930s, urban and rural Americans adapted their everyday lives to meet these new demands; their increased mobility, communication, and ethnic interaction shaping a common culture out of shared financial hardships.

Certainly the Depression economy strained budgets across the country. While prices in general dropped 20 percent between 1929 and 1932, average family income shrank from $2,300 to $1,600 over the same period—more than a 30 percent decrease. Also, by 1932 nearly 25 percent of the population was unemployed, while those still working suffered wage cuts, reduced or extended workdays, and declining job conditions. Almost all Americans had to adjust their consumption in response to lower incomes.

While the Depression caused financial distress, it also affected morale and family relationships. Psychologically, Americans accustomed to poverty suffered less than the former middle class, which expected the satisfaction of adequate and steady earnings. These "new poor"—proponents of hard work and self-reliance—struggled to maintain their self-esteem in the face of unemployment, tight budgets, and charitable handouts. Even in relatively prosperous households, the anxiety of daily life increased: men, for instance, worried that unemployment, decreased income, or the acceptance of financial assistance proved their inadequacy, while middle-class women, unable to maintain their personal appearance through purchase of cosmetics, clothes, or even dental services, sometimes feared losing their husband's affection. With birth control priced beyond their budgets, many middle-class wives also feared pregnancy and the financial strain of additional children.

At the same time, affordable technology affected the style and price of living in both city and country. Automobiles, for instance, became faster, more efficient, and so accessible that by 1935 about 50 percent of families owned a car—though often an older vehicle painstakingly nursed. Radios fell in price from $133 in 1929 to $35 in 1933, with smaller models selling for $10, so that radio audiences more than doubled during the 1930s. Ownership of household appliances, such as refrigerators and vacuum cleaners, increased slightly during the Depression, beginning a transformation in domestic labor that would continue through the 1950s. Moreover, Depression manufacturers re-created ordinary items such as dishware, combs, and radio cases in colorful, inexpensive plastics and streamlined designs, gradually changing the appearance of American households over the course of the decade. The 1930s, therefore, not only affected the American attitude; they changed the American lifestyle.

URBAN LIFE

Economic conditions forced urbanites, like most other Americans, to cope with unemployment or underemployment. As a first step, they generally cashed in any insurance policies; when they had depleted their savings and insurance monies, they pawned possessions, sought credit with their landlord and grocer, and borrowed from friends and relatives. If unable to pay their current rent, families moved to older, cramped, and less expensive tenements. Some met payments through creative approaches: for example, African Americans in New York City's Harlem sometimes raised money through "rent parties" at which, for a donation of a quarter to a dollar toward the host's monthly bill, passersby could enjoy music, dancing, and home-brewed alcohol. Other urbanites looked for competitions—such as races, pie-eating contests, and dance marathons—through which they could win enough money to cover, perhaps, the next month's expenses. Adolescents, imitating the flag-sitters of the 1920s, sometimes sat in trees for days on end in the hope that impressed passersby would toss some change into a nearby collection box.

Migrants sitting in front of their shack of a home in 1936. For many Americans in the Great Depression, daily life was a grind of poverty, joblessness, and despair. *(Brown Brothers)*

Many people garnered cash by peddling fruit or other small, inexpensive items and services. Beginning in October 1930, the International Apple Shippers Association, then burdened with a surplus of apples, allowed individuals to purchase a box of seventy-two apples for $1.75–2.25 and sell them on the city streets for five cents apiece, for a profit (in theory) of $1.35–1.85. Thousands participated, although the cost of public transportation—about five cents per trip—and the inevitable damaged pieces probably reduced the profit to a dollar or less. Other people sold surplus onions or neckties, shined shoes, or peddled items such as Bibles and brushes from door to door. Still others, slightly less enterprising, dutifully sought employment each morning and spent afternoons reading in the public library, which improved their education and occasionally inspired attempts at novel-writing.

In spite of their efforts, however, many urbanites could not make rent or mortgage payments. Evictions were common: over 20 percent of urban homeowners defaulted on their mortgages between 1929 and 1934, while, in at least eleven cities, the foreclosure rate surpassed 40 percent. Indignant neighbors sometimes protested evictions and offered to share their house or apartment with their dispossessed friends. Overcrowding grew severe as two or more families crushed into one tiny tenement dwelling, in extreme cases sleeping in shifts for lack of bedding or floor space. If unable to find lodging with relatives or friends, dispossessed families lived as vagrants or settled in the shantytowns, known as "Hoovervilles," which sprang up outside of cities. There the very poorest of urbanites lived in tiny, makeshift shacks, often lined with tarpaper. Outdoor fires provided warmth, while breadlines or nearby garbage dumps sustained the residents.

As in previous decades, urbanites of southern and eastern European ethnicity found emotional support in their cultural enclaves composed of immigrant, first-

CANADA

NEW HAMPSHIRE 5.6%
VERMONT -0.1%
MAINE 6.2%

WASHINGTON 11.1%

MONTANA 4.1%

NORTH DAKOTA -5.7%

MINNESOTA 8.9%

NEW YORK 7.1%

MASSACHUSETTS 1.6%

OREGON 14.2%

IDAHO 17.9%

SOUTH DAKOTA -7.2%

WISCONSIN 6.8%

MICHIGAN 8.5%

RHODE ISLAND 3.8%
CONNECTICUT 6.4%
NEW JERSEY -4.5%

WYOMING 11.2%

PENNSYLVANIA 2.8%

IOWA 2.7%

NEBRASKA -4.5

OHIO 3.9%

INDIANA 5.8%

WEST VIRGINIA 10.0%

DELAWARE 11.8%
MARYLAND 11.6%
D.C. 36.2%

NEVADA 21.1%

UTAH 8.4%

COLORADO 8.4%

ILLINOIS 3.5%

VIRGINIA 10.6%

CALIFORNIA 21.7%

KANSAS -4.3%

MISSOURI 4.3%

KENTUCKY 8.8%

NORTH CAROLINA 12.7%

ARIZONA 14.6%

NEW MEXICO 25.6%

OKLAHOMA -2.5%

ARKANSAS 5.1%

TENNESSEE 11.4%

SOUTH CAROLINA 9.3%

ATLANTIC OCEAN

PACIFIC OCEAN

MISSISSIPPI 8.7%

ALABAMA 7.1%

GEORGIA 7.4%

TEXAS 10.1%

LOUISIANA 12.5%

FLORIDA 29.2%

Gulf of Mexico

MEXICO

Population Growth, 1930–1940
- Above 20 percent
- 10.0–19.9 percent
- 5.0–9.9 percent
- 0–4.9 percent
- Population loss

0   250   500 Miles
0   250   500 Kilometers

(CARTO-GRAPHICS)

generation, and second-generation Americans. The immediate presence of extended family and others from the same cultural region provided residents with a sense of stability, sources of personal and financial help, community-based institutions tailored to residents' specific needs, and, in a time of failing enterprises and unemployment, sources of self-esteem that were separate from financial matters. However, in spite of the enclaves' unique benefits, their erosion, already underway, was accelerated by Depression-era conditions. Financial necessity pushed ethnics to look beyond their neighborhood for employment and cheaper housing, promoting a greater cultural mix in the workplace and in residential patterns. Institutions such as banks and mutual aid societies, though formerly the community's financial basis, suffered for lack of funding. Meanwhile, entertainment and education encouraged ethnic youth to identify less with their parent culture and increasingly with America's developing popular culture. While southern and eastern European ethnic communities resisted outside pressures and provided valuable support structures, the Depression nevertheless decreased the

communities' population and encouraged the scattering of families throughout the United States.

By contrast, urban African-American communities swelled throughout the 1920s and 1930s as rural African Americans moved north in hope of employment and greater civil liberties. Concentrated in the poorest sections of the city, many African Americans lived in small tenement apartments or basements, often infested with vermin and equipped with inadequate or nonfunctional toilet facilities. Although living in substandard structures, African Americans generally paid more for their rent than whites of the same income level and often spent 40 to 50 percent of their earnings on rent alone. Since the majority of African-American men in cities remained jobless throughout the Depression, households often relied on women's labor for basic necessities. Reportedly many women stood on street corners, waiting to be hired for a day's domestic labor at a rate of ten to twenty cents per hour. Beginning in 1933, government welfare programs assisted many; previously, African-American churches had contributed most of the charitable aid available to urban African Americans.

RURAL LIFE

Despite the twentieth-century trend toward urbanization, by 1930 nearly half of all Americans still lived in communities with a population of 8,000 or less. Rural life changed rapidly during the 1930s, however, due to a depressed economy, the mechanization of farm labor, and greater access to transportation and electricity. In the late 1920s, agricultural prices had declined sharply, so that the drought and grasshopper plagues of 1930–34 descended upon midwestern families already in financial distress. The overall scarcity of money within the economy between 1929 and 1933 further impeded farmers' efforts not only to live, but to pay off mortgages contracted in more prosperous times. By 1933, over 40 percent of farm owners, unable to make their payments, lost their land—and with it, their livelihood. Dispossessed owners or tenants migrated to neighboring or even distant states to start afresh; others, more fortunate, managed to make mortgage or rent payments through strict economy and local or federal aid. Although New Deal agricultural programs doubled farm income between 1934 and 1940, property owners enjoyed the bulk of these gains, while tenants, share-croppers, and migrant families survived on public relief or their own low incomes.

The Works Progress Administration supported many households after 1935, although the wages were paltry: an Illinois family of seven received only $780 per year of WPA work relief. Those farmers who relied on state and local aid often fared worse, receiving family incomes averaging $24 per month in the late 1930s. Between 1937 and 1938, the relief board of a rural Minnesota community allowed one family $6 for rent, $14 for groceries, and $3.60 for milk each month, stipulating that no canned milk, butter, or condiments be purchased. Coming to terms, both financially and emotionally, with welfare and charitable handouts proved difficult for many recipients who upheld traditional agrarian ideals of self-reliance and independence.

As hard times forced the younger generation to look beyond their immediate families and localities for their livelihood, rural communities became depopulated in response to poverty. While before the Depression the children of farm owners could rely on parents to help them purchase land in the same community, during the 1930s even an eldest son could expect only to inherit his parents' mortgaged farm, while other children, perhaps, might receive only farm equipment or household supplies. In addition to this disappointment, the increasing mechanization of farm work, accelerated by federal programs, demanded that young farmers make greater initial investments in agricultural machinery. New Deal crop reduction programs further discouraged agricultural careers and, in lowering the demand for farm labor, displaced many southern sharecroppers. Not surprisingly, significant numbers of rural youth chose to leave their home counties during the Depression for work in cities or other farm communities. Women in particular sought suitable jobs, education, and marriage partners outside their parents' locality. Many African Americans moved to cities in the Midwest and New England, seeking employment and civil liberties.

While automobiles helped depopulate rural areas, they also decreased the isolation of rural life. No longer was it necessary to purchase supplies and services or sell products in the nearest town if another, though somewhat more distant, place offered better prices, more variety, or unique opportunities for entertainment. Moreover, the automobile enabled farmers to travel more frequently. Instead of going to town once a week or even once a month, during the Depression many farm families habitually went twice each week, usually on Wednesday and Saturday nights, and often for amusement as well as business. This new mobility strengthened the nationwide popular culture as rural residents increasingly enjoyed the same films, music, and magazines as urbanites did. Pinups and fan magazines appeared in rural stores. Groups of young men and women learned of the new dances at halls thirty or fifty miles from their hometown, far from the supervision of their families.

As the Depression progressed, many rural households gained access to utilities, due mainly to the work of the New Deal's Tennessee Valley Authority (1933) and the Rural Electrification Administration (1935). While roughly 10 percent of all rural homes used electrical power in 1930, nine years later one in four had electrical hookups; by 1942, 40 percent and, by 1946, 50 percent, enjoyed electrical access. These families—mainly white—began to update their homes with electric irons, washing machines, refrigerators, vacuum cleaners, and other devices that increased efficiency and reduced manual labor: as one rural woman wrote, "There is just as much to do on the farm as ever, but it is a lot easier to do it." The appearance of farmhouses also improved as utilities reduced the need for cisterns, smokehouses, outdoor privies, and other satellite structures.

In spite of drastic transformations in rural economics and society, much remained unchanged in the daily life of rural families in the Midwest and South. The farm remained the center of activity, with traditional men's and women's labor conducted in roughly the same space. Generally, the workday began at four or five in the morning and lasted until eight in the evening—or, as southern sharecroppers phrased it, "good sun till good dark"—though often indoor tasks, such as bookkeeping and mending, extended the day's labor well past suppertime for both genders. Rural African-Americans in the South worked a half-day on Saturday in addition to their weekday schedule. Neighbors cooperated to perform heavy labor such as haying, threshing, or building. In secluded communities, the exchange of labor and homemade products often made monetary transactions superfluous.

Raised to accept familial authority and discipline, rural children participated in their parents' work— hoeing weeds, harvesting fruit, caring for animals, and completing household tasks as their parents dictated. Tenant farmers in the South sent children into the field as soon as they were physically able so that they might contribute to the family income and acquire the necessary life skills; in the Midwest, children graduated from housework to barn and field work as they advanced in age. Often parents would place capable children in charge of daily tasks, such as caring for poultry or watering the mules. The pattern of familial responsibility continued even after young men and women left the family farm for other opportunities: young adults often sent money or supplies to their rural parents, and men joined the Civil Conservation Corps in order to help their parents financially.

Female labor continued to increase the rural family income and well-being. In the Midwest, women tended the kitchen garden, gathered eggs, churned butter, and preserved foods for the family or for sale in town; in the South, women helped in the fields as well as managed household matters. Women's labor often provided most of the household income for poverty-stricken families in the dust bowl.

While amenities generally improved for rural residents, African Americans experienced few positive changes in their quality of life during the Depression. In the South, they were legally segregated into substandard areas of the town, often divided from the Caucasians by railroad tracks or some other symbolic barrier. Throughout the Depression, rural African Americans remained largely without electricity and plumbing: by the late 1930s, less than 2 percent of African-American households in the rural South had electricity, and only 5 percent had running water.

FOOD AND DRINK

"People don't eat in the long run . . . ; they eat every day," Harry Hopkins emphasized to President Franklin D. Roosevelt's appropriations committee in 1933. And every day throughout the Depression era Americans of both the lower and middle classes took unusual measures—whether desperate or simply creative—to ensure that their dependents had enough food, and quality food.

During the 1930s, hunger posed a daily threat to the poorest Americans, both urban and rural, in spite of the dramatic plunges in grain and dairy prices that devastated farmers. In Arkansas, for example, a widow with seven children could muster only a pint of flour and a few chicken bones to feed her family; sharecroppers in Louisiana ate the oats intended for their livestock; a boy in Nashville, Tennessee, remembered a distasteful meal of dog food and potatoes. Four single, college-educated women subsisted on bananas, having read that bananas were the cheapest and most filling food available. Across the country, Hooverville residents flavored their cornmeal mulligan stew with scraps from garbage cans. Breadlines of up to 2,000 people in San Francisco, demonstrations in Chicago and New York City, and food riots in Detroit suggest that such desperation was common among America's lower classes between 1930 and 1935.

Many who accepted food relief during the Depression assert that the experience blurred distinctions of class and race, as young and old, white and African American, educated and uneducated, all waited together in line—or jockeyed for the most favorable position within the line. Reportedly, people nearest the front received mainly broth from the top of the soup tureen; those at the back received more meat and potatoes, but waited longer.

Even employed Americans, ineligible for welfare benefits, were forced to economize in order to find grocery money, occasionally in ways that injured their sense of decency and dignity. In Milwaukee, for instance, a Catholic family skimped on funeral expenses in order to purchase food, although this failure to honor the dead according to traditional standards deeply upset family members. Moreover, nearly all income levels developed innovative tricks, techniques, and substitutions designed to stretch their food—and food allowance—as far as possible. Ketchup mixed with a cup of hot water approximated tomato soup: this, taken free from restaurant tables, along with free crackers and a five-cent cup of coffee, could pass for a meal. In rural East Texas, women often made sausage from rabbit rather than from costly pork, mixing the ground meat with plenty of lard to stretch it still further. Farmers' wives canned, pickled, and preserved more foods for future use, precluding expensive trips to the local store. In general, shoppers bought margarine instead of butter and chose poultry over more expensive red meat. Jell-O, a dessert of flavored gelatin, served as a cheap after-dinner sweet.

In spite of their economizing, middle-class Americans generally consumed a greater variety and quality of food during the Depression than they had ten or twenty years earlier. Per capita consumption of milk, citrus fruits, juices, and spinach actually increased between 1917 and 1936, while from 1935 to 1939 Americans consumed twice as much fruit juice as in the 1920s. These dietary changes were due in part to the kitchen gardens maintained in both city and country and to the growing mass manufacture of inexpensive canned and frozen foods. However, the electric refrigerator's rising popularity had probably the greatest influence on the American diet during the Depression years. Though until 1930 the annual production of refrigerators failed to exceed the production of old-fashioned iceboxes, the continued extension of electrical lines, massive advertising campaigns, and lower prices increased the refrigerator's annual sales from 800,000 in 1930 to 2,300,000 in 1937. Suddenly a fixture in the middle-class kitchen, the refrigerator encouraged both economy and nutrition in families that could afford the initial investment, plus the ongoing cost of electricity.

Americans also consumed alcohol throughout the Depression, although the Twenty-first Amendment—the repeal of Prohibition—was not fully ratified until December 1933. With bootlegged whiskey priced from two to ten dollars per bottle, some households improvised their own, less expensive alcoholic beverages. Beer, for instance, was brewed at home, accompanied by eager discussion of the varieties of malt and yeast and the proper quantity of sugar. Some Americans also created "gin" by diluting bootlegged grain alcohol with water and flavoring the mixture with juniper drops obtained from the grocer or druggist. Such home concoctions tasted terrible at the very least and often endangered the consumer—although revelers quipped that any drink was safe that did not remove a fingernail dipped into it. In spite of their preoccupation with il-legal beverages, Americans did not celebrate the repeal of Prohibition on December 5, 1933, with quite the gusto expected by urban police departments: after a long process of ratification, Americans found the repeal anticlimactic, and many establishments did not actually receive alcohol shipments until days later. In New York City, restrained celebrations did not give way to wide-spread indulgence until New Year's eve.

RECREATION

With entertainment dollars scarce during the Depression, most Americans looked for simple and inexpensive ways to pass their free time. In general, prices favored the consumer as businesses struggled to entice frugal customers. In New York City, for example, a special outing could consist of dinner at a Greenwich Village restaurant for two dollars; dancing to a popular band (thirty to fifty cents); a movie opening (about thirty-five cents); or a subway trip to the beach at Coney Island or the Rockaways. The cheapest opera tickets cost a dollar; plays, fifty cents; nice hotels, about three dollars per day. Italian and Chinese food, being relatively inexpensive, increased in popularity.

Radio, the era's most popular diversion, occupied nearly 86 percent of American families daily by 1939, with most households listening an average of 4.5 hours each day. Adventure programs, music, comedy, and, beginning in 1933, President Roosevelt's fireside chats all boosted American morale, upholding basic family values and promoting a sense of national community.

At an average ticket price of thirty-five cents throughout the decade, movie shows provided an inexpensive escape from grim realities. While the luxurious movie palaces of the 1920s had declined, their simpler replacements, eager to offset decreasing profits, enticed the passerby with double features, giveaways, an expanded selection of refreshments, and, beginning in 1935, Technicolor films. The new movie houses drew audiences of 60 million Americans each week during the early 1930s and, in 1939, 85 million per week. In rural areas, families and peer groups drove regularly as far as thirty miles to the nearest cinema to see the latest Hollywood release, already enjoyed by vast numbers of urbanites in large theaters such as New York City's Roxy and the Radio City Music Hall. Fan magazines proliferated. Movie plots and actors set the fashion nationwide, as young girls bleached their hair in imitation of Jean Harlow, while Clark Gable's appearance in *It Happened One Night* (1934) made the man's undershirt optional.

Baseball also drew crowds, although the price of seats—over a dollar in the major-league ballparks—deterred many fans from attending, in spite of the attraction of celebrity athletes such as Babe Ruth and Joe DiMaggio. Some franchises, eager to stimulate sales, introduced night games and offered women and children free admission on specified days. Fearing that sports radio broadcasts further discouraged ballpark attendance, the New York Yankees, New York Giants, and the Brooklyn Dodgers all refused to broadcast their games by radio. In spite of such efforts and precautions, however, baseball crowds did not increase to 1929 levels until 1941. Nevertheless, the sport retained its charm as fans identified strongly with their local team and its star players, who, in spite of celebrity status, appeared hardworking and accessible to ordinary Americans. Many fans gathered at railway stations to see their team off or welcome them home. Major league baseball remained segregated in the 1930s, but black athletes, such as Satchel Page and Josh Gibson, flourished in the Negro Leagues.

Besides baseball, many sporting events competed for Americans' attention, including professional and collegiate football, basketball, hockey, and boxing. The latter appealed especially to migrants from Oklahoma who, pouring into California throughout the 1930s, arranged local matches that occasionally featured female boxers. Both urban and rural African Americans closely followed the career of boxer Joe Louis through radio and newspaper accounts. In collegiate athletics, the successes of Notre Dame's football team became a point of pride for Catholics across the country.

Overall, the Great Depression's economic, social, and technological changes had tremendous impact on daily life throughout the United States, blurring class differences and encouraging the formation of a mainstream American culture. This common culture would further cohere during World War II and in time would dominate the 1950s postwar prosperity.

RAE SIKULA

Bibliography

Markowitz, Gerald, and David Rosner, eds. *"Slaves of the Depression": Workers' Letters about Life on the Job.* Ithaca, NY: Cornell University Press, 1987.

McElvaine, Robert S. *The Great Depression: America 1929–1941.* New York: Times Books, 1993.

McGovern, James R. *And a Time for Hope: Americans in the Great Depression.* Westport, CT: Praeger, 2000.

Phillips, Cabell. *The New York Times Chronicle of American Life: From the Crash to the Blitz, 1929–1939.* London: Macmillan, 1969.

Sternsher, Bernard, ed. *Hitting Home: The Great Depression in Town and Country.* Chicago: Quadrangle Books, 1970.

Terkel, Studs. *Hard Times: An Oral History of the Great Depression.* New York: Pantheon Books, 1970.

Watkins, T. H. *The Hungry Years: A Narrative History of the Great Depression in America.* New York: Henry Holt, 1999.

INTERNATIONAL AFFAIRS

World War I and the Great Depression, although separated by a decade, were inextricably linked in the minds of the American public and U.S. leaders alike. Traditional suspicion of "entangling" alliances was reasserted in response to the destructiveness of world war. The nation's dependence on and vulnerability to a free and unmanaged international economy had proven, with the crash of 1929, to be just as unstable and dangerous to peace and prosperity. The traditional view that wealth would most reliably increase if the market was left unfettered by government lost its persuasiveness when the full impact of the Great Depression hit. The atmosphere of suspicion and insecurity was reflected in the international community. Moreover, the United States had moved into more central focus in the deliberations of foreign leaders and was almost universally recognized as having become a great power. Some saw in the United States a possible alternative model to the one that had swept Europe into a war that left both winners and losers weak and vulnerable; others believed that the dramatic economic development of the United States was the result of an advantage unfairly enjoyed by a nation that had been slow to respond to the dire need of natural allies. Similarly, foreign critics claimed that the United States had pursued economic dominance without accepting the leadership responsibility believed to come with it.

All of these concerns forced policy-makers to reconsider U.S. goals and approaches to international relations. This period is often described as the high water mark of "isolationism," but this is a misnomer, as the period from 1920 to the onset of World War II witnessed a shifting approach to foreign relations, not a rejection of them.

BACKGROUND: THE 1920s

At the conclusion of World War I, the American president, Woodrow Wilson, had taken the lead in articulating the need for an international approach to conflict resolution. He believed that the growing sophistication of the international economy and an improved international infrastructure, based largely on recent advances in communication, meant that all nations would henceforth be collective victims to any international disorder. His solution was articulated in the Fourteen Points, a set of specific principles of international relations, including the formation of a League of Nations capable of collectively ensuring that the principles were honored. Wilson emphasized the importance of national self-determination, the international rule of law, and the belief that international economic development was essential to peace and could truly flourish only under nonpreferential free trade and progressive democracy. Many Americans agreed with these principles, but balked at the assertion that the League of Nations would serve as a defensive alliance. The postwar sentiment was expressly opposed to collective security arrangements that could draw the United States into European wars. In the end, Wilson was unwilling to compromise his principles to allay fears of military commitment, and the newly Republican Congress voted against U.S. participation in the League.

Despite firm opposition to collective security arrangements, the United States took an active role in defining the postwar international peace by championing strict armament reductions during the Washington Naval Conference of 1921–22 and encouraging regional collective security arrangements in Asia, Europe, and Latin America. In a series of attempts to promote a peace that meant something more permanent than the absence of war, the United States tried to alleviate the financial crisis in postwar Europe. This took the form of direct aid—as in the $66 million worth of food sent to Russia—despite the official policy of nonrecognition for the revolutionary government. At the heart of the crisis was the German economy, which had been devastated by the war and crippled by heavy reparation demands. At the 1924 London Conference, the United States effectively agreed to subsidize German recovery with an initial loan of $110 million.

This signaled the beginning of a rapid expansion of U.S. private investment abroad. The ultimate impact of this investment continues to foster a debate about developmentalism and dependency. In Europe, development and dependency seemed particularly linked, since the German war debt could be serviced only with the continued flow of dollars into the European community. In 1929, an American banker, Owen Young, devised the Young Plan, which renegotiated German reparations and demonstrated the importance of the United States to the international economy.

On the eve of the Depression, the United States had begun to take an even more active role in creating a stable international order. The early 1920s had witnessed a "Red Scare" and a general fear that revolutionary nationalism could undermine the security of a peaceful community of nations. The fears of direct attacks on U.S. capital interests abroad, the spread of Russian communism to less developed nations, and subversion of U.S. liberties at home through propaganda began to dissipate as U.S. officials sought to reach accommodations with China and Mexico. The United States further sought to reassure the world that its antagonism toward disruptive revolutions did not mean that foreign self-determination would be challenged in the name of democratic liberty, no matter how connected U.S. leaders believed the two ideas to be. The principles of Wilson's peace proposals were reaffirmed in the 1928 assertion of the undersecretary of state, J. Reuben Clark, that the Monroe Doctrine did not justify interventionism in Latin America. Charles A. Lindbergh's 1927 goodwill tour and president-elect Herbert Hoover's visit to Latin America served to articulate the idea that the United States sought to be a "good neighbor." This internationalist approach was perhaps most clearly stated in the 1928 Kellogg-Briand Pact, which condemned the recourse to war and asserted its universal unacceptability as an instrument of international relations. The fact that the Soviet Union and the United States were both signatories to the pact seemed to bode well for future peace.

FOREIGN RELATIONS AND ECONOMIC CRISIS

Efforts to establish international cooperation were dramatically challenged in October 1929. The stock market crash resulted in a destructive downturn in the U.S. economy with devastating repercussions throughout much of the world. Overproduction, irresponsible speculation, and consumer debt spending had not only spurred the collapse, but now created a crisis of faith in the basic assumptions of capitalist expansion. In any case, there was little cash available to jump-start the stalled economy, and foreign dependence on U.S. investments resulted in the spread of the economic shock. The internationalist assumption that multilateral free trade would promote peace and prosperity gave way to its opposite: protectionism, preferential blocs, and managed currencies. Not only was the U.S. economy in shambles, but so was the international order it had sought to promote.

The Republican Congress, seeing the international economy as a threat to domestic stabilization, passed the Smoot-Hawley tariff bill in June 1930. The bill raised tariff rates on most imported goods in the hope of stimulating domestic production. The tariff wall that was erected against foreign imports prevented Europe from making payments on its war debts with goods imported by the United States. Despite the overwhelmingly negative response from professional economists, who warned against the new tariff's potential to deepen the financial crisis and undermine the stabilizing effects of international economic cooperation, President Hoover did not veto it. European nations responded in kind, creating an atmosphere of competitive economic isolation. In particular, Britain created a system of imperial preference between herself and her colonies that led other nations to seek protection in economic blocs.

In 1931, the financial crisis worsened as first Austria and then Germany experienced massive failures of their banking systems, which made it impossible for those nations to continue payments on their war debts. Without German payments of reparations to France, France could not continue her own debt payments to the United States. Confronted with a mounting European crisis, Hoover proposed a one-year moratorium on all war debts and reparations. After the French were persuaded to accept this one-year "holiday," the Hoover moratorium was met with enthusiasm on both sides of the Atlantic: Europeans gained a sudden increase in purchasing power, and private U.S. investors in European war recovery had reason to hope that they might see continuing returns after all. In fact, a number of prominent U.S. businessmen urged a simple cancellation of war debts owed to the United States, but this view could not win popular support when the treasury was empty and unemployment was rising.

War debts and reparations remained a focal point, however, as Hoover met with the French premier in 1931 to discuss the possibility of reducing the debts. A group of debtor nations, meeting in Lausanne, Switzerland, in 1932 to renegotiate debt payments, recommended a reduction of German reparations from $32 billion to $714 million. This proposed reduction met with a popular outcry in the United States against a perceived foreign conspiracy to have U.S. citizens foot the bill for Germany's misdeeds. Hoover echoed public sentiment when he asserted that the war debt situation was a European problem. Later that year, Hoover met with president-elect Franklin D. Roosevelt to address the European debt problem, but Roosevelt, too, saw the problem as tangential to the real crisis at home.

In his first year in office, President Roosevelt sought to stabilize the national economy by exercising greater governmental control over foreign economic relations. The internationalist principles of the 1920s had given away to the nationalism of the Depression. No longer did the U.S. government have faith that undirected free trade would result in increasing prosperity and stability worldwide. In 1933, European leaders met in London at the World Economic Conference in the hope of cooperating in stabilizing international exchange rates. President Hoover had supported this goal and further sought to reestablish the gold standard. Roosevelt, however, rejected the notion of linking the dollar to foreign currencies because it would limit his ability to respond aggressively to the needs of the domestic economy. Later in that same year, Roosevelt rejected the efforts of his secretary of state, Cordell Hull, to promote a hemispheric free-trade system at the Pan-American Conference in Montevideo.

The private sector also moved away from the strategies of a liberal free market. In the face of protectionist tariffs, nationalist price and exchange rate regulations, quotas, and neomercantilist cartels, U.S. private interests sought to protect their foreign investments through participation in cartels designed to stabilize international prices. Investments in primary industries like mining and agriculture were hit the hardest as surpluses languished without markets. U.S. investors in foreign countries participated in international agreements that functioned as industry monopolies capable of artificially maintaining profitably high prices. At times, the high tariffs of the 1930s served to stimulate U.S. foreign investments while protecting U.S. domestic industry. For instance, high tariffs and low quotas for American oil exports promoted energy self-sufficiency at home while effectively protecting U.S. private investments in foreign oil sources. Although the value of U.S. foreign trade dropped from $9.5 billion in 1929 to $3 billion in 1932 and the U.S. government pursued economic policy designed to limit dependency on the international market, private companies found

ways to survive the Depression that had a profound impact on international affairs.

NEUTRALITY AND INTERNATIONAL DISORDER

Japan created the most immediate challenge to international security. Throughout the 1920s, the United States had been a major player in international efforts to substitute disarmament treaties for the false security of large national arsenals among the great powers. The 1921–22 Washington Conference had resulted in an agreement to establish a tonnage ratio of 10:10:6:3:3 for Britain, the United States, Japan, France, and Italy. Further, it was agreed that Japan would withdraw from Siberia and leave China open to international trade. Japan challenged this ratio as jeopardizing the security of its Pacific interests, and the major powers, meeting in London in 1930, worked out a compromise position granting part of Japan's requested quota increase. The Japanese navy, however, argued that the compromise was an unacceptable affront to national sovereignty and revealed the civilian government's weakness.

The situation grew more severe when conflicts escalated between Chinese and Japanese military forces in Manchuria. The Japanese Kwangtung army had been stationed in Manchuria since 1905, when it had wrested control over the region from Russia. When Kwangtung soldiers blew up a portion of the South Manchurian Railway in 1931, the ensuing clashes were used to justify an expanded Japanese presence in the region. The Chinese looked to the League of Nations for some action in keeping with the principle of collective security. The league proved willing to do little more than issue statements encouraging a diplomatic solution to the conflict, so the Chinese turned to the United States. Secretary of State Henry L. Stimson initially believed that the Japanese civilian government would honor the Washington Conference treaties and would be able to control the Kwangtung army. This was not the case, however, and Japan made further territorial advances into China. By 1932, the Japanese had conquered southern Manchuria. Stimson then issued his famous statement that the U.S. government would not recognize any territorial or administrative changes that the Japanese forced on China. The League of Nations, following suit, refused to recognize the legitimacy of any advances in Japanese territorial and political control of Manchuria. Japan left the league and the Kwangtung army consolidated its control in Manchuria.

The Great Depression had placed economic issues

squarely in the center of international relations. The closing of national economic borders forced the world's foreign policy makers to redefine the basic assumptions and goals of the international order. U.S. economic nationalism had been intended only as a temporary solution to a major crisis, however, that never entirely obscured the essential connections between the United States and the rest of the world. Both Hoover and Roosevelt viewed Japanese territorial aggression in China, Russian communism, increasing European nationalism, and a growing Latin American anti-Yankee orientation as matters requiring clear responses from the United States. By 1933, it seemed to U.S. policymakers that the free market and democracy were under general attack as nations around the world turned toward centralized authorities that promised to increase employment, income, security, and national pride. These, of course, were the very promises that Roosevelt himself claimed that the New Deal programs would meet. Expanded federal programs designed to alleviate the poverty caused by the Depression depended on the cooperation of party politicians and private businessmen alike in order to defend against attacks that the New Deal had undermined liberal democracy in favor of state planning. More importantly, the new regulatory activities of the government were not used to limit the basic freedoms of expression and assembly at home as totalitarian regimes were doing abroad.

During Roosevelt's first term, the United States sought less to promote peace through active cooperation than to protect itself from possible conflicts through a posture of nonintervention and neutrality. The Good Neighbor policy, neutrality acts, and withdrawal of nonrecognition as a diplomatic tool were all designed to establish that the United States did not seek to direct the political fates of foreign nations and would not be responsible for them. This approach kept the United States out of the center of the developing conflicts, but also meant that Washington was willingly relinquishing a formal leadership role.

In his first inaugural address, Roosevelt stated what came to be known as the Good Neighbor policy: "In the field of world policy I would dedicate this nation to the policy of the good neighbor—the neighbor who resolutely respects himself and, because he does so, respects the sanctity of his agreements in and with a world of neighbors." This policy had particular significance for U.S. relations with Latin America, where a long tradition of U.S. military interventions had undermined the credibility of attempts to promote liberal democracies in the hemisphere and had caused many Latin American nations to seek alternative trade partners in the belief that economic ties to the United States would bring political and military backing in their wake. Roosevelt did leave troops in the Canal Zone and Guantanamo Bay—which both belonged to the United States—but confirmed Clark's assertion that the United States would no longer invoke the Monroe Doctrine to intervene in Latin American affairs by withdrawing U.S. troops from former protectorates in order to allow Latin Americans to direct their own destinies. The United States left, however, newly established National Guard contingents officially designated to provide protection for their constitutional rights.

Efforts to reduce regional mistrust of the United States also included assurances against political interventions. In 1930, Mexico's foreign secretary, Genaro Estrada, asserted that no country should use or withhold recognition of a foreign government in order to affect the political destiny and national sovereignty of foreign nations. The policy of refusing to employ either direct military or indirect political intervention resulted in a passive response when Rafael Leonidas Trujillo Molina used the National Guard in 1930 to seize power in the Dominican Republic and Anastasio Somoza did the same in Nicaragua in 1937. Many Americans felt uncomfortable with the seeming impossibility of steering a diplomatic course between interventionism and tolerance of totalitarian regimes. Tolerance was implied by continuing trade in those countries, however, and Roosevelt contented himself with the telling observation that Somoza "may be a bastard, but he's our bastard."

The United States recognized the Soviet Union in 1933 in part to maintain a consistently neutral policy toward foreign governments, but also to encourage trade, which had declined dramatically in the previous two years. This was not a radical break with tradition, however. Despite official nonrecognition of Soviet leadership, the United States had continued a brisk trade and active investment in the Russian economy since the end of World War I. By 1928, nearly one-quarter of all foreign investments in Russia came from American interests. Trade may have been less significant to recognition than a desire to deter Japanese expansion into China. Good relations between the Soviet Union and the United States were fleeting. By 1935, political purges under Joseph Stalin created an increasingly suspicious atmosphere between the two countries, and cooperative international arrangements were unacceptable to the U.S. government. The Soviet Union tried to forge an international alliance against fascism during the Comintern Congress of 1935, but the United States viewed it as a propaganda initiative designed to grant legitimacy to international socialism.

Rising international tensions pushed the United States to declare its neutral posture formally in the Neutrality Act of 1935, which outlawed the sale of arms to belligerent nations. Despite a traditional insistence on the right of neutrals to trade freely with all nations, this new definition of neutrality was intended to keep the United States out of any possible entanglements.

THE COMING WAR

Although the Roosevelt administration continued to seek ways to protect U.S. economic interests without becoming entangled in power politics, the mounting European tension had become obvious by 1933 when Adolf Hitler came to power. Hitler and the Nazi leadership aroused a paranoid and aggressive variant of German nationalism by playing on the economic crisis fueled by the Depression and anger at what was seen as the oppressive reparations debts and moral culpability assigned to Germany by the victors of World War I. To this paranoia were added racist promises of a German destiny in which Jews and Slavs would give way before the advancing forces of Aryan supremacy. Hitler quickly withdrew Germany from the League of Nations and sought to make an advantage of the fact that international cooperative arrangements had weakened during the Depression. He did this first by blatantly defying disarmament agreements as he rapidly developed German military forces. Britain and France chose a strategy of "appeasement" in the hopes of allaying German fears, welcoming it back into the ranks of the great powers, and avoiding another world war.

The postwar dream of maintaining international organizations capable of enforcing cooperation and collective action was further challenged when Italy's Fascist dictator Benito Mussolini invaded Ethiopia in 1935. The League of Nations officially supported Haile Selassie's cause against Italian annexation and imposed an embargo against the shipment of war matériel to Italy. Again hoping to satisfy the appetite of an aggressive nation, the league lifted the embargo a year later, hoping that a sacrificed Ethiopia might allow peace in Europe. Hitler and Mussolini were convinced that the conciliatory responses from the league's great powers demonstrated their weakness and lack of resolve to protect anything beyond their own limited interests. With no viable deterrent, Hitler confidently invaded the Rhineland, a demilitarized zone between France and Belgium. The French and Belgians were unwilling

to challenge German troops in an open confrontation, and the international community did nothing. The United States, too, chose to remain outside of the conflict by claiming that German activity in the Rhineland did not directly violate the 1921 treaty that the United States had signed with Germany.

In 1936, General Francisco Franco led a nationalist uprising against the republican government of Spain, which quickly developed into a civil war of international consequences. The British and French led an international Non-Intervention Committee guaranteeing that the twenty-seven participating nations would stay out of the Spanish conflict. The United States did not participate, but did encourage the international community to assert neutrality by placing embargoes on war shipments to either faction in Spain. Nonetheless, Germany and Italy supported Franco with military supplies, the Soviet Union and Mexico supported the Republicans, and 3,000 U.S. volunteers went to Spain to support the republican cause. The Spanish Civil War catalyzed the division of the world into competing camps: By the end of 1936, Germany had allied with Italy under the Rome-Berlin Axis and with both Italy and Japan in the Anti-Comintern Pact, which identified Soviet Russia as a common enemy. Nationalist dictatorships of the Right had aligned formally against the Communist dictatorship of the Left. The liberal democracies remained uncertain how to ensure the peace. The first victory went to the Right, since continuing German and Italian support to Spain's fascist forces helped Franco win power in 1939.

Despite these signals, the newly elected prime minister of England, Neville Chamberlain, continued a conciliatory strategy with Germany. In 1938, Hitler forcibly annexed Austria and began the systematic oppression of Austrian Jews. This did not overly worry the other great powers, as Austria was seen as essentially German in national culture and political orientation. In what has become known as an infamous meeting in Munich in September 1938, Britain and France attempted, one last time, to appease Hitler's territorial appetite by allowing Germany to annex the Sudetenland. But Hitler was not appeased and conquered all of Czechoslovakia and Poland in 1939. These invasions were a death blow to the peace that had been guaranteed by the Versailles treaties. In a diplomatic coup, Hitler signed a nonaggression pact with Stalin, effectively keeping the Soviet Union out of German conflicts with France and Britain and avoiding a two-front war. Stalin had given up the role as champion of the antifascist nations, unaware that the Axis powers had a defense pact against the Soviet Union.

THE UNITED STATES AND THE ALLIES

Totalitarian states had outmaneuvered the European democracies, and the United States began to take a more assertive role in international affairs than it had in the previous decade. Roosevelt's first concern was that German and Italian colonization in Europe and Africa might soon turn to Latin America. Soon after his reelection in 1936, Roosevelt met with Latin American leaders in Buenos Aires in order to "consult for our mutual safety and our mutual good." This mention of safety as a cause for international cooperation was a small first step toward wartime collaborations. Next, Roosevelt began to build a government-sponsored system of international cultural exchange. This had been left to private enterprise during the 1920s, but the Axis propaganda strategies had shifted the exchange and production of cultural expressions into the purview of diplomacy and even national security. In 1938, the United States established the Division of Cultural Relations as an agency within the State Department and charged it with advancing cultural relations between the United States and Latin America in order to defend against Nazi propaganda there. The Mexican expropriation of U.S. oil interests that year almost led to disaster when Mexican president Lazaro Cardenas responded to U.S. economic sanctions by offering to sell Mexican oil to Germany and Italy. The United States backed down and the two countries worked out an agreement that offered fair compensation for U.S. oil companies and a Mexican promise of regional solidarity in response to European aggression.

Hitler was not concerned that the United States would intervene against his expansionist plans. He believed that U.S. neutrality was the product of American economic and social crises and that U.S. leaders were hobbled by their need for popular support of foreign policy initiatives. When European war broke out in September 1939, Roosevelt reasserted American neutrality. Privately, however, he lamented that no nation seemed able or willing to save civilization from totalitarian forces. After the attempted appeasement of Hitler in Munich in 1938, Roosevelt had begun building up the U.S. armed forces to ensure the national defense including the production of ten thousand new warplanes annually. Strict neutrality gave way to new strategies as Roosevelt secretly received orders for planes from the British and French governments, joined in a joint declaration of hemispheric defense, and loaned $25 million to China for defense against the Japanese. These strategies became overt when Congress re-sponded to the German invasion of Poland by amending the Neutrality Act to allow Britain and France to purchase U.S. arms on a cash-and-carry basis after Roosevelt had urged the nation to deter aggression through any and all means short of war.

In September 1939, after the Pan-American Conference in Panama City, the United States declared a 300-mile neutral zone off the coast from Maine to Argentina. U.S. naval patrols soon began coordinating with British naval intelligence to ensure the safe passage of merchant vessels crossing the Atlantic. The war in Europe quickly escalated as Finland fell to Soviet forces in the Winter War of 1939–1940 and France fell to Germany in the summer of 1940.

Well before the Japanese attacked Pearl Harbor, Roosevelt realized that the United States would eventually enter the war. He knew that the victors of the war, not neutrals, would have a role in forging a new international order. Roosevelt responded to Allied defeats in Europe with the lend-lease agreement, under which Britain received old U.S. destroyers in exchange for British naval bases in the Western Hemisphere. By making the exchange an executive agreement, Roosevelt avoided congressional debate on the issue. It was clear that the president was preparing for war, however, when Roosevelt initiated the first peacetime conscription in U.S. history with the 1940 Selective Training and Service Act. Nonetheless, popular sentiment was staunchly against any military commitment that went beyond national defense. The draft could be viewed as necessary preparedness against possible Nazi aggression, and the lend-lease agreement was eventually made into a bill with congressional support because the naval bases were deemed vital to hemispheric security. By 1941, Congress granted the president the right to sell, lend, or lease war supplies to any nation that the president identified as vital to national security.

Now that Congress had allowed the shipment of arms to Allied forces under naval escort, U.S. merchant vessels became a target of German submarine warfare. Germany and the United States seemed on the brink of war. When a U.S. destroyer was attacked by a German submarine in fall 1940, Roosevelt ordered the U.S. navy to fire on German and Italian vessels that ventured into the defensive zone. Undeclared warfare had begun.

It was, however, relations with Japan that led the United States to a declaration of war. While Japanese forces were establishing an independent government in Manchuria, the United States continued to trade with both China and Japan. This trade ended when Japan invaded southeast Asia in 1940. British and Dutch colonial possessions as well as Chinese borders were threatened by this bold move. The United States responded by cutting off oil sales to Japan and extending lend-lease aid to the Soviet Union in the hope of checking Japanese advances.

The dual conflicts in Europe and Asia led, in August 1941, to a secret meeting between President Roosevelt and British Prime Minister Winston Churchill in which they articulated Allied war aims and set down the foundational principles of the postwar peace. The emphasis was placed on territorial sovereignty, political self-determination, anticolonialism, open commerce, higher living standards worldwide, the freedom from want and fear, the end of Nazi tyranny, and the abandonment of force as a diplomatic tool. These principles were repeated in a note sent by Secretary of State Cordell Hull to Japan indicating that Japan should cease its pursuit of territorial aggrandizement if it hoped to avoid a war with the United States. The Japanese received the "Hull note" as an ultimatum and responded,

on December 7, 1941, with the attack on Pearl Harbor. The next day the United States declared war on Japan.

NICHOLAS MAHER

Bibliography

Dallek, Robert. *Franklin D. Roosevelt and American Foreign Policy, 1932–1945*. New York: Oxford University Press, 1995.

Gellman, Irwin. *Good Neighbor Diplomacy: United States Policies in Latin America, 1933–1945*. Baltimore: Johns Hopkins University Press, 1979.

Iriye, Akira. *The Globalizing of America, 1913–1945*. Vol. 3 of *The Cambridge History of American Foreign Relations*, New York: Cambridge University Press, 1993.

Offner, Arnold. *American Appeasement: United States Foreign Policy and Germany, 1933–1938*. New York: W. W. Norton 1969.

Rosenberg, Emily S. *Spreading the American Dream: American Economic and Cultural Expansion, 1890–1945*. New York: Hill & Wang, 1982.

PART II
GENERAL ENTRIES

INTRODUCTION TO PART II

Part II of *Encyclopedia of the Great Depression and the New Deal* contains entries on a host of different subjects. (For entries on government, see Part III; for entries on international affairs and foreign policy, see Part IV; for biographies, see Part V; and for original historical documents, see Part VI.)

Part II includes entries on population sectors, such as ethnic groups (some examples: African Americans, Native Americans), gender (women), and age groups (youth and elderly). There are entries on politics, including parties (Communist, Republican), events (fireside chats, hunger marches), advocacy groups (March on Washington Movement, Unemployed Councils), and federal elections (1930 through 1940). Labor is discussed in entries on unions and union federations (Trade Union Unity League, United Automobile Workers) and strikes (general and sit-down). Business is handled with entries on important companies (Ford, U.S. Steel), economic sectors (banking, railroads), and trade associations and groupings (Delta Council, "little steel"). And there are entries on sociological, political, and economic phenomena (charity, crime, fascism).

Finally, a significant portion of the entries in Part II is devoted to culture, in the broadest sense of the word. There are general entries on the various branches of the arts (fine art, music) and different types of media (feature films, radio). Also included are entries on specific cultural and media productions (generally, those that were created or especially popular in the 1930s). This category includes films (*Scarface, The Wizard of Oz*), comics (*Li'l Abner, Superman*), radio shows (*Amos 'n' Andy, The War of the Worlds*), fiction (*The Grapes of Wrath, Tobacco Road*) and nonfiction (*How to Win Friends and Influence People, Let Us Now Praise Famous Men*), theatrical companies and productions (*The Group Theatre, Porgy and Bess*), magazines (*Life, Saturday Evening Post*), and, to use a late twentieth-century term, media events (the Dionne quintuplets, the *Hindenburg* disaster).

As this long list indicates, the 1930s—for all of its economic woes—was one of the most dynamic and creative in the nation's history, full of new art, new politics, new organizations, and new ideas.

ADVERTISING AND CONSUMPTION

While the 1930s marked the worst economic period in United States history, the period between the stock market crash and World War II ushered in a new social culture of consumption in the United States. During this time, business, industry, advertising, and the federal government changed the population from a society of producers into a society of consumers.

The origins of Great Depression–era consumption stem from late nineteenth-century rapid industrialization. From this period through World War I, the industrial fabrication of domestic goods and later war supplies created the demand for labor and attracted a multitude of workers to the heavy manufacturing centers in the northeast. With the armistice in November 1918, U.S. industrial conditions changed dramatically. The ending of war production and a flooded labor market resulted in high unemployment and a brief economic depression. Despite this temporary economic decline, industry promptly retooled and began production and marketing of consumable goods. Earmarks of consumption during this decade of prosperity, popularly known as the Roaring Twenties, included the automobile, speakeasies, flappers, and an abundance of new domestic products—all fueled by government-endorsed unsound margin investing. While these earmarks seemed to depict the whole of American society, the majority of the population worked in either industry or agriculture and generally consumed only a nominal portion of the goods produced. Many industrial leaders such as Henry Ford encouraged employees to purchase manufactured goods by paying higher wages for longer hours and increased production. Despite these approaches, more than 70 percent of Americans were not partaking of this new wealthier and more comfortable lifestyle but were living off what they earned and saving a mere 5 percent of their earnings.

This disparity between production and consumption by the majority of Americans facilitated the nationwide economic collapse. As the total numbers of consumables reached saturation point within the market, production declined. This led to the closing of plants, increased unemployment, and the decay of consumer and investor confidence in a once robust economy. In October 1929, these factors culminated in the stock market crash. President Herbert Hoover and many economists initially believed that the sell-off was merely a necessary period of economic adjustment. Rather than an adjustment, the catalyst behind the economic collapse was the failure of the greater population to consume the goods it produced.

Nationally, between 1929 and 1935, family income dropped 35 percent, from an average of $2,300 to $1,500 annually. For the economy to stabilize, business and industry needed the population to spend its limited financial resources. Fortunately, during the 1920s, industrial production created the framework for the mass consumption of goods. By 1927, businesses and advertisers established a national identity and encouraged consumption through popular culture, easier communications, and wider product selection. Radios with standard AC plugs and the advent of national broadcasting networks provided music, news, and popular shows that surpassed regional and ethnic boundaries. The setting of the first transatlantic telephone line between New York and London and the running of overland lines between New York and San Francisco instantly connected the nation and the world. Consumer choices expanded in all areas of production, from textiles and clothing to automobiles: Henry Ford abandoned the strictly black Model T in favor of the Model A in various colors. While business, industry, and entertainment created the context for a national economy, they now faced the formidable task of changing the public's purchasing patterns in an attempt to solidify a national culture of mass consumption.

EFFORTS TO INCREASE CONSUMPTION

After 1929, the task of getting the population to spend what monies it did have fell to Madison Avenue and advertising. To accomplish this, advertisers created marketing strategies that drew upon the needs, desires, and societal views of the population. Depression marketing initially focused on providing techniques to feed the population. Magazines and newspapers maintained circulation by printing "Depression Recipes" that explained how to provide for the nutritional needs of a family of five for as little as $8 a week.

To encourage consumption beyond the basics, advertisers concentrated on the elements of limited re-

Despite the economic depression, radios continued to be a best-selling appliance in the 1930s. *(Library of Congress)*

sources, morality, and escapism. Advertising itself took on a new and distinctive look of bold lettering accentuated with two-tone or black-and-white photographs. This approach was a dramatic contrast to the smooth, flowing text and colors of the 1920s. Advertisers educated themselves as to the values and views of the population by moving to targeted areas. Ad writers moved into mining towns, industrial neighborhoods, and other communities to better understand the problems facing consumers. Termed "Advertising in Overalls" in *Advertising and Selling*, marketing directly communicated products with the appropriate lingo, diction, and style of the prospective buyer.

Another important advertising approach encouraged buyers to spend by capitalizing on society's desired return to traditional values. A common belief held that the Depression was a result of the immorality of the 1920s. This view gained popularity in light of the growing number of homeless workers and fatherless families, as well as reports of increases in abortions and premarital sexual activity. While statistics prove that these reports were unfounded, a huge percentage of the population focused on a return to traditional moral behavior. Consequently, advertising asserted the importance of returning to the family environment and embracing one's roots and community. Advertising campaigns capitalized on the high unemployment that often resulted in a personal sense of shame, worthlessness, and inadequacy for males now unable to provide for their families. Advertisers, as well as the media and entertainment industries, alleged that the return to traditional roles would assert the male as the responsible, virtuous leader of the family unit. These new social arguments therefore encouraged women to return to traditional standards of behavior and assume the supporting role within the family structure. *Selling Mrs. Consumer*, a pamphlet, marketed food products and domestic goods to women. Photo magazines, newspapers, and even specifically targeted comic strips such as "Mother Minds Her Business" presented the marketing-oriented argument that by fulfilling their household responsibilities, women could solve the family's problems with the aid of such products as Wonder Bread, Ovaltine, and Lifebuoy Soap.

In contrast to the perception that the Great Depression tore families apart, the combination of these traditional views with the scarcity of extra disposable income encouraged family togetherness. Businesses marketed family-bonding activities such as listening to the radio, reading, solving crossword puzzles, and playing cards. Parker Brothers marketed the Depression-inspired board game Monopoly, a time-consuming and escapist activity in which players could happily imagine leaving a life of poverty to become a real-estate millionaire.

While advertisers understood the importance of capitalizing on traditional values to sell their products, they also realized the benefit of marketing escapism from the Depression. Businesses and advertising initiated this process, but it was the motion-picture industry that most directly capitalized upon it in providing means of escape. Following the 1927 release of *The Jazz Singer*, film with sound became an increasingly powerful tool for guiding the direction of society. In keeping with the new social standards, the Motion Picture Producers and Distributors of America chose self-censorship in conveying only traditional values and morals. Throughout the Depression, films created specific scenarios and story lines designed to uplift, enlighten, and encourage the population to endure and succeed. Films such as Charlie Chaplin's *Modern Times* depicted the plight and success of the unemployed worker, while others featured lighthearted screenplays, Busby Berkeley's lavish sets and tightly choreographed routines, and the polished dance of stars such as Fred Astaire and Ginger Rogers. The combined purposes of the film industry to promote personal success and create an escape worked splendidly. Weekly cinema attendance rose from 60 million in 1930 to 80 million by 1940.

Although the motion-picture industry capitalized on the conditions of the era to fill theaters, businesses relied on the movies to sell products. Unlike direct advertising, films suggested that consumers could attain the same quality of life depicted in movies simply by using the same products as the stars, such as Bette Davis's vacuum cleaner or James Cagney's soap. Following these marketing and product-placement techniques, advertisers capitalized on print media in marketing escapism throughout the nation. The rags-to-riches story that portrayed a nation in which everyone was rich or about to become rich routinely appeared in numerous books, newspapers, and photo-magazines like *Colliers* and *Saturday Evening Post*.

Gradually, these marketing methods succeeded. Lower food prices, installment buying, and the production of modern and inexpensive plastic items kept sales constant and the economy going. The advertising of new commercial products—including electrical appliances, clothing, compact cameras, and kitchen goods—enticed much of the population to spend its modest earnings. While not everyone could immediately afford these new products, over time the population of producers in the 1920s started to become consumers during the 1930s. Even the sale of arguably pointless items, such Sieberling-Latex figurines of Dopey and the other Disney dwarfs, bolstered the sagging economy as Americans purchased them in abundance.

GOVERNMENT EFFORTS

While business and industry led the way in encouraging the American people to spend their earnings, President Franklin D. Roosevelt's New Deal programs mirrored this approach. During his last speech before the 1932 election, Roosevelt called for a new focus on the "consumer" in his plan to revive the failed economy. With New Deal programs, out of necessity the federal government created a national welfare state to provide for the needy population. State-sanctioned collective bargaining and a direct relationship with industry created an entirely new connection between the federal government and the national economy.

Many of the New Deal's "alphabet programs" had

consumer offices that conducted budget studies and emphasized the role of the consumer in economic recovery. One Works Progress Administration (WPA) study suggested that even the most frugal emergency budget should include money for nonnecessity items such as tobacco, games, athletic equipment, and leisure goods. The proposal argued that this would improve the population's quality of life and at the same time encourage economic growth. At the next level, the WPA's proposed "maintenance budget" included increased recreational funds that would enable each family member to attend the movies at least once a week.

Beyond such budgetary guidelines promoting nonnecessity spending from the WPA, the Bureau of Labor Statistics, and the Civil Works Administration, several programs worked to increase the population's discretionary income and thereby create the necessary infrastructure to support new products. The Agricultural Adjustment Administration provided economic support for agricultural workers by increasing farm prices through the regulation of supplies and costs. In the south, the Tennessee Valley Authority and the Rural Electrification Administration provided reasonably priced electricity to rural populations, thereby providing an improved infrastructure and encouraging the purchase of electrical appliances.

While these programs aided the levels of society hardest hit by the Depression, other programs worked to increase middle-class consumption. The Federal Deposit Insurance Corporation and the Securities and Exchange Commission regulated the sales of public stock offerings and corporate securities. As these provided financial protection and encouraged investing, the Federal Housing Administration and the Home Loan Corporation further assisted consumers by changing the structure of mortgage financing to make homes more affordable and lending more economically sound. At the local level, chambers of commerce mirrored federal recovery plans in promoting spending and the consumption of local goods. In many areas, promotion became so extreme that chambers proclaimed even moderate spenders as heroes and accused savers of being villains. Building on the industrialization and changing economy of the previous decades, these businesses and New Deal policies created a consumer-oriented economy and established the framework for the boom in production and consumption after World War II. The evolution of producers of the 1920s into consumers during the 1930s illustrates the complex relationship between the national population and the economy. Throughout the Great Depression, this process expanded the consumer base and increased the equal distribution of wealth. Further-more, through advertising, sales, and consumption, it created a "producer-capitalist culture" that remains in effect to the present.

PATRICK MOORE

See also: auto industry; films, feature; Ford Motor Company; radio; stock market; Civil Works Administration; Federal Deposit Insurance Corporation; Federal Housing Administration; Home Owners Loan Corporation; Securities and Exchange Commission; Works Progress Administration; Berkeley, Busby; Cagney, James; Ford, Henry.

Bibliography

Barnard, Rita. *The Great Depression and the Culture of Abundance: Kenneth Fearing, Nathanael West, and Mass Culture in the 1930s.* New York: Cambridge University Press, 1995.

Bauman, John F., and Thomas H. Coode. *In the Eye of the Great Depression: New Deal Reporters and the Agony of the American People.* DeKalb: Northern Illinois University Press, 1988.

Biles, Roger. *A New Deal for the American People.* DeKalb: Northern Illinois University Press, 1991.

Braeman, John, Robert H. Bremner, and David Brody, eds. *The New Deal: The National Level.* Columbus: Ohio State University Press, 1975.

Dubofsky, Melvyn, and Stephen Burwood, eds. *The New Deal: Selected Articles on the Political Response to the Great Depression.* New York: Garland, 1990.

Strasser, Susan, Charles McGovern, and Matthias Judt, eds. *Getting and Spending: European and American Consumer Societies in the Twentieth Century.* Washington, DC: The German Historical Institute, Cambridge University Press, 1998.

Watkins, T. H. *The Hungry Years: A Narrative History of the Great Depression in America.* New York: Henry Holt, 1999.

AFRICAN AMERICANS

During the Great Depression, African Americans experienced one of the most difficult sets of challenges of any segment of the population. As a result of New Deal influences, however, African Americans underwent a transition in political party loyalty, strengthened their political voice, and made several key steps toward improved civil rights.

During World War I, the Great Migration brought over a half-million African Americans from the South to urban centers in the Northeast. The combination of limited immigration from Europe, increased jobs in war-matériel production, and the departure of existing workers to the military created a demand for African-American industrial labor. At the same time, the destructive influence of the boll weevil decimated southern cotton crops and limited the demand for agricultural labor. The creation of new and concentrated African-American communities in northern cities provided new social, political, cultural, and economic opportunities. At the end of World War I, however African Americans experienced a new series of racial tensions. Upon returning from the service in Europe, white workers expecting to reclaim their jobs became outraged when they found black migrants holding their positions. Problems with racial discord over jobs intensified as unemployment surged while industry changed from the production of war matériel to domestic goods.

LABOR ISSUES

Despite this period of high unemployment and racial discord, African Americans continued moving north throughout the 1920s. They found considerable opportunities in the automobile, glass, paper, and tobacco industries. Meanwhile, African Americans in the South experienced little of the economic growth and opportunity enjoyed by those in the North. While southern textile operations grew, they employed only a very small number of blacks.

Although jobs existed, one significant challenge facing African Americans was the limited ability to improve their wages and working conditions. While total union affiliation grew dramatically during the 1920s, blacks were almost always segregated or outright barred from union membership. In an attempt to solve this problem from within, several groups such as the American Negro Labor Congress and the Brotherhood of Sleeping Car Porters and Maids formed black unions. Unfortunately, they experienced little success because of resistance within a white-controlled industrial and labor environment.

While a union voice eluded the African-American population, the number of black-owned businesses did increase after World War I. Although the total number of black businesses grew much more slowly than that of white-owned businesses, black ownership proved significant. African-American business owners developed social and political influence within the black community and increased the numbers of African Americans in the white-collar socioeconomic group.

As black northern migration continued throughout the 1920s, conditions did not improve for those who remained in the South. As soil erosion and the boll weevil continued to decimate crops, forcing a shift of cotton production to southwestern states, the total number of African-American farm owners declined, as did black agricultural employment. While the stock market soared and many Americans enjoyed the prosperity of the 1920s, few economists or politicians in Congress acknowledged the unequal distribution of wealth and the increasingly dire needs of the agrarian South. Most African Americans in agriculture, as well as those in ship building, mining, and some textiles, were facing increasing poverty and desolation. When the October 1929 stock market crash occurred, most southern African Americans were already suffering from depression conditions.

In the North, as businesses closed, banks failed, and factories and mines ceased production, African Americans were typically the first to lose their jobs. In the large black employment sectors of domestic and personal service, they too quickly lost their positions as white employers cut back on expenses.

In the rural South, where most African Americans still lived, poverty and starvation increased as their annual incomes fell to less than $200 a year. The nationwide Depression only worsened the already severe conditions. Agricultural prices dropped sharply, especially for cotton, and landowners resorted to evicting sharecroppers and tenant farmers. While local relief agencies in the North quickly mobilized to provide support for their needy populations, few such operations existed in the South to help the immediate needs of suffering blacks.

Because of worsening conditions in the South, a new wave of African Americans headed north and west in search of employment and assistance. During the 1930s, the population of Harlem more than doubled, while new African-American communities emerged in many western cities. Unfortunately, as the Depression continued, problems worsened in the North as well. Employers routinely offered what jobs did exist to white workers. Even skilled African Americans found potential positions going to unskilled white employees. Black unemployment nationwide was 20 to 50 percent higher than that in the total population. In northern industrial cities, black unemployment ran 50 to 90 percent. In 1935, 65 percent of African Americans in At-

lanta were in need of public assistance, and in Norfolk 80 percent of the black population was on relief. At the height of the Depression, over 2 million African Americans nationwide were out of work or on relief, many of whom were incapable of supporting themselves in any line of work.

While the African-American population as a whole suffered extensively during the Depression, African-American women experienced the worst conditions. In northern cities during the 1920s, they routinely held the lowest positions with the least pay. Once the Depression hit, they were the first to be pushed out of the labor force. Although unemployment for African American women was among the worst for any ethnic or gender group, they did experience minimal social gains. Southern merchants, competing for an ever decreasing number of retail dollars, began permitting African-American women to shop in their establishments and try on clothing. Sadly, this residual social improvement provided little compensation for scarce wages and high unemployment.

As African Americans faced unequal firing and hiring practices, discrimination also occurred in the distribution of relief. At the start of the Depression, relief fell to religious and charitable organizations. As a rule, these groups provided for needy whites before minority groups. Unfortunately, relief supplies rarely sufficed for even part of those in need, leaving African Americans with little or no aid. When organizations created work relief, again, the black population was the last to benefit from the opportunities. In many locations, there was often as much as a six-dollar difference in the monthly aid between white and black families, a significant amount given that rural incomes averaged about $20 per month in the 1930s. To the African-American community, these discrepancies in aid and relief illustrated deficiencies in both political and social influence.

Compounding the problems associated with discrimination were the increased racial tension and violence that African Americans also faced. These were not new problems, as blacks had routinely experienced racial intolerance in the South and suffered similar inequities in the North after World War I. During the Depression, tensions over limited employment, resources, and relief led to an increase of violence against African Americans. In an attempt to secure valuable jobs, whites used violence and intimidation to keep blacks from employment opportunities. Similar actions in respect to aid distribution and support led to widespread suffering for blacks throughout American cities.

In the 1920s, most black unionization attempts proved unsuccessful, but during the Depression groups

Several men relax at a shoe-shine stand in Selma, Alabama, in December 1935. The Great Depression sent African-American unemployment rates above 50 percent in towns and cities across America. *(Library of Congress)*

emerged to challenge the practice of open discrimination against African Americans in respect to jobs and aid. In St. Louis, the Urban League initiated a "Jobs for Negroes" movement that protested white-owned businesses whose client base was almost exclusively black, but who hired no black employees. Finding initial success in breaking the racially biased hiring practices in St. Louis, the movement spread throughout urban areas in the Midwest and East. In New York City, "Don't Buy Where You Can't Work" campaigns led to extensive picketing throughout black areas. There, too, the technique proved successful and led to hundreds of new jobs in Harlem stores and with utility operations.

The process, however, accentuated the discrepancy between whites and blacks in respect to employment, wages, and relief support. These tensions led to a 1935 race riot in Harlem. The uproar began when a white-owned business caught a black boy stealing a knife.

Although the boy managed to escape, rumors of the boy's being beaten to death spread throughout the community. Huge crowds emerged and led to attacks on white merchants and severe rioting and looting. The conflict resulted in four deaths and millions of dollars in damage. The riot, however, brought attention to bear on the situation and its inequities, leading New York Mayor Fiorello La Guardia to appoint an Interracial Committee on Conditions in Harlem. The committee found that indeed there was vastly insufficient relief to provide for the African-American population.

Picketing of white businesses continued throughout the early years of the Depression, despite various city governments' attempts to end the protests. In 1937, the final testament to the success of the technique came when the United States Supreme Court declared that picketing was a constitutionally legal method to secure relief and equality.

CANADA

WASHINGTON -0.6%
MONTANA -24.2%
NORTH DAKOTA -46.7%
MINNESOTA 7.2%
NEW HAMPSHIRE 27.2%
VERMONT -0.7%
MAINE -16.3%
OREGON 4.2%
IDAHO -27.4%
SOUTH DAKOTA -22.4%
WISCONSIN 106.5%
MICHIGAN 182.0%
NEW YORK -17.2%
MASSACHUSETTS 15.2%
RHODE ISLAND -1.2%
CONNECTICUT 22.1%
NEW JERSEY 78.3%
WYOMING -9.1%
NEBRASKA 3.9%
IOWA -8.6%
OHIO 66.1%
INDIANA 38.6%
PENNSYLVANIA 49.1%
NEVADA 49.1%
UTAH -23.4%
COLORADO 4.5%
ILLINOIS 80.5%
WEST VIRGINIA 33.1%
VIRGINIA 4.9%
DELAWARE 7.5%
MARYLAND 13.0%
D.C. 20.1%
CALIFORNIA 109.1%
KANSAS 14.5%
MISSOURI 25.6%
KENTUCKY -4.2%
NORTH CAROLINA 20.3%
ARIZONA 34.3%
NEW MEXICO -50.3%
OKLAHOMA 15.3%
ARKANSAS 1.3%
TENNESSEE 5.6%
SOUTH CAROLINA -8.2%
MISSISSIPPI 8.0%
ALABAMA 4.9%
GEORGIA -11.2%
TEXAS 15.3%
LOUISIANA 10.9%
FLORIDA 31.1%

PACIFIC OCEAN
ATLANTIC OCEAN
Gulf of Mexico
MEXICO

African-American Population Growth, 1920–1930
- Above 50 percent
- 25.0–50 percent
- 10.0–24.9 percent
- 0–9.9 percent
- Population loss

0   250   500 Miles
0   250   500 Kilometers

(CARTO-GRAPHICS)

POLITICS

In the South, Depression-exacerbated tensions led to national attention. In 1931, authorities in Scottsboro, Alabama, arrested nine African Americans and charged them with the rape of two white prostitutes. Although prosecutors could produce no physical evidence of guilt and would not question the testimony of the white women, the jury found the nine men and boys guilty. The court sentenced eight to death, but spared the ninth, a minor. Over the next several years, national attention focused on the racial inequity of the case. In an attempt to secure justice, the Supreme Court twice ordered new trials. While the courts never acquitted the nine, by 1950, all were free. The state dropped charges against four and paroled four, and one escaped to Michigan, where the governor refused to permit extradition. For African Americans, the case was a relatively small victory, but it proved significant, as the nine became champions of the struggle to change the pattern of discrimination nationwide.

The first years of the Depression made African Americans increasingly aware of the limits of black political and social control. During the 1920s, blacks developed a growing dissatisfaction with the Republican Party, which had held their allegiance since the Republican administrations of the Reconstruction era. In an attempt to bolster southern support, Republican leadership spent considerable time and resources appealing to white political and social leaders. The presidential election of 1928 fully illustrated this point as Herbert Hoover carried seven southern states into the White House. This appeal to Conservative white Southerners angered many African Americans since they recognized the willingness of the Republicans to alienate the black vote to garner white political support.

The Republican shift caused a number of African Americans to abandon the party of Lincoln. While the degradation of party loyalty created yet another challenge to the political voice of the black population, it did regenerate interest in the political process. Without a party, African Americans carefully watched their congressional representatives and used their votes to fight any action against the black population. After the start

CANADA

NEW HAMPSHIRE -47.6%
VERMONT -32.4%
MAINE 19.0%

WASHINGTON 8.5%
MONTANA 13.1%
NORTH DAKOTA 22.9%
MINNESOTA 5.1%

OREGON 14.8%
IDAHO -10.9%
SOUTH DAKOTA -26.6%
WISCONSIN 13.2%
MICHIGAN 23.0%
NEW YORK 38.4%
MASSACHUSETTS 5.8%

WYOMING -23.5%
IOWA -3.9%
PENNSYLVANIA -0.9%
RHODE ISLAND 11.2%
CONNECTICUT 12.4%
NEW JERSEY NA

NEVADA 28.7%
NEBRASKA 3.0%
OHIO 9.7%
INDIANA 8.9%
WEST VIRGINIA 54.7%
DELAWARE 10.0%
MARYLAND 9.2%

UTAH 11.5%
ILLINOIS 17.8%
VIRGINIA 1.7%
D.C. 41.8%

CALIFORNIA 53.4%
COLORADO 2.9%
KANSAS -1.8%
MISSOURI 0.2%
KENTUCKY -5.3%
NORTH CAROLINA 6.8%

ARIZONA 39.5%
NEW MEXICO 63.9%
OKLAHOMA -1.9%
ARKANSAS 0.9%
TENNESSEE 6.6%
SOUTH CAROLINA 2.6%
GEORGIA 1.3%

PACIFIC OCEAN

MISSISSIPPI 6.4%
ALABAMA 4.1%

TEXAS 8.1%
LOUISIANA 9.4%
FLORIDA 19.1%

ATLANTIC OCEAN

Gulf of Mexico

MEXICO

African-American Population Growth, 1930–1940
- Above 50 percent
- 25.0–50 percent
- 10.0–24.9 percent
- 0–9.9 percent
- Population loss

0   250   500 Miles
0   250   500 Kilometers

(CARTO-GRAPHICS)

of the Depression, remaining party loyalty further eroded. Many African Americans placed the responsibility of the economic collapse with the Republican Party and condemned Hoover's feeble attempts at viable relief.

The election of 1932 posed a difficult choice for African Americans. Despite the change to the Republicans' courting of white southerners, many blacks still supported the party of Lincoln out of respect and tradition. Furthermore, many blacks had vivid memories of President Woodrow Wilson's racially biased administration, so voting for another Democrat was not an acceptable alternative. Despite Franklin D. Roosevelt's promised changes, he generated little enthusiasm within the black population. Beyond his party affiliation, few African Americans outside of New York knew anything about the Democratic candidate. In fact, many blacks were considerably concerned over Roosevelt's poor health, as his potential demise once in the White House would result in Texan John Nance Garner's assuming the presidency.

Despite these concerns, many African Americans

voted for Roosevelt, and, once elected, his popularity among blacks quickly increased. The president's manner appealed to many blacks, as it did to most Americans. His fireside chats generated a sense of national belonging that few African Americans had ever experienced. Additionally, many African Americans related to his physical disability, which illustrated a sense of strength over adversity.

While Franklin D. Roosevelt was sensitive to the needs of African Americans and other minorities, it was Eleanor Roosevelt who championed their cause during the Great Depression. As the first politically active First Lady, Eleanor Roosevelt worked to remain connected with needy populations. Her newspaper column, "My Day," encouraged people to write in and ask for help with their problems. Although she could rarely provide any direct assistance, she was instrumental in explaining how the New Deal was working to provide for African Americans and others. Outside of public view, she constantly reminded her husband to provide for the needs of the black population. On Eleanor's urging, the Roosevelt administration worked with black educators and administrators, including Mary McLeod Bethune of the National Youth Administration, to create new opportunities for blacks.

While Eleanor Roosevelt crusaded for African-American employment opportunities, she was also diligent in her quest for social equality. When the Daughters of the American Revolution (DAR) denied black opera singer Marian Anderson the opportunity to sing in Constitution Hall, the First Lady resigned her membership in the DAR and arranged a public concert on the steps of the Lincoln Memorial. On Easter Day, 1939, Anderson's concert attracted 75,000 people.

Although African Americans increasingly supported President Roosevelt, a prejudice, discrimination, and segregation still prevailed in federal policy and within many of his New Deal programs. While Roosevelt acknowledged the needs of the African-American population, he also recognized that his continued success hinged upon support from southern white Democrats in Congress and the Democratic Party. The president therefore refused to promote civil rights legislation and even chose not to support a federal antilynching law.

The African-American political voice did, however, improve through new government appointments and presidential advisers. While previous presidents had had African-American advisers, black representation on Roosevelt's team was comparatively large. In 1936, Mary McLeod Bethune organized African Americans within the Roosevelt administration into a semiofficial advisory commission on race relations called the "black cabinet" or the "black Brain Trust." The members were not politicians, but were usually party faithful, and included Ph.D.s, J.D.s, and a college president, who provided genuine advice on race-related and relief-oriented issues. Despite the comprehensive nature of the membership, the group had a strictly advisory capacity and rarely spoke directly with the president.

Several key New Deal agency heads understood the problems of the African-American population. Among the most vocal and active was Harold Ickes, who served as secretary of the interior and director of the Public Works Administration (PWA), and Harry Hopkins, who served as the head of several New Deal programs. Both leaders pushed for racial equality throughout the programs they oversaw. Under their direction, the PWA, the Civil Works Administration, and the Works Progress Administration (WPA) were among the best at providing nondiscriminatory relief and jobs for African Americans. Under the PWA, construction of hospitals, playgrounds, colleges, and community centers provided for African-American communities. Unfortunately, even where construction was benefiting black populations, the local administration hired a disproportionately low number of African Americans for construction jobs. The WPA was among the best at equal hiring practices, supporting nearly 1 million African-Americans families. Through its operation, the program employed professional and clerical personnel as well as actors, writers, and artists.

Despite the influence of the "black cabinet" and the direction of Ickes, Hopkins, and others, many New Deal programs, as well as state and local programs, routinely limited or denied African Americans support and relief. The long-standing tradition of discrimination in the country remained unchanged in many of the programs designed to provide assistance. During the hearings to set codes for fair competition and employment for the National Industrial Recovery Act, organizers invited only a few African Americans to attend. As a result, this early New Deal program left blacks with significant shortcomings in wages and cost of living allocations. While this illustrated an early problem with New Deal discrimination, few African Americans complained for fear of losing their jobs entirely.

Under the Tennessee Valley Authority and the Rural Electrification Administration, the predominantly southern operations openly practiced segregation and discrimination. While the programs did provide benefits to African Americans, they were drastically unequal in respect to hiring or pay. Even administrators who desired to provide greater benefits and opportunities for black workers found antiblack attitudes nearly impossible to overcome.

African Americans experienced similar obstacles to relief with the Agricultural Adjustment Act. The program guidelines provided funds directly to farmers to plow under their crops and slaughter their livestock in order to raise prices. Unfortunately, dishonest white landowners worked with program administrators to either circumvent funds from reaching black farmers or simply evict tenant farmers and accept the benefits for themselves.

Between 1933 and 1942, the Civilian Conservation Corps provided jobs for 200,000 African-American youth doing conservation, reforestation, erosion control, and other projects. While black leaders outwardly criticized the CCC for its strict segregation policies and unequal work and pay, many credited its educational programs with significantly diminishing illiteracy and juvenile delinquency.

Direct-relief programs were not alone in the practice of discriminatory inequality. The Federal Housing Authority provided funds to help African Americans keep their homes and improve their living conditions. Although the federal government guaranteed the funds, banks often refused to lend to African-American applicants, citing concerns over the risk of nonpayment and diminishing property values. Elsewhere, housing funds were simply misused at the local level. After slum demolition in Cleveland, planners scrapped construction plans for low-income African-American housing and instead built segregated, middle-income residences. Rather than providing new housing for blacks, the program simply moved the location of the slums.

Even apparently balanced programs left many African Americans in need of support. Under the provisions of the 1935 Social Security Board, the government provided assistance for the elderly in need. However, the program blocked many African Americans from benefits because the guidelines excluded agricultural and domestic labor from eligibility. In Texas, this inequity was further compounded when the state legislature mandated that job skills programs could train minority women only in domestic labors such as cooking, cleaning, and sewing.

Even with the problems of discrimination and inequality, by 1938 New Deal programs provided 30 percent of African Americans with some form of federal aid. Though this was still only a small percentage of the total number of African Americans in need, most African Americans praised and supported Roosevelt and the New Deal. In 1934, the last large group of African Americans left the Republican Party and joined the Democratic Party. By 1936, this transition of African-American party affiliation was all but complete and Roosevelt received nearly 90 percent of the black vote nationwide. Despite the traditions of dis-crimination that influenced many parts of the Roosevelt administration and the New Deal, the era improved the African-American social and political voice, helped black communities survive, and created the framework for civil rights successes of later decades.

PATRICK MOORE

See also: Brotherhood of Sleeping Car Porters; Democratic Party; Republican Party; Scottsboro case; "black cabinet"; Civil Rights Section (Department of Justice); Agricultural Adjustment Act; Civil Works Administration; Federal Housing Administration; National Industrial Recovery Administration; Rural Electrification Administration; Social Security Act; Tennessee Valley Authority; Works Progress Administration; Anderson, Marion; Hoover, Herbert; Roosevelt, Eleanor; Roosevelt, Franklin D.; Document: Chief Justice Charles Evans Hughes' Opinion on Admission of a Negro Student to the University of Missouri Law School, 1938.

Bibliography

Carlton, David L., and Peter A. Coclanis, eds. *Confronting Southern Poverty in the Great Depression: The Report on Economic Conditions of the South with Related Documents.* New York: Bedford Books of St. Martin's, 1996.

Finkenbine, Roy E. *Sources of the African-American Past.* New York: Longman Publishers, 1997.

Franklin, John Hope, and Alfred A. Moss Jr. *From Slavery to Freedom: A History of Negro Americans.* New York: Knopf, 1988.

Foner, Philip S., and Ronald L. Lewis, eds. *The Era of Post-War Prosperity and the Great Depression, 1920–1936.* Vol. 6, *The Black Worker.* Philadelphia: Temple University Press, 1981.

Wolters, Raymond. *Negroes and the Great Depression: The Problem of Economic Recovery.* Westport, CT: Greenwood Press, 1970.

AGRICULTURE

The agricultural crisis in the United States during the Great Depression was as firmly rooted in the nation's agricultural development as it was the logical outcome of a "boom and bust" cycle. The 1900–14 period had been one of remarkable price stability. World War I stimulated demand and prices increased until doubling by 1920. Farmers brought more acreage into production, farm debt mounted, and overproduction created surpluses. When demand contracted in 1921, prices declined 50 percent. Continued depression of the agricultural sector ran counter to the general economic prosperity of the 1920s. In 1932, after the onset of the Great Depression, prices declined to 32 percent of the 1900–14 level. With an end to the Depression nowhere in sight, farmers searched for some practical approach to mitigating the disaster.

The Hoover administration responded by sponsoring the Agricultural Marketing Act, which became law in June 1929. The act created the Federal Farm Board, which set up entities such as the Wool Marketing Corporation and Cotton Stabilization Corporation to make purchases in the open market in order to stabilize prices. Unfortunately, the voluntary program gave farmers little incentive to reduce their acreage, and so overproduction continued.

As farmers became more frustrated, renegade dairy farmers in the Sioux City, Iowa, area stopped milk trucks and dumped supplies onto the highway, while thousands of protesters began patrolling highways into the city and picketing agricultural shipments. Law enforcement officers broke up picket lines in Council Bluffs, Iowa, and Omaha, Nebraska, after tense confrontations and arrests. The incidents underscored the futility of individual farmers' efforts to raise prices and the necessity for a national approach to restrict overproduction. New York governor Franklin D. Roosevelt, campaigning for president in Sioux City, promised farmers that when elected he would devote more time to agriculture than to any other single problem.

FIRST NEW DEAL LEGISLATION AND PROGRAMS

Roosevelt's approach to the farm problem followed the overall thrust of New Deal programs, which aimed at "relief, recovery, and reform." The Agricultural Adjustment Act of 1933, centerpiece of the administration's agricultural program, attempted to break the vicious cycle of continued overproduction in the face of decreasing demand. The act established the Agricultural Adjustment Administration (AAA), which distributed subsidies to farmers all over the country for reducing acreage and production of enumerated crops.

The Tennessee Valley Authority (TVA) marked the first comprehensive approach to regional problems in American history. The regional development authority managed and developed dams, generated hydroelectric power, supported and encouraged industry, promoted rural electrification, produced agricultural fertilizer, and promoted conservation and management of land and water resources.

Refinancing of mortgages and the making and extension of loans to farmers were facilitated by various acts, including the Farm Credit Act (June 16, 1933); creation of the Commodity Credit Corporation (October 16, 1933); passage of the Farm Mortgage Refinancing Act (January 1934), the Crop Loan Act (February 23, 1934), Farm Mortgage Foreclosure Act (June 1934), and the Federal Farm Bankruptcy (Frazier-Lemke) Act (June 28, 1934).

The Jones-Connally Farm Relief Act (April 7, 1934) and the Jones-Costigan Sugar Act (May 1934) extended the list of enumerated commodities subject to the AAA. The administration and Congress breached AAA's voluntary principle with passage of the Bankhead Cotton Control Act (April 21, 1934) and later with the Tobacco Control Act (June 28, 1935), provisions of which contained compulsory quotas for the two commodities and tax penalties for noncompliance.

SECOND NEW DEAL LEGISLATION AND PROGRAMS

In keeping with his call for social reform in his 1935 State of the Union address, President Roosevelt, by virtue of the Emergency Relief Appropriation Act (April 8, 1935) created the Resettlement Administration (RA) to help destitute farmers who had not benefited from the AAA, to administer conservation and land use projects, and to establish subsistence homesteads for impoverished farmers and "greenbelt towns" for city workers.

The Second New Deal moved toward social reform and the initiation of large-scale public works and employment projects. The Soil Conservation Act (April 27, 1935), Rural Electrification Administration (May 11, 1935), and the National Resources Board (later reorganized as the National Resources Committee) (June 30, 1934) carried out the new administration's thrust toward conservation and development programs.

After the Supreme Court invalidated the Federal Farm Bankruptcy Act, the administration passed a modified Farm Mortgage Moratorium (Frazier-Lemke) Act of 1935 (August 29, 1935). When the Supreme Court invalidated the Agricultural Adjustment Act in *United States v. Butler* in January 1936, Congress passed a measure, the Soil Conservation and Domestic Allotment Act (February 29, 1936), featuring benefit payments to farmers who voluntarily practiced sponsored soil conservation measures. The Supreme Court did uphold the constitutionality of the TVA in *Ashwander v. TVA*. The Bankhead-Jones Farm Tenant Act (July 22, 1937) established the Farm Security Administration as the new home of the RA and attempted to assist farm tenants and sharecroppers ignored by the AAA, making it possible for them to purchase a farm with generous credit terms. Passage of the Agricultural Adjustment Act of 1938 (February 1938) completed the workaround of *United States v. Butler* et al. by modifying and restoring the basic aims of the 1933 act.

The 1938 act incorporated the "parity payment principle" and established the "ever-normal granary." The system called for government loans on surpluses at below "parity prices" based on 1909–14 levels of farm purchasing power. During below-parity years, the government would store the surplus, which farmers would liquidate later in parity years. The act also established the Federal Crop Insurance Corporation under the Department of Agriculture to insure wheat crops by payment in kind. In 1939 the administration initiated a food stamp plan in Rochester, New York. The plan was operating in over 100 cities until discontinued at the outbreak of World War II.

HENRY A. WALLACE AND THE DEPARTMENT OF AGRICULTURE

Appointed secretary of agriculture by President Roosevelt, Henry Agard Wallace became the man charged with carrying out and coordinating New Deal agricultural programs. Wallace's father, Henry Cantwell Wallace, had served as secretary of agriculture in the Harding administration and created the Bureau of Agricultural Economics, a model for future federal re-

search agencies. During the New Deal, Henry A. Wallace would build on and extend his father's legacy.

In spite of threatened cutbacks by members of the Seventy-second Congress, Wallace succeeded in winning increased funding for the Department of Agriculture. While implementing various New Deal policies and directing an expanding array of programs during his tenure as secretary (1933–40), Wallace succeeded in expanding the agency's research mission. He used emergency relief funds to construct a central national agricultural research center at Beltsville, Maryland, in 1934. He secured funding in the Bankhead-Jones Act of 1934 for construction of nine regional laboratories to conduct research in farm product distribution, marketing, and water resource conservation. The Agricultural Adjustment Act of 1938 funded four more centers to investigate new industrial uses for surplus farm products.

AGRICULTURE IN THE WEST

The Great Plains region includes ten states, stretching from the Dakotas and Montana through Nebraska, Wyoming, and Colorado to Kansas, and south to include Oklahoma, Texas, and New Mexico. The nation's preeminent grain-producing and livestock region had benefited in the early 1900s from the agricultural boom and from advances in plant breeding and new plowing technology that reduced labor costs and increased production per acre. Unfortunately, the burden of higher equipment costs and credit payments increased pressures for farmers to cultivate more acreage. In 1931, overproduction resulted in a record wheat crop and subsequent price collapse. A full decade of poor land-management practices such as overgrazing and overtillage depleted soil moisture, leached nutrients, and encouraged erosion. All of these forces conspired to set the Great Plains up for agricultural, financial, and social devastation during the 1930s. As rising debts, commodity surpluses, and depressed demand and prices took their toll, the abuse of the land made the region vulnerable to drought.

What became known as the 1930s drought was actually a series of four discrete drought episodes: 1930–31, 1934, 1936, and 1939–40. It extended beyond the Great Plains. The drought of 1934 affected over 75 percent of the nation's land area, involving twenty-seven states from the Northwest and Southwest to the Midwest and even the South and Southeast. Ten years of these recurrent drought episodes and economic depression produced a whipsaw effect that foreclosed the possibility of recovery until the return of normal rainfall totals in 1938–41 and the stimulus of wartime ag-

The poverty of the nation's agricultural population in the Great Depression is captured in this photo of a migrant farm labor camp in California's Central Valley. *(Brown Brothers)*

ricultural demand. The most severe period of drought in the nation's history up to that time also helped to create one of its greatest ecological disasters and human tragedies. Both the drought and poor agricultural land management caused the "dust bowl." The physical destruction of farmland was not only a cause but also a consequence of incredibly severe dust storms that stripped areas of Kansas, Oklahoma, and Texas of topsoil. As hundreds of millions of tons of topsoil were upturned by storms and deposited by the winds in distant states, the human tragedy mounted. Thousands of communities were affected, leading to mass migration from the region. The "Okies" (dispossessed dirt farmers from Oklahoma and surrounding states) were the largest identifiable group among the uprooted.

AGRICULTURE IN THE SOUTH

In the nation's most distinctive and agriculturally dependent region, the Great Depression contributed to the acute exacerbation of a long-standing and seemingly intractable problem, yet the crisis provided the necessary stimulus to initiate a long-term strategy to provide a solution. Cotton production dominated southern agriculture in the Great Depression. The staple crop had been the underpinning of the entire southern economic and social system since long before the Civil War. After the Civil War and Reconstruction, the South had suffered sharp declines in cotton prices following contraction in world cotton consumption. From the middle 1890s until 1920, modest recovery in cotton was accompanied by the relocation of textile production from the Northeast. The stimulus of World War I had benefited the southern economy to a limited degree, but not enough to initiate systemic change away from dependence on agriculture. In fact, the region lost ground in the 1920s as agricultural prices sagged. Southerners as a whole were already impoverished when the Great Depression began, with relative income per capita amounting to only half the national average.

Franklin D. Roosevelt clearly understood the importance of the South to the nation and the need to address not only the immediate effects of the Depression in the South, but also the long-standing underdevelopment of the region. Calling the South "the nation's number one economic problem" in 1938, the president charged the National Emergency Council (NEC) to prepare a report on the problems and needs of the South with the assistance of southern leaders. The committee investigated several key problem areas: soil despoliation, the need for cheap fertilizer and cheap power, the South's capital resources and absentee ownership of those resources, lack of industrial development and absentee ownership of new industries, labor and employment, child labor, farm ownership and tenantry, farm income, taxation, education, housing, and health.

The Report on Economic Conditions of the South issued in 1938 was unrelenting. Most laborers were unskilled and lacked employment. Regional wage rate differentials existed in every category. Industries were invariably low-wage, low-skill operations. Underemployment and unemployment, long endemic to the region, had reached staggering levels during the Depression. The region had more farmers and farm laborers than any other region. Cash cropping and farm tenancy contributed to poor productivity and husbandry.

If the report produced a clear snapshot of the deplorable state of the agricultural South in 1938, the conditions it described were of long standing and not merely the result of the Great Depression. The symptoms were, however, already being addressed by several New Deal programs and agencies, including, among the most prominent, the Agricultural Adjustment Administration.

COTTON, AGRICULTURAL ADJUSTMENT, AND MODERNIZATION

The AAA aimed at raising and stabilizing farm income by limiting cash-crop acreage, removing surpluses and reducing price effects on markets, paying direct subsidies to farmers, and fostering conservation practices. Ostensibly a voluntary program, it nevertheless imposed various tax penalties for farmers producing more than specified crops on their allotted acreage. Noncompliant farmers received no subsidies.

The idea of limiting cotton acreage to reduce surpluses had been discussed in the South earlier. After the devastatingly low prices in 1931, northern Louisiana cotton planters, realizing the impracticality of a purely voluntary approach, enlisted the aid of Louisiana governor Huey P. Long in prohibiting cotton planting, gathering, and ginning in the state in 1932. The ban never took effect, however, because Long failed to convince the required three-fourths of cotton states to pass similar measures. The AAA, in contrast, was able to effect drastic reductions in cotton acreage, and the removal of surpluses caused a record low cotton export by 1938–39. The program was instrumental in reversing the previous trends of tenancy increase originating during the Civil War and ownership decrease that had begun in the 1920s.

But the program aggravated the already dismal condition of tenants and sharecroppers, forcing them out of the fields and into the cities. Black farm workers suffered most from the program. Even though white farm tenants outnumbered blacks two to one, less than one-fourth of black farm workers owned their own land. Between 1930 and 1940, the number of white farm operators remained constant, but 200,000 black owners, tenants, and sharecroppers had been driven out of agriculture. The New Deal responded by initiating resettlement and rehabilitation efforts under various agencies, including the Interior Department's Division of Subsistence Homesteads, the Federal Emergency Relief Administration, the Resettlement Administration, and the Farm Security Administration. Most of these projects were of limited scope and funding, and the resettlement projects in particular leaned toward social experimentation rather than relief.

In short, the New Deal policy focused on reducing farm production and the number of farmers, rather than increasing the welfare of most agricultural workers. The reduction of acreage reduced labor requirements, and federal payments grossly favored landowners. Placing the majority of AAA payments in the hands of the planters encouraged agricultural mechanization because payments could be spent on machinery, but landowners benefited more from payments by reducing the number of tenants.

The Southern Tenant Farmers Union (STFU) organized resulting tenant protest. The STFU, whose membership included both black and white tenants, spotlighted the plight of tenants and helped pass the Bankhead Farm Tenant Act in 1937. Unfortunately, this act provided scant relief for tenants late in the crisis.

The AAA struck at what modernizers perceived to be the primary cause of "southern backwardness"—the endemic oversupply of low-wage agricultural labor. Farm labor was exempted from minimum-wage legislation, unemployment insurance, and Social Security.

New Deal programs did not deal with the South's lack of industrial development or directly address documented regional imbalances.

NEW DEAL PROGRAMS AND REGIONAL DISPARITIES

New Deal relief and reform measures were primarily designed to address national rather than regional problems. New Deal agricultural programs mainly involved loans and expenditures by such agencies as the Federal Emergency Relief Administration, Reconstruction Finance Corporation, Public Works Administration, Works Progress Administration, Rural Electrification Administration, Civilian Conservation Corps, and Civil Works Administration. It is clear that these programs aimed at relief rather than reform, recovery, or income redistribution because some regions and states obtained greater per capita shares of New Deal relief compared to others. Western states received more relief in the form of loans and expenditures from 1933 to 1939 because the high-wage and high-income region experienced the largest absolute and percentage decreases in farm income from 1929 to 1932. The West received an average $535 per capita in relief between 1933 and 1939, compared to $182 for the Southeast.

The largest differential split between high-and-low receiving areas followed an east-west rather than a north-south axis. The eastern half of the nation, which included the more industrialized Northeast, received only one-third of the benefits. The South, with its low wages and staple cash production, received 60 percent less per capita than the West. Statistically, the greater the proportion of blacks in agriculture in a given state, the lower the per capita benefits. The 1938 *Report on Conditions of the South* apparently came too late in the decade to be of much help to southern farmers.

CONRAD L. REIN

See also: dust bowl; Farm Holiday Association; Okies; Southern Tenants Farmers Union; Agricultural Adjustment Act (1933); Civilian Conservation Corps; Commodity Credit Corporation; Farm Security Administration; Federal Surplus Relief Corporation/Commodities Corporation; Jones-Connally Farm Relief Act; Resettlement Administration; Rural Electrification Administration; Soil Conservation and Domestic Allotment Act; Soil Erosion Service/Soil Conservation Service; *United States v. Butler et al.*; Documents: Agricultural Adjustment Act, May 12, 1933; *United States v. Butler et al.*, 1936.

Bibliography

Arrington, Leonard J. "Western Agriculture and the New Deal." *Agricultural History* 44:4 (October 1970): 337–54.

Atack, Jeremy, and Peter Passell. *A New Economic View of American History from Colonial Times to 1940.* New York: W. W. Norton, 1994.

Carl, Thomas, Stanley A. Changnon Jr., and William E. Risbane Jr. *Drought and Natural Resources Management in the United States: Impacts and Implications of the 1987–89 Drought.* Boulder, CO: Westview Press, 1991.

Grubs, Donald. "Jackson, That 'Socialist Tenant Farmers' Union, and the New Deal." *Agricultural History* 42:2 (April 1968): 125–37.

Holley, Donald. "The Negro in the New Deal Resettlement Program." *Agricultural History* 45:3 (July 1971): 179–95.

Myrdal, Gunnar. *An American Dilemma: The Negro Problem and Modern Democracy*, vol. 1. New York: Harper & Row, 1962.

National Emergency Council: Report on Economic Conditions of the South. Washington, DC: Government Printing office, 1938.

Neimi, Albert W., Jr. *U.S. Economic History: A Survey of the Major Issues.* Chicago: Rand McNally, 1975.

Purcell, Carol W., Jr. "The Administration of Science in the Department of Agriculture, 1933–1940." *Agricultural History* 42:3 (July 1968): 231–40.

Rein, Conrad L. *From Southland to Sunbelt: The Legacy of Dependent Development in New Orleans and Louisiana*, 1930–1990. Ann Arbor: University of Michigan Press, 1998.

Salutos, Theodore. "The New Deal and Farm Policy in the Great Plains." *Agricultural History* 43:3 (July 1969): 51–74.

Shideler, James H. "The Development of the Parity Price Formula for Agriculture, 1919–1923." *Agricultural History* 27:3 (July 1953): 445–55.

Shover, John L. "The Farmers' Holiday Association Strike, August 1932." *Agricultural History* 39:4 (October 1965): 197–203.

United States Department of Agriculture. *USDA Yearbook of Agriculture.* Washington, DC: Government Printing Office, 1929–41.

Warrick, Richard A. "Drought in the Great Plains: A Case Study of Research on Climate and Society in the USA." In *IIASA Proceedings Series: Climate Constraints and Human Activities*, ed. Jessee Ausubel and Asit K. Biswas. New York: Pergamon Press, 1980.

Williams, T. Harry. *Huey Long.* New York: Knopf, 1969.

Winters, Donald L. "The Persistence of Progressivism: Henry Cantwell Wallace and the Movement for Agricultural Economics." *Agricultural History* 41:2 (April 1967): 109–20.

Wright, Gavin. *The Political Economy of the Cotton South: Households, Markets and Wealth in the Nineteenth Century.* New York: W. W. Norton, 1978.

ALCOHOLICS ANONYMOUS

Alcoholics Anonymous (AA), the self-help group designed to assist those suffering from alcohol addiction, was founded in New York City in 1935 by stockbroker William G. Wilson and surgeon Robert Holbrook Smith of Akron, Ohio. Alcoholics themselves, they too saw addiction spreading among Americans hard hit by the Great Depression and freed from the strictures of Prohibition, which had ended in 1933.

Wilson and Smith—known, as would become the AA tradition, by their first names and last initials—believed that alcoholics were not getting the help they needed. Often blamed for their addiction, alcoholics—the two founders believed—needed to reach out to others for help, and the best people to help them were their fellow sufferers. The program, which combines self-help psychology, group social dynamics, and a nondenominational spirituality, soon gained thousands of adherents and, in 1939, Wilson and Smith published the outlines of their program in a book with the same title, *Alcoholics Anonymous*.

Over the following decades, the group has gained millions of members, spread to over 100 countries, and spawned a variety of similar programs for people suffering from other social problems, such as drug abuse, obesity, and gambling.

See also: Prohibition.

Bibliography

Kurtz, Ernest. *A.A.: The Story*. San Francisco: Harper & Row, 1988.

Robertson, Nan. *Getting Better: Inside Alcoholics Anonymous*. New York: William Morrow, 1988.

AMERICAN FEDERATION OF LABOR

Founded in 1886 by Samuel Gompers, the American Federation of Labor (AFL) was originally styled according to the British "new union" model, which emphasized benefit systems, high dues, centralized control over local unions, and collective bargaining. The AFL distinguished itself from the Knights of Labor, another large working-class organization of the time, by restricting membership to skilled workers and by not organizing on the basis of sex, race, or color. Moreover, the AFL was dedicated to what its leaders called "pure-and-simple" unionism, which focused on short-term objectives, relied on economic power rather than politics, limited membership to workers, and organized strictly on occupational lines. The goal of this conservative agenda was to create a common ground, albeit a narrow one, on which workers of varying nationalities might unite. The American Federation of Labor was quite successful and, by the 1930s, 85 percent of all union workers were under its aegis. Furthermore, despite the challenge presented by the Congress of Industrial Organizations, the federation remained the largest and most powerful union during the age of Franklin D. Roosevelt. The AFL accomplished this not by being a static organization, as is sometimes charged, but by being dynamic and willing to change with the times.

Even so, by 1930, despite periods of growth, the AFL faced problems that, at times, made it a weaker union than it had been in 1900. For the AFL, pure-and-simple unionism worked best during the first two decades of the twentieth century. While facing the constant anti-union activities of the National Association of Manufacturers (NAM), the federation's membership grew from over 1.6 million in 1904 to 2.6 million by 1914. During World War I, the federation made gains but advances were offset by growth in the numbers of nonunion workers and unions that were not affiliated with the AFL. In part, the problem lay with the racist and nativist mind-set of the union's leadership and rank-and-file members. The AFL often refused to organize or to allow as members African Americans, Chinese, and other minorities. When the AFL granted charters to unions with minority workers, it did so begrudgingly, as with the case of the Brotherhood of Sleeping Car Porters. Additionally, the union's conservative leadership was stifling to those of a more radical bent. As a result, new unions, such as the Amalgamated Clothing Workers, founded in 1914 under the leadership of Sidney Hillman, formed successful organizations outside of the AFL. More significant problems arose in the 1920s. Successes in the NAM-led open-shop movement, violence against unionists, the Supreme Court's anti-labor decisions, and challenges by the Communist Trade Union Education League led to a major decline in membership. By 1933, the AFL was back to pre–World War I membership levels.

Initially, the Great Depression made things worse for the AFL. Unemployment, which in some cities was as high as 80 percent, translated into a rapid decrease in overall membership and economic power. At first, the federation's leadership was at a loss for solutions to the crisis. AFL leaders had long supported the Republican Party, which encouraged volunteerism and associationism rather than direct federal involvement in the economy. But soon after the election of Franklin D. Roosevelt, the AFL developed a more radical language. In late 1932, AFL president William Green called for a universal strike if the new government did not take steps to end the Depression. Roosevelt and the New Deal responded to the demand for change with the National Industrial Recovery Act (NIRA), which created several alphabet agencies whose task it was to reverse the economic downturn. More important for the federation was the NIRA's Section 7, which gave workers the right to organize unions and bargain collectively. In essence, Roosevelt had provided the AFL and other unions with his imprimatur to fight for recognition, wages, and benefits. "The president wants you to join the union," organizers told recruits, who responded by the thousands. By 1934, the federation had added almost a million members. These gains were not lost when the Supreme Court overturned the NIRA in 1935 but were solidified under the National Labor Relations (Wagner) Act passed immediately after the Court's decision.

The dramatic resurgence of the labor movement in the 1930s was a mixed blessing for the AFL. New unions and mobilized workers quickly ran afoul of the more staid federation leadership. The AFL was not blindly committed to craft unionism. In the 1910s and 1920s, it did reorganize itself to encourage craft-industrial unions to make it easier for workers in new industries to join. The AFL's departments, such as the Metal Trades Department, were designed to allow for more union collaboration and growth. Yet as auto-

TABLE 1

MEMBERSHIP OF AMERICAN LABOR ORGANIZATIONS, 1933–1945 (IN THOUSANDS)

	All organizations	*AFL affiliates*	*CIO affiliates*	*Independent unions*
1933	2,973.0	2,317.5	–	655.5
1934	3,608.6	3,030.0	–	578.6
1935	3,753.3	3,218.4	–	534.9
1936	4,107.1	3,516.4	1,204.6	590.7
1937	5,780.1	3,179.7	1,991.2	609.2
1938	6,080.5	3,547.4	1,957.7	575.4
1939	6,555.5	3,878.0	1,837.7	839.8
1940	7,282.0	4,343.0	2,154.1	784.7
1941	8,698.0	5,178.8	2,653.9	865.3
1942	10,199.7	6,075.7	2,492.7	1,631.3
1943	11,811.7	6,779.2	3,303.4	1,729.1
1944	12,628.0	6,876.5	3,937.1	1,814.4
1945	12,562.1	6,890.4	3,927.9	1,743.8

Source: Leo Troy, *Trade Union Membership, 1897–1962* (New York: National Bureau of Economic Research, 1965).

motive, mine, and rubber workers began to spontaneously form unions and strike, the AFL's leaders failed to react quickly enough. Rather than recognize the new unions and give leadership roles to the militants, Green and the department heads wanted organizers to turn over the new recruits to established affiliates, which had the potential to divide workers along occupational lines. In 1935, a radical cadre within the federation led by the United Mine Workers' John L. Lewis created the Committee for Industrial Organization (CIO) to pursue industrial unionism irrespective of craft lines. Immediately, the AFL denounced the committee and in 1936 suspended the unions that made up the CIO. Taking full advantage of the opportunity, the CIO—which soon changed its name to the Congress of Industrial Organizations—expanded its membership to the detriment of the AFL.

Although the AFL proved powerless to organize workers in industries of mass production, it made other gains in the 1930s. In the construction, transportation, communication, and service industries, the federation grew dramatically. The AFL was flexible enough to expand where the CIO offered no competition. Between 1937 and 1945, the AFL affiliates added 3.7 million new members (see Table 1). In this same period, only 3,900 (8 percent) of the 47,600 cases brought before the National Labor Relations Board (NLRB) involved direct electoral competition between the AFL and the CIO. In other words, while the CIO used the Wagner Act and the NLRB to its advantage in the mass production industries, the AFL similarly adopted modern union methods, thus increasing its influence dramatically during the 1930s, becoming not only an economic power but a political one as well.

ANDREW E. KERSTEN

See also: Brotherhood of Sleeping Car Porters; Congress of Industrial Organizations; National Labor Relations Act; Section 7 (National Industrial Recovery Act); strikes, general; unions and union organizing; United Mine Workers; Green, William; Lewis, John L.

Bibliography

Green, James R. *The World of the Worker: Labor in Twentieth-Century America.* Urbana: University of Illinois Press, 1980.

Taft, Philip. *The A.F. of L. from the Death of Gompers to the Merger.* New York: Harper & Brothers, 1959.

Tomlins, Christopher L. "AFL Unions in the 1930s: Their Performance in Historical Perspective." *Journal of American History* 65:4 (March 1979): 1021–1042.

Zieger, Robert H. *American Workers, American Unions.* Baltimore: Johns Hopkins University Press, 1986.

AMERICAN GUIDE SERIES

The American Guide Series was the major achievement of the Federal Writers' Project, an agency established in 1935 by the federal government to provide work for jobless writers, researchers, and editors. The series—inspired by the internationally famous travel guidebook series by Karl Baedeker—included books covering every state in the union and all U.S. territories at the time, except Hawaii. In addition, the series included volumes on major cities—including Los Angeles, New Orleans, New York, Philadelphia, San Francisco, and Washington. There were also books and pamphlets on important highways and trails such as U.S. Route 1, the Ocean Highway, and the Oregon Trail, as well as numerous volumes on counties, towns, and even some historically significant villages. The larger state books combined travel and tourist information with essays on geography and geology, local fauna and flora, art and architecture, history, and the local economy. Those employed on the project included professors, graduate students, librarians, lawyers, and a variety of white-collar professionals who claimed to qualify as writers. While the results were uneven, many of the guide books—particularly the one commissioned on New York City—were masterpieces of travel and encyclopedic literature. Among the writers involved in the series were such notables as Conrad Aiken, John Cheever, Ralph Ellison, Zora Neale Hurston, and Richard Wright.

See also: Federal Writers' Project; Aiken, Conrad; Hurston, Zora Neale; Wright, Richard.

Bibliography

Bold, Christine. *The WPA Guides: Mapping America.* Jackson: University Press of Mississippi, 1999.

Among the many publications of the Federal Writers' Project was this late 1930s guide to ski resorts in the eastern United States. (*Library of Congress*)

Hobson, Archie, ed. *Remembering America: A Sampler of the WPA American Guide Series.* New York: Columbia University Press, 1985.

Weisenberger, Bernard A., ed. *The WPA Guides to America: The Best of 1930s America as Seen by the Federal Writers' Project.* New York: Pantheon Books, 1985.

AMERICAN LABOR PARTY

The American Labor Party (ALP) was founded in New York in 1936 as a leftist party that supported Franklin D. Roosevelt's reelection bid. The ALP was critical in the reelection efforts of Mayor Fiorello La Guardia in the late 1930s and in the election of radical congressman Vito Marcantonio. Essentially socialist in orientation, though an adamant supporter of the New Deal as well, the ALP was strongly backed by many of the city's labor unions, who saw it primarily as labor's political vehicle in New York state. It was also heavily supported by many of the city's Communists.

While the ALP elected several city councilpersons and state legislators in the 1930s, its real impact was in endorsing major party candidates under the state's fusion rules, whereby a candidate can run at the head of more than one party ticket. La Guardia, for example, won 22 percent of the vote for mayor as head of the ALP ticket in 1937, a significant part of his overall winning majority of 58 percent. While red-baited, or attacked as communistic in the 1930s, the ALP remained popular with leftist and liberal voters. But as anticommunism intensified in the late 1940s, the ALP found itself increasingly isolated and its leadership voted to disband the party in 1956.

See also: La Guardia, Fiorello; Marcantonio, Vito.

Bibliography

Meyer, Gerald. "American Labor Party." In *Encyclopedia of Third Parties in America*, ed. Immanuel Ness and James Ciment. Armonk, NY: M.E. Sharpe, 2000.

Waltzer, Kenneth. "The Party and the Polling Place: American Communism and the American Labor Party in the 1930s." *Radical History Review* (Spring 1980).

AMERICAN NEWSPAPER GUILD

Among the first white-collar unions in the history of the United States, the American Newspaper Guild (ANG) was founded in 1933 to fight for higher wages, better working conditions, and more job security among salaried newspaper reporters.

Traditionally, newspaper reporters worked long hours, were poorly paid, and could be fired on the whims of dictatorial editors. So impoverished were many reporters that they were discouraged from getting married and frequently took bribes to slant stories from a certain angle.

The onset of the Great Depression made things even worse, as newspapers failed and advertising revenue fell by 40 percent between 1929 and 1933. Thousands of reporters were laid off and those who kept their jobs saw their wages cut. Reporters were especially vulnerable to such cost-cutting measures because, unlike typesetters and most other technical people on newspapers staffs, they had no union and therefore could not bargain collectively or strike.

The triggering event for the founding of the ANG was the National Industrial Recovery Act of 1933. Under that act, many newspapers were granted immunity from antitrust actions (during the Depression, the closure of newspapers left many towns with only one daily paper) in exchange for accepting the act's Section 7, which allowed for the formation of unions. During the course of the year, regional ANG bodies were established, leading to the formation of a national organization in December, under the leadership of syndicated columnist Heywood Broun.

Citing Section 7, the ANG demanded union recognition as well as a forty-hour week, overtime, vacations, a minimum wage, and advance notice of layoffs. The American Newspaper Publishers Association (ANPA) responded with a slander campaign, charging that the ANG was communist inspired and led. Using loopholes in Section 7, newspaper publishers and editors also began firing ANG organizers.

In summer 1934, the first ANG-organized strikes began, against several small New York City-area dailies. While mostly ineffective, the strikes established the idea of reporters bargaining collectively for their working conditions. In February 1936, the Scripps-Howard chain of papers agreed to recognize the ANG.

But one of the biggest newspaper chains—led by William Randolph Hearst—resisted. In early 1936, reporters went on strike against the Hearst paper in Milwaukee. Injunctions were issued against picketers, and Broun, among others, was arrested. Soon, reporters in other cities—most notably, Seattle—organized sympathy strikes. In September, the strike ended in a victory for the ANG. That same year, the union affiliated with the American Federation of Labor, but left for the Committee for Industrial Organizations in 1937.

The ANG continues to be the leading union of newspaper reporters in the United States.

See also: American Federation of Labor; Congress of Industrial Organizations; newspapers and magazines; unions and union organizing; National Recovery Administration; Section 7; Hearst, William Randolph.

Bibliography

Leab, Daniel J. *A Union of Individuals: The Formation of the American Newspaper Guild, 1933–1936.* New York: Columbia University Press, 1970.

AMOS 'N' ANDY

Perhaps the most popular radio show in America during the Great Depression, *Amos 'n' Andy* depicted the lives of African Americans living in Harlem. Created in Chicago in 1926 as the *Sam 'n' Henry* show, the program was acquired by the National Broadcasting Company (NBC) in 1929 and broadcast nationally under its new name *Amos 'n' Andy*. The two main characters—Amos, browbeaten and subservient, and Andy, lazy and pompous—were played by white radio entertainers Freeman Gosden and Charles Correll, who parodied, in stereotypical fashion, the accents and manners of urban blacks who had recently migrated from the rural South. A third character—the Kingfish—was depicted as conniving and corrupt, providing a nickname for the ambitious populist Louisiana senator and governor Huey P. Long.

Almost from the very beginning, the caricatures of African Americans conveyed on the program raised protests in the black community. In 1931, the *Pittsburgh Courier* gathered 750,000 signatures on a petition demanding that NBC cancel the program. However, the campaign—along with frequent protests by the National Association for the Advancement of Colored People (NAACP)—failed to get the series off the air. In 1951, the show was acquired by the Columbia Broadcasting System and put on television with black actors. Poor ratings after the first season and continued black protests forced the program off the air in 1953, though it remained in syndication until 1966.

See also: radio; Long, Huey P.

Bibliography

Andrews, Bart, and Ahrgus Juilliard. *Holy Mackerel! The Amos 'n' Andy Show.* New York: E.P. Dutton, 1986.

Ely, Melvin Patrick. *The Adventures of Amos 'n' Andy: A Social History of an American Phenomenon.* New York: Free Press, 1991.

ARTS, FINE

PAINTING

Depression and Conservatism

The economic crash of 1929 was attended by a sharp new interest by Americans in their own art, to the general exclusion of all other styles. This interest may have been under way before the Depression, but hard times appear to have driven the country into deep introspection, even to the point of artistic jingoism. We *needed* an art of our own, said painters like Thomas Hart Benton, and lacked one. Or if we ever had it, it was lost. Was our country on its knees for the very reason that our culture was not robust? President Franklin D. Roosevelt may have thought so when he delivered his first inaugural address. The money changers have fled from their high seats in the temple of our civilization, he thundered, and we may now restore that temple to the ancient truths. Conservative jeremiads like this played well in a decade of isolationism and fear. Art in media besides painting was socially conscious and nativist too. John Steinbeck wrote about dust bowl heroism, for example, and Aaron Copland was busy setting cowboy mythology to music. Painters, for the most part, also looked backward in time, for essentially American themes, whether they meant to praise antique agrarian virtues or to denounce the contemporary opposite.

Their assertion of traditional ideals, real or imagined, took the form of resolute, almost cartoonish realism. Collectively—though this is only a generality—the conservative realists' work is spoken of as American Scene painting. The name may derive from the title *The American Scene*, a 1907 essay by Henry James, about his rediscovery of the spiritual values of his homeland. Within the American Scene there are two broad camps: regionalism and social realism. It was the regionalists who articulated our fondest myths, setting them usually in the midwestern farmland. The social realists, preoccupied with social reform, painted the grimmest tableaux of Depression life, as they themselves often knew it. There are antecedents to both these movements in the Ashcan school of social commentary, in folk art, and in the Hudson River school.

Realism in the manner of the American Scene presupposed an interest in community participation. Artists were inclined to remove themselves from their work as best they could and explore wide themes of social change, history, political motivation, and spiritual insight. As well, they organized among themselves and asserted their artistic teaching license, as it were, in exhibitions and new print venues. In 1931, the Whitney Museum of American Art opened, the very first of its kind.

This was not a good time to be an abstract artist in America or to be interested in erudite European formalism. In the face of real chauvinism, cubism and fauvism were gone from the mainstream by the 1930–31 exhibition season. Ideologues like Thomas Craven thought that the European sensibilities that had obtained for so long were worn-out and sterile, an assortment of pointless techniques instead of a form of meaningful communication. They also smacked of bohemianism and Parisian libertinism, rarely popular among Americans historically. Worst of all, the academic artistic techniques were not meant to be egalitarian, accessible to everyone; American Scene painters were adamant on the notion that art was for public edification—so much so that many of them sympathized with leftist and politically charged aesthetic systems like the Soviet Communists' antielitist socialist realism and Mexican mural painting. These were clear examples of art with a didactic, public-service purpose.

New Deal Intervention

The Works Progress Administration (WPA) came to the rescue of American artists in a big way, particularly the American Scene painters. Numerous smaller initiatives like New York's Gibson Committee had organized relief projects for artists already. But after petitioning from influential groups like the American Federation of Arts, the government acted to form a federal art program that would support a national style, accessible to the ordinary citizen, and that would support democratic sensibilities generally.

There were four projects. The Public Works of Art Project ran from December 1933 to June 1934, directed by Edward Bruce and Forbes Watson. It affirmed a basic nationalism in contemporary art in America. Next was the Treasury Department's Section of Painting and

Sculpture, a sponsor of competitions more than a relief program. It was disliked by artists generally, who thought it either elitist or bland—with some reason, too: the murals it commissioned had to conform with local tastes and be approved by Washington. This project lasted until 1943. Third was the Federal Art Project (FAP), under the aegis of the WPA. Begun in May 1935, it included support for design labs, exhibitions, bibliographies, and the recording of artifacts, such as in the Index of American Design. This was the most ambitious of the government projects, and it lasted until 1943. Fourth, the Treasury Relief Art Project, running from 1935 to 1939, underwrote the decoration of public buildings for which money had not already been allocated. This was financed through the FAP and was the smallest of the four relief undertakings. The American Scene lay at the center of all the art relief projects, at least from the standpoint of aesthetics. The political content was surprisingly minimal.

More surprising was the artistic consensus over the relief programs. Even archleftist elements usually approved of the WPA's art initiatives. The American Artists' Congress, for example, founded in 1936 in sympathy with the call by the Popular Front and the American Communist Party for literary and artistic action against fascism, endorsed the government's programs and lobbied for their permanency.

Regionalism

Regionalism in painting paralleled analogous trends in literature, such as in the Vanderbilt University circle around Robert Penn Warren, and in the various social sciences as well. Despite their differences here and there, they all sought to use indigenous types and themes in systematic affirmation of the American spirit. Three of the best-known regionalists were Thomas Hart Benton, John Steuart Curry, and Grant Wood, all born in the Midwest, but each distinguishable from the other: Benton for elongated, curvilinear depictions of farmers at work, Curry for his animals and country landscapes with blurred edges, and Wood for his tight, folkist renderings. Benton is especially famous for a 1930 cycle of murals on the theme of modern technology for the New School for Social Research in New York City, called *America Today*, presented as a montage of images of the working class.

Other forms of regionalism include those of Charles Burchfield, whose brooding psychological crises inform a very dark construction of small-town America, and Edward Hopper, the New Yorker who rejected his colleagues' "caricatures" of the American

experience. He focused on vernacular architecture and was a favorite among all the regionalist factions. Two self-taught members of the regionalist school were Anna Mary Robertson Moses, also known as Grandma Moses, and Horace Pippin, both steeped in the traditions of folk art. Grandma Moses moved to oil painting after learning to render nostalgic country scenes in yarn. Pippin drew on his army experience in World War I and on his life as a black artist in Pennsylvania to paint on a large range of subjects, most famously the life of the antislavery leader John Brown.

Social Realists

The socially conscious faction within American Scene painting, the social realists, disliked artistic elitism, as the regionalists did, and renounced academic artifice too. But unlike the regionalists, they fixated on the horrors of disenfranchisement among parts of the population, the migrant laborers most notably. For the social realists, classic regionalism approached the nationalist hyperbole of Hitlerian propaganda, and they fought bitterly about this in the public forum. The social realist movement was too democratic to be a true cousin of socialist realism, the official art form of the Stalinist USSR, but its preoccupation with the lower classes probably does make it a more international style than regionalism, its ancestors including European realists like Jean Courbet and Jean-François Millet and groups like the Artists International Association and the Kitchen Sink school.

The most prominent of the social realists in the 1930s was Ben Shahn, whose paintings, murals, and posters inveighed against fascism, social dissonance, and economic injustice. He is most famous for his work on the theme of the kangaroo convictions of anarchists Sacco and Vanzetti, a cause célébre of the 1920s. Other prominent figures were Raphael Soyer and Isabel Bishop, who depicted the anonymous toil of New York crowds. Black artists made enormous contributions to social realism. Jacob Lawrence, the most famous painter of the 1920s Harlem Renaissance, produced enormously influential treatments of major social issues, culminating in his sixty panels on the theme of migration from the South after World War I.

The Influence of Mexican Muralists

Public murals like Thomas Hart Benton's were central to the teaching of democratic values in the 1930s. They were heavily influenced by Mexican muralists who worked in the United States. Narrative murals in the

YEARS OF DUST

RESETTLEMENT ADMINISTRATION
Rescues Victims
Restores Land to Proper Use

Many American artists in the 1930s—including Ben Shahn, the creator of this 1936 poster for the Resettlement Administration—produced works for the federal government during the Great Depression. *(Library of Congress)*

Spanish-speaking Americas had long been conventional didactic tools. Diego Rivera produced a fresco cycle on industry for the Detroit Institute of Arts. He was hamstrung by his communist sympathies and saw a mural at Rockefeller Center destroyed for this reason. José Clemente Orozco produced an apocalyptic mural in Dartmouth College's Baker Library on the human capacity for greed, deception, and violence. David Alfaro Siqueiros, also limited by his radical politics, taught in the United States during the '30s and numbered among his students the young Jackson Pollock.

Outside the American Scene

There were artists in the 1930s who followed the School of Paris, who were not motivated by environmental or representational concerns, and who ignored the American landscape, the Depression, and social issues overall. Mild dissenters like Stuart Davis were neither provincial nor academic and exotic. At the other end, however, were abstractionists, whose work survived all the blizzards of popular opprobrium. Numerous modernist cells had actually done very well all this time. And, in fact, the Federal Art Project even supported a number of experimental artists. New York's Museum of Modern Art, which opened in 1929, mounted many exhibitions in cubism, fantastic art, dada, and surrealism. The Whitney Museum exhibited American abstract painting in 1936. And in 1939 Solomon R. Guggenheim founded the core collection of nonobjective work that would move to the famous Frank Lloyd Wright building on Fifth Avenue in 1959. There were even forums and interest groups for modernists, like the American Abstract Artists (AAA), formed in New York in 1936 along the lines of the Abstraction-Création group in Europe. They sponsored exhibitions, publications, and lectures and were generally associated with synthetic cubism, though to the exclusion of expressionism and surrealism.

The prominent American modernists in the 1930s include Stuart Davis, whose collages and paintings of consumer-product packaging in the manner of synthetic cubism are an important forerunner of the 1960s. It was just before the 1930s that he developed his famous *Egg Beater* series. Burgoyne Diller, one of the AAA artists, was the first American to work up an abstract style based on the Dutch art movement known as *de Stijl*. Irene Rice Pereira tried to wed art and technology in a manner inspired primarily by the Bauhaus. Milton Avery produced thin, broad planes of color much in the style of Henri Matisse. And Augustus Vincent Tack, the decade's modernist maverick, fused nonobjective and figural modes into coherent and enormous abstractions.

PHOTOGRAPHY

Photography during the 1930s responded to the same documentary impulse that drove the muralists. The Farm Security Administration (FSA) in particular sponsored numerous journalistic exercises to educate the public about the damage done by the Depression. The driving figure behind these was economist Roy Stryker, who did much of the hiring of the FSA photographers. Two of these were Dorothea Lange, famous for her 1936 *Migrant Mother*, Niporno, California photo, which was known sometimes as the Madonna of the Depression, and Walker Evans, who worked to counter the culture of salon photography. He collaborated late in the decade with his friend James Agee on an influential book about Alabama sharecropper families, published in 1941 as *Let Us Now Praise Famous Men*. Margaret Bourke-White, a photojournalist for Henry Luce's *Fortune* magazine, chronicled midwestern misery among migrants and produced a famous cover photo of the Fort Peck Dam. Another Luce photographer, Alfred Eisenstaedt, a refugee from Germany, became famous for an image of a West Point cadet's hazing and later for the well-known Victory Day kiss on Times Square. Berenice Abbott, a one-time disciple of surrealist artist Man Ray, did numerous artistic photos of New York for the WPA, working in modernist, abstract style instead of strict photojournalism. At the torrid other end, Arthur Felling ("Weegee") snapped voyeuristic freelance news photos of sensational public events. James van der Zee, trained during the Harlem Renaissance, produced a distinct style of portraiture, with retouched prints and painted backgrounds.

Art photography, distinct from the journalistic kind, flourished in the 1930s too. Alfred Stieglitz, the founder of modern photography in the United States at the turn of the century, was still active in the 1930s, known by now for an ethereal series of black-and-white cloud photographs. (Kodachrome color film, made by Kodak, first appeared in 1935, replacing Louis Lumière's 1907 "autochrome" technique, but it passed nearly without notice by artistic photographers.) Stieglitz's artistic descendant (though he was never a student), Edward Weston, pursued a fused path of abstraction and realism, culminating in 1930 with the famous *Pepper*. Weston, and his colleague Ansel Adams, worked with the smallest possible camera lens openings, and they helped found the West Coast society known accordingly as Group f/64 in 1932. Adams soon became the foremost nature photographer in the country, a gifted technician capable of producing a full range of tonal subtlety. Two other photographers associated with this school are Imogen Cunningham and Paul Strand.

SCULPTURE

American sculpture during the 1930s lacked the vitality of painting and photography. European work was more abundant and probably better. In the United States, imitative academic styles were the norm, and few sculptors developed either modernist or regionalist themes or techniques. Alexander Calder, the best-

known American sculptor before World War II, worked in a European context, having based himself in Paris since 1926. Like Calder, John Storrs, who geometricized figurative sculpture in stone in the manner of the Indian art he collected and who won commissions for art deco building decoration, expatriated to France. Lesser-known artists during the 1930s, whose reputations would blossom after World War II, included David Smith and Isamu Noguchi. In the first wave of modern American sculptors already known in the 1930s were two important immigrants from Europe, Gaston Lachaise and Elie Nadelman. Lachaise is famous for his theme of the large female nude with tapering limbs, and Nadelman for his primitivist take on contemporary life. There was constructivist sculpture in the 1930s in America, but only in the hands of a minority. Polish-born Theodore Roszak is famous for this and, later in the decade, for his interest in machine-inspired industrial design. He was best known for his *Construction in White* (1937), a whitewashed plywood and plastic collage of intersecting circles. Significantly, Roszak did much work for the WPA.

ARCHITECTURE AND DESIGN

American building design during the 1930s was nearly untouched by any of the trends that swept Europe in the 1920s. George Howe and William E. Lescaze's Philadelphia Savings Fund Society building (1931–32) was the first and most important example in the country of the International Style. Generally speaking, though, the famous skyscrapers of the 1930s, such as the Empire State Building in New York, which so epitomized the American spirit of urban building, were in fact done in the various revivalist traditions of the 1890s—merely bigger—and not usually along the modernist lines of the likes of Gropius and Mies van der Rohe that prevailed overseas.

Art deco is the most identifiable design style of the decade, a decorative motif from Dutch architecture of the 1920s, extremely popular in the United States in the 1930s. Art deco design adorns buildings such as the Union Trust Company in Detroit and all manner of domestic appliances and automobiles as well.

Duncan Fisher

See also: Empire State Building; *Let Us Now Praise Famous Men*; Farm Security Administration; Federal Art Project; Public Works of Art Program; Works Progress Administration; Agee, James; Benton, Thomas Hart; Bourke-White, Margaret; Copland,

Aaron; Evans, Walker; Rivera, Diego; Steinbeck, John; Wood, Grant.

Bibliography

Agee, William C. *The 1930's: Painting and Sculpture in America.* New York: Whitney Museum of American Art, 1968.

Baigell, Matthew. *The American Scene: American Painting of the 1930s.* New York: Praeger, 1974.

Baigell, Matthew, and Julie Williams, eds. *Artists Against War and Fascism: Papers of the First American Artists' Congress.* New Brunswick, NJ: Rutgers University Press, 1986.

Boswell, Peyton, Jr. *Modern American Painting.* New York: Dodd, Mead, 1939.

Corn, W. M. *Grant Wood: The Regionalist Vision.* New Haven: Yale University Press, 1983.

Dennis, J. M. *Grant Wood: A Study in American Art and Culture.* New York: Viking Press, 1975.

Ekirch, Arthur A., Jr. *Ideologies and Utopias: The Impact of the New Deal on American Thought.* Chicago: Quadrangle Books, 1969.

Heller, Nancy, and Julia Williams. *The Regionalists: Painters of the American Scene.* New York: Galahad, 1976.

Jones, A. H. "The Search for a Usable American Past in the New Deal Era." *American Quarterly* 23 (1971): 710–24.

McKinzie, Richard D. *The New Deal for Artists.* Princeton: Princeton University Press, 1973.

Marling, K. A. *Wall-to-Wall America: A Cultural History of Post Office Murals in the Great Depression.* Minneapolis: University of Minnesota Press, 1982.

O'Connor, F. V. ed. *Art for the Millions: Essays from the 1930's.* Boston: New York Graphic Society, 1973.

O'Connor, F. V., ed. *The New Deal Art Projects: An Anthology of Memoirs.* Washington, DC: Smithsonian Institution Press, 1972.

Odum, Howard W., and Harry E. Moore. *American Regionalism.* New York: Henry Holt, 1938.

Turner, Jane, ed. *The Dictionary of Art.* New York: Macmillan, 1996.

Watson, Forbes. *American Painting Today.* Washington, DC: The American Federation of Art, 1939.

ASIAN AMERICANS

For the United States's Asian-American population, the Great Depression's hardships merely intensified the segregation, economic discrimination, and general white hostility they already faced. Numbering only a few hundred thousand, the great majority of people of Asian ancestry lived on the Pacific Coast, mostly in California, and in Hawaii. During the 1930s, federal law barred most Asian immigrants from citizenship because of their race. Asian Americans born in the United States were automatically entitled to citizenship but found that this status opened few doors.

Japanese Americans comprised the largest group of Asian-ancestry people in the continental United States and Hawaii. On the West Coast, most worked in industries linked to agriculture in some way: Farming, gardening, and retail fruit and vegetable sales were common occupations. But second-generation Japanese Americans, or "nisei," found few opportunities outside this ethnic economic niche. Most whites would not hire them or use their professional services. Given the large Asian-ancestry population in Hawaii, the second generation there experienced greater general acceptance. Still, they found most occupations aside from agriculture closed to them. And in both places, agriculture was hardly a stable or remunerative industry in the midst of the Great Depression.

Like other Asian Americans, Japanese Americans living on the West Coast also experienced a web of private and public prejudice designed to keep them in their place. Those who wished to purchase a decent home in most urban areas found that segregationist homeowners' organizations and restrictive deeds made this almost impossible. Instead, urban Japanese Americans lived in substandard and slum housing. Many businesses and public facilities, including swimming pools, public parks, theaters, barber shops, restaurants, and golf courses, remained segregated either partially or completely. In rural areas, numerous state laws prevented the first generation, or "issei," from purchasing or leasing property in their own names or even for their children. Although in practice numerous issei broke such laws with the help of white neighbors or older nisei, their livelihoods depended on the honesty of such people rather than legal protection. Organizations like the American Legion and the American Federation of Labor vigilantly guarded against any attempt by the nisei or issei to better their lot through changing racist laws.

The Chinese-American population in the United

As with other ethnic minorities, Asian Americans, like this farm family in Los Angeles County, faced discrimination as well as economic hard times during the Great Depression. *(Library of Congress)*

States, which had been shrinking since the passage of exclusionary laws in the nineteenth century, finally began to grow slowly in the 1930s. The American public's general perception of Chinese and Chinese Americans also started to improve, in large part because of books like Pearl Buck's *The Good Earth*. Many whites on the West Coast, nervous about Japanese ambitions in Asia and Japanese-American success in farming, also compared Chinese Americans favorably to their Japanese-American neighbors. However, the largely urban Chinese-American population hardly benefited from such comparisons, for, in most cities, they lived either in segregated ghettos like San Francisco's Chinatown or in cramped back rooms of the laundries and restaurants that still made up the bulk of their ethnic niche economy. Like their Japanese-American peers, second-generation Chinese Americans, no matter how well educated, found few job opportunities, especially on the West Coast where the majority lived. Many even traveled to China, hoping to find better jobs and more acceptance, as well as to help that country in its struggle to modernize under the new nationalist government.

As relative newcomers to the United States, Filipinos, the vast majority young, single, and male, had not created any real economic niches comparable to those of Japanese and Chinese Americans. But like their Asian-American peers, they found well-paying careers closed to them, whatever their education or intelligence. In the cities of the West Coast and a few other areas such as New York and Chicago, Filipinos worked in the service industry as bellboys, doormen, waiters, and sometimes Pullman porters. In rural areas, most toiled as farm laborers, following the harvest from northern Washington to southern California. As white migrants from dust bowl states like Oklahoma, Missouri, and Texas poured into the Pacific Coast states during the Depression, they sometimes competed with Filipinos for such jobs and complained about such competition. However, this did not stop the American-educated Filipinos from trying to unionize and from striking against bad conditions. Their skin color and their willingness to fight for decent treatment won them many enemies, however. Heeding white critics, the U.S. government attempted to buy off many Filipinos, offering them a free return passage to the Philippines; when this effort largely failed, Congress voted to grant the Philippines eventual independence and to curb Filipino immigration afterward.

On the West Coast, then, Asian Americans, including small communities of Koreans and Sikh Indians, lived under a quasi–jim crow system that branded them second-class people. Opportunities for them were hardly better in Hawaii. While many people of Asian descent began to organize to oppose this system during the Depression, legal recognition and approval of segregation and racism limited the success of such ventures. Citizenship requirements kept many first-generation poor from taking advantage of the increasing number of New Deal government jobs and programs created to alleviate widespread poverty. Farmworkers in particular could not participate in the new Social Security pension program. Still, during these years the Japanese American Citizens League, the Chinese Hand Laundry Alliance of New York, the Chinese American Citizens Alliance, and various anti-Japanese Korean nationalist groups fought for greater recognition and respect.

Such organizations, as well as simple demographics, helped plant the seeds for the eventual postwar dismantling of legalized racial inequality on the West Coast and in Hawaii. Exclusionary laws had shaped and in some cases retarded Asian-American family growth and reproduction, but in the 1930s, a large proportion of both the Chinese- and Japanese-American population were native-born and just coming of age. They were largely American-educated and thoroughly familiar with the freedoms they were supposed to enjoy. And in cities from Los Angeles to Honolulu, they were just beginning to consider the possibility of using their political voices to claim these freedoms.

CHARLOTTE BROOKS

See also: agriculture; *The Good Earth*; China; Japan.

Bibliography

Chan, Sucheng. *Asian Americans: An Interpretive History*. New York: Twayne, 1991.

Chun, Gloria Heyung. *Of Orphans and Warriors: Inventing Chinese American Culture and Identity*. New Brunswick, NJ: Rutgers University Press, 2000.

Thomas, Dorothy Swaine. *Japanese American Evacuation and Resettlement: The Salvage*. Berkeley: University of California Press, 1952.

Yu, Renqiu. *To Save China, To Save Ourselves: The Chinese Hand Laundry Alliance of New York*. Philadelphia: Temple University Press, 1992.

AUTOMOBILE INDUSTRY

Within the span of one generation, the auto industry had fundamentally transformed the American economy and society. In 1899, fewer than 4,000 vehicles were made by just over 2,000 workers. By 1929, over 5 million vehicles were produced, and almost 500,000 workers were employed making motor vehicles and motor vehicle parts. With the rapid growth of the industry came a corresponding expansion in the ownership of passenger cars. In 1913, the first year motor vehicle registration figures were compiled, there were approximately 1.25 million cars on the road, by 1920 there were 10 million, and by 1930 there were 25 million. Although the rate of increase slowed with the Great Depression, by the 1930s autos were already the largest industry in the United States, and General Motors (GM) was the largest industrial corporation in the world, producing over 40 percent of the passenger cars sold at the time. GM was also the largest producer of trucks and buses.

Broad ownership of cars was a uniquely American experience in the 1930s. Approximately 70 percent of all the world's motor vehicles were registered in the United States. Not surprisingly, the U.S. auto industry dominated world production. In 1929, the U.S. automakers manufactured 85 percent of the world's vehicles, of which 10 percent were exported.

ECONOMIC DOWNTURN

Auto producers, including part makers, suffered a greater drop in gross and net income than the average for all manufacturing corporations between 1929 and 1934. Despite this, the industry lost money only in 1932 (and GM never did), while overall the corporate sector sustained losses in 1931, 1932, and 1933. The industry's greater exposure to the collapse in the economy was due to its large fixed investment in plant and equipment, which made it especially vulnerable to economic downturns when many car owners put off buying a new car and kept repairing the cars they already owned. The fall in demand for new cars was dramatic. After hitting a record high in sales of new vehicles of 5,294,087 in 1929, sales plummeted to 1,848,013 in 1933. Employment in the industry followed a similar trend, with 447,448 workers in 1929 falling to 243,614 in 1933. Average wages for those who remained employed dropped by 37 percent because of wage cuts and fewer hours. Yet autoworkers on average were paid 24 percent more than workers in manufacturing as a whole. Many businesses related to autos also were hit hard by the Depression. The number of new car dealers dropped from approximately 42,000 in 1929 to just over 30,000 in 1935. Employment by dealers also dropped from 1929, when it stood at almost 550,000, to a low in 1933 at just over 200,000. The total dollar value of new and used car sales followed the trends in sales: in 1929, this figure peaked at almost $6.5 billion, while in 1933 it hit a Depression low at just over $2 billion.

VEHICLE USAGE AND ROAD BUILDING

In the 1920s, sociologists were already documenting the transformation of social relations that resulted as car usage expanded. Increasingly reliant on the automobile, Americans drove more miles each year. While there were 198 billion miles of motor vehicle travel in 1929, the Depression low in 1932 and 1933 was 206 billion miles. By 1941, there were 334 billion miles traveled. Revenues from special motor vehicle taxes increased correspondingly from $849 million in 1929 to $1.693 billion in 1940. New Deal public works projects often took the form of road building, indirectly subsidizing the industry. Half of the 2 million workers involved in these projects built roads and streets. Between June 1933 and April 1934, the Civil Works Administration built or repaired 500,000 miles of roads. During the next three years, relief officials and the Bureau of Public Roads spent $2.8 billion on roads. Overall, the number of miles of surfaced roads doubled between 1930 and 1940, totaling 1,367,000.

TRENDS TOWARD CONCENTRATION

The evolution of the industry from its initial competitive stage to a tight oligopoly controlled by three firms began in the 1920s and continued during the Depression. As many as eighty-eight firms were involved in manufacturing in 1921, but within a few years forty-three firms left the industry. By 1929, the Big Three (General Motors, Ford, and Chrysler) accounted for almost 75 percent of production, and by 1937 they accounted for 85 percent. Five other companies shared most of the rest of sales: Hudson, Nash, Packard, Studebaker, and Willys-Overland. During the Depression, a number of widely known automakers went under: Locomobile, Moon, Peerless, Franklin, and Jordan. Key to this trend toward concentration was the introduction of the annual style change. Initiated by GM in 1923, mostly cosmetic changes were made to each year's new cars. Smaller producers could not afford the capital or advertising costs that came with updating models each year. In 1939, the Federal Trade Commission confirmed that the annual style change favored large producers over smaller ones and spurred the trend toward concentration.

NEW DEAL LEGISLATION

Two prominent pieces of New Deal legislation deserve special mention: the National Industry Recovery Act (NIRA), which attempted to regulate competition, and the Wagner Act, which provided for workers' rights to unionize. The NIRA was not seen as necessary by the automakers because they were well organized, with a powerful trade association, the National Automobile Chamber of Commerce (NACC), which administered cross-licensing of patents. Unlike in many industries, price cutting was not a problem. Already highly concentrated, automakers followed the price-setting benchmarks of Ford and geared their production to sales forecasts, which were essential for annual model changes. Nevertheless, a committee of the NACC drew up the industry code for prices, wages, hours, and conditions of labor, varying little from industry practice and proving to be relatively ineffective. Henry Ford ignored the code altogether, but due to his popularity was never prosecuted. During its short life, the NIRA's provisions that ostensibly guaranteed workers the right to organize were ignored by industry officials.

Even after the passage of the Wagner Act, putting teeth in the government's ability to protect workers' efforts to unionize, industry officials fought unionization efforts in some of the most bitterly fought contests between workers and big business. Autoworkers borrowed from the French the use of sit-down strikes, which became a signature tactic of the times. Violence was common as workers struggled to unionize. Ford became notorious for the "Battle of the Overpass" at its River Rouge plant in Michigan, in which union leaders were beaten by company thugs, while GM fought unionization by spending almost $1 million between 1933 and 1937 on espionage and munitions to prevent workers from organizing. Finally, in early 1937, both GM and Chrysler recognized the United Auto Workers as the collective bargaining agent for the industry. Ford would not be unionized until 1941.

REORGANIZING GROUND TRANSPORTATION

Auto industry officials realized that the continued profitability and growth of the industry depended on more than economic recovery because by the late 1920s the market for automobiles was saturated, with most new car purchases going to those who already owned a vehicle. Overall, the existing stock of vehicles was sufficient for the nation's transportation needs. GM led the way in organizing industry efforts to remake the system of ground transportation in order to spur new car sales. In 1933, Alfred Sloan, GM's president, brought together the auto, oil, and rubber industries to form the National Highway User's Conference (NHUC) to lobby for highway construction and for a system of taxation that would dedicate revenues for this purpose. To shape public perceptions of the future of transportation and housing patterns at the 1939 World's Fair in New York, GM's exhibit presented a picture of how American society would look in 1960. With superhighways and cars at its core, the image foreshadowed the subsequent postwar suburban development and was the most popular exhibit of the fair. Meanwhile, the Bureau of Public Roads issued its 1939 report, *Toll Roads and Free Roads*, which weighed the feasibility of three east-west and three north-south national toll roads. Although the report argued against such a plan, it did lead President Franklin D. Roosevelt to appoint the National Inter-

regional Highway Committee, whose 1943 report, *Interregional Highways*, mapped what became the Interstate Highway System.

In the quest to transform the nation's transportation system, GM was not content simply to lobby government officials or to shape public opinion. Beginning in 1932, the company went about buying municipal electric trolley lines, dismantling them, substituting diesel buses in their place, and then reselling the systems. (By this time, GM was already the largest producer of buses.) The high cost and slow speed of buses contributed, in turn, to the collapse of hundreds of public transit systems, making it increasingly necessary for Americans to own a car. This conscious effort to create an auto-dependent nation was not accomplished without a public outcry. In 1935, the American Transit Association censured GM for its attempt to motorize Portland's electric streetcar system. In response, GM set up a holding company to continue its efforts, bringing together the same set of corporate interests (i.e., oil and rubber) as it had in the NHUC. By 1949, more than 100 electric transit systems in forty-five cities and 90 percent of the nation's trolley network were gone. That same year, a federal jury convicted GM and it partners of conspiring to dismantle trolley lines throughout the nation and levied a meager $5,000 fine.

SAFETY ON THE NATION'S ROADS

As more miles were driven each year, the death and injury toll mounted on the nation's roads. By the mid-1930s, annual traffic deaths exceeded 30,000, and industry officials worried about a backlash against the automobile. In 1937, industry officials set up the Automobile Safety Foundation (ASF) headed by Paul Hoffman, president of Studebaker. (Hoffman had earlier tried to get the industry's trade association involved in highway safety, but was unsuccessful until a *Reader's Digest* story, "And Sudden Death," detailed the suffering that resulted from vehicle crashes. Reprinted in approximately 2,000 newspapers and magazines, the story's total printed circulation reached 35 million.) Simply an extension of the industry, the ASF directed public attention away from unsafe cars to driver behavior and improved road engineering as the solution to highway safety. No attention was given to injury prevention and, in fact, there were no medical doctors or academic researchers on the ASF's board or among its officers. For the automakers themselves, styling took precedence over safety.

FOREIGN HOLDINGS AND WORLD WAR II

Although the Big Three were primarily domestic companies, each did have foreign holdings by the 1930s. In 1929, GM, in fact, acquired Adam Opel, Germany's largest automaker. Together, the German subsidiaries of Ford and GM controlled 70 percent of the German car market by the end of the decade. With the coming of World War II, GM and Ford, in particular, were integral to the war efforts of both the Allied and Axis powers. Widely known as the arsenals of democracy for their contribution to U.S. war efforts, Ford and GM cooperated with the Nazis in converting their German plants to military use. After the war, each received reparations from the U.S. government for damages done to their plants by Allied bombing.

With America's entry into World War II, the U.S. auto industry converted its plants to war production and virtually no passenger cars were produced for the duration of the war. It was not until 1948 that sales matched the level achieved in 1929.

STAN LUGER

See also: Ford Motor Company; General Motors; United Automobile Workers; National Industrial Recovery Act; National Labor Relations Act; World War II, early history of; Sloan, Alfred.

Bibliography

Eastman, Joel. *Styling vs. Safety: The American Automobile Industry and the Development of Automotive Safety, 1900–1966.* Lanham, MD: University Press of America, 1984.

Fine, Sidney. *The Automobile Under the Blue Eagle.* Ann Arbor: University of Michigan Press, 1963.

Kay, Jane Holtz. *Asphalt Nation: How the Automobile Took Over America and How We Can Take It Back.* New York: Crown, 1997.

Lichtenstein, Nelson. *The Most Dangerous Man in Detroit: Walter Reuther and the Fate of American Labor.* New York: Basic Books, 1995.

Luger, Stan. *Corporate Power, American Democracy and the Automobile Industry.* New York: Cambridge University Press, 2000.

Rae, John. *The American Automobile: A Brief History.* Chicago: University of Chicago Press, 1965.

St. Clair, Jeffrey. *The Motorization of American Cities.* New York: Praeger, 1987.

Senate, Committee on the Judiciary. *American Ground Transport: A Proposal for Restructuring the Automobile, Truck, Bus and Rail Industries.* A report by Bradford Snell to the subcommittee on Antitrust and Monopoly. 93rd Cong., 2nd sess., 1974.

United States Federal Trade Commission. *Report on Motor Vehicle Industry.* Washington, DC: Government Printing Office, 1939.

Whitney, Simon. *Antitrust Policies,* vol. 1. New York: The Twentieth Century Fund, 1958.

BANKING

It is hard to gain a true understanding of the Great Depression without taking into account the banking industry's decline. In fact, there was a symbiotic effect between the collapse of the economy in the Great Depression years and the decaying banking sector. The two would have a profound effect on how Americans viewed banks and the regulation of banking, setting banking policy for three decades after the the Great Depression. The events also influenced Americans' general views on regulation.

PRECURSORS TO COLLAPSE

The seeds of the banking crisis of 1929 and, by extension, of the Great Depression lie in an era of prosperity—1920s America. The 1920s in many ways marked the expansion of American banking. Previously, there had been little in the way of consumer debt financing by American banks. For example, it was almost unheard of for a commercial bank to lend money for a home mortgage. Most people had to buy their homes with cash. Much of this tight-fisted lending changed in the heated post–World War I economy. Banks (particularly small local banks) began to increase their lending to start-up farms. However, when food prices fell following the war, farmers began defaulting on loans and a large number of "country" banks that had made marginal loans quickly found themselves in trouble. This led to a limited crisis in banking that would be the harbinger for the greater collapse to come.

The 1920s prosperity kindled an unprecedented consolidation of American business—particularly the manufacturing sector. This only exacerbated the problems of local banks because their customer base of small businesses was eroding. Combined with the situation in the farm industry, it was inevitable that the small bank sector would suffer. As small banks failed, larger banks captured their customer base. The banking industry was following the same wave of consolidation that engulfed other sectors in the economy. In addition to the need to meet the demands of customers who were not being served by the now faltering small bank industry, merger mania in the banking industry was fueled by cost-saving considerations. Certain banking operations, such as management responsibilities, could be consolidated and their cost reduced by spreading it over a larger enterprise. A measure of the consolidation is found in the following statistics: from 1923 through 1928, the number of banks was reduced from 30,178 (with $54 billion in resources) to 26,213 (with $71 billion in resources).

The banks that remained took part in one of the greatest economic booms in American history. There was a great expansion of wealth on the national level. However, it was distributed, for the most part, to the upper classes. Those who had a stake in or managed big business in America benefited splendidly. In addition, due to increases in labor productivity, consumer prices had actually gone down. Finally, with the federal coffers bulging with surplus, Americans, particularly the wealthy, were privileged with federal income tax reductions as well. The result was that the American elite was awash in money.

THE SPECULATIVE BUBBLE

The logical thing to do was to invest even more into the very businesses that had created the wealth. The problem was that this investment was increasingly fueled by debt. In addition to increased consumer debt, there was an unprecedented number of loans (commonly referred to as margin accounts) being taken out specifically to invest in the stock market. An estimated $6 billion was loaned to investors to engage in stock market speculation. Instead of this wealth being distributed throughout the population, which might have lent some stability to the system, it was disproportionately being circulated back into the hands of the wealthy and large business interests.

The speculative house of cards held up until 1929, when a credit crunch, caused in part by the collapse of foreign banks, led to a reduction in the demand for goods and forced price reductions. Businesses that earlier seemed impervious began losing money and as a consequence began cutting down on production, slash-

ing wages, and reducing their labor force. This had the inevitable consequence of further reducing the demand for goods and exacerbating the recession. A healthy banking industry might have survived and indeed contributed to pulling the country out of this recession, staving off a depression. However, the industry was fundamentally flawed and ended up contributing to the problem.

Banks had become increasingly engaged in long-term business financing, as opposed to their traditional function of providing short-term loans to finance business and trade. They began to get involved in the underwriting of securities. An underwriter helps businesses sell company stock (ownership) to investors. Such activities were generally engaged in by investment banks. National banks, as opposed to state banks, were prohibited by law from engaging in investment banking activities. However, through appeals to the courts, national banks began making incursions into investment banking. In the end, the chief regulator of national banks, the comptroller of the currency, relaxed regulations, allowing banks to gain an even greater foothold in the field. Later, Congress stepped in with specific legislation, the 1927 McFadden Act, granting commercial banks permission to engage in investment banking. This was partly the result of bank pressure applied by circumventing existing regulation and structuring deals so that they would not fall under the umbrella of national banking regulation. By the end of the 1920s, commercial banks were fully ensconced in the investment banking field, offering corporate securities to the public. Even people of modest means began investing in the market. Of course, this was done for the most part to meet the legitimate needs of a growing industrial nation. However, it set the stage for systemic bank failures when businesses began to default on loans and the interest collected could not keep up with promised payments to depositors.

In an effort to attract ever more capital to fuel the business boom, banks offered higher interest rates on deposits, not only on direct consumer deposits but on "interbank" deposits as well (the interest larger banks grant to smaller banks for deposits held on their behalf). Ultimately, the larger banks used the monies they gathered from smaller institutions to lend to stock market speculators. The banks would run into trouble once the stock market failed and loan obligations could not be met. Federal authorities, including President Herbert Hoover and officials at the Federal Reserve, tried to put a halt to the speculation, but it had taken on a life of its own.

THE BEGINNING OF THE END

In September 1929, stock markets in Europe, including the heavily influential London stock exchange, began collapsing. It was only a matter of days before the financial plague spread to America. The crash came on October 24, 1929, with subsequent dips on October 26 and 29. The panic in the stock market quickly spread to other sectors of the economy. In particular, the farming industry was, again, especially hard hit with falling prices for farm products. This led to an increase in loan defaults, with the predictable negative effects on banks. However, the more significant consequence to banks came from defaults in the loans lent out for stock speculation. When the price of stocks decreased in their margin accounts customers were required to make payments. Of course, some were not able to do so, given the dire times. Moreover, to the extent that customers made payments on margin accounts, it had the negative effect of withdrawing money from the system that might otherwise have been devoted to funding new business ventures. Businesses were faltering given the lack of consumer demand for products. This led to increased layoffs and production cutbacks. There was a spiraling downward cycle—the Great Depression.

Banks suffered as a consequence of the Depression—deposits dried up and loans that would have been sound in good economic times turned out to be bad investments in the hard economic times. Unlike the failures that occurred earlier in the century, bank failures following the Great Depression were not limited to small, rural institutions. In fact, two of the largest banks in America, Bank of the United States and Bankers Trust Company, failed during this period. Between them, they represented $650 million in deposits—a very significant sum at the time. When depositors realized that banks, even those of considerable size, were facing financial ruin, they rushed to remove their deposits. This not only triggered what is commonly referred to as a "run" on troubled banks but a "panic" that also encompassed healthy banks.

Once the smell of bank failure permeated the air, customers believed that the only way to protect themselves from losing their deposits was to withdraw funds—even if there was no indication that their bank was in trouble. The fallout from the Bank of the United States collapse illustrates how often irrational instincts took over. The Bank of the United States was actually a privately owned New York state bank with no direct connection to the national government. However, once

Americans heard that the "Bank of the United States" had failed, they assumed that the system was ruined nationwide.

Unfortunately, the collective paranoia became a self-fulfilling prophecy because banks operate under a system of fractional reserves. When customers deposit money at a bank, even today, the bank does not merely lock it up in a vault. The bank keeps a portion of the money on reserve to meet depositor demand for withdrawals but lends the bulk of it out in order to make a profit. This is standard and usually prudent banking policy because, under most circumstances, only a fraction of depositors will demand their funds at any particular time. However, if all customers do in fact demand their monies at once, which happens in a panic, even the most fiscally sound institution can be ruined.

GOVERNMENT RESCUE AND REFORM

There clearly was a crisis in the industry, and stopgap measures, such as the Reconstruction Finance Corporation (authorized to lend to failing banks), were inadequate to resolve the deep-set problems: draconian measures had to be taken. The first such measure in an effort to stop the hemorrhaging was the declaration of a banking holiday. A "banking holiday" is a euphemism for a closure. The idea was that banks would close temporarily, go on "holiday," so that regulators could determine which institutions had a realistic chance of survival and take whatever measures necessary to support viable firms. There was an early effort to have a nationwide holiday, but this was thwarted by President Hoover's reluctance to take such drastic action. However, beginning with New York, individual states began taking it upon themselves to declare statewide banking holidays. This all happened so quickly that, by the time President Franklin D. Roosevelt declared a national banking holiday on March 6, 1933, forty-eight states had already done so on a state-by-state basis. Some state holiday lasted several days; others dragged on for a week or more.

In conjunction with the banking holiday, Congress passed the Emergency Banking Act of 1933. The purpose of the act was to provide a mechanism for sorting through the rubble. Banks would be categorized based on their relative weakness. Banks that could not survive due to severe financial deterioration would not reopen and their assets would be liquidated. If an institution was financially weak, yet could be sustained if given financial help, assistance was provided. When the holiday was over, only banks that were fiscally sound would reopen. Institutions that were in good fiscal condition before the holiday would benefit from the respite because, once there were assurances that the banking system was sound, there would be no impetus for customers to rush to remove their deposits from healthy banks in a panic. Part of the reassurance came in the form of President Roosevelt's March 12 fireside chat, in which he explained the reasoning behind the holiday and its public benefits.

The banking holiday and Emergency Banking Act were clearly only temporary measures. Policy-makers needed to devise long-term solutions to the structural issues highlighted by the collapsed banking system. In fashioning these remedies, Congress set up a structure that would govern American banking well into the remainder of the twentieth century. There were three principal areas that had to be addressed. First, the American people had to once again feel a sense of trust that if they deposited their money into banks it would be there when requested. Second, banks had to be prevented from engaging in the types of risky securities operations that contributed to the crisis. Finally, there needed to be a cap on interests rates so that banks would not feel pressured to engage in risky ventures in order to meet interest rate demands.

The first goal was met with the creation of the Federal Deposit Insurance Corporation (FDIC). Again, as with the banking holiday, President Roosevelt discussed its benefits in a fireside chat to sooth the nation's fears. The FDIC was established as part of the principal legislation responding to the crisis, the Banking Act of 1933 (more popularly referred to as the Glass-Steagall Act). Through the FDIC the federal government pledged to insure that any bank depositor would be paid in full up to the amount, initially, of $2,500. If a bank failed and could not pay, the federal government would step in and make up the difference. The insured amount was quickly raised to $5,000 and eventually to the current $100,000. This measure may indeed be the most important, and certainly the most enduring, legacy of the banking crisis. Since its establishment, Americans have had confidence in the banking system and, even when times have been rough in the industry, there has been no recurrence of the panics that marked the period of crisis.

The Glass-Steagall Act also prohibited commercial banks from engaging in investment banking activities. This meant that banks could no longer participate in the types of underwriting and securities operations that were in part responsible for the industry's poor condition in the 1920s.

Interest rates were also regulated under the Glass-Steagall Act. Banks were forbidden to offer interest on checking deposits. In addition, regulations were passed that limited the interest that could be paid on savings accounts.

There is an inextricable link between the banking industry's fate in the 1920s and the Great Depression. The Great Depression and responses to the banking crisis led to the public policy choices that defined the banking industry for the next six decades. However, as memories of the Great Depression and the banking crisis have faded, so too have many of the laws that were passed as a response to both phenomena. Interest rates have been deregulated and, more dramatically, the separation between the commercial and investment banking industry has been obliterated. The only major piece of the Banking Act of 1933 still intact is deposit insurance.

JAMES HACKNEY

See also: banking holidays; Insurance; Emergency Banking Act; Federal Deposit Insurance Corporation; Federal Reserve Bank; New Deal, first; Reconstruction Finance Corporation; Dawes, Charles; Eccles, Marriner; Glass, Carter; Documents: Hoover's Outline of Program to Secure Cooperation of Bankers to Relieve Financial Difficulties, October 6, 1931; Fireside Chat on the Banking Crisis, March 12, 1933

Bibliography

Brandeis, Louis. *Other People's Money and How Bankers Use It.* Boston: Bedford Books of St. Martin's, 1913.

Deuss, Jean. *Banking in the U.S.: An Annotated Bibliography.* Metuchen, NJ: The Scarecrow Press, 1990.

Eccles, George. *The Politics of Banking.* Salt Lake City: University of Utah, 1982.

Klebaner, Benjamin. *American Banking: A History.* Boston: Twayne, 1990.

Krooss, Herman, ed. *Documentary History of Banking and Currency in the United States.* New York: Chelsea House, 1969.

BLACK LEGION

Also known as the Invisible Eye of Labor, the Black Legion was the Michigan branch of the Ku Klux Klan (KKK). It was given its anti-labor moniker because—unlike other KKK organizations that focused on anti-black, anti-Semitic, and anti-immigrant activities—the Black Legion made a name for itself when it harassed union officials and unionizing workers during the organizational struggles in the automobile industry during the mid- and late 1930s. While few members of the secretive organization were ever prosecuted, the Black Legion was implicated in numerous beatings, several kidnappings, and at least one murder.

See also: auto industry; United Automobile Workers; Reuther, Walter.

Bibliography

Kraus, Henry. *Heroes of Unwritten Story: The UAW, 1934–1939.* Urbana: University of Illinois Press, 1993.

Lichtenstein, Nelson. *The Most Dangerous Man in Detroit: Walter Reuther and the Fate of American Labor.* New York: Basic Books, 1995.

BONUS ARMY

The Bonus Army, or Bonus Expeditionary Force, was comprised of a group of World War I veterans and their families who moved to Washington, D.C., to request the bonuses that had been promised to them under the World War Adjusted Compensation Act of 1924. As a partial compensation for their service, veterans of World War I were to have bonus payments extended to them beginning in 1945. When the full impact of the Great Depression began reaching the country, veterans were especially affected. Many lost their jobs and their homes. With nowhere else to go, no foreseeable end to the Depression in sight, and without much prior arrangement, veterans alone and in groups began to migrate to the nation's capital in an effort to demand early payment of their bonuses.

The first bonus march took place in late 1931 when a group of veterans from Oregon rode boxcars to Washington, D.C., to request that Congress release the bonus payments early. This group of approximately forty men engaged in courtesy visits with members of Congress and even had their trip home paid for by their representative, but few tangible goals were achieved as a result of these meetings. Although there was little communication between this group of men and the group that eventually became the bonus marchers, some consider this first group a precursor to the actual Bonus Army march.

While the bonus march itself was rather disorganized, most historians agree that it began in Oregon. Approximately two hundred men, led mainly by an ex-medic named Walter W. Waters, began their journey to the nation's capital riding boxcars and freight trains for free. Riding the rails was a common practice at this time, and, while it was frowned upon by railroad companies, those who actually conducted and worked on the trains were unlikely to remove anyone, especially veterans with nowhere else to go.

After about three weeks, the first group from Oregon finally arrived in Washington in spring 1932. At least one group had arrived previous to the Oregon bonus marchers. This group, from Tennessee, had parked their vehicles near the White House with signs declaring "We want our bonus." Both this group of veterans and those who came from Oregon received press coverage, and, by the time the group from Oregon arrived, numerous other groups had already begun to travel to the capital.

The sporadic arrivals of veterans soon became a constant flow until thousands had moved to Washington, D.C. Most groups had ridden in boxcars or broken-down vehicles and had depended on veterans and service organizations for food and other essentials. Once in the nation's capital, the veterans built a makeshift camp in Anacostia, a section of the city, by moving into partially destroyed and abandoned buildings or us-

In July 1932, members of the Bonus Army marched in Washington, D.C., to demand immediate payment for their services in World War I. *(Brown Brothers)*

ing whatever materials they could find to construct shacks and hovels for themselves and their families. During their time in Washington, the Bonus Army received food and supplies from organizations and supporters around the country.

From the beginning, the government, in particular the War Department, was not pleased with the Bonus Army and made no attempt to hide its opinions about the marchers. On July 28, 1932, Pelham D. Glassford, the police superintendent for the District of Columbia, began removing some veterans from abandoned buildings. Two men, William Huska and Eric Carlson, were killed in a struggle with the police. The facts surrounding this situation remain unclear, but both men were unarmed. Shortly afterward, under several erroneous presumptions including the guise of removing Com-

munists from the ranks of the Bonus Army, General Douglas MacArthur commanded troops to remove all veterans and their families from the makeshift camp. Whether or not President Herbert Hoover approved of MacArthur's actions has always remained somewhat of a mystery. Although records indicate that Hoover was not fond of the Bonus Army, certain historical documents indicate that he was not pleased with MacArthur's course of action.

The actual removal of the Bonus Army was a rather simple task militarily. Under MacArthur, the cavalry, infantry, and tanks forced the veterans and their families out of their ''homes'' and into nearby Maryland. The shacks and hovels were then burned and the entire camp was completely destroyed in a matter of hours.

The results of the bonus march were mixed. Politically, the quick and hostile removal of the veterans and their families left many people upset and disappointed with the administration and its handling of the situation. This incident illustrated the often precarious relationship between veterans and the Hoover administration. Many observers, including the president himself, believed it contributed to Hoover's defeat for reelection in Novermber 1932.

In May 1933, a second Bonus Army of some 3,000 veterans gathered in Washington. Unlike Hoover, President Franklin D. Roosevelt treated them well, providing the veterans with food and medical services. First Lady Eleanor Roosevelt met with them and the veterans soon dispersed. Although they did not receive their bonuses, many found employment with the newly created Civilian Conservation Corps. In 1936, Congress enacted a bonus bill over President Roosevelt's veto.

SHANNON HARRIS

See also: Bonus Bill, Douglas MacArthur; election of 1932.

Bibliography

Bartlett, John H. *The Bonus March and the New Deal*. New York: M.A. Donohue & Company, 1937.

Daniels, Roger. *The Bonus March: An Episode of the Great Depression*. Westport, CT: Greenwood Press, 1971.

Keene, Jennifer. *Doughboys, the Great War, and the Remaking of America*. Baltimore: Johns Hopkins University Press, 2000.

Liebovich, Louis. *Press Reaction to the Bonus March of 1932: A Re-evaluation of the Impact of an American Tragedy*. Columbia, SC: Association for Education in Journalism and Mass Communication, 1990.

Waters, Walter W. *B.E.F.: the Whole Story of the Bonus Army, by W. W. Waters as told to William C. White*. New York: AMS Press, 1970.

BROTHERHOOD OF SLEEPING CAR PORTERS

The Brotherhood of Sleeping Car Porters (BSCP), founded in 1925 by A. Philip Randolph, was the largest and most influential predominantly African-American labor union of the 1930s. Not only did it help raise wages and improve working conditions in the cars of the Pullman Palace Car Company (PPCC)—the number one employer of blacks in the United States at the time—it also proved critical in the fight for fair racial employment practices throughout American industry.

To be a sleeping car porter in the 1930s was, by the standards of black employment in the Great Depression, a prestige job; many of the union's members were college-educated. Yet because of their race, they were forced to work serving an almost entirely white clientele, often doing tasks far beneath their skills and educational abilities.

Randolph was not the first to attempt to unionize sleeping car porters. An earlier effort involving the Railway Men's Association, a union of black workers throughout the railroad industry, was blocked by George Pullman, founder and president of the PPCC, and his company union, the Employee Representation Plan. Beginning with 2,500 workers, Randolph signed up nearly 5,000 porters by 1928. But it was the passage of the Railway Labor Act of 1934 that finally forced Pullman to recognize the BSCP. In 1937, the union won its first contract and continued to serve as the sole organized representative of sleeping car porters and railway conductors until its amalgamation into the Brotherhood of Railway and Airline Clerks in 1979.

In 1941, the BSCP provided the organizational locus for Randolph's March on Washington to integrate the armed forces and defense industry. The march was ultimately called off, but only after Randolph had forced the Franklin D. Roosevelt administration to establish the Fair Labor Standards Act, guaranteeing racial equality in defense industry hiring.

See also: March on Washington Movement; railroads; Fair Labor Standards Art; Randolph, A. Philip.

Bibliography

Harris, William Hamilton. *Keeping the Faith: A. Philip Randolph, Milton P. Webster, and the Brotherhood of Sleeping Car Porters, 1925–37*. Urbana: University of Illinois Press, 1991.

Santino, Jack. *Miles of Smiles, Years of Struggle: Stories of Black Pullman Porters*. Urbana: University of Illinois Press, 1989.

The Brotherhood of Sleeping Car Porters was the nation's largest African-American union during the Great Depression era. Here, union officers, including president A. Philip Randolph (to left of the union banner), display their allegiance to union and country. *(Brown Brothers)*

CHARITY AND PHILANTHROPY

Prior to the Great Depression, the American people believed that charity would lead to the pauperization of the poor. Before 1929, only those who experienced extreme hardships, such as the loss of their home or starvation, qualified for assistance, and even then many eligible individuals found it difficult to ask for help. The wealthy established philanthropic foundations but rarely donated money for direct distribution of food or other essential daily items. In 1928, foundations received over 500 gifts of 1 million dollars or more from the wealthy.

As the financial crisis spread, the negative attitude toward charities changed dramatically. By 1930, within one year of the stock market crash, businesses and wealthy individuals supported charities by contributing or raising funds for the needy. Nuns, YMCA directors, newspaper owners, manufacturers, private individuals such as wealthy "high society" ladies, and even Al Capone established breadlines. Assisting those in dire straits became a "community service," a sense of duty to neighbors fostered by rhetoric that linked benevolence with a strong spiritual responsibility. The term "community" emphasized the importance of assistance remaining at the local level.

Charitable organizations successfully reached their fund-raising goals during 1930 and helped many people without the aid of the federal government. The American Red Cross distributed $15 million worth of food and supplies to approximately 2.5 million people throughout a twenty-three state area hardest hit by drought: Some $5 million came from the organization's disaster relief fund, and another $10 million was collected in a special fund-raising drive. Congress allocated a grant of $25 million to the Red Cross for its relief efforts, but the offer was refused. The directors of the organization believed that the federal government played no role in providing relief for the people; that responsibility belonged to private individuals and organizations.

As the number of unemployed continued to rise, the federal government decided to coordinate the efforts of the business community to benefit charities on a national level. In August 1931, President Herbert Hoover appointed Walter S. Gifford, president of America Telephone and Telegraph, as the head of the Organization for Unemployment Relief with a goal of raising $175 million. Gifford worked with the top executives of some of the largest corporations in the country, including United States Steel, General Motors, and Ford Motor Company, and with their suggestions developed a campaign plan that could be applied as a model in each city. Just before the public announcement to kick off the drive, several of the manufacturers cut the wages of their workers by 10 percent or more. News of the pay reductions resulted in some initial criticism that quickly dissipated once the advertising program commenced. Throughout October and November, movie theaters showed clips, newspapers ran articles and advertising, and radio played commercials promoting charitable giving. Advertisements stated that morale could win wars, beat depressions, and lay the foundation for prosperity and that in just one month the American people "shall have met the worst threat the Depression can offer; and we shall have won." Spurred on by the belief that the Depression could be beat by giving during a one-month period, ordinary citizens contributed over $100 million for victims of the economic crisis. Community chests in cities and towns received a share of the donations.

The realization that a systematic approach would provide a safety net for all Americans created another shift in attitude toward charity. During congressional hearings on the effectiveness of the fund-raising efforts, Gifford assured senators that the program was working. Social workers and other witnesses painted a different picture. They stated that the needs of the inhabitants of rural areas and small towns without an established charity remained unaddressed, that the problem continued despite the best advertising efforts, and that only federal relief programs could adequately meet the needs of the American people. Their testimonies resulted in an outpouring of criticism toward private charities.

The public condemnation of charities and philanthropies focused on the motivation of the wealthy. According to critics, the rich donated money as a means of avoiding the payment of taxes on their vast fortunes. By appearing to be benevolent, they could avoid class warfare, a major consideration in a period following the Bolshevik revolution in Russia, and at the same time maintain control over society. Charges that Wall Street controlled these charitable organizations appeared to validate this attitude of distrust and disapproval.

Within months of the congressional hearings, state governments assumed control over relief efforts despite strong opposition. Franklin Delano Roosevelt, then governor of New York, persuaded his constituents that helping the unemployed remained their social duty. By providing funds for the destitute, business would reap the benefits of increased consumer spending and that would lead to an economic recovery. During his administration, the state of New York administered state funds for the relief of the unemployed. Other states implemented similar programs within a short time. The Chamber of Commerce of the United States and other groups unsuccessfully opposed the use of public funds for private assistance. Charity no longer began at home.

By 1932, the Hoover administration implemented two programs that would eventually lead to federal control over relief efforts. Under the first program, the Red Cross, an organization that had previously refused government assistance, accepted the responsibility of distributing surplus wheat and cotton to the needy. That same year, the Reconstruction Finance Corporation offered loans to the states for their relief efforts. When Roosevelt moved into the White House, the administration decided to centralize assistance under a federal program that would tax the wealthy and borrow extensively to provide national welfare benefits.

Once the federal government assumed responsibility for relief efforts, philanthropic foundations shifted all their attention back to research and cultural issues but on a more limited scale. From 1929 to 1932, foundations received only half the usual funding. The stock market crash directly affected their revenue-generating stock portfolios, causing the decline. For instance, the Julius Rosenwald Fund invested heavily in Sears, Roebuck, and Company. As the price of that stock plummeted from $200 to $10 a share between 1929 and 1932, the fund's revenue declined accordingly. Foundations began limiting the size of their grants and fellowships. But even during the early years of the Depression, the rich established new foundations such as the A. W. Mellon Charitable and Educational Trust and the Kellogg Foundation. Hospitals and universities received a large portion of the grants during this time. The Rockefeller Foundation invested heavily in medical and health research and applied new medicines and programs throughout the world. The foundation contributed $1.5 million to study ways to quickly end the Depression and also set up programs to teach the Russian, Japanese, and Chinese languages in the United States. A major cultural issue involved the historic preservation of sites like Colonial Williamsburg, another project of the Rockefeller family. Some of the national parks, such as the Grand Tetons, also received funding. Henry Ford created Greenfield Village and the Ford Museum in Dearborn, Michigan, with its early American village and collection of buildings that included Thomas Edison's laboratory, the Wright brothers' cycle shop, and the building in which Ford built his first automobile. Ford designed the entire complex to reflect the old-fashioned American way of doing business in an attempt to encourage people to pursue traditional means of supporting themselves.

Roosevelt's New Deal policies altered the pattern of charitable and philanthropic contributions, raising fresh criticism. Under the Revenue Act of 1935, the government allowed corporations to deduct up to 5 percent of their taxable income as charitable donations. At the same time, taxes increased and benefactors changed their wills, leaving more of their wealth to family and less to foundations. Jesse Isidore Straus, the chief executive of Macy's, eliminated bequests to eighteen different institutions because of high taxes. Eventually, some individuals realized the tax benefits and giving once again increased. Through restrictions on their gifts, the wealthy could specify that the foundations receiving funds from them would be required to pay the estate taxes on the balance of the assets designated for family members. Lawyers utilized every loophole possible to secure the maximum benefit for their clients, including the deduction of up to 15 percent of their individual taxable income for donations. Liberals argued that philanthropists continued to contribute funds for selfish reasons; since they could not spend or invest all their money, they used it to control society by influencing how people thought.

Despite this criticism, the wealthy continued to give, and, by the mid-1930s, charities and philanthropies surpassed pre-Depression receipts. In 1935, American foundations received over $2.5 billion in gifts. In 1936, the A. W. Mellon Charitable and Educational Trust gave the largest gift in American history. Under the terms of the bequest, the federal government received Mellon's art collection, enough money to build the National Gallery, and an endowment fund, all amounting to $80 million. When the museum opened in 1941, the curator included an exhibition of over 20,000 watercolors painted by artists under New Deal programs to refute the argument that the National Gallery would not include American artists. In 1937, the Red Cross, in a campaign to assist victims of the Ohio-Mississippi flood, raised over $25 million. The following year, private agencies and the federal government coordinated efforts to assist New Englanders hit by a hurricane. Ordinary citizens involved themselves in programs such as the March of Dimes, while President Roosevelt raised funds for polio victims during his annual Birthday Balls.

Charitable giving continued in the late 1930s as the world situation changed. After European leaders unsuccessfully attempted to avert a second world war, the United States required charities providing relief to belligerent countries to register with the federal government. Gradually, the campaigns for fund-raising turned into war drives as the United States entered the conflict. The Depression and the New Deal slowly receded as government expenditures and programs like lend-lease stimulated the economy. Unemployment declined and prosperity returned, leaving far fewer people who actually needed assistance.

Throughout the Great Depression and the New Deal, the nature and direction of charities changed course several times. Charities, frowned upon just months earlier, regained the support of the American public during the first years of the financial crisis. By 1932, the number of unemployed and the severity of the problem required the intervention of the state governments. Within a year, the federal government, at first slowly and then aggressively, assumed control over relief efforts on a national basis. Once this shift of responsibility transpired, many Americans, having lost confidence in the ability of charities to address the problems, began criticizing them because of their ties to Wall Street financiers. By the end of the New Deal, the attitude of the American public toward charities had once again turned favorable as these organizations and the federal government cooperated to assist victims of natural disasters and disease.

Philanthropies, like charities, experienced many twists and turns during the 1930s. The wealthy, diverging from their pattern of large foundation gifts, donated heavily to charities from 1929 to 1932. After the federal government relieved both charities and philanthropic organizations of the burden of relief assistance, these foundations returned to their more traditional educational, health, and cultural goals. Although the wealthy donated some of the largest gifts in American history during this period, the American people remained critical at worst and apathetic at best toward philanthropic endeavors.

CYNTHIA NORTHRUP

See also: Ford Motor Company; General Motors; United States Steel; Reconstruction Finance Corporation; Capone, Al; Ford, Henry; Hoover, Herbert.

Bibliography

Bremner, Robert H. *American Philanthropy*. Chicago: University of Chicago Press, 1960.

Sealander, Judith. *Private Wealth and Public Life: Foundation Philanthropy and the Reshaping of American Social Policy from the Progressive Era to the New Deal*. Baltimore: Johns Hopkins University Press, 1997.

CHRISTIAN FRONT

An anti-Semitic and anticommunist organization, the Christian Front (CF) was founded in 1938 and lasted until America's entry into World War II. Openly pro-Nazi, the CF encouraged the harassment and boycott of Jewish businesses. With its slogan "Buy Christian," it published a directory of non-Jewish businesses in the New York City area called the *Christian Index*. By 1939, the organization was being openly supported by the demagogic radio preacher Charles E. Coughlin. The organization's highpoint was a New York City rally in May 1939 that attracted thousands of followers. But after America's declaration of war against Nazi Germany in 1941, the group was abandoned by many of its supporters and was soon drowned in anti-Nazi sentiment and disbanded.

See also: fascism, domestic; Liberty League; Coughlin, Father Charles.

Bibliography

Mintz, Frank P. *The Liberty Lobby and the American Right: Race, Conspiracy, and Culture*. Westport, CT: Greenwood Press, 1985.

Ribuffo, Leo. *The Old Christian Right: The Protestant Far Right from the Great Depression to the Cold War*. Philadelphia: Temple University Press, 1983.

CITIZEN KANE

Frequently voted by film critics as the greatest American film ever made, *Citizen Kane* was co-written and directed by Orson Welles, who also starred in the title role. Telling the fictionalized story of the rise and fall of newspaper magnate William Randolph Hearst, the 1941 film was an immediate critical and box office success.

Using pathbreaking cinematographic effects and unknown stars from his Mercury Theatre Company, Welles got the film made for RKO Studios despite enormous pressure from Hearst, who tried to stop its release. Coming at the tail end of the Depression—and on the eve of World War II—the film's portrayal of the overly ambitious Charles Kane, who is destroyed by his greed, has remained a timeless cinematic classic.

The film, co-written by Herman Mankiewicz, also featured Joseph Cotten and Agnes Moorehead.

See also: films, feature; Hearst, William Randolph; Welles, Orson.

Bibliography

Carringer, Robert L. *The Making of Citizen Kane*. Berkeley: University of California Press, 1996.

Harlan, Lebo. *Citizen Kane: The Fiftieth-Anniversary Album*. New York: Doubleday, 1990.

COMMONWEALTH CLUB SPEECH

Among the seminal orations of Franklin D. Roosevelt's 1932 campaign for the presidency, the speech to the Commonwealth Club of San Francisco in September laid out many of the issues and ideas that dominated New Deal thinking.

Roosevelt argued that America had reached the end of the "frontier" stage of its development, when citizens could anticipate endless economic growth: "Our industrial plant is built; the problem just now is whether under existing conditions it is not overbuilt. Our last frontier has long since been reached." With fewer opportunities for small business owners, there was the very real danger, he said, that big corporations would consolidate their hold over the American economy. This combination of circumstances had the potential to leave Americans mired in poverty.

To counter this sober and depressing future, Roosevelt argued, Americans had to rethink their values. The federal government had to step in to regulate economic affairs, not so much to spur competition, but to regulate the existing economic system in order to make sure its products were distributed fairly. "The day of the great promoter or the financial Titan, to whom we granted everything if only he would build, or develop, is over," Roosevelt declared. "Our task now is not discovery, or exploitation of natural resources, or necessarily producing more goods. It is the soberer, less dramatic business of administering resources and plants already in hand, of seeking to reestablish foreign markets for our surplus production, of meeting the problem of underconsumption, of adjusting production to consumption, of distributing wealth and products more equitably."

The speech is particularly noteworthy as it reveals the sober thinking behind Roosevelt's ever-sunny and optimistic exterior. Many historians suggest that the speech reflects the thinking of Roosevelt's advisers, including Adolf Berle Jr., rather than of the presidential candidate himself.

See also: election of 1932; New Deal, first; Berle, Adolf, Jr.; Roosevelt, Franklin D.

Bibliography

Davis, Kenneth S. *FDR: The New York Years, 1928–1933*. New York: Random House, 1985.

Schlesinger, Arthur A., Jr. *The Age of Roosevelt: The Crisis of the Old Order, 1919–1933*. Boston: Houghton Mifflin, 1957.

COMMUNIST PARTY

The Communist Party (CP) entered the Depression severely weakened both by government oppression and by its own response to that oppression, having spent the 1920s as an underground movement. As a result of this secrecy, in 1929, there were only about 13,000 members, of whom only 5,000 spoke English, 9,000 paid dues, and under half were in any sort of trade union organization. While the party literature reached far more people than its actual membership, 1929 still represented one of the lowest points in the CP's history.

The Party's expansion really began in the very early 1930s, during what is sometimes called the Third Period of communist ideology. During this period, party members were expected to rigidly support Russia and to strongly oppose all political enemies, ranging from right-wing fascists and supporters of liberal capitalism to members of the noncommunist Socialist Party, called "social fascists" in party literature.

Since socialists and even some outright conservatives led many of the locals in the American Federation of Labor (AFL), the most important labor union of the early 1930s, party activists set up their own trade unions under the Trade Union Unity League (TUUL). The TUUL was a mixed success at best; AFL workers generally proved unwilling to leave their established unions to join the fledgling organization. The only places where the TUUL was even mildly successful were in the garment industry, where the communists had always retained a number of supporters, and in those areas where the AFL had never made any real headway, particularly among unskilled workers and low-paid white-collar workers. Even in these industries, however, the TUUL's numbers remained extremely small.

Despite tactics like this "dual unionism," which tended to isolate the CP from other leftists and reformers, the economic crisis of the early Depression, with high levels of unemployment, large numbers of unorganized workers, mass evictions, and overwhelming poverty, meant that the Party was quite successful in recruiting large numbers of supporters. Party demonstrations consistently attracted crowds of thousands, and on March 6, 1930, which the Communists labeled International Unemployment Day, they were able to claim over 1 million demonstrators in cities across the country. Even more important were the smaller, daily struggles; evictions and strikes could easily lead to protests, and members of the CP, as well as their rivals in the Socialist Party, often led these struggles.

One of the most important single issues for the Party in this early period, outside of poverty and unemployment, was the Scottsboro case, in which nine young African-American men and boys were arrested for rape in Alabama in 1931, and sentenced to death on flimsy evidence. The CP-led International Labor Defense immediately challenged the verdicts and offered legal advice and aid to the defendants. Communists, who had strongly opposed racism for much of the Party's existence, suddenly found themselves leading a movement against racism, and as a result they won great support in the African-American community, even among those who, before the Scottsboro campaign began, had shown no interest whatsoever in radical politics.

If the Scottsboro campaign was a success for the Party, it was not the only one. Communists participated in the 1934 International Longshoremen's Association strike, which closed down the Pacific Coast from May until June of that year and ended only after the great San Francisco General Strike, in which Communists also played key roles. Indeed, throughout the strike wave of 1934, from the southern textile workers strike to smaller strikes in cities and towns across the country, Communists participated both as organizers and supporters.

It was during this period also that the Party began to build up its infrastructure, particularly with the International Workers Order (IWO). The IWO was no innovation when it was founded in 1930; it was simply the Party's answer to the socialist-led Jewish workingmen's association, the Workmen's Circle. Unlike the Workmen's Circle, however, IWO leaders decided to open the organization to people of all ethnicities and races, organized into branches that were still divided primarily along ethnic lines. They did this both by providing cheap life insurance and by giving working-class people in the communist orbit places for much-needed leisure. The IWO sponsored orchestras, sports teams, theater groups, and children's camps, as well as attracting numerous celebrities to perform for the various branches. While not every IWO member was involved with the Communist Party's political issues, it proved to be an excellent ally, a fundraiser for party events, and a way for the Party to network with its numerous members and supporters.

By 1934, then, the Party was clearly becoming a major force in American life, working on issues ranging from strikes to lynchings. It had better than doubled its membership, now claiming 26,000 members, and in the intervening years since 1929, some 20,000 others had joined and then left again. Despite this growth spurt, it was in many ways still a small and isolated movement, something which changed during the Popular Front period.

THE POPULAR FRONT: AMERICANISM OF THE TWENTIETH CENTURY

By the mid-1930s, it was extremely clear that the Third Period strategies were not going to be adequate. Communist union organizers criticizing President Roosevelt's policies found themselves nonetheless benefiting greatly from the National Industrial Recovery Act's Section 7. In addition, the various government-sponsored employment programs of the early New Deal, while far from the unemployment insurance that Communists were demanding, were at least an indication that the federal government was attempting to respond to the crisis.

At the same time, international issues made it even harder to deny the need for unity with other leftists. With the increased threat of fascism represented by Hitler and Mussolini, Communists worldwide began recognizing the need to work alongside other leftists in the struggle against it. Russian policy—and CP policy—began to shift accordingly in the mid-1930s, culminating first in the formation of the Popular Front in 1935, when communists attempted to form alliances with the Socialist Party, and then in the formation of the Democratic Front in early 1938, when Communists united with liberal Democrats against the Right.

Many Communists found the new turn initially unsettling. After years of opposing Roosevelt and the New Deal, they were now expected to unite with the New Dealers. After years of branding Socialists as "social fascists," they now attempted to unite with Socialists against fascism. However, it quickly became clear that the Popular Front period, from 1935–39, would turn out to be one of the most important moments in the Party's history.

During this period, party leaders began to alter the CP's image, consciously placing the Party in the tradition of American revolution. Washington, Jefferson, and Lincoln became figures worthy of celebration in CP circles. Party leader Earl Browder made the statement, ironic in light of later events, that communism was the "Americanism of the twentieth century." Membership rolls grew exponentially in this environment. By 1938, the CP had some 55,000 members, far more than it had claimed at any earlier time in its history.

But more important than either of these was the leadership of Communists in the mainstream industrial unionism represented by the Congress of Industrial Organizations, (CIO). While many CIO leaders continued to be staunch anti-Communists, they were often willing to use Communists as organizers due to the singular dedication and experience that CP activism provided. In particular, the Transport Workers Union and the extremely large United Electrical, Radio, and Machine Workers Union were both Communist-led. Communists, many of them ex-TUUL activists, also occupied key positions in the Steel Workers Organizing Committee, the United Auto Workers (in which they helped to organize the Flint sit-down strikes), the United Office and Professional Workers Association, and the Retail, Wholesale and Department Store Union.

The Party also made important headway in recruiting artists and intellectuals during this period. Writers like Lillian Hellman, Dashiell Hammett, Richard Wright, and Langston Hughes all associated closely with the Party, whether they actually joined or not. Musicians also became involved; Woody Guthrie, the most famous American folk musician, was a longtime supporter of CP causes, and composer Aaron Copland, though not as close to the Party as Guthrie, was involved in Party activity during these years. In addition, the opening nights of party-supported theater productions, such as Clifford Odets's *Waiting for Lefty* and Marc Blitzstein's *The Cradle Will Rock*, became occasions for protests and socializing among party members.

Perhaps the most important party role during this period was its strong support for the Loyalists in the Spanish Civil War. Many of the Communists' newfound allies found themselves much more willing to work with the CP due to the Loyalists' own united front against fascism, and party members were key in organizing, supporting, and volunteering for the Abraham Lincoln Brigade, the American soldiers who went to fight alongside the Loyalists.

By the middle of 1939, therefore, the Party had become a mass organization, with people of widespread political beliefs all working together against fascism. That year of 1939, however, would see a fundamental

Communist Party members display their commitment to peace and their solidarity with the Soviet Union at a New York City May Day rally in 1936. *(Brown Brothers)*

realignment of party policy that shook much of the CP's support.

THE NONAGGRESSION PACT, THE DIES COMMITTEE, AND THE WAR

At the end of August 1939, Soviet Russia signed a non-aggression pact with Nazi Germany. To Communists in the United States, this came as a shock; Earl Browder and other party leaders had spent much of that year insisting that, rumors to the contrary, no such pact was being negotiated. Indeed, weeks after the pact was signed, the Communists remained part of the Popular Front; it was only in mid-September that the CP finally

came out against U.S. participation in World War II, calling it an imperialist war and downplaying the dangers posed by Hitler and Mussolini.

Party policy changed very quickly after the new line was established. Communists, some of whom had always been uneasy in their alliances with Roosevelt and the Democrats, now turned on their allies, attacking Roosevelt as a dictator and a deceiver of the masses and alienating many of their previous supporters. Other party activists, however, tried their best to downplay issues of foreign policy, instead attacking, more fiercely than they had during the Popular Front, America's domestic problems, such as racism and capitalism.

Contributing to the Party's growing isolation were renewed governmental attacks. The infamous House

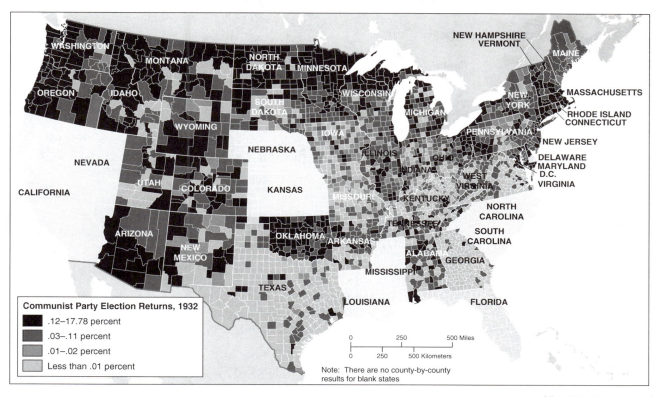

Communist Party Election Returns, 1932
- .12–17.78 percent
- .03–.11 percent
- .01–.02 percent
- Less than .01 percent

Note: There are no county-by-county results for blank states

(CARTO-GRAPHICS)

Un-American Activities Committee (HUAC), which began in 1938 as the Dies Committee, by 1939 was clearly gaining ground. Before the nonaggression pact, those CP members who were targeted by HUAC could reasonably expect, and often received, a certain degree of support from a broad-based liberal movement, including members of the Roosevelt administration. After September 1939, however, Roosevelt and his supporters were actually backing HUAC against their former allies.

The next year brought clear evidence of the new broad-based anticommunist movement. First, a systematic campaign began on the local and state levels to attack Communists wherever they might lurk. The Communist Party was removed from the ballot in a number of states, and Communists became the frequent targets of vigilante as well as local police attacks. More disturbingly, however, the U.S. Congress passed the Smith Act in 1940, which required all aliens to be registered and fingerprinted, made illegal any discussion of the violent overthrow of the government, and allowed the government to deport any immigrants who had ever belonged to an organization that might support such an overthrow.

Perhaps luckily for the Communist Party in the United States, Hitler invaded Russia in June 1941, which meant that party supporters could cease their attacks on the Roosevelt administration's pro-war policies. Even more fortuitous, in December 1941, Japan bombed Pearl Harbor. The Party, which had been supporting stepping up the war effort for six months by that time, was now in a position to grow exponentially. Due to its strong support for the war effort, the Party would achieve membership numbers during the war far greater than those achieved at any time during the Depression.

DANIEL OPLER

See also: American Labor Party; Congress of Industrial Organizations; Popular Front; Trade Union Unity League; Unemployed Councils; House Un-American Activities Committee; Smith Act; Abraham Lincoln Brigade; Nazi-Soviet nonaggression pact; Soviet Union; Spanish Civil War; Bridges, Harry; Browder, Earl; Dies, Martin; Foster, William Z.; Marcantonio, Vito; Robeson, Paul; Stalin, Joseph

Bibliography

Denning, Michael. *The Cultural Front: The Laboring of American Culture.* London: Verso, 1996.

Kelley, Robin. *Hammer and Hoe: Alabama Communists During the Great Depression*. Chapel Hill: University of North Carolina Press, 1990.

Klehr, Harvey. *The Heyday of American Communism: The Depression Decade*. New York: Basic Books, 1984.

Naison, Mark. *Communists in Harlem During the Depression*. New York: Grove Press, 1983.

Schrecker, Ellen. *Many Were the Crimes: McCarthyism in America*. Princeton: Princeton University Press, 1998.

CONGRESS OF INDUSTRIAL ORGANIZATIONS

Created in 1935 by members of the American Federation of Labor (AFL) committed to expanding the labor movement to all workers, the Congress of Industrial Organizations (CIO) formed permanent labor unions in numerous industries and contributed to an unprecedented rise in working-class organizing. The organization relied on widespread worker disenchantment during the Depression, dramatic tactics such as sit-down strikes, and the political and legal support of the Franklin D. Roosevelt administration to organize millions of American workers. Despite violent resistance, insufficient resources, and internal conflicts, the CIO guaranteed that organized labor played a significant role in political and economic decisions during both the crises of the 1930s and later wartime mobilization.

The origins of the CIO stemmed from numerous factors. Above all, 90 percent of nonagricultural labor in the United States lacked union representation in 1935. Most workers faced harsh discipline; increasing mechanization; few legal rights; age, gender, and racial discrimination; and, after 1930, increasing anxiety about falling wages and rising unemployment. Second, many industrial laborers grew skeptical of the AFL by 1935. Despite gains in membership after 1933, the AFL appeared cautious and unable to take advantage of the opportunities of the New Deal. Furthermore, millions of workers toiled in occupations outside of the AFL's traditional focus on craftsmen. Capitalizing on the twin enemies of hostile corporate management and an ineffective AFL, individuals such as John L. Lewis of the United Mine Workers (UMW) argued for a more comprehensive industrial unionism that included more than skilled workers in a few select industries. Lewis punctuated his passionate call for industrial unionism at the 1935 AFL convention when he decked William Hutchinson, a more conservative rival from the Carpenter's Union. The next day, Lewis organized what was then referred to as the AFL's Committee for Industrial Organization, the precursor of the Congress of Industrial Organizations. A former coal miner and experienced labor organizer, Lewis formed an alliance with former adversaries within the AFL such as David Dubinsky and Sidney Hillman of the garment trades, as well as representatives from the United Textile Workers and Oil Workers. While many perceived the CIO as a means of reforming the AFL, the dynamic and aggressive Lewis envisioned a more inclusive labor movement capable of preserving American democracy and economic justice in the industrial age.

SUCCESSES AND LIMITATIONS

Lewis' aggressive advocacy and the enthusiastic response of workers brought the CIO significant gains during the latter half of the decade. The often violent opposition of the unpopular AFL also enhanced the reputation of the fledgling CIO. Early successes included negotiating contracts for striking rubber workers in Akron, Ohio, and the formation of the Steel Workers Organizing Committee (SWOC) to bring U.S. Steel to the bargaining table in 1937. One of the most dramatic efforts involved the innovative use of sit-down strikes by the United Auto Workers (UAW) in Flint, Michigan. The strikes at the General Motors and Chrysler plants had numerous advantages: the strategy allowed a small number of workers to shut down production, protected workers from the violence of the picket line, and fostered an esprit de corps among workers and their families. By the beginning of World War II, the CIO claimed contracts with over 3,000 companies, including Ford Motor Company, Goodyear, and Westinghouse. The years 1936 to 1938 brought campaigns for longshoremen as well as workers in such areas as electrical appliances, lumber, mining, textiles, meatpacking, food and canneries, cemeteries, hotels, and restaurants. While the CIO's exact membership figures were always suspect, in 1937 the organization claimed over 4 million workers throughout the nation, 6,000 affiliated unions, an expanding national office in Washington, D.C., and over

C.I.O.
vs
A.F. of L.

LABOR

ROLLIN KIRBY,

HOUSE IN DANGER?

As this 1940 cartoon indicates, the increasingly bitter relations between the American Federation of Labor (AFL) and the upstart Congress of Industrial Organizations (CIO) in the late 1930s was seen as endangering interests of the labor movement during the Great Depression. *(Library of Congress)*

60,000 local officials. In 1938, the CIO, which had existed independently from the AFL in everything but name for years, broke with the older organization. Now larger than the AFL in terms of membership, the CIO formally changed its name to the Congress of Industrial Organizations.

The CIO owed much of its success to its relationship with the federal government during the Roosevelt administration. Beginning with the National Industrial Relations Act in 1933 and especially the National Labor Relations (or Wagner) Act of 1935, organized labor found allies in the federal government. The Wagner Act protected the rights of workers to organize and bargain collectively, and the National Labor Relations Board (NLRB) penalized companies guilty of unfair labor practices. In the United States Senate, Robert La Follette Jr.'s (R-WI) Civil Liberties Committee investigated the corporate espionage and violent intimidation that continued to characterize labor relations. After decades

of defeats and relatively little political power, organized labor, led by the CIO, also played an active role in the 1936 presidential election. Lewis campaigned for Roosevelt's reelection, and the CIO formed labor's Non-Partisan League to funnel campaign contributions to sympathetic Democratic candidates throughout the nation. While the CIO received much of its publicity from its fiery leader and dramatic confrontations, Lewis and the organization continually worked to move labor conflict from the streets to the political arena, the courtroom, and the negotiating table. Not surprisingly, union membership increased after Roosevelt's impressive reelection and a stronger economy in 1936. In turn, the rulings of the NLRB proved crucial in protecting the CIO's tenuous progress after the economic recession of late 1937.

Despite its successes, the CIO was always a vulnerable organization, overly dependent on the leadership of Lewis and the financial resources of his powerful United Mine Workers. While some CIO affiliates such as the UAW and the Textile Workers Union were solvent, many others, such as the SWOC, were millions of dollars in debt by the late '30s. As a result, the UMW provided over 40 percent of the entire CIO budget during its early years and many affiliates relied on loans from the UMW. Moreover, worker loyalty to employers and widespread violence—uniformed policemen killed ten labor supporters in Chicago's "Memorial Day Massacre" in 1937—kept the majority of workers from joining the CIO. Affiliates depended on a handful of dedicated activists. Most of the nation's workers, although sympathetic to the political left, were understandably more cautious than radical or revolutionary. In addition, many of the workers whom the CIO claimed as part of its membership totals were excused from paying dues because of unemployment. Other workers simply remained committed to the AFL. The rival organization limited the effectiveness of the CIO through its own organizing campaigns, boycotts of goods produced by CIO workers, and occasional confrontations.

RACE AND GENDER

The CIO's experiences with race and gender were illustrative of the successes and limitations of the young organization. Unlike earlier unions, including the AFL, the CIO committed itself to biracial organizing. Blacks, many of whom were recent migrants to the North, made up an increasing percentage of industrial workers by the Great Depression, with large numbers in the steel industries and 25 percent of all workers in meatpacking. Trapped in the most dangerous segments of the labor force with the lowest pay and least security, black workers were often militant supporters of industrial unionism. Regardless of its progressive position on race relations, the CIO kept its focus on the rights of workers, failing to confront American racism. For example, the CIO's organizing drive in the South emphasized campaigns in all-white textile mills in the hope of insulating the CIO from debilitating racial conflict. It was not until the more prosperous 1940s that the CIO, then a much stronger organization, took a more aggressive stance against racial discrimination in employment.

According to labor historian Raymond Marshall, statistics on black union membership are hard to come by for the 1930s. Altogether, there were roughly 600,000 African-American union members in 1940, but which unions they belonged to is not clear. By 1945, blacks made up about 3.4 percent of the membership of the AFL and 6.7 percent of CIO's. Whether that reflected the CIO's more aggressive approach to black organizing or simply that there were more black workers in the kinds of industries organized by the CIO is not known.

Women workers joined blacks as relatively new members of the industrial work force in the 1930s. Over 30,000 women worked in the automobile industry, with many more in electrical appliances, textiles, and the garment industry. Although gender discrimination and low wages made female workers likely supporters of CIO efforts and although women played important supportive roles during strikes, the organization rarely strayed from traditional notions of gender and work. Men dominated leadership roles as well as CIO priorities and perspectives. Partly due to its origin among exclusively male mine workers, the CIO, at least before the wartime mobilization of the 1940s, was unable to transcend the idea of labor activism as a masculine effort to protect the rights of American men.

RADICALISM AND INTERNAL CONFLICTS

While the CIO's split with the AFL shattered any notion of a monolithic labor movement, the specter of political radicalism within the movement always threatened to weaken the CIO's fragile gains. Communists and Socialists in the United States enjoyed small but unprecedented popularity during the Great Depression, and many radicals played active roles in organized labor. Communists were often the first Americans to call for the mass mobilization of the unemployed. The CIO's emergence coincided with increased cooperation

between radicals and New Deal liberals, and many Communists held top positions within some unions, such as meatpacking. In California, the CIO's director was Harry Bridges, a leader among groups of longshoremen who were strong supporters of the Soviet Union. Elsewhere, southern blacks working in both industrial and agricultural jobs blended their rich heritage of resistance to racial oppression and labor exploitation with a communist critique of American capitalism. Many of these southern radicals soon became attracted to the CIO because of its relative strength and stability and its potential for interracial unity among workers. Such relationships between the CIO and political radicals fueled fierce opposition among American conservatives and worried those within the labor movement who perceived labor reform as a way to avoid the political extremism of Nazi Germany and the Soviet Union. After the Nazi-Soviet nonaggression pact of August 1939, the presence of Communists became even more problematic. Lewis was far from a radical, but the movement needed the grassroots organizing of Communists and Socialists and he always believed that the CIO could control its more militant factions.

As a fragile organization faced with anticommunist critics, hostile management, and a rival AFL, the CIO responded with an unprecedented level of cooperation and support for the federal government. Sidney Hillman, one of the original founders of the CIO and head of the Amalgamated Clothing Workers of America, became chief representative for labor in the war-related mobilization effort. While Hillman and others campaigned for Democrats, Lewis became an ardent isolationist and resigned as CIO president in 1939. He publicly condemned Roosevelt for assigning government contracts to companies with poor records of labor management and criticized the CIO for its new role within the emerging national security state. In contrast to the CIO's unequivocal support of the New Deal in 1936, the fractured CIO, now led by Philip Murray but still heavily influenced by Lewis and the UMW, offered no official endorsement or financial support during the presidential election of 1940.

Regardless, public and congressional support for labor militancy eroded as the American economy shifted to wartime mobilization. The CIO gained 1.5 million additional workers in the years immediately preceding Pearl Harbor, but national security, combined with rising wages and full employment, gave extra weight to the need for cooperation and stability. This approach and the wartime economic recovery gave the CIO its greatest strength during the 1940s.

While labor conflicts continued through the postwar years, the CIO's initial struggles to create a larger, more inclusive labor movement during the Great Depression resulted in higher wages and improved working conditions for millions of American workers. The CIO's efforts, together with other factors such as the New Deal, ensured that future political and economic leaders could no longer ignore the perspectives and power of organized workers.

RICHARD HUGHES

See also: American Federation of Labor; American Newspaper Guild; auto industry; Communist Party; Ford Motor Company; General Motors; manufacturing and construction; mining; Steel Industry; Steel Workers Organizing Committee; strikes, general; strikes, sit-down; unions and union organizing; United Automobile Workers; United Mine Workers; United States Steel; National Labor Relations Act; New Deal, second; *NLRB v. Jones & Laughlin; West Coast Hotel v. Parrish*; Bennett, Harry; Bridges, Harry; Dubinsky, David; Hillman, Sidney; Lewis, John L.; Murray, Philip; Reuther, Walter; Documents: National Labor Relations Act, July 5, 1935; *National Labor Relations Board v. Jones & Laughlin Steel Corporation*, 1937; *West Coast Hotel Company v. Oregon*, 1937; *West Coast Hotel v. Parrish*.

Bibliography

Dubofsky, Melvyn, and Warren Van Time. *John L. Lewis: A Biography*. Urbana: University of Illinois Press, 1986.

Kelley, Robin. *Hammer and Hoe: Alabama Communists During the Great Depression*. Chapel Hill: University of North Carolina Press, 1990.

Marshall, Raymond. *The Negro and Organized Labor*. New York: John Wiley and Sons, 1965.

———. *The Negro Worker*. New York: Random House, 1967.

Zieger, Robert H. *The CIO: 1935–1955*. Chapel Hill: University of North Carolina Press, 1995.

———. "Toward a History of the CIO: A Bibliographic Report." *Labor History* 26:4 (Fall 1985): 487–516.

COURT-PACKING PLAN

Frustrated by a conservative Supreme Court's rulings that eviscerated many of his New Deal programs—including *Schechter Poultry Corporation v. United States*, which ruled the National Industrial Recovery Act unconstitutional in 1935—President Franklin D. Roosevelt announced he would reorganize the Supreme Court shortly after his second inauguration in March 1937.

The centerpiece of the program was Roosevelt's decision to add one justice to the Court for every sitting justice over the age of seventy. While the president argued that the measure was designed to lighten the workload of the aging justices, his political opponents argued that it was a dictatorial attempt to make the court more amenable to a variety of New Deal laws and programs like the Wagner Act (also known as the National Labor Relations Act), the Tennessee Valley Authority, and Social Security, all of which were to be ruled on in the Court's coming sessions. Despite his popularity, Roosevelt was eventually forced to back off what his political opponents called the court-packing plan. And the public, fearful that Roosevelt's move represented an assault on the constitutional separation of powers, largely agreed with the president's detractors.

This 1937 illustration by *Los Angeles Times* cartoonist Bruce Russell captures President Franklin D. Roosevelt's difficulty in convincing Congress to go along with his plan to add justices to the Supreme Court. *(Brown Brothers)*

Many contemporaries saw Roosevelt's decision to back off his plan as his first major political defeat.

Still, it is argued that, while forced to back down from his plan, Roosevelt achieved his ultimate goals. The Court moved to the left, upholding key New Deal laws, including the Wagner Act, and, by the end of his second administration, Roosevelt had been able to select four new liberal justices—Hugo Black, Felix Frankfurter, Stanley Reed, and William Douglas.

See also: National Labor Relations Act; Supreme Court; Black, Hugo; Frankfurter, Felix; Roosevelt, Franklin D. Documents: Reform of the Federal Judiciary, 1937; Adverse Report on Reform of the Federal Judiciary from the Senate Committee on the Judiciary, June 7, 1937.

Bibliography

Alsop, Joseph. *The 168 Days*. New York: Da Capo Press, 1973.

Baker, Leonard. *Back to Back: The Duel between FDR and the Supreme Court*. New York: Macmillan, 1967.

CRIME

Standing on the running board of a getaway car, with a blazing tommy-gun in his hands and a beautiful gun moll waiting for him in the hideaway, the gangster of the 1930s cut a dashing figure. Cars, guns, and women were his to command, and, unlike most men of the day, this man had money to burn. As the decade opened, the romance that had been attached to bank robbers since the days of Jesse James continued to reign. But public worship gradually turned to public disgust. Fueled by anger at the Lindbergh baby kidnapping and by a New Deal–inspired confidence in government, citizens demanded better law enforcement. With the creation of a national crime laboratory, a national registry of fingerprints, and the expansion of federal policing powers, the decade witnessed the professionalization of law enforcement.

When the decade began, the Prohibition experiment had already failed. The illegal manufacture and sale of intoxicating beverages had increased far beyond the power of officials to control them. The bootlegging of alcohol, as the *Saturday Evening Post* declared, furnished the funds for the organization of crime and the corruption of law enforcement officials on an unprecedented scale. No man had greater success in bootlegging during the 1920s than Al Capone. In 1930, the Chicago Crime Commission published a list of public enemies and Capone headed it. A year later, with local authorities unable or unwilling to prosecute him for murder, agents of the Treasury Department sent Capone to prison for evading federal income taxes on his gains from bootlegging.

Capone had been linked to the Mafia, a secret criminal society composed largely of men of Italian extraction. Although the existence of the Mafia remained a subject of debate throughout the 1930s, a number of

men did unquestionably run organized criminal conspiracies. When Prohibition ended in 1933, the large sums of money that had flowed into the hands of bootleggers offered opportunities for many of these criminals to invest in new illegal activities. Charles "Lucky" Luciano, one of these men, headed syndicates dealing with gambling, narcotics, and prostitution. He purged the "Old Mafia" in New York by killing several of its members in 1931 and, in 1937, was linked by New York District Attorney Thomas E. Dewey to political corruption. Louis "Lepke" Buchalter, another New York syndicate leader, sometimes dealt in narcotics but was known mostly for his extortion of laborers in the garment industry. Other syndicates specialized in narcotics, with morphine, opium, marijuana, cocaine, and heroin being the most popular drugs in the 1930s.

With income scarce and debts high during the Great Depression, it is not surprising that loan-sharking became a major source of revenue for organized criminals. Loan sharks made fast money available to those who needed it and were willing to pay high rates of interest. Those who did not pay suffered broken bones, shattered kneecaps, and, occasionally, violent death. Despite the growing clout of syndicates, relatively few people had contact with organized crime. For most people, the picture of a criminal was a bank robber.

The crash of the stock market in 1929 did little to improve the image of banks. By foreclosing on farms and homes, bankers and banks became more unpopular than ever, and the prevailing view came to romanticize criminals as latter-day Robin Hoods. Woody Guthrie, a folk singer, expressed the view of the common man in his 1939 song "The Ballad of Pretty Boy Floyd" with the line,

wherever you may roam,
  You won't ever see an outlaw drive
    a family from their home

Though there is no evidence that any bank robber ever donated his loot to the poor, their habit of stealing from the rich delighted many people. During the 1930s, bank robberies multiplied across the nation. The South and Midwest witnessed the most crime, with those who had mortgages foreclosed cheering at the distress of the bankers and those who had their life savings on deposit praying for the capture of the robbers. In an era before the federal government insured bank deposits, a bank robbery meant the loss of life savings. But with money increasingly hard to get, fewer and fewer people sympathized with the bankers. It was the men warring with the banks who garnered the applause.

No bank robber ever managed to steal as many hearts as did John Dillinger. Once a farmboy from Indiana, Dillinger had made fools of lawmen all over the Midwest during a ten-month period. When not mocking the authorities, he and his gang found time to kill ten men, wound seven others, rob four banks and three police arsenals, and stage three jailbreaks, killing a sheriff in one and wounding two guards in another. Yet, after Federal Bureau of Investigation (FBI) agents shot Dillinger to death in front of the Biograph Theater on the night of July 22, 1934, newspaper letters-to-the-editor columns were filled with protests. Despite his labeling by the FBI as Public Enemy Number One, people howled against the brutality of the bureau and wailed about the end of a "misunderstood boy."

Despite his love for gunplay, Dillinger did not prove to be the most violent of the bank robbers. According to J. Edgar Hoover, the Missouri-based Barker gang held the title for viciousness. Arizona Barker, better known as Kate or Ma Barker, and her boys, Herman, Freddie, Lloyd, and Arthur (known as Doc), robbed and killed at random throughout the Midwest, aided by Alvin "Creepy" Karpis, who joined the Barkers in 1930 after befriending Freddie in prison. Seeking to branch out, the Barkers moved from robbery to kidnapping and began their downfall. By grabbing Edward G. Bremer Sr. of St. Paul, Minnesota, in January 1934, the gang received a ransom of $300,000.

They also sparked FBI interest. Kidnapping had become a federal offense, and Hoover's men managed to find a fingerprint left on a gasoline can. Hoover says that the FBI traced the fingerprint to Doc Barker via his prison record, and the FBI started to close in on the gang. Karpis tried to disguise himself through plastic surgery after the jailing of several men who had

exchanged ransom money. He was caught in New Orleans in 1936 and soon found himself in Alcatraz prison for life. Lloyd and Doc also returned to prison, but Kate and Freddie never joined them. After Doc was captured in Chicago with a map of their Oklawaha, Florida, hideaway, the two remaining Barkers decided to fight rather than surrender. Well-equipped with two machine guns with hundred-shot drums, two shotguns, three automatic pistols, cartons of ammunition, a rifle, and five bulletproof vests, Kate began the gun-battle with the FBI by firing a machine gun from an upstairs window. A few minutes later, both Barkers lay dead.

The publicity from the demise of the Barker gang enhanced the reputation of the FBI for skillful and brave police work. The FBI had demonstrated that, unlike local lawmen who were often cowed by the heavy firepower of robbers, they would not stop until they got their suspects. The case of George "Machine Gun" Kelly gave the government men more public esteem and a new nickname. A habitual criminal, Kelly came to prominence as a society bootlegger in Memphis during the days of Prohibition. Linked with organized crime, he was suspected of involvement in the June 1933 Kansas City Massacre, in which two police detectives, a chief of police, and an FBI agent were killed in an attempt to liberate a gangster named Frank Nash. A month later, Kelly kidnapped oilman Charles F. Urschel of Oklahoma City. The public had been advised by the Justice Department to report any kidnapping personally to Hoover since 1924. Urschel's wife promptly awakened Hoover from his slumber, and the FBI soon arrived in Oklahoma. Meanwhile, Urschel had managed to keep his wits about him and he noted every noise, every step, and every conversation during his ordeal. Released unharmed, Urschel's information led the FBI to a farmhouse owned by Kelly's relatives. Captured in Memphis, Kelly surrendered, shouting, "Don't shoot, G-Men! Don't shoot!"

As Kelly learned, the government men had a new approach to kidnapping. Although abductions had taken place before the Great Depression, the 1930s was the era of kidnapping. In the peak period from 1933 to 1936, forty-eight cases—an average of twelve a year—provoked an outcry of public revulsion and demands for tougher laws. No case of kidnapping sparked as much universal rage as the snatching of Charles A. Lindbergh Jr.

Stolen from his crib on the second floor of his New Jersey home on the night of March 1, 1932, one-year-old Charlie was the first child of the famed aviator who had flown solo from New York to Paris across the Atlantic Ocean. Hampered by poor evidence collection, poor police strategy, and enormous publicity, the case was badly botched from the beginning. Instead of a photo of the child with a recent newspaper, Charlie's sleeping suit was accepted as proof that he was still alive. He was not. Soon after the ransom had been paid, the badly decomposed body of the toddler was found on May 12, 1932. The baby had apparently been killed shortly after his disappearance, perhaps on the same night. The public, to which Lindbergh had made numerous appeals for the return of his son, demanded action. The FBI had no authority to investigate or take action against criminals who flitted from state to state to avoid arrest and prosecution. The bureau had to work with both the New York City police and the New Jersey state police to solve the crime. On September 19, 1934, a German-born carpenter named Bruno Richard Hauptmann found himself under arrest by the three police agencies. Convicted on the basis of testimony (later described as "fabricated" by the FBI) that the wood from his attic matched the wood on a ladder found at the crime scene, Hauptmann was sentenced to death and electrocuted on April 3, 1936. Seen at the time as a triumph for scientific evidence, Hauptmann's guilt was questionable.

Public demands that the national police force, the FBI, should possess all the powers necessary to arrest those responsible for abductions led to the passage, in 1934 of the Federal Kidnapping Statute. Popularly known as the Lindbergh Law, the act gave the FBI exclusive jurisdiction for the federal government over all violations of the statute. The accumulation and analysis of all the facts relating to a kidnapping could now take place under one roof: that of the FBI.

The powers of the FBI continued to expand. In 1930, Congress had authorized the FBI to keep a file of all fingerprints taken in the nation. The FBI laboratory opened in 1932 to handle ballistics as well as physical evidence from blood, hair, soil, dust, and me-

tallic traces. Eager to use Hoover's G-men against gangsters, in the 1930s Congress made it a federal crime to transport stolen money, to flee prosecution for major crimes across state lines, or to kill a federal officer.

As the nation began to develop a centralized police force, more demands for changes in law enforcement arose. During Herbert Hoover's presidency, he had commissioned an unprecedented study of law enforcement. The resulting Wickersham Commission report, issued beginning 1931, summed up the prevailing wisdom about crime and criminality, police, prosecution, prison, and parole. In response to Wickersham, the FBI began something that chiefs of police had been requesting for years: the collection of Uniform Crime Reports based on the number of incidents reported to police departments across the country.

Although the decade had begun amidst the lawlessness created by Prohibition and economic collapse, the 1930s proved a watershed for law enforcement. The United States began to move toward a national system of criminal justice. Advances in criminal detection and prosecution led to a steady decline in the crime rate in the later half of the decade, a drop that continued into the war years.

CARYN E. NEUMANN

See also: Lindbergh kidnapping; Prohibition; Federal Bureau of Investigation; Capone, Al; Dewey, Thomas; Dillinger, John; Floyd, "Pretty Boy"; Hoover, J. Edgar.

Bibliography

Albini, Joseph. *The American Mafia*. New York: Meredith, 1971.

Bles, Mark, and Robert Low. *The Kidnap Business*. London: Pelham, 1987.

Hoover, J. Edgar. *Persons in Hiding*. Boston: Little, Brown, 1938.

Lane, Roger. *Murder in America*. Columbus: Ohio State University Press, 1997.

DAMS

Major floods in the Mississippi River basin in the 1920s, demands for more electric power throughout the country, and the need for major public works projects that would soak up the millions of unemployed workers led the federal government to embark on an ambitious dam building program during the New Deal years of the 1930s.

Aside from the numerous hydroelectric projects of the Tennessee Valley Authority, the major dams of the New Deal era were confined to the western states. The Fort Peck Dam, a Public Works Administration project, straddled the upper Missouri River in northeastern Montana. Among the largest earth-fill dams in the world—at 21,432 feet in length—the Fort Peck Dam was finished in 1937.

The Grand Coulee Dam, while not finished until 1942, was begun during the New Deal. Situated astride the Columbia River in Washington state, it was constructed under the aegis of the Federal Bureau of Reclamation. With 11,975,500 cubic yards of concrete and generators capable of producing 6,494 megawatts of electricity, it is the largest dam in the Pacific Northwest.

While not part of the New Deal, construction on the Hoover Dam was inaugurated in 1930 and finished in 1936. The highest concrete arch dam in the United States, the Hoover Dam is located on the Colorado River, between Arizona and Nevada. Originally called the Boulder Dam, it was renamed in 1947 for the ex-president who first ordered it built.

See also: public works; Public Works Administration; Tennessee Valley Authority.

Bibliography

Jackson, Donald C. *Great American Bridges and Dams*. New York: John Wiley, 1996.

DELTA COUNCIL

The national Depression of the early 1930s deepened an agricultural crisis in the farmlands along the lower Mississippi River second in its devastating effects only to the midwestern dust bowl. The Great Flood of 1927 had nearly crippled agribusinesses over millions of acres in the Midwest and in Mississippi, Arkansas, and Louisiana. The effects of flood and depression were particularly acute in the highly agrarian world of the Mississippi Delta, the farming lands in eighteen counties in northwestern Mississippi within the river flood plain.

In an effort to reverse the economic tide, a private organization of plantation owners, civic leaders, and agriculture extension agents was formed in 1935. Named the Delta Council, this group depended solely on private, municipal, and county funds to promote a variety of private and public initiatives for flood control, agricultural development and research, land utilization planning, forestry and game preserves, and highway development.

Its headquarters was established in Stoneville, Mississippi, near an existing agricultural extension laboratory, and the council was initially very active in providing private funds for expanded agricultural research, particularly in combating the boll weevil and in developing improved mechanical forms of cultivation. It also promoted educational programs in crop diversification and other forms of modern agriculture, as well as acting as a lobbying organization for public funds for regional development of transportation links and industrial sites. Perhaps most successfully, it evolved a series of marketing schemes to promote the consumption of regional crops, particularly cotton, soybeans, and catfish.

The Delta Council was unusual in being a private cooperative response to regional economic disaster. Its successes, particularly in developing private market solutions with limited public assistance, have contributed to its longevity. In the year 2000, the Delta Council was still active in many of its initial missions, encouraging increased efficiency in agribusiness through such tools as satellite technology, aerial planting, and biotechnology and encouraging increased markets for its products through such efforts as its Cotton USA program, which has successfully enlarged the international and domestic market for cotton-based fibers in consumer goods and apparel.

STEPHEN SHEPPARD

See also: agriculture.

Bibliography

Cash, William M., and R. Daryl Lewis. *The Delta Council: Fifty Years of Service to the Mississippi Delta.* Stoneville, MS: Delta Council, 1986.

DEMOCRATIC PARTY

On the eve of the Great Depression, the Democratic Party, excluded from power for almost a decade, and the minority party in the United States for much of the previous thirty years, gave little evidence of political strength. The brief ascendancy of Woodrow Wilson's presidency (1913–1921) had been achieved only with the support of dissident Republicans and collapsed under the social and political strains of World War I. During the 1920s, party leaders sought to overcome the cultural tension that prevailed between the big-city machine politicians of the North and rural Democrats of the South and West on issues such as national Prohibition and the Ku Klux Klan. At the 1924 Democratic convention, these divisions split the party into warring camps, forcing the nomination of a conservative with little appeal to the country. In the general election, Progressive Party candidate Robert M. La Follette actually led Democrat John W. Davis in twelve western states, and President Calvin Coolidge won a sweeping victory, capturing 15.7 million votes to Davis's 8.4 million. In 1928, rural Democrats handed a doomed nomination to Governor Alfred E. Smith of New York. Herbert Hoover trounced Smith 444 to 87 in the electoral college and 21.3 million to 15.0 million in the general election. The Democrats had hit rock bottom.

The weakness of the party organization further hampered efforts to effect a political recovery during the 1920s. The Democratic National Committee (DNC) proved too large and unwieldy to formulate policy, and its unpaid chairmen were at the mercy of the state leaders. Franklin Delano Roosevelt, a rising Democratic politician, advocated the establishment of a permanent party headquarters and a more democratic policy-making process. After the ascent of John J. Raskob to the chairmanship of the DNC in 1928, some of these reforms were instituted and an executive committee and publicity department established.

Raskob, however, remained a vocal conservative, fundamentally opposed to government interference in the economy or excessive public expenditure, even as he embraced repeal of national Prohibition.

The declining fortunes of the Republican Party in the early 1930s, as President Hoover's administration staggered from crisis to crisis, made the 1932 Democratic presidential nomination a most desirable commodity. In 1930, the party had gained a majority in the House of Representatives and came within one seat of control of the Senate. Raskob's efforts to secure support for his program (including a higher tariff for American industry) and the presidential candidacy of Al Smith were blocked by Southern conservatives. Both factions, however, were united in their hostility to New York governor Franklin D. Roosevelt, around whom had gathered a group of liberal, pro-government activists from the Wilson era. In April 1932, Roosevelt delivered his "Forgotten Man" radio address, which criticized President Hoover's efforts to spur recovery as inadequate and identified underconsumption in rural areas as the nation's principal economic problem, which required some redistribution of national income. Entering the party primaries, Roosevelt won a majority of the delegates, but he lacked sufficient votes for nomination at the convention in Chicago, thanks to the party's two-thirds rule (a device intended to assure the South of control over the process of selection). His supporters were nevertheless able to secure the key posts of keynote speaker and permanent chairman for members of his faction. When, after three ballots, it became clear that Roosevelt's nomination would require outside support, Representative John Nance Garner of Texas was persuaded by Democrats from the West, including newspaper publisher William Randolph Hearst, to release his California delegates and give Roosevelt the nomination. The nominee, despite his advocacy of the need to reduce government expenditures and bureaucracy, confirmed the fears of many conservatives by his pledges of guaranteed economic security and federal regulation of business. This blunt assertion of the virtues of the regulatory state signaled a new departure that would fundamentally reshape the party of Thomas Jefferson and Grover Cleveland.

A NEW POLITICAL ORGANIZATION, 1932–1936

After receiving the nomination on June 30, 1932, Roosevelt made a dramatic, unprecedented move. He flew from Albany to Chicago to deliver an acceptance speech to the convention. No nominee had ever before addressed the convention that had nominated him. "I pledge you, I pledge myself," he told the assembled Democrats on July 2, "to a new deal for the American people."

In launching his fight for the presidency, Roosevelt sought to broaden the base of his party rather than make a purely partisan appeal, defining his crusade in terms of "liberalism" in order to encourage dissident Republicans to break ranks with President Hoover. The Democratic campaign sought to build upon the successes achieved by Al Smith among the urban immigrant population in 1928, when more than a hundred counties in the Northeast had switched from the Republican Party to the Democratic Party. It also attempted to connect with voters in the West, with assertions of the need for a planned economy—as embodied in Roosevelt's address to San Francisco's Commonwealth Club—and the need for government to foster the expansion of public utilities. Despite these promises, the party platform was vague and did not commit the new administration to a specific blueprint for the future. The future president was able to preserve

No one epitomized the Democratic Party during the Great Depression better than Franklin D. Roosevelt, who served as president from 1933 to 1945. Here he is shown tapping a telegraph key in the White House on November 12, 1936, officially opening the San Francisco-Oakland Bay Bridge, a New Deal public works project. (*Brown Brothers*)

his freedom of maneuver and still win 57 percent of the popular vote, even as his party won sizable majorities in Congress. There was, as yet, no ideological transformation of the party, and support for Roosevelt remained comparatively evenly distributed between rural and urban areas and among different ethnic groups and social classes.

Though the New Deal evolved into a plan to restructure the national economy, it also served as an effective means of cementing political loyalties. This may help to explain why many conservatives in Congress were less hostile to the early phase of government expansion, given their desire to satisfy the needs of their constituents. Despite the nonpartisan criteria initially adopted for allocating and staffing federal projects, government administrators soon embraced a more cooperative relationship with local Democratic organizations. Sixty of the sixty-five new federal agencies were exempted from the civil service laws, and party chairman James A. Farley—an aggressive organization Democrat—pressed for patronage jobs to go

to those Democrats who had been loyal campaigners and were certified by their local congressman. To facilitate this task, Farley pressed for greater centralization of the party organization. During the 1932 campaign, a list of 160,000 Democratic activists throughout the nation and their campaign duties was compiled by the DNC, and literature was directed to these activists rather than to state committees. Financially, the party also saw a shift away from business contributions to small donations. Bankers and stockholders, who provided 24 percent of the party's funds in 1932, provided 3 percent by 1936, and, by 1940, only 13 percent of individual contributions exceeded $5,000.

The rise of specialist party divisions also constituted a new element in political thinking. Under Mary Dewson, the Women's Division established a system of county "reporters" to comment on the progress and problems of federal agencies and distribute information on the benefits of such programs as Social Security. The Labor Division enjoyed a less influential status within

Governors by Party Affiliation, 1928
Democrat
Republican

(CARTO-GRAPHICS)

Governors by Party Affiliation, 1936

Democrat
Republican
Third Party

(CARTO-GRAPHICS)

the party, since organized labor—while backing Roosevelt—preferred to maintain its autonomy and by the mid-1930s was itself divided between the American Federation of Labor and the newly formed and more radical Congress of Industrial Organizations (CIO). By contrast, the Young Democratic Clubs served as a forum for liberal college students, which strengthened Roosevelt's hand at the end of the 1930s, when party regulars were pressing for a more conservative approach. Despite these changes, it is essential to acknowledge historian David Plotke's argument that the Democratic Party remained dependent on Roosevelt for its image and vision. Often, the party leadership sought to bypass state and local Democratic organizations that were unfriendly, rather than build a new mass party. Liberal intellectuals continued to set policy, and the rush of new recruits to the party at the ballot box did not lead to marked increases in membership. In an arena in which both the national government and the Democratic Party were expanding, the former enjoyed a clear advantage.

PARTY POLITICS AT THE GRASSROOTS, 1933–1937

At the state level, New Deal programs often became entangled in existing Democratic factional conflicts. In Pennsylvania, Democratic governor George Earle was charged by his opponents with playing politics with relief, while governors in Idaho, Nebraska, and Louisiana all sought to use federal aid to consolidate their own political positions. Federal programs did, however, provide a model for some Democratic gubernatorial administrations. In New York, Governor Herbert Lehman secured passage of a minimum-wage law and persuaded voters to endorse a $40 million bond to support relief. Governor Frank Murphy of Michigan backed old-age pension legislation and workers' compensation, while George Earle's administration secured restrictions on company policy and established a bureau of civil liberties and the regulation of public utilities. In Texas, New Deal development aid was channeled through liberal politicians hostile to Wall Street's control of the economy, including Representatives Sam Rayburn (D-TX) and Lyndon B. Johnson (D-TX). Sometimes there could be confusion, as when Roosevelt's ideological sympathy for Minnesota's Farmer-Labor Party conflicted with party loyalty to the state's Democrats, some of whom backed the Republican gubernatorial candidate in 1938 in protest at their lack of access to federal patronage. Democratic strength at the state level was also no necessary guarantee of liberal sympathies, for the governors of Oregon, Washington, and West Virginia during the 1930s were all vocal conservatives.

By contrast, certain social and ethnic groups did find their niche within the Democratic Party during this period. The rise of a new semiskilled workforce and the philosophy of the "new unionism" both favored the policies of the Roosevelt administration and inclined the labor movement to the Democratic Party. After the Supreme Court outlawed the National Recovery Administration in 1935, Senator Robert Wagner (D-NY) came to serve as the spokesman for labor legislation in Congress, not just for the National Labor Relations Act, but also for social welfare and public housing legislation. In New York City, Roosevelt endorsed the creation of the American Labor Party to attract New Deal supporters who opposed the Tammany Hall Democratic machine, while in traditionally Republican Pennsylvania and California, voter registration drives in 1934 and 1936 secured large increases in membership. Prominent union leaders, such as Sidney Hillman and John L. Lewis, who did not belong to the Democratic Party, helped found Labor's Non-Partisan League to win the president additional support. The CIO's abandonment of support for a national third party and its endorsement of the federalization of industrial unions marked a new phase in the evolving relationship between the Democratic Party and the American working class.

An equally significant gain for the New Deal coalition was the rise of black Democrats within the party. The existence of the "black cabinet," a group of black advisers in the Roosevelt administration, called into question the party's traditional stand on race. By the 1930s, moreover, African Americans increasingly sought to make both national parties compete for their votes. In St. Louis, a younger black generation endorsed a Democratic mayoral candidate in 1933, who responded by building a hospital for black indigents and appointing many African Americans to public office. The number of African Americans in state legislatures and local offices grew steadily in the course of the decade, and, for the first time, accredited black del-

egates were present at the 1936 Democratic convention, where Representative Arthur Mitchell (D-IL), the only African American in the House of Representatives, gave the welcoming speech. The 1936 presidential campaign made direct appeals in the black press, emphasizing the benefits of federal relief. The federal government established the first Civilian Conservation Corps camp commanded by black officers in 1936, and Roosevelt delivered his first address to a largely black audience at Howard University that same year. Black turnout increased dramatically in the years that followed, with particularly strong support manifested for President Roosevelt.

THE CONSERVATIVE RESPONSE, 1935–1938

The presidential election of 1936 marked the apogee of Democratic political fortunes, as Roosevelt far outpaced the Republican candidate, Alfred Landon of Kansas. He won 61 percent of the vote and crushed Landon—who carried only Maine and Vermont—523 to 8 in the electoral college. The strong support for the party by poor voters was clearly evident, and Roosevelt also drew black and Jewish voters from their traditional Republican allegiances. The campaign of 1936 served to create a voting bloc in the country and established links with voters—particularly in the West and Midwest—who had previously backed third-party tickets. Urban voters were strongly supportive of the Democrats, consolidating a trend begun by Al Smith in 1928, and the country's twelve largest cities turned in substantial margins for the party, margins that would grow more important in the 1940s as the Democratic majority shrank. Economic needs met by federal aid had now created a voting bloc that looked to Washington, D.C., for its salvation. The national administration's relationship with the traditional power brokers in America's big cities, however, remained more ambiguous. Most urban leaders were initially skeptical of the rural Democrat coalition that backed Roosevelt, and only Tom Pendergast of Kansas City endorsed him in 1932. As the New Deal wore on and the cities gained from the new process of cooperative federalism (particularly the projects of the Works Progress Administration), the party bosses became better disposed, and leaders like Frank Hague of Jersey City mobilized voters for Roosevelt in 1936. In New York City, Edward Flynn, boss of the Bronx, helped restructure the Tammany machine to make it more appealing to independent voters who had backed progressive Republican Mayor Fiorello

LaGuardia. Nevertheless, the relationship was always uneasy. The administration tolerated the machines only when it could not afford to challenge them, and when Pendergast's power declined in the late 1930s, the White House supported his Missouri opponents.

If the city bosses were ambivalent toward the administration, ideological conservatives viewed with alarm the shift to the left. Repeal of the two-thirds rule at the 1936 convention suggested that the conservative South would no longer be able to exercise its hold on the affairs of the Democratic Party. In early 1937, the president responded to a series of judicial defeats on key items of New Deal legislation by seeking to reorganize the Supreme Court. This action united conservatives and many moderates who supported the administration's legislative ends but not its means. When the court-packing reform legislation was blocked, Roosevelt departed from his previous neutrality in intraparty disputes and opposed conservative Democratic incumbents in the 1938 primary season. Following the victories of New Deal partisans Lister Hill and Claude Pepper in Senate primaries in the South, the New Dealers embarked upon a strategy of making the Democratic Party a liberal bastion. Their tactics and outlook, however, were often inconsistent, and they chose to target some opponents of court reform whose overall record was far from conservative. Government workers on relief projects were mobilized in support of liberal politicians, and in Kentucky they provided a critical source of support for Senate majority leader Alben Barkley. Elsewhere in the South, however, local bases of support proved far more resistant to liberal overtures, and many Democrats resented the attempt at dictation by the national administration. Ultimately, Representative John J. O'Connor of New York was the only incumbent to be defeated, even though many conservative victories did not necessarily represent voters' repudiation of the New Deal. The purge campaign aided the rise of the conservative coalition, as conservative Democrats and Republicans in Congress found an element of common cause, but it also intensified the ideological struggle within the Democratic Party, where liberals had come to exercise a far more pervasive influence.

LIBERALISM RESURGENT, 1938–1941

Though an economic recession and public protests over attempts to unionize the steel industry in 1937 represented a setback for the New Dealers and a gain for congressional conservatives, liberals continued to

put their faith in the Democratic Party. Passage of the Fair Labor Standards Act in June 1938 convinced most unionists that their future was irrevocably bound up with the fate of the Democratic coalition. At the same time, a number of progressives, including Senator Joseph O'Mahoney (D-WY), began to push for federal licensing of corporations in an effort to reduce the concentration of economic power, and the Temporary National Economic Committee (TNEC) was created to hold hearings on the issue. In the California race for governor, Culbert Olson, one of the few Democratic challengers elected in 1938, pledged his administration to solving the problem of distribution of economic resources identified by the TNEC and to providing for the collective welfare. Olson's program, however, was blocked in the state legislature, and he secured only minor reforms in the penal system and the appointment of a number of liberal judges before his defeat in 1942. With the outbreak of the Spanish Civil War in 1936, moreover, the national administration came to focus more directly on a foreign policy designed to counter the rise of fascism. In 1940, in an effort to win bipartisan support for his internationalist policy, President Roosevelt appointed Republicans to the posts of secretary of the navy and secretary of defense. At home, moderate Democrats like James Farley concluded from the results of purge elections of 1938 that there was a need to ensure greater intraparty harmony and avoid interference in local affairs. The president, by contrast, defended the need to consolidate the liberal voting bloc and serve the cause of labor, and he opposed the nomination of a conservative candidate in 1940.

The president's anticipated retirement revealed the extent to which Democratic success had rested on one man. Roosevelt's favored choice for a liberal successor was Harry Hopkins, former head of the Federal Emergency Relief Administration and the Works Progress Administration, but Hopkins was unpopular with party regulars. Both James Farley and Vice President John Nance Garner enjoyed conservative support, but the former had little elective experience, while the latter was anathema to liberals. Ultimately, Roosevelt decided to ignore tradition and run for a third term, though he found himself far more dependent on the city bosses, particularly Ed Kelly of Chicago, than in 1932 or 1936. Most Democrats acknowledged, however, that only Roosevelt could unite the various conflicting factions of their party, and they finally agreed to endorse his selection of ultraliberal Henry A. Wallace of Iowa as his running mate. The campaign quickly developed into a clash between two liberal and internationalist candidates, after the Republicans nominated utility executive Wendell L. Willkie, a maverick Democrat turned Republican. Willkie hoped to benefit from an endorsement by labor leader John L. Lewis—and he did carry the state of Michigan—but over two-thirds of the labor vote went to Roosevelt on election day. Though the president won only 55 percent of the popular vote, somewhat down from his performance during the 1930s, he still won convincingly, and the split between rich and poor voters persisted, especially in urban areas. In the final analysis, Roosevelt had succeeded in adding a class component to the Democratic coalition and had achieved his objective of a more ideologically liberal party. This liberal ascendancy, especially on such issues as government intervention in the economy and growing support for civil rights legislation, would mark the Democratic Party for more than a generation to come.

JEREMY BONNER

See also: American Federation of Labor; Commonwealth Club speech; Congress of Industrial Organizations; election of 1932; election of 1934; election of 1936; election of 1938; election of 1940; "Forgotten Man" radio address; "black cabinet"; Fair Labor Standards Act; Federal Emergency Relief Administration; Works Progress Administration; Barkley, Alben; Farley, James; Garner, John Nance; Hearst, William Randolph; Hillman, Sidney; Hopkins, Harry; La Guardia, Fiorello; Lewis, John L.; Murphy, Frank; Pepper, Claude; Raskob, John J.; Rayburn, Sam; Roosevelt, Franklin D.; Smith, Al; Wagner, Robert; Documents: Democratic Party platform, 1932; Roosevelt's New Deal speech to Democratic Convention, July 2, 1932; Democratic party platform, 1936; Roosevelt campaign speech, October 14, 1936; Democratic Party platform, 1940.

Bibliography

Allswang, John. *The New Deal and American Politics: A Study in Political Change.* New York: John Wiley, 1978.

Burner, David. *The Politics of Provincialism: The Democratic Party in Transition, 1918–1932.* New York: W. W. Norton, 1967.

Fraser, Steve. "The 'Labor Question.'" In *The Rise and Fall of the New Deal Order, 1930–1980,* ed. Steve Fraser and Gary Gerstle, pp. 55–84. Princeton: Princeton University Press, 1989.

Patterson, James T. *Congressional Conservatism and the New Deal: The Growth of the Conservative Coalition in Congress, 1933–1939.* Lexington: University Press of Kentucky, 1967.

———. *The New Deal and the States: Federalism in Transition.* Princeton: Princeton University Press, 1969.

Plotke, David. *Building a Democratic Political Order: Reshaping American Liberalism in the 1930s and 1940s.* New York: Cambridge University Press, 1996.

Rosen, Elliott. *Hoover, Roosevelt and the Brains Trust: From Depression to New Deal.* New York: Columbia University Press, 1977.

Savage, Sean. *Roosevelt: The Party Leader, 1932–1945.* Lexington: University Press of Kentucky, 1991.

Schwarz, Jordan. *The New Dealers: Power Politics in the Age of Roosevelt.* New York: Vintage Books, 1993.

Weiss, Nancy. *Farewell to the Party of Lincoln: Black Politics in the Age of FDR.* Princeton: Princeton University Press, 1983.

DIONNE QUINTUPLETS

The Dionne quintuplets were born to Oliva and Elzire Dionne in Ontario, Canada, on May 28, 1934. From the moment they were born prematurely, the quintuplets became an international human interest story, being the only set of five births in which all survived for more than a few days. The five girls—Émilie, Yvonne, Cécile, Marie, and Annette—ended up making three feature films for Twentieth-Century Fox and provided endorsements for products from cars to cod-liver oil. The town of Callandar, near where they were born, became a major tourist attraction during the 1930s, and the attending physician, Allan Roy Dafoe, became a minor media star. Because of the poverty of the parents—and the fact that the Dionnes already had nine other children—the government of Ontario made the quints wards of the province, though the father regained legal control in 1941.

See also: Canada.

Bibliography

Blatz, William E. *The Five Sisters: A Study of Child Psychology.* New York: William Morrow, 1938.

Tesher, Ellie. *The Dionnes.* Toronto: Doubleday Canada, 1999.

DUST BOWL

From 1930 to 1941, severe drought, heat, and high winds created almost intolerable living conditions for residents of Oklahoma, Texas, New Mexico, Colorado, and Kansas. Labeled the dust bowl, this region received a double dose of hard luck in not only extreme weather but also the Great Depression. The epicenter of the dust bowl lay in the Oklahoma panhandle, and the area of drought, heat and wind radiated outward from there in all directions.

The origin of the dust bowl lies in a combination of greed, ignorance and environmental factors. Following World War I much of the population of Europe depended heavily on U.S. farmers and ranchers for its survival. This almost total reliance on U.S. agriculture created high demand, resulting in an agricultural boom time that swept over the Great Plains. Farmers on the Great Plains, seeing an opportunity for large profit, began cultivating as much land as possible. Acre upon acre of marginal and submarginal land was plowed to make way for wheat and other high-profit crops. Worrying little or not at all about soil or water conservation, most farmers and ranchers ignored warnings from government officials and continued with wasteful, old-fashioned farming methods.

In the late 1920s as severe drought and high heat hit the plains, strong winds began to carry the topsoil from the fragile newly plowed lands. Huge dust storms resulting from severe soil erosion filled the sky, covering towns and farms. Combined with environmental factors, economic woes as well began to hit the Great Plains. Farmers were glutting the market with overproduction and crop and livestock prices began falling to record lows. Arching over all was the economic turmoil of the Great Depression; the farmers and ranchers of the Great Plains were in serious trouble.

For residents of the dust bowl the election of Franklin Delano Roosevelt in 1932 brought a renewed hope for improvement. With his talk of a New Deal for the American people, Roosevelt appeared to many dust bowl residents as their last chance to save their homes, families and farms. Historians sometimes speak of the New Deal as having three main elements: relief, recovery and reform. These three terms can also be used as a framework with which to discuss the New Deal as it affected the dust bowl.

RELIEF

Several of Roosevelt's programs, especially in the early days of the New Deal, were intended to bring immediate and direct aid to those dust bowl residents with the most need. While a few of these needy allowed pride and independence to stand in the way of such offers of help, critical conditions on the plains soon forced even the most reluctant of them into acceptance.

On June 9, 1934 Roosevelt asked Congress for $525 million in drought relief for the farmers and ranchers of the dust bowl. Approved in the Emergency Relief Appropriation Act in 1935, the relief funds were used for emergency livestock feed loans, to purchase livestock for feeding those starving in urban areas, government jobs for out-of-work farmers, seed for farmers and the construction of work camps for out-of-work youths.

Also in 1935, the Resettlement Administration was enacted and placed under the supervision of Rexford Tugwell, an agriculturist and one of Roosevelt's advisers on the dust bowl issue. Like many of Tugwell's plans, the resettlement idea was considered too radical by most farmers and many politicians.

Under Tugwell's plan, farmers living on submarginal lands, or even those families who were merely too far in debt to pull themselves out, would be bought out of the farms they inhabited and relocated to more profitable areas. Farmers who feared resettlement often armed themselves and vowed to fight to the death to stay on their land regardless of how unprofitable it was. Other opponents of the Resettlement Administration included large-scale farmers who feared that the government, by resettling families on profitable land, would merely create more competition. Although attempted for several years, the resettlement program never attained even a moderate level of success.

Other New Deal programs, such as the Farm Security Administration and Federal Emergency Relief Administration, made sure that families and individuals received food, clothing, shelter and other necessities. Families or individuals who refused to accept the donations outright, could enroll in a work project improving roads, building dams or doing some other work in their area.

A farm family flees a dust storm on the lower Great Plains in the early 1930s. *(Brown Brothers)*

Direct federal relief was the least desired of the government programs, because for many farmers, receiving the aid was the final admission of defeat or failure. Despite the stigma attached to such aid, it was estimated that at one point over 90 percent of the farmers in Oklahoma alone were receiving some type of direct government aid. While Oklahoma is considered the state most affected by the dust bowl, the numbers of aid recipients for surrounding states was almost as high.

RECOVERY

In addition to direct relief, Roosevelt and his advisers designed programs based mainly on incentives that

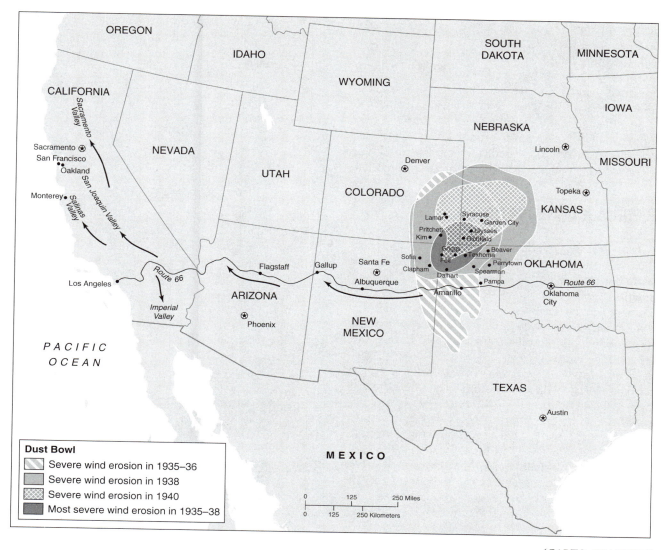

Dust Bowl

- Severe wind erosion in 1935–36
- Severe wind erosion in 1938
- Severe wind erosion in 1940
- Most severe wind erosion in 1935–38

(CARTO-GRAPHICS)

would help farmers and ranchers in their recovery from the drought and Depression. Most of these recovery programs fell under the auspices of the Agricultural Adjustment Administration, (AAA) created in 1933, and worked on the theory of "planned scarcity." These recovery plans provided funds to purchase livestock from ranchers and to pay farmers a certain amount for every acre left uncultivated. The goal of planned scarcity was to reduce the amount of grain and food on the market, theoretically raising prices and benefiting farmers, ranchers, and those who depended on their success.

The amount of livestock purchased by the U.S. Government increased drastically as rainfall and production throughout the dust bowl decreased. By 1935, the federal government had become the largest cattle owner in the world. In 1934, almost $1 million dollars

in subsidies was paid to Cimarron County farmers in Oklahoma to cut back on the amount of crops raised in their fields. By the end of the 1930s the AAA had enrolled a majority of the dust bowl farmers into these cutback programs. In Haskell County, Kansas, more than 90 percent of the farmers were receiving farm subsidies for leaving a portion of their fields uncultivated.

These government subsidy programs were never meant as a permanent solution to problems. Ultimately, it was hoped that the cutback and livestock buyout programs would help in the recovery of the agriculture markets, whereupon the farmers and ranchers would be set on their own independent means again. In the end, most of the AAA reduction schemes must be considered a failure. If some farmers did agree to decrease production, inevitably others increased production, hoping to take advantage of the expected higher crop prices. Also, these plans tended to favor the large-scale wealthier farmers. The more land they held, the more land they could leave uncultivated and the more money they received, while farmers holding only small bits of land were paid relatively small subsidies, provided they could afford to leave any land at all uncultivated. Later research revealed that under the programs of the AAA crop production in most dust bowl states actually increased, thereby insuring lower prices and further damage to the already weakened soil.

REFORM (CONSERVATION)

It was perhaps in the area of conservation that Roosevelt and his New Deal advisers achieved their greatest success. With the introduction of the Soil Conservation Service (SCS) in 1935, the federal government began educating farmers in environmentally friendly farming techniques, such as shelterbelts, crop rotation, the introduction of soil-stabilizing grasses, terracing, and contour plowing.

The shelterbelt program was a pet project of Roosevelt's that, with the creation of the SCS, he was able to see come to fruition in 1937. Shelterbelts, essentially rows of trees used to block damaging winds, had been used with great success during European droughts and Roosevelt and his advisers felt the concept would work equally well in the United States. The first shelterbelts were planted in Oklahoma. In a line extending from northern Texas to the Canadian border, rows upon rows of trees were planted around and along arid farm fields. The belts proved effective where planted, but the vast areas encompassed by the dust bowl and the expense of shelterbelt construction—an estimated $75 million over twelve years—ultimately limited the use and appeal of the concept.

Another dust bowl experiment of the New Deal involved the "listing" of fields. The lister, a large double-sided plow, created huge furrows in the land that disrupted the flow of wind. Farmers received federal funds to aid them in the listing project. Participants were paid either twenty cents for every acre they themselves listed or forty cents for every acre if they had someone else do the work. By working with farmers in the listing project, government advisers could also educate farmers in the concepts of terracing and contour plowing. The listing project proved extremely successful: it saved vast sections of farmland from destruction, educated farmers in techniques that are still in used today, such as contouring and terracing, and at the very least helped farmers to maintain their equipment and keep things in running order.

Elements of listing, contouring, and terracing were utilized throughout the 1930s and the number of farmers involved in the projects increased annually as the techniques proved successful. Throughout the decade an average of 8 million acres a year were plowed according to the tenets of the SCS, saving them from the ravages of wind and erosion. These conservation elements were considered such an important asset in the battle against the dust bowl elements that in Kansas and Texas fines were levied against farmers not complying with the SCS measures.

Similar to Tugwell's resettlement plans was the idea behind the Land Use Planning Division and the Tri-State Land Utilization and Conservation Project. Under these two subbranches of the AAA, land that had been entirely consumed by the roving dunes of sand was purchased outright from the resident families. Although initially garnering very few takers, by the late 1930s hundreds of families had accepted the government buyout programs and headed, they hoped, for greener pastures. By 1947, when submarginal purchase officially ended, over $47.5 million had been spent and acreage equal to that of Vermont and Massachusetts had been purchased. The acquired lands were later added to Indian reservations or turned into wildlife refuges or national grasslands.

CONCLUSION

In the end, the agricultural plans implemented by Roosevelt and his advisers never achieved the sweeping changes hoped for. Relief programs fed, sheltered, and clothed the needy but did little to permanently improve conditions. The most radical relief plan and perhaps the one that held the greatest chance for success, the Resettlement Administration, was one of the most despised of all New Deal policies. Farmers and politicians alike refused to support or cooperate with Roosevelt on this matter. The recovery concept of planned scarcity also had little effect on Great Plains residents. Under the plan, some farmers did indeed leave fields fallow or slaughtered livestock in order to receive government aid, but ultimately production increased under this plan negating any good that might have been achieved.

The policies promoting soil and water conservation were arguably the only elements of Roosevelt's agricultural plans that had any lasting effect. Elements of conservation such as terracing, contour plowing, and listing reduced topsoil erosion during the 1930s and are still used on present-day farms. The government purchase of submarginal lands and lands totally consumed by sand resulted in millions of acres being turned over to Native Americans or reserved for public use.

The return of rains and cooler temperatures gradually brought an end to drought conditions on the plains. Historians cite 1941 as the official end of the dust bowl era. While rain settled the dust on the plains, entry of the United States into World War II settled the matter of the Great Depression. Jobs and good wages sparked by wartime production turned an economic bust into a boom. While Roosevelt's New Deal policies for the dust bowl actually did, in the end, very little for most residents of the plains, the hope and trust that he inspired with his programs undoubtedly helped people to endure and persevere during a time of desolation and tragedy.

STEVEN KITE

See also: agriculture; *Grapes of Wrath, The;* Okies; Agricultural Adjustment Act (1933); Hickok, Lorena; Lange, Dorothea; Steinbeck, John; Document: Agricultural Adjustment Act, May 12, 1933.

Bibliography

Biles, Roger. *A New Deal for the American People.* Dekalb: Northern Illinois University Press, 1991.

Hamilton, David E. *From New Day to New Deal: American Farm Policy from Hoover to Roosevelt, 1928–1933.* Chapel Hill: University of North Carolina Press, 1991.

Hendrickson, Kenneth D., ed. *Hard Times in Oklahoma: The Depression Years.* Oklahoma City: The Oklahoma State Historical Society, 1983.

Saloutos, Theodore. *The American Farmer and the New Deal.* Ames: The Iowa State University Press, 1982.

Worster, Donald. *Dust Bowl: The Southern Plains in the 1930's.* New York: Oxford University Press, 1979.

EDUCATION

America's educational system was in dire shape when Franklin D. Roosevelt took office in March 1933. In Alabama, 85 percent of the public schools were closed as tax revenues evaporated. Dr. A. F. Harmon, the state superintendent of education, reported, "Despite all the sacrifices by teachers, the schools of fifty counties [out of Alabama's sixty-seven] were closed." As of the first of April, he noted that "7,000 teachers were out of work, and the doors of 2,400 school buildings were closed in the faces of 265,000" students. Many of the unemployed teachers had not been paid for three to eight months and others not for a year.

Dr. Harmon also remarked that average annual salaries of $140 had been paid partly in cash and partly in scrip for two years, but merchants had increasingly balked at accepting the latter. Evoking echoes of the district schools of the 1830s, a century earlier, some teachers in Alabama were working simply for room and board in a community round robin.

Urban schools fared somewhat better. In New York City, the first response by the board of education was to slash salaries from 6 to 33 percent, effective January 1933. The second response was to cut salaries indirectly by the introduction in 1934 of "payless furloughs," that is, working without pay for one or several weeks.

As elsewhere in the country, Chicago's teachers were subject to the litany of pay cuts, payless furloughs, increased work loads, and fear of unemployment. Like their colleagues in New York, moments of desperation aroused teachers. In April 1933, 5,000 militant Chicago teachers, wearing armbands signifying that they had not been paid for ten months, stormed five city banks to negotiate their warrants—to no avail. Nonpayment of teachers' salaries stretched out to two years.

In Seattle, along with pay cuts, teachers received sporadic pay warrants that were often discounted by merchants and at other times nonnegotiable. As local tax collections diminished, the warrants drawn on the county treasury became essentially promissory notes. Monthly pay consisted for a time of a $50 warrant and the remainder in $10 denominations to facilitate payment of bills without receiving change in cash. In addition, a clause was inserted into the 1933 teacher's contract that each teacher would not be paid for three weeks during the school year as an economy measure. The payless furlough had arrived in Seattle, too.

DUNNING OF TEACHERS

Adding insult to teachers' salary slashes and payless furloughs was the role of involuntary teacher philanthropy. Throughout the decade, the dunning of teach-

This old one-room schoolhouse in Crossville, Tennessee, was replaced with a modern facility as part of the Tennessee Valley Authority project in the 1930s. *(Brown Brothers)*

ers for charitable contributions was a recurring motif, especially in New York, led by Superintendent William O'Shea and his successor, Harold Campbell. Again and again, the two superintendents in New York City called upon teachers to divest themselves of contributions from their shrunken paychecks.

As in New York City, teachers in Seattle were asked to "donate" a part of their pay, their time, and their good will on top of salary cuts. Seattle's new superintendent of schools, Worth McClure, volunteered the teachers' free time, for example, in teaching literacy classes to the unemployed.

WOMEN TEACHERS

Aside from salary cuts, payless furloughs, and involuntary contributions, teachers were subjected to other disabilities. In the name of economy and efficiency, women teachers were dismissed on the basis of mar-

riage, health, or some violation of a bureaucratic rule. The marriage rule was typical in the Depression; jobs, it was believed, should be reserved for men first and then single women.

Across the land one out of four women teachers were wed, officially. How many concealed their marriages is unknown. A researcher discovered in a 1939 study of nearly 1,500 cities that only 23.4 percent of the school districts had hired married women teachers as new teachers. Repeatedly, the researcher increasingly found educational administrators saying, "married teachers not wanted."

Another criterion for denying women teaching positions was the charge of being overweight. One New York City teacher, Rose Freistater, reduced her weight from 180 to 154 pounds. Despite this accomplishment, an attorney for the board of education averred that her normal weight should have been 122 pounds and thus he considered her a "sub-standard risk."

Still another method of cost reduction by school boards involved the early retirement or dismissal of senior teachers in favor of novice ones. New York City led the way in this process, with its own chief medical officer and staff ordering teachers to come to the headquarters for medical examinations.

DR. EMIL ALTMAN'S LIST

In March 1934, Dr. Emil Altman, New York City schools' chief medical officer, charged that the incidence of mental disorder among teachers was about the same, about 3 percent, as in the general population. Accordingly, he asserted that 1,500 teachers currently employed were emotionally unstable or insane. After this time bomb, Mayor Fiorello La Guardia felt compelled the following day to call for the removal of unbalanced teachers and of any unfit city employees. But, by the next day, the numbers game took another turn when Dr. Altman reduced the number in question to 700 teachers. Disingenuously, he declared that "there was no reason for a rumpus being stirred up." Despite having created a rumpus from a statistical average, he went on to insist it was "not unnatural that such cases exist, but they should not exist in the schools." A day later, Dr. Altman insisted that there were emotionally unstable teachers, he repudiated "the impression that these people are insane." Days later, following teacher protests, Dr. Altman virtually retracted his sensational charges of insane teachers.

While Dr. Altman was withdrawing his allegations, the *New York Times* chose to pick up La Guardia's call that 700 unfit teachers had to go for "even this rate is too high if only we can find a satisfactory test."

NEW DEAL

President Roosevelt, in an address before the 1938 annual convention of the National Education Association, spoke of the need not to be bound by the narrow keeping of financial books. There was a need, he instructed, for future as well as immediate balancing of the books. Roosevelt asserted that the most important element of a democratic society was the wise husbanding of natural and human resources. Using language that anticipated later economists' concerns with the effects of schooling on economic growth, Roosevelt noted, "Man's present day control of the affairs of nature is the very direct result of investment in education." Thus, in Roosevelt's view, prudent use of both natural

and human resources would redound to the nation's benefit.

Roosevelt went on to note the wide disparity of per capita income among the states and the corresponding differences in educational expenditures. The president observed, "We all know that the best schools are, in most cases, located in those communities which can afford to spend the most money." Since federal dollars, like all other dollars, were in short supply, Roosevelt proposed that assistance be given to the poorer communities in order to lift "the level at the bottom" rather than giving aid to "the top."

Given the president's support, many believed general federal aid to education might be forthcoming. The issue was pertinent, since the administration the preceding year had decided to reduce overall federal expenditures, thereby ushering in the economic recession of 1937.

As to the fate of the particular educational bill in Congress introduced by Mississippi Senator Pat Harrison, Turner Catledge of the *New York Times* wrote that the budget decisions of the New Deal "implied that the President had set his face against certain extraordinary projects, such as federal aid to education" and other domestic programs. The Harrison bill offered $100 million in educational block grants to the states. Accordingly the bill was sidetracked while the president continued to espouse the cause of education.

But if explicit general federal aid to education lay dormant, actual federal expenditures were numerous and substantial, if often under the guise of "emergency" programs. Various alphabet agencies, such as the Civilian Conservation Corps, National Youth Administration, Works Progress Administration, and Public Works Administration, either had educational components or worked in conjunction with public schools. Necessity often overruled the debate over the "principle" of federal aid.

Consider, for example, the construction of schools. Alice Barrows, of the Office of Education, noted, "Public Works Administration has been a life saver for the schools. In four years from 1934 to 1938, the PWA has made grants and loans for school buildings amounting to $452,444,344."

But given the New Deal's budget decisions in 1937 and the subsequent recession, a cutoff date of January 1939 had been established for further PWA funds for school projects. Altogether, federal funds for school construction from 1934 to 1939 amounted to $1.7 billion, with a matching state and local component of approximately $300 million. For these expenditures, by

School children study their readers outside a rural schoolhouse in Scottsboro, Alabama in June 1936. *(Library of Congress)*

1939, the nation obtained 59,614 classrooms for schools and colleges, and 102 public libraries.

WORKS PROGRESS ADMINISTRATION

But it was the Works Progress Administration (WPA) that provided badly needed *operating* funds to the schools. While the WPA, of all the alphabet agencies spawned by the New Deal, suffered from the notoriety as a "boondoggle" enterprise of leaf raking, it created much of social value.

Aside from school construction and job creation, the WPA had an impact on the public schools in other ways. Reviewing its accomplishments in 1938, Aubrey Williams, deputy administrator of the agency, observed that the WPA had initiated new educational programs, such as adult education and nursery schools. "The WPA nursery school program, for example, has focused the attention of many educators on the importance of the pre-school years for the later physical and social development of the child. Defects in health and nutrition . . . may be corrected with comparative ease . . . whereas their correction in later years may be costly, if not impossible." The WPA operated 1,500 nursery programs across the country, some as demonstration projects.

Williams added that under the rubric of "emergency education" begun by the Federal Emergency Relief Administration and continued by his agency, the WPA had provided jobs, reduced illiteracy, and stimulated state and private agencies to set up comparable programs for the young and the old. One hundred thousand teachers had been employed to instruct 4 million men and women as well as 150,000 preschool children. In 1938 alone, 30,000 teachers had been employed and 1.25 million adults enrolled in various programs in all forty-eight states. For the school year 1937–38, approximately 1.5 million adults had been enrolled nationally in classes that ran the gamut from cooking and nutrition to family budgeting, personal hygiene, care of the sick, and other family welfare concerns. All the more remarkable was the fact that, despite reductions in the numbers of classes and teachers, enrollment continued to climb. One WPA official observed in 1938 that a million adults since 1933 had been taught to read—a feat of no mean political, economic, and social significance. In addition, as wave after wave of immigrants fleeing Nazi Europe arrived, they immediately sought out classes in English and citizenship training.

Rose A. Cohan, a specialist in parent education, noted at a conference in New York City that the WPA was "blazing the trail" in nursery and parent education. Implicitly, she recognized that it was the WPA that outlined a de facto family policy during the Depression with the schools in a supporting role. More often than not, school officials saw WPA funds simply as supplements to their status quo efforts and saw servicing new clienteles as a sideline. Meanwhile students who failed their subjects during the regular school year could avail themselves of remedial classes during the summer under WPA auspices.

Confirming Cohan's observation, an unusual experiment was forthcoming. In New York City, as a result of population shifts, a junior high school on the lower east side of Manhattan became surplus for disposition or conversion to other purposes. Fortunately under both WPA and the New York City Board of Education sponsorship, a free adult day and night school opened that was believed to be the first of its kind in the nation. In this predominantly Jewish and Italian neighborhood, immigrant mothers were offered English and citizenship courses by day while their children received nursery care.

At night workers could attend classes. Worthy of mention too was the WPA nutrition project in New York City that supplied 119,000 free hot lunches daily to needy children. For the most part, the WPA lunch consisted of a sandwich and a half, a hot dish, one piece of fruit or pudding, and milk. Instead of teacher philanthropy, the WPA had institutionalized since 1935 the provision of this social necessity. Of course, this did not preclude true "voluntary" giving by teachers if they chose.

Another WPA innovation was the use of the storefront to supplement the work of the schools. In Brooklyn, one storefront offered a ten-week course in retail training. In another direction, the WPA opened the first boarding school for girls in Chicago, accommodating about 130 youngsters between the ages of 16 and 25 for a three-month course in "community leadership." The candidates were restricted to youngsters whose parents were either on relief or worked for the WPA.

On the political front, Representative Emanuel Celler (D-NY), taking a leaf from the President's Advisory Committee on Education, proposed in his bill that the WPA's educational services be made permanent. Second, he proposed the establishment of a National Advisory Committee of Five to assist the commissioner of education in administering the proposed act. Finally, he proposed funding levels of $70 million for 1939 rising to $250 million by 1943. Apparently, this was the sole attempt to bestow the mantle of legitimacy on the wide range of WPA programs in education and to use these programs as the vehicle for permanent federal aid.

TUSHER AFFAIR

Despite construction of new schools and classrooms in New York City using federal funds, obsolete school buildings, triple sessions in some schools, and high student/teacher ratios remained. Therefore, school officials sought to shut down the worst facilities and elsewhere to consolidate classes and to reduce enrollments. The result was mandatory reassignments of students to other schools.

In response, early in February 1939, the parents of students of PS 97 in the Bronx and of PS 116 in Queens launched a parent/student strike. Shortly thereafter, PS 40 and PS 123 saw picketing by parents and teachers. Approximately 130 students and their parents walked the picket lines with placards: "This is not a strike, this is a lockout," "We want our 3Rs," and "PS 97 is our school—let us in."

One school official saw no reason for parental objections and predicted that the strike would soon collapse. But the strike, led by the brothers William and Benjamin Tusher, parents of school children, entered its second, third, and fourth weeks. Repeatedly, the Tushers sought the intervention of the mayor, to no avail, as well as putting out feelers to the American Civil Liberties Union. Even the *New York Times* reporter admitted that the strike, viewed lightly at first, had become a serious matter. After two weeks of picketing, "the parents and children ha[d] experienced an undue amount of rain, snow, sleet and slush."

When not condescending toward the parents as unruly children in need of discipline, school officials attempted to invoke the truancy laws. When parents did not attend quietly at these truancy hearings, the school officials turned the matter over to the courts.

In domestic relations court, the judge found the parents guilty as charged under the truancy laws and complimented the school officials for holding the best interests of students paramount. But Benjamin Tusher demurred: "After all, if a father hasn't got the right to look after his son, who has?" Under threat of fines and jail, most parents complied and the strike fizzled out. But Benjamin Tusher chose three days in jail while William Tusher rallied the remnant of parents into the sixth week. Brought before another judge, the parents finally capitulated.

Having discovered that he could not fight city hall, William Tusher concluded that the strike had served the purpose of alerting the board of education to first consult "the people involved" before imposing future student reassignments.

NEW LONDON, TEXAS

In March 1937 in New London, Texas, twenty minutes before the close of the school day, an accidental gas explosion ripped apart a new school, the London Consolidated High School, killing close to five hundred students and teachers.

Days later, a military inquiry, convened to determine the cause of the explosion, concluded that an electrical spark was the likely cause. Witnesses included the superintendent of schools, W. C. Shaw. In that oil-rich county in east Texas, Shaw testified that, for econ-

omy's sake, the school had been permitted to tap, gratis, a residual gas line of the Parade Oil Company with the tacit approval of an oil official.

Despite warnings from school architects of abnormal gas pressure under the school and from Parade personnel of potential danger, Shaw dismissed these criticisms out of hand merely as attempts to force the school district to purchase the gas. When a school board member was asked if this failed economy had been necessary, he replied, no, but he saw no reason to make unnecessary expenditures when the gas had been free. As a result, 455 children and teachers lay dead, including Superintendent Shaw's son, Sam, 17.

DOMINIC W. MOREO

See also: youth; National Youth Administration: Williams, Aubrey.

Bibliography

"Hint Switch Spark Set School Blast." *New York Times*, March 23, 1937, p. 3.

Berger, Meyer. "500 Pupils & Teachers Killed in Explosion of Gas in Texas School; 100 Injured Taken From Debris." *New York Times*, March 19, 1937, pp. 1, 14.

———. "School Deaths Under 500; Some Families Have Lost All Their Children." *New York Times*, March 20, 1937, pp. 1, 2, 3.

Moreo, Dominic W. *Schools in the Great Depression.* New York: Garland, 1996.

Tyack, David B. *Great Depression and Recent Years.* Cambridge: Harvard University Press, 1984.

ELDERLY, THE

The elderly in the Great Depression and New Deal were a small but powerful force in the United States. They faced many of the same problems and challenges that other Americans faced during this time, yet they shaped and were shaped by the times.

In 1930, according to the U.S. Census Bureau, almost 5.5 percent of the U.S. population, or 6,633,805 individuals (3,325,211 men and 3,308,594 women), were 65 or older. By 1940, this number had grown to 9,019,314 (4,406,120 men and 4,613,194 women). Although the average life expectancy in 1929 was only in the low sixties for whites and high forties for blacks, these figures partly reflected early deaths from child-

hood illnesses and accidents. It was estimated that, once an individual reached the age of 65, the average African-American man could expect to live another 12.0 years; African-American woman, another 12.7 years; white man, another 11.9 years; and white woman, another 13.1 years. Life expectancy increased by 1940 to an average of 66.2 years for whites and 53.8 for nonwhites.

Only a slightly higher number of aged individuals lived in rural rather than urban areas. In fact, the greatest numbers of the elderly were concentrated in large states with a mix of farming and industrial jobs. In 1930, New York had 667,325 citizens over 65; Pennsylvania, 508,278; Illinois, 421,073; Ohio, 414,836; and California, 366,125. States with predominantly ranching and mining industries had the lowest number of elderly: Wyoming had 8,707 elderly people and Nevada had 4,814. Not surprisingly, of the 58.4 percent of men over 65 still employed in 1930 almost 75 percent were employed in some aspect of agricultural work. Well under 1 percent of women over 65 continued to work, primarily in the agricultural and domestic trades. By 1940, only 41.8 percent of all men over 65 were still employed.

About two-thirds of the elderly male population, 2,116,537 individuals, were married in 1930, 883,680 were widowed, and 37,371 were divorced. Females over 65 showed lower marriage rates of 1,147,200 married, 1,869,034 widowed, and 17,893 divorced. By 1940, the numbers remained comparable except for the women's divorce rate, which shot up to almost double the 1930s rates. In 1940, there were 57,367 divorced men over 65 and 33,221 divorced women 65 and older.

Perhaps the most immense change the elderly faced during this time was adapting to the concept of retirement from employment and the acceptance of government financial assistance to survive. Prior to the Great Depression, the elderly supported themselves via employment and savings or relied on their families or private charity for assistance. There were also a limited number of business pensions that continued to function during the Depression.

Although some elderly people remained employed throughout the Depression, many employed and unemployed elders advocated the new plans for government-supported pensions proposed in the Townsend Plan and Share Our Wealth. So vocal was the support for these plans that it was no surprise that the 1935 Social Security plan provided both an insurance section to deal with the needs of future retirees and also an old-age assistance section to provide immediate financial assistance for those in need. Under the old-age assistance programs, payments varied from state to state with annual payments of $79 to $434. Approximately 20 percent of all over the age of 65 received benefits at any given time. This was fifteen times the level of aid given in 1930, and approximately 50 percent of the aid went to support those 65 and older. The insurance aspect of the Social Security program did not really begin until after 1941.

Freed from the necessity of maintaining themselves via employment, the elderly in the 1930s began to look for activities to fill their leisure hours. Either as groups or individuals, they soon claimed the time of public recreation directors and workers hired by cities to deal with the young. In the late 1930s, large numbers of senior citizens created groups in which they played softball, formed glee clubs, gave concerts, attended dances, went on field trips, staged horseshoe contests, and went hiking. Before the acceptance of leisure time activity for older people, a walk around the house was considered an adequate outing for the elderly, with games and organized activities reserved for the young. But these newly retired elders adopted any number of leisure time activities in officially sanctioned groups and centers for the elderly.

SUSAN B. STAWICKI-VROBEL

See also: Share Our Wealth Society; Townsend Plan; Social Security Act; Townsend, Francis; Document: Social Security acts, August 15, 1935.

Bibliography

Achenbaum, W. Andrew. *Old Age in a New Land: The American Experiences Since 1790*. Baltimore: Johns Hopkins University Press, 1978.

Bureau of the Census. *Historical Statistics of the United States: Colonial Times to 1970, Part 1*. Washington, DC: Government Printing Office, 1970.

Fischer, David Hackett. *Growing Old in America*. New York: Oxford University Press, 1977.

Giles, Ray. "A Step Toward Livelier Old Age." *Reader's Digest*, August 1937, 26–28.

Graebner, William. *A History of Retirement: The Meaning and Function of an American Institution, 1885–1978*. New Haven: Yale University Press, 1980.

Haber, Carole. *Beyond Sixty-five: The Dilemmas of Old Age in America's Past*. Cambridge, UK: Cambridge University Press, 1983.

Haber, Carole, and Brian Gratton. *Old Age and the Search for Security: An American Social History*. Bloomington: Indiana University Press, 1994.

Kurian, George Thomas. *Datapedia of the United States, 1790–2000: America Year by Year*. Lanham, MD: Bernan Press, 1994.

Patterson, Donald O. "Male Retirement Behavior in the United States, 1930–1950." *Journal of Economic History* 51:3 (September 1991): 657–74.

"Play Past Sixty." *Recreation* (September 1936): 301–02.

Sachs, Bernard. "Recreation After Fifty." *Recreation* (August 1937): 308, 332–33.

Smith, Daniel Scott. "Accounting for the Change in the Families of the Elderly in the United States, 1900–Present." In *Old Age in a Bureaucratic Society*, ed. David Van Tassel and Peter N. Stearns. Westport, CT: Greenwood Press, 1986.

ELECTION OF 1930

The election of 1930 was the first congressional election following the Wall Street crash of 1929 and the onset of the Great Depression. With rising numbers of bankruptcies, a deepening farm crisis, and an unemployment rate fast approaching 10 percent by November 1930, the election was seen as a referendum on President Herbert Hoover and the Republican-led Congress's handling of the economic crisis. Not surprisingly, the results were discouraging for the GOP, even though the party managed to maintain a bare control over both houses of Congress.

In the party's worst setback since the recession year election of 1922, the Republicans lost fifty-three seats in the House, even though they won 54.1 percent of the popular vote, just six-tenths of a percent below their margin in the prosperous election year of 1928, when Hoover swept to power over Democrat Al Smith. Still, the Republicans' margin in the House was so paper-thin that it was erased in the few by-elections held between November 1930 and the election of 1932. In the Senate, the Republicans' losses were equally catastrophic, with their majority whittled down from seventeen seats to one. Moreover, progressives in both parties tended to win out over more conservative candidates.

Because the margins were so small, and because he privately hoped to spread the blame for the continued economic depression, Hoover suggested that the Democrats—though in the minority—organize the new Congress. But the idea was squelched by leaders of both parties. Republican congressmen did not want to give up their hold on committee chairmanships, and the Democrats—looking forward to victory in the 1932 election—wanted to maintain their role as congressional dissenters.

See also: Democratic Party; election of 1932; Republican Party; Hoover, Herbert.

Bibliography

Schwarz, Jordan A. *The Interregnum of Despair: Hoover, Congress, and the Depression*. Urbana: University of Illinois Press, 1970.

Smith, Gene. *The Shattered Dream: Herbert Hoover and the Great Depression*. New York: Morrow, 1970.

ELECTION OF 1932

The election of November 8, 1932, occurring in the midst of the Great Depression, marked a dramatic realignment in both presidential and congressional politics. The overwhelming victory of the Democratic nominee and governor of New York, Franklin Delano Roosevelt, over Herbert Hoover, the one-term incumbent Republican president, ended twelve years of Republican control of the White House and began the first of five successive Democratic administrations. In addition, the impressive victories of Democratic candidates in Congress introduced Democratic control of both the House and the Senate, which lasted until the election of 1946, when the Democrats lost both houses of Congress. However, despite the large victory for the Democrats, the 1932 election represented a desire on the part of the American voters for change in general, rather than the specific endorsement of the Democratic Party.

THE CONVENTIONS

The Republicans held their convention in Chicago, Illinois, from June 14 to June 16. President Hoover was easily renominated on the first ballot, but the GOP was not optimistic about his chances in November. The 1932 Republican convention saw the beginning of the GOP tradition of appointing the party leader from the House of Representatives as the permanent convention chair. The atmosphere at the convention was subdued as the delegates discussed their platform. The most serious controversy centered on the issue of Prohibition. A minority of delegates called for outright repeal, but the majority recommended and won the call for a referendum on Prohibition in the party plank. Otherwise, controversy at the convention was limited to an aborted attempt by Maryland senator Joseph I. France to have Calvin Coolidge nominated as the party's candidate, and vigorous, but brief, opposition to Vice President Charles Curtis's place on the ticket. Curtis was eventually and unanimously renominated on the first ballot. The GOP platform blamed the nation's economic crisis on international factors and called for local and private unemployment relief, the reduction of public expenditures, the cooperative organization of farm-

ers to plan production, continuation of the tariff, and a referendum on Prohibition.

The Democrats also held their convention in Chicago, Illinois, later that month, from June 27 to July 2. The crisis of the Great Depression provided the Democrats with their best opportunity to win the presidency since 1912, when Woodrow Wilson was elected to his first term. When the Democrats began their convention, they did not yet have a nominee, but they were confident that whoever was nominated would defeat Hoover in the November election. Roosevelt entered the convention with a majority of the delegates' support, but was short of the two-thirds necessary for nomination. Roosevelt's main opponents at the con-

Even some members of the normally pro-Republican business community supported Democratic presidential candidate Franklin D. Roosevelt in 1932, as this New York City banner makes clear. By the 1936 election, most of that support had evaporated. *(Brown Brothers)*

A Most Vicious Circle
—Costello in the Albany "News."

As this editorial cartoon from the early 1930s illustrates, many Americans held President Herbert Hoover responsible for the Great Depression. *(Brown Brothers)*

vention were Al Smith, former New York governor and 1928 Democratic Party nominee, and House Speaker John Nance Garner of Texas. The delegates finally nominated Roosevelt on the fourth ballot, after the California delegation, led by William Gibbs McAdoo, announced that it was shifting its support to Roosevelt from Garner, who was soon nominated as Roosevelt's running mate.

The Democrats' platform was not significantly different from that of the Republicans. The Democrats blamed the Republicans for the Great Depression and called for drastic reduction of governmental expenditures, a balanced budget, the extension of federal credits to the states to provide unemployment relief, the repeal of Prohibition, and the enactment of agricultural price reforms. Roosevelt was the first major party candidate to accept his nomination personally at the convention. In his acceptance speech, Roosevelt promised "a new deal for the American people." This phrase, the "New Deal," came to define his approach to solving the crisis of the Great Depression during his adminis-

tration, but neither Roosevelt nor the Democrats articulated what this meant at the convention.

THE CAMPAIGN

Although the Republicans narrowly outspent the Democrats in the campaign (the Republicans spent $2,900,000 and the Democrats $2,379,000), Hoover was no match for Roosevelt. Out on the campaign trail, Roosevelt spoke only vaguely about the "New Deal" and of experimenting with different ways of solving the nation's economic crisis. He more often criticized Hoover's shortcomings and called for the repeal of Prohibition.

Roosevelt's campaign, coordinated by James Farley of New York, the Democratic National Committee chair, was the first truly modern presidential campaign. Farley had developed an extremely effective and extensive national direct mail campaign within the Democratic Party. These direct mailings, often including photographs of Roosevelt, were then supplemented by telegrams and telephone calls. Roosevelt also used the radio much more effectively than his opponent. Roosevelt's broadcasts impressed voters as warm, understanding, humorous, and optimistic. In addition, Roosevelt toured the nation, making twenty-three major addresses, in order to demonstrate to voters that he was not incapacitated by polio.

Hoover initially preferred to remain in Washington after the Republican convention, hoping that voters would regard his attention to the economic crisis as an indication of his fitness to continue in the office. However, an angry Hoover eventually took to the campaign trail in October as the Democrats continually referred to the "Hoover Depression" in their campaign. Hoover's campaigning at this point would make little difference in the outcome of the election. Nevertheless, Hoover considered every issue with seriousness; he was the last president to write his own speeches. In a series of nine major addresses, Hoover tried to explain that the economic crisis originated abroad and that Roosevelt's proposals for remedy, being either too radical or socialistic, would leave the country in even worse shape than it was at the time. Hoover's ineffective use of radio in the campaign only reinforced many voters' perception of him as depressing and shrill.

THE PRESIDENTIAL ELECTION RESULTS

Roosevelt won the presidential election in a popular and electoral landslide. For three-quarters of a century, Democrats had had difficulty winning the White House.

Roosevelt was the first Democrat elected to the presidency with a majority of the popular vote since the election of Franklin Pierce in 1852. Out of a total of 531 possible electoral votes, Roosevelt won 472 to Hoover's 59. Roosevelt carried the popular vote for all but six states; Hoover carried only Pennsylvania, Maine, Connecticut, Delaware, New Hampshire, and Vermont. Of a total popular vote of 39,758,759, Roosevelt won 22,829,501 votes, or 57.5%; Hoover won only 15,760,684, or 39.6% of the vote. Even in the midst of the Great Depression, only 52.4 percent of eligible voters cast votes for the office of president and only 33.7 percent cast votes for congressional candidates.

A number of minor candidates and parties, in addition to the Democrats and Republicans, also ran in the 1932 election. Norman M. Thomas (Socialist), who ran on the ballot in forty-five states, won 888,649 votes, or 2.2 percent of the popular vote. William Z. Foster (Communist), on the ballot in thirty-nine states, won 103,253 votes, or 0.3% of the popular vote. The remaining 180,672 votes cast, or 0.5% of the popular vote, were distributed among eight other candidates and parties, who were not on the ballots in all forty-eight states: William David Upshaw (Prohibition), William Hope Harvey (Liberty), Verne L. Reynolds (Socialist Labor), Jacob S. Coxey (Farmer Labor), John Zahland (Na-tional), James R. Cox (Jobless), and the Jacksonian and Arizona Progressive Democrat parties.

Much of Roosevelt's support came from voters who had abandoned the GOP. Roosevelt gained strength from new farm and working-class voters, building upon traditional support from urban, ethnic, and white southern voters. Otherwise, in absolute numbers, the Democrats did not significantly increase their support among African Americans, nonsouthern rural, and northeastern urban voters (these gains were more noticeable in the 1928 and 1936 elections). However, while a majority of African Americans voted for the GOP, as they had traditionally since the end of the Civil War, never before had so many voted for the Democrats as they did in 1932. The 1932 election marked the beginning of important voter realignment in favor of the Democrats for years to come.

CONGRESSIONAL ELECTIONS

The election of 1932 revealed that the electorate's dissatisfaction with the status quo extended not only to the presidential race, but also to House and Senate races. The Democrats won a stunning victory in Congress, gaining seventy new congressmen and thirteen

Presidential Election, 1932
Herbert Hoover
Franklin D. Roosevelt

(CARTO-GRAPHICS)

senators. Eliminating the Republicans' bare majority in the Senate and significantly improving upon the Democrats' bare majority in the House, the election brought an overwhelming majority of 310 Democrats to 117 Republicans in the House and 60 Democrats to 35 Republicans in the Senate (a ratio of nearly three to one in the House and two to one in the Senate). With the exception of the 1946 and 1952 elections, when the Republicans gained control of both the House and the Senate, the election of 1932 decisively ended Republican dominance of Congress, which had lasted since the 1890s, and marked the beginning of Democratic control of Congress, which lasted until the election of 1994. The Democrats created a major political realignment by maintaining their southern electoral base and expanding to other regions in the nation, especially northern, industrial, and urban districts.

When John Nance Garner, who had been the previous speaker of the house, became vice president in 1933, the Democrats elevated Henry T. Rainey of Illinois to the position of Speaker. Rainey, who died in office on August 19, 1934, was succeeded by William B. Bankhead of Alabama. In the Senate, Key Pittman of Nevada was raised to the position of Senate majority leader. The Republican leader of the Senate was Charles L. McNary of Oregon, and Bertrand H. Snell of New York was the Republican leader of the House.

ERIC PULLIN

See also: Commonwealth Club speech; Communist Party; Democratic Party; Farmer-Labor Party; Jackson Day speech (FDR); Republican Party; Socialist Party; Baruch, Bernard; Foster, William Z.; Garner, John Nance; Hoover, Herbert; Raskob, John; Roosevelt, Franklin D.; Smith, Al; Thomas, Norman; Documents: Democratic Party platform, 1932; Roosevelt's New Deal speech to Democratic Convention, July 2, 1932; Republican Party platform, 1932; Hoover campaign speech, October 31, 1932.

Bibliography

Boller, Paul. *Presidential Campaigns.* Oxford, UK: Oxford University Press, 1984.

Freidel, Frank. "Election of 1932." In *History of American Presidential Elections, 1789–1968*, vol. 3, ed. Arthur M. Schlesinger Jr. and Fred L. Israel, pp. 2707–2806. New York: McGraw-Hill, 1971.

Kendall, Kathleen. *Communication in the Presidential Primaries: Candidates and the Media, 1912–2000.* Westport, CT: Praeger, 2000.

Roseboom, Eugene, and Alfred Eckes. *A History of Presidential Elections from George Washington to Jimmy Carter.* New York: Macmillan, 1979.

ELECTION OF 1934

Labeled by the *New York Times* as the "most overwhelming victory in the history of American politics," the election of 1934—a referendum on the early New Deal and President Franklin D. Roosevelt's first two years in office—provided a landslide for the Democrats in Congress. Although unemployment remained above 20 percent throughout the year, voters expressed their general satisfaction with the numerous anti–economic depression programs initiated by the administration and passed by the Democratic Congress.

In the Senate, Democrats won 26 of the 35 seats up for grabs, raising their lead over the Republicans from 69 to 25, with the remaining two seats being held by independents or third-party candidates. In the House, the results were somewhat less spectacular, with the Democrats winning 322 of the 435 seats, a gain of 9. While this increase was modest, it nevertheless bucked an important trend in American electoral politics, whereby the party holding the White House usually loses seats in off-year elections. In fact, the Democrat majority was made even more effective because members of the Progressive and Farmer-Labor parties—who generally voted with the Democrats—won 7 and 3 seats, respectively. This gave the Democrats and liberals in Congress control of more than 78 percent of the seats in the House. Moreover, the mandate given to Roosevelt and the Democrats was bolstered by the fact that the election witnessed a record turnout for an nonpresidential poll.

Ultimately, the huge Democratic majority made it possible for Roosevelt to introduce and pass even more liberal New Deal legislation, including the National Labor Relations Act and the Social Security Act. But there were warning signs for Roosevelt and the Democrats in the results coming out of a number of states such as California, Minnesota, and Wisconsin, where winning congressional candidates—and, in California, radical Upton Sinclair and his nearly successful End Poverty in California campaign—staked out positions substantially to the left of Roosevelt's on income redistribution and corporate regulation.

See also: Democratic Party; election of 1932; election of 1936; End Poverty in California; Farmer-Labor Party; New Deal, first; New Deal, second; Republican Party; Wisconsin Progressive Party; Roosevelt, Franklin D.

Bibliography

McElvaine, Robert S. *The Great Depression: America, 1929–1941*. New York: Times Books, 1993.

Romasco, Albert U. *The Politics of Recovery: Roosevelt's New Deal*. New York: Oxford University Press, 1983.

ELECTION OF 1936

The presidential election of 1936 featured Republican candidate Alfred M. Landon, the governor of Kansas, and incumbent Democrat Franklin Delano Roosevelt. The United States was still recovering from the Great Depression, and the upcoming election would test how the American people felt about Roosevelt's comprehensive New Deal program.

Roosevelt believed it was the government's responsibility to take over economic controls if the private sector failed. Roosevelt's New Deal policy contributed to both recovery and reform, but it also interfered with freedom of business enterprise, established far-reaching controls over labor and farming, encouraged growth of bureaucracy, created administrative confusion, impaired the merit system, encouraged a fear of dictatorship, and at some points conflicted with the Constitution. Those who opposed Roosevelt condemned the philosophy of the New Deal. Roosevelt was attacked by both conservatives and progressives, conservatives arguing that he had gone too far, progressives arguing that he had not gone far enough. The New Deal survived over obstacles and criticism, and the nation was on the way toward recovery when the time came for the nominating conventions.

THE REPUBLICAN CONVENTION

The Republican convention took place in Cleveland. The Republicans had four contenders for the nomination: Alf Landon, Senator William E. Borah of Idaho, Senator Arthur H. Vandenberg of Michigan, and W. Franklin Knox, publisher of the *Chicago Daily News*. Before the balloting, Vandenberg and Knox withdrew, leaving the nomination to Landon, who defeated Borah in the balloting. Roosevelt's cross-party war secretary Frank Knox, once Landon's rival for the Republican nomination, became the Republican vice presidential candidate.

The Republican platform criticized the New Deal for dishonoring American traditions and betraying the promises upon which the Democrats received support in 1932. According to the Republicans, the president had usurped powers of Congress, threatened the integ-

At the 1936 Republican convention, delegates cheer the presidential and vice presidential nominations of Alf Landon and Frank Knox. The ticket won only eight electoral votes, however, suffering one of the biggest electoral defeats in American history. *(Brown Brothers)*

(CARTO-GRAPHICS)

rity of the Supreme Court, violated the rights and liberties of the American people, and threatened the tradition of free enterprise. They promised to maintain the American system of constitutional and local self-government, preserve free enterprise, stop uncontrolled government spending, and keep America out of the League of Nations. The Republicans were not all that enthusiastic about their state, however, because they realized that they probably could not beat Roosevelt.

THE DEMOCRATIC CONVENTION

Roosevelt was unanimously renominated by the Democratic Party. No other name but Roosevelt's was put forth at the Democratic convention held in Philadelphia. He pledged to continue supporting New Deal policies. There was some opposition from more conservative Democrats, but none that substantially threatened Roosevelt's renomination. Roosevelt traveled to Philadelphia that same night to accept the nomination. The vice presidential candidate was John Nance Garner, Roosevelt's current vice president.

OTHER CANDIDATES

The minor candidates in 1936 included North Dakota representative William Lemke for the Union Party, who was supported by Father Charles E. Coughlin, radio personality and leading spirit of Native Union for Social Justice. The Socialist Party nominated Norman Thomas, the Communist Party nominated Earl Browder, the Socialist-Labor Party chose John W. Aiken, and the Prohibitionists nominated David L. Colvin.

Celebrated people in both the Democratic and Republican parties crossed party lines. Prominent Democrat Alfred E. Smith supported Landon and became a member of the Liberty League, an anti-New Deal group opposing what it viewed as the bureaucracy and autocracy of the Roosevelt administration. On the Republican side, Senator George W. Norris ran as an independent and Senator Robert La Follette endorsed Roosevelt.

REPUBLICAN STRATEGY

Landon emphasized his ability to balance the country's budget. The Republicans attempted to present Landon

President Franklin D. Roosevelt reads congratulatory telegrams at his Hyde Park, New York, home, after his landslide re-election victory in 1936. *(Brown Brothers)*

as a plain country boy with a good heart and honest purpose who would save the country from the anti-business and proradical Roosevelt. Under Landon's leadership, the United States would abandon the New Deal and embrace free enterprise. "Life, Liberty, and Landon" became his principal campaign slogan.

DEMOCRATIC STRATEGY

Landon's lackluster personality could not compare to Roosevelt's charisma. Roosevelt was at the height of his popularity and was cheered by huge crowds wherever he spoke. He defended New Deal policies and pledged to continue and expand them.

Even though the public adored him, most newspapers denounced him. Roosevelt had the support of only 36 percent of the nation's press. Newspaper magnate William Randolph Hearst, a leader in the anti-Roosevelt crusade, published an editorial about Roosevelt's communist entourage leading the nation towards radicalism. The *Chicago Tribune* stated that a Roosevelt victory would mean "Moscow in the White House." Yet the *New York Times* supported Roosevelt, believing that Landon offered little in comparison.

In the final weeks of the campaign, normally pragmatic men accused both Roosevelt and Landon of fascism, communism, and Nazism. Roosevelt's reelection was certain, although a *Literary Digest* poll predicted Landon would win with 370 electoral votes to Roosevelt's 161. A Gallup poll more accurately predicted that Roosevelt would receive 389 electoral votes to Landon's 141.

THE ELECTION

Landon was badly beaten, carrying only Maine and Vermont and winning eight electoral votes. Roosevelt won the greatest plurality ever received in a national election, nearly 5 million larger than in 1932, and won 523 electoral votes. In Congress, the Democrats increased their numbers in both the House of Representatives and the Senate.

At the time of Roosevelt's inauguration, which was now held on January 20, 1937, the date having been changed in 1933 by the Twentieth Amendment, the *New York Times* favorably compared the position of the United States with that of four years before. Stocks were up, prices were down, and the nation seemed poised for recuperation. The people had voted in favor of Roosevelt and the New Deal.

ELIZABETH KEANE

See also: Communist Party; Democratic Party; Farmer-Labor Party; Republican Party; Socialist Party; Union Party; Browder, Earl; Landon, Alfred; Lemke, William; Roosevelt, Franklin D.; Thomas, Norman; Documents: Democratic Party platform, 1936; Republican Party platform, 1936; Roosevelt campaign speech, October 14, 1936

Bibliography

Goodwin, Doris Kearns. *No Ordinary Time: Franklin and Eleanor Roosevelt and the Home Front in World War II.* New York: Simon & Schuster, 1994.

Lorant, Stefan. *The Presidency: A Pictorial History of Presidential Elections from Washington to Truman.* New York: Macmillan, 1951.

ELECTION OF 1938

After suffering setbacks in every election since 1928, the Republicans made their first gains in a decade in the congressional elections of 1938. Aided by the uproar over President Franklin D. Roosevelt's ham-handed efforts to pack the Supreme Court with pro–New Deal judges, the sharp recession of 1937–38, and continuing high unemployment rates of nearly 20 percent, Republicans made substantial gains in both houses of Congress, albeit from extraordinarily low numbers.

In the 1938 elections, Republicans gained eighty-one seats, nearly doubling their record low total of eighty-eight seats following the 1936 poll. Moreover, the GOP gained eight new senators, increasing their number by more than half to twenty-three. In state elections as well, the revival of the nearly moribund Republican Party was unmistakable. Republicans won an additional thirteen governorships, more than tripling their number to eighteen. The election also saw the rise of future Republican Party presidential candidate Thomas Dewey, who nearly beat New York Governor Herbert Lehman, the popular and seemingly invincible Democratic incumbent.

Still, not too much should be made of this Republican resurgence. In Congress, Republicans held barely 40 percent of the House and, despite some gains, still managed to lose twenty-four of the thirty-two Senate seats in contention. This continuing weakness on the part of the Republican Party—particularly its more conservative, strongly anti–New Deal wing—would shift the party somewhat to the left in the 1940 election, when it would nominate the pro–New Deal, internationalist Wendell Willkie.

See also: court-packing plan; Democratic Party; election of 1936; election of 1940; New Deal, second; Republican Party; Roosevelt, Franklin D.

Bibliography

McElvaine, Robert S. *The Great Depression: America, 1929–1941.* New York: Times Books, 1993.

Romasco, Albert U. *The Politics of Recovery: Roosevelt's New Deal.* New York: Oxford University Press, 1983.

ELECTION OF 1940

The election of 1940 involved Republican candidate Wendell Willkie and Democratic incumbent Franklin Delano Roosevelt. The election was notable because American voters elected their first third-term president.

The small Republican minority in Washington had not been successful in its opposition to the New Deal. Its only hope for any reversal of New Deal policies lay in the Supreme Court, which had nullified some key New Deal legislation. President Roosevelt, feeling that the Court was behind the times, formulated a plan to enlarge it. A group of Democratic senators did not support the administration on this issue, and Roosevelt suffered his first major defeat in Congress. Protest followed his proposal to add to the Court; Roosevelt was accused of "packing the court" and denounced as a dictator. Middle-class support for the New Deal began to slip away in 1937 and 1938. In addition, the so-called Roosevelt recession began with another stock market crash in 1937. In the mid-term elections of 1938, the Republicans increased their congressional representation.

As the election year approached, domestic issues seemed to fade in importance as the country focused on the possibility of American involvement in the war in Europe and the Pacific. Many Americans did not believe that Roosevelt would run for another term. The Constitution did not limit the number of terms a president could serve, but it was an unwritten tradition in American politics for presidents to follow a two-term limit.

THE REPUBLICAN CONVENTION

Republican gains in Congress had given the party some hope for the presidential election. The favorites for the nomination were New York's district attorney Thomas E. Dewey, Senator Robert A. Taft of Ohio, son of former President William Howard Taft, and Senator Arthur Vandenberg of Michigan. As the convention in Philadelphia progressed, Dewey remained the leading candidate, but in the months before the convention, political outsider Wendell Willkie, a utilities executive and corporate lawyer, had gained a following. Willkie campaigned actively and, when it became clear that neither Dewey nor Taft could muster up enough support, he won enough votes to secure the nomination. He had never held public office, but he had the backing of big business and the people who wanted a new face. The Republicans chose Charles L. McNary, the Senate minority leader as the vice presidential nominee. McNary was an isolationist who favored high tariffs and drew support from conservatives, a direct contrast to Willkie. The party hoped that Willkie would appeal to liberal Republicans and anti-Roosevelt New Dealers while McNary would appeal to isolationist conservatives who favored high tariffs. The Republican platform, pledging "American preparedness and peace," promised aid to democratic victims of aggression which would not be in violation of neutrality law.

THE DEMOCRATIC CONVENTION

It seemed that Roosevelt was against a third term; some even believed that he was grooming Secretary of Commerce Harry Hopkins as his successor. But the situation in Europe led him to reconsider; a new candidate could increase division in the Democratic ranks and weaken the party. Roosevelt believed that no other candidate could carry the Democrats to victory in 1940. Some Democrats, however, were opposed to a third term for Roosevelt and suggested Postmaster General James Farley, Vice President John Nance Garner, or Maryland Senator Millard Tydings. At the Democratic convention in Chicago, three-fourths of the electorate chose Roosevelt to run for a precedent-breaking third term.

Roosevelt pledged to help farmers, workers, and businessmen, developing and expanding some New Deal policies. Roosevelt promised to keep America out of foreign entanglements unless the nation was attacked and to extend aid to democracies under attack.

The vice presidential candidate was Henry A. Wallace, Roosevelt's secretary of agriculture. He was Roosevelt's choice, and Roosevelt was quite firm about having Wallace on the ticket. Some Democrats objected because Wallace had been a Republican as late as 1928. After a bitter struggle, the Democrats nomi-

(CARTO-GRAPHICS)

nated him, replacing the more conservative John Nance Garner.

OTHER CANDIDATES

The Socialist Party nominated Norman Thomas for the fourth time. The Communist Party nominated Earl Browder, and the Prohibitionists chose Roger Babson.

REPUBLICAN STRATEGY

Willkie endorsed most of Roosevelt's New Deal policies as well as supporting Roosevelt's foreign policies, but he criticized the president for seeming to incite the nation toward war. He challenged Roosevelt to a series of debates, but presidential spokesman Harold Ickes stated that wartime concerns prevented the president from taking part.

Willkie ran a traditional campaign. His main allegation was that Roosevelt wanted to perpetuate totalitarianism by running for a third term. Roosevelt took little interest in the campaign, maintaining that leading the country through troubled times was far more im-

portant. This silence frustrated Willkie and led to harsher campaign tactics, such as Willkie's assertion that, if Roosevelt were reelected, it would mean wooden crosses for the nation's brothers, sons, and sweethearts. Willkie stated that the New Deal had floundered and left the nation without an adequate defense.

DEMOCRATIC STRATEGY

Roosevelt finally replied to Willkie's charges on October 23 in Philadelphia by saying that it was Republican opposition in Congress that made the United States unprepared for war. The president praised his administration's aims of preparing the country and keeping it out of war. Roosevelt's lack of interest in the campaign helped the Democrats because it appeared that he was acting in the interests of the nation.

THE ELECTION

Apparently, the American people were not afraid of Roosevelt becoming a dictator and they elected him for

Republican Wendell Willkie, shown here campaigning in Ohio (standing in car), ran a spirited campaign against President Franklin D. Roosevelt in 1940, but Willkie lost by nearly 5 million votes. *(Brown Brothers)*

a third term. Roosevelt won 449 electoral votes to Wilkie's 82, and America had its first and last third-term president. Roosevelt would win an unprecedented fourth term in 1944, and die in office the following year. In 1947, a Constitutional amendment was proposed that set a two-term limit on the presidency. The Twenty-second Amendment was ratified in 1951.

ELIZABETH KEANE

See also: Communist Party; Democratic Party; Farmer-Labor Party; Liberty League; Republican Party; Socialist Party; Browder, Earl; Roosevelt, Franklin D.; Thomas, Norman; Willkie, Wendell; Documents: Democratic Party platform, 1940; Republican Party platform, 1940.

Bibliography

Goodwin, Doris Kearns. *No Ordinary Time: Franklin and Eleanor Roosevelt and the Home Front in World War II.* New York: Simon & Schuster, 1994.

Lorant, Stefan. *The Presidency: A Pictorial History of Presidential Elections from Washington to Truman.* New York: Macmillan, 1951.

EMPIRE STATE BUILDING

At 1,250 feet, the tallest skyscraper in the world at the time, New York City's Empire State Building was completed on May 1, 1931, and represented the last great project of the construction boom of the 1920s.

Built in just nineteen months between October 1929 and May 1931, the Empire State Building was the tallest building in the world for more than thirty years. Here, the building appears as it was before a 200-foot television tower was erected on top in 1953. *(Brown Brothers)*

Contracts for the structure at Thirty-fourth Street and Fifth Avenue were signed in September 1929, just one month before the Wall Street crash. Yet despite the downward turn of the economy, building promoters John J. Raskob, a self-made millionaire, Al Smith, the former governor of New York and 1928 Democratic Party candidate for president, and industrialist Pierre S. du Pont proceeded with the project. With unemployment approaching record levels, workers were not hard to find. That, and new building techniques, allowed construction to proceed at breakneck speed. Demolition of the old Waldorf-Astoria Hotel, which stood on the site, began in December 1929, and the first steel columns were set into place just five months later. With up to 3,500 persons employed on the construction site, the building grew by about a floor a day during the peak of construction activity.

Although intended to represent a brave front in the face of economic uncertainty—and perhaps help reverse the tide of unemployment in New York City—the Empire State Building remained in financial trouble through the end of World War II, with nearly half the offices unoccupied as late as 1945, earning it the nickname, the "empty state building."

See also: manufacturing and construction; Raskob, John; Smith, Al.

Bibliography

Tauranac, John. *The Empire State Building: The Making of a Landmark.* New York: Scribner, 1995.

Willis, Carol. "Empire State Building." In *The Encyclopedia of New York City*, ed. Kenneth Jackson. New Haven, CT: Yale University Press, 1995.

END POVERTY IN CALIFORNIA

By 1934, Franklin D. Roosevelt's New Deal faced pressure from many who wished to pull it farther to the Left. Minnesota governor Floyd Olson, Louisiana senator Huey P. Long, and Francis Townsend all built enthusiastic bases of support for their plans to heighten the government's involvement in the private sector. One of the most intriguing of these challenges was Upton Sinclair's 1934 California gubernatorial bid as the head of the End Poverty in California (EPIC) movement. Sinclair was a famous muckraking novelist who was best known for his exposés of the meatpacking industry (*The Jungle*, 1906), the Teapot Dome Scandal (*Oil!*, 1927), and the Sacco-Vanzetti case (*Boston*, 1928). Sinclair, a registered Socialist, approved of the New Deal but felt that it did not do enough to solve the fundamental structural problems in the American economy. In September 1933, like-minded California Democrats persuaded the author to change his registration to Democrat and run for governor for the third time—in two earlier campaigns he had failed to amass more than 60,000 votes while running as a Socialist.

Sinclair kicked off his crusade with the October 1933 publication of a slim volume entitled *I, Governor of California, and How I Ended Poverty: A True Story of the Future*, which described how he would be nominated and elected and laid out his EPIC plan for creating prosperity for all Californians within four years. Sinclair argued that the profit system, which increased production while lowering wages, was responsible for the Depression and created conditions in which people starved even though there were surpluses of food. EPIC would remedy this system by allowing the state to take over idle land and factories and turn them over to the unemployed, who would in turn use them to produce goods for their own consumption. Sinclair proposed to generate the funds needed for these purchases by imposing high taxes on the rich, corporations, banks, and insurance companies. Under his "production for use" (as opposed to production for profit) scheme, workers in the agricultural colonies would trade their surplus food for manufactured commodities made in state-owned factories, thus ensuring that everyone had enough to survive and, not coincidentally, spelling the end of the capitalist system.

I, Governor of California electrified the state, which had well over 1 million people on the unemployment rolls. The book sold 225,000 copies in one year and sparked the formation of EPIC clubs across California. Members went door-to-door to raise funds for their candidate and snapped up copies of the *EPIC News*, a weekly publication that had a circulation of about 1.4 million. On August 24, 1934, Sinclair triumphed in the Democratic primary, winning over half the vote in a field of nine candidates. His strong performance, built on a coalition of laborers, the unemployed, and a surprisingly large middle-class contingent, made him the clear favorite against incumbent governor Frank Merriam, a staunchly anti-Roosevelt conservative Republican.

The nomination secured, Sinclair made a pilgrimage to Hyde Park in the hopes of gaining a presidential endorsement. Roosevelt was at his charming best with the candidate, laughing, telling stories, and implying that he would come out in favor of production for use, but never making any firm commitments to Sinclair and EPIC. Indeed, Roosevelt refused to offer an opinion on the controversial candidate during the election and never backed EPIC. Following the president's cue, many California Democrats abandoned their candidate and reluctantly supported Governor Merriam.

REPUBLICANS FIGHT BACK

The general election was marred by unprecedented levels of deception, smearing, and vicious attacks. California Republicans, already on edge after a general strike in San Francisco earlier in 1934, were determined not to allow the radical Sinclair to win the election. The GOP hired Campaigns, Inc., the nation's first political consulting firm, to run its campaign. Independent of the party's machinery, the firm established budgets and battle plans, generated themes and concocted slogans, and wrote speeches and arranged itineraries. Campaigns, Inc., also pored over Sinclair's novels in an effort to use his own words against him in state newspapers. By lifting lines out of context and applying some creative editing, the firm convinced many that the author was antichurch, a Communist, and a free-love advocate—none of which was true.

A former author and socialist, End Poverty in California leader Upton Sinclair is shown during a campaign rally at the Hollywood Bowl. *(Brown Brothers)*

Other organizations, mostly led by California businessmen, launched their own crusades against EPIC. The California Real Estate Association gloomily warned residents trying to sell their homes that no one would buy if Sinclair won, and many California-based corporations warned their stockholders that a Sinclair win would threaten future dividends. United for California, another front for businessmen, hired advertising executive Don Francisco to manufacture anti-EPIC propaganda for newspapers and radio. Francisco also pioneered the use of direct mail in a political campaign, littering mailboxes throughout California with pamphlets that distorted Sinclair's record and goals. Most major newspapers, which were run by conservatives, were more than willing to participate in the smear-Sinclair drive. Led by the *Los Angeles Times* and the *San Francisco Chronicle*, papers either ignored EPIC altogether or printed column after column of negative articles, editorials, and cartoons, many fed to them by anti-EPIC organizations.

Some of the most effective propaganda came from Hollywood. Although many actors and screenwriters favored Sinclair, MGM's Louis B. Mayer and other executives clamped down on their studios and turned them into pro-Merriam tools. The film magnates pressured their stars to issue anti-Sinclair statements, forced their employees to contribute to Merriam's campaign, and threatened publicly to leave California if Sinclair won. MGM also produced three "documentary" films, entitled *California Election News*, to educate voters on the dangers of Sinclairism. The slickly produced shorts, which were shown in theaters all over the state, followed a supposedly nonpartisan "Inquiring Cameraman" as he interviewed California voters. The series portrayed Sinclair supporters (played by actors) as bums, foreigners, or radicals. On camera, many expressed doubts that EPIC would work, while others looked forward to Sinclair's Sovietization of California. Backers of Merriam—more actors—were depicted as sober, thoughtful, and respectable citizens who felt confident that the Republican candidate could bring stability and prosperity back to California.

With this onslaught of negative propaganda, it is surprising that EPIC did as well as it did. Governor Merriam won 1,138,620 votes, while Sinclair captured 879,537. Progressive candidate Raymond Haight received 302,519 votes, which may have kept Sinclair from winning. Even though Sinclair lost, twenty-four EPIC candidates were elected to the state legislature. Sinclair vowed to fight on, but EPIC quickly fragmented between those who wanted to join the Democratic mainstream and those who wanted to form a separate party. The movement lingered on until the 1940s, but never came close to matching its success in 1934. Besides establishing many of the methods that would be used in later elections—political consultants, widespread negative ads, and the extensive use of mass media—the EPIC campaign helped to galvanize liberals in Hollywood and also deserves some credit for the New Deal's leftward swing in 1935.

DAVID WELKY

See also: election of 1934; Socialist Party; Sinclair, Upton.

Bibliography

Mitchell, Greg. *The Campaign of the Century: Upton Sinclair's Race for Governor of California and the Birth of Media Politics.* New York: Random House, 1992.

Sinclair, Upton. *I, Governor of California, and How I Ended Poverty: A True Story of the Future.* Published by the author, 1933.

Watkins, T. H. *The Great Depression: America in the 1930s.* Boston: Little, Brown, 1993.

ESQUIRE

Although it was born during the depths of the Great Depression, *Esquire* magazine from the beginning was oriented toward middle-class men with time and money to spend on leisure activities.

Esquire was founded in October 1933 as a men's fashion magazine by three staffers at *Apparel Arts*, a trade magazine for the garment business. Originally a quarterly, the magazine did extremely well from its very beginning, selling tens of thousands of its first issue. By the time it became a weekly in January 1934, it was selling 60,000 copies an issue, a figure that rose to 700,000 by 1938.

As media historians note, the success of the magazine suggests that even during the Great Depression, America could sustain a large middle class with disposable income.

With its mix of "girlie" pictures, tips for sophisticated male lifestyles, and fiction by some of the top writers of the day—including Dashiell Hammett, Ring Lardner, and Ernest Hemingway—*Esquire* became a model for post-World War II magazines like *Playboy* and *Sports Illustrated*.

See also: newspapers and magazines; Hammett, Dashiell; Hemingway, Ernest.

Bibliography

Gingrich, Arnold. *Nothing but People: The Early Days at* Esquire: *A Personal History, 1928–1958*. New York: Crown, 1973.

Merrill, Hugh. *Esky: The Early Years at* Esquire. New Brunswick, NJ: Rutgers University Press, 1995.

FAMILY CIRCLE

Founded in 1932 as a magazine for married women, with articles primarily on housekeeping and parenting, *Family Circle* was the first periodical to be primarily sold through stores of various sorts, rather than by subscription or on newsstands.

During its first fourteen years in circulation, the magazine was offered free and met its costs through advertising. Its first issue was twenty-four pages in length and featured articles on beauty, fashion, and cooking, as well as on movies, books, radio shows, and other cultural subjects. Its practical articles offered its largely middle-class readership a way to economize during hard times.

Featuring political, cultural, and international celebrities on its cover, *Family Circle* was an immediate success. Its initial run was 350,000 and rose to over one million by early 1934, being distributed largely through thousands of grocery stores around the country.

The magazine continues to be one of the best-selling periodicals in America, with a current worldwide circulation of more than 20 million copies per issue.

See also: newspapers and magazines.

Bibliography

Peterson, Theodore. *Magazines in the Twentieth Century*. Urbana: University of Illinois Press, 1964.

Wolseley, Roland E. *The Changing Magazine*. New York: Hasting House, 1973.

FANTASIA

One of the most popular and critically acclaimed animated films of all time, *Fantasia*, featuring fantastical imagery and a distinctive nineteenth- and twentieth-century classical score, was produced by Walt Disney in 1940.

The idea for the film originated with Philadelphia Orchestra conductor Leopold Stokowski, who approached Disney with the idea of a creative collaboration. Disney was receptive as he was looking for a way to revive the character of Mickey Mouse, introduced in the late 1920s. At first, Disney wanted to make a short, but Stokowski convinced him that a feature-length film would be better.

Both Stokowski and Disney were fascinated with the latest in technological innovations, and they incorporated one of the first stereophonic scores into the film. Perhaps the film's most famous scene is "The Sorcerer's Apprentice," featuring Mickey Mouse.

The film was not an immediate box office or critical success. Audiences, expecting a more conventional animated movie, like Disney's previous *Snow White*, were disappointed with a movie that lacked a central narrative. Critics decried what they considered the misuse of classical music, especially the very loose interpretation of Igor Stravinsky's *Rite of Spring* ballet. But later audiences, often unaware of the controversy, have continued to fill theaters whenever *Fantasia* is revived.

See also: films, feature; music; Disney, Walt.

Bibliography

Culhane, John. *Walt Disney's* Fantasia. New York: Abradale Press, 1983.

Taylor, Deems. *Walt Disney's* Fantasia. New York: Simon & Schuster, 1940.

FARMER-LABOR PARTY

The Farmer-Labor Party—also known as the Minnesota Farmer-Labor Party (FLP)—was a liberal-left party of Minnesota that, as its name implies, represented the interests of farmers and workers in the upper Midwest state.

The party arose in the years immediately after World War I, when farm prices crashed and the national economy went into a brief but very deep recession, accompanied by widespread labor unrest. Originally, the FLP was an amalgamation of several political and labor organizations, including the Minneapolis Socialist Party, the Minnesota State Federation of Labor, and the state branch of the Non-Partisan League, a rural protest and political movement that arose in neighboring North Dakota shortly before World War I.

During the economically troubled first half of the 1920s, the FLP grew rapidly, building on the liberalism of the state's Scandinavian immigrant population and the grievances of factory workers and small farmers. It

even elected several members of the state's congressional delegation. In 1924, it was active in the strong third-party presidential campaign of progressive Robert La Follette of neighboring Wisconsin. But the conservative turn that embraced the region and nation in the late 1920s sank the hopes of the FLP, until the Wall Street crash of 1929 and the subsequent national economic depression revived them.

In 1930, with the Depression just under way, the party elected its candidate, Floyd Olson, as governor with nearly 60 percent of the vote. The FLP also elected 10 percent of Minnesota's House of Representatives delegation and one U.S. Senator. In 1932, it once again took the governorship and increased its House representation to 55 percent of Minnesota's delegation. By 1936, its members held two-thirds of Minnesota's House of Representative seats and both seats in the U.S. Senate.

The accomplishments of the party were many. It made collective bargaining for Minnesota workers easier and it dramatically slowed the state's rate of small farm foreclosures, inaugurating a program that anticipated the New Deal's federal Agricultural Adjustment Act.

By the late 1930s, however, the party was in political trouble, as the alliance between farmers and laborers broke down over support for various New Deal programs. It struggled during the early years of World War II, winning about one-third of the gubernatorial vote, and was fused with the Democratic Party in 1944 to become the Democratic-Farmer-Labor Party.

See also: Wisconsin Progressive Party; Agricultural Adjustment Act; Olson, Floyd.

Bibliography

Gieske, Millard. *Minnesota Farmer-Laborism: The Third Party Alternative.* Minneapolis: University of Minnesota Press, 1979.

Haynes, John Earl. *Dubious Alliance: The Making of Minnesota's DFL Party.* Minneapolis: University of Minnesota Press, 1984.

Valelly, Richard M. *Radicalism in the States: The Minnesota Farmer-Labor Party and the American Political Economy.* Chicago: University of Chicago Press, 1989.

FARM HOLIDAY ASSOCIATION

The Farm Holiday Association (FHA)—sometimes referred to as the Farmers Holiday Association—was an organization that used the tactics of boycott and protest to raise farm prices and protect the small farmer from bankruptcy and foreclosure in the early years of the Great Depression.

The FHA was founded during a national convention of small farmers organized by the Iowa Farmers' Union in May 1932. Electing as its first president a radical minister named Milo Reno, the organization called for a farmers' "holiday" with the slogan "Stay at Home—Buy Nothing—Sell Nothing." Modeled after the bank "holidays" of the Depression years, when banks closed to prevent runs on their deposits, the farmers' holiday involved farmers refusing to sell or distribute their goods, thereby raising prices. During the early Depression, already low prices for crops, livestock, and dairy goods plummeted around the nation.

While the opening of the holiday was scheduled for July 4, it took until late August to organize the farmers of other midwestern states. Reno and other FHA leaders had hoped to keep things peaceful and for the most part succeeded. But when some members of the FHA tried to blockade highways to prevent the delivery of farm goods, battles broke out between the boycotters and police. The most violent incident occurred outside Sioux City, Iowa, where one striker was killed and another five were wounded by police gunfire.

While the FHA attracted much national press attention, it was never able to enroll much more than 10 percent of the farmers in the region, thus failing to accomplish its main mission of raising farm prices. By late 1933, the FHA had largely stopped trying to prevent the delivery of farm goods and shifted to the prevention of farm foreclosures. At foreclosure auctions, FHA members would intimidate outsiders to prevent them from bidding, allowing an FHA member to win the farm by bidding a penny. The mortgage would then be returned to the original farmer. This tactic was somewhat more successful than the highway blockades and even pushed midwestern state legislatures to pass farm mortgage foreclosure moratoriums.

Eventually, Milo and other FHA leaders demanded a kind of National Industrial Recovery Act—which regulated business in the interest of maintaining nondestructive competition—for farmers. The Agricultural Adjustment Act of 1933 partially satisfied those demands and, with government checks beginning to arrive in farmers' mailboxes in late 1933 and 1934, the FHA soon disbanded.

See also: Document: Agricultural Adjustment Act, May 12, 1933.

Bibliography

Saloutos, Theodore, and John D. Hicks. *Agricultural Discontent in the Middle West, 1900–1939.* Madison: University of Wisconsin Press, 1951.

Stock, Catherine McNicol. *Main Street in Crisis: The Great Depression and the Old Middle Class on the Northern Plains.* Chapel Hill: University of North Carolina Press, 1992.

Watkins, T. H. *The Hungry Years: A Narrative History of the Great Depression in America.* New York: Henry Holt, 1999.

FASCISM, DOMESTIC

Fears of fascism arising from the misery of the Depression prompted novelist Sinclair Lewis to write *It Can't Happen Here* (1935), a fictional account of how fascism could come to America. On Broadway, a young actor-director and antifascist named Orson Welles clothed his 1937 Mercury Theatre production of *Julius Caesar* in the costumes of Mussolini's Blackshirts and emphasized the ineffectuality of Brutus's liberalism against the totalitarian state. Many went beyond fictional representations and looked for real-life Hitlers in American life. Some saw him in Senator Huey P. Long of Louisiana (Long himself predicted that fascism would arise in the United States under the guise of "Americanism"). Others saw the potential for fascism in newspaper publisher William Randolph Hearst or the probusiness, anti–New Deal group, the Liberty League. All of these individuals denied any sympathy for fascism, but there were plenty of figures in this era who publicly asserted their desires to be the American Hitler.

LAWRENCE DENNIS: PHILOSOPHER OF AMERICAN FASCISM

Unlike most American fascists, Lawrence Dennis was independently wealthy and well educated and had an impressive résumé. He had held positions of responsibility, including seven years with the State Department and six with New York banking firms. He was also published in some of the most respectable journals in America, such as the *New Republic, Foreign Affairs,* the *Nation,* and the *Saturday Review of Literature.* From 1935 on, his themes were the communist threat, the weakness of liberalism, and the championing of fascism. In three books, Dennis defined fascism as pragmatic, as creating its own truths and values on a daily basis to suits its changing purposes. Dennis traveled to Nazi Germany in 1936, stating that he would like nothing better than to be a follower of Hitler.

SEWARD COLLINS AND *THE AMERICAN REVIEW*

A journal of American fascism, *The American Review,* appeared shortly after Franklin D. Roosevelt took office as president in 1933. Its editor, Seward Collins, a Princeton graduate and vociferous anti-Communist, was a fervent admirer of Hitler, seeing in his victory the end of the communist threat. Collins proudly labeled himself an anti-Semite and, like Hitler, desired the ousting of Jews from national political life. But Collins did not desire a new order as much as a revival of older forms of monarchical government.

EZRA POUND: LOST GENERATION FASCIST

The only authentic American intellectual the fascists could claim, the poet Ezra Pound saw the future in Mussolini's Italy. Pound instructed readers in his version of American history, with heavy doses of anti-Semitism thrown in. According to Pound, America had been strong until the mid-nineteenth century, when the money power, personified by capitalists of Jewish origin, took over, bringing with them poverty and degeneracy. Pound saw in Roosevelt's New Deal merely a continuation of Jewish moneyed control. To Pound, the capitalists' reign was like a cancer and only fascism would be able to cut it out. The heritage denied America by the Jewish moneyed houses had reappeared in fascist Italy; Pound compared Mussolini himself to Thomas Jefferson. Pound emigrated to Italy until his capture by American troops in 1945.

GERALD WINROD: THE FASCIST AS MAN OF GOD

Gerald Winrod, a Kansas fundamentalist minister, wedded his theory of fascism to apocalyptic themes in the Bible. He saw Jews as an incarnation of the anti-Christ and the New Deal as their vehicle for evil, while Hitler was the sword arm of Christ. Winrod predicted he would become dictator of the country after quelling a communist revolution. In 1938, he ran for the U.S. Senate in the Republican primary election and placed third in a four-man race.

FASCIST GROUPS IN AMERICA

Founded and organized by German nationals living in the United States, the German-American Bund had as its purpose the unification of German-American citizens against what they perceived to be the monopoly of power by American Jews. To those fearful of Nazism, the sight of this group in Madison Square Garden, with the American flag beside the Nazi one and a portrait of George Washington alongside one of Hitler, was chilling. The movement was headed by Fritz Kuhn, a former World War I soldier on the German side, who proclaimed himself the "American fuehrer." Kuhn attacked the New Deal as a tool of both Moscow and the Jews.

Like Hitler's Brownshirts, some homegrown American fascists sprang from World War I veterans' groups. General Art Smith's Khaki Shirts was a splinter group of the Bonus Expeditionary Force that had demanded from the government advance bonus payments for their service in World War I. A soldier who had fought in Africa and China, Smith clearly saw his model as Mussolini, whose march on Rome had resulted in his one-man rule. Smith planned a march on Washington, composed of a million and a half veterans. But before the march could occur, Smith was imprisoned on a charge of perjury.

William Dudley Pelley's Silver Shirts was consciously modeled on Hitler's SS. Pelley, a former screenwriter, claimed divine inspiration for his movement: In a vision from God, he was told to begin the movement after a young house painter became head of the German people. Pelley was obsessed with the idea of an international Jewish conspiracy, seeing in Roosevelt's New Deal government its American branch.

His ultimate goal was to remove Jews from national office and replace them with Silver Shirters. It is estimated that there were Silver Shirts organizations in forty-six states.

The Black Legion, headquartered in Michigan, was an offshoot of the Ku Klux Klan, even sporting similar, albeit different-colored, robes. The Legion gained power in Detroit, an industrial city hard hit by the Depression. It listed the usual enemies: Jews, Catholics, African Americans, and Communists. It infiltrated units of the United Auto Workers, established an informal employment agency by terrorizing minor executives in the automobile industry, and became an influence in allotting Works Progress Administration jobs. The Legion's power was broken when thirteen of the membership were given life sentences for murder and thirty-seven more were imprisoned for terms up to twenty years for terrorist activities.

RON CAPSHAW

See also: Black Legion; Christian Front; German-American Bund; Liberty League; National Union for Social Justice; Share Our Wealth Society; Silver Shirts; Union Party; House Un-American Activities Committee; Smith Act; America First Committee; fascism, Italy; Nazi Germany; Coughlin, Father Charles; Dies, Martin; Hearst, William Randolph; Hitler, Adolf; Lindbergh, Charles A.; Long, Huey P.; Mussolini, Benito; Smith, Gerald L.K.; Document: Huey P. Long's "Every Man a King" speech, 1934.

Bibliography

Schlesinger, Arthur, Jr. *Years of Upheaval.* Boston: Houghton Mifflin, 1958.

Schonbach, Morris. *Native American Fascism During the 1930s and 1940s.* New York: Garland, 1985.

FILMS, DOCUMENTARY AND NEWSREEL

The first American newsreel was produced by the French film company Pathé in 1911. One of the very first stories was a stunt: a daredevil of renown named Rodeman Law who was engaged to jump off the Statue of Liberty wearing a parachute. Throughout the 1910s and early 1920s, many small companies came and went, and by the late 1920s there were five silent newsreels in production, each associated with one of the five major studios. These five newsreels were Pathé News (released independently before 1931 and by RKO after); Universal News; Hearst Metrotone

News (later called News of the Day), released by MGM; Fox Movietone News; and Paramount News. However, there were some minor differences in the content and style of these newsreels. The Fox reel was presented as a series of departments, each of which had its own commentator. Fox, the largest newsreel company, had sound equipment before any of the other reels. Pathé News used a lot of sports material and several narrators. Hearst Metrotone was widely considered the most conservative (mainly because its owner William Randolph Hearst was a pro-German sympathizer before

World War II). Paramount News was considered the most aggressive news gatherer, using a panel of three editors rather than just one. Universal News was remarkable for its use of a dubbed voice-over, or voice recorded separately and added later to the film, eschewing synchronous sound, or sound recorded at the same time that the subject was filmed, and was known as "The Five Cent Weekly."

While there were slight distinctions between the newsreels, what is remarkable is their obvious similarity. Popular press articles consistently refer to them simply as "the newsreels" without distinguishing between companies. A 1935 article went so far as to refer to the "five standard brands" of newsreel. In more recent histories of documentary films, the term "newsreel" has been used just as broadly. The similarity was reinforced because the five companies tended to rent footage from one another if they had missed getting film on a major story. In 1936, it was noted that if "one of Pathé's cameras had broken down at Governor [Alfred] Landon's notification ceremonies in Topeka, probably Fox or Universal would have helped out with an extra print." Film historian Raymond Fielding has written of the situation after about 1930, "A monotonous similarity of newsreel content crept into the newsreel programs throughout the industry—to an increasing extent each of the five newsreel companies began screening identical footage." Scholars Siegfried Kracauer wrote Joseph Lyfold in 1948 about "a newsreel format that hasn't changed appreciably in the past twenty years. . . . The photographic techniques used by the five major newsreel companies . . . are as predictable as days of the week."

Newsreels that drew on a popular appreciation of historical pageants were produced in 1937 on 8mm and 16mm film by Castle Films for home viewing as well. As many as 2 million amateur American movie makers owned 8mm and 16mm projectors at this time. The first two subjects available were the coronation of King George VI and the *Hindenberg* disaster. The coronation film was the more popular of the two. "The response to these two pictures has been so overwhelming," producer Eugene W. Castle noted. "This is a parade that can march through every home in the land."

It must be stressed that the newsreels were first and foremost a kind of entertainment. In the words of one historian, "The newsreels always maintained a remarkable silence on social issues." Louis de Rochemont, in fact, created *The March of Time* out of the frustration he felt with the newsreel, saying that newsreels "never

get behind the news [that is, explain] . . . [or] what has led up to a given event."

In order to give a sense of the freshness of an event, it was important for newsreel companies to be the first to have the picture. The sense was that the first picture on display was the authentic one, the rest being only paltry imitations. So, newsreel companies went to great lengths to have the first image. In a 1930 newsreel about the coronation of Haile Selassie I, Emperor of Ethiopia, Fox Movietone exhibited the film with the following editorial note prominently displayed at the head of the segment:

> Fox Movietone makes it possible for you to see these remarkable pictures 17 days after the event by means of a 5,000 mile airplane flight of great hardship from the east coast of Africa to France by Captain Lawrence Hope, English Ace.

The notion of performance extended to personalities as well. Political figures were seen as variations on the screen idol. Even the serious newsreel followers who attended the all-newsreel theater in New York tended to see real political figures as celebrities. A 1931 article called "Matinee Idols of the News Reels" listed some of the "ten outstanding movie actors among public figures of the world." Among those were: Admiral Byrd, Calvin Coolidge, Benito Mussolini, General Pershing, Charles Schwab, the Prince of Wales, and Thomas Edison. Another favorite with the public was President Franklin D. Roosevelt, who was described by historian Guiliana Muscio as "the best actor in talking pictures" and "the greatest single attraction" in newsreels: "for box office attraction [he left] Clark Gable gasping for breath." This feature contributed greatly to his popularity.

Film scholar Giuliana Muscio argues that the role of cinema and audiovisual communication in disseminating the particular messages of the New Deal was similar to their uses in the totalitarian regimes of Germany and Italy. While there exist striking differences in style of implementation, the similarity lies in the way that audiences were encouraged to recognize themselves as one people with similar goals. The general effect, says Muscio, was that "social cooperation and nationalism went together, in the name of national identity, of the people, of national culture."

Before his election, Roosevelt had appeared frequently in the Hearst newsreel because Hearst supported Roosevelt's candidacy. Such campaign period segments would show Roosevelt sitting casually outdoors in a wicker chair with his campaign manager, swimming with his grandchildren, or introducing his family to newsreel viewers—and letting his little grand-daughter announce that the campaign's song was "Happy Days Are Here Again." While Hoover might be shown in a long shot, in a long black coat at a public event, Roosevelt would be shown yachting under a voice-over announcing, "Rough or smooth—it's all the same to the governor who faces another journey on the stormy seas of politics."

After Roosevelt won the election, his inauguration warranted an entire issue of the Hearst reel, including a large inauguration parade. The reel begins with a cavalcade of flags held aloft by soldiers marching in formation, followed by planes flying in formation above the Capitol, followed again by phalanxes of troops marching down the avenue. The President's inaugural address asked for "broad executive privilege to wage war on the Emergency, as great as the power would be if in fact we were invaded by a foreign foe." This special inauguration reel began a cycle of presidential appearances in Hearst Metrotone News and unambiguous support for his early New Deal policies. The other newsreel companies enthusiastically filmed the inauguration as well.

Initially a strong supporter of Roosevelt, Hearst was instrumental in his nomination, and avidly supported his policies in the period of the first New Deal. Hearst's production company, Cosmopolitan Pictures, also produced a film in 1932 called *Gabriel Over the White House*, which was about a benign dictator with heavenly guidance. This dictator calls up the images of Washington, Jefferson, and Lincoln as he goes about eliminating Congress and single-handedly dispatching problems in a distinctly martial manner. It is believed that much of the dictator's dialogue was written by Hearst and that Hearst had intended to release the film on Inauguration Day. However, it was not released until about a month later due to Metro-Goldwyn-Mayer studio head Louis Mayer's reservations about the political message of the film.

Universal, also, had a special relationship with the presidency, as much for the sake of having images of the president to show as anything else. Apparently, Carl Laemmle, the founder of Universal Pictures, had assured the president that in the public interest Universal News was entirely at his disposal: "I am ready to follow your precedent of breaking any precedents which stand in the way of action toward national recovery. While the printed word is effective the talking motion picture is more so, and our newsreel is ever and always at your command."

During his tenure in office, Roosevelt held 998 press conferences, had all 5,000 to 8,000 letters per day from citizens answered, and staged twenty-eight fireside chats by radio. He also made himself available to both the newsreels and to newspaper photographers. By his use of communications and the media, Roosevelt conveyed his image and words throughout the entire country.

On 13 March, 1933, Roosevelt appeared in all the newsreels to appeal to the public. In huge letters the title for the Hearst coverage read, "President Urges Confidence in Nation's Banks." This is followed by an "editorial note": "This is a special message from the White House addressed particularly to the motion picture audience by President Roosevelt. It is of vital import to every American citizen." In this early newsreel of his presidency, Roosevelt discussed the banking crisis and calmly informed viewers of how the government aimed to solve the problem. "I want to tell you what has been done," the President explained, "and why it has been done." He goes on to explain why the banks had failed earlier and why they are now secure. Four months later, Roosevelt again used the newsreels to directly address audiences and ask them to support the National Industrial Recovery Act (NIRA).

This representation of enthusiasm for the (NIRA) was congruent with endorsements found in fiction films which were also produced by the same film companies that produced the newsreels. Warner Studios, though not a newsreel company was most dedicated to boosting the New Deal in its fiction films. *Footlight Parade*, for example, ends "with sailors dancing and marching. By firing their rifles, images are formed of both the NRA eagle and FDR's face." For the film *Breadline*, Warner Studios head Jack Warner requested permission to use the president's voice and photograph. "You people must have faith," Roosevelt tells viewers. "Let us unite in vanquishing fear. It is your problem, my friends, no less than it is mine. Together we cannot fail." Warner's 1933 movie *The Road Is Open* features an unsubtle dialogue between George Washington, Abraham Lincoln, and Woodrow Wilson, and Roosevelt—"There isn't a person in America," Washington remarks, "who won't benefit by the NRA [National Recovery Administration], if every man, woman, and child does his part"—once again emphasizing the mythic theme of national unity. Each of the other studios included varying degrees of pro-Roosevelt sentiment in their early New Deal productions although permission to use the president's voice or face in fiction films was systematically denied.

The earlier silent newsreels had presented "views" of places and happenings, giving audiences the sense that they could see "the thing" (sea, battle, building, street—whatever it was) with their own eyes in the same way that a circus let them see animals, wax museums let them see visages of famous people, and funerals let them view bodies. Early sound newsreels enhanced the audience's sense of seeing for themselves by adding sounds to the images. The sound newsreel fully emerged by 1931 and, dominated by a voice-over, quickly became established as the standard newsreel form. Newsreels played a major role in disseminating information in the 1930s by showing viewers current events in a brand new format. The newsreels thrived for the next two decades, until the rise of television in the 1950s advanced its demise in 1967.

JANE COLLINGS

See also: photography; Metro-Goldwyn-Mayer (MGM); Hearst, William Randolph

Bibliography

Barnouw, Erik. *Documentary: A History of the Non-Fiction Film.* New York: Oxford University Press, 1983.

Barsam, Richard. *Nonfiction Film: A Critical History.* Bloomington: Indiana University Press, 1973.

Blake, Nelson Manfred. *A Short History of American Life.* New York: McGraw Hill, 1952.

Cashman, Sean. *America in the Twenties and Thirties: The Olympian Age of Franklin Delano Roosevelt.* New York: New York University Press, 1989.

Fielding, Raymond. *The American Newsreel 1911–1967.* Norman: University of Oklahoma Press, 1972.

Jacobs, Lewis. *The Documentary Tradition.* New York: W. W. Norton, 1979.

Kracauer, Siegfried, and Joseph Lyford. "A Duck Crossed Main Street." *New Republic* 13 (December 1948): 13.

"Matinee Idols of the News Reels." *Literary Digest* 5 (September 1931): 32.

Menefee, Selden. "The Movies Join Hearst." *New Republic* 9 (October 1935): 241.

Moyers, Bill. "Profile of Edward R. Murrow." *American Masters,* Public Broadcasting Systems, February 21, 1991, pt. 2.

Muscio, Giuliana. *Film, Industry, and the New Deal.* Ph.D. diss., University of California, 1992.

Pryor, Thomas M. "Newsreels for the Home." *New York Times,* July 4, 1937: 4.

Rollins, Peter C. "Ideology and Film Rhetoric: Three Documentaries of the New Deal Era (1936–1941)." In *Hollywood as Historian: American Film in a Cultural Context,* ed. Peter C. Rollins. Lexington: University Press of Kentucky, 1983.

FILMS, FEATURE

Hollywood entered the 1930s under the most unfavorable of circumstances. Most of the movie-going public had little to spend on anything but necessities, and the industry was still experimenting with the new medium of sound. Nevertheless, the Great Depression era would be the golden age of Hollywood. The nation not only went to movies in droves, but it ranked movie stars as important as presidents (so did President Franklin D. Roosevelt, who once said that Shirley Temple's smile was as effective as a relief program in lifting America's spirits). America was clearly fascinated with Hollywood. Popular songs featured lyrics about Gary Cooper and Clark Gable. Fan magazine sales were high, and thousands of letters poured in from all over the nation declaring who should play Rhett Butler and Scarlett O'Hara. The movie industry wielded incredible power in this period. According to one studio executive, studio heads could get a conference at the White House anytime they wanted. But the Depression would leave its mark on the film industry in ways other than just giving it enormous prestige. In this period, film had to adjust to the changing tastes of Depression-era America.

STARS

The casting of a star forecast the type of picture it would be. Cary Grant meant romantic comedy, Errol Flynn meant a swashbuckler, and Bette Davis meant drama. Stars in the 1930s conveyed a specific image. On-screen, Gary Cooper was earnest and taciturn, Clark Gable roguish, and Basil Rathbone villainous. Off-screen, the studios constructed an image for their stars that meshed with their cinematic personas. Thus, cinematic he-man Clark Gable hunted in his spare time, and swashbuckler Errol Flynn sailed in his yacht.

Hollywood stars lived like royalty while the rest of

the country labored in misery. Screen stars owned yachts and mink coats and commanded high salaries. Despite their high living, stars were expected to be moral. A paternity suit or divorce could hurt a star's box office. Thus, character actor Lionel Atwill was relegated to the status of B movie actor because of his sexual escapades; actress Paulette Goddard lost the part of Scarlett O'Hara in *Gone With the Wind* because she lived with Charlie Chaplin. Studio publicists worked overtime covering up a star's drunk driving accidents, abortions, or drug habits, and fashioning a moral image for the star in question.

ESCAPISM

A variety of genres arose in cinema in the 1930s. Many of these could be labeled escapist in that their purpose was merely to make the audience forget momentarily the breadlines and the soup kitchens and entertain or transport them into another age or another world.

Although horror films had been around since the silent era, the genre would experience widespread popularity in the early 1930s. *Dracula* (1931) was based on Bram Stoker's 1897 novel about a vampire nobleman attacking the wives of a group of Englishmen. The film starred Bela Lugosi, who reprised his critically acclaimed stage role. Lugosi would be typecast in horror films for the rest of his life because of this portrayal. That same year, Universal released *Frankenstein*, which made a star of Boris Karloff, who played the monster with the help of heavy makeup. Clearly the studio king of horror films, Universal hit its stride in the 1932–35 period. *The Invisible Man* (1933) introduced British actor Claude Rains to American audiences. But audiences began to see horror films as moving beyond the boundaries of entertainment and into the realm of indecency. Todd Browning's *Freaks* (1932), which used real-life armless and legless circus freaks in a tale of revenge and murder, shocked audiences and was withdrawn from circulation after a few showings; so too was *Island of Lost Souls* (1932), in which the mad scientist played by Charles Laughton tries to get a shipwrecked man to mate with a female leopard. Films such as these contributed much to getting the notorious Hays Code installed in 1934. Will Hays was a censor of films, and anything he deemed unacceptable or indecent was not shown until the studios had taken out the offending parts.

A blend of horror, adventure, and morality tale was RKO's *King Kong* (1933), in which a giant gorilla is captured by a newsreel crew and put on display in New York City. The tale ends with Kong's spectacular battle with biplanes atop the Empire State Building, after the ape has destroyed large sections of the city. Even though this film was intended to provide an escape from the dire atmosphere of the day, the Depression nevertheless makes an appearance in the film: the film's heroine is recruited for the expedition out of a breadline.

Adventure movies were equally popular in the Depression. Some merely added sound to material used in the silent era of cinema. Cinematic versions of Edgar Rice Burroughs's *Tarzan* had begun as early as 1918. The 1930s series, starring Olympic swimmer Johnny Weissmuller, spawned sequels until the late 1940s. A jungle hero who lives off the land and is answerable to no authority, Tarzan inhabits a world remote from breadlines and bosses. Equally popular were expedition movies such as *Trader Horn* (1931), *The Lost Jungle* (1934) (featuring real-life animal trainer Clyde Beatty), *Jungle Menace* (1937), and *King Solomon's Mines* (1937). RKO's *Gunga Din* (1939) was a cinematic retelling of Rudyard Kipling's pre–World War I "Three Soldiers."

Films that took viewers back to the past were also tailored to appeal to the dream fantasies of Depression-era America. MGM's *Mutiny on the Bounty* (1935) had as its theme rebellion against the boss in the form of Clark Gable taking over the ship from the tyrannical Charles Laughton. The most popular star of adventure movies featuring heroes defying authority was Errol Flynn. Classically handsome and athletic, Flynn was the undisputed king of swashbucklers. In films like *Captain Blood* (1935) and *The Adventures of Robin Hood* (1938), Flynn not only rebelled against authority (usually in the form of a corrupt king), but also was rewarded for doing so, usually with a title and the hand of Olivia de Havilland.

COMEDIES

Comedies had in common with escapist films the intention of making audiences forget their woes by making them laugh.

Comedic attacks on the establishment were highly popular forms of cinematic entertainment in the 1930s. By far the most popular representatives of anti-establishment humor were the Marx Brothers. Groucho is the parvenu interested only in money and sex, Chico is the Italian con man who mangles the English language, and Harpo is a silent mime who steals from the rich and gives to himself. All three flout convention and attack, verbally and otherwise, everything cherished by society: the opera, which in one film they destroy, football, racetracks, colleges, and garden parties. They physically attack upper-class women, cheat them at cards, and steal and wear their dresses. Unlike the escapist films, the Marx Brothers were not shy about confronting the Depression: in one film, Groucho refers to stowaways as the stockholders of yesteryear; in another, Harpo responds to an unemployed man's request for help to get a cup of coffee by withdrawing a cup of coffee from his pocket. However, audiences drew the line at the Marx Brothers' subversiveness when the Brothers mocked the government in the film *Duck Soup* (1933, which, ironically, is now considered the Brothers' masterpiece), and eventually the Brothers were tamed and transformed into destroyers for a good cause (usually to aid a young couple).

The thirties spawned a new genre of comedy: the screwball variety. In screwball comedy, the romantic couple at the center of the story are eccentrics, often portrayed through slapstick. The films are usually set among wealthy people who can afford to behave oddly. But often the romantic couple is the result of a crossing of class lines.

The film that began the screwball comedy cycle was Frank Capra's *It Happened One Night* (1934), which won Oscars for Best Picture, Best Director, Best Actor (Clark Gable), and Best Actress (Claudette Colbert). In the film, class lines are crossed when a spoiled heroine escapes her father in order to marry a superficial playboy and meets up with a down-to-earth reporter, who frequently tells her off for being a spoiled, rich brat.

Capra contributed again to this genre with *Mr. Deeds Goes to Town* (1936), starring Gary Cooper. In the film, a small-town man becomes a national idol when he uses his unexpected inheritance to help dispossessed farmers. Corrupt lawyers try to have him declared insane, although, true to the genre form, he is only eccentric.

Frank Capra's *You Can't Take It With You* (1938) combined his well-worn sentimentalization of the common folk and championing of Americanism with a view of work designed to appeal to Depression-era audiences. The family in the movie pick occupations that they enjoy doing; by contrast, the other family under examination work to make money and do not enjoy their occupation. Class lines are crossed when the rich son of the business family marries the daughter of the eccentric one.

Other screwball films were there simply to entertain rather than feature a slice of Americana. Leo McCarey's *The Awful Truth* (1937) transformed divorce into comedy with the couple battling over visitation rights to the dog. Howard Hawks's *Bringing Up Baby* (1938), starring Cary Grant and Katharine Hepburn, featured rapid-fire dialogue and dizzyingly fast plot changes.

The Thin Man series mixed screwball and mystery (the series was based on a story by mystery author Dashiell Hammett). Nick Charles is a former detective who comes into money and martinis when he marries Nora, a society girl, who repeatedly urges him to solve a mystery. The series combined the witty repartee and high-class surroundings of the screwball genre with an actual mystery.

Ernst Lubitsch's *Ninotchka* (1939) both poked fun at and denounced Stalinism as serious, repressive, and unenjoyable. Playing the title character, Greta Garbo discovers, courtesy of playboy Melvyn Douglas, that capitalism can be fun.

THE SOCIAL COMMENTARIES

Not all films in this era were escapist or optimistic. Many addressed the hard realities of the era. The dangers of domestic fascism were addressed in the Warner Bros.' film *The Black Legion* (1936). The plight of the Okies was the topic of *The Grapes of Wrath* (1940). Political corruption was the theme of Frank Capra's *Mr. Smith Goes to Washington* (1939). *Boys Town* (1938) addressed the criminalizing effect of poverty on children.

GANGSTER MOVIES

Gangster films were popular forms of social commentary in this era that borrowed from the headlines. *Little Caesar* (1930) was based on the life of real-life gangster Al Capone, and *The Petrified Forest* (1936) featured a character modeled on John Dillinger. The genre introduced audiences to a new type of cinematic leading man: the tough guy who disdains chivalry for violence. The cultivated leading man of the 1920s was replaced by a coarser, low-class version who wields a gun rather than a cocktail shaker. Now leading men rough up women (an obligatory scene in a James Cagney movie), engage in shoot-outs with cops, and drink bootleg liquor. The formula for this kind of film was cautionary: the gangster rejects the pleas from his mother to go straight, rises to the top of the underworld through

The Petrified Forest, a popular 1936 thriller about a drifter, starred (from left) Humphrey Bogart, Leslie Howard, and Bette Davis. *(Brown Brothers)*

violence, eventually has to kill his best friend, and then dies a violent death. Crime does not pay.

OVERSEAS MARKETS

Regarding events overseas, studio bosses were fearful of alienating their foreign markets. Hence, anti-Nazi films were not in evidence until the eve of America's entry into World War II. Out of fear of alienating Catholic voters, the film *Blockade* (1938) toned down the politics behind the Spanish Civil War and left the audience in doubt as to which side the protagonists represented. However, Warner Bros., nicknamed the New Deal studio for its message movies, made the first American anti-Nazi movie *Confessions of a Nazi Spy* (1939), which detailed the dangers of fifth columns in the United States.

Films that combined the elements of comedy and social commentary were those made by Charlie Chaplin in the 1930s. In *Modern Times*, Chaplin poked fun at the machine age and factory work for turning workers into robots. In *The Great Dictator*, Chaplin mocked Adolf Hitler and the bullying tactics of the Nazis. His Tramp character of silent days was given a voice with which to denounce the Nazis.

Stars were expected to be apolitical in this era. When Errol Flynn visited war-torn Spain in 1937, both pro-Franco Catholics and Loyalist supporters in the United States denounced him. Despite this demand, many stars were political in the Depression. Fredric

March and Melvyn Douglas spearheaded the Hollywood Anti-Nazi League, which raised funds for German refugees and donated ambulances to Loyalists in Spain. Because Hollywood Stalinists were members of some of these antifascist organizations, Congress would investigate Hollywood stars in 1940.

1939: THE PINNACLE YEAR

Nineteen thirty-nine was a banner year for cinema. In that year, MGM released *The Wizard of Oz*, which pioneered new uses of color. In director John Ford's hands, the western, long considered juvenile fare, received an adult treatment in *Stagecoach*. By far the most impressive offering that year was David O. Selznick's *Gone With the Wind*. Based on Margaret Mitchell's best-selling novel about the Old South during the Civil War, the film was the result of a three-year nationwide casting call for the characters. Practically every actress in Hollywood lobbied for the role of Scarlett O'Hara. The part of Rhett Butler was solved by a nationwide poll that selected Clark Gable. The film was the first blockbuster, breaking box office records and earning eleven Academy Award nominations. It also broke new controversial ground with a rape scene and the insertion of profanity into the dialogue.

Ironically, a shift in thematic content occurred this same year. Antiestablishment comedies were abandoned for the safe antics of Abbott and Costello; serious social commentaries were eschewed for patriotic war movies and musicals. No longer were American gangsters the villains; their place was now filled by the Nazis and Japanese. But apart from the foreignness of the villains, the films featured little serious ideological content. But the 1940s would not be devoid of all serious filmmaking. Orson Welles' *Citizen Kane*, considered by many film critics the best American film ever made, appeared in 1941. An exploration of the corrupting effects of wealth, the film was based loosely on real-life publisher William Randolph Hearst. Nevertheless, audiences wanted lighthearted musicals or simplistically patriotic war films. And throughout the war era, that was what they got.

RON CAPSHAW

See also: *Citizen Kane*; *Gone With the Wind*; *Grapes of Wrath, The*; *It Happened One Night*; *King Kong*; *Little Caesar*; Metro-Goldwyn-Mayer (MGM); Motion Picture Production Code/Production Code Administration; *Mr. Smith Goes to Washington*; Okies; *Stagecoach*; *Wizard of Oz, The*; Spanish Civil War; Cagney, James; Capra, Frank; Cooper, Gary; Flynn, Errol; Ford, John; Gable, Clark; Garbo, Greta; Grant, Cary; Hawks, Howard; Hays, Will; Hearst, William Randolph; Hepburn, Katharine; Marx Brothers; Temple, Shirley; Weissmuller, Johnny; Welles, Orson.

Bibliography

Baxter, John. *Hollywood in the Thirties*. New York: Barnes, 1968.

Roddick, Nick. *A New Deal in Entertainment: Warner Brothers in the 1930s*. London: British Film Institute, 1983.

Rubin, Martin. *Busby Berkeley and the Tradition of Spectacle*. New York: Columbia University Press, 1993.

Sklar, Robert. *Movie-Made America: A Cultural History of the American Movies*. New York: Random House, 1975.

Thomas, Tony. *The Films of Errol Flynn*. New York: Citadel Press, 1969.

FIRESIDE CHATS

The "fireside chats" were a series of radio talks that President Franklin Delano Roosevelt delivered to the American people during the Great Depression and World War II. Roosevelt is widely viewed by historians as the first president to make effective use of radio as a mass medium. As the name implies, the fireside chats were not speeches, but seemingly personal conversations in which Roosevelt tried to achieve the illusion that he was speaking directly to Americans in their living rooms.

The first of the chats was delivered on Sunday, March 12, 1933—just one week after Roosevelt took office—and was designed to explain, in layman's terms, the reasons why the president had closed the nation's banks, following a series of depositor runs in the weeks leading up to the inauguration. "I can assure you that it is safer to keep your money in a reopened bank than it is to keep it under the mattress," he explained in a confident and cheerful voice. "You people must have faith; you must not be stampeded by rumors or guesses. Let us unite in banishing fear." The address worked; when the banks opened the following day, the runs had stopped and deposits actually outran withdrawals.

Other fireside chats were delivered to explain the National Industrial Recovery Act and other major New Deal programs. The last of the New Deal chats, delivered on September 3, 1939, was meant to reassure Americans after the Nazi invasion of Poland and the declaration of war by France and England against Germany. "I hope the United States will keep out of this war," Roosevelt said. "I believe that it will. And I give you assurance and reassurance that every effort of your government will be directed toward that end."

See also: radio; Roosevelt, Franklin D. Documents: Fireside Chat on the Banking Crisis, March 12, 1933; Fireside Chat on the National Recovery Administration, July 24, 1933; Fireside Chat on Social Security Acts, January 17, 1935; Fireside Chat on work relief programs, April 28, 1935.

Bibliography

Buhite, Russell D., and David W. Levy, eds. *FDR's Fireside Chats.* Norman: University of Oklahoma Press, 1992.

Freidel, Frank B. *Franklin D. Roosevelt: A Rendezvous with Destiny.* Boston: Little, Brown, 1990.

FLASH GORDON

One of the most popular science fiction comic strips and serial movies introduced during the Great Depression, *Flash Gordon* featured the eponymous hero and his beautiful companion, Dale Arden, trapped on the planet Mongo, where they battled evil rulers and strange monsters.

Flash Gordon, drawn by commercial artist Alex Raymond and written by pulp magazine editor Don Moore, was introduced into the Sunday comics in 1934. Modeled closely after *Buck Rogers,* which had come out in the late 1920s, the strip had wooden writing, but the illustrations grew increasingly skilled and sophisticated over the years.

While the technology featured in the strip now seems ludicrously dated, young audiences loved the primitive-looking ray-guns and rocket ships. An almost immediate hit, the cartoon hero was soon found in comic books and, after 1936, in movie serials as well.

Three *Flash Gordon* films were produced during the Great Depression: *Flash Gordon* (1936), *Flash Gordon's Trip to Mars* (1938), and *Flash Gordon Conquers the Universe* (1940).

By the late 1930s, the comic strip had gone daily, though this ended in 1944 and revived again in the 1950s and 1960s. With various artists doing the strip, *Flash Gordon* is still featured in a dwindling number of Sunday comic sections.

See also: films, feature; newspapers and magazines.

Bibliography

Barry, Dan, and Harvey Kurtzman. *Flash Gordon.* Princeton, NJ: Kitchen Sink Press, 1988.

Raymond, Alex. *Flash Gordon.* Franklin Square, PA: Nostalgia Press, 1967.

FOOTLIGHT PARADE

One of the first of the movie musical spectaculars choreographed by Busby Berkeley in the 1930s, *Footlight Parade* (1933) told the story of a producer of musical stage numbers designed to be performed between double features at a major movie house. Starring James Cagney as the producer, the film featured dozens of dancers and musicians. Directed by Lloyd Bacon, *Footlight Parade* also starred Joan Blondell, Ruby Keeler, Guy Kibbee, and Dick Powell. Song and dance extravaganzas included "Shanghai Lil," "By a Waterfall," and "Honeymoon Hotel." Like other musicals choreographed by Busby Berkeley, the lavish sets and the upbeat mood of the film were popular with Depression-era audiences looking for escapist entertainment.

Still, the movie did bring in current events and, arguably, served as a propaganda film for the New Deal. At the beginning of the film, Cagney finds himself jobless and hungry and, as he sings, one step from the breadline. At the end of the film, Cagney and Keeler dance a number while they hold up placards promoting the "blue eagle" symbol of the New Deal's National Industrial Recovery Act.

See also: films, feature; *Gold Diggers of 1933;* National Industrial Recovery Act; Berkeley, Busby; Cagney, James.

Bibliography

Pike, Bob. *The Genius of Busby Berkeley.* Reseda, CA: CFS Books, 1973.

Rubin, Martin. *Busby Berkeley and the Tradition of Spectacle.* New York: Columbia University Press, 1993.

FORD MOTOR COMPANY

The second largest automobile company in the United States in the 1930s, after General Motors, the Ford Motor Company was troubled during the Great Depression years by declining sales, a limited line of products, and numerous—and occasionally violent—labor confrontations.

The Ford Motor Company was founded by Henry Ford in 1903. Five years later, it introduced the Model T, the most successful car of the pre–World War II era. Using techniques borrowed from the meatpacking industry, cars and parts were brought to stationary workers along a moving assembly line, thereby cutting production and labor costs enormously. The cheap and reliable car sold by the millions and made Ford the number one auto seller in the world through the early 1920s, producing nearly half the cars made in the United States. By the end of the 1920s, Ford had more than twenty assembly plants on five continents, including the massive River Rouge plant in Dearborn, an independent city inside of Detroit.

To encourage the company's workers to buy the products of their own labor, Henry Ford introduced the unprecedented $5 per day wage in 1914, although, to get the wage, workers had to put up with intrusive company monitoring of their home life.

But the Great Depression hit the company, and its workers, hard. Between 1930 and 1931, annual sales of the Model A, which had replaced the Model T in 1927, had declined from $1.4 million to $620,000. The company lost $37 million and was forced to lay off tens of thousands of workers. For those who continued to work, pay was cut to $4 a day and the assembly line speeded up. Meanwhile, the company's euphemistically named Service Department, led by Harry Bennett, head of Ford's security force, operated an elaborate spy network against its workers, looking out for signs of labor organizing and firing any worker who made trouble.

The prominence of the company's owner—and its increasingly tough anti-labor tactics—made Ford a target for leftist protest. In March 1932, the communist-affiliated Detroit Unemployed Council organized the nation's largest hunger strike at the River Rouge plant. As 3,000 demonstrators marched, demanding the right to organize and better working conditions, they were attacked by Bennett's security force and the Dearborn

Although the Ford Motor Company was eclipsed as the world's largest automaker by General Motors in the 1930s, it still produced millions of cars. Here company founder Henry Ford, standing with his son Edsel Ford, presents the twenty-seven millionth automobile manufactured by Ford, February 1939. (*Brown Brothers*)

police. Four marchers were killed and dozens were injured.

But it was General Motors that was first targeted by the United Automobile Workers (UAW) during the great upsurge in labor organizing in 1937, following the passage of the pro-labor National Labor Relations Act of 1935. Indeed, even after GM had agreed to negotiate with the union, Henry Ford held out. Just as he believed that the stock market crash had been caused by a cabal of Jewish bankers, so he believed—in an ideological contradiction—that the unions were a Jewish-communist conspiracy to destroy American industry. Not until 1941, when war manufacturing profits made the idea more palatable and the federal government's demand for uninterrupted production had forced

Ford's hand, did the company agree to recognize the UAW.

See also: auto industry; strikes, sit-down; United Automobile Workers; National Labor Relations Act; Bennett, Harry; Ford, Henry; Reuther, Walter. Document: National Labor Relations Act, July 5, 1935.

Bibliography

Bryan, Ford R. *Henry's Lieutenants*. Detroit: Wayne State University Press, 1993.

Collier, Peter. *The Fords: An American Epic*. New York: Summit Books, 1987.

Lacey, Robert. *Ford, the Men and the Machine*. Boston: Little, Brown, 1986.

"FORGOTTEN MAN" RADIO ADDRESS

A radio address delivered by Franklin D. Roosevelt at the beginning of the 1932 campaign for the presidency, the so-called "Forgotten Man" address is widely viewed by historians as the speech that set the tone for both the election campaign and the New Deal policies of the Roosevelt administration.

Seen by conservatives as a radical and even socialistic departure from mainstream politics, the address emphasized the need for a heightened federal government role in the economy. Roosevelt called for "plans like those of 1917 [i.e. World War I federal government direction of the economy] that build from the bottom up and not from the top down of the economic pyramid."

In the April address, which was collaborated on by liberal adviser Raymond Moley, Roosevelt argued that the cause of the Great Depression lay in under-consumption—a view advocated by the political left—rather than overproduction, as President Herbert Hoover and the Republicans argued. But more than about mere policy, the address was full of sympathetic utterances about the plight of the common man and woman and contrasted sharply with Hoover's speeches and their cool aloofness toward the nation's unemployed and impoverished millions.

See also: election of 1932; fireside chats; radio; Hoover, Herbert; Moley, Raymond; Roosevelt, Franklin D.

Bibliography

Leuchtenberg, William E. *FDR and the New Deal: 1932–1940*. New York: Harper Torchbooks, 1963.

Schlesinger, Arthur M. Jr. *The Politics of Upheaval*. Boston: Houghton Mifflin, 1988.

42ND STREET

A rguably the most popular musical movie extravaganza of the 1930s, *42nd Street* was produced by Busby Berkeley and directed by Lloyd Bacon in 1933. A classic example of Depression-Era moviemaking, *42nd Street* is the story of a young understudy who goes on stage after the star of the show breaks her leg a few hours before opening night. This sudden streak of good luck—leading to fame and fortune—was a popular theme in the escapist spectacles of the 1930s. The film featured a number of catchy tunes and large-scale dance production numbers. It starred Warner Baxter, Ruby Keeler, Una Merkel, Dick Powell, and Ginger Rogers.

See also: *Footlight Parade; Gold Diggers of 1933*; movies, feature.

Bibliography

Pike, Bob. *The Genius of Busby Berkeley*. Reseda, CA: CFS Books, 1973.

Rubin, Martin. *Busby Berkeley and the Tradition of Spectacle*. New York: Columbia University Press, 1993.

GENERAL MOTORS

Founded in 1908, General Motors (GM) passed the Ford Motor Company in 1929 to become the largest automobile manufacturing company in the United States and the world during the 1930s. By 1941, GM was producing 44 percent of all cars manufactured in the United States. At the same time, hit by a number of sit-down strikes in the latter half of the decade, GM was also the first major auto manufacturer to recognize the United Automobile Workers (UAW) as the union representative for its factory workers.

Under the aegis of wealthy carriage maker William C. Durant, GM came together as an amalgamation of several independent auto and truck manufacturers, including Buick, Cadillac, Oldsmobile, Oakland (later Pontiac), Marquette, Reliance, and Rapid. The Chevrolet company and Delco Products joined in 1918, and Fisher Body Company and Frigidaire came under the GM umbrella in 1919.

Under Durant and, after 1920, his successor, former GM vice president Alfred P. Sloan Jr., General Motors introduced a number of technological and marketing innovations. Key to GM's success was its ability to offer a wide variety of makes and models, appealing to various tastes and pocketbooks. In addition, the company introduced the yearly model, in which various makes of car were retooled and redesigned annually, making it desirable for customers to buy new cars long before their old ones aged.

Like other industrial corporations, GM was hit hard by the Great Depression. Between the first quarters of 1929 and 1930, earnings fell by 27.4 percent, from $61.9 to $44.9 million, and they continued to go down through the end of 1932. But after that, sales for GM and other auto manufacturers recovered. Between 1932 and 1935, auto sales went from 1.1 million units, valued at $616 million, to 3.8 million units, worth $1.7 billion. In 1936, GM's profits were up to $240 million. At the same time, however, thousands of workers were laid off or put on part-time by GM, and wages for the 250,000 who remained at work by 1936 were cut by 10 percent or more. Speedups also occurred at GM's sixty-nine separate plants.

The discrepancy between the renewed sales and continuing wage depression angered many auto workers. With the passage of the National Labor Relations Act of 1935, which made industrial organizing easier, many GM workers flocked to join the UAW. GM responded by setting up spy networks and even, it was alleged by some critics, secretly cooperating with anti-labor thugs from the Black Legion, the Michigan branch of the Ku Klux Klan.

The first major strike against GM occurred at its Chevrolet plant in Toledo, Ohio, and was essentially broken by the company's security force, which employed guns, tear gas, and even hand grenades. In 1936, the newly formed UAW decided to target GM for its first offensive, using the new labor weapon of the sit-down strike, whereby striking workers remained in the plant rather than picketing outside. This, of course, made it much more difficult for the company to employ strikebreakers. Choosing Fisher Body Plant Number One in Flint, Michigan—key to virtually all of GM's operations—the UAW launched the sit-down at the end of December 1936.

The company immediately demanded that the government remove the workers. But pro–New Deal and pro-labor Michigan governor Frank Murphy—inaugurated in January 1937—refused. Soon, other GM plants were shut down by sit-down strikes. On February 16, the company caved in to the workers' demands and, among other concessions, recognized the UAW as the workers' representative in collective bargaining. This success boosted UAW ranks from 88,000 in February 1937 to over 400,000 by the end of the year. The strikes also inspired workers in other industries.

The UAW's decision to strike at GM first was based on the strategy that once the biggest auto manufacturer had agreed to recognize the union, others would follow. This was true for Chrysler and some of the other smaller companies, but Ford held out until 1941.

See also: auto industry; Ford Motor Company; sit-down strikes; United Automobile Workers; Raskob, John J.; Reuther, Walter; Sloan Alfred; Document: National Labor Relations Act, July 5, 1935.

Bibliography

Cray, Ed. *The Chrome Colossus: General Motors and Its Times.* New York: McGraw-Hill, 1980.

Fine, Sidney. *The Automobile Under the Blue Eagle.* Ann Arbor: University of Michigan Press, 1963.

Lichtenstein, Nelson. *The Most Dangerous Man in Detroit: Walter Reuther and the Fate of American Labor.* New York: Basic Books, 1995.

GERMAN-AMERICAN BUND

The German-American Bund, also known as the Friends of the New Germany, was a pro-Nazi, anti-Semitic organization founded in 1933, with the rise of Adolf Hitler to power in Germany. A quasi-military group that received secret funding and guidance from the German government, the Bund membership largely consisted of American citizens of German ancestry.

Members of the German-American Bund, a pro-Nazi organization, march in New York City in October 1939. (*Library of Congress*)

The Bund had its greatest strength in the mid-Atlantic states and would engage in military drills at a number of training camps, including Camp Siegfried in New York, Camp Nordland in New Jersey, the Deutschhorst Country Club in Pennsylvania, and elsewhere. There, youths and adults were organized into paramility units, wearing uniforms modeled after the German Nazi storm troopers.

Reaching its peak in 1939 with some 20,000 members, the organization soon collapsed under scandal and the rush of international events. First, Bund national leader Fritz Julius Kuh was prosecuted for forgery and misappropriating organization funds. Then, in 1940, national secretary James Wheeler-Hill was convicted of perjury. With America's declaration of war against Germany in December 1941, the Bund disappeared.

See also: Black Legion; fascism, domestic; Nazi Germany; Silver Shirts; World War II, early history of; Hitler, Adolf.

Bibliography

Canedy, Susan. *America's Nazis: A Democratic Dilemma: A History of the German American Bund.* Menlo Park, CA: Markgraf Publications Group, 1990.

Diamond, Sander A. *The Nazi Movement in the United States, 1924–1941.* Ithaca, NY: Cornell University Press, 1974.

GOLD DIGGERS OF 1933

Gold Diggers of 1933, a Busby Berkeley production, was a classic Depression-era musical movie extravaganza. Directed by Mervyn Le Roy, the 1933 film followed the standard plot of its genre. The movie opens backstage at a musical theater, where cast members are singing "We're in the Money." The local sheriff enters to tell them that, because of a lack of funds, he is forced to close down the theater. But an "angel," or financial backer, arrives in the person of Brad (played by Dick Powell). A renegade from a wealthy family that disapproves of show business, Brad joins the production and saves it from ruin. While the movie did not indict the rich as a class, it did insinuate that their value system was wrongheaded. The movie also starred Joan Blondell, Ruby Keeler, Ginger Rogers, and Warren William. It inspired two sequels, *Gold Diggers of 1935* and *Gold Diggers of 1937*, both of which were considered by critics much inferior to the original.

See also: films, feature; *Footlight Parade; 42nd Street;* Berkeley, Busby.

Bibliography

Pike, Bob. *The Genius of Busby Berkeley.* Reseda, CA: CFS Books, 1973.

Rubin, Martin. *Busby Berkeley and the Tradition of Spectacle.* New York: Columbia University Press, 1993.

GONE WITH THE WIND

The best-selling book in the history of American publishing through its debut in 1936, *Gone With the Wind* told the story of Scarlett O'Hara, the daughter of a wealthy southern planter, as her fortunes rise and fall before, during, and after the Civil War. Written by Margaret Mitchell, a former journalist from Atlanta, over a period of ten years, the book was an immediate hit, selling 1 million copies within six months and 8 million by the author's death in 1949.

The movie rights were sold in 1936 to Hollywood producer David O. Selznick. The 1939 movie version, starring Vivien Leigh as Scarlett and Clark Gable as her ne'er-do-well lover Rhett Butler, was as enormous a hit as the book. Picking up a record eleven Academy Awards in 1940, *Gone With the Wind* went on to become the highest grossing Hollywood movie through the 1960s. At the same time, both the book and the movie perpetuated myths about the Old South, including the general contentedness of the slaves and the benevolence of the masters.

See also: films, feature; literature; Gable, Clark.

Clark Gable played Rhett Butler and Vivien Leigh starred as Scarlett O'Hara in the 1939 *Gone With the Wind*, the number one box office draw of the 1930s. *(Brown Brothers)*

Bibliography

Bridges, Herb. Gone With the Wind: *The Definitive Illustrated History of the Book, the Movie, and the Legend.* New York: Simon & Schuster, 1989.

Harwell, Richard, ed. Gone With the Wind *as Book and Film.* Columbia: University of South Carolina Press, 1992.

GOOD EARTH, THE

One of the five best-selling novels of the Great Depression, *The Good Earth* was written by Pearl S. Buck, the daughter of American Presbyterian ministers who had served in China, and published in 1931. Telling the story of a Chinese peasant and his slave-wife who escape famine and plague in their search for land, *The Good Earth* captured the Depression-era longing for financial security among its hundreds of thousands of readers. Buck went on to publish two more related novels—*Sons* in 1932 and *A House Divided* in 1935—which completed *The House of Earth* trilogy. But it was largely on the reputation of *The Good Earth* that Buck won the Nobel Prize for Literature in 1938. The novel was then made into a popular movie, starring Paul Muni and Luise Rainer, in 1937.

See also: films, feature; literature; Buck, Pearl; Muni, Paul.

Bibliography

Conn, Peter J. *Pearl S. Buck: A Cultural Biography*. New York: Cambridge University Press, 1996.

Doyle, Paul A. *Pearl S. Buck*. Boston: Twayne, 1980.

GRAPES OF WRATH, THE

Written by John Steinbeck, *The Grapes of Wrath* was published in 1939 and tells the story of the Joads, an impoverished Oklahoma family that migrates to California in search of work during the Great Depression. In the best-selling novel, Steinbeck, a political leftist in the 1930s, portrayed how the brutal California agricultural industry ruthlessly exploited farmers escaping the miseries of the dust bowl of the Midwest in the early 1930s. The novel was an immediate critical as well as popular success, winning Steinbeck a Pulitzer Prize and a National Book Award. Widely considered his greatest novel, *The Grapes of Wrath* also helped earned Steinbeck the Nobel Prize for Literature in 1962. In 1940, the book was turned into a movie directed by John Ford and starring Henry Fonda. Like the book, the film was both a popular and critical success.

See also: films, feature; literature; Ford, John; Steinbeck, John.

Bibliography

Owens, Louis. *John Steinbeck's Re-vision of America*. Athens: University of Georgia Press, 1985.

Parini, Jay. *John Steinbeck: A Biography*. New York: Henry Holt, 1995.

Impoverished Okies, like this family fleeing to California with its meager possessions, served as the model for the Joad family in John Steinbeck's 1939 Pulitzer Prize–winning novel *The Grapes of Wrath*. *(Brown Brothers)*

GROUP THEATRE

One of the most influential companies in American theatrical history, the Group Theatre—founded in 1931 by theatrical personalities Harold Clurman, Cheryl Crawford, and Lee Strasberg—introduced American actors and audiences to the revolutionary Stanislavskian acting technique, first developed at the Moscow Art Theater.

The Group Theatre, based in New York City, grew out of a 1920s theatrical company known as the American Laboratory Theater. The Group Theatre included twenty-eight members who not only worked but lived together. The theater remained in existence for about a decade and, during that time, had enormous impact on the American theater, especially through its introduction of the Stanislavskian approach to acting. Also known as method acting, it involved the use of emotional memory and has since become the dominant school of theatrical acting in the United States.

The Group Theatre produced a string of formally experimental and political controversial Broadway hit shows, including *Men in White* (1933), *Awake and Sing!* (1934), and *Waiting for Lefty* (1934). Among the actors, directors, and writers in the company who went on to great fame on the stage and screen are Stella Adler, John Garfield, Lee J. Cobb, Karl Malden, Howard Da Silva, and Irwin Shaw.

See also: films, feature; Mercury Theatre.

Bibliography

Clurman, Harold. *The Fervent Years: The Story of the Group Theatre and the Thirties.* New York: Harcourt Brace Jovanovich, 1975.

Smith, Wendy. *Real Life: The Group Theatre and America, 1931–1940.* New York: Knopf, 1990.

HARLEM RIOT (1935)

A one-day, violent civil disturbance triggered by the arrest of a dark-skinned Latino youth, but caused by long-term economic problems, the Harlem riot of 1935 resulted in the deaths of three African Americans and $2 million in property damage.

The riot began on March 19, 1935, when a white Harlem store owner accused ten-year-old Diego Rivera of shoplifting a knife. After the boy struck a clerk, he was arrested by police. Rumors soon spread that Rivera had been beaten and even killed by the police. The store where Rivera had been arrested was attacked by rioters and then the violence spread to nearby blocks.

Long-term causes included high unemployment rates and economic frustration. Boycotts and pickets against stores that refused to hire blacks—which had started in 1933—were banned by a court injunction shortly before the riot. Many in the neighborhood said that the police used unnecessary violence to break up the pickets.

In the wake of the riot, Mayor Fiorello La Guardia established the Mayor's Commission on Conditions in Harlem. The biracial commission issued "The Negro in Harlem: A Report on Social and Economic Conditions Responsible for the Outbreak of March 19, 1935," which recommended antidiscrimination measures such as increased African-American access to public housing, relief programs, and city jobs, including jobs in the police department.

See also: African Americans; La Guardia, Fiorello.

Bibliography

Kirby, John B. *Black Americans in the Roosevelt Era: Liberalism and Race.* Knoxville: University of Tennessee Press, 1980.

Sitkoff, Harvard. *A New Deal for Blacks: The Emergence of Civil Rights as a National Issue.* Vol. 1, *The Depression Years.* New York: Oxford University Press, 1978.

Wolters, Raymond. *Negroes and the Great Depression: The Problem of Economic Recovery.* Westport, CT: Greenwood Press, 1970.

HINDENBURG DISASTER

One of the most memorable disasters of the Great Depression, the explosion of the German zeppelin, or rigid-frame airship, *Hindenburg* killed thirty-six people as it docked in Lakehurst, New Jersey, after its first trans-Atlantic flight on May 6, 1937.

Ever since they had been used for military purposes in World War I, zeppelins—named after their designer, Ferdinand, Graf von Zeppelin, a German military officer—had caught the fancy of the well-to-do traveling public, since they offered a comfortable and faster way to travel than ship and even railroad.

By the late 1920s, several of the airships were transporting passengers across the Atlantic in high style. The *Hindenburg*, launched in April 1936, was the pride of the Zeppelin Company's airship fleet and the largest rigid airship ever built. It measured over 800 feet in length, could reach speeds of eighty miles an hour, and carried up to a hundred passengers.

After a rather dramatic departure in Germany in late April 1937—rumors of a saboteur aboard were investigated by Nazi authorities and passengers carefully vetted—the *Hindenburg* enjoyed an uneventful trip across the Atlantic. As newsreel cameras rolled, it pulled up to the docking tower at the naval air station at Lakehurst. Suddenly, the ship's giant, hydrogen-filled cells exploded into flame and the ship came

The spectacular crash of the German airship *Hindenburg* in May 1937, which left thirty-six dead, virtually ended commercial airship travel. *(Brown Brothers)*

crashing to the ground as a radio announcer, describing the scene to the listeners of his Chicago radio station, broke down in tears. Of the ninety-seven passengers and crew members on board, thirty-six were killed.

Several causes of the disaster were immediately suggested: a hydrogen leak, electrostatic atmospheric sparks igniting the ship's flammable skin, or an anti-Nazi act of sabotage. Modern engineers believe that the probable cause was the second—atmospheric charges. Besides becoming an icon of technological hubris, as the airship was supposed to be invulnerable to disasters, the *Hindenburg* explosion doomed the future of mass airship travel, opening up the skies to heavier-than-air plane travel. It also proved an embarrassment for Nazi claims of technological prowess. And, finally, it ended the use of hydrogen in lighter-than-air craft; nonflammable helium has been used ever since.

See also: Nazi Germany.

Bibliography

Hoehling, A. A. *Who Destroyed the Hindenburg?* Boston: Little, Brown, 1962.

Stacey, Thomas. *The Hindenburg.* San Diego: Lucent Books, 1990.

HISPANIC AMERICANS

Americans did not use the ethnic identifier "Hispanic" in the 1930s, save possibly in reference to the "Hispanos" of New Mexico. Hispanic today refers to the millions of Spanish-speaking Americans derived by birth or ancestry from the regions formerly under Spanish colonial rule. In the 1930s, however, Mexican Americans made up the greatest part of the Spanish-speaking population of the United States. The 1930 United States Population Census reported more than 1.4 million Mexican Americans. By way of comparison, the 1930 census enumerated 32,685 Cubans, 10,822 Central Americans and 48,338 South Americans. By 1940, fewer than 70,000 Puerto Ricans resided in the continental United States. The discussion that follows thus concentrates exclusively on the Mexican-American experience during the Great Depression and the New Deal.

More than half of the 1.4 million Mexican-American men and women enumerated in the 1930 census were born in the United States (805,535 born in the United States; 616,998 born in Mexico). Many of the native born were, however, children: 60 percent of the 277,000 Mexican-American families enumerated in 1930 included between one and six children under ten years of age.

The great majority of the foreign-born Mexican-American population came during the Great Migration from 1900 to 1930. During these three decades, more than 1.5 million Mexicans crossed the border seeking greater opportunity in America. Many of these migrants returned after a brief sojourn; many came and went repeatedly; hundreds of thousands returned to Mexico during the Great Depression, victims of shrinking opportunity and xenophobia. By the start of World War II, however, a generation of American-born or -raised Mexican-American men and women came of age. Having known no other home but the United States, they took a far more active role in American cultural and political institutions, integrated their community into the larger Anglo-American society, and carved out a unique Mexican-American identity.

THE GREAT MIGRATION

Although the Hispanic presence in the American Southwest dates back to the seventeenth century, perhaps only 100,000 Mexican men and women populated the region when it became part of the United States following the Mexican-American War (1846–47). Relatively few Mexicans migrated north during the rest of the nineteenth century. The 1900 census found only 103,410 Mexican-born U.S. residents.

Beginning in 1900, however, waves of Mexican migrants dwarfed the existing population. Push and pull factors contributed to one of the largest migrations in American history. In Mexico, economic change and political revolution dislocated millions of people in a population that soared from 9.2 million in 1870 to 13.6 million in 1910. Nearly 1.5 million Mexicans—10 percent of Mexico's population—responded to these crises with their feet and headed north to the American Southwest.

A number of factors also pulled immigrants north. Long-established kin and village networks in the immediate border regions greatly facilitated migration. More important, however, jobs beckoned Mexicans north. Southwestern agriculture, railroads, and mines employed thousands of Mexicans during this period. Agriculture was specially important in this regard. The Newlands Reclamation Act of 1902 transformed millions of acres in the Southwest. By 1929, huge irrigated farms worked by Mexican migrants provided 40 percent of the total U.S. fruit and vegetable production. During this period, farmers greatly increased their cultivation of labor-intensive crops such as cotton.

Mexico supplied the majority of America's low-wage immigrant laborers in the 1920s. The Chinese Exclusion Act (1882) and the gentleman's agreement with Japan (1907–08) impaired Asian migration. The Reed-Johnson Immigration Act of 1924 imposed racial quotas on migrants from outside the Western Hemisphere and virtually halted southern- and eastern-European migration. Subsequent legislation sought to impair the entry of Mexicans, but border authorities seldom enforced it, especially during labor shortages.

Thus, at the start of the Great Depression, Mexican Americans were an important demographic and economic part of the American Southwest. Tens of thousands of Mexicans also penetrated into the Midwest, finding places in thriving industrial cities like Chicago and Detroit. Still, the Southwest remained the center of the Mexican-American population, and agriculture the main business of Mexican-American workers. Once the Great Depression set in, however, increased competition for scarce resources injured Mexican Americans.

THE GREAT DEPRESSION

The advent of international economic depression boded ill for Mexican-American workers. Agricultural labor declined, and what jobs remained were harder to get as thousands of farm families fled Oklahoma's dust bowls for California and parts in between. As many as 350,000 "Okies" settled in California alone. Racial discrimination disrupted decades-long patterns of seasonal migration as farmers hired "white" families instead of Mexican Americans. Many Mexican Americans moved to urban centers where there was greater opportunity to subsist. Urban barrios grew in cities like Los Angeles, San Antonio, El Paso, and even Denver. In New Mexico, many Mexican Americans retreated into their mountain villages as opportunities in Colorado beet farms dried up.

There was, however, as historian Sarah Deutsch writes, "no place of refuge." Unemployment soared quickly following the crash of the stock market, and by 1933, 15 million Americans (25 percent of the workforce) were unemployed. In the Southwest, legislation barred Mexican "aliens" from local public works. Private charities, the primary source of relief before Roosevelt's New Deal programs, excluded or discriminated against Mexican Americans. For many Mexican Americans, the United States was suddenly an inhospitable environment.

REPATRIATION

While most Mexican Americans remained in the United States throughout the Depression, increased discrimination and job competition encouraged many to repatriate. As many as 500,000 Mexican Americans returned to Mexico between 1929 and 1935. Diverse interests aided and abetted repatriation. Astute and mobile Mexican Americans were part of the first wave of repatriates. Many of these economically successful men and women saw opportunities evaporate, packed up, and drove to Mexico with their valuables and sav-

Like other minorities, Hispanic Americans, like these California grape pickers, were hard hit by falling wages during the Great Depression. *(Brown Brothers)*

ings shortly after the 1929 stock market crash. Most Mexican Americans, however, remained. Many of them joined the millions of Americans who quickly exhausted their resources. Swelled relief rolls stretched local agencies. In the early 1930s, welfare agencies in cities like Los Angeles and Denver found it cheaper to buy a one-way ticket to Mexico than to feed a family indefinitely. Trains sponsored by municipal relief authorities repatriated thousands of poverty-stricken Mexicans tired of increased racist hostility and discouraged by economic hardship.

The Mexican government also promoted repatriation through a series of largely unfulfilled promises that attracted thousands of desperately poor men and women angry at the hostility of their host nation. Many others, whose immigration status was ambiguous (only

in 1924 was a formal border patrol established—previously, Mexicans often crossed the border undocumented), feared legal deportation and voluntarily left. Highly visible and sensational raids scared men and women living in marginal financial and legal conditions. On February 26, 1931, for example, Department of Labor Bureau of Immigration agents (they became the Immigration and Naturalization Service in 1933) detained 400 men and women in a daylight raid on a popular square in downtown Los Angeles. Agents took into custody only eleven Mexicans, five Chinese, and one Japanese, but the message was loud and clear. Altogether, authorities officially deported only 300 Mexicans; many more were coerced or deceived into leaving. The majority of the 400,000 to 500,000 Mexican Americans who left, however, many with

American-born children, repatriated voluntarily out of frustration and anger.

Repatriation waned for a number of reasons. By 1933, the majority of those inclined to leave had done so; the Mexican Americans who stayed often had property and established roots in the area. As well, reports of conditions in Mexico discouraged many. Repatriated Mexican Americans fared poorly upon return, and government promises of land and assistance never materialized. Finally, Franklin D. Roosevelt's election provided hope and confidence for all Americans. New Deal relief and work programs improved the material existence of all Americans.

THE NEW DEAL

New Deal programs, however, left an ambivalent legacy within the Mexican-American community. While thousands of families benefited from the introduction of federal aid, the Federal Civil Works Program excluded thousands more who failed to meet residence requirements or were undocumented. Furthermore, programs to help farmers often injured Mexican farmworkers. For example, the Agricultural Adjustment Administration pulled thousands of acres out of production to stabilize prices. While farmers received compensation for their losses, farmworkers had few alternatives. Other New Deal programs, such as the Works Progress Administration, encouraged an arts-and-crafts revival in northern New Mexico that subsequently committed villagers to the tourist trade and offered little to prepare them for a market-based industrial economy. Federal interventions also disrupted generations-old survival strategies and precipitated profound social and cultural change.

Still, local authorities could not deny federally funded direct relief on the basis of legal status. Nor could they use these funds to further repatriation objectives. These monies improved the lives of thousands of Mexican-American families. As well, many New Deal programs clearly targeted Mexican-American communities. More than 32,000 young men from New Mexico participated in Civilian Conservation Corps projects in that state. This program greatly supplemented local incomes and furthered the education and confidence of a generation of young Mexican Americans. New Deal land reforms also helped many New Mexico villagers. The Interdepartmental Rio Grande Board acquired and distributed 1 million acres of marginal land in an effort to replace lost traditional cattle and sheep pastures. In San Antonio, Texas, the Alazan-Apache Courts housing project provided 2,554 single-family dwellings for impoverished Mexican Americans. The project derived in large part from the Wagner-Steagall Act of 1937, which created the United States Housing Authority and earmarked federal funds for low-income housing.

THE CREATION OF A MEXICAN-AMERICAN IDENTITY

Of course, the shock of repatriation and the hostility experienced throughout the Depression traumatized the community, overshadowing the positive effects of the New Deal. Ironically, however, repatriation shifted the generational balance of power within the community and empowered a generation of American-born or -raised Mexican Americans. These young men and women did not look to Mexico and determined to enjoy their rights as Americans.

American-born or -raised Mexican Americans empowered the community through their increased role in a number of American organizations and institutions. In particular, the numerous labor struggles stimulated by Section 7 of the National Recovery Administration Charter (National Industrial Recovery Act, 1933) attracted their energy. Mexican-American men and women participated as organizers and rank and file in numerous American Federation of Labor and Congress of Industrial Organizations affiliates: the International Ladies' Garment Workers' Union, the Independent Furniture Workers' Local, the Carpenters Union, the Steel Workers Organizing Committee, the International Longshoremen's and Warehousemen's Union, the United Cannery, Agricultural, Packing and Allied Workers of America, and other, sanctioned and unsanctioned organizations. Many of these young men and women became ardent critics of American political economy. These political and labor struggles "Americanized" thousands of workers and labor leaders. Whereas in the 1920s, a community dominated by recent arrivals looked to Mexico for its identity, by the 1940s, Mexican Americans, the overwhelming majority American-born or -raised, looked to full participation in American social, political, economic, and cultural life for individual and group fulfillment.

Joe Torre

See also: agriculture; Mexico; Cárdenas, Lázaro

Bibliography

Bureau of the Census. *Fifteenth Census of the United States: 1930. Population.* Washington, DC: Government Printing Office, 1931–33.

Deutsch, Sarah. *No Separate Refuge: Culture, Class and Gender on an Anglo-Hispanic Frontier in the American Southwest, 1880–1940.* New York: Oxford University Press, 1987.

Dinwoodie, David H. "Indians, Hispanos and Land Reform: A New Deal Struggle in New Mexico." *Western Historical Quarterly* 17:3 (July 1986): 291–323.

Forrest, Suzanne. *The Preservation of the Village: New Mexico Hispanics and the New Deal.* Albuquerque: University of New Mexico Press, 1989.

Gonzales, Manuel G. *Mexicanos: A History of Mexicans in the United States.* Bloomington: Indiana University Press, 1999.

Hoffman, Abraham. *Unwanted Mexican Americans in the Great Depression.* Tucson: University of Arizona Press, 1974.

Monroy, Douglas. *Rebirth: Mexican Los Angeles from the Great Migration to the Great Depression.* Berkeley and Los Angeles: University of California Press, 1999.

Montoya, Maria E. "The Roots of Economic and Ethnic Divisions in Northern New Mexico: The Case of the Civilian Conservation Corps." *Western Historical Quarterly* 26:1 (Spring 1995): 14–34.

Sanchez, George J. *Becoming Mexican American: Ethnicity, Culture and Identity in Chicano Los Angeles, 1900–1945.* New York: Oxford University Press, 1993.

Weber, Debra. *Dark Sweat, White Gold: California Farm Workers, Cotton and the New Deal.* Berkeley and Los Angeles: University of California Press, 1994.

Zelman, Donald L. "Alazan-Apache Courts: A New Deal Response to Mexican American Housing Conditions in San Antonio." *Southwestern Historical Quarterly* 87:2 (October 1983): 123–50.

HOBOES AND TRANSIENTS

The serious economic problems that plagued the United States during the Great Depression led men, women, teenagers, and children to abandon their hometowns and look for work and prosperity elsewhere. Wandering was not new, but the nation's worst depression exacerbated it. The size of the transient population is unknown, but during Herbert Hoover's presidency, officials estimated that between 400,000 and 2 million Americans traveled from place to place in search of opportunity. A one-day census of 765 cities conducted in March 1933 counted more than 201,000 transients. The actual number of transients was undoubtedly higher than recorded in 1933 and 1934, because the wandering populace was difficult to measure. Especially during the early years of the Depression, families were often seen wandering America in their cars. A significant number of teens, particularly young men, traveled from place to place seeking not only work but also adventure. The majority of transients, however, were white men between the ages of twenty and forty-five who traveled alone. Railroad freight cars were the men's preferred mode of transportation because they were free and fast.

Private charitable organizations, cities, and towns across the United States faced serious challenges from the wanderers, because transients not only stopped and asked for work, but required food, clothing, and shelter. As the burden of caring for unemployed and needy local residents increased, wanderers found municipalities less willing to help them. Residents of cities and towns preferred that local funds be used to assist needy neighbors, not people from out of town—and especially not hoboes, whom they considered professional wanderers. It was usual for localities to offer an evening meal, overnight accommodations in the city jail, and breakfast before placing drifters on the first train out of town. In many places, local laws legitimated this attitude, so transients had no legal right to receive assistance.

THE NEW DEAL TO THE RESCUE

The New Deal came to the rescue of transients, relief organizations, and localities in 1933. The Federal Emergency Relief Act provided for assisting wanderers and lifted the burden of their care from charities and municipalities. In July, the Federal Emergency Relief Administration encouraged state relief officials to begin planning for nonresident care and the Federal Transient Program was born. Washington defined transients as nonresidents who had been in a state for fewer than twelve months. It agreed to fund all expenses for the care of this unwanted and needy group. Each state's Emergency Relief branch was to devise a plan and submit it to the federal government for approval. Some

Itinerants, known as hoboes, illegally rode freight trains looking for work in the Great Depression. Here, two men ride boxcars on a rail line along the West Side of Manhattan. *(Brown Brothers)*

states, however, were slow to take advantage of the New Deal's offer, because they were afraid that providing the necessities of life for transients would encourage more people to take to the nation's roads and invade cities and towns that had transient bureaus. Nevertheless, by fall 1934, 340 transient bureaus were spread across the nation in every state except Vermont. The first facilities appeared in larger cities and transportation centers. Urban bureaus offered lodging, well-balanced meals, medical care, recreation and educational opportunities, and work for which lodgers received a small stipend each week. At most bureaus, each male applicant was registered, met with a social worker, and received a physical examination, clean clothes, and a bed to call his own.

There were different arrangements for women traveling alone, families, and blacks. Unattached women were often given greater care and protection more than their male counterparts. Rather than provide them with long-term care, social workers tried to return them to their legal residences. Families were rarely housed in transient bureaus, but provided with private accommodations when possible or enough gas money to reach their destination. The black transient population also presented special problems. Although segregation within the bureaus was common throughout the nation, southern states usually had separate bureaus for African Americans.

The emergency nature of the transient program meant that states and localities scrambled to establish bureaus in makeshift quarters in order to meet Washington's requirements and begin caring for the drifters who were burdening their relief resources. Many municipalities converted old warehouses, hotels, and business buildings into transient centers, resulting in lodgings of varying quality. Harry Hopkins, President Franklin D. Roosevelt's chief relief administrator, referred to some of the bureaus as "thinly disguised flophouses." In an effort to remove transients from cities and to provide them with long-term care, the federal government encouraged states to establish transient camps. Each camp, affiliated with one or more urban bureaus from which it received clients, was a community unto itself. At the camps, transients worked on a variety of projects, from reforestation to publishing camp magazines and teaching fellow camp inhabitants how to read and write.

THE NEW DEAL ABANDONS TRANSIENTS

In January 1935, during his State of the Union address, President Roosevelt announced his desire that Washington "quit this business of relief," put people to work, and return the responsibility for work and relief to the localities. The Federal Transient Program was one of the casualties of the New Deal's different focus. By December 1935, the transients were integrated into the Works Projects Administration's activities near the bureaus where they had been living or they were returned to their hometowns. During the transient division's twenty-eight-month tenure, the federal government had expended $86 million to care for the nation's wandering population. The New Deal explored uncharted territory when it provided transients with the right to relief. In addition, Washington replaced the usual methods of dealing with nonresidents, such as passing them from one locality to the next, with a system that sought to discourage wandering. The transient system had benefited drifters, states, and localities. When the program ended, however, transients suffered the most. Once again, they found themselves unwelcome in towns and cities across America and without legal claims to relief.

JEFFREY S. COLE

See also: dust bowl; Okies; unemployment.

Bibliography

Crouse, Joan M. *The Homeless Transient in the Great Depression: New York State, 1929–1941.* Albany: State University of New York Press, 1986.

Hopkins, Harry. *Spending to Save: The Complete Story of Relief.* New York: W. W. Norton, 1936; reprint, Seattle: University of Washington Press, Americana Library, 1972.

Uys, Errol Lincoln. *Riding the Rails: Teenagers on the Move During the Great Depression.* New York: TV Books, 1999.

HOW TO WIN FRIENDS AND INFLUENCE PEOPLE

Written by a public speaking teacher named Dale Carnegie and published in 1936, *How to Win Friends and Influence People* was one of the five best-selling books of the 1930s. Over 750,000 copies were sold in the first year of publication.

Like many of the other self-help books published in the Great Depression, the book offered readable, simplified lessons in basic human psychology. Carnegie emphasized the importance of attitude in a person's success and stressed that readers should view their own shortcomings as advantages. Despite the hard times of the 1930s, *How to Win Friends* is often cited by historians to show that, despite the economic downturn and the collectivist solutions offered by the New Deal, many Americans retained their faith in individualist enterprise during the Great Depression.

See also: literature; Carnegie, Dale.

Bibliography

Kemp, Giles. *Dale Carnegie: The Man Who Influenced Millions.* New York: St. Martin's, 1989.

HUNGER MARCHES

A series of demonstrations between 1930 and 1932 that were designed to highlight unemployment and economic want, the hunger marches were often organized by Communists and met with stiff resistance by local officials and police in the towns and cities where they occurred.

The first series of organized hunger marches came on March 6, 1930. Spearheaded by communist organizations, including the Trade Union Unity League, the marches occurred in cities from California to New York and brought an estimated 500,000 persons into the streets.

While several marches took place throughout 1930, their number grew in the spring and summer of 1931 to the point where the Central Committee of the Communist Party of the United States decided to coordinate these activities through the creation of the National Hunger March Committee of the Unemployed Councils in August. The committee called for nationwide demonstrations that culminated in a march on Washington on December 7.

To dissuade the 1,620 delegates trucked into the city for the march, Police Chief Pelham Glassford laid out an extra-long route, designed to exhaust the

So-called hunger marches, like this 1936 demonstration in Harrisburg, Pennsylvania, were a popular form of protest in the Great Depression, when many Americans faced food shortages even as farmers destroyed crops to keep up agricultural prices. *(Brown Brothers)*

marchers, and surrounded both the Capitol and the White House with large contingents of officers.

A second hunger march on Washington occurred in early January, 1932. Angered that Communists had led the earlier march, Father James Cox, a Pittsburgh priest and homeless advocate, brought some 15,000 "real American citizens" to the capital. Meeting with President Herbert Hoover, Cox pleaded for a $5 billion public works and farm loan program to help the nation's poor, but was told that existing programs were sufficient to meet the problems of the Depression.

The last of the great hunger marches—aside from the Bonus Army march in the spring and summer of 1932—took place on March 7, 1932, and was organized by the Communist-led Detroit Unemployed Council. The march on the Ford Motor Company's giant River

Rouge plant was met by police and Ford security forces, who attacked the marchers, leaving four dead and dozens injured.

See also: Bonus Army; Communist Party; Ford Motor Company; Trade Union Unity League; Unemployed Councils; Hoover, Herbert.

Bibliography

Baskin, Alex. "The Ford Hunger March—1932." *Labor History* (Summer 1972).

Lisio, Donald J. *The President and Protest: Hoover, Conspiracy, and the Bonus Riot.* Columbia: University of Missouri Press, 1974.

Heineman, Kenneth. *A Catholic New Deal: Religion and Reform in Depression Pittsburgh.* University Park: Pennsylvania State University Press, 1999.

I AM A FUGITIVE FROM A CHAIN GANG

A 1932 film starring Paul Muni, *I Am a Fugitive from a Chain Gang* tells the story of an occasionally employed World War I veteran who—somewhat innocently—gets caught up in an acquaintance's robbery of a diner in the South. The hero of the film soon finds himself on a chain gang, from which he escapes. Moving to Chicago, he falls in with a woman of the streets. When he refuses to marry her, she turns him in and, although many citizens rise up in his defense, the Illinois authorities extradite him to the unnamed southern state. A powerful indictment of the chain gang system, *Fugitive* is often cited by film

critics as the definitive statement about Depression-era values whereby innocent people were punished by a brutal and unjust system. The film was directed by Mervyn Le Roy and was a critical and box office success.

See also: crime; films, feature; Muni, Paul.

Bibliography

Baxter, John. *Hollywood in the Thirties.* New York: Barnes, 1968.

Sklar, Robert. *Movie-Made America: A Cultural History of the American Movies.* New York: Random House, 1975.

INSURANCE INDUSTRY

During the first decades of the twentieth century, the insurance industry in the United States experienced rapid growth as many Americans, especially in the 1920s, accrued the wealth necessary to purchase life, property, or burial coverage. From 1900 to 1925, the amount of life insurance in force increased 737 percent and the number of life insurance companies grew 364 percent. As in most other industries, however, the onset of the Great Depression reversed that growth. As some firms failed and others lost private and corporate clients, employment in the sector

including insurance decreased about 15 percent (from 1.5 million to 1.3 million) from 1929 through 1933. In the latter year, the Northwestern Mutual Life Insurance Company, based in Milwaukee, sold only $191 million of new insurance, making it the worst year for the company since 1918. Two things particularly endangered American insurers: increased defaults on policy premiums and expanded loans to distressed clients. By March 1933, almost one-third of Northwestern Mutual's policyholders had borrowed against their equity. The combination of defaults and loans decreased customer confidence in the stability of many firms, some of which were threatened with runs during winter 1932–33. One a run, in which policyholders rushed to withdraw their cash investments, resulted in the failure of one of the largest insurance companies in New Orleans in February 1933. Such failures, could threaten a larger run on other local financial institutions.

In comparison to other sectors, however, the insurance industry weathered the Depression relatively well. As did most other industries, insurance faced its most difficult challenges from 1929 to early 1933. Even taking those years into account, however, during the entire decade of the 1930s only thirty-nine life insurance companies, less than 2 percent of the national total, failed. Some smaller firms managed to scrape by. The American Life and Accident Insurance Company of Kentucky survived on profits from the sale of a Louisville radio station in which the company's owner also held an interest, while the African-American-owned Chicago Metropolitan Funeral System Association remained in operation only on the strength of its owner's personal gambling winnings. As a whole, the industry persevered because it had been well regulated at the state level since before the turn of the century and because, at least after the crisis of 1932–33, consumers increasingly regarded the purchase or maintenance of life insurance as a stable investment compared with banks or the stock market. By 1934, the industry began a slow and relatively steady recovery that attained pre-Depression levels of employment and sales by the end of the decade.

STATE ENCROACHMENT

Although insurers achieved some measure of financial stability by 1934, they were threatened by state encroachment throughout the 1930s and particularly during the New Deal. Although life insurance remained the most widespread form of coverage, two relatively new kinds of policies—unemployment and health insurance—were being written. After the Depression's beginning, private insurers began to underwrite the corporate unemployment plans of such firms as General Electric when they suddenly proved too costly. This proved a poor risk for insurers, however, who subsequently joined industrialists in calling for state-mandated unemployment insurance from 1929 through 1935. Insurers expected that states, including Wisconsin, which passed the first such measure, would require and regulate unemployment coverage, but would not create state insurance monopolies. That held

true until the national Social Security Act (1935), which created unemployment insurance funded by employer and employee contributions and administered by the federal government, eliminated an emerging market for insurers. On other occasions, the insurance industry was more successful in forestalling federal encroachment. In response to a campaign led by labor and reformers, the progressive New York Senator Robert F. Wagner submitted a bill to create national health insurance in February 1939. Believing that the proposed measure, in creating state-administered coverage, would eliminate consumers' needs for private health insurance, the industry, along with the American Medical Association, successfully opposed Wagner's bill.

WOMEN AND AFRICAN AMERICANS IN THE INDUSTRY

By the beginning of the Great Depression, the insurance industry was racially segregated. White-owned firms, especially such well-capitalized ones as Prudential, dominated the field. Although these firms would and did write policies for African-American consumers, they charged blacks higher rates compared to whites. Further, racial segregation in both the southern and northern states, where the Great Migration had deposited millions of southern African Americans, had the unintended effect of producing large and underinsured clienteles. During the early twentieth century and the Depression years, black entrepreneurs filled their communities' needs for affordable insurance. In addition to the aforementioned Chicago Metropolitan Funeral System, which sold policies that insured a proper burial after a customer's death, the North Carolina Mutual Life Insurance Company offered a wider range of services to southern blacks. These insurers helped form the core of an emerging black middle class in such cities as Chicago, Durham, and Atlanta.

Finally, women, both white and black, had moved into the insurance business in great numbers by the Depression's commencement. In 1910, insurance had been an almost exclusively male preserve. By 1930, however, about one-third of all employees in the industry were women. Most females worked as stenographers, typists, clerks, and bookkeepers. Although underrepresented, about 10 percent of all women in insurance nevertheless worked as managers, accountants, auditors, and sales agents.

TODD BENNETT

See also: banking; Social Security Act; Documents: Fireside Chat on Social Security Acts, January 17, 1935; Social Security acts, August 15, 1935.

Bibliography

Davis, Audrey B. "Life Insurance and the Physical Examination: A Chapter in the Rise of American Medical Technology." *Bulletin of the History of Medicine* 55:3 (1981): 392–406.

Edsforth, Ronald. *The New Deal: America's Response to the Great Depression.* Malden, MA: Blackwell, 2000.

Gordon, Colin. *New Deals: Business, Labor, and Politics in America, 1920–1935.* New York: Cambridge University Press, 1994.

Gurda, John. *The Quiet Company: A Modern History of Northwestern Mutual Life.* Milwaukee: The Northwestern Mutual Life Insurance Company, 1983.

Kirkwood, James Trace. "Corporate Profile: The American Life and Accident Insurance Company of Kentucky." *Filson Club History Quarterly* 66:2 (1992): 265–69.

Kwolek-Follan, Angel. *Engendering Business: Men and Women in the Corporate Office, 1870–1930.* Baltimore: Johns Hopkins University Press, 1994.

Mulcahy, C. Richard. "Working Against the Odds: Josephine Roche, The New Deal, and the Drive for National Health Insurance." *Maryland Historian* 25:2 (1994): 1–21.

Stone, Mildred F. *A Short History of Life Insurance.* Indianapolis: The Insurance Research and Review Service, 1942.

Weare, Walter B. *Black Business in the New South: A Social History of the North Carolina Mutual Life Insurance Company.* Urbana: University of Illinois Press, 1973.

Weems, Robert E., Jr. "The Chicago Metropolitan Mutual Assurance Company: A Profile of a Black-Owned Enterprise." *Illinois Historical Journal* 86:1 (1993): 15–26.

Yates, JoAnne. "Information Technology and Business Processes in the Twentieth Century Insurance Industry." *Business and Economic History* 21 (1992): 317–25.

INTERNATIONAL LADIES' GARMENT WORKERS' UNION

Founded in 1901, the International Ladies' Garment Workers' Union (ILGWU), led by David Dubinsky, was one of the most important mass industry unions in America in the early twentieth century and played a crucial role in the formation of the Committee for Industrial Organization (forerunner of the Congress of Industrial Organizations, CIO) in 1935.

The origins of the ILGWU go back to the various socialist-oriented garment trade unions of the late nineteenth century. Largely made up of Italian and Jewish immigrant workers, the ILGWU was involved in several important strikes against garment sweatshops in the first decade of the twentieth century.

In the late 1920s and early 1930s, the union got caught up in the internecine struggles within the left, especially after the Communist Party divided into two branches in 1928—a left wing oriented toward Moscow and a right wing with an independent American focus. Most of the ILGWU membership and leadership sided with the latter, especially after the leftists formed the competing Needle Trades Workers Industrial Union (NTWIU), a member organization of the communist-oriented Trade Union Unity League.

By the mid-1930s, the failure of the communist union and a Moscow-issued appeal for all Communists to join other liberal and left organizations in the fight against conservatism and fascism had led most of the NTWIU workers back into the ILGWU fold. United, the ILGWU followed Dubinsky into supporting the leftist American Labor Party (ALP), which ran independent candidates for local and state office, but supported Franklin D. Roosevelt for president in 1936.

Meanwhile, on the industrial front, Dubinsky joined United Mine Worker president John L. Lewis in 1935 in forming the Committee for Industrial Organization, a group within the American Federation of Labor (AFL)—of which the ILGWU was a member union—that pushed for more aggressive organizing of the mass industries like automobiles and steel.

But soon, Dubinsky found himself at odds with other leaders of the Committee for Industrial Organization. Upset at the influence that radical Sidney Hillman, head of the rival Amalgamated Clothing Workers Union (ACWU), had over the organization, the more conservative Dubinsky pulled the ILGWU out in 1938 and returned to the AFL. He also did not like the ALP's decision to nominate Hillman as its senatorial candidate in 1938 and so distanced the ILGWU from the ALP.

During the 1940s, Dubinsky spurned Hillman's efforts to unite the AFL and the CIO, although a merger was eventually achieved in 1955. With ILGWU membership falling sharply after the 1960s, the union joined with the ACWU and virtually all other garment and textile worker unions in 1995 to create the Union of Needletrades, Industrial and Textile Employees, better known by its acronym, UNITE!

See also: American Federation of Labor; American Labor Party; Congress of Industrial Organizations; Trade Union Unity League; unions and union organizing; Dubinsky, David; Hillman, Sidney; Lewis, John L.

Bibliography

Dubinsky, David, and A. H. Raskin. *David Dubinsky: A Life with Labor.* New York: Simon & Schuster, 1977.

Tyler, Gus. *Look for the Union Label: A History of the International Ladies Garment Workers Union.* Armonk, NY: M. E. Sharpe, 1995.

IT HAPPENED ONE NIGHT

The first and arguably the most popular of the so-called screwball comedies of the 1930s, *It Happened One Night* combined the talents of some of Hollywood's favorite personalities, including stars Clark Gable and Claudette Colbert, as well as director Frank Capra.

Screwball comedies featured high-velocity plots, rapid-fire dialogue, preposterously confused situations and scenes, and upper-class characters who were a bit eccentric. *It Happened One Night* featured all of these elements as it told the story of a wealthy heiress (Colbert) making her first venture into the world of ordinary people as she tries to escape an unhappy arranged—but unconsummated—marriage. On her trail is a tough-talking reporter (Gable) out to cover the human interest story.

Screwball comedies, say film historians, were popular in the 1930s because they provided perfect escapist entertainment—lighthearted plots, ritzy scenes, and the inevitable love match between rich and ordinary Americans, which helped to ease the deep class tensions of the era.

See also: films, feature; Capra, Frank; Gable, Clark.

Bibliography

Carney, Raymond. *American Vision: The Films of Frank Capra.* New York: Cambridge University Press, 1987.

Tornabene, Lyn. *Long Live the King: A Biography of Clark Gable.* New York: Putnam, 1976.

The definitive screwball comedy of the Great Depression era, the 1934 Frank Capra film *It Happened One Night* featured Clark Gable and Claudette Colbert. *(Brown Brothers)*

JACKSON DAY SPEECH

Delivered on Jackson Day, an annual Democratic Party event celebrating Andrew Jackson, the seventh president of the United States and one of Franklin D. Roosevelt's self-declared heroes, this speech marked the beginning of Roosevelt's 1936 reelection run. The speech, broadcast to some 3,000 Jackson Day dinner audiences around the country, strongly attacked the "forces of privilege and greed" and is often cited by historians as marking a new and more radical phase in the rhetoric of the New Deal.

While Roosevelt offered little in the way of concrete proposals, the speech had an immediate and galvanizing effect on Americans. Republicans denounced it as a rallying cry for class warfare. But many Americans seemed moved. More than 95 percent of the those who wrote the president about the speech approved of what he said. Still, Roosevelt did not put his rhetoric into action, as he soon ordered spending cuts in public works programs and called for the balancing of the federal budget.

See also: election of 1936; Roosevelt, Franklin D.

Bibliography

Schlesinger, Arthur. *The Politics of Upheaval*. Boston: Houghton Mifflin, 1960.

Zevin, B. D. *Nothing to Fear: The Selected Addresses of Franklin Delano Roosevelt, 1932–1945*. Boston: Houghton Mifflin, 1946.

KEYNESIAN ECONOMICS

John Maynard Keynes (1883–1946), graduate of Cambridge University, developed the most important set of economic principles within the capitalist school of economics since eighteenth century Adam Smith, who described the basic rules of capitalism. Like Smith, Keynes realized that one can best understand economics by consulting history and not by looking for "natural laws." As economic adviser to Britain's delegation at the Versailles conference of 1919, Keynes knew that the victorious nations, in saddling Germany with reparations, would inevitably bring on economic disaster for Europe, which would in turn have grave political consequences. He outlined his understanding of the results of World War I in two books, *The Economic Consequences of the Peace* (1919) and *The End of Laissez Faire* (1926).

After the stock marked crashed in 1929, Keynes outlined his ideas in various lectures and magazine articles, advising the British government how to shorten the slump and avoid a deeper depression. He pointed out that laissez-faire principles were deficient in at least seven ways. First, unlike Adam Smith, Keynes said investments did not automatically equal savings. Second, bankers were oversaving, because, as oligopolists, they had refused to lower interest rates; instead, they had contracted loans. Third, short on credit, the industrial sector then cut costs by curbing production and laying off workers. Fourth, for the next year, as the workers spent less, businesses and the government cut investment, contracting employment, incomes, and investments even further. The world market then spiraled down to its low point in 1933.

Fifth, because markets were global, devaluing currency to make a single nation's exports cheaper, or raising tariffs to keep imports out, were only short-term remedies. Powerful competing foreign nations could always retaliate, leading to ad hoc devaluation by each competing nation. So Keynes as a political economist called upon the finance ministers of the major countries at the London Economic Conference in 1933 to agree internationally to cancel the war debts and reparations remaining from World War I.

Devaluing money and raising tariffs had already been tried by most governments. France devalued the franc in 1928, followed by the British pound in 1931 and the U.S. dollar in 1933. Later, France devalued its money for a second round in September 1936. For political reasons, President Franklin D. Roosevelt pressed the British not to retaliate, and he refused on behalf of the United States to retaliate.

As the new president in 1933, Roosevelt had said "no" to an international financial agreement. He had his own national recovery plans and would not try to help Europe recover from its economic problems. By September 1936, he was willing to bail out France but not all of Europe. Keynes won over the U.S. government to his global ideas by 1944, when the Bretton Woods Conference assembled to plan financially for the postwar international capitalist world.

Keynes's sixth reason why laissez-faire principles were deficient was that during the Depression, agriculture was in worse shape than industry because farmers were less able than industry to restrict production in order to raise prices. Telling farmers to depend on the "invisible hand" of the market, when large corporate industry did not do so itself, only depressed the price of food to all-time lows. Keynes did not oppose an agricultural subsidy providing a floor under farmers' incomes. Farmers had the least amount of bargaining power in the oligopolistic system called the "free market."

Keynes's seventh reason was that the weakness of the old, "perfect competition" model that was in place in 1929 led governments to demand balanced budgets. Keynes argued that if governments could run deficits to fight wars, they could run deficits to fight unemployment, the so-called economic "pump-priming" idea. Keynes argued that laissez-faire principles were deficient in the 1930s, because governments were trying to balance their budgets and pay off the high debts of the World War I era when production had been high.

All seven of Keynes's ideas were rejected by the conservative governments and businesses that had slashed costs by firing workers and foreclosing on small farms. Keynes invented the concept of effective demand; that is, the poorer classes naturally had the desire to consume more goods and services, but they had no product to sell in the temporarily overglutted industrial sector. The government had to stimulate purchasing power by the working classes through tax cuts and subsidies to encourage private industry to invest again in manufacturing. If the banks lowered interest rates, they could encourage industrialists to borrow more and invest more. Investment was the key to increasing jobs.

The Roosevelt administration tried many Keynesian ideas, such as pushing for lower interest rates at the Federal Reserve Banks, creating the Social Security Administration, encouraging collective bargaining by the establishment of the National Labor Relations

Board (NLRB), and creating jobs through the Agricultural Adjustment Administration (AAA), Works Progress Administration (WPA), Public Works Administration (PWA), Civilian Conservation Corps (CCC), Federal Deposit Insurance Corporation (FDIC), Federal Housing Administration (FHA), Tennessee Valley Authority (TVA), Security and Exchange Commission (SEC), and several other pump-priming programs. Employment rates improved gradually from 1933 to 1939.

Roosevelt himself met Keynes in the White House in May 1934. As a politician, Roosevelt was not going to call himself a "Keynesian," but the British economist clearly influenced many of the president's top advisers, including Felix Frankfurter, Adolf Berle, Henry Wallace, Henry Morganthau, Thurman Arnold, Rexford Tugwell, and Harry Dexter White. Professional academic economists like Alvin Hansen and Gardiner Means, who shared many of Keynes's ideas, influenced many other lesser known bureaucrats throughout the administration. America's top journalist, Walter Lippman, publicized the ideas of Keynes.

Of course, Adolf Hitler's rearmament programs provided full employment for Germany by 1939, at an even faster rate than the recovery in the United States. During World War II, the American military grew greatly. Consequently, government spending, as Keynes had suggested, stimulated the private economy to grow even faster than during the earlier period of modest welfare stimulus programs. In 1944, the nation had only a 2 percent unemployment rate, a rate never again matched. Hitler and the Japanese imperialists in effect speeded up the New Deal recovery and boosted production and jobs to new highs until the 1949 recession. The economy of Hitler's Third Reich, after booming in 1939, paid a heavy price in wartime physical destruction by 1945.

The lessons of the warfare economies of Germany, Japan, and Italy, as well as the British experience in two world wars, showed Americans that the so-called radical measures of the Roosevelt administration had actually been too modest. A great deal of productive capacity that had been underutilized in the United States from 1933 to 1941 had been wasted because of stubborn adherence to the old free market principle of demanding a balanced budget and waiting for the natural free market to take effect. Throughout history, the military in all countries has never hesitated to suggest deficit finance. Keynes actually invented a substitute for war as a method for stimulating prosperity. Keynes proved that governments can behave in constructive or destructive ways to encourage further prosperity, depression, or recovery. With all its shortcomings, the welfare state is preferable to the warfare state.

Markets, according to Keynes, are not like a seesaw, but rather like an elevator or a well of water. When income, consumption, and savings all go down, they will stay down unless some noneconomic factors induce businesspeople to invest on the basis of speculation. Increase in population, natural disasters, preparation for war, or new technology can all stimulate growth in production and thus create fuller employment. This philosophy guided most western democracies after World War II and is attributed by many economic historians as one of the main sources of the unprecedented prosperity of the global economy between the late 1940s and early 1970s.

ROBERT WHEALEY

See also: Agricultural Adjustment Administration; Civilian Conservation Corps; Federal Deposit Insurance Corporation; Federal Housing Administration; Federal Reserve Board; National Labor Relations Act; Public Works Administration; Securities and Exchange Commission; Tennessee Valley Authority; Works Progress Administration; London Economic Conference (1933); Arnold, Thurman; Berle, Adolf; Frankfurter, Felix; Lippman, Walter; Morgenthau, Henry Jr.; Tugwell, Rexford; Wallace, Henry A.

Bibliography

Heilbroner, Robert L. *The Worldly Philosophers: The Lives and Ideas of the Great Economic Thinkers.* 7th ed. [1st ed. 1953] New York: Simon & Schuster, 1999.

Keynes, John Maynard. *The Collected Writings of John Maynard Keynes.* New York: St. Martin's, 1971.

———. *Essays in Persuasion.* Rev. ed. [1st ed. 1931] New York: W.W. Norton, 1963.

———. *General Theory of Employment, Interest and Money.* New York: Harcourt Brace, 1936.

Rosenof, Theodore. *Economics in the Long Run: New Deal Theorists and their Legacies, 1933–1993.* Chapel Hill: University of North Carolina Press, 1997.

Skidelsky, Robert Jacob Alexander. *Keynes.* Oxford, UK: Oxford University Press, 1996.

———. *John Maynard Keynes: A Biography.* 2 vol. London: Macmillan, 1983.

KING KONG

The original and still most recognizable monster film of all time, *King Kong* (1933) left one of the most indelible images in the history of American cinema: a giant ape, clutching the blond heroine, fighting off airplanes as he clings to the top of the Empire State Building.

The film combines two classic plots: Beauty and the Beast and the "bring-'em-back-alive" jungle story. It begins with a journey to Skull Island, where primitive natives live separated by a giant wall from dinosaurs, monsters, and Kong himself.

A rescue scene ensues after the natives offer the heroine (played by Fay Wray) as a bride to Kong. Eventually the beast is tamed and brought to New York for display. But the giant ape, desperate for Wray, breaks loose, finds her, and takes her to the top of the Empire State Building, itself constructed only two years before the film was made, where he is eventually brought down by fighter airplanes.

While *King Kong* did not receive a single Academy Award nomination, it has nevertheless left some of the most recognized images in the history of cinema.

See also: Empire State Building; films, feature.

Bibliography

Goldner, Orville, and George E. Turner. *The Making of King Kong.* New York: Ballantine, 1976.

Gottesman, Ronald, and Harry Geduld. *The Girl in the Hairy Paw: King Kong as Myth, Movie, and Monster.* New York: Avon, 1976.

LEGION OF DECENCY

Founded by a group of American Roman Catholic bishops in 1933, the Legion of Decency was an organization designed to reduce the level of sexuality and profanity in Hollywood films through a boycott by Catholic movie-goers. Rather than government censorship boards, which were then being considered, the bishops hoped that their organization could achieve the same ends through popular protest.

In April 1934, the legion began distributing pamphlets to Catholic dioceses across the country, calling on parishioners to observe the boycott. The bishops claimed that petitions supporting their cause were signed by over 11 million Americans, including many Protestants and Jews.

The movie studios, already hard hit by the Depression-era drops in attendance, readily succumbed to the pressure. That year, they established the Production Code Administration within the Motion Picture Producers and Distributors Association (MPPDA) in 1934, the trade organization for the industry run by former Republican National Committee Chairman Will Hays, and placed Catholic newsman Joseph Breen at its head. The MPPDA, or Hays office as it was popularly known, had been installed to tone down the sexuality in movies in the early 1920s, in response to a number of Hollywood scandals. But the legion did not believe the Hays office went far enough. The Production Code Administration, however, satisfied most of the legion's demands by quickly getting all of the major Hollywood studios to agree to avoid a variety of topics in their movies, including abortion, drugs, homosexuality, incest, and profanity.

See also: films, feature; Motion Picture Production Code/Production Code Administration, Hays, Will.

Bibliography

Baxter, John. *Hollywood in the Thirties.* New York: Barnes, 1968.

Sklar, Robert. *Movie-Made America: A Cultural History of the American Movies.* New York: Random House, 1975.

LET US NOW PRAISE FAMOUS MEN

A collaborative book effort between writer James Agee and photographer Walker Evans, *Let Us Now Praise Famous Men* (1941) chronicles the story of three impoverished southern sharecropper families during the Great Depression.

Let Us Now Praise Famous Men began as a photo and essay story for *Fortune*—owned by Henry Luce—in 1936. Agee, a cultural critic and essayist, and Evans, a staff photographer with the Farm Security Administration, were hired to travel the South that summer to capture rural living conditions.

But when the piece came back ten times longer, and far bleaker in perspective than the *Fortune* editors had asked for, it was killed after a year of editing attempts. The magazine released the article to Agee, who then signed it as a book with the publisher Harper and Brothers. But Harper, too, turned it down when Agee refused to make certain editing changes. Finally, in 1941, Agee sold it to Houghton Mifflin, who went ahead and published it.

Aside from Evans's exquisitely harrowing black-and-white photographs, one of the most interesting aspects of the book is the narrative voice taken by Agee, which constantly questions the very act of trying to tell a story about people so very different from the author. This self-reflective quality, say literary critics, has given the book a staying power that more earnest and straightforward documentary efforts from the 1930s do not have. Thus, it has been in print almost continuously since it was first published.

See also: Farm Security Administration; Agee, James; Evans, Walker.

Bibliography

Staub, Michael E. *Voices of Persuasion: Politics of Representation in 1930s America*. New York: Cambridge University Press, 1994.

Stott, William. *Documentary Expression and Thirties America*. Chicago: University of Chicago Press, 1973.

LIBERTY LEAGUE

Formed in 1934 by conservative Democrats and corporate leaders, the Liberty League—also known as the American Liberty League—attacked President Franklin Delano Roosevelt as a socialist and the New Deal as a "communistic" plot. Its chief spokesperson was Al Smith, the 1928 Democratic candidate for president.

In 1936, Smith rallied a number of disaffected Democrats to back Georgia governor Eugene Talmadge as a black horse candidate for the Democratic presidential nomination. When Roosevelt won the nomination, Smith and the Liberty League turned to the popular and increasingly anti-Roosevelt radio preacher Father Charles Coughlin to rally his listeners to support a third-party candidate. Newspaper mogul William Randolph Hearst, who had also turned on Roosevelt, was recruited as well. The failure to mount an effective third-party campaign, along with Roosevelt's landslide victory in the 1936 general election, however, sounded the death knell for the league.

See also: election of 1936; Coughlin, Father Charles; Hearst, William Randolph; Smith, Al.

Bibliography

Brinkley, Alan. *Voices of Protest: Huey Long, Father Coughlin, and the Great Depression*. New York: Knopf, 1982.

Mintz, Frank P. *The Liberty Lobby and the American Right: Race, Conspiracy, and Culture*. Westport, CT: Greenwood Press, 1985.

LIFE

The most influential photography-based mass circulation magazine in American history, *Life* hit the newsstands for the first time on November 23, 1936, with a cover photograph of the Fort Peck dam by Margaret Bourke-White and inside, a photo of a newborn baby captioned, in a double entendre, "Life Begins."

Life magazine was the brainchild of Henry Luce, who had introduced the successful newsweekly, *Time* in 1923 and the business magazine *Fortune* in 1931. The inspiration for the new weekly magazine was the increasingly popular newsreels of the cinema and European photography magazines like the French *Vu* and the English *Illustrated London News*.

To launch the magazine, Luce assembled a team of some of the best photographers in America. Besides Bourke-White, these included Alfred Eisenstaedt, Robert Capa, and Peter Stackpole. Their goal was to capture American life in all its diversity and present it in bold, stylistically innovative photography.

Sometimes, that boldness got the magazine into trouble. An April 1938 issue featuring scenes from an educational film entitled *Birth of a Baby* was banned in many areas because of its explicit depiction of a mother in labor. After protests by a number of public figures—including First Lady Eleanor Roosevelt—obscenity charges were dropped.

Despite—or, more likely, because of—such controversy, the magazine was an immediate popular success. It quickly sold out its first run of 250,000 copies and, within a year, was typically selling a million copies per issue. At its peak in the 1950s, it was selling over 8 million copies.

By the early 1970s, however, the spread of television and a host of specialized market magazines had undermined *Life*'s circulation numbers and it closed down in 1972. It was reissued as a semiannual from 1973 to 1977 and as a monthly from 1979 through the late 1990s, when it was terminated once again.

See also: newspapers and magazines; *Time*; Bourke-White, Margaret; Luce, Henry.

Bibliography

Hamblin, Dora Jane. *That Was the Life*. New York: W. W. Norton, 1977.

Wainwright, Loudon. *The Great American Magazine: An Inside History of Life*. New York: Knopf, 1986.

LI'L ABNER

L*i'l Abner*, a popular cartoon strip featuring the goings-on in the hillbilly community of Dogpatch—was introduced to the newspaper-reading public in 1934 and became an immediate success. By the end of the decade it was printed in hundreds of newspapers.

Created by cartoonist Al Capp and syndicated by United Features Syndicate, *Li'l Abner* starred Abner Yokum, a rather dense and naive hillbilly who lived with his Mammy in a log cabin and who, despite his name, was not li'l (little) but large in stature. Many of the cartoons featured the romantically challenged Abner who was chased down by the buxom, half-undressed Daisy Mae.

Indeed, in the late 1930s, Capp introduced the idea of Sadie Hawkins Day, when Daisy Mae and other single women were given the opportunity to initiate romances with the obtuse bachelors of the community. A woman who caught her man had the right to drag him to a preacher and marry him. The idea, modified to a dance party, caught on with high schools and colleges and has been an annual event on many campuses ever since.

Aside from romance, *Li'l Abner* also featured commentary on public events of the day, with characters who personified greedy businessmen and fast-talking politicians, among others. There were also constant references to events in the popular culture of the time.

Though the strip was enormously successful from the 1930s through the 1950s, its hillbilly milieu began to feel increasingly dated in the 1960s, and *Li'l Abner* ceased publication in 1977, two years before the death of Capp himself.

See also: newspapers and magazines.

Bibliography

Berger, Arthur Asa. *Li'l Abner: A Study in American Satire*. New York: Twayne, 1969.

Capp, Al. *The Best of Li'l Abner*. New York: Holt, Rinehart, and Winston, 1978.

LINDBERGH KIDNAPPING

C*alled* the "crime of the century," the Lindbergh baby kidnapping case was watched by the whole world in the early 1930s. The kidnapping and resulting trial shocked the nation and led to changes in kidnapping laws.

Charles A. Lindbergh, a celebrated American aviator and engineer, was the first person to make a nonstop solo flight across the Atlantic Ocean from New York to Paris in 1927. His achievement won the admiration and acclaim of the world, and he was hailed as a hero in Europe and the United States.

THE KIDNAPPING

On March 1, 1932, Charles and Anne Lindbergh were staying at Hopewell, New Jersey, in their new home that was under construction. At approximately 10:00 P.M. Charles A. Lindbergh Jr.'s nursemaid, Betty Gow, entered the nursery to make sure he was sleeping peacefully, but the baby was missing. After confirming that no one else in the house had the baby, the Lindberghs called the New Jersey State Police.

Colonel H. Norman Schwarzkopf, the chief of the New Jersey State Police, took charge of the investigation. At the Lindbergh home, the police discovered four pieces of key physical evidence: a white envelope containing a ransom note found in the nursery; a broken, homemade extension ladder found about seventy-five feet from the Lindbergh estate; a footprint left in the soft dirt underneath the nursery window; and a three-quarter-inch chisel also found underneath the nursery window. The footprint lost most of its value as evidence because no plaster casting was taken of it. The police estimated that it was a size nine footprint.

The ransom note bore no fingerprints. It did contain a "signature" that consisted of two interlocking circles both slightly bigger than a quarter. In the oval form where the circles overlapped, was a solid red mark the size of a nickel. Three small holes had been punched through the logo. One was in the center of the red mark, and the other two were in line with it, just outside the larger circles. This signature appeared on all the notes that the kidnappers sent.

Letters expressing public support, sympathy, and many leads poured in. Many of these leads turned out to be hoaxes. Dr. John F. Condon, a retired Bronx educator, volunteered his help by putting a notice in the *Bronx Home News* seeking contact with the kidnapper. In reply, he received notes declaring that the child was safe and demanding $70,000. The sleeping suit that the baby had been wearing on the night of March 1 was delivered to Dr. Condon as proof. On April 2, at a meeting in a Bronx cemetery, Dr. Condon, accompanied by Lindbergh, gave a box of marked bills, U.S. gold certificates, to a shadowy figure with a reputedly German accent.

Lindbergh's baby was found dead on May 12, 1932, by a truck driver. The child had been buried a mile from Hopewell and approximately four and one-half miles from the Lindbergh home. An autopsy found that death had occurred two or three months previously and was the result of a fractured skull.

THE TRIAL

Two and a half years of frustrating investigations and rumors passed before the first real clues led to the arrest of Bruno Richard Hauptmann, a Bronx carpenter who had no regular job but who seemed to be living better than most people were in the middle of the Depression. In 1932, Hauptmann retired from carpentry and became an investor in the stock market. In Sep-

tember 1934, some of the marked ransom bills began showing up in the New York area. One had been used to buy gasoline at a service station whose owner, thinking it might be a counterfeit, wrote the car's license number on the bill. The license turned out to be Hauptmann's.

When questioned, Hauptmann denied knowing anything about the Lindbergh kidnapping or the ransom money. But when the police searched his garage, they discovered a box full of the money, totaling $14,600. Hauptmann's explanation for this money was that Isidor Fisch, an old business partner, had left the box in Hauptmann's possession when Fisch had gone back to Germany in 1933. Not knowing that money was inside, Hauptmann had placed the box in his broom closet. It remained there until one day Hauptmann accidentally bumped the shelf with a broom and the box was opened. Since Fisch owed him $7,000, Hauptmann felt privileged to spend some of the money. As for the chisel, no fingerprints were recovered from it, but it was later used against Hauptmann in the trial because of the absence of a three-quarter-inch chisel in Hauptmann's toolbox. Additionally, authorities found Condon's address and telephone number written on the door trim inside Hauptmann's son's closet. These pieces of evidence led to Hauptmann being charged with the kidnapping and murder of the Lindbergh baby. From the beginning, the press labeled Hauptmann as guilty.

On the witness stand, Hauptmann denied any involvement in the kidnapping, insisting that he had made money in the stock market and that Fisch had left the bills at his house. But the jury found the Lindbergh money to be one of the most compelling pieces of evidence produced by prosecutor David Wilentz. They also believed handwriting experts who said the ransom notes matched Hauptmann's handwriting. Woodwork and forestry experts said North Carolina pine from a lumberyard near Hauptmann's home, and a board cut from his floor, were used in the kidnapping ladder. Rounding out Wilentz's case were eyewitnesses who placed Hauptmann near the Lindbergh estate on the day of the crime.

Defense counsel Edward Reilly was hired by the Hearst newspapers to add some color to a trial whose outcome appeared to be a foregone conclusion. Reilly ridiculed the evidence against Hauptmann and implied that the true culprits could have been the Lindberghs' servants, gangsters, Hauptmann's friend Fisch, or Dr. Condon. He attacked the police as inept and accused them of planting evidence and botching the investigation.

Prosecutor Wilentz in his five-hour summation urged the jurors not to bring a recommendation of mercy. Their choice was to acquit "this animal, this Public Enemy Number One of the World" or find him guilty of murder in the first degree.

The presiding justice, Thomas Trenchard, reviewed the evidence and charged the jury, giving them detailed instructions. Some observers had speculated that the Lindbergh child died when accidentally dropped from the ladder. But the jury was warned that even an accidental death, during commission of a burglary, meant "felony murder" and the death penalty. The jury of eight men and four women took eleven hours to reach a unanimous verdict of guilty. Despite appeals, despite stays of execution by New Jersey governor Harold Hoffman, Bruno Richard Hauptmann, refusing to confess, went to the electric chair at Trenton State Prison on April 3, 1936.

AFTERMATH

The Lindbergh baby kidnapping case has been a subject of interest for many years, since many doubts exist as to the guilt of Bruno Hauptmann. Most scholars, however, believe that Hauptmann was guilty or at least in-

volved in the kidnapping, extortion, or both. Kidnapping became a federal crime by a congressional act known as "the Lindbergh Law."

The media attention surrounding the trial was excessive even by today's trial standards. Newspapers ran thousands of articles and photos, often filling several pages with trial coverage. The conclusion of the trial did not end the press's pursuit of the Lindbergh family. After the trial, the Lindberghs' wanted to build a new life with peace and safety for their newborn son, Jon. The Lindberghs' moved to England, where they lived for about two years. With the growing threat of war, they returned to the United States. However, Charles A. Lindbergh's controversial stance against American entry into World War II led to criticism among many of his countrymen.

ELIZABETH KEANE

See also: Crime; Hoover, J. Edgar; Lindbergh, Charles A.

Bibliography

Berg, A. Scott. *Lindbergh.* New York: Berkley, 1998.

Davis, Kenneth S. *The Hero.* London: Longmans, 1959.

Kennedy, Ludovic. *The Airman and the Carpenter: The Lindbergh Kidnapping and the Framing of Richard Hauptmann.* New York: Viking, 1985.

LITERATURE

The Great Depression had a profound effect on American citizens and American writers. The widespread poverty and depression provided writers with a wealth of topics and emotions. It also served as a turning point, or an epiphany of sorts, for many writers who spent the 1920s in other countries, isolating themselves from America and enjoying the decadent, carefree lifestyle the twenties created. With the stock market crash of 1929 and the ensuing financial and cultural changes, many writers returned to American soil and shifted their writing style to focus on this new world of the Great Depression.

Another change brought about by the Depression occurred in American libraries. As money became scarce during the Depression, more Americans began using the libraries as a way to enjoy themselves. Library circulation

increased 40 percent from 1929 to 1933. Owning books was a luxury many Americans could not afford, and libraries proved to be a feasible solution to this problem. This increased interest in libraries caused a marked decrease in book sales. From 1929 to 1933, overall book sales in the United States dropped by nearly half. This decrease helped spawn many changes in the publishing industry, including the increased popularity of mail order book clubs. Also, hardcover sales of reprints of previous best-sellers increased. The element of the market that suffered the greatest during this time was new authors. They had a more difficult time than ever attempting to be published and then selling their work.

Despite waning book sales and nationwide poverty, some of America's most recognized writers were working during the 1930s. Some of the century's greatest works, both in fiction and nonfiction, were written and published during the decade. The fiction best-seller lists were filled with both "high" literature and popular fiction works.

WILLIAM FAULKNER

In the fiction market, writers such as William Faulkner, John Steinbeck, Ernest Hemingway, John Dos Passos, Thomas Wolfe, James T. Farrell, and Pearl S. Buck were turning out works. Faulkner experienced a creative boom during this era, writing his acclaimed Yoknapatawpha saga, including *Sartoris* (1929), *The Sound and the Fury* (1929), *As I Lay Dying* (1930), *Sanctuary* (1931), *Light in August* (1932), *Absalom, Absalom* (1936), and the collection of stories *The Unvanquished* (1938). He also wrote two other novels during this time, *Pylon* (1935) and *The Wild Palms* (1939); and two volumes of stories, *These Thirteen* (1931) and *Dr. Martino* (1934). This incredible output of work embodied many of the ideals and themes that were popular during the Great Depression. Faulkner specialized in criticism of the industrial society (a theme that would be found in a majority of novels during the 1930s). He also focused on the individual person's isolation in his novels. Faulkner was considered one of the most prevalent writers from the South, and his works still stand today as literature. Readers reacted and still react strongly to his works since he was fond of creating grotesque characters and experimenting freely with the medium of writing. He was regarded as an undisciplined but prolific writer, not only a voice of the South, but a voice of the Depression, though not so much as John Steinbeck would prove to be.

JOHN STEINBECK

John Steinbeck is best known as the author of the most recognized novel of the American's plight during the Great Depression. *The Grapes of Wrath* (1939) was and is still considered *the* novel of the Great Depression. Steinbeck wrote many great novels, but *The Grapes of Wrath* was the one that made him a respected author. Four other works of Steinbeck's were published during the 1930s, including *Pastures of Heaven* (1932), *Tortilla Flats* (1935), *In Dubious Battle* (1936), and *Of Mice and Men* (1937), Steinbeck's success perhaps, lies in his connection with the average American or, even more, with the plight of the poor American. His first best-seller, *Of Mice and Men* (1937), dealt with average

Americans' desires similar to those of many Americans during the Great Depression. Steinbeck's protagonists wanted only enough food to eat and a place to sleep. As many Americans lost their incomes, jobs, and homes, these basic requirements became the desires of a nation. Steinbeck recognized this and made his works connect to the readers with this understanding. Following the financial and critical success of *Of Mice and Men*, Steinbeck was poised to capture the market with *The Grapes of Wrath*. It was wildly successful, selling more than 300,000 copies in 1939 and continuing as a best-seller into 1940. Readers connected with the Joad family more than with any other novel's characters of the 1930s. This book was not without its detractors, as some critics claimed it to be no more than a social tract and not a literary work. Still, even the occasional criticism of the novel could not lessen its popularity. Although Steinbeck did not write nearly as much as Faulkner during this period, his work marked him as the voice of the common man during the Depression.

ERNEST HEMINGWAY

Ernest Hemingway spent the 1920s isolated in Europe, writing, drinking, and passing the time with friends. He felt that a writer has to isolate himself from his homeland in order to more clearly observe himself and his writing subjects and to write better. Isolation to him meant being not a hermit, but a stranger in a strange land, adapting to a new culture. But the crash of 1929 changed his views. As the world began to feel the effects of the Depression, Hemingway, like many writers, was forced to realize that isolation was a thing of the past and that ignoring the world's social problems was wrong. Hemingway ended his self-imposed isolation, returned to the United States, and began writing about common men and common problems. His output was not high, nor were his works of this time considered his greatest, but his voice and his change in style and belief had a lasting effect on the literary world. Hemingway published only one novel during the 1930s, *To Have and Have Not* (1937), two nonfiction works, *Death in the Afternoon* (1932) and *The Green Hills of Africa* (1935), and some short works of fiction. He flanked the decade with two of his most famous works, *A Farewell to Arms* (1929) and *For Whom the Bell Tolls* (1940). He was considered one of the last writers of the lost generation syndrome, a forefather of sorts for disillusioned, critical writers to come. This is not to say that Hemingway was bitter or a writer controlled by feeling. He was an observer with a sharp eye for detail and a cynical outlook on life. It was this style that was considered Hemingway's strongest tool for other writers. He struggled to achieve a mastery of words and language, and his simplicity, though often admired and mimicked, is rarely duplicated with any success. This deceivingly simple style became increasingly popular during the 1930s. Most writers, especially new writers, were looking to write simply, yet strongly, like Hemingway. His change of opinions, from isolationist to social observer and commentator of sorts, was a profoundly important change. His style and strength as a writer were his great contributions to the literary world during the Great Depression.

JOHN DOS PASSOS

John Dos Passos has often been considered the writer that bridged authors from the 1920s to the 1930s. Like Hemingway, Dos Passos had to learn how to shift the focus from the individual to society. This was a common shift during the Depression, as writers emphasized the effect of society on an individual, or, more to the point, how society, especially industrialized society, frequently failed the individual in a variety of ways. Dos Passos focused specifically on society's failure to create a healthy environment in which the individual can develop. His trilogy, *U.S.A.* (1937), created a bleak picture of modern industrial society in America. These three novels were originally published as *The 42nd Parallel* (1930), *1919* (1932), and *The Big Money* (1936). He also wrote *The Ground We Stand On* (1941). Dos Passos was an innovative writer with his *U.S.A.* trilogy. He used "Newsreels," "Camera Eye," and "Biographies" to create an omniscient narrator and to slowly show the separation of individual from society and reality. Society appeared bleak, hopeless, and without true direction or compassion. Dos Passos also attacked capitalism and berated the hollowness of the ideal of success in America. Each novel in the series is more bleak, yet superior to its predecessor. *U.S.A.* is considered a landmark series among social novels and is still widely read today.

THOMAS WOLFE

One writer whose style stands out in the 1930s was Thomas Wolfe. His verbose, prosaic writing style was in direct contrast to the pared down, stark style of Hemingway and Steinbeck. Wolfe wrote four lengthy books before his death in 1938. The works contain over 1 million words and are considered to be somewhat autobiographical. *Look Homeward, Angel* (1929), *Of Time and the River* (1935), *The Web and the Rock* (1939), and *You Can't Go Home Again* (1940) are considered to be one work, much like Dos Passos's *U.S.A.* The latter two novels were published after Wolfe's death, but still sold well. Wolfe was considered the voice of the younger generation, and his style of language was out of fashion in a time when simplicity and spareness of language were the norm. His novels relied on emotion and lyricism as opposed to artistic strength and consistency, as many critics noted, but this criticism did not faze Wolfe. He staunchly supported his use of language and his immersion in emotion and detail. His novels are still read today.

JAMES T. FARRELL

James T. Farrell's most famous work, *Studs Lonigan: A Trilogy* (1935) was a lengthy work like Wolfe's, but a social piece like Dos Passos's. It is, in fact, a trilogy of novels: *Young Lonigan* (1932), *The Young Manhood of Studs Lonigan* (1934), and *Judgment Day* (1935). *Studs Lonigan* was considered classic Depression literature. The story dealt with corruption in the Irish-Catholic section of Chicago, but its broader theme was how society failed the individual, most notably, young men. The collection reiterated, through the protagonist, Studs, that industrialized society did not care for or nurture its people and, in fact, debased them. This novel is often compared to Theodore Dreiser's *An American Tragedy*. Farrell also wrote two other novels during the Great Depression, *A World I Never Made* (1936) and *No Star Is Lost* (1938), but neither achieved the success or acclaim of *Studs Lonigan*. In fact, Farrell soon lost many readers, as his subject matter and writing style never left South Side Chicago and this lack of variation and experimentation and a heavy hand with word usage proved tedious to many readers. Even so, *Studs Lonigan* is still considered an important paean to Depression-era literature.

PEARL S. BUCK

In 1938, Pearl S. Buck won the Nobel Prize (for literature) for her novel *The Good Earth* (1931). The story revolved around the plight of a Chinese family fighting flood, drought, and economic deprivation. The novel's success is usually attributed to two factors: the reader's interest in foreign locales and the common struggles the family faced, similar to those many Americans faced during the Great Depression. So it was both escapist literature and social commentary.

OTHER WRITERS

A great number of new authors emerged during the Depression; even under the shadow of literary giants like Faulkner and Steinbeck, and despite waning book sales, some budding writers managed to endure and triumph over the Great Depression's effect on the publishing industry. Under Hemingway's influence, a number of writers adopted his hard, sharp writing style, including John O'Hara, James M. Cain, and Jerome Weidman. O'Hara wrote *Appointment in Samarra* (1934) and *Butterfield 8* (1935); the former was a scathing, passionate novel about the country club culture. James M. Cain's *The Postman Always Rings Twice* (1934) and *Serenade* (1937) were bitter, brutal novels, the first dealing with adultery and crime. Jerome Weidman's *I Can Get It for You Wholesale* (1937) and its sequel *What's in It for Me* (1938) focus on corruption in the New York clothing industry. Erskine Caldwell, another scholar of the Hemingway and O'Hara style, wrote *God's Little Acre* (1933) and *Tobacco Road* (1932), another bleak, searing piece of Great Depression literature. Caldwell's *God's Little Acre* not only made his career; it also marked the start of a new trend in the publishing industry, pushing the envelope in regard to censorship. It was a novel that turned toward sensuality and also railed against an industrial, capitalist society. There were also books by young writers influenced by a more proletarian style, such as Thomas Bell's *All Brides Are Beautiful* (1936), Robert Cantwell's *Land of Plenty* (1934), and Leane Zugsmith's *A Time to Remember* (1936). Richard Wright wrote his famous work on racial violence and tension, *Native Son* (1940) and *Uncle Tom's Children* (1936). Marjorie Kinnan Rawlings published two novels, *South Moon Under* (1933) and *The Yearling* (1938), which, like Faulkner's works, dealt with Southerners, but Rawlings's books portrayed the people of backwoods Florida. Horace McCoy's *They Shoot Horses, Don't They?* (1935) was set at a marathon dance contest and still has a strong following to this day as a satirical and existential work. John Marquand started his career as a serious novelist after years as a writer for magazines with *The Late George Apley* (1937) and *Wickford Point* (1939). Katherine Anne Porter published two successful collections of stories during the 1930s, *Flowering Judas* (1930) and *Pale Horse, Pale Rider* (1939). Another novelist who experienced success

during the 1930s with short story collections was William Saroyan, who wrote *The Daring Young Man on the Flying Trapeze* (1934), *Inhale, Exhale* (1936), *Love, Here Is My Hat* (1938), and *The Trouble with Tigers* (1938). The Great Depression saw many other budding writers emerge, including Conrad Richter, Jesse Stuart, and James Gould Cozzens. A number of other established writers also continued to publish during the 1930s, such as Robert Nathan, Stephen Vincent Benet, Thornton Wilder, Sinclair Lewis, Ellen Glasgow, and Elizabeth Madox Roberts.

The best-seller lists for fiction were not only filled with social novels that were considered literature; there was also a fair amount of pulp fiction that captivated readers. Historical romances flourished, including such works as Kenneth Roberts's *Northwest Passage* (1937) and *Oliver Wiswell* (1940) and Walter D. Edmonds's *Drums Along the Mohawk* (1936). This decade also saw the publication of one of the most famous historical romances of popular fiction: Margaret Mitchell's *Gone With the Wind*. Another popular work that received strong, if fleeting, praise was Hervey Allen's *Anthony Adverse* (1933). Released in June, it became a summer best-seller. It was a lengthy book set in the Napoleonic age and, although it is not considered a literary work, it is still thought of as a solid piece of popular fiction.

The year 1933 marked a boon for the literary world when Judge John M. Woolsey lifted the censorship plaguing James Joyce's *Ulysses* and American readers were allowed to purchase unabridged copies at $3.50 a copy. *Ulysses* was actually begun in 1914, published in part in the *Little Review* in 1918 and smuggled into the United States for a number of years. The unabridged edition had been banned from the United States for content since publication nearly two decades earlier, but a federal case was not made until 1933, when U.S. Customs seized an unabridged copy of *Ulysses* en route to American publisher Bennet A. Cerf. Chief Assistant U.S. Attorney Samuel C. Coleman fought to keep the unabriged *Ulysses* out of the hands of American citizens because he found it "obscene." Woolsey himself read the book and found it to be fit for American readers. The novel with such a torrid past was finally available in the United States.

ERIN AUSK

See also: *Good Earth, The; Grapes of Wrath, The; Tobacco Road;* Caldwell, Erskine; Dos Passos, John; Faulker, William; Hemingway, Ernest; Steinbeck, John; Document: *United States v. One Book Called "Ulysses", 1993.*

Bibliography

Conn, Peter J. *Pearl S. Buck: A Cultural Biography*. New York: Cambridge University Press, 1996.

Minter, David. *William Faulkner, His Life and Work*. Baltimore: Johns Hopkins University Press, 1980.

Reynolds, Michael S. *Hemingway: The American Homecoming*. Cambridge, MA: Blackwell, 1992.

Steinbeck, Elaine, and Robert Wallsten, eds. *Steinbeck: A Life in Letters*. New York: Viking, 1975.

LITTLE CAESAR

Considered by film historians to be the prototypical gangster film, *Little Caesar* tells the story of Caesar "Rico" Bandello, played by Edward G. Robinson, a ruthless and ambitious mobster whose only goal is to make money and who will stop at nothing to get it, destroying all those who stand in his way.

Released in 1930, as the Depression was just getting under way, the film, directed by Mervyn Le Roy, was an immediate box office and even critical success. By depicting Bandello as a money-grubbing gangster, the movie—say many film scholars—equated criminal activity with business and thereby captured the political mood of Depression-era audiences.

See also: crime; films, feature; Robinson, Edward G.

Bibliography

Baxter, John. *Hollywood in the Thirties*. New York: Barnes, 1968.

Sklar, Robert. *Movie-Made America: A Cultural History of the American Movies*. New York: Random House, 1975.

"LITTLE STEEL"

A term popularly applied to a number of steel firms competing with America's largest steel manufacturer, U.S. Steel, "little steel" included Jones & Laughlin, Bethlehem Steel, Republic Steel, Inland Steel, and other small companies. Unlike U.S. Steel, which agreed to accept the Steel Workers Organizing Committee (SWOC) of the Congress of Industrial Organizations as the union representative for its workers in March 1937, the "little steel" companies refused to negotiate, with the exception of Jones & Laughlin, which recognized SWOC in May.

At first, the leaders of SWOC were reticent about calling a strike against the remaining steel companies, since they feared that union resources—and favorable public opinion—were depleted after months of strike activities in several industries. But the rank and file insisted, and a strike was called in May. Company executives, including Republic Steel head Tom Girdler, hired hundreds of security men and brought in thousands of nonunion workers to break the strike.

On Memorial Day, thousands of workers and their families held a picnic outside Republic Steel's plant on the south side of Chicago. Security guards and local police opened an assault on the picnickers, leaving ten dead and dozens wounded. Over the next few weeks, similarly violent confrontations occurred at a number of "little steel" plants in Ohio, leaving another eight persons dead. With their strike funds depleted, SWOC was able to win a contract only from Inland Steel. Union recognition from the rest of the "little steel" companies would have to wait for 1941 and the upturn of business due to World War II preparation.

See also: Congress of Industrial Organizations; steel industry; Steel Workers Organizing Committee; United States Steel Corporation. Document: *National Labor Relations Board v. Jones & Laughlin Steel Corporation*, 1937.

Bibliography

Bertin, Amy. *Competition and Productivity in the Depression-Era Steel Industry*. Thesis, Harvard University, 1994.

Reutter, Mark. *Sparrows Point: Making Steel, the Rise and Ruin of American Industrial Might*. New York: Summit Books, 1989.

LONE RANGER, THE

One of the most enduring of American western radio serials, *The Lone Ranger* was the brainchild of Detroit radio station owner George W. Trendle, who introduced the Robin Hood-type character in January 1933.

Looking for new and innovative programming for his independent WXYZ station, Trendle assembled a team of radio producers, along with radio writer Fran Striker, to come up with a new type of western hero with a strong moral code. A law student, Earl Graser, was hired to be the voice of the Lone Ranger, and Tonto was played by a Shakespearean actor named John Todd. In 1941, Graser died in a car accident and was replaced by radio announcer Brace Beemer.

Popular in Michigan, the show, named *The Lone Ranger* after its hero, was picked up by stations in Chicago and New York in early 1934. The half-hour show was broadcast three times a week on Monday, Wednesday, and Friday evenings at 6:30.

The Lone Ranger came with his own origin myth. Part of a group of six Texas Rangers gunned down by an outlaw gang, the Lone Ranger was rescued by an Indian boyhood friend named Tonto. The only one to survive—hence, the name—the Lone Ranger wore a mask as a means to secure his identity against any possible retribution by the gang that killed the other rangers. In the first few months of the show, the Lone Ranger also acquired his famous mount, Silver.

Trendle wanted the Lone Ranger to be a role model for his juvenile audience, and so he never drank, smoked, gambled, or used bad language during his various adventures rescuing the innocent and chasing down the guilty.

In 1937, *The Lone Ranger* made the transition from radio to film, with Clayton Moore in the title role and Jay Silverheels as Tonto. The fifteen-part radio series of that year was followed by another in 1939. Later films based on the series appeared in the 1950s and 1980s, although the producers of the latter garnered bad publicity when they refused to let Moore who was not the star of the movie, don the Lone Ranger mask in public; they said he was too old and fat and would ruin the image of the character for younger audiences. *The Lone Ranger* also became a popular TV series, beginning in 1949 and lasting until 1957.

See also: films, feature; radio.

Bibliography

Moore, Clayton, and Frank Thompson. *I Was That Masked Man.* Dallas: Taylor Publishing, 1996.

Van Hise, James. *Who Was That Masked Man? The Story of the Lone Ranger.* Las Vegas: Pioneer Books, 1990.

LYNCHING

Lynching—the extrajudicial murder of persons suspected of crimes—remained a prominent problem in America in the 1930s, even if the numbers of persons lynched during the Great Depression fell off dramatically from the highs recorded in the period between the 1890s and the 1920s. As in previous decades, the vast majority of lynching victims were black males living in the South.

The number of lynchings during the 1930s ranged from a high of twenty-eight in 1933 to a low of eight in 1937, part of a continuing downward trend that had begun in the early 1920s. (For comparison, the most lynchings in any year in U.S. history was 230 in 1892.) In 1933, the Commission on Interracial Cooperation sponsored a Southern Commission on the Study of Lynching, which published a report called *The Tragedy of Lynching.*

The report noted that most lynching victims were accused of crimes such as murder and rape (particularly of white women), but that "causes" might include

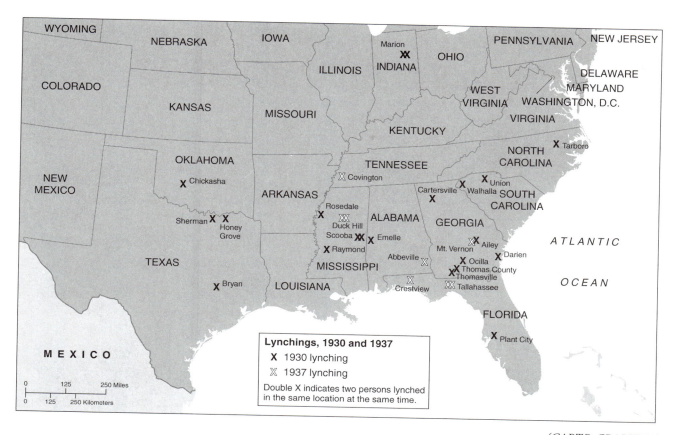

Lynchings, 1930 and 1937
X 1930 lynching
X 1937 lynching
Double X indicates two persons lynched in the same location at the same time.

(CARTO-GRAPHICS)

"crimes" as innocuous as "insults to whites." Lynchings, the report found, often involved torture and mutilation of the corpse.

In 1934, the National Association for the Advancement of Colored People, the nation's oldest and largest civil rights organization, used the report to urge passage of an antilynching bill in Congress, sponsored by Senator Joseph Costigan (D-CO). The bill would have made lynching a federal crime if state and local officials failed to act within thirty days. Like similar bills discussed in 1935, 1936, and 1937, the Costigan legislation never made it out of committee. A 1938 bill, sponsored by Costigan and New York Senator Robert Wagner (D-NY), was killed in a six-week filibuster by southern senators.

While President Franklin D. Roosevelt was on rec- ord deploring lynchings—and his wife Eleanor was an outspoken antiracist advocate—the president made no effort to push the legislation through, fearing that a too aggressive approach might alienate southern Democrats in Congress and thereby jeopardize New Deal legislation.

See also: African Americans; National Association for the Advancement of Colored People; Scottsboro case; Wagner, Robert.

Bibliography

Raper, Arthur Franklin. *The Tragedy of Lynching.* Westport, CT: Greenwood, 1933. Reprint, New York: Dover, 1970.

Zangrando, Robert L. *The NAACP Crusade Against Lynching, 1909–1950.* Philadelphia: Temple University Press, 1980.

MARCH ON WASHINGTON MOVEMENT

The March on Washington Movement (MOWM) was an organization, created by Brotherhood of Sleeping Car Porters president A. Philip Randolph, that planned to host a massive demonstration in Washington in 1941 to demand racial equality in defense industry hiring.

The march, which also called for the desegregation of the armed forces, was the first planned mass demonstration in African-American history. It showed, said black activist and scholar Ralph Bunche, a supporter of the march, that blacks were ready to take control of their own political destiny, rather than accept New Deal handouts from whites.

Ultimately, the march was called off after President Franklin D. Roosevelt met with Randolph and agreed to issue Executive Order 8802, establishing a Fair Employment Practices Committee (FEPC) to look into charges of racism in the defense industries. While the FEPC proved less than effective, the MOWM was an inspiration for the massive 1963 pro–civil rights March on Washington.

See also: African Americans; Brotherhood of Sleeping Car Porters; Randolph, A. Philip.

The 1941 March on Washington Movement, which aimed to desegregate the military and end discrimination in the nation's defense industries, earned some of its money through the sale of books and pamphlets. *(Library of Congress)*

Bibliography

Garfinkel, Herbert. *When Negroes March: The March on Washington Movement in the Organizational Politics for FEPC.* New York: Atheneum, 1959.

Pfeffer, Paula. *A. Philip Randolph: Pioneer of the Civil Rights Movement.* Baton Rouge: Louisiana State University Press, 1990.

MEMORIAL DAY MASSACRE

The Memorial Day massacre refers to the shooting of dozens of laborers and their families who had peacefully assembled outside the Republic Steel plant in South Chicago on the Memorial Day holiday in 1937. Ten demonstrators were killed by police during the attack and dozens more wounded.

The massacre occurred during a period of heightened labor tensions in the steel industry. To take advantage of the National Labor Relations Act—legislation that encouraged union activities—a number of labor groups had begun to organize the steel industry. Among these groups was the Steel Workers Organizing Committee (SWOC) within the Congress of Industrial Organizations.

In March 1937, SWOC won union recognition by the nation's largest steel company, the U.S. Steel Corporation. But a number of smaller companies—known popularly as "little steel" and including Republic—failed to accept this arrangement. When labor protesters organized a Memorial Day picnic at the South Chicago Republic plant, both company security guards and local police opened fire. Further violence at other "little steel" plants around the Midwest ended in the deaths of eight more workers.

See also: Congress of Industrial Organizations; "little steel"; National Labor Relations Act; steel industry; Steel Workers Organizing Committee. Document: National Labor Relations Act, July 5, 1935.

Bibliography

Bertin, Amy. *Competition and Productivity in the Depression-Era Steel Industry.* Thesis, Harvard University, 1994.

Cohen, Lizabeth. *Making a New Deal: Industrial Workers in Chicago.* New York: Cambridge University Press, 1990.

MERCURY THEATRE

Although in existence for a short three years from 1937 to 1940, the Mercury Theatre was one of the most influential theatrical companies of the 1930s and, indeed, in all of American theater history.

It was formed as an act of protest after actor John Houseman and director Orson Welles had their Federal Theater Project production of Marc Blitzstein's radical, pro-labor play *The Cradle Will Rock* postponed because of conservative protest in Congress and elsewhere. Rather than giving up on the drama, Houseman and Welles formed the Mercury Theatre and produced the play. So successful was the production that the Mercury continued putting on plays, becoming famous for its innovative and flamboyant stagings. Its production of Shakespeare's *Julius Caesar* in modern garb—with strong references to dictators Benito Mussolini of Italy and Adolf Hitler of Germany—was critically acclaimed. Other famed productions of the Mercury Theatre included George Bernard Shaw's *Heartbreak House* and the company's last staging, Richard Wright and Paul Green's adaptation of Wright's novel about black life in the South, *Native Son.* The Mercury Theatre also broadcast productions for the radio.

See also: radio; Federal Theater Project; Blitzstein, Marc; Welles, Orson; Wright, Richard.

Bibliography

Thomson, David. *Rosebud: The Story of Orson Welles.* New York: Knopf, 1996.

Welles, Orson. *Orson Welles on Shakespeare: The W.P.A. and Mercury Theatre Playscripts.* ed. Richard France. Westport, CT: Greenwood Press, 1990.

METRO-GOLDWYN-MAYER

The most successful Hollywood film studio of the 1930s, Metro-Goldwyn-Mayer—better known by its initials MGM—was crucial in the development of the so-called studio system, whereby major studios held the most popular stars under exclusive contract. And with its motto "More Stars Than There Are in the Heavens," MGM had more top personalities under contract than any other studio in Hollywood.

MGM was founded in 1924 by theater chain owner Marcus Loewe by combining Goldwyn Pictures Corporation—once owned by Samuel Goldwyn—and Louis B. Mayer Pictures and Metro Pictures Corporation—both owned by Louis B. Mayer—into a single subsidiary of Loewe's Incorporated.

MGM, with its identifying corporate mascot Leo, roaring at the beginning of each picture the studio made, changed the way Hollywood operated. In the 1920s, stars who operated independently of studios dominated. But from the very beginning, MGM placed its stars under contract and by the early 1930s had developed the most impressive roster in Hollywood, including Joan Crawford, Clark Gable, Greta Garbo, William Powell, and Spencer Tracy.

Under the leadership of Irving Thalberg, MGM developed its signature style of fancy costumes, elaborate sets, and glossy cinematography. Among the films produced during the 1930s by MGM were *Anna Christie* (1930), *Dinner at Eight* (1933), *The Thin Man* (1934), *The Great Ziegfeld* (1936), *The Good Earth* (1937), and *Goodbye Mr. Chips* (1939).

MGM continues to be a major studio in Hollywood, although its ownership has changed hands somewhat and the company has branched out into other forms of entertainment, most notably Las Vegas gambling.

See also: films, feature; *Good Earth, The*; Gable, Clark; Garbo, Greta; Goldwyn, Samuel; Mayer, Louis B.; Powell, William; Tracy, Spencer.

Bibliography

Eames, John Douglas. *The MGM Story*. New York: Crown Publishers, 1976.

Hay, Peter. *MGM: When the Lion Roars*. Atlanta: Turner Publishing, 1991.

MINING

Mining, especially coal mining, was considered a "sick" industry before the Great Depression. During the 1920s, 70 percent of the nation's supply of bituminous (soft) coal as opposed to anthracite, or hard, coal, was produced by four states: West Virginia, Pennsylvania, Illinois, and Kentucky. Illinois differed from the three Appalachian states not only by geography, but also by its higher number of mechanized mines and stronger United Mine Workers' presence. Still, mining regions shared common problems. Coal production had fallen throughout the 1920s. In 1927, bituminous coal production was 60 million tons less than in 1920. During the same period, the number of miners dropped from 700,000 to 575,000. Wages declined as mine operators shifted production from unionized northern mines to nonunionized southern mines. Mining was also inconsistent: periodic coal surpluses brought halts in production and mine closings.

These, in turn, brought unemployment or reduced wages to miners.

Bituminous coal mining was unstable during the 1920s. The industry was dominated by numerous small companies locked in tight competition. To stabilize the volatile industry, mine owners turned to local and state governments, often seeking special legislation. In 1924, under the leadership of Secretary of Commerce Herbert Hoover, the United Mine Workers and the coal industry struck a deal intended to bring order to the industry by setting wage and production levels. The deal, known as the Jacksonville agreement, collapsed under regional competition and failed to solve the problems facing the industry. As business leaders saw it, their problems grew from glutted markets, declining profits, and wage cuts.

The Great Depression compounded the problems of the mining industry. By depressing the demand for consumer goods, inhibiting construction, and reducing railroad transportation, it further decreased the demand for coal. As the industry collapsed, miners suffered. Many miners were unemployed or working part-time; by 1932, the average pay for coal miners reached fifty cents an hour. Some families left the mines to seek employment elsewhere, an often futile effort given the scope of the economic crisis. Families in some communities compensated for reduced wages by growing more food in garden plots and by sharing resources. Many miners pursued a course different from that of most other workers during the early years of the Depression: They went on strike. The number of coal strikes soared with the Depression. In 1930, 46,877 miners participated in strikes: in 1931, this number mushroomed to 113,808. Although the number of strikers dropped slightly in 1932, the amount of work time lost to strikes in the coal industry continued to increase.

As the Depression deepened, business and labor leaders sought solutions. Business leaders blamed excessive competition for undermining profits. Led by the National Association of Manufacturers, the extractive industries sought to form economic cartels modeled after those in Europe. Business leaders first turned to the individual states for legal reforms but found working with each state cumbersome and ineffective; they next turned to the national government. As president, Herbert Hoover continued to encourage voluntary cooperation, a course he had pursued as secretary of commerce. These efforts fell apart under the pressure of the economic collapse.

THE NEW DEAL AND THE NIRA

Franklin D. Roosevelt's 1932 election as president marked an important turning point for the mining industry. In some ways, Roosevelt's early New Deal policies resembled Hoover's policies, with the emphasis on business-government cooperation and the desire to reduce competition in order to increase prices, profits, and wages for workers. These policies were embodied in the National Industrial Recovery Act (NIRA), which created the National Recovery Administration (NRA). Industry and labor leaders hailed the act as a way out of the economic troubles that had plagued the industry for over a decade.

At the heart of the NIRA were industrial codes written by committees composed of representatives from business, labor, and government. NIRA codes essentially eliminated competition and established minimum prices. The initial codes tended to favor business, in part because business interests dominated the process of code writing. One observer described the early process as a "bargain between business leaders on the one hand and businessmen in the guise of government officials on the other."

While NIRA codes were written for almost every industry, mining held a special position as an extractive industry. NIRA codes governing extractive industries contained authority for direct price fixing. Mining codes contained these exceptional provisions because of the belief among some reformers that coal should be treated like a public utility, the concerns of environmentalists, and the feeling that mining as a sick industry needed additional protection from the forces of competition. The codes helped to increase prices and granted some relief for the industry. Farmers and consumers hurt by the increased cost of coal objected to the codes, arguing that they allowed industrialists to fix prices and form cartels—thus harming the average person. Also, NIRA codes were generally criticized for favoring big business over small economic concerns. In 1935, Congress passed the Guffey-Snyder Coal Stabilization Act to address problems of the bituminous coal industry. The act guaranteed the miners' right to organize and bargain collectively, mandated minimum wages and maximum hours, and created a federal commission to fix prices and allocate production. Although industry leaders had lobbied for the legislation, noncompliance with the codes was widespread. The government responded by tightening control over the mining industry—unlike its response to similar acts of noncompliance in other industries.

Industrial leaders had welcomed the NIRA and its codes, but they adamantly opposed the act's Section 7, which allowed labor representatives at the bargaining table and recognized the right of workers to unionize. Although the Supreme Court declared the NIRA unconstitutional in May 1935, Section 7 and its successor, the Wagner Act, dramatically changed mining by speeding the rise of industrial unionism. Like most other industries, however, the coal industry experienced prosperity only with the economic revival that accompanied World War II.

PHILLIP PAYNE

See also: United Mine Workers; National Industrial Recovery Act; Section 7; Hoover, Herbert; Lewis, John L.; Documents: National Industrial Recovery Act, June 16, 1933.

Bibliography

Shifflett, Crandall A. *Coal Towns: Life, Work and Culture in Company Towns of Southern Appalachia, 1880–1906*. The Knoxville: The University of Tennessee Press, 1991.

Dubofsky, Melvin and Warren Van Tyne. *John L. Lewis: A Biography*. New York: Quadrangle/New York Times Book Co. 1977.

Hawley, Ellis W. *The New Deal and the Problem of Monopoly*. New York: Fordham University Press, 1995.

MOTION PICTURE PRODUCTION CODE/ PRODUCTION CODE ADMINISTRATION

The Motion Picture Production Code was written in 1930, under pressure from Catholic church officials and others who believed that Hollywood films had become too sexually explicit. However, it was not implemented until 1934 in response to pressure from the newly formed Legion of Decency and public protest over the sexual and violent nature of some sound films.

The code, written by an influential Catholic layman and film trade publisher named Martin Quigley, applied a rigorous set of standards to make sure that movies adhered to what the church considered a morally righteous plot, in which sin was punished and virtue rewarded by film's end. Assisting Quigley with the codes authorship was a Jesuit priest and St. Louis University professor named Daniel A. Lord.

Will Hays, a former Republican National Committee chairman and Presbyterian elder who headed the Motion Picture Producers and Distributors Association, popularly known as the Hays office, immediately approved the code. However, the studios largely chose to ignore the code during the early 1930s, which resulted in the founding of the Legion of Decency, a new Catholic protest organization aimed at curbing what it saw to be the immoral excesses of Hollywood movies. This new anti-Hollywood campaign led to the even more restrictive Production Code Administration of 1934. Codes were replaced in the 1960s with the rating system.

See also: films, feature; Legion of Decency; Hays, Will.

Bibliography

Baxter, John. *Hollywood in the Thirties*. New York: Barnes, 1968.

Sklar, Robert. *Movie-Made America: A Cultural History of the American Movies*. New York: Random House, 1975.

MR. SMITH GOES TO WASHINGTON

Mr. Smith Goes to Washington (1939) is considered by many film critics to be the most representative of Hollywood director Frank Capra's style of celebratory, all-American cinematic storytelling.

Featuring James Stewart in the title role, the film tells the tale of an earnest but naive young man from a small town who is appointed by a corrupt governor to serve out the term of a recently deceased U.S. senator. The governor—himself controlled by an evil media mogul—believes that the innocent "Boy Scout" Jefferson Smith will be unable to recognize what is going on in Washington, thereby allowing the governor's backers to have their way. But Smith—advised by his savvy but good-hearted assistant, played by Jean Arthur—proves himself incorruptible and far smarter than the governor had anticipated, eventually thwarting the nefarious plans of the media tycoon.

The story surrounding the film is, perhaps, even more interesting than the movie's own plot. It had an elaborate premiere in Washington in October 1939 with an audience filled with congressmen, cabinet officials, and Supreme Court justices. Afterward, however, many of the politicians complained that the film depicted the nation's representatives in a venal and self-serving light, albeit in fictional form. At a time when fascism was on the rise in Europe, the film, they felt, ridiculed America and the idea of democracy.

In fact, Capra celebrated both by telling the story of an everyman who defeats the vested interests. The public and the film community agreed. A box office hit, the film garnered eleven Academy Award nominations in a year that also saw the release of *Gone With the Wind*, *Stagecoach*, and *The Wizard of Oz*.

See also: films, feature; Capra, Frank.

Bibliography

Capra, Frank. *The Name Above the Title: An Autobiography*. New York: Macmillan, 1971.

Carney, Raymond. *American Vision: The Films of Frank Capra*. New York: Cambridge University Press, 1986.

MUSIC

In early 1929, an NBC survey showed that one-third of American homes owned a radio. This translated into a potential audience of 41.4 million listeners. By 1934, 60 percent of American homes were influenced by radio. The popularity of radio among its listeners proved to be the greatest asset of the music of this era. Both popular and classical music found vast numbers of listeners thanks to radio. Its influence on Americans as an influential medium would not be challenged until the spread of television in the 1950s.

The music of the Great Depression had a profound effect on popular and classical music for years to come. Popular music was marked by the influx of swing music into the mainstream. A music style that had been seen as predominantly African American, mainly due to its strong ties to jazz, it became *the* popular style of the 1930s. The bouncy rhythms and carefree lyrics of many swing songs paved the way for the style of music that would become rock and roll.

SWING

Swing created its own world, which reached beyond radio and music and became part of the cultural landscape. It even had its own language known as "jive talk." Popular radio shows like *Let's Dance* showcased the music of many swing bands. Every Saturday, listeners could learn the top ten songs in the nation by tuning in to *Your Hit Parade*. Fans could read about their favorite bands in trade journals such as *Metronome* and *Downbeat*. Swing influenced a number of dances with names like the lindy hop, the jitterbug, and the big apple, among others.

Some of the leading musicians of the swing style were Benny Goodman, Artie Shaw, Tommy and Jimmy Dorsey, Harry James, Bob Crosby, Chick Webb, Duke Ellington, Count Basie, Jimmie Lunceford, and Cab Calloway. Benny Goodman was known as "The King of Swing," due to popularity, frequent radio appearances, and a part in the movie *The Big Broadcast of 1937*. Artie Shaw, a clarinetist and composer, formed his band in 1936. His band's notable difference from other swing bands was its makeup. Shaw had a unique mix of strings, clarinet, and rhythm section. He later added a singer to his group and, over the years, developed a reputation that rivaled Benny Goodman's. The Dorsey brothers originally played together as the Dorsey Brothers Band, but creative and personal differences led them to split in 1935 and form separate bands. Jimmy Dorsey had a fondness for Dixieland music and fluctuated between this music style and the modern swing sound. Brother Tommy, a trombonist, favored a brassier sound when he took over leadership of a band originally known as the Joe Haymes orchestra. Another swing musician, Harry James, originally worked as a trumpet soloist for Benny Goodman before leaving to front his own band, with Goodman's blessings. Bob Crosby, younger brother of the famed singer Bing Crosby, worked with the Dorsey brothers, but left to join a Dixieland band. Another accomplished bandleader, Chick Webb, led a swing band at the popular Savoy Ballroom in Harlem in the 1920s and 1930s. Duke Ellington, Count Basie, and Cab Calloway (along with Jimmie Lunceford) were popular African-American bandleaders who helped create and promote the swing sound. Duke Ellington had a noted jazz sound to his music, which he referred to as "jungle music." His sound was more sophisticated and less flashy than that of many other swing bands. Count Basie played piano in his own band and often had male crooners, along with the usual female singers. Jimmie Lunceford's band was considered one of the most dynamic of the 1930s. It reveled in showmanship and improvisation and was drawn to the bouncy beat of swing. An important and well-remembered figure in the world of swing music was Cab Calloway. A singer and bandleader whose dynamic personality led to movie appearances and a role in George Gershwin's *Porgy and Bess*, Calloway formed the group The Missourians in 1929. This group became the house band at New York's famous Cotton Club, where Calloway helped preserve the swing sound and the roots from which it came.

Most swing bands were drawn to Tin Pan Alley songs and relied on musical improvisation during performances. Almost every element of swing was adapted from African-American culture: the size of the bands, the songs, the dances, and the music itself. Early swing music relied on exact playing and a method known as the call-and-response pattern, in which one section of the band would play a passage of music and then another section would play in response to the first. In musical terms, swing music tended to have an even stress on the four beats of the bar. What this means is that the beat of most swing songs was steady, heavy, and almost driving throughout the music. The wild, more energetic swing style developed later, as the music and performers adapted to a young audience that wanted music to dance to.

Performers such as Count Basie and Glenn Miller were not the only ones to benefit from the popularity of swing music. Their lead singers (known as "canaries" in jive talk) enjoyed fame in their own right. Ella Fitzgerald worked with Chick Webb's band and made the song "A-Tisket A-Tasket" the number two song of 1938. Fitzgerald briefly took over the band after Webb's death. Billie Holiday, one of the greatest jazz vocalists of the twentieth century, joined Artie Shaw's band in 1938. Holiday also recorded with Benny Goodman, Teddy Wilson, and Count Basie. Martha Tilton sang with Benny Goodman and made "And the Angels Sing" a number one hit in 1939. Helen O'Connell sang with Jimmie Dorsey, and Marion Hutton joined forces with the Glenn Miller Band. Most lead singers enjoyed success due to their talent and their work with swing bands.

One noticeable change from the beginning of the Great Depression to its demise was the change in musical tastes. A more mellow sound and bigger bands became popular and acts like the Andrews Sisters were more sought after as the 1940s neared. Just as the musical taste of the Roaring Twenties tended toward the blues, a nation locked in a depression (financially and emotionally) sought solace in the happier sounds of swing. As financial burdens eased, but the war loomed in the distance, popular taste began to fluctuate again, from wild, dancing swing music to mellow, heartfelt ballads. Both were popular in the late 1930s, but the swing style was definitely evolving into something new.

Two very popular jazz clubs helped create and foster the swing sound during the Great Depression: the Savoy Ballroom and the Cotton Club. Harlem's Savoy Ballroom remained open from 1926 to 1959. It boasted some 250 bands playing there during those years, including Ellington's and Webb's. It also inspired the swing song "Stompin' at the Savoy." The Cotton Club was another Harlem nightclub that was made famous by a variety of performers, particularly Ellington and Calloway. The club, popular during the 1920s and 1930s, closed in 1940. A strong number of talented musicians were nurtured in the Cotton Club and the Savoy, and the swing style itself is said to have originated in the Harlem nightclubs.

OTHER POPULAR MUSIC

Although swing was known as "the" sound of the 1930s Depression era, it was not the only music that existed at the time. Woodrow Wilson Guthrie (known as Woody Guthrie), who would come to fame in the 1940s, was a street performer during the Great Depression. Guthrie spent his time traveling the United States, performing and honing his folk singing and songwriting skills. One could argue that swing, with its infectious, happy beat and carefree attitude, was quite opposite to the somber mood gripping the struggling nation throughout the Depression and that, therefore, Guthrie's raw, American folk sound was more the voice of a nation and a social class than swing was. His works include such songs as "This Train Is Bound for Glory," "So Long, It's Been Good to Know You," and "This Land Is Your Land."

Another style of music often grouped with swing was the dance band sound. Not to be confused with swing, this style was more waltz-like and by the note— no improvisation. This style was popular with an older, more affluent crowd. One of the most noted acts of the Depression was Guy Lombardo and His Royal Canadians. Lombardo was a Canadian-born musician who formed his band in 1917. The group had a distinctly "older" sound than that of the newer swing bands that began appearing in the late 1920s. Although scorned by fans of swing, Lombardo and his band toured and recorded extensively, and their New Year's Eve performances became an annual favorite for many radio listeners.

CLASSICAL MUSIC

Popular music was not the only music evolving during the difficult Depression days; classical music was seeing its own changes throughout the 1930s. As the world was changing between the two World Wars, so was classical music. Classical music between 1910 and 1930 was highly experimental, mimicking the volatile nature of worldwide politics during this time. Music such as this was labeled "the new music." Due to social and technological changes (most notably, radio), music evolved very quickly during the twentieth century to meet with changing tastes and influences. Some of the most notable composers and musicians who created new work during the Great Depression were Aaron Copland, George Gershwin, Béla Bartók, Sergey Prokofiev, Dmitry Shostakovich, Igor Stravinsky, and Carl Orff. In America, Aaron Copland composed his noted ballet *Billy the Kid* in 1938 and devoted some time to studying Mexican folk songs for his orchestral suite *El Salon Mexico*, composed in 1936. He also composed the school opera *The Second Hurricane* in 1936 and scored music for a number of films. George Gershwin, known as a pianist, conductor, and composer, opened his opera, *Porgy and Bess*, in New York in 1935.

The common feature among most composers creating new work during the Depression was the interest in regional folk music. While Copland was studying Mexican folk songs, Béla Bartók, a Hungarian scholar-composer, was collecting, recording, and publishing over 2,000 native folk songs of Hungary, Romania, and Yugoslavia. Folk music intrigued Bartók, and he spent a great deal of time writing books, compositions, and articles based on folk style, even developing a unique musical technique incorporating folk elements. His 1936 work, *Cantata Profana*, showcases this folk technique and a variety of folk song themes.

Three Russian composers influenced the world of classical music during the Great Depression: Prokofiev, Shostakovich, and Stravinsky. Prokofiev released his ballet, *Romeo and Juliet*, in 1935 and composed his popular work *Peter and the Wolf* in 1936. Shostakovich's symphonies were his most enduring works of the 1930s, including his fifth, widely considered the most popular. Stravinsky was known as a neoclassic composer, which is not a style directly associated with this period in history. However, he did create a number of important works between 1929 and 1940. His ballet-melodrama *Persephone* was composed in 1934. He also wrote chamber music at this time, including *Duo Concertant* in 1932, a *Concerto for Two Pianos* in 1935, and the *Dumbarton Oaks Concerto in E* in 1938. He wrote *Cappriccio* in 1929 and the *Violin Concerto* in 1931.

One other classical composer, Carl Orff, experienced creative peaks during the Great Depression. A German-born composer, he created his famous work *Carmina Burana* in 1936 or 1937. The driving rhythm and foreboding, primitive force in the work typifies his style. Orff was also an influential teacher and creator of a number of teaching aids still used today.

ERIN AUSK

See also: films, feature; *42nd Street; Gold Diggers of 1933; Porgy and Bess;* Federal Music Project; Anderson, Marion; Armstrong, Louis; Astaire (Fred) and Rogers (Ginger); Autry, Gene; Basie, Count; Berkeley, Busby; Berlin, Irving; Calloway, Cab; Copland, Aaron; Ellington, Duke; Gershwins, George and Ira; Goodman, Benny; Guthrie, Woody; Holiday, Billie; Ledbetter, Hudson William "Leadbelly"; Porter, Cole; Robeson, Paul; Rodgers (Richard) and Hart (Lorenz); Smith, Kate; Temple, Shirley; Vallée, Rudy.

Bibliography

Bowen, Ezra, ed. *This Fabulous Century, Volume III, 1920–1930.* New York: Time-Life Books, 1970.

———. *This Fabulous Century, Volume IV, 1930–1940.* New York: Time-Life Books, 1970.

Congdon, Don, ed. *The 30's: A Time to Remember.* New York: Simon & Schuster, 1962.

Dunning, John. *On the Air: The Encyclopedia of Old-Time Radio.* New York: Oxford University Press, 1998.

Marquis, Alice G. *Hope and Ashes: The Birth of Modern Times 1929–1939.* New York: Free Press, 1986.

Morehead, Philip D., with Anne MacNeil. *The New International Dictionary of Music.* New York: Penguin Books USA, 1992.

Sherrow, Victoria. *Hardship and Hope: America and the Great Depression.* New York: Twenty-First Century Books, 1997.

NATION, THE

Founded by former abolitionist Edwin L. Godkin as a pro–civil rights magazine in 1865, *The Nation* became increasingly left-leaning during the course of the Great Depression.

Under the editorship of Ernest Gruening, the magazine was reticent of Franklin D. Roosevelt during the 1932 campaign, but became an outspoken supporter of the New Deal programs. In addition, *The Nation* was an ardent backer of normalized U.S. relations with the Soviet Union and loudly supported the antifascist loyalist government in Spain during that country's civil war in the late 1930s.

During the Popular Front period, in which Communists joined with other left-liberal forces in the mid- to late 1930s, the magazine was open in its praise of the achievements of the communist regime in the Soviet Union.

See also: newspapers and magazines; The *New Republic*; Soviet Union; Spanish Civil War.

Bibliography

The Best of The Nation: *A Selection of the Best Articles of Lasting Value to Appear in* The Nation *During the Recent Past.* New York: The Nation Associates, 1952.

Boroff, David, ed. The Nation *One Hundredth Anniversary Issue.* New York: Nation Co., 1965.

NATIONAL ASSOCIATION FOR THE ADVANCMENT OF COLORED PEOPLE

The nation's oldest civil rights organization, the National Association for the Advancement of Colored People (NAACP) was founded in 1909 by black intellectual W. E. B. Du Bois and others. Once at the cutting edge of racial politics, the organization had become a bulwark of mainstream black politics by the 1930s.

Under the leadership of national secretary Walter White, the NAACP was outspokenly anticommunist and slow to support such causes as the Scottsboro defendants—a number of young black men accused of raping two white women in Alabama in 1931—and A. Philip Randolph's March on Washington, which demanded equality in hiring at the nation's defense plants in 1941.

On other issues, however, the organization remained an outspoken advocate of black interests, continuing to pursue its antilynching campaign. While a strong supporter of Franklin D. Roosevelt, marking the 1930s transition of the black electorate from the Republican to the Democratic Party, the NAACP was critical of the way a number of New Deal programs were implemented. According to the NAACP, New Deal jobs programs like the Works Progress Administration failed to hire enough unemployed black workers. In addition, the organization argued, some New Deal programs were actually having a negative effect on black economic prospects. For example, by paying southern, white, land-owning farmers not to grow crops, the 1933 Agricultural Adjustment Act forced black sharecroppers off the land. By enforcing the union shop, the National Labor Relations Act jeopardized the jobs of blacks, since unions often refused to organize them.

See also: African Americans; March on Washington Movement; Randolph, A. Philip.

Bibliography

Ross, Barbara Joyce. *J. E. Spingarn and the Rise of the NAACP, 1911–1939.* New York: Atheneum, 1972.

Zangrando, Robert L. *The NAACP Crusade Against Lynching, 1909–1950.* Philadelphia: Temple University Press, 1980.

NATIONAL UNION FOR SOCIAL JUSTICE

The National Union for Social Justice (NUSJ) was founded by radio preacher Father Charles Coughlin in November 1934 as a liberal lobbying group and support organization for Franklin D. Roosevelt and the New Deal. It was also a personal political vehicle for Coughlin and his economic ideas, which included, most notably, a demand for inflationary monetary policies.

Promoted on Coughlin's enormously popular radio program, the organization grew quickly, though it was not as big as the preacher insisted. Although Coughlin told listeners that there were over 5 million members by late 1935, the figure was probably more like 1 million. Regardless of the actual number, the organization had many sympathizers and was actively courted by many politicians.

Early in 1936, however, Coughlin and the NUSJ changed political directions entirely. Where once the organization's slogan had been "Roosevelt or ruin," it was now, said a bitter Coughlin, "Roosevelt and ruin." Like its founder, the NUSJ became increasingly anti-Semitic in the late 1930s and slowly lost support, as Coughlin himself faded from the scene.

See also: fascism, domestic; Coughlin, Father Charles.

Bibliography

Brinkley, Alan. *Voices of Protest: Huey Long, Father Coughlin, and the Great Depression.* New York: Vintage Books, 1982.

Warren, Donald I. *Radio Priest: Charles Coughlin, the Father of Hate Radio.* New York: Free Press, 1996.

NATIONAL URBAN LEAGUE

The National Urban League was founded in 1911 as a social service organization with a mission to help the growing number of African-American migrants moving from the rural South to cities in the North. This was done by providing health, education, and welfare services.

Under the leadership of Lester Granger, the league became increasingly political, especially after Franklin D. Roosevelt took office in 1933. At the top of its agenda was advocacy of African-American inclusion in New Deal programs. The organization was highly critical of various federal public works programs for their failure to hire a proportionately equivalent number of unemployed black workers.

See also: African Americans; National Association for the Advancement of Colored People.

Bibliography

Moore, Jesse Thomas. *A Search for Equality: The National Urban League, 1910–1961.* University Park: Pennsylvania State University Press, 1981.

Weiss, Nancy Joan. *The National Urban League, 1910–1940.* New York: Oxford University Press, 1974.

NATIVE AMERICANS

In 1928, one year before the stock market crash devastated the American economy and signaled the onset of the Great Depression, a congressionally appointed investigative group issued *The Problem of Indian Administration*. Known as the Meriam Report after the team's leader, Lewis Meriam, the document detailed the abysmal conditions then prevalent on the nation's reservations. Indians, the report found, suffered from rampant disease, poor health, and the crushing burden of extreme poverty. In short, they had already been living in a depression long before the coming of the Great Depression. Conditions for Native Americans had been rapidly declining for decades following forced assimilation programs, such as allotment of Indian lands under the terms of the 1887 Dawes Act and off-reservation boarding schools. (The allotment process divided collective Indian lands into private holdings, which led to loss of Indian lands through sales to non-Indians.) The report placed the blame squarely on federal Indian policies and recommended wide-ranging reforms.

Although Native Americans shared the economic suffering that befell other Americans in the Depression years, the 1930s paradoxically signaled new hope for Indians. Under President Franklin Delano Roosevelt, Indians too would have a New Deal. The Indian New Deal emphasized a return to tribalism and Indian identity, improved reservation economies, and increased participation of Native American reformers and intellectuals in the cultural life of the United States.

One of the non-Indian reformers disturbed by the conclusions of the Meriam Report was John Collier. Collier came from a social worker background in New York and had become increasingly active in Indian reform in the 1920s. When Roosevelt's secretary of the interior, Harold Ickes, chose Collier as his new commissioner of Indian Affairs, Collier brought with him a reformist zeal unprecedented in that particular office. Collier carried a pluralist vision of American society, in which the Indian was not forced to conform with "white" culture. Collier openly criticized federal assimilationist policies and sought to end the allotment process. Moreover, he attempted to revivify Native-American cultural life through a series of programs, such as an Indian Arts and Crafts Board.

Prompted by Collier, Indians were included in key New Deal relief programs such as the Civilian Conservation Corps, the Agricultural Adjustment Administration, the Resettlement Administration, and the Works Progress Administration (WPA). But the centerpiece of Collier's program was the Indian Reorganization Act of 1934. This wide-ranging legislation authorized tribes to organize governments, encouraged the strengthening of Indian cultural life, and, most significantly, ended allotment.

Although hailed by many tribal communities, Collier's zeal angered others. Among Navajos, Collier is remembered as the person who imposed the devastating stock reduction program on them. The program was an effort to reduce the sheep in the Navajo Nation in order to stem overgrazing and subsequent soil erosion. But sheep were more than a commodity: They formed part of the traditional cultural existence of Navajo society. It is not surprising, therefore, that Navajos were shocked at the slaughter and dumping of thousands of sheep.

Collier also attempted to increase Indian participation at the federal level. He asked D'Arcy McNickle, a Chippewa-Cree, to serve in the Bureau of Indian Affairs. McNickle had been working with the WPA's Federal Writers Project. A writer and intellectual, he was the author of *The Surrounded* (1936), a major breakthrough in Native-American fiction.

Other Indian intellectuals joined McNickle in giving voice to native peoples in the United States in the 1930s. Lakota author Luther Standing Bear wrote *My Indian Boyhood* (1931), *Land of the Spotted Eagle* (1933), and *Stories of the Sioux* (1934) before his death in 1939. *Land of the Spotted Eagle* included painful reflections on his boarding school experiences at Carlisle Indian Industrial School. Osage author John Mathews published several works in the 1930s, including *The Osages: Children of the Middle Waters* and *Talking to the Moon*. Although it would be several more decades until Indian intellectuals found a wider acceptance in American society, Standing Bear, McNickle, and Mathews paved the way for later writers such as N. Scott Momaday and Vine Deloria Jr.

Just as World War II ended the Great Depression, so too did it mark the end of the renewed tribalism of the 1930s. In the years following the war, federal

Native American craftspeople exhibiting their handiwork in New York in the 1930s. *(Library of Congress)*

bureaucrats effectively dismantled Indian New Deal programs. A sea-change in policy placed the federal government on a course called termination, which sought to finally solve the "Indian problem" by breaking up reservations, terminating the responsibilities of the Bureau of Indian Affairs, and rapidly assimilating Indians into white American culture. In many ways, the policy harked back to the grim days of the late nineteenth century. Yet the war experience also initiated what would eventually come to be called self-determination. Native-American veterans returned home from service to find that their sacrifices abroad did not translate into greater rights or respect for Indian cultures at home. Many of these veterans later assumed leadership in organizations like the National Congress of American Indians and in the renewed call for Indian rights in the decades following the war.

Scott C. Zeman

See also: Agricultural Adjustment Administration; Civilian Conversation Corps; Indian Reorganization Act; Resettlement Administration; Works Progress Administration.

Bibliography

Hoxie, Frederick, ed. *Encyclopedia of North American Indians.* Arlington Heights, IL: Harlan Davidson, 1988.

Hoxie, Frederick, and Peter Iverson. *Indians in American History.* Arlington Heights, IL: Harlan Davidson, 1988.

Philip, Kenneth. *John Collier's Crusade for Indian Reform, 1920–1954.* Tucson: University of Arizona Press, 1981.

NEW DEAL, SECOND

Midway through Franklin D. Roosevelt's first presidential administration, cracks had begun to weaken his alliances of farmers, business, and labor on which the major New Deal programs of 1933 and 1934 had rested: the National Industrial Recovery Act (NIRA) and Agricultural Adjustment Act, the Tennessee Valley Authority (TVA) and Civilian Conservation Corps, and new regulations over banks, mortgages, and securities. These and their allied programs had largely been based on a bootstrap philosophy of economic recovery—providing incentives and capital to restart the businesses that had stalled. With the exception of the creation of the TVA, few of these programs promoted fundamental social or economic reform. By 1935, the leaders of labor and the intellectual Left were frustrated with the collaboration of the administration with business leaders, who the Left thought benefited inordinately from New Deal price supports and job creation schemes and whose greed had been the problem all along. Further, the businessmen were increasingly frustrated with the growing burdens of regulation and labor protection.

As if these political problems were not enough to unsettle the New Deal, its economic effects were modest at best. While the crisis had not worsened, the Depression had only slightly abated. Unemployment had fallen from its 1933 peak of 25 percent but was still at 20 percent. Industrial production in 1935 was only at the same level it had held during a brief peak in 1933, still far below its precrash levels. Wholesale prices and industrial growth had both stabilized, at last, but were still only 80 percent of their levels in 1929.

The final blows, however, came in Supreme Court decisions overturning key elements of Roosevelt's plan. In January, in *Panama Refining Co. v. Ryan* (1935), the NIRA's provisions relating to oil were overturned. The Railroad Pension Act was struck down in March in *R.R. Retirement Board v. Alton R.R.* (1935).

The girder that broke the camel's back came on May 27, when the court handed down *Schechter Poultry v. United States* (1935); the Schechter brothers' appeal of their convictions for selling sick chickens in violation of the poultry code established by the National Recovery Act under the NIRA was successful, and their convictions were overturned. The reasoning by Justice Cardozo, who pointed out not only that the NIRA delegated too much congressional power to an agency but also that the Schechters' business was intrastate and thus not reachable by Congress's power over interstate commerce, seemed to mortally wound the structure not just of the NIRA but of most of the 1933–34 New Deal legislation. The *Schechter* opinion also led to Roosevelt's battle with the Supreme Court, including his plan to pack the Court, and to his acceptance of a new approach to the New Deal.

OVERTURES TO REFORM

Roosevelt's Brain Trust had long expected that the Supreme Court would overturn the New Deal, at least in part, and many of its members had chafed under the conciliatory view Roosevelt had taken of business from the beginning. In early meetings, some consideration of more fundamental economic reforms had been mooted. From these discussions, Eleanor Roosevelt's reports on national conditions of the workers, and Franklin Roosevelt's private concern to succeed in overcoming the Depression, the president had shown considerable early interest in reforms broader than those of his early bills.

His 1935 State of the Union message contrasted sharply with his 1933 inaugural pledge to help "this great nation . . . revive and prosper." He now looked to constitutional means to co-opt the desire for reform that he believed had toppled governments in Europe, using both the tools of recovery and of economic and social reform: "The attempt to make a distinction between recovery and reform is a narrowly conceived effort to substitute the appearance of reality for reality itself. When a man is convalescing from illness, wisdom dictates not only cure of the symptoms but also removal of their cause." Among the cures Roosevelt argued for was a system of Social Security to provide "old-age insurance" and protection for unsupported dependents.

Even so, the immediate public agenda he announced in his January address was still limited to the elements of recovery legislation already enacted. Most of the specifics he outlined were designed to move people from relief lines to public employment. More generally, for the year he sought only "the consolidation of Federal regulatory administration over all forms of transportation, the renewal and clarification of the general purposes of the National Industrial Recovery Act, the strengthening of our facilities for the prevention, detection, and treatment of crime and criminals, the restoration of sound conditions in the public-utilities field through abolition of the evil features of holding companies, the gradual tapering off of the emergency credit activities of the Government, and improvement in our taxation forms and methods."

Toward these ends, Roosevelt sent some bills to Congress and acted on his own authority to strengthen the earlier programs. In April, Congress passed the Emergency Relief Appropriations Act, which was designed to create federal jobs programs. It also passed the Soil Conservation Act, creating the Soil Conservation Service as an arm of the Department of Agriculture, with the intent of halting the erosion that had created the great dust bowl of the Midwest and stripped much of the country's farmland of its fertility. In May, Roosevelt signed executive orders creating the Works Progress Administration (WPA), including the National Youth Administration (NYA), and the Rural Electrification Administration (REA), and signed a bill reforming bankruptcy procedures for farmers.

In private, however, Roosevelt was entertaining more and more arguments for wider reform. The lead in such arguments fell to Supreme Court Justice Louis Brandeis and, more often, his lieutenants and Roosevelt legal advisers, Felix Frankfurter, Ben Cohen, and Tommy Corcoran, who had been the administration's drafters and lobbyists in the First Hundred Days. Their views, especially their view that no cooperation with the leaders of business would succeed in reform, began to triumph with Roosevelt as the winter progressed, helped no doubt by the announcement in early May that the U.S. Chamber of Commerce had denounced the New Deal.

In mid-May, Senate progressives, led by Wisconsin Senator Robert La Follette Jr., met at the White House and demanded greater reforms from Roosevelt. Their strongest argument was the overwhelming mandate that Roosevelt had earned from the people in the elections the November before. The 1934 midterm election had strengthened Roosevelt's hand in Congress, a rare gift for any president. The Democrats had won nine more seats in both the Senate and in the House, for majorities of 69–25 and 310–117, respectively. Such arguments were not lost on Roosevelt.

Thus, when the *Schechter* decision fell, Roosevelt was angry. In his press meeting four days later, he attacked the "horse and buggy" definition of commerce applied by the Supreme Court and began his counteroffensive against the "nine old men." More tellingly, though, he was already poised on the brink of a new chapter in the New Deal.

THE SECOND HUNDRED DAYS

After months of idleness, Congress was prodded into action by the president. Roosevelt summoned the leaders of both houses to the White House and insisted on the passage of four bills before adjournment: the Social Security bill, the Wagner labor act, a utilities bill, and a banking bill. To this list, he later added a tax reform bill and other economic legislation salvaged from the ruins of the NIRA. Thus, rather than enjoying their customary summer adjournment, congressmen found themselves at their desks through Washington's steamy June and July, swarmed around by Roosevelt's lieutenants, with the voice of the fireside chat only a phone call away.

The first success was the Wagner Act, known for its sponsor, New York Senator Robert F. Wagner (D-NY), and officially titled the National Labor Relations Act (NLRA) (1935). Roosevelt had initially resisted the law, which established a permanent right of labor to collective bargaining and put the government in the role of arbitrator in labor disputes. The Senate had passed the bill on May 20 and it was out of committee in the House by the time Roosevelt adopted it as a program of his own. Roosevelt summoned Wagner for meetings in the While House to settle concerns raised by Labor Secretary Frances Perkins and then gave the act his blessing. It established a new agency, the National Labor Relations Board, tasked with protecting the rights of workers (except agricultural and domestic laborers) to organize unions of their own choice and to engage in collective bargaining. The NLRA barred employers from certain unfair labor practices, such as setting up a company union and firing or discriminating against unionized workers. Congress passed the act on June 27, and Roosevelt signed it on July 5.

On July 19, Roosevelt's tax plan arrived on the Hill, demanding an increase in the estate tax, new gift taxes, and a graduated tax on the incomes of individuals and corporations, so that those with more money paid at a higher rate. It was immediately denounced by the newspapers as a plan to soak the rich in order to steal the left-wing thunder of populists like Huey P. Long. Indeed, Long, then in the U.S. Senate, rose after the bill was read to say, "I just wish to say 'Amen.'" Roosevelt, however, did not back the bill as consistently as his progressive aides in the Congress would have liked, and, in the end, Congress passed the so-called Wealth Tax Act of 1935, actually the Revenue Act of 1935, without the inheritance tax and corporate graduations but with significant increases on wealthier individuals, through surtaxes and increased rates, to a highest level of 75 percent for incomes over $5 million. The act passed on August 30.

In a move that Roosevelt had long entertained—and that echoed the philosophy of Franklin's trust-busting cousin Theodore—the president also moved against the huge public utility holding corporations, the combines. The combines had not only built local monopolies to end competition but then inflated their rates and bribed legislators to help them gouge consumers and evade regulation. The bill, drafted by Cohen and Corcoran, included a death-knell line that would dissolve any holding company that could not justify its existence by January 1, 1940, but it also gave the Securities and Exchange Commission (SEC) the power to prove that the holding companies should be dissolved by courts. Over huge opposition by the money-dripping utilities, the Senate passed the bill intact, by a margin of a single vote. The House, however, passed the bill without the death-knell clause, on a vote that split party discipline on both sides. Roosevelt's men organized a countercampaign that included an investigation of the utility lobby. Lead Senate investigator Hugo Black found that telegrams has been sent to the Senate from Pennsylvania under forged names, after which the Western Union office from which they had come was burned; he also found evidence of bribery of certain congressmen. Despite the revelations and Roosevelt's pitched battle for the whole bill, the compromise bill with its powers for the SEC to investigate and to dismantle holding companies went through. The Public Utility Holding Company Act of 1935 was passed on August 26.

The Eccles Bill, or the Banking Act of 1935, was the product of a Roosevelt appointee to the Federal Reserve Board, Marriner Eccles, a Utah banker. Exposed to the economic thoughts of John Maynard

Keynes, Eccles sought to end the control of private bankers over the governors of the Federal Reserve, giving it more autonomy and more control by the White House. His bill was introduced in February and put on Roosevelt's June wish-list by Roosevelt staffers. Roosevelt himself was limited in his support for the bill, which passed primarily because of personal lobbying by Eccles and the support of Western bankers who saw control of the Federal Reserve by the government as better than control by Wall Street. The law, in a much altered version, passed on August 23, giving the president power to appoint the seven governors of the board, which would have more control over regional banks and rates.

In the wake of the sinking of the NIRA, the New Dealers revived portions of the old programs of the NRA industrial codes in the form of individual statutes. The most far-reaching of these was the regulation of coal mining through the Guffey-Snyder Act, which set minimum wage and hour laws for miners and created a commission to review the operation of marginal mines, close those that ought to be closed, and ensure rehabilitation of displaced miners. Although this act would be struck down by the Supreme Court in 1936, much of it would be reenacted in 1937.

Despite the vast new scope of these initiatives, by far the most significant bill of the whole plan was the Social Security Act. The bill was born as a response to criticisms that Roosevelt's relief packages were too stingy to widows, to the elderly, and to those unfit for work. Roosevelt created a Committee on Economic Security in June 1934, chaired by Secretary of Labor Frances Perkins, to study methods of permanent social insurance. That committee embraced a plan modeled on the existing social insurance plan in Wisconsin, largely crafted by legal expert Paul Rauschenbusch and his wife, Elizabeth Brandeis (Louis's daughter). The committee's plan called for compulsory insurance, in which the payments of current workers financed the retirement annuities vested in retirees over age sixty-five. It also established federal/state programs for the support of the blind and crippled, for dependent mothers and children, for public health, and for unemployment insurance.

Social Security bills were introduced in both houses on January 17, sponsored by Robert Wagner in the Senate and Marylander David Lewis in the House, with Roosevelt's strong endorsement. Opposition came from both the Left, which thought the benefits too stingy, and the Right, which abhorred the whole idea of redistribution as supporting the idle. The Social Security Act passed along party lines, in April in the

House and in June in the Senate and Roosevelt signed it into law on August 15.

The exhausted Congress adjourned on Tuesday, August 27.

INFLUENCE ON REFORM AND GOVERNMENT

The legislation passed in the Second Hundred Days is the most dramatic element of the Roosevelt plan of 1935, yet this monumental achievement should not obscure the many other components of the New Deal during this period. Many of the bills had been long in the works, spurred by reformers outside the White House and its Brain Trust. Agencies created by executive order were as important to recovery and reform as were those created by the new statutes. Furthermore, the final significance of many of these programs depended on the imaginative construction of their broad tasks given by individual administrators at all levels. The results were the combination of reform planning, legislative authorization, administrative creation, and personal initiative.

The effects of this new governmental synthesis were far-reaching. The WPA, headed by Harry Hopkins, and its NYA arm, including young administrators like Lyndon B. Johnson in Texas, not only employed millions of citizens on collective projects but also altered the scope of the federal bureaucracy. The REA and the revitalized TVA extended public services to tens of millions. The new Social Security Administration became the backbone of individual retirement for the next century. Taken together, the new agencies and laws represented an important shift in both aim and method from the early focus of the New Deal.

What type of shift, and what the new focus really was, has been the subject of debate since at least 1934. The very term "Second New Deal" gained significance in scholarly discourse only after Basil Rauch's *History of the New Deal* in 1944. The nature of the shift between the First and the Second New Deal has been deeply controversial. Whether the Second New Deal was more about socialism, reconstruction, reform, regulation, bureaucracy, federalism, or economics, and whether its moves were authored by Roosevelt, the Progressives, the Brain Trusters, Brandeis's men, or a host of disparate and transient allies, have been debated without resolution ever since. Regardless, the national agencies created during this period set in place a new form of national government and created new expectations in the citizenry of what government could, and should, do.

Steve Sheppard

See also: Agricultural Adjustment Act; Civilian Conservation Corps; National Labor Relations Act; *Schechter Poultry Corporation v. United States*; Securities and Exchange Commission; Social Security Act; Soil Conservation and Domestic Allotment Act; Tennessee Valley Authority; Wealth Tax Act; Works Progress Administration; Black, Hugo; Brandeis, Louis; Cohen, Benjamin; Corcoran, Thomas G.; Frankfurter, Felix; La Follette brothers; Roosevelt, Franklin D.; Documents: National Labor Relations Act, July 5, 1935; Social Security acts, August 15, 1935; Fireside Chat on Social Security Acts, January 17, 1935; Fireside Chat on work relief programs, April 28, 1935; *National Labor Relations Board v. Jones & Laughlin Steel Corporation*, 1937.

Bibliography

Ackerman, Bruce. *We the People: Transformations.* Cambridge: Harvard University Press, 1998.

Burns, James McGregor. *Roosevelt, 1882–1940: The Lion and the Fox.* San Diego: Harcourt, Brace, 1956.

Cushman, Barry. *Rethinking the New Deal Court: The Structure of a Constitutional Revolution.* New York: Oxford University Press, 1998.

Friedel, Frank. *Roosevelt: A Rendezvous with Destiny.* Boston: Little, Brown, 1990.

Graham, Otis L. *An Encore for Reform: The Old Progressives and the New Deal.* New York: Oxford University Press, 1967.

Kennedy, David M. *Freedom from Fear: The American People in Depression and War, 1929–1945.* New York: Oxford University Press, 1999.

Konefsky, S. J. *The Legacy of Holmes and Brandeis: A Study in the Influence of Ideas.* New York: Macmillan, 1956.

Leuchtenberg, William E. *Franklin D. Roosevelt and the New Deal.* New York: Harper & Row, 1963.

———. *The Supreme Court Reborn: Constitutional Revolution in the Age of Roosevelt.* New York: Oxford University Press, 1995.

Louchheim, Katie. *The Making of the New Deal: The Insiders Speak.* Cambridge: Harvard University Press, 1983.

McElvaine, Robert S. *The Great Depression: America, 1929–1941.* New York: Times Books, 1993.

Mitchell, Broadus. *Depression Decade: From New Era Through New Deal, 1929–1941.* New York: Harper & Row, 1947.

Rauch, Basil. *The History of the New Deal, 1933–1938.* New York: Creative Age Press, 1944.

Romasco, Albert U. *The Politics of Recovery: Roosevelt's New Deal.* New York: Oxford University Press, 1983.

Roosevelt, Franklin. *The Public Papers and Addresses of Franklin D. Roosevelt.* Compiled by Samuel I. Rosenman. 13 vols. New York: Random House, 1950.

Schlesinger, Arthur M. *The Coming of the New Deal.* Cambridge, MA.: Houghton Mifflin, 1958.

———. *The Politics of Upheaval.* Cambridge, MA.: Houghton Mifflin, 1960.

U.S. Statutes at Large. 1935–36. Volume 49.

NEW MASSES

While it never had a large circulation, *New Masses*, a magazine closely affiliated with the Communist Party, was influential beyond its size, publishing some of the most important leftist writers, intellectuals, and artists of the Great Depression era.

Following in the tradition of *Masses* (1911–17), *New Masses* came out as a monthly from 1926 through 1933 and then was turned into a weekly from 1934 through 1948. In the late 1920s, the magazine was run by independent leftist journalists like Max Eastman. But in 1930, *New Masses* was directed by the International Union of Revolutionary Writers, then meeting in the Soviet Union, to become "the cultural organ of the class-conscious workers and revolutionary intellectuals" of the United States.

New Masses soon found itself with a host of major writers—steered leftward by the effects of the Great Depression—eager to contribute pieces, including James Agee, Erskine Caldwell, Ernest Hemingway, Langston Hughes, and Richard Wright. The magazine was also known for its elegant yet powerful graphics and illustrations.

As a product of American communism, *New Masses* followed all of the twists and turns of the communist movement in the 1930s. In the early 1930s, the magazine remained critical of liberals and socialists, a position which it dropped during the Popular Front phase of the mid-1930s. At that time, the magazine focused on the struggle against fascism in the Spanish Civil War. Then, after the 1939 Nazi-Soviet nonaggression pact, the magazine became increasingly hostile to those liberal and leftist forces in the United States that advocated intervention on behalf of the anti-Nazi cause in Europe. This last shift alienated many on the Left within the United States, diminishing the magazine's already small circulation further and undermining its influence among intellectuals.

New Masses continued through World War II and after, then merged with another magazine to become *Masses and Mainstream* in 1948.

See also: Communist Party; newspapers and magazines; Nazi-Soviet nonaggression pact; Spanish Civil War; Agee, James; Cald-well, Erskine; Hemingway, Ernest; Hughes, Langston; Wright, Richard.

Bibliography

Fitzgerald, Richard. "*New Masses*: New York, 1926–1948." In *The American Radical Press, 1880–1960* ed. Joseph R. Conlin, Vol. 2. Westport, CT: Greenwood Press, 1974.

North, Joseph, ed. *New Masses: An Anthology of the Rebel Thirties.* New York: International Publishers, 1969.

NEW REPUBLIC, THE

The *New Republic*, founded by Progressive Era journalist Willard Straight in 1911, was among the most widely read and influential left-liberal magazines in 1930s America, featuring contributions by Walter Lippmann, Malcolm Cowley, and others.

While circulation declined in the conservative 1920s, it picked up again in the early 1930s with the onset of the Depression. Initially, the magazine was critical of Franklin D. Roosevelt and the New Deal, criticizing the president and his program for not going far enough in shifting the country to the Left. Still, *The New Republic* strongly supported the National Recovery Administration. In addition, the magazine was an out-spoken supporter of civil rights, publishing many articles on the subject.

Like *The Nation*, the other major leftist magazine of the 1930s, *The New Republic* attempted to find a way to fuse Marxist thought and the American liberal political tradition.

See also: magazines and newspapers; *The Nation*.

Bibliography

Peterson, Merrill D. *Coming of Age with* The New Republic, *1938–1950*. Columbia: University of Missouri Press, 1999.

Seideman, David. The New Republic: *A Voice of Modern Liberalism.* New York: Praeger, 1986.

NEWSPAPERS AND MAGAZINES

The 1930s were a time of great upheaval in the newspaper and magazine industries. Some of these changes were merely continuations of long-term trends, but others were intimately connected to the larger issues that surround the Great Depression.

NEWSPAPERS AND THE GREAT DEPRESSION

The economic dislocation of the 1930s took a toll on newspapers. Circulation declined sharply from 1929, when Americans purchased 42 million papers every day of the workweek and 29 million on Sundays. In 1933, Americans bought 37.6 million daily papers and 25.5 million Sunday editions. More important, advertising income, which accounted for about two-thirds of newspapers' revenue, fell 45% from 1929 to 1933. Circulation recovered quickly, surpassing 1929 levels by 1935, but advertising was much slower to return. The loss of revenue forced some papers, like the *New York World*, to fold, and required the ones that survived to slash costs by cutting wages, stretching supplies, and printing smaller issues.

The uncertain economy also encouraged the continuation of the trend toward consolidation, a process that grew up alongside the incorporation of American business. The creation of newspaper chains began in the late nineteenth century. By 1932, there were sixty-five chains operating 342 daily sheets, which accounted for about two-fifths of America's circulation. Some of these chains, such as Scripps-Howard and Gannett, worked as rough democracies, granting local papers a great deal of autonomy and determining editorial policy by a vote of the editors. Others, including the McCormick-Patterson chain, which ran the immensely influential *Chicago Tribune* and *New York Daily News*, and William Randolph Hearst, who operated twenty-eight dailies at his peak of power in the mid-1930s, were run strictly as dictatorships, with editorial control lodged firmly within the publisher's office. The increasing consolidation of the newspaper industry and the emergence of these publishing titans led to attacks from critics who believed that newspapers had become boring and standardized and feared that information could eventually be controlled by an autocratic cabal of elitist publishers. Ominously, by 1930, over 1,000 towns and cities had only one daily paper, about twice as many as in 1910. The increased use of press association reports and syndicated features brought on even more complaints about the perceived uniformity of opinion.

Initially, many papers chose to ignore the Depression. Hearst insisted that his papers be "prosperity papers," and others were also slow to print any explanation or analysis of the crisis. By 1932, however, most publishers were willing to admit that America faced major problems, and the newspaper industry welcomed Franklin D. Roosevelt into office as a savior. Roosevelt's winning personality and his willingness to speak openly with reporters made him very popular with the press, and many newspaper elites believed that his leadership would lift the country out of the doldrums.

But it was not long before newspapers turned on the president. Many editors and publishers feared that the New Deal's expensive reform and employment programs would bankrupt the nation. In addition, Roosevelt's insistence on drawing up an National Recovery Adminstration code for the newspaper industry infuriated press magnates. Publishers viewed the NRA as the first step toward government licensing of newspapers and the destruction of the free press. In private, they also complained about the code's provisions for a minimum wage, maximum hours, and regulation of child labor, in the form of newsboys.

The gap between the press and the president widened throughout the 1930s. Many newspapers opposed the Social Security Act of 1935—Richard McCormick, the viciously anti–New Deal publisher of the *Chicago Tribune*, ran a scare piece in his paper claiming that

the act would require all Americans to wear dog tags. Most newspapers opposed Roosevelt's court-packing plan, which smacked of creeping dictatorship. Isolationists like McCormick and Hearst were horrified by Roosevelt's halting steps toward intervention in the European war.

Newspapers expressed their discontent by overwhelmingly supporting Republican candidates in the 1936 and 1940 presidential elections. In 1936, about two-thirds of all dailies that endorsed a candidate, accounting for 70 percent of circulation, backed Republican Alf Landon. The only major paper that supported Roosevelt was the *New York Daily News*. Even fewer papers favored Roosevelt 1940. One survey of urban dailies revealed that only 9 percent were for the president. The papers' stance drew additional criticism from detractors and bolstered the conception that newspapers were losing influence with the public.

Newspaper publishers also perceived threats from within the industry, most explicitly in the form of a new union, the American Newspaper Guild. The Guild, which was comprised of writers and other editorial workers, appeared in 1933 and, like many other unions, grew increasingly militant in the mid- and late 1930s. In 1936, it affiliated itself with the American Federation of Labor. In 1937, it jumped to the maverick Committee for Industrial Organization. Swelling to around 20,000 members by 1940, the guild struck repeatedly for better hours and wages and began taking positions on political issues. The guild openly supported the Spanish Loyalists, called for new job-creation programs, and backed the court-packing plan. The guild alerted publishers to the underlying divisions between management and labor in the newspaper industry, disillusioning them of their long-held belief that they were benevolent, paternal figures who were loved by their employees. The guild's activism, combined with the publishers' innate conservatism, also caused many non-union editors to slant their papers' coverage of labor issues in favor of management.

MAGAZINES AND THE GREAT DEPRESSION

Although the 1930s were hardly an easy time for magazines, they did have a smoother road than the newspapers. While many people had only one local newspaper available, they could easily find a magazine whose views coincided with their own, thereby lessening the need for strident attacks on editorial slanting and sparing magazine editors some of the abuse that newspaper owners absorbed. Magazines were, however, hit hard economically. From 1929 to 1933, the number of magazines plummeted from 5,157 to 3,450, and readership dropped by over 13 percent. Advertising revenues, which accounted for well over half of magazine income, fell by almost one-third as some businesses cut costs and others shifted their advertising toward the radio. Economic indicators turned around after 1933, but the Depression claimed a number of long-running, well-respected magazines, including the *North American Review, St. Nicholas*, and *Living Age*, and forced a number of others, including *Century* and *Forum*, to merge in order to survive.

There were, however, a number of successful periodicals launched during the Depression. Most notable of these were two inspirations of *Time* publisher Henry Luce: *Fortune* and *Life*. First appearing in 1930, *Fortune* quickly became required reading for American businessmen. *Life* was even more significant. Debuting in 1936, *Life* applied new printing technologies that allowed for rapid, high-quality reproduction of photographs in magazines to capitalize on America's growing fascination with the camera, a fad fueled by the development of inexpensive and portable cameras like the Leica. By 1941, *Life* had a circulation of over 3 million. Its success inspired a host of imitators, including *Look* (1937) and *Click* (1938), and accelerated the trend toward replacing drawings with photographs for illustration.

But most of the successful magazines of the 1930s had been established well before the Depression. For example, *Reader's Digest* and *Time*, two products of the 1920s, found great favor among middle-class readers. Both publications reflected a desire for magazines that digested and interpreted major news stories in small, quickly read pieces, thereby creating the illusion that one could be informed about all the important events of the day with very little effort. Both of these periodicals had a conservative slant and were boisterously pro-American.

Like the newspaper industry, magazines became increasingly consolidated in the 1930s, again continuing a process that had begun decades before. Most of the big-selling magazines were products of publishing companies, like Crowell-Collier and Street and Smith, that printed a number of periodicals. The biggest conglomerate, however, was the mighty Curtis Publishing Company, whose magazines took in as much as two-fifths of all magazine advertising revenue in the United States. Curtis's flagship publication, the *Saturday Evening Post*, was the most beloved of all American magazines. Editor George Horace Lorimer was a vocal

exponent of rugged individualism and viewed Roosevelt as a traitor to his class. Consequently, the *Post* offered a conservative, probusiness perspective in both its fiction and nonfiction. But even the *Post*, which boasted a subscription of around 3 million, struggled. As ad revenue declined, the magazine shrank from over 200 pages per issue to around sixty before starting to recover in the late 1930s.

Curtis also published the *Ladies' Home Journal*, the most powerful of the "Big Six" women's magazines—the *Journal, Delineator*, Hearst's *Good Housekeeping, McCall's, Pictorial Review*, and Crowell-Collier's *Woman's Home Companion*. More than general-interest magazines, these publications tried to establish a close relationship with their readers by offering advice and tips and by encouraging readers to write in with questions or problems. These publications, some more than others, viewed the home as women's proper place and focused on housekeeping, child rearing, and cooking. Their fiction often leaned toward the sentimental and featured good-hearted women falling in love or dealing with problems related to their relationships with men.

As a class, the pulp magazines were the 1930s' biggest success story. Although scorned by intellectuals, the pulps contained some of the finest short-story fiction produced during the Depression, along with a great deal of rubbish. Pulps varied widely, but shared a few characteristics. Extremely cost-conscious, they were printed on cheap ("pulp") paper that was of such low quality that illustrations often printed poorly. Pulp editors, therefore, filled their pages with densely packed words and used few adornments. Advertisers were reluctant to spend money in pulps, which had low reputations and a reputedly lower-class audience, so these magazines were more dependent upon revenue from subscriptions than most. Each pulp had its own theme, ranging from the steamy, slightly seamy stories in Bernarr Macfadden's *True Story* and a host of other love pulps to the action-filled tales in *True Detective Mysteries, Western Stories*, and *War Aces*. The pulps also pioneered in the field of science fiction, a niche served by, among others, *Amazing Stories* and *Wonder Stories*. The pulps were put out by a handful of companies, including Munsey, Dell, Fawcett, and Street and Smith, which closely followed audience trends and were quick to imitate any new, successful pulp or to kill a pulp that had passed its prime.

The Depression created no major new trends in either newspapers or magazines. Rather, the 1930s were a time of continuing evolution within these industries.

Old favorites died, new leaders emerged, and most had to make sacrifices in order to weather the economic storm.

DAVID WELKY

See also: advertising and consumption; American Newspaper Guild; *Esquire; Family Circle; Let Us Now Praise Famous Men; Life; Nation, The; New Masses; New Republic, The; Newsweek;* Photography; *Saturday Evening Post; Time;* Adamic, Louis; Agee, James; Bourke-White, Margaret; Broun, Heywood; Hearst, William Randolph; Hopper, Hedda; Lippman, Walter; McCormick, Robert; Murrow, Edward R.; Parsons, Louella; Rogers, Will; Roosevelt, Eleanor; Winchell, Walter

Bibliography

Brendon, Piers. *The Life and Death of the Press Barons.* New York: Atheneum, 1983.

Peterson, Theodore. *Magazines in the Twentieth Century.* Urbana: University of Illinois Press, 1964.

Tebbel, John, and Mary Ellen Zuckerman. *The Magazine in America, 1741–1990.* New York: Oxford University Press, 1991.

———. *The Compact History of the American Newspaper.* New York: Hawthorn Books, 1969.

White, Graham. *FDR and the Press.* Chicago: University of Chicago Press, 1979.

NEWSWEEK

One of the most important news magazines in the United States since its founding in 1933, *Newsweek,* consciously created to be an alternative to the popular *Time,* was first conceived of by *Time's* first foreign editor, Thomas J. C. Martyn.

Originally named *News-Week,* the magazine suffered from relatively low circulation during its early years. In 1937, it merged with *Today* magazine, founded by Raymond Moley, a former member of Franklin D. Roosevelt's Brain Trust. With the more streamlined name *Newsweek,* it now reflected Moley's liberalism, thereby becoming ideologically distinct from the more conservative *Time,* published by media ty-

coon Henry Luce. The magazine also tried to distinguish itself by publishing signed articles and emphasizing a more sober style of writing.

In 1961, the magazine was purchased by the *Washington Post* Company, which beefed up its reportorial staff. *Newsweek* remains the second best-selling newsweekly magazine in the United States, after *Time.*

See also: Brain Trust; newspapers and magazines; *Time;* Luce, Henry; Moley, Raymond.

Bibliography

Tebbel, John. *The American Magazine: A Compact History.* New York: Hawthorn Books, 1969.

OKIES

Okies was the popular—and derogatory—term for the impoverished farmers who were driven out of Oklahoma and other midwestern states by drought, low crop prices, and foreclosures.

Throughout the 1920s, while the urban economy boomed, rural America was mired in an economic slump caused by overproduction and deflated crop prices. Attempting to maximize output, many midwestern farmers practiced unsustainable agricultural methods, including straight-line plowing.

A decade-long drought that began in 1930 turned much of the farmland in western Oklahoma, northern Texas, southern Kansas, and eastern Colorado to dust. When winds picked up, millions of tons of topsoil were stripped from the land to form vast dust storms that deposited dirt as far away as the Atlantic seaboard. At the same time, a further collapse of crop prices set off by the Great Depression resulted in the foreclosure of thousands of farms by local banks that were themselves facing a crisis of declining deposits.

This combination of natural and economic catas-

Known popularly as Okies, economic refugees from the Great Plains worked in the fields of California during the Great Depression. Here, an Okie family rests in a migrant farm camp in Blythe, California, in 1936. *(Library of Congress)*

trophes forced thousands of Great Plains farmers off the land. Desperate for sustenance, many headed to California to find wage work as migrant farmworkers. Living in poverty in temporary camps, they were feared and loathed by many Californians. Eventually, a number of New Deal programs, including the Agricultural Adjustment Act and Resettlement Administration, began to take effect, slowing the exodus to the West Coast. In 1939, writer John Steinbeck captured the hard lives of the Okies in his best-selling novel *The Grapes of Wrath*, which was turned into a popular movie the following year.

See also: agriculture; dust bowl; *Grapes of Wrath, The*; Agricultural Adjustment Act; Resettlement Administration.

Bibliography

Hendrickson, Kenneth D., ed. *Hard Times in Oklahoma: The Depression Years*. Oklahoma City: The Oklahoma State Historical Society, 1983.

Worster, Donald. *Dust Bowl: The Southern Plains in the 1930's*. New York: Oxford University Press, 1979.

PHOTOGRAPHY

In many ways, the 1930s was the decade in which photography came of age in the United States. Technological innovations intersected with social concerns and changing aesthetics to allow photography to find an important niche in American culture. Although it may have been an expensive hobby, given the economic constraints of the Depression, there was a vigorous amateur market for photography, which added to the overall increase in interest in photography. During the first half of the twentieth century, the United States increasingly became an image-oriented society, spurred partly by the growth of the motion picture industry and the advances in photomechanical reproductions of photographs, including the development of "wireless" transmissions of photographs that brought photographic images to an ever widening audience. Additional technological advances included higher quality camera lenses and the development of 35-millimeter film for small, handheld cameras, and improved chemistry for "fast" films that allowed for low-light and stop-action photographs.

Recognizing the increased interest in photography, the administration of President Franklin D. Roosevelt was eager to utilize photography's potential for recording and promoting the New Deal. Throughout the Depression, virtually every department and agency of the federal government made extensive photographic records of their activities. New Deal photographers generally used a documentary aesthetic, which presented images as an objective record of social conditions, unmanipulated by the photographer. By publishing and exhibiting these photographs, the government hoped to gain the support of the American public for the New Deal. In addition to their public relations roles, photographers working for New Deal agencies served as "visual historians," creating an extensive archive of images, most of which are now located in the National Archives.

Paralleling the documentary photography of the New Deal, the 1930s also saw the development of the new discipline of photojournalism and the proliferation of magazines that gave as much, and sometimes more, weight to photographs as they did to words. These illustrated magazines, which frequently carried stories about the effects of the Great Depression, presented readers with much higher quality images than those found in newspapers. The most successful of the illustrated magazines was *Life*, a weekly magazine founded in 1936 by Henry Luce, who also published *Time* and *Fortune*. The principal rival of *Life* was *Look*, a biweekly magazine first published in 1937. Both magazines had high circulation figures, and both were important outlets for government-sponsored photography, as well as images made by members of the Photo League, an important organization based in New York City. The very first cover of *Life*, published on November 23, 1936, was a photograph of the Works Progress Administration's Fort Peck Dam, shot by Margaret Bourke-White, a leading photojournalist. *Life* and *Look* frequently published photographs by various New Deal agencies, especially the Farm Security Administration. This practice benefited both parties, giving these new magazines respectability while giving the Roosevelt administration a means of presenting the work of the New Deal to a national audience. With the rise of the illustrated magazines, photojournalism became an increasingly important form of mass communication. From 1936 until the 1960s, *Life* was the preeminent printed source of information and entertainment in the United States. No other magazine before or since was as popular or as influential.

Photography also found its way into art museums in the 1930s, particularly in New York City's Museum of Modern Art (MoMA). In 1932, MoMA mounted its first exhibition to include photographs, "Murals by American Painters and Photographers." The next year, MoMA held its first solo exhibition of a photographer's work, "Walker Evans: Photographs of Nineteenth-Century Houses." In 1938, MoMA held a major exhibition of Walker Evans's "American Photographs," which included many images made by Evans while he was employed by the Resettlement Administration (RA). In 1940, MoMA established a Department of Photography and named Beaumont Newhall, a strong supporter of the Photo League, as curator. The 1930s thus saw a merging of the interests of photographers, publishers, museums, and the federal government for advancing the cause of photography as an important force in American arts and society. The following three groups of photographers illustrate some of the more significant dimensions of photography during the Great Depression.

One of the most memorable images from the 1930s, this photograph by Dorothea Lange captures the fear and despair of rural families caught in the economic depression. *(Corbis)*

RESETTLEMENT ADMINISTRATION/FARM SECURITY ADMINISTRATION

The most famous body of photographs to come out of Depression-era America is the work produced by the photographers of the Resettlement Administration (RA) and the Farm Security Administration (FSA), collectively referred to as the FSA photographers. Many of the images that were made by the FSA photographers have become icons of the Great Depression, due to both the skill of the individual photographers and the vision of Roy Stryker, who directed the FSA photographic project, which resulted in roughly 270,000 prints and negatives. In 1935, Rexford Tugwell, the administrator of the RA, appointed Stryker (a former student of Tugwell's) to be the chief of the Historical Section for the Information Division of the Resettlement Administration, a position Stryker kept when the RA was renamed the FSA. Stryker was directed to hire photographers to record the rural rehabilitation projects of the FSA, including images both of deprivation and of relief efforts. Although primarily concerned with rural America, the FSA photographers also traveled to the nation's cities, where many displaced farmers went in search of industrial jobs. Consequently, the FSA photographers documented a wide cross section of American society.

Stryker hired both well-known and novice photographers, including Walker Evans, Arthur Rothstein, Dorothea Lange, Ben Shahn, Marion Post Wolcott, Gordon Parks, Carl Mydans, John Vachon, Russell Lee, Jack Delano, John Collier, and Marjory Collins. At any given time, only a few photographers were on his staff. Stryker provided his photographers with detailed shooting scripts and encouraged the photographers to learn about the history, economy, and social structures of the communities where they were sent on assignment. When out on assignment, the photographers would send their negatives back to Washington, D.C., where Stryker's staff would print the images that Stryker wanted to use to promote the activities of the FSA. Stryker maintained a tight control over the FSA project, including the right to destroy negatives. Stryker's insistence on control sometimes led to conflict with his photographers. For example, Walker Evans worked for the FSA for just eighteen months and left because of significant philosophical differences with Stryker.

The FSA photographs provide a good mirror of the concerns of many Americans during the Great Depression. The photographs from the first years of the FSA project tended to exemplify traditional social documentary photography, with an emphasis on the dignity of the poor and displaced farmers and a celebration of agrarian society. As the United States approached World War II, however, Stryker told the photographers to seek out more positive images of American life, including the strength of American industry. Ironically, both the grim and the optimistic photographs were sometimes met with charges that they were propaganda.

The photographs of the FSA were seen widely during the Depression. By 1938, FSA photographs had been published in many national magazines and newspapers and were included in a major photography exhibition at the Grand Central Palace. The popularity of the images continued to grow, and, by 1940, nearly a dozen books containing FSA photographs had been published. Stryker's unit was transferred to the Office of War Information in 1942. In 1943, Stryker left government service and went to work in the public relations department of Standard Oil of New Jersey. The FSA file is stored in the Library of Congress.

Dorothea Lange, who photographed for *Life* magazine and the Farm Security Administration, poses atop her car, which served as a portable darkroom, in 1936. *(Library of Congress)*

WORKS PROGRESS ADMINISTRATION

The Works Progress Administration's Federal Art Project (WPA/FAP), active from 1935 to 1943, employed artists who were on government relief. The WPA/FAP marked the first time that the federal government directly supported the nation's art activities, which was controversial because many Americans did not feel that the government had any role in supporting the arts. The work of the WPA/FAP was concentrated in urban areas, where most of the country's artists lived, and the art produced was available at the state and local level. The 1930s was a time when artists believed that they had an important role to play in society and that their art could have a positive impact on people's lives. Photographers were routinely employed to record WPA/FAP art projects, such as recording artists at their easels or teaching young students, or performers and dancers on stage. Photography was also sometimes included in collaborative projects, including the creation of murals, a popular public art form in the 1930s.

Although photography was primarily used to record the activities of the WPA/FAP, some projects used photography for its own potential as a means of recording social reality or of creative expression. Berenice Abbott, Minor White, and Clarence John Laughlin used photography to record the changing urban environments of three American cities, revealing a retrospective spirit that could also be found in the photography of the FSA. Abbott's project, "Changing New York," which recorded the physical transformation of New York City from 1935 to 1938, was one of the most successful and best-known of the WPA/FAP projects. White photographed Portland, Oregon, and said that he wanted to "document by nostalgia." Laughlin documented the architecture of the old South, seeking arrangements that visually linked modern signs and products with Victorian-era buildings of New Orleans. A WPA/FAP project in California that included Edward and Brett Weston was concerned primarily with creative self-expression and carried no designs for documenting any existing social conditions.

THE PHOTO LEAGUE

The Photo League was a loosely knit group of photographers who came together in New York City in the 1930s. Most league members were the children of working-class Jewish immigrants living in Brooklyn, the Bronx, or Manhattan's Lower East Side; among the members were Aaron Siskind, Lisette Model, Walter Rosenblum, Sol Libsohn, and Sid Grossman. The Photo League was founded in 1936 as a spin-off of the radical Workers' Film and Photography League, which was founded in 1930 in Berlin as a part of the Workers' International Relief, itself an arm of the Communist International. Inspired by the pioneering social documentary photography of Lewis Hine, much of the energy of the Photo League came from radical Depression-era politics. For fifteen years, the Photo League was a vibrant center of activity in American documentary photography, offering classes in photography (Paul Strand was one of the teachers) as well as exhibition space, lectures by leading photographers and critics, and social and financial support for its members.

Although the Photo League was not a government-sponsored organization, league members shared many of the same social concerns as the photographers of the FSA, and some FSA photographers were also league members. Other league members worked on projects for the WPA/FAP. The Photo League actively sought to present the informational and social concerns of documentary photography in aesthetically pleasing compositions, with careful attention paid to the quality of the final print. Less nostalgic than either the FSA or the WPA/FAP, the Photo League had an activist orientation that sought change in the present instead of longing for a simpler past.

Photo League photographers were concerned with issues of poverty and racial inequality, and they concentrated their work primarily in the slum areas of New York City, areas with which many of them were familiar. As part of its political philosophy, the Photo League insisted that photographers record the social conditions of their surroundings through carefully made photographs. Not surprisingly, many of the photographs produced by league members are similar to FSA photography, both in subject matter and photographic style. However, the ability to control both the printing and the context of the photographs set the Photo League apart from the photographers of the FSA, who had little control over how their photographs were used. In 1947, amid an increasingly conservative political environment, the Photo League was blacklisted. By 1951, the Photo League disbanded, though its influence continued for many years, its former members continuing to publish and exhibit and to teach a younger generation of photographers.

MARK RICE

See also: Farm Security Administration; Federal Art Project; *Life*; *Look*; Resettlement Administration; Works Progress Administration; Bourke-White, Margaret; Evans, Walker; Lange, Dorothea; Shahn, Ben.

Bibliography

Bezner, Lili Corbus. *Photography and Politics in America: From the New Deal into the Cold War.* Baltimore: Johns Hopkins University Press, 1999.

Curtis, James. *Mind's Eye, Mind's Truth: FSA Photography Reconsidered.* Philadelphia: Temple University Press, 1989.

Daniel, Pete, et al. *Official Images: New Deal Photography.* Washington: Smithsonian Institution Press, 1987.

Fleischhauer, Carl, and Beverly W. Brannan, eds. *Documenting America, 1935–1943.* Berkeley: University of California Press, 1988.

Kozol, Wendy. *Life's America.* Philadelphia: Temple University Press, 1994.

Stott, William. *Documentary Expression and Thirties America.* New York: Oxford University Press, 1973.

POPULAR FRONT

The Popular Front is the term used to describe the alliance between the Communist Party of the United States, the Socialist Party, progressives, and liberals within the Democratic Party in the middle and late 1930s.

During the 1920s and early 1930s, American Communists kept their distance from other leftist and liberal groups and parties. Following the lead of the Soviet Communist Party, American Communists viewed Socialists and liberals as insufficiently radical in their fight against capitalist excesses.

But by the mid-1930s, events both in America and abroad had forced a rethinking of this strategy. The rise of the stridently anticommunist Nazi regime in Germany led Moscow to seek democratic allies in Western Europe in the struggle against fascism. This was known as the Popular Front strategy, and its slogan was "no enemies on the left." In America, the Popular Front was both antifascist and pro–New Deal.

During the middle and late 1930s, Communists joined with labor and liberal political organizations to promote union organizing and government job programs, fight domestic fascism, and support the government of Spain, which was fighting fascists in that country's civil war. But in 1939, when the Soviet Union signed a nonaggression treaty with Nazi Germany, the Popular Front was abandoned in both Western Europe and the United States. Hitler's invasion of the Soviet Union in June 1941—and America's entry into the war and alliance with the Soviet Union after December 1941—revived the Popular Front for the duration.

See also: Communist Party; Democratic Party; fascism, domestic; Socialist Party; Soviet Union; Spanish Civil War.

Bibliography

Klehr, Harvey, and John Earl Haynes. *The American Communist Movement: Storming Heaven Itself.* New York: Twayne, 1992.

Ottanelli, Fraser. *The Communist Party of the United States: From the Depression to World War II.* New Brunswick, NJ: Rutgers University Press, 1991.

A temporary alliance between the Communist Party and other leftist forces, the Popular Front of the 1930s was intended by Communist leaders to ward off conservative politicians in America and defeat fascist movements abroad. *(Brown Brothers)*

PORGY AND BESS

One of the greatest achievements of the American musical theater, *Porgy and Bess* (1935) was called a "folk opera" by its creators, composer George Gershwin and lyricists Ira Gershwin and DuBose Heyward.

With its story of the tragic love of a crippled man named Porgy for a beautiful young woman named Bess, the musical is set amidst a rural southern black community, and both the music and lyrics borrow heavily from the African-American gospel and blues tradition. Many of the songs in *Porgy and Bess* have become all-American classics, including "Summertime," "I Got Plenty o' Nuttin'," and "It Ain't Necessarily So."

The three-act opera was first performed by the Theatre Guild at New York's Alvin Theater on October 10, 1935, and went through 124 performances. It has been revived several times since, including a huge production at Radio City Music Hall in 1983.

See also: music; Gershwin, George and Ira.

Bibliography

Alpert, Hollis. *The Life and Times of* Porgy and Bess: *The Story of an American Classic.* New York: Knopf, 1990.

Rosenberg, Deena. *Fascinating Rhythm: The Collaboration of George and Ira Gershwin.* New York: Dutton, 1991.

PROHIBITION

The era of Prohibition lasted from January 1920 to April 1933, during which the Eighteenth Amendment to the Constitution and the National Prohibition Act (Volstead Act) outlawed the "manufacture, sale, or transportation of intoxicating liquors" that contained more than 0.5 percent alcohol.

THE PROHIBITION ERA: 1920–33

By the time the states had ratified the Eighteenth Amendment in 1919 (the ratification process was completed in record time) and the Volstead Act was passed in 1920 (an act that was written by the head of the Anti-Saloon League), most states had enacted laws that banned the manufacture and sale of alcohol. Supporters of Prohibition, primarily women's temperance groups, progressive reformers, and rural Protestants, predicted the dawn of a new era for the nation's moral character. Urban crime, political corruption, and family violence would become distant memories.

Yet supporters of Prohibition failed to appreciate not only the complexity of the nation's problems, but also just how difficult it would be to regulate private behavior. Enforcement of Prohibition, the responsibility of which was given to the Treasury Department in 1925 under the Volstead Act, proved to be an immense challenge. Only 1,500 federal agents were allotted for the daunting job of patrolling the entire nation: about one agent for every 200,000 square miles, not including 12,000 miles of coastline and borders. Faced with a near impossible task and paid a miserly income, many agents succumbed to the enticement of easy money— 10 percent of Prohibition agents were fired for corruption during the 1920s.

For criminals, or for others who simply sought adventure and enjoyed flaunting the law, Prohibition offered a wealth of opportunities. From the isolated backcountry of Tennessee to the urban center of Chicago, citizens devised ingenious ways of skirting Prohibition. They distilled liquor from corn, squash, and potatoes, as well as from industrial alcohol, antifreeze, and paint. Many consumers, understandably, became ill or died from drinking products such as Jackass Brandy, Soda Pop Moon, Jake, and Pebble Ford. Not all alcohol was unsafe: rumrunner Bill McCoy smuggled good quality liquor from the Caribbean and Europe, prompting drinkers to ask for "the real McCoy," while distilleries in Mexico, the West Indies, and Canada, in particular, enjoyed a brisk business as they willingly sold liquor to contrabandists. Customers interested in entertainment and music with their drinks could frequent one of the thousands of speakeasies that cropped up across the country; New York, for example, boasted at least 30,000 speakeasies by 1927. According to legend, the easiest way for a stranger to locate a speakeasy in New York (a "city on a still") or San Francisco was to "ask the nearest cop," who could usually point out one just a few doors away. Loopholes in the law allowed the selling of alcohol for medicinal or religious purposes. The sale of sacramental wine increased dramatically, while one enterprising criminal bought a chain of drugstores so he could order alcohol legally and then hijacked his own delivery trucks.

Prohibition also encouraged the growth of organized crime. Many of those who had operated gambling and prostitution rings now took the logical next step and entered the lucrative market of liquor trafficking. Chicago's Al "Scarface" Capone, in particular, reaped huge profits from the liquor business—one estimate put Capone's take in 1927 at $60 million. As Capone remarked matter-of-factly, "If people didn't want beer and wouldn't drink it, a fellow would be crazy for going around trying to sell it . . . I've always regarded it as a public benefaction if people were given decent liquor and square games." The business of crime often included violence, as rival gangs confronted each other to protect their respective turfs. In Chicago, for instance, over 200 gang-related killings occurred during the first four years of prohibition.

REPEAL: 1929–33

In the early 1920s, supporters of Prohibition could note with satisfaction that alcohol consumption had decreased, particularly among the working class (probably due to the exorbitant price of bootleg liquor—the price of a quart of beer increased 600 percent between 1916 and 1928). In 1910, per capita consumption of alcohol was 2.6 gallons; by 1934, it was less than a gallon. Ar-

In an illustration entitled "Beer is Back," workers and consumers outside the Falstaff Brewing Company in St. Louis celebrate the relegalization of beer on April 7, 1933. *(Library of Congress)*

rests for drunkenness fell, and alcohol-related diseases declined.

Yet, by the end of the decade, it was clear that Prohibition had failed to eliminate drinking and create a more orderly and moral society, especially within major urban areas. While the law was successful in virtually eliminating the working-class saloons, it encouraged the growth of new drinking establishments, such as cafés, restaurants, and nightclubs, that catered to the middle class. Law enforcement was ineffective; moreover, no politician seriously considered shutting down the Mexican and Canadian borders or erecting a naval blockade along the coastlines to stop the flow of thousands of gallons of liquor into the United States. Finally, the progressive zeal to impose order on society and to improve moral character had dissipated by the end of the decade. In its place arose a new consumer

culture that emphasized youth, entertainment, and materialism, which allowed little room for the reformist impulse.

As Americans began to question the effectiveness of the "noble experiment," a movement for repeal of the Eighteenth Amendment emerged. Organized opposition had appeared as early as 1922 in the Association Against the Prohibition Amendment (AAPA), which consisted of wealthy industrialists opposed to a powerful federal government. After the stock market crash in 1929, the AAPA also argued that repeal of Prohibition would create new jobs and the legal manufacture and sale of alcohol would create a new source of tax revenue. The AAPA was joined by the Women's Organization for National Prohibition Reform (WONPR) in 1929. Like the AAPA, the WONPR believed that the government had no business in dictating the habits of private individuals. The WONPR grew into a formidable opponent of Prohibition and counted chapters in forty-four states by 1933. As its official pamphlet to potential members stated, "National Prohibition has incited crime, increased lawlessness, hypocrisy, and corruption among all classes of citizens and . . . the cause of real temperance has been retarded."

In politics, President Herbert Hoover, who had reached the White House in 1928 on a dry platform, refused to endorse the repeal of Prohibition in 1932, although his advisers were pleading with him to change his stance. Most delegates to the Democratic convention in 1932 were openly calling for repeal, and Franklin D. Roosevelt, who had not taken a strong stand either way, took up the cause. After Roosevelt assumed the White House, he applauded the new Congress as members amended the Volstead Act to allow the sale of wine and beer containing 3.2 percent alcohol. On December 5, 1933, the Twenty-first Amendment repealed the Eighteenth Amendment and sent the responsibility of Prohibition back to the states and to local communities. Not all states followed the federal example. Kansas remained dry until 1948, Oklahoma until 1957, and Mississippi until 1966. Many states also allowed local governments to enact Prohibition laws in their own communities.

CHRISTINE K. ERICKSON

See also: Alcoholics Anonymous; Crime; election of 1932; *Scarface*; Capone, Al; Document: Democratic Party platform, 1932; Republican Party platform, 1932

Bibliography

Kerr, K. Austin. *Organized for Prohibition: A New History of the Anti-Saloon League.* New Haven: Yale University Press, 1985.

Lender, Mark Edward, and James Kirby Martin. *Drinking in America: A History.* New York: Free Press, 1982.

Neumann, Caryn E. "The End of Gender Solidarity: The History of the Women's Organization for National Prohibition Reform in the United States, 1929–1933." *Journal of Women's History* 9:2 (Summer 1997): 31–51.

Parrish, Michael E. *Anxious Decades: America in Prosperity and Depression, 1920–1941.* New York: W. W. Norton, 1992.

Pegram, Thomas R. *Battling Demon Rum: The Struggle for a Dry America, 1800–1933.* Chicago: Ivan R. Dee, 1998.

http://www.history.ohio-state.edu/projects/prohibition/contents.htm

http://www.wpl.lib.oh.us:80/AntiSaloon/

PUBLIC ENEMY

Among the most popular gangster movies of the 1930s, *Public Enemy* was directed by William Wellman and starred the young James Cagney.

Like others of its genre, including *Little Caesar* and *Scarface*, *Public Enemy* depicted men who had gone bad and turned against society. Yet the movie also suggested that that same society was harsh and chaotic, somehow part of the reason why the movie's hero had gone bad. While never overt, this message, say film historians, was picked up and appreciated by Depression-era audiences.

The 1931 film also starred Jean Harlow, Joan Blondell, Beryl Mercer, and Mae Clarke. Like many other gangster films, *Public Enemy* was produced by the Warner Brothers studio.

See also: films, feature; *Little Caesar*; *Scarface*; Cagney, James.

Bibliography

Baxter, John. *Hollywood in the Thirties.* New York: A. S. Barnes, 1968.

Sklar, Robert. *Movie-Made America: A Cultural History of the American Movies.* New York: Random House, 1975.

RADIO

People listened to radio differently in the 1930s from the way they do today. If the medium now is the domain of background music, call-in talk shows, and commuter headlines, it was once the central source for news, entertainment, and general opinion. Radio's influence far outweighed that of the newspapers; roughly, it filled the roles in family life that television and the Internet fill today. That is, beyond informing people and entertaining them, it socialized them. Radio was part of an enormous public dialogue that standardized people's beliefs about themselves. Largely in this medium people formed their notions of family life, civic structure, and national mission. Radio was the backbone of popular culture in a way that it no longer is.

RADIO CULTURE

Nor had it started that way. Less than a generation before, experimental stations playing to hobbyists and eccentrics improvised schedules as best they could, from some humble sound sources. There were local dance orchestras, blackface minstrel acts, sometimes election results, and assortments of sopranos and learned lecturers. Professional broadcasting was still so undifferentiated from garage tinkering in the early 1920s that commercial stations were required to go off the air—and did—whenever a maritime distress signal was heard.

By the mid-1930s, however, broadcasting (and tinkering too) was widely organized, capitalized, and regulated. Americans had grown used to the medium and accepted what they heard on commercial radio as weighty journalism and solid performance. Production standards were much improved, to be sure, but the listening public was remarkably prepared to hear radio content as Truth, with a capital "T." Emblematic of this credulity was the public response to dramatist Orson Welles's adaptation of H. G. Wells's piece of Victoriana, *The War of the Worlds*, broadcast on NBC by his Mercury Theatre on Halloween eve 1938. This was a simulated as-it-happens account of a landing in New Jersey by an invasion force from Mars. Such was radio's authority that people by the thousands fled their homes and abandoned their jobs. By some estimates, over a

million Americans believed that an invasion was under way. Highway patrols were overwhelmed by refugees, particularly on the eastern seaboard. Telephone exchanges jammed with frantic calls to relatives and police. National Guardsmen trooped to their armories in some New Jersey counties to report in. Even off-duty doctors and nurses turned out to tend to the casualties of Martian weapons.

It is not documented that anyone was killed in the panic, folklore to the contrary, but there was an aftermath of indignation. The National Broadcasting Corporation was sued. Ontario authorities considered censorship of programs originating in the United States. British pundits politely discounted American gullibility, while German and Italian ones shrilled that only a cowardly and decadent democracy would fall for tall tales of Martian—or Axis—atrocities. Radio and movie scripts bore traces of the event for a decade, in dialogue that alluded to hoax broadcasts and public overreaction. America's perplexity at its own frenzy drove investigations such as the Princeton University Project, led by psychologist Hadley Cantril, and CBS's own study, directed by sociologist Herta Herzog. What made radio able to disrupt the national peace? According to these probes, it was a combination of the novelty of sound effects, overall jitters about war in Europe (reported nearly live by radio correspondents), the presence of exotic science in public imagination (partly radio's own achievement), and the accident of tuning in late, when listeners missed the dramatic disclaimers and the station breaks. But mostly, the studies concluded, behind the panic was the sheer habit of assuming radio's general authority. This habit was of the essence of the 1930s, when it was even illegal for radio comedians to imitate the president on the air, as both a matter of respect for the office and a surety against panicky misunderstandings.

BROADCAST TECHNIQUES

It was in the 1930s that the medium jumped to the center of American household life, but the leaps in ingenuity that made possible the box in the living room had mostly been made by the 1920s. Guglielmo Marconi's improvements on the early 1900s wireless apparatus of Heinrich Hertz and his colleagues had produced a rudimentary design for sending and receiving continuous-wave signals adaptable to Morse code. Crystal detectors made receivers capable of detecting the fluctuations of speech; these or the more sophisticated magnetic, electrolytic, and vacuum tube detectors were the heart of radio receivers until after World War II. Reginald Fessenden's remarkable principle of heterodyne reception, made practical by Edwin Armstrong's circuit design and Lee De Forest's thermionic grid-triode tube, put sensitive, wide-band receivers in the hands of the public by the end of World War I. Transmitters, originally based on an arcing "spark-gap" technique, were improved with tuned circuits, alternators, arc oscillators, and triode oscillators, and by the early 1920s stable signals across the band, with power ratings as high as 500 kilowatts, were common. Power generators for microwave frequencies were on paper at least by 1924 and became workable when Russell and Sigurd Varian invented the klystron in 1939.

There were specialized uses for radio technology in the 1930s besides broadcasting, of course. There were ship-to-shore telegraphy and telephony. Jamming of opponents' signals was conducted by the Nazis and the Soviet Union before World War II. Rudimentary facsimile transmission had been possible since 1925. Commercial radiophotos were available for newspapers soon after.

Ordinary broadcasting was chiefly conducted in the medium-wave, amplitude-modulated (AM) manner familiar to us, but not exclusively so. Edwin Armstrong, who responded to the industrialist David Sarnoff's call for a static-free signal, spent ten years at Columbia University developing a frequency-modulated (FM) signal, which he demonstrated with great effect to specialists and business executives in 1935. In evangelizing for commercial use of this emergent technology he faced terrific opposition from entrenched AM broadcast elements, a bitter patent fight with his underwriters, Radio Corporation of America (RCA), and resistance from the Federal Communications Commission (FCC), more interested in spectrum allocations for television than for FM. Armstrong's salesmanship finally prevailed, and the Yankee Network in Boston Massachusetts and Hartford, Connecticut's station WDRC began commercial FM transmission in 1939.

Shortwave broadcasting, common worldwide in the late 1930s, was surprisingly absent in the United States. President Franklin D. Roosevelt thought it reasonable to have an overseas voice on these long-range bands, but business interests balked, fearing either government meddling in private broadcasting or private broadcasting that lent itself poorly to selling things. Some thirty-five licenses were issued at last in 1939—Britain, Germany, and the Soviet Union having been in the overseas broadcast business for a decade already. When war came, these American stations were gradually commandeered by the government.

The emergent medium that one day would rival radio broadcasting in general was television, but it posed no commercial threat to radio during the 1930s, even though the decade was a frenzied one for television experimenters, policy-makers, and entrepreneurs. In 1939, David Sarnoff unveiled NBC's TV effort at the New York World's Fair. President Roosevelt went on the air himself. (Herbert Hoover had also been in an AT&T telecast experiment in 1927, before his tenure as president.) There were modest scheduled transmissions from the NBC studios for the rest of the year.

Where did the money come from for all this development in radio? Paradoxically, the poor economy helped. Families liked cheap entertainment in this decade, during which something close to one-third of the nation's cinemas went bankrupt. Citizens in the famous *Middletown* study of Muncie, Indiana, conducted by sociologists Robert and Helen Lynd, were dramatically more likely to spend time around the radio in 1936 than they were even seven years before, when radio listening was statistically insignificant. There had been 3 million radio sets in the country in 1924; ten years later, there were nearly 30 million. This stunning growth continued, and by World War II practically every house in the country had at least one radio set. People were willing to forgo paying for food and rent in order to have radio sets in their homes. Car radios and battery-powered portable sets lengthened broadcasters' reach into the countryside as well. The spending public's appetite for receivers, transmitters, and programming content was simply voracious. To satisfy it, more than 275 new stations went on the air between 1935 and 1941. Nearly half of all midsized municipalities had their own stations by mid-decade. Technology and consumer demographics live in symbiosis, after all. This is a principle that shows even in contemporary radio design. Where modern televisions are boxy appliances as a rule, 1930s radios were typically encased in fine cabinetry, like other furniture, or in studiously artistic moulded plastic. Radio culture was, in its fashion, serious business.

In the days before television, Americans, like this Texas couple, relaxed in the evening to listen to their favorite music, comedy, and dramatic radio programs. *(Library of Congress)*

MASS POLITICS

Radio in the 1930s was a melding of technology and popular opinion in another way. As Roosevelt was visionary in his use of airplanes during his political campaigns, so he worked the radio into his political life as well. Media politics may be conventional to us today, but during the Depression—at least on the Rooseveltian scale on which it was managed—this was new. In about thirty intimate broadcast addresses, known as "fireside chats," he was able to win over the bulk of the country to his fairly radical political and socioeconomic vision for combating first the Depression at home and then Axis aggression abroad. Thanks to radio, he was the first president to have his voice recognized instantly by millions of Americans nationwide.

Radio, Roosevelt believed, was good for democ-racy. It could knit together cultural factions otherwise alien to each other, principally those geographically separated. Newspapers were less available for this purpose. The big ones, especially those belonging to the Hearst and McCormick empires, were hostile to New Deal economics; here was demagoguery in the service of the safely rich. The president understandably discouraged ownership of radio stations by newspapers and was largely able to sanitize the medium of the press bias that continued to obtain in print. Not that radio confidence-building was not the convention among totalitarian leaders as well. Radio could promote fascism as well as democracy. Adolf Hitler planned for cheap and low-powered sets in Germany to spread Nazi Party propaganda. Propaganda Minister Joseph Goebbels could preempt regular programming for Hitler right from his desk. Democratic governments abroad were getting used to politicking through the microphone too. Winston Churchill and Charles de Gaulle were abler and more enthusiastic than their predecessors had been in this respect, and it worked well for their popularity.

Roosevelt's partnership with the broadcast industry was clear. He promised no government interference, he appointed FCC commissioners who were sympathetic to business, and he gave radio reporters free access to halls of power. For this his addresses got right-of-way on the networks—networks that even offered to build landlines to independent stations who would air the addresses. Roosevelt was also friends with men like David Sarnoff, founder and head of NBC, and William Paley, head of CBS.

The president had a clear partnership with his audience as well. He talked slowly and simply, without arrays of figures. He anchored his economic talk in the issue of each household's standard of living—was it better last year or worse?—and he did not withhold secrets if he could help it, even in his private comings and goings. (The polio in his legs was taboo, however, and journalists respected that taboo, as they did his possibly adulterous relationship with his secretary.) He even liked to come to his constituency on Sunday evenings at around ten, just when households were quietest and most indulgent. And he worked at the theatrical aspects of his scripts. For he had to compete with a dial full of professional actors and comedians. Thus he labored at easy delivery in a neutral accent, even listening to recordings of himself for practice. Older statesmen groused that his folksy delivery was displacing the grand platform oratory of the nineteenth century. Presidents Wilson, Harding, and Coolidge had all tried radio themselves, but without enthusiasm or good results; so did Hoover, but he was so poor a performer that his broadcasts may have been counterproductive.

Radio delivery mattered in campaigning. Republican presidential candidate Wendell Willkie was effectively laughed offstage and out of Roosevelt's way after his intractable on-air clumsiness in 1940. Delivery mattered even more in rallying Americans to practical political doctrine. Roosevelt's first inaugural address, full of military euphemisms calculated to appeal to the generation that had fought in World War I, worked astonishingly well at calming public jitters. Fear itself, he told them, was the only enemy, and concerted action by all would restore the nation's prosperity. So attentively did the public begin to follow the network coverage of movements on Capitol Hill that Congress—whose debates were now broadcast—enacted important legislation in favor of the New Deal. This was a direct function of presidential personality on the air.

A classic case of 1930s radio manipulation of public opinion was Roosevelt's handling of the banking crisis in March 1933, when he declared an emergency holiday for four days and offered loans to all the banks that were solvent but overwhelmed. Roosevelt went on the air quickly to explain what he had done, ignoring a speech drafted for him by the Treasury Department and using his own, straightforward script instead. The public's response was so supportive that Congress found itself obliged in June to pass a landmark law governing accountability among the members of the Federal Reserve Bank. In the banking affair and in all others, Roosevelt simply styled the radio as his medium for reporting back to the people who elected him. This report-card spirit of on-air address was reliably good for his popularity and hence for his effectiveness in office. His four critical fireside chats of 1933 are universally acknowledged to have secured the public's acceptance of New Deal doctrine.

NETWORKS AND REGULATION

The FCC commissioners appointed by President Roosevelt came into office under the aegis of the Communications Act of 1934, which updated the 1927 Radio Act that created the five-man Federal Radio Commission (FRC). Much had changed in radio technology, and the equipment was being put to many more uses. Congress grouped radio matters under the new commission as it had grouped transportation matters under the Interstate Commerce Commission and power matters under the Federal Power Commission. The commission's method of regulating was codified now, replacing the FRC's fiat system of General Orders.

Even updated, however, the law supporting the FCC was still unwieldy. Its chief assumption, that broadcasting was a local matter and could be licensed as such, was flatly untrue, since by the 1930s the networks controlled the bulk of what the public heard. This was clear when a minor war over content broke out. Senators Robert Wagner (D-NY) and Henry Hatfield (R-WV) led a constituency worried by the gradual displacement of educational programs by commercial ones, and they proposed a bill to amend the act accordingly. Commercial radio, they argued, was a cultural cataclysm. Since the act's real goal had been to move telephone matters into the same domain as radio and off the desk of the Interstate Commerce Commission, too busy with railroad crises to manage phone lines well, no one had given much thought to content at all. There probably was room for amendment. But the campaign dissipated in a few years. The faction's core of thirty-odd low-powered, daytime, usually college-run stations were no match for the lobbying front for the network executives either, to whom simple profits were the only good reason for being in the broadcast business.

Each network trod carefully around antitrust law, but together they formed a near monopoly on broadcast content during the 1930s. NBC had operated two networks, the Red and the Blue, since the 1920s. (In 1943, the FCC forced it to sell one of them to the fledgling ABC.) CBS came into being in 1927, and the Mutual Broadcasting System in 1934. AT&T, skirting antitrust law itself, was the principal supplier of landlines to them all.

PROGRAMS AND PERSONALITIES

Educational programming may not have done well during the 1930s, but the decade did have some triumphs. Radio drama was strong, helped by New Deal programs like the Works Progress Administration's Federal Theater Project. (This program's conservatism, however, annoyed Orson Welles enough to form the breakaway *Mercury Theatre on the Air*.) *Columbia Workshop* and *Lights Out* in particular were two very popular shows. Norman Corwin's *We Hold These Truths* played to an audience of more than 40 million a week after Pearl Harbor. Even more popular were comedy and variety shows, featuring entertainers like Jack Benny and Bing Crosby. *Amos 'n' Andy*, a black-face act on NBC, was so popular that restaurants and factories were known to adjust their shift schedules to accommodate it. As today, 1930s broadcasting tolerated some excesses, such as the rabid "coverage" of Bruno Hauptmann's 1935 trial for allegedly kidnapping Charles A. Lindbergh's baby. On the other hand, civic-minded restraint also obtained, in programs like *America's Town Meeting of the Air* and *The University of Chicago Round Table*. NBC also sponsored its own orchestra, under the famous and capable direction of Arturo Toscanini. The big achievement of the 1930s was the sober institution of the news, a pet project at CBS.

THE AMATEUR VOICE

If commercial forces drove the elevation of the art of broadcasting, the private experimenters also played a role. One cannot understand 1930s radio culture without understanding amateur radio operators, or "hams," still tinkering in their attics. They were extremely large in the popular eye; the Spencer Tracy film *Boys Town* depicts a shortwave station, for example. By now the hams were quasi professionals, organized nationally under voluntary groups like the American Radio Relay League and cooperating with the military and with public agencies in all manner of disaster relief and message-handling tasks. The 40,000 or so licensed amateurs who performed these errands of altruism also made up an enormously useful pool of technical skill when the armed forces later mobilized against the Axis powers. Meanwhile, all through the 1930s, they continued to refine their hobby, to advise policy regulators in Washington, and to keep alive for subsequent generations the great mystique of radio.

DUNCAN FISHER

See also: *Amos 'n' Andy*; fireside chats; Lindbergh kidnapping; Mercury Theatre; world's fairs; Federal Communications Commission; *War of the Worlds*; Roosevelt, Franklin D.; Wagner, Robert; Welles, Orson. Documents: Fireside Chat on the Banking Crisis, March 12, 1933; Fireside Chat on the National Recovery Administration, July 24, 1933; Fireside Chat on Social Security Acts, January 17, 1935; Fireside Chat on work relief programs, April 28, 1935.

Bibliography

Barfield, Ray E. *Listening to Radio, 1920–1950*. Westport, CT: Praeger, 1996.

Barnouw, Eric. *A History of Broadcasting in the United States*. Vol. 1, *A Tower in Babel* [to 1933]; vol. 2, *The Golden Web* [1933–1953]. New York: Oxford University Press, 1966–1968.

Brown, Robert J. *Manipulating the Ether: The Power of Broadcast Radio in Thirties America*. Jefferson, NC: McFarland, 1998.

Culbert, David Holbrook. *News for Everyman: Radio and Foreign Affairs in Thirties America*. Westport, CT: Greenwood Press, 1976.

DeSoto, Clinton B. *200 Meters & Down: The Story of Amateur Radio*. West Hartford, CT: American Radio Relay League, 1936.

Dunning, John. *On the Air: The Encyclopedia of Old-Time Radio*. New York: Oxford University Press, 1998.

Godfrey, Donald G., and Frederic A. Leigh, eds. *Historical Dictionary of American Radio*. Westport, CT: Greenwood Press, 1998.

Head, Sydney W. *Broadcasting in America: A Survey of Radio and Television*. 3rd ed. Boston: Houghton Mifflin, 1976.

Hilmes, Michele. *Radio Voices: American Broadcasting, 1922–1952*. Minneapolis: University of Minnesota Press, 1997.

Hosley, David. *As Good as Any Foreign Correspondent on American Radio, 1930–1940*. Contributions to the Study of Mass Media and Communications, 2. Westport, CT: Greenwood Press, 1984.

RAILROADS

The years of the Great Depression and the New Deal were extremely difficult for the railroad industry. Because they needed to maintain expensive rolling stock and rights-of-way, railroads were a high-fixed-cost industry; even a small drop in traffic could result in net revenue deficits. During the 1920s, most railways had invested heavily in equipment and track improvements despite facing increasingly stiff competition for freight and passenger traffic from the rapid diffusion of automobiles, trucks, and buses. They spent approximately $765 million on 15,000 new steam locomotives, $1.7 billion on 850,000 new freight cars, and additional capital to improve the tracks and roadbeds. However, while these capital improvements greatly increased the efficiency and financial health of the industry, rapidly declining demand after the stock market crash virtually crippled the industry. Operating revenues in 1933 were less than half of their 1929 level, and the industry suffered net income deficits in 1932, 1933, 1934, and 1938. Despite a variety of attempts by both the industry and the federal government to stimulate a recovery, the economic health of the railroads improved only with the coming of World War II.

FREIGHT TRAFFIC

Accounting for approximately 70 to 80 percent of railroad revenues during the 1920s, freight traffic formed the core of the early twentieth-century railroad business but was already demonstrating signs of weakness long before the stock market crash in 1929. Taking advantage of the millions of miles of new highways, trucks began to significantly erode the freight business of the railroads by offering much greater flexibility of service, less damage to valuable merchandise freight and animals, and often lower rates. While the railroads were weighed down by extremely high fixed costs, the trucking industry was able to take advantage of publicly maintained roadways to substantially reduce costs. Ironically, early twentieth-century railway executives and farmers had been the primary promoters of highway development as a means of improving connections between the railroad and local farms.

In addition to the emerging competition from trucks, depressed prices for agricultural commodities during the 1920s kept railroad freight tonnage and revenues virtually stagnant, especially in the Midwest, South, and Southwest. As farm prices collapsed in 1930–1931, railroad tonnage and revenues plummeted by almost 50 percent. The railroads responded by making moderate reductions in freight rates (continuing a trend begun in the 1920s) in combination with drastic reductions in operating costs; employment levels dropped by over 40 percent between 1929 and 1933. Additionally, in the fall of 1932, management was able to negotiate a 10 percent cut in the basic pay rate for all remaining employees, a reduction that prevailed until 1935, when railway labor leaders successfully bargained for a return to the earlier pay rates.

Despite these efforts to cut costs, the railroads remained in serious financial trouble throughout the 1930s and sought federal intervention to relieve their plight. Progress was made in 1935 when Congress passed the Motor Carrier Act, which regulated the rates and services of trucks for the first time. This proved to be a Pyrrhic victory for the railroads, however, as the new regulation actually helped the trucking industry to earn much needed profits without undercutting its competitive advantage over the railways. While the act eliminated ruinous price competition between truck carriers by establishing minimum rates, the trucking industry quickly realized that its greater flexibility allowed it to charge the same high rates as the railroads without losing traffic. As their freight business continued to languish, the railroads turned to their passenger lines with the hope of reviving revenues.

PASSENGER TRAVEL

The total number of railroad passengers, the number of passenger-miles traveled, and revenue from passenger trains all peaked in 1920 before beginning a steady downward trend for the remainder of the decade. The growing popularity of the automobile combined with improvements in the highway network accounted for a large proportion of this loss in passenger traffic; by 1929, the automobile transported three-quarters of all intercity travelers. This declining demand for passenger service was further exacerbated by the emergence of the Greyhound bus network in 1929. By the end of 1929, the number of passenger-miles traveled by train had declined by 34 percent from its 1920 peak; by the trough in 1933, total passenger-miles were only one-third of their 1920 level. Railway passenger service operated with annual deficits in every year from 1930 to 1941.

The railways attempted to reverse this trend by improving passenger train service and speed. In 1930, air-conditioned passenger trains were introduced and rail service between New York City and Los Angeles was reduced to three days (although that same year airlines flew the distance in only thirty-six hours). However, the downward trend in demand for passenger service was reversed only with the introduction of the first streamlined diesel locomotives. In 1934, Ralph Budd, president of the Chicago, Burlington & Quincy Railroad, introduced the stainless steel *Zephyr*, while Carl R. Gray, president of the Union Pacific, built the *City of Salina* out of a lightweight aluminum alloy. The sleek lines, fast speeds, and noiseless ride of these diesel locomotives—free of the smoke and cinders of the old steam engines—caught the fancy of the riding public, and other railroads quickly followed suit with streamliners of their own. The introduction of these new trains was accompanied by a great deal of advertising—both by the individual lines as well as by the Association of American Railroads—aimed at informing potential passengers of the fast, cheap, pleasant, and reliable service now offered on diesel streamliners.

Costing between $125,000 and $200,000 each, these new locomotives were extremely expensive, but the costs were quickly recouped: In direct contrast to the older steam locomotives, the diesel engines could be turned on to full-power almost immediately, operated thousands of miles without servicing, needed little water, were at least one-third more fuel-efficient than steam engines, and exerted less wear and tear on the track. The new streamliners cut travel times between cities by 20 to 40 percent. The average daily miles traveled by passenger trains at speeds over 60 miles per hour increased from only 1,100 miles in 1930 to more than 75,000 by 1940, 10 percent of which were at or above 70 miles per hour. In addition to these dramatic increases in speed, railroad safety was also greatly improved as fatalities per 100 million passenger-miles declined from 0.28 during the decade of the 1920s to just over 0.14 for the 1930s—many times safer than either the airplane or the automobile. And yet, despite the popularity and efficiency of the new streamliners, most of the passenger trains of the 1930s were unable to turn a profit. Although the new services did slow the rate of decline in revenues, passenger deficits still averaged almost $250 million from 1935 until the eve of World War II.

LABOR RELATIONS

One of the major advantages of the use of the diesel engine was the reduction in travel times and maintenance needs while the trains were in service. Whereas steam locomotives required firemen to feed fuel into the engine's firebox, this position was no longer needed on diesel locomotives. The Brotherhood of Locomotive Firemen and Enginemen, however, battled fiercely against the elimination of this position, emerging victorious with the signing of the Diesel Locomotive Agreement on February 28, 1937. The railroads estimated that this agreement to require firemen on most locomotives added approximately $445,000 to their annual payroll costs. Additionally, although dieselization also greatly shortened travel times, a 1919 agreement based wages on distance and not hours; all locomotive crews received a day's wages every 100 miles, regardless of the time required for the trip. Thus, the increased speed of the diesel engines forced railroads to pay full wages to crews who worked only three or four hours; management proved unable to expunge this agreement during the Depression.

Labor's position was further strengthened by New Deal legislation. The Railway Labor Act of 1934 guaranteed workers similar rights to those granted to workers in the manufacturing sector under Section 7 of the National Industrial Recovery Act. The act preserved the right of railroad workers to organize and bargain collectively, as well as enumerating extensive arbitration and mediation regulations. The National Railroad Adjustment Board, established by the act, possessed the power to penalize either labor or management if they refused to settle mutual disputes.

In 1934, Congress also passed the first Railroad Retirement Act, which created a pension program administered by the government. The act established a mandatory retirement age of sixty-five and provided pensions for all current and future workers, as well as those who had been employed by a railroad within one year of the law's enactment. The act was declared unconstitutional, however, in the 1935 decision of *Railroad Retirement Board et al. v. Alton Railroad Company* when the Supreme Court ruled that the act did not fall within the purview of the interstate commerce clause and that granting pensions to former employees violated the due process clause of the Fifth Amendment. This court ruling was immediately followed by the Railroad Retirement Act of 1935, which was likewise declared unconstitutional in 1936 by a United States District Court. Finally, the Railroad Retirement Act of 1937, representing a joint proposal between management and the railway brotherhoods, provided for a revised employee pension plan.

NEW DEAL ATTEMPTS TO REVIVE THE RAILROAD INDUSTRY

As deficits in railway revenues grew in the early 1930s, President Franklin D. Roosevelt solicited cost reduction proposals from the business community. The most important proposal, drawn up by John W. Barriger III of Kuhn-Loeb and backed by Boston banker and financier Frederick H. Prince, recommended the voluntary consolidation of the nation's railroads into seven systems to eliminate waste resulting from competition. Proponents estimated that the Prince Plan of Railroad Consolidation would save the industry $740,000 per year, largely through a reduction in railway workers. Not surprisingly, primary opposition to this plan came from the railway brotherhoods, who objected to such a drastic reduction in the workforce. By the end of 1933, the Roosevelt administration had abandoned this plan and sought less drastic remedies.

As an alternative, Congress passed the Emergency Transportation Act of 1933 on the recommendation of the Interstate Commerce Commission (ICC). This act was designed to promote operating efficiency by establishing a Federal Coordinator of Transportation to eliminate redundancies in services and facilities, lower expenses, and reduce fixed charges. However, the act proved virtually ineffective due to a clause prohibiting economies obtained through a reduction in workers

below May 1933 levels. The main long-term outcome of the act was the establishment of the Association of American Railroads in 1934. The association addressed issues of mutual concern to the railroads, including questions of safety, interactions with regulatory agencies, Congress, and the federal courts, and the promotion of a favorable public attitude toward the railroads.

Although the Emergency Transportation Act provided little relief for the industry, eighty-one railroads were aided by over $512 million in loans for the refinancing of debt and the purchase of new equipment from the Reconstruction Finance Corporation. Nevertheless, the industry suffered net income deficits in 1932, 1933, 1934, and 1938, with an average rate of return on net property investment of only 2.25 percent for the entire decade; railways accounting for almost one-third of the nation's total mileage were either bankrupt or in receivership by 1938. The ICC therefore encouraged Congress to form a committee of railway representatives and brotherhood representatives to consider new legislation. The resulting Transportation Act of 1940 called for the coordination of all competing forms of transportation, including railroads, trucks, and water carriers, under the jurisdiction of the ICC.

What ultimately allowed the railroad industry to recover from the Great Depression, however, was the rearmament program begun at the end of the 1930s. Increased demand for coal, steel, and petroleum products for American defense preparations, as well as the passage of the Lend-Lease Act, reinvigorated economic activity throughout the nation. For example, freight tonnage on the Illinois Central rose 59 percent in just four months during the summer of 1939. Overall, freight traffic hit record levels by 1942 and even passenger traffic experienced a resurgence, with revenues doubling between 1941 and 1942. The war experience of the railroad industry provided it with false hopes of strong future growth and renewed dominance of the nation's transportation network.

SHARON ANN MURPHY

See also: National Industrial Recovery Act; Reconstruction Finance Corporation; Section 7; Lend-Lease Act.

Bibliography

Bryant, Keith L., Jr., ed. *Railroads in the Age of Regulation, 1900–1980.* New York: Bruccoli Clark Layman, 1988.

Childs, William R. "The Infrastructure." In *Encyclopedia of the United States in the Twentieth Century*, ed. Stanley I. Kutler, pp. 1331–1355. New York: Simon & Schuster, 1996.

Historical Statistics of the United States: From Colonial Times to 1970, pp. 723–741. Washington, DC: Department of Commerce, Bureau of the Census, 1975.

Jones, Harry E. *Railroad Wages and Labor Relations, 1900–1952.*

New York: Bureau of Information of the Eastern Railways, 1953.

Martin, Albro. *Railroads Triumphant: The Growth, Rejection, and Rebirth of a Vital American Force.* New York: Oxford University Press, 1992.

Stover, John F. *American Railroads.* Chicago: University of Chicago Press, 1961.

———. *The Life and Decline of the American Railroad.* New York: Oxford University Press, 1970.

REPUBLICAN PARTY

The era of the Great Depression witnessed one of the great political watersheds in American history. By the end of the 1930s, Franklin D. Roosevelt's New Deal had substantially remade the political structure that had persisted in the United States since Reconstruction, transforming his Democratic Party from an uneasy alliance of southern farmers and northern immigrants into a powerful national coalition representing a broad range of political and social interests. In so doing, Roosevelt helped to relegate the Republican Party, which had enjoyed great electoral success for more than thirty years, to a marginal opposition, incapable of carrying national elections or mustering legislative initiatives on its own. Yet out of this nadir of Republican influence came a chastened party that would refurbish its traditional tenets and summon a renewed era of Republican popularity in the 1950s.

THE 1920s

When Herbert Hoover defeated Al Smith in the 1928 presidential race, it seemed yet another in a long line of Republican victories. Since 1896, the Republicans had held a lock on the presidency—except in 1912 when a temporary rupture in the party handed a victory to Woodrow Wilson—and the election of Warren G. Harding in 1920 and Calvin Coolidge in 1924 seemed to certify that the GOP was the party of national leadership. Hoover's personal disdain for partisanship confirmed for many that a new stasis had indeed been reached, whereby Republicans controlled national elections and the Democrats growled as a permanent loyal opposition. The stock market crash of 1929 upset this equilibrium and began the transformative processes that would topple the Republican ascendancy.

For nearly a decade, the GOP had closely associated itself with the glittering prosperity for which the 1920s are widely remembered. Exemplified by Treasury secretary Andrew Mellon's supply-side tax cuts and Commerce secretary Hoover's aggressive pursuit of business-government partnerships, the Republican Party had cast itself as the political collaborator of American capitalism. Assurance in prosperity ran so high that Hoover boasted in his 1928 nomination acceptance speech that soon "poverty will be banished from this nation." Shortly over a year later, however, the stock market crash of October 1929 undid the confidence that many Americans held in the GOP as the party of prosperity. They saw Hoover's conservative policies as wholly inadequate to restore the economy, especially his seemingly callous opposition to poor relief. Assigned blame for the Depression, the Republicans were crushed in the 1932 presidential election. Roosevelt carried 42 of 48 states, garnered a 472 to 59 edge in the electoral college, and captured nearly 300 counties that had never gone Democratic. The rout of congressional Republicans was similarly complete.

REPUBLICANS AND THE NEW DEAL

Initially, the GOP found it hard to articulate a clear alternative to the New Deal. Vague and ineffective charges of "radicalism" and "experimentalism" were all Republicans could muster against the New Deal's wide-ranging, aggressive, and less-than-ideologically-coherent policies. For most of Roosevelt's first term, Republicans offered not solutions or programs, but nostrums alluding to fiscal conservatism, rugged individualism, and laissez-faire, precisely the formulas that the crash of 1929 seemed so decisively to discredit. Ironically, many New Deal programs echoed the business-government associations that Hoover and the GOP had championed in the 1920s, stymieing Republican efforts to push alternatives. The National Industrial Recovery Act (NIRA), for example, passed early in the first Roosevelt administration, contained a number of provisions that business interests had supported for years. The NIRA's attempt to establish industry-wide codes for regulating competition were largely borrowed from earlier business arguments that the marketplace ought to be rationalized to dispense with inefficient and cutthroat competition. Typically, conservative Republicans pressed for a softening of New Deal legislation, such as the Social Security Act of 1935, rather than risk outright conflict with the popular president. Other New Deal programs, such as the Reconstruction Finance Corporation, which sought to spur business by subsidizing the credit machinery of the nation, were actually begun under the Hoover administration.

But many New Deal initiatives represented significant departures from received wisdom and attracted large segments of previously loyal Republican support. Where conservatives favored high tariffs to protect American farm produce, Roosevelt sought and won an aggressive program that encouraged farmers to limit production and thereby raise prices. Such reversals of orthodox economic thinking outraged many on the Right, but the desperate plight of American farmers made passage of the bill, known as the Agricultural Adjustment Act, a foregone conclusion. Such innovative policies stood in stark contrast to conservative doctrines of self-reliance and limited government involvement in economic matters and led to a marked shift in the social base for each party. Agricultural support for the GOP, which had been strong in the West, fractured as producers flocked to the New Deal's promise of price supports. Progressive elements in the GOP associated with the old insurgency of Theodore Roosevelt and Robert LaFollette often abandoned traditional Republican laissez-faire and actively solicited government aid for farmers, labor, and the poor. With much of its progressive wing defecting to vote for domestic New Deal programs, opposition to Roosevelt was left in the hands of conservative Republicans loyal to business and corporate interests.

Nowhere is the political transformation of the period more evident than in the racial support given the respective parties. From the end of the Civil War, the Republican Party could take African-American support for granted, at least in those areas where blacks were permitted to vote. But beginning in 1932, blacks increasingly turned their backs on the "party of Lincoln" and became a part of the emerging New Deal coalition. Like other voters, blacks, who were especially hard hit by the Depression, embraced Roosevelt's promises of poor relief and federal spending on jobs for the unemployed. While the New Deal offered little in the way of race-specific programs, its dynamism attracted many black Americans alienated from Hoover's apparent lethargy. Franklin and Eleanor Roosevelt appeared sensitive to the plight of black Americans and were legitimately committed to social progressivism despite the absence of significant legislative gains for African Americans. The GOP was never able to fully exploit this chink in the New Deal armor. Black support for the Democrats remained strong and symbolized the enduring political transformations of the period.

The defeat of Republican presidential candidate Alf Landon in 1936 was even more complete than Hoover's had been four years earlier. By Roosevelt's second term, however, a more effective Republican critique was taking shape. Earlier Supreme Court reversals of much New Deal legislation signaled the beginning of a re-emergent political confrontation between the president and his critics in Congress that had been stifled in the early days of the New Deal. Lapses in Roosevelt's second administration, like the so-called Roosevelt Recession of 1937, the infamous court-packing plan, and Roosevelt's heavy-handed purge of his party's conservatives, as well as his more general move to the Left throughout his early second term, allowed the Republicans to portray Roosevelt as a man out of touch and determined to lead the country to ruin. Because so much of Roosevelt's appeal was based on his personal charisma, the charges began to stick. The 1938 off-term elections returned another solid Democratic majority to Congress, but the gap narrowed considerably, giving the Republicans their largest minority until the bipartisanship of the war years.

ISOLATIONISM

Foreign affairs too began to give shape to a more unified Republican posture. The Italian invasion of Ethiopia in 1935 and the Hitler-backed forces of General Francisco Franco in the Spanish Civil War of 1936 brought home the reality of the fascist threat and gave the GOP a renewed voice in national policy-making. Likewise, the growing power and prestige on the international stage of Joseph Stalin's Soviet Union offered another reason to fear for the American future. Many Republicans advised a conventional prescription of isolationism, which sought to preserve peace by quarantining the nation from foreign entanglements. Where many on the Left seemed eager to engage in international cooperation—including with Communists—in the fight against fascism, the Republican Party stood as a bastion of noninvolvement. Popular figures like Charles A. Lindbergh and prominent senators like progressive Republicans Gerald Nye and Hiram Johnson urged the United States to remain aloof from international developments and avoid embroiling the nation in a costly and meaningless war. These isolationists were highly influential precisely until Pearl Harbor made the point moot, when they loyally supported the president in the war effort. Yet even this reversal would yield fruit for a later generation of Republicans. The uncompromising clarity of the prewar isolationist position would allow the GOP to present itself in staunchly nationalist terms after the war when the Democratic administration of Harry Truman appeared to be insufficiently guarded against the internal and external threats posed by communism in the Cold War.

Ideological divisions on foreign policy between the two parties were never neat, as exemplified in Republican Senator Arthur Vandenberg's move from committed isolationism to spirited internationalism. Still, those who favored isolationism tended to cluster in the Republican Party. It is little wonder, then, that conservative concern over foreign influences became a political tactic to wound the president. Isolationism found its domestic corollary in the growing fear among conservatives that an overfondness for internationalism or a romantic view of the Soviet Union might lead some Americans to betray national security. Many Republicans pushed for heightened surveillance of domestic groups whose patriotism there was reason to question. The American Communist Party was an obvious target, but in an age when Russian-American cooperation was on the agenda of many on the Left, conservatives did not have to search hard to find possible sources of disloyalty. Increasingly, conservatives used these alliances between liberals and the more extreme Left to disparage Roosevelt's liberal agenda. The GOP's primary weapons were in the form of legislation, such as the Smith Act (1940), which prosecuted aliens charged with subversion, or congressional investigating committees, such as the House Un-American Activities Committee (HUAC). This committee in particular was a powerful political tool, charging that the Roosevelt ad-

ministration's flirtations with the Soviet Union had allowed communist spies to penetrate various agencies of the government. In one famous episode, HUAC was able to kill part of Roosevelt's Works Progress Administration by alleging that communists had infiltrated the Federal Theater Project. HUAC had not yet uncovered Communists in more sensitive areas, as it would after the war, but the precedent for fierce patriotism that Republicans had earned as a result of efforts like HUAC would serve as one of the party's primary points of credibility after the war. It should be noted that many conservative Democrats supported efforts to root out Communists: HUAC was originally chaired by a conservative Democrat, Martin Dies, and California legislator Jack Tenney chaired a state version of HUAC during and immediately after the war.

AFTER THE NEW DEAL

Rather than move ideologically to the Left to siphon off New Deal support, the Republican Party increasingly throughout the 1930s tacked more firmly to the Right, offering itself as a clear alternative to Roosevelt, whether by opposing New Deal governmental intervention with laissez-faire and self-reliance or countering liberal internationalism with firm isolationism. While this strategy would cost the GOP electoral success as long as most Americans favored the New Deal, such an ideologically consistent approach served the Republicans well after 1948, when Truman and the Democratic party were called by the voters to answer for their apparent cooperation with Communists in the 1930s. As prosperity once again returned to postwar America and people increasingly saw the Depression as an aberration, Democrats had difficulty defending themselves from charges that New Deal policies had undermined Americans' traditional work ethic by making them dependent on government largesse and perhaps opening the door to communist influence in the process. The hard-line stance of much of the Republican Party may not have generated much voter enthusiasm in the dark days of the Depression, but it did speak to a new generation of voters that rewarded the GOP with election-day victories throughout the 1950s.

JONATHAN SNYDER

See also: Democratic Party; election of 1930; election of 1932; election of 1934; election of 1936; election of 1938; election of 1940; End Poverty in California; House Un-American Activities Committee; Hoover, Herbert; Landon, Alfred; Willkie, Wendell.

Bibliography

Brinkley, Alan. *The End of Reform: New Deal Liberalism in Recession and War.* New York: Vintage Books, 1995.

Burns, James MacGregor. *Roosevelt: The Lion and the Fox, 1882–1940.* New York: Harcourt Brace Jovanovich, 1956.

Hoff-Wilson, Joan. *Herbert Hoover: Forgotten Progressive.* Boston: Little, Brown, 1975.

Hofstadter, Richard. *The Age of Reform: From Bryan to F.D.R.* New York: Vintage Books, 1955.

Leuchtenburg, William E. *Franklin D. Roosevelt and the New Deal, 1932–1940.* New York: Harper Torchbooks, 1963.

Marcus, Robert D. *Grand Old Party: Political Structure in the Gilded Age, 1880–1896.* New York: Oxford University Press, 1971.

McElvaine, Robert S. *The Great Depression: America, 1929–1941.* New York: Times Books, 1993.

Schwarz, Jordan A. *The Interregnum of Despair: Hoover, Congress, and the Depression.* Urbana: University of Illinois Press, 1970.

Thelan, David P. *Robert M. LaFollette and the Insurgent Spirit.* Boston: Little, Brown, 1976.

Weed, Clyde P. *The Nemesis of Reform: The Republican Party During the New Deal.* New York: Columbia University Press, 1994.

Weiss, Nancy J. *Farewell to the Party of Lincoln: Black Politics in the Age of FDR.* Princeton: Princeton University Press, 1983.

SATURDAY EVENING POST

Although founded just before the turn of the twentieth century, the *Saturday Evening Post* reached its peak of circulation in the 1930s, having transformed itself from a general interest and entertainment magazine into a more overtly political organ with a strong anti–New Deal editorial stance.

In its early years, the *Post* lacked a distinctive style or content and languished on the newsstand until its owner, press magnate Cyrus H. K. Curtis, hired a young editor named George Horace Lorimer. A preacher's son and a product of nineteenth-century middle-class America, Lorimer celebrated the Republican Party and the country's business culture.

He also created an immensely popular formula for the magazine, mixing articles on business, politics, popular culture, sports, and humor, as well as adding illustrations and cartoons for color. Circulation grew enormously, reaching a million by 1910, 2 million by 1920, and over 3 million by the late 1930s.

But, with the stock market crash, the Depression, and the rise of Franklin D. Roosevelt, the tone of the magazine changed dramatically. Lorimer deplored the New Deal programs, which he felt were undermining the individualism and self-reliance of the American people, and he called for a return to "old values."

While popular with many Americans, Lorimer was bitterly attacked by Democrats and other supporters of the New Deal. Gradually, the political struggle affected his health and he resigned in 1937, just as the magazine was reaching its largest audience to date. Its circulation fell off during World War II because of its isolationist stance and anti-Semitic undertones.

It revived after the war, with circulation peaking in the mid-1950s at about 5 million issues a week. By the 1960s, with its readership aging, the magazine began to lose money and closed down in 1969. It was revived in 1971 and continues to be published, but it no longer enjoys a wide circulation.

See also: newspapers and magazines, Rockwell, Norman.

Bibliography

Cohn, Jan. *Creating America: George Horace Lorimer and the* Saturday Evening Post. Pittsburgh: University of Pittsburgh Press, 1989.

Tebbel, John. *George Horace Lorimer and the* Saturday Evening Post. Garden City, NY: Doubleday, 1948.

SCARFACE: THE SHAME OF A NATION

One of the most popular films of the gangster genre of the Depression era, *Scarface: The Shame of a Nation* (1932) was directed by Howard Hawks and starred Paul Muni in the title role as a thuggish but comic low-level member of the mob whose only redeeming feature is his love for his sister, played by Ann Dvorak.

Like *Little Caesar, Public Enemy*, and other films of the genre, *Scarface* tried to explain the activities of gangsters as a phenomenon linked to a chaotic and unjust society. This theme was popular with Depression movie audiences who, while not exactly sympathizing with the gangsters, appreciated the dramatized social commentary of these films.

See also: films, feature; *Little Caesar; Public Enemy;* Hawks, Howard; Muni, Paul.

Bibliography

Baxter, John. *Hollywood in the Thirties.* New York: Barnes, 1968.

Sklar, Robert. *Movie-Made America: A Cultural History of the American Movies.* New York: Random House, 1975.

SCOTTSBORO CASE

The Scottsboro Case was one of the first significant national civil rights cases of the twentieth century and the most tragic miscarriage of racial justice of the Depression era. It signaled the beginning of a more aggressive challenge to racial discrimination in the United States by African Americans and their allies, and it brought the Communist Party to the attention of many in the black community.

The case began in spring 1931, when nine African-American youths caught a freight train from Chattanooga to Memphis, Tennessee, in search of work in the Depression-ravaged South. On the night of March 25, a group of young white hobos accosted the African Americans and a fight broke out. During the altercation, the black youths succeeded in removing the white youths from the train. The whites filed a complaint with the Scottsboro, Alabama, sheriff charging that the African-American youths had viciously attacked them without provocation. The sheriff ordered his deputies to round up all black passengers on the train. The sweep netted the nine black men and boys, ranging in age from thirteen to nineteen: Ozie Powell, Clarence Norris, Charlie Weems, Olen Montgomery, Willie Roberson, Haywood Patterson, Eugene Williams, Andy Wright, and Roy Wright. The police also discovered two white, working-class women from northern Alabama, Ruby Bates and Victoria Price. Fearful of being arrested for vagrancy and perhaps ashamed of being women hobos, the women accused the nine black youths of rape.

Based on that accusation, the "Scottsboro boys," as they came to be known, were given a hasty trial before an all-white jury. In quick succession, each of the defendants, except the youngest, was found guilty of rape and sentenced to death. The youngest defendant was also found guilty, but received a sentence of life in prison. The swift and harsh verdicts were hardly surprising given the long-standing southern tradition prohibiting interracial sex. Other factors further compromised the proceedings: defense attorney had scant time to prepare for the trial and often came to court drunk; the local press printed inflammatory accounts of the alleged rape before and during the trial; and hundreds of white mountaineers and villagers assembled outside the courthouse the day of the trial and staged a demonstration of approval, complete with band, when the verdicts were announced.

The Scottsboro Case did not initially receive national attention and might have been forgotten if the Communist Party's legal arm, the International Labor Defense (ILD), had not taken up the youths' defense after the trial. The ILD, already in the midst of an anti-lynching campaign, turned the Scottsboro Case into a legal and political crusade. The group publicly fought for control of the case with the National Association for the Advancement of Colored People (NAACP),

In the Scottsboro case, one of the most controversial trials of the 1930s, nine African-American boys and men were accused of raping two white women on a train in Alabama. Here the defendants are shown with their lawyer Samuel Liebowitz, who took on the case after appeals from the International Labor Defense, the legal wing of the Communist Party. *(Brown Brothers)*

which accused the ILD of manipulating and using the defendants for its own propaganda purposes. For its part, the NAACP originally resisted involvement in the case because of the nature of the charges. Fearing that the ILD's actions might undermine the association's support within the African-American community, however, the NAACP became increasingly involved in the youths' cause, although the ILD remained lead counsel.

Public reaction to the original verdicts was also quick and vocal. The day after the defendants were sentenced to death, the first large-scale demonstration took place at St. Luke's Hall in Harlem. Soon after, a distinguished collection of intellectuals and scientists from around the globe, including Albert Einstein, signed a petition demanding the release of the Scottsboro defendants. Several prominent legal professionals, including Clarence Darrow, considered the verdicts un-

founded and brought about by racial bias. Protests and press coverage quickly spread across the United States and Europe, making the case an international cause célèbre.

Meanwhile, the legal wrangling continued. In 1932, the U.S. Supreme Court overturned the Scottsboro convictions on the ground that the defendants' constitutional right to counsel had been denied. The second trial opened in Decatur, Alabama, on April 3, 1933, on a bit more even ground. The ILD hired famed New York defense attorney Samuel Leibowitz, who mounted a vigorous legal challenge to the charges. During the trial, Ruby Bates recanted the rape allegations and explained that she and Victoria Price had made up the story to avoid arrest for vagrancy. She also revealed that authorities seized the nine African Americans from different locations on the forty-two car train. In addition, a Huntsville detective challenged the prosecution's portrayal of the two women as virtuous examples of southern white womanhood by confirming that they worked as prostitutes and served black clients. Despite these damaging new revelations, however, an all-white jury again convicted the youths, this time sentencing two to death and the others to lengthy prison terms. In 1935, the Supreme Court set aside the convictions for a second time, claiming that state practices systematically and arbitrarily excluded African Americans from jury lists, thereby violating the equal protection clause of the Fourteenth Amendment of the Constitution. Finally, in 1937, the state of Alabama dropped charges against four of the defendants and agreed to consider parole for the five others who had been retried and convicted. Four were paroled in the 1940s. The fifth escaped to Michigan, where state officials refused to return him to Alabama.

The Scottsboro Case illustrates the way sectional, class, sexual, and racial tensions, already heightened by the Depression, could be exacerbated by explosive claims of interracial sex. It also highlights the important role the Communist Party played in the struggle for racial justice during the 1930s. Neither as sinister nor as opportunistic as its critics have claimed, the Communist Party in the United States at this time was a generally sympathetic and genuine ally of the African-American struggle for freedom. Perhaps most important, the Scottsboro Case provided a spark that ignited of black protest and activism on a national scale in the 1930s. It inspired two major civil rights rulings by the Supreme Court and signaled the start of an era when African Americans were no longer willing to tolerate economic, legal, or political injustice in the United States For these reasons, the Scottsboro Case is considered one of the first significant civil rights cases of the twentieth century.

PATRICK JONES

See also: African Americans; Communist Party; National Association for the Advancement of Colored People.

Bibliography

Carter, Dan. *Scottsboro: A Tragedy of the American South*. Baton Rouge: Louisiana State University Press, 1979.

Goodman, James. *Stories of Scottsboro*. New York: Vintage, 1995.

SERGEANT YORK

The late years of the Depression and New Deal spawned a number of highly popular socially conscious films. Among these was *Sergeant York*, the 1941 film that told the story of Alvin York, America's greatest World War I hero.

In the film, York—played by Gary Cooper—has a religious experience that converts him to pacifism and to the desire to oppose greed and violence in all their forms. When the World War breaks out, York applies for the status of a conscientious objector. After a heartfelt talk from a recruiting officer, however, York decides to join the army in order to save lives.

Film historians see *Sergeant York*, which was directed by Howard Hawks, as a movie that captured the transitional values of the late Depression. While advocating pacifism and fairness, it also shows that those things sometimes need to be defended by a resort to arms.

See also: films, feature; *Grapes of Wrath The;* Cooper, Gary; Hawks, Howard.

Bibliography

Meyers, Jeffrey. *Gary Cooper: American Hero*. New York: William Morrow, 1998.

Willis, Donald C. *The Films of Howard Hawks*. Metuchen, NJ: Scarecrow Press, 1975.

SERVICE SECTOR

A shift was already occurring from heavy production to a services-oriented economy before 1929. There was a rise in the service industries during the Depression, in areas such as transportation, trade, finance, and government operations, and a decline in the industrial sectors of the economy. From 1929 to 1938, the adjusted annual estimates by the Department of Commerce show 11.1 percent of national income originating in the service industries. Service jobs that required contact with the general public emphasized the importance of age, race, education, experience, appearance, and marital status in the tight market conditions of the Depression. Age played an important role in domestic service, public service, and clerical jobs.

Over the decade of the Depression, the hours of actual work time increased for the same or less pay. Workers in many service sector jobs were forced by irregular hours and lack of hours to live at subsistence level. After 1933, real wages increased for some sections of the service sector despite double-digit unemployment.

The clerical and sales sectors of the economy lost few jobs overall throughout the Depression. The female service sector nationwide gained a quarter of a million jobs from 1929 to 1940. Unemployment in the labor force generally affected the younger or much older worker, those who had fewer skills and were less educated than those employed. The unemployed at this time generally stayed unemployed for longer periods of time than in previous decades. There was more sharing of workers' jobs, reducing actual hours worked rather than employing a greater number of people.

In urban areas, black women were restricted to work in the service sector. The only area of increase for black female workers during the Depression was beauty service. In 1930, 50 to 60 percent of black women workers were employed in domestic or personal service. This figure declined when out-of-work white workers replaced them in their jobs.

WHOLESALE TRADE

Despite the retracting economy, expenditures rose for nondurable and service goods. These increases included personal and small shop services such as domestic services, personal appearance services, moving expenses and repairs, tailoring, and clothes pressing. They also included large-scale commercial services such as laundries, dry-cleaning companies, theaters, and hotels. In addition, relative expenditures rose in other services such as tuition, contributions, dues, postage, and public utility services, including street railway and local transportation agencies, electricity and gas companies, and telephone companies.

RETAIL TRADE

By 1930, approximately 40 percent of the jobs in the service sector were in the public sphere. Specialized businesses provided these services for cash payments, as opposed to barter or family service. The majority of working women were employed in sales, service, and clerical work. The service sector engaged all racial groups of women in excessively high numbers, with the exception of native-born, young, single, white women, who were generally employed as clerical workers. Waitresses were the largest group of service sector employees.

MISCELLANEOUS BUSINESS

A long-term trend continued as increasing numbers of married women left their traditional work in the home in order to work in clerical and service occupations. Between 1930 and 1940, women increased in the labor force by almost 50 percent, yet their numbers increased in the population by only 15 percent. In 1940, married women were 35 percent of the labor force, compared to 29 percent in 1930. Not as dramatic as in previous decades, their increase in the labor force is telling in the economically stagnant decade. Most women agreed that clerical jobs were more desirable than domestic work. Held in high status, clerical work was steadier and paid comparatively high wages ($22 to $23 a week).

A job for a husband with the Work Projects Administration (WPA), with its low wages, was generally better than the wages of a wife. "Marriage bars" in the government and private sector firms discouraged job opportunities for married women. Marriage bars were generally concentrated in service sector jobs such as clerical or office work (e.g., insurance, banking) and public sector jobs like schoolteaching. Marriage bars did not make work in the labor force impossible for women, just difficult.

AMUSEMENT, RECREATION, HOTELS, AND LODGING

Because rapid deflation increased purchasing power by 1932, demand for nonessential services such as entertainment and tourism rose. Businesses associated with amusement and entertainment, including vacations, were seasonal. Most waitresses and chambermaids disliked the fact that they had to work on Sundays, unlike in other jobs. Automobiles, radio, and the movies were some of the few growing industries during the Great Depression. An increase in the sales and service of these products affected the service sector in a positive way.

MEDICAL AND HEALTH SERVICES

The Great Depression left many Americans, employed or unemployed, too poor to afford surgical, hospital, or medical care. In 1934, it was estimated that between 75 and 90 percent of the population were unable to afford medical care services. The Social Security Act of 1935 provided some insurance protection for workers, however, this bill did not include the domestic service sector at the time. Service workers at hospitals were generally required to live on the premises.

DOMESTIC SERVICE SECTORS OF THE ECONOMY

Personalized domestic service was generally hard work with low pay, intense supervision by the employer, and longer hours than most other industries. Domestic labor was changing in scope. In the decades before the Depression, living-in had been replaced by living-out. This movement was, for the time being, overturned by employers wanting cheap round-the-clock service. They took advantage of the desperation of some workers to have a place to live. The room and board threat was an efficient corrective instrument to keep staff in line.

The houseworker's workday during the 1930s was twelve to sixteen hours. Some households with multiple domestic servants cut back and expected one servant to do the work that two had done previously. Employees were required to perform the services of chauffeur-butler-houseman or lady's maid-waitress-chambermaid, combining multiple positions into one. Households that had not previously been able to afford help and could now afford it because of the depressed wages burdened their new workers with massive workloads. Domestic service workers gave in to the new workload in order to keep their jobs.

Women held most of the domestic service jobs. Ninety percent of all domestic servants were women. Domestic service ranked highest in number of working American women throughout the 1930s. Out of 13 million working women, 1.4 million were in service industries. As women aged, they were restrained to service occupations. The domestic service sector was the highest urban sector where formerly married (widowed and divorced) women were employed. Domestic service was the usual entry-level position for adolescent girls in urban areas. When young women quit high school to help support the family, often the only position open to them was domestic work.

Male domestic service workers had the highest percentage of wives in the labor force (56 percent). Most likely, the wives were in domestic service as well. Generally, there were not many husbands in the occupations of domestic or protective service worker.

After working eight-hour days, domestic servants usually had half days off on Thursdays and Sundays. If in a live-in position, the worker's hours were twenty-four hours a day if they had to care for children or an invalid in the house. Female domestic work in 1930 paid $13 a week living-out and $3 a day for day-work. (Depending on location, race, age, and experience) They could work for several employers as day-work or as a housekeeper for one household. Live-in house workers normally earned $10 to $15 a week in urban areas (except in the south). Some worked for room and board only. A number of employers would not pay their workers for weeks, especially if they were live-in. Employees would feel obligated to accept these terms in order to have a place to live. Specially trained workers such as fancy cooks, private duty nurses, or skilled nursemaids might earn as much as $25 to $35 a week, but this was out of the ordinary.

There was little privacy in a live-in situation. Some employees had no room of their own and slept in the kitchen or on a couch in the dining room, or living room, in the children's room, or with a sick member of the household. Sharing a room with a sick individual or the children could be damaging to the worker's health. The frustrations of the housewife about the Depression were commonly taken out physically, emotionally, and financially on the domestic servant. Most servants resented the lack of personal freedom even more than the hard physical labor and the low wages. Moreover, people entertained at home to save money during the Depression and domestic workers were expected to work extra hours during their employer's parties.

The Great Depression brought a flood of workers who had never had to work before or who had been laid off from more desirable sectors of the economy into the domestic service sector. Older women who were widowed or divorced often found that the only option for them was housework. Similarly, the only recourse of clerical workers who were laid off was to move down into the service sector. Diverse groups of people thus were in competition for the available jobs in the overcrowded service sector even though these were the least desirable occupations. Contention was fierce between experienced house workers and the new flood of inexperienced workers wanting to make inroads into their segment of the economy. This intensified competition led to decreased wages and required higher standards from employees. One advantage for women was that much domestic service was considered "women's work" that men did not apply for, which provided a shelter for women during the midst of the Depression.

PERSONAL AND PROFESSIONAL SERVICES

Many service occupations were damaging to the health of the worker and were dangerous for their safety because of the hard physical labor. Laundries with their hard concrete floors and moist, steamy environment had some of the unhealthiest conditions in the workplace. Employees commonly had resultant rheumatism when they worked in the industry over a long period of time. The laundry business had a characteristically cyclical schedule with steady work in the winter and irregular work in the summer. During the Depression, all the seasons were erratic.

NONPROFIT AND EDUCATIONAL SERVICES

The WPA spent 14.9 percent of its funds on professional and service projects from 1936 to 1940. Women were restricted from large construction programs and limited to domestic service programs. WPA service projects in Atlanta in 1935 and 1936 included clerical jobs, providing supplemental teachers, indexing tax records, library assistance and book rebinding, medical laboratory work, nursing, sewing rooms, and surplus food distribution. The WPA expanded its divisions within the service sector by 1940 to include Women's Work (named Women's and Professional Division, then Professional and Service Division, then Division of Community Service Programs). This Women's Work Division administered service projects, placing women in traditionally female areas such as nursing, teaching, laundry work, and domestic service. This was similar to the forms of discrimination women faced with the NRA, where household workers were excluded from the National Industrial Recovery Act (NIRA). This generated a large amount of protest mail at the time.

In the late '30s, the WPA supported local governments that were faced with decreasing revenues to maintain library services. These new library and employment opportunities resulted in the expansion of services to readers and greater library awareness. Other nonprofit services such as the Friendly Service Bureau of Cleveland, part of the YWCA, and the Chicago Service Bureau took applications from people looking for work during the Depression and helped them find positions.

The Great Depression did not halt the long-term increase to the service sector in the American economy, though conditions worsened in areas of decreased pay and longer hours. The service sector as a whole increased, especially in the areas of entertainment and tourism. Decreases in overall prices brought increased sales in service goods. More family members were required to work during the Great Depression so these first-time recruits in the workplace filled the new nonskilled service jobs. White women benefited from the expansion in the service sector, to the detriment of black workers as a group.

MICHELLE MORMUL

See also: advertising and consumption; Women; *West Coast Hotel v. Parrish;* Document: *West Coast Hotel Company v. Parrish,* 1937.

Bibliography

Argersinger, Jo Ann E. *Toward a New Deal in Baltimore: People and Government in the Great Depression.* Chapel Hill: University of North Carolina Press, 1988.

Bernstein, Michael A. *The Great Depression: Delayed Recovery and Economic Change in America, 1929–1939.* Cambridge: Cambridge University Press, 1987.

Bureau of the Census. *Historical Statistics of the United States: Colonial Times to 1970.* Washington: Kraus International Publishing, 1989.

Cowan, Ruth Schartz. "Two Washes in the Morning and a Bridge Party at Night: The American Housewife Between the Wars." *Women's Studies* 3:2 (1976): 147–72.

Derickson, Alan. "Health Security for All? Social Unionism and Universal Health Insurance, 1935–1958" *Journal of American History* 80:4 (1994): 1333–56.

Finegan, T. Aldrich, and Robert A. Margo. "Work Relief and the Labor Force Participation of Married Women in 1940." *Journal of Economic History* 54:1 (1994): 64–84.

Fleming, Douglas L. "The New Deal in Atlanta: A Review of the Major Programs." In ed. Bernard Sternsher, pp. 7–31. Chicago: Ivan R. Dee, 1999.

Helmbold, Lois Rita. "Downward Occupational Mobility During the Great Depression: Urban Black and White Working Women." *Labor History* 29:2 (1988): 135–72.

———. *Making Choices, Making Do: Black and White Working Class Women's Lives and Work During the Great Depression.* Ph.D. diss., Stanford University, 1983.

Helmbold, Lois Rita, and Ann Schofield. "Women's Labor History, 1790–1945." *Reviews in American History.* 17:4 (1989): 501–18.

Margo, Robert A. "Labor and the Labor Markets in the 1930s." In *The Economics of the Great Depression,* ed. Mark Wheele, pp. 9–27. Kalamazoo, Michigan: W. E. Upjohn Institute for Employment Research, 1998.

Sparks, Randy J. "Heavenly Houston or Hellish Houston? Black Unemployment and Relief Efforts, 1929–1936." In *Hope Restored: How The New Deal Worked in Town and Country.* ed. Bernard Sternsher, pp. 182–195. Chicago: Ivan R. Dee, 1999.

Stock, Catherine McNicol. *Main Street in Crisis: The Great Depression and the Old Middle Class on the Northern Plains.* Chapel Hill: University of North Carolina Press, 1992.

Swain, Martha H. "A New Deal in Libraries: Federal Relief Work and Library Service, 1933–1943." *Libraries & Culture* 30:3 (1995): 265–83.

Tidd, James Frances, Jr. "Stitching and Striking: WPA Sewing Rooms and the 1937 Relief Strike in Hillsborough County." In *Hope Restored: How the New Deal Worked in Town and Country.* ed., Bernard Sternsher pp. 207–220. Chicago: Ivan R. Dee, Publisher, 1999.

Veysey, Laurence. "A Postmortem on Daniel Bell's Postindustrialism." *American Quarterly.* 34:1 (1982): 49–69.

Wandersee Bolin, Winifred D. "The Economics of Middle-Income Family Life: Working Women During the Great Depression." *Journal of American History* 65:1 (1978): 60–74.

Ware, Susan. *Holding Their Own: American Women in the 1930's.* Boston: Twayne, 1982.

SHARE OUR WEALTH SOCIETY

The explosive growth of the Share Our Wealth Society in the mid-1930s was part of a broader movement toward radicalism that caused disillusioned Americans to support the sweeping reform programs of messianic figures like Father Charles Coughlin, Francis E. Townsend, and Upton Sinclair. The Share Our Wealth Society was the brainchild of U.S. senator Huey P. Long (D-LA), a skillful orator and a crafty politician who had built up an unprecedented political organization in Louisiana during his time as governor of that state. Long had been an enthusiastic supporter of President Franklin D. Roosevelt but, giving in to his own presidential ambitions and feeling that Roosevelt's New Deal would not fundamentally reform America's economy and society, he broke with him in mid-1933. In February 1934, he took to the airwaves to announce the formation of the Share Our Wealth Society, which he intended to use as an independent political organization to boost his own political aspirations.

Share Our Wealth was based on Long's notion that wealth was finite, meaning that the only way to raise the fortunes of the poor was to take from the rich. Accordingly, the centerpiece of his plan was a call to appropriate all accumulated wealth above $5 million and all annual earnings over $1 million. The money raised from this tax would be used to provide every American family with a "homestead," which included a house, a car, and a radio, and to guarantee everyone an annual income of between $2000 and $2,500. Besides this confiscatory tax, which was the only constant element of Share Our Wealth, Long proposed a number of sweeping reforms, many of which quickly lost his interest, as part of his package. At various times, he added old-age pensions, free college education for students who passed entrance exams, and veterans' bonuses to his program. Long also toyed with the idea of a thirty-hour workweek, supported an eleven-month work year, and called for an ambitious program to combat disease and drug addiction. He did not leave farmers out of his plan; he suggested that the government could ease agricultural overproduction by limiting acreage, storing surpluses, and employing farmers on public works projects.

With his typical bombastic fervor, Long declared that his comprehensive reform program had been culled from the ideas of Plato, the Pilgrims, Theodore Roosevelt, and Pope Pius XI and urged supporters to form local Share Our Wealth Clubs to help promote his cause. Within two months, 200,000 people had signed up. By the end of 1934, membership shot up to 3 million. It crested in spring 1935 at 7.7 million. In February 1935, officials claimed that there were 27,500 clubs in operation. Much of the credit for the society's growth belongs to Long's lieutenant, Gerald L. K. Smith, a former Disciples of Christ minister whose slavish devotion to the senator and fierce hatred of Roosevelt fueled his fiery rhetoric on his national recruitment drives. Share Our Wealth was especially popular in Long's native South, but it was a truly national movement that had strength all over the United States. African Americans, the most downtrodden on the economic and social ladder, were strongly drawn to Share Our Wealth. Some northern clubs were integrated, but in the South they were segregated and blacks could stand only on the fringes of club rallies. Long's movement also found agricultural and union backers, but it was primarily a lower-middle-class movement. Small-business leaders and professionals, many of whom had raised themselves up to some level of success, were terrified that the Depression would shove them into economic privation and, believing that Share Our Wealth could preserve their modest stability, clung to Long. The society made Long a famous man. His national radio broadcasts scored outstanding ratings, and he received more mail than the other ninety-five U.S. senators combined. In April 1935, he averaged 60,000 letters per week. As his popularity peaked, many Democrats feared that Long's society could topple Roosevelt in the 1936 election. While polls showed that Long did not have enough backers to win the presidency, he certainly was a threat to swing the campaign to the Republicans.

But Long's fame and the swelling membership of the Share Our Wealth Society masked fundamental problems within the movement. Economists quickly ridiculed his plan. Noting that there were only forty-three Americans who made more than $1 million a year, they figured that families which made under $5,000 a year would receive only $400 under Long's plan, far below the magnificent sums he had promised.

(CARTO-GRAPHICS)

Further, critics contended, since Share Our Wealth would kill all incentive to make over $1 million, there would be nothing to confiscate after the first year. In addition, Long failed to explain how he would deal with nonliquid assets, such as stocks, bonds, and buildings, that could not be easily transferred to the poor. Long himself was more interested in creating his own national organization than in pressing for his proposed reforms, a fact that he conceded in private meetings with close friends, and he responded with cooked-up or misleading statistics and vague suggestions that the details of his plan still needed to be worked out.

Moreover, the Share Our Wealth Society was never a coherent movement. People could form locals simply by writing to Long, declaring themselves president of a chapter, and providing a list of names and addresses of members, which the senator used to build up a massive mailing list in preparation for his presidential bid. Clubs charged no dues and were so loosely organized that the society's national headquarters could not control local leaders. Meeting in homes, churches, and lodge halls, some locals did discuss how to implement Long's program, but many did not. Some local clubs were indistinguishable from other local organizations

and spent the bulk of their time discussing local issues. Others became vehicles for local interest groups or politicians. A few existed solely to make a profit by selling copies of Long's autobiography, *Every Man a King* (the slogan of the society), and other speeches and tracts that he sent to locals under his senatorial franking privilege—writings that were supposed to be distributed for free to his followers. Clubs in Louisiana existed more to bolster Long's statewide machine than to work for national reforms.

The society disintegrated after Long was cut down by an assassin in 1935. Long's henchmen, most of whom believed in Share Our Wealth no more than their boss had, were eager to mend their fences with Roosevelt, who had been withholding federal funds from Louisiana as punishment for its senator's disloyalty. The fanatical Gerald Smith tried to take up the reins of power, but Long's machine, which survived the senator, denied him access to the precious mailing list, effectively ending his chances of taking over. Roosevelt's 1935 Wealth Tax bill and the passage of the Social Security Act co-opted some of Long's thunder and hastened the demise of the Share Our Wealth Society.

DAVID WELKY

See also: election of 1936; Long, Huey P.; Smith, Gerald L. K.

Bibliography

Brinkley, Alan. *Voices of Protest: Huey Long, Father Coughlin, and the Great Depression.* New York: Knopf, 1982.

Jeansonne, Glen. *Messiah of the Masses: Huey P. Long and the Great Depression.* New York: HarperCollins, 1993.

Williams, T. Harry. *Huey Long.* New York: Knopf, 1969.

SILVER SHIRTS

One of the most extreme of the American right-wing hate groups that were inspired in the 1930s by the rise of the Fascists in Italy and the Nazis in Germany, the Silver Shirts were founded by journalist William Pelley in 1933. Their name was a conscious imitation of the Blackshirts of Italy and the Brownshirts of Germany, paramilitary groups who enforced the political will of Benito Mussolini and Adolf Hitler, respectively.

Pelley claimed divine inspiration for the organization, saying that in 1928 he had died for seven minutes and gone to heaven, where he was told to create the Silver Shirts in order to build support for Hitler and his ideas in the United States.

A strident anti-Semite, Pelley was also virulently anti–Franklin D. Roosevelt and anti–New Deal, saying that one was a secret communist agent and the other was a program for socializing the United States. Arrested for fraud in 1934, Pelley was soon released, but in 1942 he was convicted on charges of sedition and sent to prison for eight years. That—and America's entry into the war against Nazi Germany—led to the demise of the Silver Shirts.

See also: fascism, domestic; fascism, Italy; Nazi Germany.

Bibliography

Diamond, Sander A. *The Nazi Movement in the United States, 1924–1941.* Ithaca, NY: Cornell University Press, 1974.

SOCIALIST PARTY

The Socialist Party (SP) entered the Great Depression as a mere shadow of its earlier strength in the pre–World War I era. By the late 1920s, when the Depression began, party membership was at an all-time low, with a mere 7,800 members, as compared to 100,000 in 1912.

The dwindling numbers, however, were not the only problem the SP faced in the late 1920s. Throughout the decade, the Communist Party had posed a threat to the Socialists; it was, after all, more radical than the Socialist Party, and, unlike the SP, the Communists had the authority of the Russian Revolution behind them. As a result, many young Socialists left the SP throughout the 1920s to join the Communist Party.

In addition to the external threat of Communism, the party was also ideologically divided throughout the early years of the Depression. The Old Guard, the older and more conservative leaders, many of them in the garment unions, who had been running the party since the split between the Socialists and Communists in 1919, continued to control most of the party apparatus. It was the Old Guard who continued to push the SP into backing the American Federation of Labor (AFL), despite the increasing conservatism of AFL leadership.

At the same time, there was growing internal opposition to the Old Guard by the Militants, a younger group of SP activists. The Militants were more united by their dissatisfaction with the Old Guard than by any coherent ideology, but they tended to favor more radical programs, including an increased commitment to industrial unionism and a less centralized leadership of the SP.

These difficulties, though obviously serious, did not present insurmountable obstacles, particularly when the Depression hit. The SP was in fact to find the Depression a great aid to their efforts, at least at

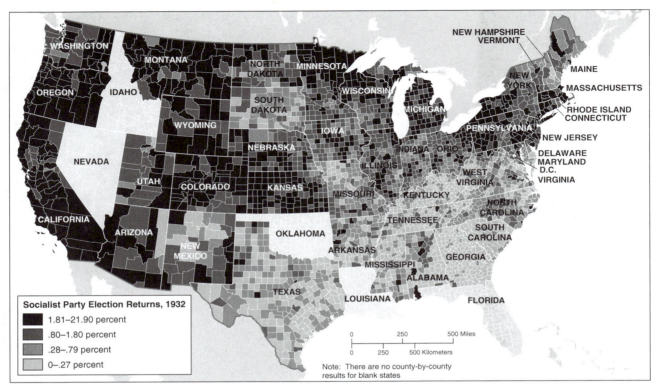

Socialist Party Election Returns, 1932
- 1.81–21.90 percent
- .80–1.80 percent
- .28–.79 percent
- 0–.27 percent

Note: There are no county-by-county results for blank states

(CARTO-GRAPHICS)

first. Capitalism appeared to be discredited, and seemed to have crumbled just the way Marxists had long said it would. The Socialist Party's alternative to capitalism, democratic socialism, seemed to many more achievable than the Communist method of worker revolution. Membership rolls quickly expanded; by 1933, the SP had more than doubled its membership to 18,600. In addition, membership in the Socialist Party was no longer a mere formality. SP members were now expected to be actively involved in the organization's daily life, to attend marches and rallies and participate in rent strikes and antieviction protests.

As a result, the party grew not only in numbers, but in diversity. It had always had a base in the garment trade and certain industrial centers (Milwaukee, for example, had long been a Socialist stronghold by the early 1930s). During the early Depression, however, the SP spread to rural areas as well; the Socialist-led Southern Tenant Farmers Union even extended into the jim crow South, where Socialists bravely challenged segregation and the exploitation of African-American rural workers.

Just as important as the growth and new diversity was the emergence, in the late 1920s, of a charismatic leader. Norman Thomas, a Militant Socialist who first appeared as the Socialist candidate for president in

1928, became a major drawing card for the SP, consistently getting votes far in excess of party membership. Even more important, Thomas's charisma and the openness of the SP to people with fairly diverse beliefs (at a time when the Communist Party was trying to attract members who strictly followed the party line) especially appealed to students and young people, and this served to revive, at least for the time being, the SP's youth movement, the Young People's Socialist League.

A PARTY DIVIDED, 1932–35

In a way, it was the very strengths of the SP that doomed it to failure. The May 1932 national convention was large and diverse, but also filled with factional infighting, particularly between the Militants and the Old Guard. The two factions agreed that Norman Thomas should continue to serve as the SP candidate for president, but they had little else in common by this time, disagreeing on the recognition of Russia, repeal of prohibition and, as always, the SP's strategy in dealing with trade unions.

However, it was the elections of SP officials that led to the most bitter debates, particularly the election

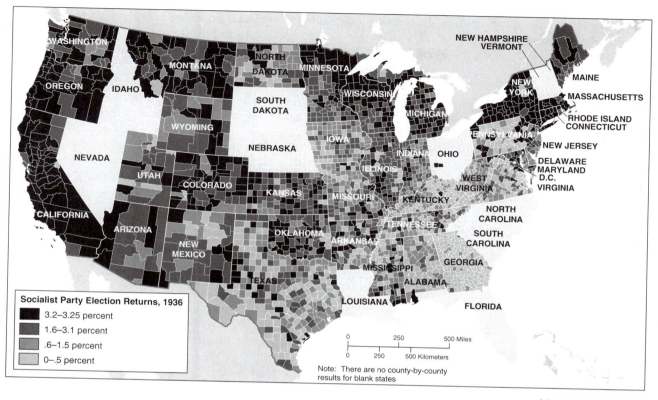

Socialist Party Election Returns, 1936

- 3.2–3.25 percent
- 1.6–3.1 percent
- .6–1.5 percent
- 0–.5 percent

Note: There are no county-by-county results for blank states

(CARTO-GRAPHICS)

of the national chairman, an honorary position which the Old Guard won. The Militants, however, won control of the powerful SP Executive Committee and found victory also in Thomas's nomination.

Although Thomas did relatively well in the 1932 presidential election, polling around 900,000 votes, he did far worse than many Socialists had hoped, and his defeat by Franklin Delano Roosevelt was a major blow to the Socialists, especially since Roosevelt's New Deal came to resemble, in some respects at least, Thomas's 1932 presidential platform. Thomas had won great respect among voters by calling for a minimum wage, maximum-hour laws, unemployment insurance, and old-age pensions. While the early New Deal in particular did not contain many of these provisions, the Roosevelt administration was clearly attentive to the needs of working- and lower-class Americans. By late 1933, in fact, Thomas, previously one of Roosevelt's strongest opponents, admitted that the Roosevelt administration was doing a surprisingly good job, although he continued to criticize New Deal programs as giving too much power to the president.

The Socialists, as always, were more successful in local politics than in national elections. Fiorello La Guardia, though himself not a Socialist, recruited a number of Socialists to serve on his staff (including, in a volunteer position, Thomas himself), and the SP did win in a number of smaller cities across the country, including Bridgeport, Connecticut, and Toledo, Ohio.

By 1935, however, these small victories, important though they were, were quickly overshadowed by other failures. By that time it was clear that Roosevelt had won the support of the traditional Socialist base, particularly the trade unions. In addition, Hitler's rise to power in Germany and the destruction of Socialism there were extremely distressing to many American Socialists. The rise of fascism and Nazism meant new challenges, and problems. The SP's continued commitment to pacifism meant that it faced many contradictions on international issues during this era; Socialist support for the Loyalists in the Spanish Civil War was combined with opposition to any U.S. sanctions against Mussolini's Italy after to the invasion of Ethiopia.

In addition, the Communist Party's sudden call in 1935 for a united front with the Socialists and Democrats alike greatly disconcerted the Socialists, who had previously opposed the Communists for being too radical and the Democrats for being too conservative. This call also contributed to the SP's continuing problem with factionalism; though few Socialists actively supported the Communists, a number of Militants at least tried to be open to the possibility of working together, a tactic that earned them great animosity from the Old Guard, whose dissatisfaction with the SP was quickly growing.

COLLAPSE, 1936–40

All of these problems came together at the Socialist Party's May 1936 convention. A number of party members, including party national chairman Leo Krzycki, resigned from the SP to support Roosevelt and the New Deal. The number of defections was staggering; by mid-1936, the SP had under 12,000 members, close to its pre-Depression nadir; and by the end of that year, the numbers had sunk even further, to nearly 6,000. At that same 1936 convention, the Militants and Old Guard finally had the confrontation that had been building for years.

Both the Militants and the Old Guard had significant followings in New York state, and both recruited delegates for the convention. The convention, led primarily by Militants like Thomas, refused to seat the Old Guard delegates after two days of debates, and the Old Guard formally left the Socialist Party.

The ousting of the Old Guard not only deprived the SP of a number of members; it also opened the door for supporters of Leon Trotsky to enter the SP. As long as the Old Guard had been part of the Socialist Party, it had vigorously opposed Communists and Trotskyists alike, making certain that neither was welcome in the party. However, now that the Old Guard was gone, the Trotskyists flocked to the SP.

At least in theory, the Trotskyists and Socialists had much in common, particularly their dislike of Stalin's Russia. Norman Thomas and a number of other Socialists had also come out against Stalin's persecution of Trotsky and his supporters, and the SP still prided itself on being open to people with a wide range of political opinions, including Trotskyists. In practice, however, the Trotskyists' interest in the SP was opportunistic—they entered not to support the party, necessarily, but to gain the Socialists' support for their own version of Marxism. The coalition was therefore short-lived. In mid-1937, the Trotskyists were expelled from the SP for sectarianism; when they left, however, they took with them a large number of members, particularly of the Young People's Socialist League, in which they had won a significant following. The SP was devastated by the loss; by 1938, its membership had sunk further still, to approximately 3,000 people.

Despite declining numbers, the SP did have some minor victories in the late 1930s. An attempted collaboration with the American Labor Party (ALP) in 1938 and 1939, for example, brought the party some benefits, including a seat for Socialist Harry Laidler on the New York City Council in 1939, but it was mostly a frustrating experience, especially as the ALP put its firm support behind war preparations, which the SP had long opposed. By 1940, Thomas campaigned on the SP ticket, against the ALP, which supported Roosevelt.

The SP's antiwar stance was now its greatest liability. In 1938, while the threat of war grew, Americans as diverse as New Deal Democrats and Communists united in their support for collective security and war preparations. However, most Socialists, Norman Thomas in particular, continued to oppose the coming war, criticizing Communists and liberals alike for their willingness to support actions that could easily lead to war.

This antiwar stance put the SP in a strange position, especially after the Hitler-Stalin pact of August 1939. At that time, Socialists, Communists, and political conservatives were all united in their opposition to the war. Little else united them, however; the SP vigorously attacked the CP's antiwar activism, even going so far as to set up an organization, the Keep America Out of War Congress (KAOWC), which actively worked against the Communists' own antiwar campaigns. At the same time, the KAOWC often worked together with the anti-Semitic and extremely right-wing America First Committee, led by noted Hitler supporter and aviator Charles A. Lindbergh, among others. The relationship was never an easy one, particularly with America First members constantly insisting that Jewish Americans were steadily manipulating the United States into a needless war. Partially in response to this argument, a growing pro-war faction of Socialists came to believe that military intervention was necessary. While some remained a sort of loyal opposition within the party, others were expelled from the SP for their open criticism of the party line, and isolationists and interventionists had extreme struggles reminiscent in some ways of the sort of factional infighting between the Militants and the Old Guard.

Thus the Socialist Party's brief emergence as a major political force during the early 1930s did not develop. The Socialists left the decade much as they had begun it, with a charismatic leader, but with a movement that was small, marginal, and rife with internal divisions that threatened the very existence of the party.

DANIEL OPLER

See also: Popular Front; House Un-American Activities Committee; Smith Act; Thomas, Norman.

Bibliography

Johnpoll, Bernard. *Pacifist's Progress: Norman Thomas and the Decline of American Socialism.* Chicago: Quadrangle Books, 1970.

Seidler, Murray B. *Norman Thomas: Respectable Rebel.* 2d ed. Syracuse: Syracuse University Press, 1967.

Warren, Frank. *An Alternative Vision: The Socialist Party in the 1930s.* Bloomington: University of Indiana Press, 1974.

SOUTHERN TENANT FARMERS UNION

The Southern Tenant Farmers Union (STFU) was established in the 1930s in response to the conditions of tenant farming and sharecropping and to inequities created by the Agricultural Adjustment Administration (AAA) of the New Deal. The AAA came into being in spring 1933 as part of President Franklin D. Roosevelt's onslaught of programs known as the New Deal, which were meant to correct the economic problems of the nation. The AAA was created to assist farmers suffering from crop gluts and low prices. The goal was to provide financial assistance to farmers while imposing crop limits in order to reduce production. This effectively drove prices up but also created some unfortunate side effects.

THE BIRTH OF THE SOUTHERN TENANT FARMERS UNION

Tenant farmers and sharecroppers worked much of the agricultural land in the South. Through this labor system, which emerged following the Civil War, these farm laborers were paid a certain portion of the product they grew on the landowner's property. Tenant farmers provided their own tools and received a larger percentage of the crop as payment than sharecroppers, who provided only their labor and used the landowner's equipment. Tenant farmers and sharecroppers primarily grew cotton, an important and popular cash crop in the South in the 1930s; they farmed almost three-quarters of the cotton crop. These agricultural workers—both black and white—worked and lived in deplorable conditions, surviving on incomes much lower than the national average. Unsanitary conditions, standing water, and malnutrition contributed to diseases such as typhoid, dysentery, hookworm, and malaria. Sharecroppers were the poorest, averaging roughly $415 a year, while tenant farmers averaged closer to $800; both groups endured a hand-to-mouth existence while producing crops for landowners.

Through the AAA, landowners were paid subsidies to limit production of certain crops, such as cotton, wheat, hogs, and corn, with two requirements: (1) some of the funds were to be distributed among the sharecroppers and tenant farmers, and (2) the landowners had to maintain the same number of tenant farmers and sharecroppers on their land as were there at the beginning of the Depression. Violations of these requirements were investigated by committees staffed by large landowners, so, not surprisingly, little response was made to complaints. Landowners used the subsidies to purchase mechanical equipment and put land used by tenant farmers out of production, thereby displacing tenant farmers. Roughly 200,000 black and over 900,000 white tenant farmers and sharecroppers were displaced as a result of AAA policies during the Great Depression. Many of these displaced farmers migrated to the West or to northern industrial cities.

The STFU was created in 1934 in Arkansas in an effort to deal with the inequities of the AAA program as well as the general conditions of tenant farming and sharecropping. Strongest in the delta region of Arkansas, it also garnered a following in Missouri, Mississippi, Alabama, Oklahoma, and Texas. The biracial union included black and white tenant farmers and sharecroppers, with members of both races serving in the leadership and recruiting.

INITIAL SUCCESSES OF THE STFU AND THE LANDOWNERS' RESPONSE

The union achieved some successes, most notably a cotton strike for higher wages in fall 1935, bringing a national spotlight on the plight of tenant farmers and sharecroppers. This attention pressured the federal government to take some limited steps to improve the situation through the creation of the Resettlement Administration and later the Farm Security Administration.

An evicted Arkansas sharecropper and organizer for the Southern Tenant Farmers Union relaxes with his family at a federal housing project in Hill House, Mississippi. *(Library of Congress)*

The landowners recognized the threat represented by the STFU and responded with intimidation and violence. Vigilante committees were organized to put down the organizing efforts of the union. These groups used threats, beatings, and gunfire to suppress the tenant farmers as well as continued eviction of tenant farmers and sharecroppers from the land. Moreover, local communities passed ordinances against public speaking and organizing. Landowners who demonstrated sympathy for tenant farmers' concerns faced extreme pressure from their peers to evict STFU tenant farmers. The winter of 1936 marked a period in which many union members were evicted from the land.

Violence was the most effective tool for landowners. Landowners increasingly targeted STFU gatherings and meetings. When dynamite was thrown into a tent colony, local law enforcement officials refused to investigate the incident. In January 1936, a union meeting taking place in a church in Earle, Arkansas, was interrupted by two deputies entering without warrants. A brawl broke out and the two white deputies hauled one African-American member to jail, returned to the church, and opened fire on the remaining union members, injuring two and arresting three more. A cloaked lynch mob later murdered a black witness who intended to testify against the deputies. Landowners and their managers attacked a union gathering, beating men, women, and children with ax handles and nearly lynching a white STFU attorney and a white STFU organizer.

This violence generated support for tenant farmers within the Roosevelt administration. An effort by the administration to create an agency entrusted with the task of providing homes and land to tenant farmers was weakened by congressional resistance. The resulting Farm Security Administration was stymied by seriously weakened political power and small appropriations. Although Americans were increasingly aware of the plight of sharecroppers and tenant farmers, the strength of the southern landowners and their importance to the Democratic Party precluded any real efforts to reform the southern agricultural system. In a final, limited effort at reform, the Roosevelt administration forced landowners in 1938 to distribute funds to tenant farmers.

The STFU faded into obscurity in the final years of the Depression, having achieved little in the way of significant legislation changing the conditions of tenant farmer and sharecropper life. In evaluating the success of the STFU, one is forced to conclude that while it managed to successfully publicize and educate Americans on the plight of tenant farmers, it achieved little real change. Although many tenant farmers and sharecroppers learned to fight for themselves and work with

members of other racial groups, many were still forced off the land and forced to find work far from home.

JEFF CRANE

See also: African Americans; agriculture; unions and union organizing; Agricultural Adjustment Act (1933); Farm Security Administration; Alexander, Will; Document: Agricultural Adjustment Act, May 12, 1933.

Bibliography

Cantor, Louis. *A Prologue to the Protest Movement: The Missouri Sharecropper Roadside Demonstration of 1939*. Durham, NC: Duke University Press, 1969.

Grubbs, Donald H. *Cry From the Cotton: The Southern Tenant Farmers' Union and the New Deal*. Chapel Hill: The University of North Carolina Press, 1971.

Venkataramani, M. S. "Norman Thomas, Arkansas Sharecroppers, and the Roosevelt Agricultural Policies, 1933–37." *Mississippi Valley Historical Review* 47:2 (September 1960): 225–46.

SPORTS

In 1930, as the nation's economy continued to plunge and millions of Americans struggled against poverty and unemployment, Babe Ruth held out for an increase of his already lofty $80,000 salary. According to legend, when a reporter pointed out that Ruth earned more than President Herbert Hoover, Ruth replied, "I had a better year than he did." Indeed he did. While Hoover's reputation plunged along with the stock market, Ruth remained the nation's most recognized sports hero. Throughout the decade, sports figures such as Ruth provided entertainment for the suffering masses, and participation in athletics provided a welcome diversion to the hardships of the Depression.

Spectator sports in America were hard-hit by the failing economy. Crowds at professional baseball games, which normally packed huge stadiums, dwindled. Minor league teams suffered even more, and several leagues, along with the teams in them, went out of business. Collegiate athletic programs withered as attendance at college football games dropped. Without this valuable income, many colleges eliminated lesser sports such as swimming, tennis, gymnastics, and golf from their curriculum. As most Americans struggled to make ends meet, extra cash for gambling at the horse

track disappeared, and the racetracks barely survived. The average purses at the Preakness, Kentucky Derby, and Belmont Stakes, racing's Triple Crown, shrank by nearly half between 1930 and 1935, from roughly $56,000 to $33,000. Boxing endured not only smaller crowds and decreased gambling interest, but also a drought of quality champions; only Joe Louis in the late 1930s revived interest in the sport. Private sporting interests suffered as well, as golf and tennis clubs struggled to stay afloat, and equipment sales dropped. The athletes participating in these sports felt the bite of the Depression, as salaries and prize money in virtually every sport were reduced. The average salary for major-league baseball players dropped from a high of $7,000 in 1929 to $4,500 in 1936. Even Babe Ruth was forced to take a pay cut.

Coaches and owners employed unique and creative means to soften the effects of the Depression. In 1933, professional baseball added an All-Star Game showcasing the game's greatest stars in an effort to draw more fans. Led by the general manager of the Cincinnati Reds, Larry MacPhail, baseball executives appealed to the fans by playing night games, adding color to their uniforms, having "ball girls" scoop up foul balls,

Major League and Negro League Teams, 1930s

◪ National League

⌂ American League

◢ Negro League

Most Negro league teams existed in some but not all years of the 1930s.

(CARTO-GRAPHICS)

and broadcasting their games over the radio. College football added the Orange, Sugar, and Cotton Bowls to their New Year's Day slate of bowl games, and college basketball introduced the National Invitation Tournament (NIT) in 1938 and the NCAA Tournament the following year. Schools attempted to increase interest in their sports by promoting charitable causes and auctioning off equipment. Professional football increased the number of teams making the playoffs each year and incorporated a number of rule changes, including the addition of the forward pass. The era also featured the growth of sports that naturally emphasized theatrics, such as wrestling, ice-skating shows, soap-box derbies, airplane races, and rodeos.

While such innovations contributed to the survival of sports during the Depression, the skills of the athletes and the thrill of the sporting events themselves kept the fans coming to the ballpark. A number of athletes of that era are remembered as among the finest of all time. In addition to Babe Ruth, baseball fans thrilled to watch the

The New York Yankees play in a 1930s World Series game in the "house that Babe Ruth built," Yankee Stadium. *(Brown Brothers)*

exploits of superstars such as Lou Gehrig, Joe DiMaggio, "Dizzy" Dean, Hank Greenberg, and Carl Hubbell. The stars of college football included Don Hutson, Sammy Baugh, Whizzer White, Sid Luckman, and Tom Harmon. The boxer Joe Louis, track stars such as Jesse Owens and Mildred "Babe" Didrikson, college basketball's Hank Luisetti, and the golfer Bobby Jones all rank among the finest ever to play their sports.

These athletes showcased their talents in many memorable sporting events. The decade was highlighted by the 1932 and 1936 Olympic Games, which established traditions of pageantry and athletic achievement that continue today. The United States hosted the 1932 Winter Games, held in Lake Placid, New York, and the Summer Games in Los Angeles. The Summer Games surpassed all previous Olympics in splendor and expense, as the city went deep into debt to hide all signs of the Depression. Organizers constructed an elaborate

village to house the athletes and staged a stunning opening ceremony. The nation was introduced to Didrikson, perhaps the greatest female athlete of the twentieth century, who set world records in the javelin throw and eighty-meter hurdles and matched the record in the high jump only to finish second. She went on to have a splendid career in basketball and golf, while excelling in exhibitions of many other games, such as bowling, swimming, football, and baseball.

The 1936 Games were held in Germany. Only after a long and bitter struggle to boycott the "Nazi Olympics" ended in failure did American athletes sail for Europe. In an effort to demonstrate the superiority of the German intellect and body, Hitler authorized a spectacle to that point unmatched in Olympic history. The city of Berlin received a face-lift for the Summer Games, and the Germans improved upon innovations that had been introduced in Los Angeles. Nazi athletic superiority suffered a blow, however, as the unquestioned star of the Games was the black American athlete, Jesse Owens. Owens won four gold medals, in the 100-and 200-meter sprints, the broad jump, and the 400 meter relay. His outstanding achievements, coupled with the medal-winning efforts of other black track stars such as Cornelius Johnson (high jump), Ralph Metcalfe (100 meters) and Mack Robinson (200 meters), dealt a serious blow to the myth of Aryan supremacy.

These Olympians comprise only a small part of a group of black athletes who marked many achievements during the 1930s. Joe Louis, boxing's "Brown Bomber," became the heavyweight champion in 1935 by knocking out the Italian Primo Carnera. Louis's bouts against Max Schmeling, the German champion, became a showcase for the battle between democracy and Nazism. The German won their first fight in 1936, knocking out Louis in the twelfth round. The rematch, held in Yankee Stadium on June 22, 1938, was an even greater spectacle. The match itself did not live up to its hype, as Louis won easily with a knockout in the first round.

While Owens and Louis achieved national fame by besting the Nazis, hundreds of other black athletes toiled in near anonymity in the black baseball leagues. Negro League baseball games were an important social event in the black community, and they provided not only entertainment to a group largely at the bottom of the economic ladder, but also a source of hope for escaping the Depression. The black ballplayers brought their game to cities across the country throughout the 1930s, frequently barnstorming against, and defeating, all-white teams. They played quality baseball, emphasizing speed and smart baserunning over power, and several of the stars of the 1930s ultimately reached the Baseball Hall of Fame. Some of the top players of the era were James "Cool Papa" Bell, Josh Gibson, Leroy "Satchel" Paige, Walter "Buck" Leonard, and Ray Dandridge.

If the exploits of athletes such as these allowed sports in America to survive the darkest days of the Depression, Franklin D. Roosevelt's New Deal programs helped strengthen American interest in sport and laid the foundation for the sports craze of the late twentieth century. The Works Progress Administration and other relief agencies devoted much money and manpower to the construction of sporting facilities, such as gymnasiums, swimming pools, and tennis courts. The federal government aided in the building of parks and playgrounds, and encouraged citizens to play and exercise. Civic programs, church groups, youth clubs, the YMCA, and many other local organizations grew in support of sports. New Deal projects

to create ski trails and promote winter sports led to a boom in the skiing industry. Between 1930 and 1940, the number of skiers in the United States grew from only a few thousand to some 2 million. Horse racing enjoyed a revival in the late 1930s, fueled in part by the abundance of new or remodeled tracks, built with federal aid. The government sponsored the growth of public sporting grounds, golf courses, tennis and basketball courts, and baseball and softball fields. Sports such as golf and tennis moved from the realm of the elite to the public domain as a result of these programs.

Not all citizens responded positively to Roosevelt and the New Deal. The decade was marred by labor strife, strikes, and violence, as downtrodden workers struggled to escape the Depression. Worker unrest spilled over into the world of sports. A sporting movement within the working class, which flourished in Europe, took root in many urban areas in America. Many workers, first- or-second-generation immigrants, preferred to play the sports of their native countries instead of American baseball or football. International workers' sport groups included the Socialist Workers Sport International and its communist rival, the Red Sport International. Both groups emphasized mass participation, group discipline, and physical fitness over competition and profits. Their athletic festivals featured swimming, cycling, soccer, running, and gymnastics. They opposed the cutthroat competition and selfish exploitation of professional athletics, and on a number of occasions they held alternative sporting festivals. While these international groups staged huge events in Europe and Russia, labor sports groups in the United States held smaller alternative Olympiads in 1932 in Chicago and in 1936 in both Cleveland and New York City. While similar festivals in Europe attracted hundreds of thousands of spectators, those in America struggled to draw several thousand. This failure might be attributed to the general aversion to communism and socialism in the United States and to the popularity of sports such as baseball, which attracted many immigrant participants. Still, this nascent worker sport movement, ultimately undone by the American nationalism of World War II, did provide an alternative sporting venue for the worker of the Depression era.

Sport in America during the Great Depression bridged a gap between the golden age of the 1920s and the postwar boom of the late 1940s. Owners and managers longed for the huge crowds and gate receipts of the 1920s, and fans looked in vain for athletic heroes in the towering tradition of Babe Ruth and Red Grange. Still, the 1930s looked forward more than back. Black athletes competed against, and bested, white athletes with greater frequency, anticipating the successful integration of major sports that would follow in the 1940s. Female athletes, led by "Babe" Didrikson, achieved greatness on the athletic fields, at the same time inspiring talk of sexual ambiguity and lesbianism that would resurface in female athletics even late in the twentieth century. Perhaps most important, in the 1930s fewer people watched sporting events, and more people participated. Aided by funding from New Deal programs, sports such as golf, tennis, skiing, and bowling attracted millions of Americans. This mass participation in sports presaged the fitness craze of the 1980s and 1990s. The Great Depression challenged athletes, coaches, and owners with poor attendance and reduced salaries, threatening them with destitution themselves. In adapting to survive these troubled times, they laid the foundation for trends in athletics that would reach prominence in the postwar era.

KEVIN WITHERSPOON

See also: Olympics (Berlin, 1936); Didrikson, Babe; DiMaggio, Joe; Gehrig, Lou; Greenburg, Hank; Louis, Joe; Owens, Jesse; Paige, Leroy "Satchel"; Ruth, Babe.

Bibliography

Baker, William. *Sports in the Western World.* Urbana: University of Illinois Press, 1988.

Betts, John Richard. *America's Sporting Heritage: 1850–1950.* Reading, MA: Addison-Wesley, 1974.

Rader, Benjamin. *American Sports.* Englewood Cliffs, NJ: Prentice-Hall, 1990.

STAGECOACH

The silent movie era of the 1920s saw Hollywood producing a number of high-quality, or A-movie, westerns. But during the 1930s, the western slipped in quality, relegated largely to serials and B-movie status. *Stagecoach* (1939) reversed the trend and returned the western to the A-movie list. At the same time, it established John Ford as the premier director of top-quality westerns and made a star of John Wayne.

As the title indicates, the movie is largely set in a stagecoach carrying a collection of characters who represent different social types, even if they are somewhat clichéd: the drunken doctor, the big-talking businessman, the gentleman gambler, the rich lady snob, the timid traveling salesman, the kind hearted prostitute, and the young, revengeful outlaw named Ringo (played by Wayne).

As the passengers make their way across the desert, the rich lady gives birth prematurely and Indians attack the stagecoach. These crises bring the squabbling and mutually distrustful characters together. Enormously popular, the film conveyed to Great Depression audiences that they must stick together if they were to make it through their own crisis.

The film enhanced the acting career of Wayne, who had spent most of the 1930s in B-westerns.

See also: films, feature; Ford, John; Wayne, John.

Bibliography

Davis, Ronald L. *John Ford: Hollywood's Old Master.* Norman: University of Oklahoma Press, 1995.

Gallagher, Tag. *John Ford: The Man and His Films.* Berkeley: University of California Press, 1986.

STEEL INDUSTRY

Like most industries in 1929, the steel industry suffered tremendous losses in the stock market failure. The demand for steel relied on the general business climate. The complex industry had a unique structure with massive overhead costs, unequal distribution, and a lack of production concentration, all of which affected its pricing policy. The steel producers did not function under a free competition system until 1924, and they controlled a large pool of unorganized labor with little or no representation. In addition, a few firms concentrated in the northeast and Midwest dominated the industry.

Since the dawn of the machine age, most economic indicators measured the success of the nation by its iron, and then steel output. In 1929, the iron and steel industries had the third highest number of employees (440,000) and were second in the value created by the manufacturing process. After the 1929 market crash, the industry limped along by cutting hours and wages for its workers, but maintained high prices for its product. The Smoot-Hawley Act (1930) drastically increased tariffs, which decreased the amount of steel exports. A ripple effect worked through the industry. The high price of steel contributed to a decreased demand and lowered the amount of work done at steel-dependent businesses, and less demand at steel-dependent businesses translated into low production for the steel industry. The industry had expanded in the post—World War I era, but, by 1931, steel production fell to 29 million tons. The industry produced at only 15 percent of its 71-million-ton capacity in 1932–33. The steel industry had shunned earlier efforts to establish unemployment compensation and other actions that it saw as detrimental to the status quo. The workers had no effective representation since the most recognized union, the Amalgamated Association of Iron, Steel, and Tin Workers (AAISTW), had suffered considerable defeats during the Homestead strike (1892) and steel strike of 1919.

In 1930, President Herbert Hoover, a proponent of laissez-faire capitalism, made agreements with the steel industry to hold wages at their current level. Hoover's Reconstruction Finance Corporation, established in January 1932, awarded emergency financing to certain major institutions, including railroads, insurance, banks, and building and loan associations, in the hopes of creating a trickle-down effect that would spur industries such as steel. When the institutions did not use the funds to invest in new ventures, steel producers did not follow through on wage agreements.

THE ELECTION OF ROOSEVELT AND THE NEW DEAL

The election of Franklin D. Roosevelt in 1932 brought a drastic change in the role of government in the steel industry. Roosevelt's New Deal policies sought to create a floor on wages and a ceiling on hours to increase employment across the board. The National Industrial Recovery Act (NIRA) of 1933 called for industrial codes to set up fair labor practices, recognition of employee representation through trade unions, and public works appropriations. The NIRA was an effort to rationalize the industrial economy and redress the imbalance between large corporations and wage earners. The individual industries created their own codes, which had to meet the approval of the National Recovery Administration (NRA). The companies attempted to adjust the language in Section 7 of NIRA, which called for employee representation, in order to sanction employee representation programs (ERPs), or company unions, as the workers' bargaining agent. Heads of the major companies, such as Myron C. Taylor of United States Steel and Charles Schwab of Bethlehem Steel Corporation, balked at the inclusion of labor leaders in the code negotiations. Following a walkout by the steel company representatives during a negotiations meeting with Secretary of Labor Frances Perkins, President Roosevelt called Taylor and Schwab to the White House, where, after some coercion, they agreed to sign the Steel Code in August 1933. The code called for an eight-hour day, a forty-hour week, and a forty-eight-hour-per-week cap, and set a minimum wage which varied by region. Also under the code, prices became fixed under a basing point system that set the cost of steel regionally. The code allowed price-fixing and exclusions from some antitrust laws in return for wage

Steel workers greet Secretary of Labor Frances Perkins at a Pittsburgh factory. *(Brown Brothers)*

increases and other concessions, but only if the steel industry operated at at least 60 percent capacity. The Steel Code also gave the industry tremendous self-regulatory powers since the American Iron and Steel Institute, an industry-dominated entity, enforced the code. By June 1934, President Roosevelt established the Steel Labor Relations Board (SLRB) to investigate accusations that companies ignored the workers' right to choose their representatives. A lack of enforcing power and legal maneuvering by companies kept the SLRB from being effective. The companies maintained the status quo in labor by not allowing the ERPs to negotiate wages or call strikes. When the SLRB sought to hold representation elections at some plants, the companies challenged its power to call such elections. Roosevelt attempted to intervene, but failed to resolve the conflict.

THE END OF THE NRA AND THE WAGNER ACT

The Supreme Court ruled the NIRA unconstitutional in *Schechter Poultry v. United States* (1935), and gradually all industry codes expired. Learning from the shortcomings of the NIRA, the federal government passed the National Labor Relations Act (NLRA), also known as the Wagner Act, on July 5, 1935. The act created a three-person labor panel, the National Labor Relations Board (NLRB), with increased powers in order to guarantee workers' right to self-organization. Legislators gave the NLRA more enforcement power in bringing unions and industry to negotiate, and made it constitutional by characterizing unfair labor practices as obstructions to interstate commerce since they usually led to labor disputes. The Supreme Court upheld the NLRB as constitutional in *NLRB v. Jones & Laughlin Steel* (1937). The NLRB had subpoena power, an investigative staff, and far-reaching enforcement powers.

The new government backing of labor unions and the inactivity of craft-based unions prompted John L. Lewis, of the newly formed Congress of Industrial Organizations (CIO), to propose an organizing drive in the steel industry. After its expulsion from the American Federation of Labor (AFL), the CIO joined with the Amalgamated Association of Iron, Steel and Tin Workers (AAISTW) to form the Steel Workers Organizing Committee (SWOC). The United Mine Workers (UMW) provided $500,000 for an organizing drive in the historically union-opposed steel industry, which had long used the ERPs to stifle labor unrest and refused to negotiate with labor unions.

Soon after the passage of NLRA, the formation of SWOC, and the establishment of the La Follette Civil Liberties Committee, organized labor began to see union membership increases in the steel industry. The 1936 election brought many pro–New Deal politicians into federal, state, and local office, including a UMW officer as lieutenant governor of Pennsylvania, a crucial state for the steel industry. The steel industry risked losing government contracts when the forty-hour-week clause of the Walsh-Healey Act (1936) prompted the federal government to consider building munitions plants rather than contract to private corporations. In December 1936, Myron C. Taylor began secret negotiations with John L. Lewis. The industry reeled in March 1937 when its largest producer, U.S. Steel, signed a contract through its Carnegie-Illinois branch with the SWOC. While the agreement granted representation only to the SWOC members, not all employees, the contract shattered the illusion that the steel industry could not be organized along industrial lines. By spring 1937, the SWOC claimed contracts with over 100 companies, including Jones & Laughlin, Crucible, Sharon, Wheeling, and Allegheny Steel.

TOM GIRDLER AND THE LITTLE STEEL STRIKE

Unorganized steel companies quickly adopted defensive strategies to avoid unionization, and Republic's Tom Girdler became the figurehead of anti-unionism in the industry. The four companies known as "little steel"— Bethlehem, Republic, National, and Youngstown Sheet and Tube—quickly instituted the concessions of the (SWOC–Carnegie-Illinois agreement), but did not recognize an independent representation. By lauding the

ERPs for these concessions, the companies hoped to solidify support for the company unions and stop the independent drive. When the SWOC demanded contract negotiations, Girdler countered by shutting down Republic's Massillion, Ohio, works. With the help of spies from the Pinkerton National Detective Agency, Republic infiltrated the SWOC in company towns and rallied citizens into Back-to-Work groups and Citizens Councils. The La Follette Committee later uncovered that the "little steel" companies influenced the anti-SWOC citizens groups and stockpiled weapons and tear gas in preparation for a standoff with the SWOC.

The SWOC called a strike against Republic and Youngstown on May 26, 1937. During a peaceful rally at Republic's Chicago mill on Memorial Day, May 30, city police attacked the workers, killing ten people. The police beat many of the marchers, including women and children, and those killed were shot in the back. The La Follette Civil Liberties Committee investigated the incident, known as the Memorial Day Massacre, and accused the police of attacking the crowd after newsreel footage provided evidence against the officers.

After the SWOC called strikes against Youngstown Sheet and Tube and Bethlehem-Johnstown works, President Roosevelt appointed the Steel Mediation Board to settle the disputes. The steel companies refused to allow the NLRB to hold elections that would put the SWOC–Carnegie-Illinois agreement in place if the SWOC won a majority. Soon after, the country fell into a recession, and the companies and organizers suffered setbacks. The "little steel" companies lost an unfair labor practices suit brought by the SWOC via the NLRB that forced the reinstatement with back pay of workers fired during the "little steel" strike. The most damaging aspect of the suit came when the NLRB ruled ERPs to be unfair. The companies fought the ruling through the courts as steel production and worker organization increased in 1939–40.

As the war in Europe escalated, President Roosevelt called for increased steel capacity including new plants, in the United States. Steel manufacturers balked at the request since most believed the war would be a short one and steel makers feared a postwar increase in European and Japanese steel production. The great expense of expansion in the steel industry made steel makers leery of the costly endeavor without a sure increase in demand. To entice the steel companies, the federal government offered $1.1 billion in public money to fund the increase in capacity. The money came with the terms that the private companies would operate the mills, but the government would own them. After the war, the mills would be sold to the companies at a reduced rate. Meanwhile, the courts upheld the NLRB's ruling on the ERPs, and facing increased union membership in 1940–41, Bethlehem granted the SWOC representation elections at its plants. After the SWOC achieved a majority at Bethlehem, other steel companies agreed to payroll cross-checks with SWOC membership rolls instead of a formed election. The NLRB listed the SWOC as the official bargaining agent of all major steel companies.

With the U.S. involvement in World War II, President Roosevelt established the National War Labor Board in 1942 to determine procedures for settling labor disputes. In July 1942, the War Labor Board announced a steel labor agreement, and the open-shop policy in the steel industry ended.

VINCENT T. BROOKS

See also: American Federation of Labor; Congress of Industrial Organizations; "little steel"; manufacturing and construction; Memorial Day massacre; Steel Workers Organizing Committee; unions and union organizing; United States Steel; National Labor Relations Act; *NLRB v. Jones & Laughlin*; Murray, Philip; Documents: National Labor Relations Act, July 5, 1935; *National Labor Relations Board v. Jones & Laughlin Steel Corporation*, 1937.

Bibliography

Bertin, Amy. *Competition and Productivity in the Depression-Era Steel Industry.* Thesis, Harvard University, 1994.

Brooks, Robert, and Romano Ravi. *As Steel Goes,..: Unionism in a Basic Industry.* New Haven and London: Oxford University Press, 1940.

Galeston, Walter. *The Unionization of the American Steel Industry.* Berkeley: University of California Press, 1956.

Hogan, William Thomas. *Economic History of the Iron and Steel Industry in the United States.* Lexington, MA: Heath, 1971.

Reutter, Mark. *Sparrows Point: Making Steel, the Rise and Ruin of American Industrial Might.* New York: Summit Books, 1989.

Seely, Bruce Edsall. "Iron and Steel in the Twentieth Century." *Encyclopedia of American Business History and Biography.* New York: Facts on File, 1994.

Stewart, Maxwell Slutz. *Steel: Problems of a Great Industry.* New York: Public Affairs Committee, 1937.

STEEL WORKERS ORGANIZING COMMITTEE

The Steel Workers Organizing Committee (SWOC) originated in a June 13, 1936, memorandum of agreement signed by the newly created Congress of Industrial Organizations (CIO) and the established, but ineffective, Amalgamated Association of Iron, Steel, and Tin Workers (AAISTW). The CIO, under the orchestration of United Mine Workers (UMW) president John L. Lewis, had severed relations with the craft union–based American Federation of Labor (AFL) in an effort to organize the staunchly anti-union steel industry along industrial lines. The CIO hoped to take advantage of the National Labor Relations Act of 1935 (Wagner Act), which gave workers the right to collectively bargain using the representative of their choice. The SWOC-AAISTW agreement essentially eliminated the Amalgamated's organizing activities and limited its responsibilities to issuing charters and executing trade agreements. Philip Murray, vice president of the UMW, became the SWOC's first director. Members of the CIO, UMW, and affiliated unions made up the majority of the SWOC. Only two members of the AAISTW sat on the original committee. With a $500,000 pledge from Lewis and the UMW, the SWOC set out on an organizational drive in the steel industry.

Most major steel industries used employee representation programs (ERPs) formed at the time of World War I. Often called company unions, these groups were meant to comply with the Wagner Act mandate for union representation. As a first step, the SWOC planned to recruit ERP members to establish an independent union mentality. The SWOC began with the nation's largest steel producer and the bastion of the industry's open-shop policy, United States Steel (U.S. Steel). U.S. Steel officially formed in 1901, but it and its predecessors had a long history of anti-union activities beginning with the 1892 strike in Homestead, Pennsylvania, that ended in the defeat of the AAISTW. The steel strike of 1919, the first national strike in the industry, further illustrated the company's resolve and its adherence to the ERP standard. By December 1936, after successful membership drives in the U.S. Steel plants, Lewis secretly met with U.S. Steel chairman Myron C. Taylor to discuss a contract. The announcement of an agreement between Carnegie-Illinois Steel, the largest subsidiary of U.S. Steel, and the Steel Workers Organizing Committee on March 2, 1937, surprised the nation. Taylor, prompted by the desire to sustain economic recovery, influenced by the results of the recent United Auto Workers–General Motors strike, and surprised by the rapid organization of the SWOC, signed a "members only" contract. While the "members only" status did not allow the SWOC to represent all Carnegie-Illinois workers, it signified the SWOC's emerging power. The contract called for a wage increase to sixty-two-and-a-half cents per hour, a forty-hour workweek, time-and-a-half overtime, and the creation of grievance procedures. By spring 1937, the SWOC claimed contracts with 100 companies, mostly smaller steel producers following U.S. Steel.

THE LITTLE STEEL STRIKE AND RENEWED DRIVE

Steel producers such as Bethlehem, Republic, National, Inland, and Youngstown Sheet and Tube, known as "little steel", quickly reacted to the U.S. Steel–SWOC contract by instituting similar wage and hour concessions within the ERP system without a formal contract. The "little steel" companies controlled a 38 percent portion of the industry's capacity, second only to U.S. Steel. Strengthened by the U.S. Steel agreement, the SWOC called its first strike in May 1937 after failing to reach an agreement with Jones & Laughlin (J&L) Steel. The strike lasted only two days and the resulting contract gave the SWOC its first exclusive bargaining rights for a major steel producer. Next, the SWOC moved against "little steel" and called for contract negotiations, but the companies ignored the requests. In an act of defiance, on May 20, 1937, Republic shut down its Massillon, Ohio, works and, six days later, the SWOC called a strike against the company. On May 30, 1937, during a pro-union rally at Republic's mill in Chicago, city policemen fired on the unarmed crowd, killing ten and wounding over 100 in the so-called Memorial Day Massacre. After further violence at "little steel" plants and failed intercession by the Steel Mediation Board, the SWOC strike faltered and the mills reopened. In an effort to capture some form of victory, the SWOC filed an unfair labor practices report with the NLRB against Republic. The decision forced the "little steel" companies to reinstate 5,000 strikers with back pay and to eliminate ERPs.

The 1937–38 recession slowed the SWOC's membership drive. War contracts brought increased steel production in 1939–40 that prompted an upswing in the SWOC membership. Van A. Bittner took over the organizing responsibilities for the SWOC and renewed the membership drive. In 1940, the SWOC negotiated a new contract with U.S. Steel, the first since 1937. While the company agreed to major concessions in grievance procedures, vacation time, and holiday pay, the contract remained a "members only" agreement. The NLRB called for secret elections at Bethlehem Steel plants during 1940–41, and the SWOC won a majority vote. After the success at Bethlehem's plants, other Little Steel companies agreed to cross-checks of the SWOC membership lists with company payrolls in lieu of a formal election. The results showed a majority in favor of the SWOC and therefore entitled it to become the exclusive collective bargaining agent for Little Steel workers. Prolonged "little steel"–SWOC negotiations and the outbreak of World War II prompted the newly formed War Labor Board (WLB) to consider the matter of union representation among the "little steel" companies. The WLB called for a five-and-a-half cent wage increase, maintenance of membership, and checkoff of union dues. In March 1942, the NLRB issued a call for elections at U.S. Steel plants after the SWOC filed petitions claiming it had been denied bargaining status guaranteed under the Wagner Act. The elections gave the SWOC exclusive bargaining rights at U.S. Steel, thus effectively ending the long-standing open-shop policy in the steel industry.

In May 1942, the SWOC and the AAISTW held a joint convention in Cleveland, Ohio. The AAISTW officially disbanded, and the rank and file voted to adopt a constitution and transform the SWOC into the United Steel Workers of America (USWA).

VINCENT T. BROOKS

See also: American Federation of Labor; Congress of Industrial Organizations; "little steel"; Memorial Day Massacre; steel industry; unions and union organizing; U.S. Steel; Lewis, John L.; Murray, Philip; Documents: Section 7 (National Industrial Recovery act); National Labor Relations Act, July 5, 1935.

Bibliography

Brooks, Robert, and Romano Ravi. *As Steel Goes, . . . :Unionism in a Basic Industry*. New Haven: Oxford University Press, 1940.

Galeston, Walter. *The Unionization of the American Steel Industry*. Berkeley: University of California Press, 1956.

Lages, John David. *The CIO-SWOC Attempt to Organize the Steel Industry, 1936–1942: A Restatement and Economic Analysis*. Thesis, Iowa State University of Science and Technology, 1967.

Reutter, Mark. *Sparrows Point: Making Steel, the Rise and Ruin of American Industrial Might*. New York: Summit Books, 1989.

Seely, Bruce Edsall. "Iron and Steel in the Twentieth Century." *Encyclopedia of American Business History and Biography*. New York: Facts on File, 1994.

STOCK MARKET

Few people, when asked to indicate the start of the Great Depression, would point to anything other than the collapse of the stock market in October 1929. Both the general decline of stock prices in the fall of that year, and the precipitous drops in stock values on both October 24 and October 29 ("Black Thursday" and "Black Tuesday," respectively) mark a clear transition between the booming economy of the "New Era" and the decade of decline, stagnation, and underproduction of the 1930s. Ironically, Black Tuesday may have been the high point in importance for the stock market during the Depression. Although the actions of those who operated the market came under a great deal of scrutiny during the 1930s, the history of America's stock market during the 1930s was one of consistent decline, institutional depression, and a slide toward relative cultural irrelevance. Ultimately, the stock market and the brokers who operated it suffered a longer and more protracted decline both financially and in prestige than did many of America's main industries.

THE STOCK MARKET CRASH AND THE DEPRESSION

Although long seen as the precipitating event in both America's and the world economy's decline, the stock market crash now plays a relatively limited role in historians' understandings of the causes of the Depression. While scholars disagree on the precise role that the stock market played in the onset of economic hard times, the crash is seen as at most only a single factor in a series of causes producing the Great Depression. Subsequent stock market crashes have shown that rapid declines in market value in an otherwise healthy economy do not cause widespread or protracted depression. Moreover, the Great Depression was a near decade-long time of widespread economic failure involving massive unemployment, a decline to pre–World War I levels of production, and long-term disinvestment. Despite the initial attention naturally paid to the stock market, the collapse of stock values is simply too limited and confined a factor to explain the extensive economic problems of an entire decade. Finally, in the later stages of the Depression, especially in the recession of 1937–38, the stock market was clearly subordinate to larger macroeconomic changes, influenced by recession, not driving it.

It is both logical and technically inaccurate to think in terms of a single market. To most Americans in the 1930s, the "stock market" was the New York Stock Exchange (NYSE), with its cathedral-like building on Wall Street and the "big board" listing the stock prices and issues. However, while most of public attention was focused on the activities on the floor of the NYSE, America's stock market was in practice a series of similar but structurally unrelated institutions. Just down the street from the NYSE was the curbside where independent traders had carried on a vigorous, open-air trade of their own from the late nineteenth century on. In 1921, this outdoor market had moved into its own building, and by the time of the New Deal the "Curb Exchange," although outdated in name, paralleled if it did not challenge the NYSE. Finally, in addition to these two New York-based institutions, a number of regional stock exchanges in Boston, San Francisco, and other cities in between, as well as the "over-the-counter market" (unregulated, independent dealers spread all over the country), collectively made up America's "stock market" during the New Deal. While most Americans would not have been able to draw such particular distinctions, the divisions within the larger stock market played important roles in both New Deal regulation of stock sales and the course of the "market" throughout the 1930s.

THE DECLINE OF THE STOCK MARKET DURING THE DEPRESSION

Perhaps no institutions suffered a greater relative decline in importance during the Depression than did America's stock markets. From the leading edge of

The stock market crash of 1929 ushered in the Great Depression and led to panic at the New York Stock Exchange (*shown in inset*). (*Brown Brothers*)

1920s prosperity, the brokers, speculators, and investors who populated the American stock markets fought not to regain prosperity, but simply to remain relevant in the 1930s. After losing approximately 50 percent of index value in a two-month period in the fall of 1929, stock values settled into a slow decline over the next three years. By 1932, standard stock indexes were worth only one-quarter of their 1929 levels. Even more important for those who made their livings in the market, volume (the number of shares sold) declined markedly. By 1934, annual volume had been reduced to 324 million shares, roughly one-third of the 1.1 billion shares that had changed hands at the height of prosperity in 1929. For personal speculators, this meant fewer opportunities for profit, while for the "specialists" (traders who controlled a large number of shares in a single company and made their living on a

percentage basis by selling stock for a slightly higher price than they bought it) and the commission brokers (who received a small percentage of each sale), declining volume meant declining income. Finally, at its worst, loss of volume meant the loss of jobs. Some brokerage houses, unable to put all of their traders to work, put junior members on "scotch holidays," essentially laying them off indefinitely until better times came along.

Even more telling than the general decline in market values and volume was the changing role of the market in macroeconomic development. In the 1920s, the market had seemed to drive the economy, as rising stock values presaged rising economic performance. This pattern remained constant even in recession, as the declines of 1929–30 pushed America's economy downward. However, from the mid-1930s on, the pattern reversed itself as the market seemed to follow the trends in the American economy, rather than leading it. Measurements of stock values after 1933 roughly parallel the rise in macroeconomic indicators. In 1937, the withdrawal of federal spending led to sharp declines in investment and employment. In response to these autonomous developments, the stock market declined. Stock indexes fell from a Depression-era high of 57.8 (with 1929 as 100) down to 43.8 in 1938. If the stock market had been the tail wagging the dog in the 1920s, by the late 1930s the relationship had been reversed.

However, the place of the stock market in New Deal society should be understood beyond macroeconomic and statistical measurements. This decline in importance can also be seen in stock exchange interaction with New Deal bureaucrats and regulators. As the presumed cause of both the booming economy and the emphasis on wealth during the Coolidge and Hoover years, the stock market was perhaps the leading economic cultural symbol of 1920s society. And as America turned from celebration to a more critical assessment of the 1920s, the stock market remained at center stage while the public perception of stock brokers changed from promoters of prosperity to pirates who had robbed their clients blind and driven the economy into collapse.

INVESTIGATIONS AND REGULATION

Between 1932 and 1934, the Senate, under the direction of investigator Ferdinand Pecora, carried out a public investigation of America's stock markets. Similarly, in 1933, New York Attorney General John J. Bennett Jr. investigated the practices of the Curb Exchange. Both of these probes revealed the questionable, if not fraudulent operations of America's stock market. These practices included sales on narrow margins (stocks could be purchased with as little as 10 percent of the listing price in cash and the other 90 percent borrowed "on margin"), fraudulent pricing (brokers would sell or buy a stock at one price and then report it to their client at a slightly different figure, thereby making a small profit on each trade), specialists' ability to create a "market" for stocks in which they were interested by offering misleading information, and the seemingly irresponsible speculation that took place regularly. Furthermore, the companies whose stock was the focus of all this activity did not even need to report basic financial information to investors. All told, stock exchanges were entirely private and operated more as

clubs in which members rarely chose to punish or even comment on the misbehavior of powerful members. Collectively, the revelations confirmed the popular sense that the stock market was badly in need of reform and a central cause of the failure of the American economy. While the public approval of stock brokers declined as the public became aware of the depth of manipulation involved in the stock market, the attention paid to these practices confirmed the central, if nefarious role that the stock market played in American society.

Consequently, despite declining economic importance, the stock market played a central role as a New Deal foe in the first term of Franklin D. Roosevelt's presidency. Roosevelt's attacks on "the unscrupulous moneychangers" and his references to the "failure" and "incompetence" of the "rulers of the exchange of mankind's goods" were clearly aimed at the men who operated and controlled America's stock exchanges. The early course of New Deal regulation of the stock market confirmed this importance. The Federal Securities Act (May 1933) required corporations that sold stock to provide accurate financial information to potential investors and allowed investors who could prove overt fraud to collect compensatory damages. This law however, required only the most basic reporting of information and did little to address the rules of operation of the NYSE and other stock markets.

Consequently, in 1934 Congress passed the Securities Exchange Act. This law gave the federal government power to regulate the stock exchanges through the creation of a new regulatory board—the Securities Exchange Commission (SEC). That Roosevelt intended the SEC to work with the market, rather than force market leaders around, was clear from his appointment of Joseph Kennedy as head of the SEC. Kennedy was well known for his own market speculation in the 1920s, which suggested that he would take market operators' opinions into account in any regulation. However, despite this olive branch, market leaders resisted regulation in a number of ways. NYSE President Richard Whitney was outspoken in his obduracy, commenting in 1933 that "the Exchange is a perfect institution." While many other exchange members were not as open in their hostility, most looked upon federal intervention with misgiving.

NYSE leaders, who held the most prestige in the stock market and also drew the greatest public attention, took the hardest line against the federal government. In the early years of the SEC, NYSE leaders proposed a series of internal reforms that were intended to keep the exchange a privately controlled and regulated market. Charles Gay, who followed Whitney as NYSE president and was expected to provide a more cooperative leadership, ultimately took a similar hard line, claiming that it was the SEC and not the NYSE that had lived past its time. However, neither resistance nor token reforms were enough, and with the selection of a more aggressive SEC chairman, William O. Douglas, the pressure increased for reform within the NYSE. In 1938, the exchange announced a series of new rules that required its members to maintain higher assets-to-liabilities balances to forestall widespread failures in future panics, provide significantly clearer and more detailed financial reports on trades and loans, submit to public audits, and agree to prohibitions on insider loans that allowed insolvent brokerages and traders to mask their financial trouble. While these changes staved off federal operation of the NYSE itself, they were a significant retreat from the belief that the NYSE was a "perfect institution" that would be damaged by government intervention. The market ultimately remained "private," at least in definition, but the rule changes brought on a new openness that made the exchange far less a private club than it had been in 1929.

Government involvement in stock trading also revealed splits within the market itself. While the NYSE focused on keeping government regulators out of its market, Curb Exchange leaders accommodated federal regulation. In 1934, Curb Exchange president E. Burd Grubb publicly supported federal regulation of brokerage houses, noting that his exchange had a long history of public trading. This independent stance was driven by the Curb Exchange's self-interest, particularly its niche in unlisted stock trading. The vast majority of stock sold at the Curb Exchange was unlisted (previously issued stock, sold either privately or initially through another exchange and now being resold from one investor to another purely for speculative purposes, not to raise investment capital). If Congress outlawed unlisted trading or required extensive financial disclosure of unlisted stocks, the Curb Exchange would be out of business. Ultimately, Congress did not do so, as Curb Exchange leaders found a middle position between the NYSE and the federal government. Although one could never truly speak of a single "stock market," federal intervention forced divisions into the open, further reducing the ability of stock traders to operate as a coherent entity.

THE STOCK MARKET AND WAR PREPAREDNESS

By the time America entered World War II, the stock market had declined significantly in public attention and importance. Questions of business/government planning, federal use of the antitrust laws, revival of the power of labor unions, and direct federal intervention into both the industrial and agricultural economies all captured far more attention than did the actions of stock traders or the conditions of the stock market. The focus of investment and the economy had shifted from New York to Washington, D.C.

In perhaps the clearest sign of the declining economic and cultural importance of the stock market in the New Deal, recovery came far earlier for most other sectors of the economy than it did for America's stock brokers and traders. With the increase in demand produced by war orders, America's economy began to rise after 1939 as production, employment, and consumer consumption all increased significantly. Furthermore, with the emphasis on rapid production to supply war matériel to both Britain and the Soviet Union, American businessmen took on a renewed cultural and political importance. However, the stock market and its leaders continued to stagnate. Even as late as 1942, by which time most Americans had found jobs, the stock market continued to lag. The Dow Jones Index declined throughout the first four months of the year, hitting bottom in April 1942. At the Curb Exchange, volume declined even as the war started in Europe. In 1942, it had dropped more than half of its level in the last full year before the war. The war also ushered in a new kind of industrial financing—government contracts. With cost-plus contracts and federal funds being raised through taxes and government bonds, public issues of stock played a relatively minor role in driving the economy forward. The masters of the new economy were men who used federal contracts to stimulate private business, and the old-time financiers of Wall Street seemed outdated. Stocks rose in both volume and value in the second half of the war, but by the time the war came to an end America's stock markets were shells of what they had been only a decade and a half earlier. In short, the New Deal was a bear market for everyone associated with America's stock markets.

BRETT FLEHINGER

See also: Securities and Exchange Commission; Douglas, William O.; Kennedy, Joseph P.; Roosevelt, Franklin D.; Whitney, Richard.

Bibliography

Fearon, Peter. *War, Prosperity and Depression: The US Economy 1917–1945.* Oxford: Philip Alan, 1987.

McCraw, Thomas K. *Prophets of Regulation: Charles Francis Adams, Louis D. Brandeis, James M. Landis, Alfred E. Kahn.*

Cambridge: Belknap Press of Harvard University Press, 1984.

McElvaine, Robert S. *The Depression and New Deal: A History in Documents.* New York: Oxford University Press, 2000.

Sobel, Robert. *AMEX: A History of the American Stock Exchange, 1921–1971.* New York: Weybright and Talley, 1972.

———. *NYSE: A History of the New York Stock Exchange 1935–1975.* New York: Weybright and Talley, 1975.

STRIKES, GENERAL

The year 1934 was pivotal for labor relations in the United States. The advent of the National Industrial Recovery Act (NIRA) in 1933 with its Section 7 provision for labor's right to have union representation and to bargain collectively gave rise to heightened expectations on the part of workers. Employers still believed that they could defeat unionization with a strong offensive. In three cities—Toledo, Minneapolis, and San Francisco—labor's rights to unionize were tested in massive strikes.

All of these strikes resulted in urban violence with people killed, wounded, and maimed. Radical leadership and substantial support from other workers were also characteristic. Employers were especially recalcitrant, willing to use any weapon to stop union recognition. In the end, the support of sympathetic unions, the work of federal government mediators, and the effectiveness of the strikes aided their successful resolution. In all three strikes, labor achieved the right to organize unions and the right to represent their members in negotiations with managers. In San Francisco, the union won the all-important right to control the hiring hall for longshoremen. The three major strikes were an important stepping-stone on the road to unionization and the National Labor Relations Act of 1935.

TOLEDO

Toledo was called "little Detroit" because it manufactured autos as well as many of the auto parts upon which the auto manufacturers in Detroit depended. The Depression hit the city so hard that it could not meet the municipal payroll. Willys-Overland, a vehicle manufacturer, had gone bankrupt in 1929, causing 28,000 people to lose their jobs. One of the companies that survived was Electric Auto-Lite, a manufacturer of auto parts. Dissatisfaction was high on the assembly line at Auto-Lite because of low wages. Another company whose workers smoldered with resentment was Toledo Edison, the power company, where wages had been cut 20 percent and stock purchases made by the workers at the urging of the company had dropped in value to a small percentage of what the workers had paid for them. In both companies, the workers were encouraged to organize by the passage of Section 7 of the NIRA. Workes at Electric Auto-Lite organized Federal Labor Union 18384, while workers at Toledo Edison organized the International Brotherhood of Electrical Workers (IBEW). In both cases, employers were determined to defeat union organization.

At Electric Auto-Lite, the union demanded a 10 percent wage increase, seniority rules, and union recognition. These demands were met with contempt. On February 23, 1934, 4,000 employees—union and non-union members members alike—went on strike. The employers offered a 5 percent pay increase and the right to discuss the setting up of rules for future negotiations. The strikers voted to accept this pact, believing that their union would soon be recognized.

After a month of management recalcitrance, it was clear that company officials did not intend to bargain with the union, and the workers went out on strike a second time on April 12. Electric Auto-Lite hired strikebreakers to work the assembly lines. This inflammatory action drew the battle lines tightly. A. J. Muste of the American Workers' Party (AWP) came to the support of the local. The AWP advocated organization of the unemployed so they would not become strikebreakers and, to this end, organized the Lucas County Unemployed League.

Local 18384, with the help of the AWP, organized mass demonstrations and picketing at the plant entrances. The company asked for and received a court injunction that limited picketers to twenty-five at each entrance. Ted Selander and Tom Pollock of Toledo were arrested for defying the injunction. In May, the company was still operating and had demonstrated its determination to resist the union by hiring armed guards to protect the plant and the strikebreakers. Passions were heightened by these actions, and on May 21, a crowd of 1,000 gathered outside the plant. The next day there were 4,000 and two days later, 6,000. Unrest among the municipal workers led the company to believe that the police might not be on its side so the sheriff deputized a force, paid by Electric Auto-Lite, to protect the plant.

The workers exploded when a deputy beat up an old man in the street. Street fighting continued from afternoon until midnight on March 23. Deputies fought with tear gas, iron bars, and guns. Demonstrators piled rocks and bricks on the streets and hurled them toward deputies and plant windows. Cars were overturned and set aflame. At this point, no one had been killed, but many had been seriously injured.

Meanwhile the strikebreakers were trapped in the plant with the doors locked against the crowd. Adjutant General Frank D. Henderson of the Ohio National Guard sent 900 men armed with rifles and machine guns on Thursday. They released the strikebreakers from their imprisonment. During the afternoon, the crowd grew larger and taunted the guardsmen. Tear gas was fired to disperse the crowd. The strikers hurled the tear gas canisters back and moved forward. The troops fired their guns into the air. The crowd continued to charge and the guard now fired into the human line. Two were killed and fifteen were wounded. Bricks injured ten guardsmen. Later that night, the guardsmen fired again, wounding two more. By the time the melee ended more than 200 had been injured.

The Labor Department sent out a special mediator, Charles P. Taft. The Auto-Lite plant was closed and negotiations began. The strikebreakers came in with their own union, demanding to be hired first. On June 1, an agreement was finally reached: workers would receive a five cents per hour increase in pay; there would be recognition of the union as the representative of the workers; and seniority for reemployment would place prestrike employees who worked during the strike first, strikers, second, and strikebreakers, last.

On May 24, 1934, Toledo Edison was facing challenges similar to those at Auto-Lite. The IBEW asked for union recognition and a 30 percent raise in wages: 20 percent restoration of wages cut from 1920s levels and a 10 percent new wage increase. Out of 103 unions represented in the Central Labor Union of Toledo, eighty-five were willing to go out on a general strike with the Toledo Edison workers. Realizing that a power outage would be devastating to an already angry and dispirited city, the company came to terms on June 1. The workers received a 22 percent wage increase, and IBEW received recognition as the representative of the workers. The battle for union representation was successful.

MINNEAPOLIS

As in Toledo, conditions in Minneapolis were particularly difficult during the Depression. Minneapolis was a major interstate distribution center with trucking as its mainstay. Employers in Minneapolis were diehard enemies of organized labor. The Citizens' Alliance, consisting of the main employers of the city, was willing to use rough tactics, including espionage and violence, to keep labor from organizing.

On the side of the workers was the Farmer-Labor governor, Floyd Olson. In addition, they had the skilled leadership of the Irish-American Dunne brothers, who were masterful organizers with a pronounced radical disposition. Ray Dunne, after successfully organizing the Minneapolis coal yards, set about to organize the truckers of the city in Teamsters Local 574. On April 30, 1934, the union made demands for a closed shop, wages of $27.50 per week, and better working conditions. The employers refused the demands, particularly the closed shop. The union gave up on the closed shop issue, but the employers still would not come to terms. The union called a strike on May 12 and went out three days later.

Union strike headquarters was extremely well organized. Leaders posted observers throughout the city and had four telephone lines for receiving reports of movements by trucking firms. A kitchen served thousands of meals a day to strikers' families. For the first few days, little happened, but on the fourth day, the employers launched a propaganda campaign, calling the union workers communistic, and tried to provoke them. A union infiltrator caused two trucks filled with workers and their families to be lured into an alley, where the occupants were seriously beaten. From then on, the picketers were armed with lead pipes, clubs, and baseball bats. The Citizens' Alliance recruited and deputized supporters to go out on the streets to protect employers' rights.

On May 21, the first melee took place in the central square, but no one was seriously injured. On Tuesday, May 22, the employers announced that they would be sending out perishables by truck, leading to a strikers' decision that no trucks would be allowed to move. Twenty thousand people crowded the central marketplace. The two sides faced each other. When a crate of tomatoes was thrown through a window, the fighting began. The strikers gained control of the city in a short time and no produce was moved. Two of the Citizens' Alliance men were killed. The governor threatened martial law if the two sides did not come to the table. Both ostensibly accepted the terms, the strike was called off, and trucks began to roll.

It was apparent by May 26 that the employers would not recognize the union and negotiate in good faith. Both sides prepared for a siege. The employers raised $50,000 and for their propaganda campaign against the union. The union held a mass meeting on July 5 and called for a shutdown. On July 16, the strike was resumed. The National Labor Relations Board (NLRB) sent Francis J. Haas to mediate the strike. He submitted a proposal that the union accepted, but the employers refused to sign.

The employers decided to try to break the strike. First, they sent out a shipment of hospital supplies, which was delivered without incident. A second truck escorted by armed police moved out. The strikers put a vehicle in the path of the truck, a crowd gathered, and the police began to shoot at the picketers, leaving two dead and sixty-seven wounded. Most were shot in the back.

At this point, the governor threatened martial law again if the two sides did not agree to the NLRB proposal. The strikers agreed, but the employers, who would benefit from martial law, still refused to settle. Though Governor Olson sympathized with the strikers, he felt that his first duty was to preserve order. Martial law was declared on July 26. The strikers were forbidden to picket and all shipments were required to have military permits, although permits were issued generously and were poorly enforced. The union decided to stop the trucks by force. This defiance of the law was met with the arrest and imprisonment of three union leaders.

Strikers were outraged. The governor decided to release the prisoners and to put more pressure on the employers. He offered them permits to make shipments if they would sign on to the NLRB proposal. Meanwhile the employer holdouts were hoping for a court injunction against the strict permit system, but the U.S. District Court rejected their motion.

With nowhere else to go, the employers accepted the NLRB proposal on August 21, 1934. The agreement specified that strikers would receive preference for reemployment; elections for employee representation would be held within ten days; wages for drivers would be fifty cents per hour and for helpers and others, forty cents; National Recovery Administration (NRA) codes would govern hours and overtime. The great Minneapolis strike was over, and labor had made important gains.

SAN FRANCISCO

The one major strike that could be most accurately described as a general strike was the dockworkers' strike in San Francisco in 1934. The grievances of the longshoremen were numerous: long hours, dangerous work, and low wages. The most crucial issue for these workers, however, was the "shape-up," when employers chose their favorite workers each day at the Ferry Building on the Embarcadero. Workers had to arrive at 6:00 A.M. to compete with thousands of others for work that was to begin at 8:00 A.M. In order to curry favor with the companies, the workers had to do all manner of hard and dangerous work without complaint or they would not be hired again the next day. These conditions were greatly exacerbated by the Depression.

When Section 7 of the NIRA became known, there was a great desire among longshoremen for a union to represent them and bargain collectively on the docks. The International Longshoremen's Association (ILA), which had been broken in 1919, was resuscitated. In February 1934, the ILA asked for the abolition of the shape-up, a six-hour day, and a raise in wages. If these terms were not met, the longshoremen planned to go on strike in mid-March. President Franklin D. Roosevelt intervened and established a Longshoremen's Board, obtaining a postponement of the strike. The proposals of the board did not give adequate control of the hiring hall to the workers so they went on strike on May 9. Dockworkers from Los Angeles to Seattle stopped work.

The employers tried to operate with inexperienced workers, bringing in college students and clerks to handle the rigorous physical labor. Strikebreakers caught alone away from the docks were likely to have their teeth knocked out or their legs broken. Teamsters Local 85 in San Francisco refused to carry goods to the port.

Other maritime unions also went on strike. Essentially, the strike was effective for 2,000 miles of coastline. The governors of California and Washington asked the federal government to intervene. An assistant secretary of labor was sent out but was unsuccessful in obtaining an agreement. The San Francisco ILA insisted upon control of the hiring hall and a closed shop. The head of the ILA from New York came to negotiate. The newspapers heralded the end of the strike, but the workers would not accept the terms of the negotiation. At the same time, the police and pickets were clashing at Pier 18. The longshoremen were fighting with fists and bricks and the police with guns and tear gas. No one was killed, but some were wounded.

The Industrial Association, which represented the employers, pictured the workers as Communists, particularly Harry Bridges, chair of the Joint Marine Strike Committee. On July 3, the Industrial Association determined to open the port by force. Pickets and spectators came out in huge numbers. In the afternoon, the police cleared another pier, number 38. The steel doors were opened and five trucks driven by strikebreakers entered. The pier exploded in violence. Pickets and police battled for four hours. Many were hospitalized though there were no fatalities. Confrontations were suspended for the Fourth of July.

On July 5, loading was to resume at 8:00 A.M. The police were well armed against the thousands of picketers, but the "Battle of Rincon Hill" raged the entire morning. In the afternoon, when picketers tried to get control of the Embarcadero, the area erupted in violence. Police opened fire, killing two and wounding sixty-seven. Governor Frank Merriam of California called out the National Guard to restore order.

Over the weekend, the workers held a huge funeral procession with thousands walking silently. Workers outside the maritime industry were beginning to consider joining in a general strike. The Central Labor Council requested that all the unions represented go out on strike on July 16. Panic reigned in the city. The newspapers decided to curtail the general strike by creating a Red Scare, which they thought would bring in government at all levels to break the strike. The mayor, Angelo Rossi put together a group of 500 business associates to take charge of the situation. The governor ordered in more troops. While local and state governments reacted hysterically, the Roosevelt administration refused to fall victim to the panic. The president was on a ship in the Pacific, leaving Secretary of Labor Frances Perkins in charge. She refused to call the situation more than a labor dispute.

Altogether, 130,000 workers went out on strike, but for the most part there were no disturbances during most of the walk out. By July 19, the general strike was losing steam, so the strike committee instructed the sympathetic unions to return to work. The next day, the marine workers agreed to arbitration and the longshoremen voted to accept arbitration by the Longshoremen's Board.

The arbitration resulted in a major victory for the longshoremen. The hiring hall was to be jointly run by employers and union, but the dispatcher was to be chosen by the union. This gave control over the hiring to the workers. Wages were set at ninety-five cents per hour and $1.40 for overtime. The workers gained six-hour days and thirty-hour weeks. Any work over six hours was to be paid by overtime.

CONCLUSION

Companies in Toledo, Minneapolis, and San Francisco had wielded all their weapons to stop unionization. They used spies, hired guns, and strikebreakers to break the strikes; they put on propaganda campaigns that painted union leaders as dangerous radicals to gain the sympathy of the citizenry; they formed citizens' organizations to go out on the streets to stop picketers; and they enlisted the local police and National Guard to preserve order, lessening the chances that the strikes would be successful. Despite these all-out efforts to defeat unionization, the unions in these three cities were successful in winning their rights to represent workers. The strikes were important lessons for the New Deal and played a role in convincing President Roosevelt to support the National Labor Relations Act of 1935, which would guarantee labor's rights to organize.

BONNIE FORD

See also: auto industry; Communist Party; unemployment; unions and union organizing; National Industrial Recovery Act; National Labor Relations Act; Bridges, Harry; Olson, Floyd; Perkins, Francis; Documents: Section 7 (National Industrial Recovery Act); National Labor Relations Act, July 5, 1935

Bibliography

Bernstein, Irving. *Turbulent Years: A History of the American Worker, 1933–1941.* Boston: Houghton Mifflin, 1971.

Biles, Roger. *A New Deal for the American People.* DeKalb: Northern Illinois University Press, 1991.

Braeman, John, Robert H. Bremner, and David Brody. *The New Deal.* Vol. 1. Columbus: Ohio State University Press, 1975.

Broadus, Mitchell. *Depression Decade: From New Era through New Deal, 1929–1941.* New York: Harper & Row, 1947.

McElvaine, Robert S. *The Great Depression.* New York: Times Books, 1984.

Schlesinger, Arthur M. *The Coming of the New Deal.* Vol. 2. Boston: Houghton Mifflin, 1958.

STRIKES, SIT-DOWN

From 1936 to 1938, workers across the nation sought greater control over their lives by staging a wave of sit-down strikes. In that "sit-down era," workers struck for better working conditions and official recognition of their industrial unions. The two largest strikes during this sit-down wave targeted the Akron, Ohio, rubber industry and the General Motors (GM) automotive plants in Flint, Michigan. By the end of the sit-down era, workers had forced industrial management to provide better working conditions, gained widespread recognition of labor unions, and increased the political and economic power of organized labor.

In contrast to a traditional walkout, in which strikers stay away from their jobs, workers remain in their place of employment during a sit-down strike—often at their job posts—yet refuse to work. During the sit-down era of the Great Depression, workers mounted five types of sit-down strikes. First, they staged "quickie" sit-downs, in which a small number of workers refused to work for brief periods of time. In a second type of strike, quickie sit-downs turned into plant-wide strikes as significant numbers of workers sat down in sympathy. Third, quickie strikes sometimes became lockouts when plant management refused to deal with obstinate workers. Fourth, during some sit-downs, workers reported to work, sat idly at their positions, and then left upon completion of their regular shift. This last tactic could go on for a period of days. Finally, in the most dramatic and important form of sit-down strikes, also known as the "stay-in," large numbers of workers seized control of a plant, halted its operation, and occupied it for days, weeks, or even months. Workers staged a barrage of these stay-in strikes from 1936 through 1938, bringing sweeping changes to American labor, business, and politics during the Great Depression.

The sit-down tactic held several advantages over the traditional walkout. The sit-down allowed a small group of militant workers to tie up production in a large plant or series of interdependent plants. In complex industries such as rubber, textiles, and automobiles, work stoppages on a crucial area of the assembly line could freeze production throughout the factory almost instantaneously. Workers who sat down also enjoyed more safety than picketers. They were able to construct defenses within the plants. Management and police frequently expressed reluctance to extricate sit-down strikers out of fear of damaging valuable buildings and machinery. In addition, because sit-down strikers occupied their places of employment, they prevented employers from hiring replacements or continuing production on skeleton staffs. Finally, the sit-down strike gave workers a tremendous sense of power as they sat beside idle machines that had previously seemed to dictate their daily existence.

THE COMING OF THE SIT-DOWN ERA

Workers staged very few sit-down strikes before 1936. The first documented sit-down in the United States occurred in the late nineteenth century among brewery workers in Cincinnati, Ohio. The Industrial Workers of the World staged a sit-down at a General Electric plant in Schenectady, New York, in 1905. In 1933, meatpackers at the Hormel Packing Company in Austin, Minnesota, sat down in protest. Although these strikes were successful in meeting workers' immediate goals, labor leaders and the press did not note the importance or value of the sit-down tactic.

Developments in federal politics and the day-to-day lives of workers during the Depression created the conditions that led to the sit-down movement. In 1933, Congress passed the National Industrial Recovery Act (NIRA). Section 7 of that law guaranteed workers the right to join unions. In 1935, Congress passed the Wagner Act, which forbade employers to fire workers for joining unions and from fostering employer-dominated company unions. In addition, Franklin Delano Roosevelt's 1936 presidential campaign drew heavily on labor support and encouraged a political climate gen-

Sit-Down Strikes at General Motors,
1936–1937

(CARTO-GRAPHICS)

erally friendly to workers and labor organizations. Hundreds of thousands of previously unorganized workers formed local unions. These new locals in turn flooded the ranks of the American Federation of Labor (AFL), an umbrella organization made up of various smaller unions. In late 1935, a group of militant unionists led by John L. Lewis, president of the United Mine Workers, broke away from the conservative AFL to form the Committee for Industrial Organization, which would later become the Congress of Industrial Organizations (CIO). The CIO quickly became a rival of the AFL, as many unions chose to affiliate with the new organization.

Yet despite the growing labor movement, many employers ignored the Wagner Act, refusing to allow their employees to join or bargain through unions. The sit-down wave, a product of both spontaneous worker unrest and union planning, forced management to recognize the burgeoning industrial unions. The sit-down era commenced with a series of spontaneous work stoppages in early 1936 at the Firestone, Goodrich, and Goodyear rubber plants in Akron, Ohio. Later in 1936, sit-down strikes broke out in several GM plants, setting off a nationwide sit-down wave. During that wave, workers won improvements in working conditions and affirmed their right to join and bargain through industrial unions.

THE AKRON RUBBER STRIKES

The tire and rubber industries dominated the economy of Akron, Ohio, during the 1930s, with Firestone, Goodrich, and Goodyear operating the largest production plants. During the 1920s, the Akron rubber industry thrived on the growth of the American automobile industry, and rubber workers developed into a relatively well-paid elite among industrial laborers. The Great Depression undermined the booming rubber industry and brought widespread layoffs, unemployment, and pay reductions to Akron's workforce. These downwardly mobile laborers organized the United Rubber Workers (URW) in 1933 under the banner of the AFL, but the militant URW rank and file became increasingly dissatisfied with the conservative tactics of the AFL. On January 29, 1936, without AFL approval, Akron's Firestone employees sat down and halted production throughout the plant in response to management's attempts to increase the pace of production without raising wages.

The strike quickly spread to the city's Goodyear and Goodrich plants, where workers suffered under similar working conditions. At Goodyear, employees had been shocked to learn that the company intended to lay off one-quarter of its labor force. On February 14, 137 tire builders shut off the power at the Goodyear plant and sat down, effectively halting the nation's rubber production. The militant tactics soon mobilized the entire workforce behind the strike, and although URW leaders persuaded the sit-downers to evacuate the occupied plant, the momentum generated by the initial sit-down kept workers on picket lines for the next month. Local union leaders severed their affiliation with the AFL and joined the more militant CIO. On March 21, Goodyear agreed to halt layoffs and recognized the URW-CIO as the bargaining agent for its workers.

From April through November 1936, a wave of sit-downs continued to rock the Akron rubber industry. By mid-1936, conflict developed between shop-floor militants and union leaders, who argued that the frequent spontaneous strikes undermined the union's credibility with management. Yet quickie strikes simultaneously reminded management that workers could and would exercise their power to halt production. Despite the conflict that developed within the URW, the Akron sit-downs of early 1936 established both the URW and the CIO as powerful industrial unions and marked the beginning of the widespread use of the sit-down tactic.

THE FLINT GENERAL MOTORS STRIKE

Several months after the Akron strike, a series of sit-down strikes swept General Motors plants across the country. In late December 1936, workers occupied several critical GM plants in Flint, Michigan, causing a company-wide shutdown. By the end of the forty-four-day strike in February 1937, the fledgling United Auto Workers (UAW) had won a victory over the largest corporation in the world and established labor as a powerful political force.

General Motors housed a large percentage of its production in Flint. GM had come to the town in 1905, when Buick established a plant there. Over the next twenty-five years, the company erected two Chevrolet assembly plants and numerous body and parts manufacturers. By 1930, four out of every five family heads in Flint worked for General Motors. Yet despite the corporation's tremendous wealth, many of its workers struggled to survive on low wages. In 1936, the average autoworker earned less than $25 dollars per week. Workers also objected to the industry's deplorable working conditions. Throughout the 1930s, GM supervisors increased the pace of production. Tired and harried workers were forced to labor without many time-consuming safety guards, and, as a result, job safety deteriorated. Workers often complained that they were too tired to move after working an entire shift. Given these conditions, UAW-CIO organizers successfully recruited workers in the Flint GM plants throughout 1936, particularly in the Fisher Body Plants One and Two—makers of auto bodies for a large percentage of GM cars—where conditions were worst.

In late 1936, the Flint GM strike began to take shape. Several strikes broke out in isolated GM plants across the country. Homer Martin, the president of the UAW, requested an immediate general conference between national union leaders and GM management, but the manufacturer wanted to meet with leaders at each plant individually. When workers at Cleveland's Fisher Body plant sat down on December 28, UAW leaders saw their opportunity to mount a general attack against GM. Organizers rushed to the scene of the spontaneous strike in Cleveland and urged the strikers to hold out until the union could reach a national settlement. On December 30, workers at the Fisher Body Plant Number One in Flint sat down on the job, bringing the strike to the heart of the GM empire and effectively paralyzing the company.

With the seizure of the Fisher One plant, the strike quickly spread throughout the corporation. Almost immediately, workers at the Flint Fisher Two plant staged a sit-down strike. Several of the city's Chevrolet and Buick assembly plants, dependent on the Flint Fisher plants for their auto bodies, halted production. Over the next week, the strike spread to include a total of nineteen plants in Georgia, Missouri, Indiana, Ohio, and Michigan. The UAW quickly evacuated many of the plants because of the logistical problems of feeding the sit-downers; however, workers occupied the Fisher One and Two plants in Flint throughout the strike. On January 3, 1937, a group of two hundred UAW delegates formally articulated two major demands: the recognition of UAW-CIO as the sole bargaining agent for GM workers and worker control over the speed of production. Management refused to meet their demands, believing it could extricate workers from the occupied plants.

The most dramatic moment of the strike occurred on January 11, 1937, in what was called the Battle of the Running Bulls. On that night, company guards refused to allow strike supporters to bring food to the sit-downers in the Fisher Two plant. The strikers, worried that management might be attempting to starve them out, marched to the plant gate. They encountered the contingent of guards who had refused to allow food into the plant. The strikers charged the guards, who fled to safety. The gate splintered open and the sit-downers piled into the street to the cheers of a crowd of supporters gathered outside. The cheers soon turned to howls of pain and confusion as city police arrived on the scene. The sit-downers retreated into the factory as the police beat them and hurled gas grenades into the crowd and the plant. Yet the strikers managed to secure the plant, turn fire hoses on the police, and send them scurrying under a hail of car hinges, springs, and bottles. The retreating police fired into the crowd, wounding thirteen strikers and supporters. This successful defense of Fisher Two marked the turning point in the strike, rousing the strikers' sagging morale and winning the sympathy of many workers and community members who had not taken sides to that point.

In addition, the Battle of the Running Bulls brought evenhanded government mediation and demonstrated to GM that it would need to bargain with, rather than strong-arm, the union. Michigan governor Frank Murphy ordered in the National Guard and proceeded to act as peacekeeper and mediator, rather than siding with GM. On January 15, the company and the union signed a truce in which the union agreed to evacuate all GM plants in exchange for the company's agreement to bargain with the UAW-CIO for a strike settlement; however, after hearing rumors that GM

A crowd of supporters gathers as sit-down strikers refuse to evacuate the Fisher Body Plant Number Two in Flint, Michigan, in January 1937. *(Brown Brothers)*

would attempt to bargain with the company-controlled Flint Alliance—made up of business leaders and non-UAW workers—the Flint strikers remained inside. On February 1, the union staged another dramatic event, seizing the critical Flint Chevy Four assembly plant. By closing Chevy Four, the strikers again revived their morale, demonstrating once and for all that they would not be removed from the Flint plants.

The company and union reached an agreement on February 11, 1937. In total, the strike affected over fifty GM plants and 140,000 employees. Production dropped from 50,000 cars in December 1936 to just 125 cars in the first week of February 1937. With Chrysler and Ford still producing at maximum capacity and its own production dismally sagging, GM yielded to many of the union's major demands. In exchange for ending the strike, the UAW gained sole bargaining rights in seventeen of the company's plants for six months. Although the agreement represented a compromise of the UAW's goal of company-wide exclusive bargaining, union leaders believed that the excitement and prestige generated by the strike would allow the union to become firmly entrenched within six months. Indeed, between February and October 1937, the UAW saw its ranks swell from 88,000 to over 200,000 autoworkers.

THE POST-FLINT SIT-DOWN WAVE

Heartened by labor's victory over GM, a wide range of industrial and service workers across the country mounted a barrage of sit-down strikes in 1937 and 1938. Between March and June 1937, there were 170 sit-down strikes in GM plants alone as workers sought to exercise the control over the pace and conditions of work that the union had earned in the Flint settlement. This wave of quickie sit-downs proved a mixed blessing for the newly formed UAW. The strikes served as powerful and effective organizers, bringing more workers into the union and solidifying the loyalty of the already unionized. For example, the sit-down wave spread from GM to Chrysler in March 1937, helping the union to win a settlement with that company in April. Yet at the same time, quickie strikes undermined the authority of national union leaders, who appeared to have little control over the rank and file. As early as February 1937, UAW leadership attempted to curb the sit-down tide by restricting the authority of local leaders and purging the most militant hotheads.

The strike wave also spread beyond the auto industry, causing the *Detroit News* to lament, "Sitting down has replaced baseball as a national pastime, and sitter-downers clutter up the landscape in every direction." In March 1937, over 167,000 workers participated in 170 sit-down strikes. By the end of the year, over 400,000 workers had engaged in 474 sit-downs. The state of Michigan, especially the city of Detroit, was hardest hit by the sit-down wave. The strikers in that state were most directly inspired by the Flint victory and were also heartened by Governor Murphy's relatively evenhanded treatment of the Flint strikers. In March 1937, with the Chrysler sit-down strike underway, workers also sat down in Detroit's laundries, cigar factories, warehouses, packing houses, and hotels. Retail workers, who could normally be replaced during conventional strikes, found the sit-down tactic particularly effective.

The sit-down tide receded almost as quickly as it had risen. Although there had been little government opposition to the sit-down tactic during the Flint strike—President Roosevelt had remained silent, while Secretary of Labor Frances Perkins had approved of the technique—public opinion turned against the sit-downers as the tide reached its height in mid-1937. The public criticized the strikes as a threat to both private property and public order. In late March, police broke up many of Detroit's sit-down strikes after discovering that professional agitators, not employees, had driven the strikes in the hotel industry. The AFL condemned sit-down strikes outright during the same month, while CIO leaders sought to curb their use. In April 1937, the U.S. Supreme Court upheld the Wagner Act, for-

mally solidifying labor's right to collective bargaining, thus removing much of the impetus for the sit-down strikes. Finally, in the 1939 Fansteel Metallurgical Corporation decision, the federal court declared the sit-down tactic illegal.

THE LEGACY OF THE SIT-DOWN ERA

The sit-down wave from 1936 through 1938 ushered in a new era of work conditions, labor organization, and national politics. First, the sit-down era contributed to the reorganization of authority in the workplace. As workers demonstrated they would no longer heed the whims of shop-floor supervisors, decisions about factory management were removed from the factory floor, and personnel managers worked with union officials to systematize working conditions, hiring practices, and wages. Wages and working conditions frequently saw marked improvement. Second, the Flint sit-down paved the way for CIO organization in other industries. For example, U.S. Steel recognized the Steel Workers Organizing Committee (SWOC) without a fight, largely out of fear of repeating the disastrous mistakes GM had made. In two short years, the membership of the fledgling CIO eclipsed that of the AFL. By backing and helping to guide the sit-down strikes, the CIO achieved a position of power unparalleled by any other labor organization. Finally, the quick growth of the CIO and the mobilization of masses of workers encouraged Roosevelt and other New Deal Democrats to continue to court the labor vote. Unions and workers would retain significant political influence throughout the New Deal and beyond. However, while the sit-down era augmented and affirmed the power of both labor leaders and individual workers, it also left a legacy of conflict between these two groups. After 1938, workers continued to stage periodic quickie sit-down strikes. Union leaders, however, increasingly labeled these strikes as unauthorized "wildcats." Although the initial sit-down wave had won tremendous victories and swelled union ranks, labor leaders would find rank-and-file militancy increasingly troublesome as they sought to establish productive relationships with business and government leadership.

STEVEN T. SHEEHAN

See also: American Federation of Labor; Congress of Industrial Organizations; General Motors; United Automobile Workers; National Labor Relations Act; National Industrial Recovery Act;

Murphy, Frank; Perkins, Frances; Reuther, Walter; Document: National Labor Relations Act, July 5, 1935.

Bibliography

Fine, Sidney. *Sit-Down: The General Motors Strike of 1936–1937.* Ann Arbor: The University of Michigan Press, 1969.

Kraus, Henry. *The Many and the Few: A Chronicle of the Dynamic Auto Workers.* 2d ed. Urbana: University of Illinois Press, 1985.

———. *Heroes of Unwritten Story: The UAW, 1934–1939.* Urbana: University of Illinois Press, 1993.

Nelson, Daniel. "Origins of the Sit-Down Era: Worker Militancy and Innovation in the Rubber Industry, 1934–1938." *Labor History* 23:2 (1982): 198–225.

———. "The Great Goodyear Strike of 1936." *Ohio History* 92: (1983): 6–36.

Schwantes, Carlos A. " 'We've Got 'Em on the Run, Brothers': The 1937 Non-Automotive Sit Down Strikes in Detroit." *Michigan History* 56:3 (1972): 179–99.

West, Kenneth B. " 'On the Line': Rank and File Reminiscences of Working Conditions and the General Motors Sit-Down Strike of 1936–37." *Michigan Historical Review* 12:1 (1986): 57–82.

SUPERMAN

The first of the superhero cartoon characters, Superman was originally conceived by Jerry Siegel and Joe Shuster, two Cleveland teenagers, in 1934. The original comic strip featured Superman and his newspaperman cover character, Clark Kent, who worked for the fictional *Daily Planet* newspaper, situated in the made-up city of Metropolis; his fellow reporter Lois Lane; copyboy Jimmy; and a host of other characters.

While superheroes were nothing new in the comic book industry, the character of Superman had a number of unique traits that made him especially appealing to young males—the primary readership of comic books—and Depression-era audiences. He had tremendous strength, the ability to fly, the capacity for x-ray vision, and other superhuman powers.

First, there was the character's dual personality as Superman and Clark Kent. This dichotomy offered insecure teen-age boys the idea that they could overcome their own limitations. At the same time, Kent was an average man at a time when mass culture was promoting the idea that the common man was at the center of the social order.

Second, Kent/Superman was able to overcome any obstacle and any crisis, a message of great appeal to Depression-era readers. Third, Superman was also an immigrant of sorts (from the planet Krypton) who had adopted the American way of life; this also appealed to readers at a time when the great wave of turn-of-the-century immigrants and their children were becoming fully integrated into American society.

And finally, Superman—in his red, white, and blue outfit—was an all-American hero, defending democracy and the American way in the 1930s, a time when everything the country stood for seemed to be threatened by the rise of fascism and communism abroad.

But, despite all of these appealing traits, Siegel and Shuster had a hard time selling the idea.

After trying it out in their high school newspaper, Siegel and Shuster tried to market it around to cartoon syndicates. Repeatedly turned down, they finally sold the concept to a new comic book company called Detective Comics, better known by its initials DC, in 1938. But the deal they agreed to—giving up all rights to the character for a mere $130—is considered one of the most notorious intellectual copyright contracts ever signed. In 1947, Siegel and Shuster sued to get some of the enormous earnings DC made on the character, but the case went against them.

The character of Superman has been featured in two television shows: *Adventures of Superman* in the 1950s and *Lois and Clark* in the 1990s. In addition, Superman was the hero of several films in the 1970s and 1980s.

See also: newspapers and magazines.

Bibliography

Daniels, Les. *DC Comics: Sixty Years of the World's Favorite Comic Book Heroes.* Boston: Little, Brown, 1995.

Dooley, Dennis, and Gary Engle. *Superman at Fifty: The Persistence of a Legend.* Cleveland: Octavia, 1987.

TIME

Among the most influential news magazines in America in the 1930s, *Time* magazine was founded in 1923 by publisher Henry Luce as a unique weekly digest of news, divided into various departments and written in an easy-to-read, breezy style.

A probusiness, pro-Republican magazine in the 1920s, this slant became even more apparent after 1929, when Luce took over the day-to-day management of the periodical after the sudden death of its previous editor, Briton Hadden.

In the 1930s, Luce brought *Time* to radio broadcasting, inaugurating a program called *Newscasting*, which essentially repeated the magazine's contents over the air. *Newscasting* soon evolved into *NewsActing*, whereby news items were dramatized with sound effects. Ultimately, this program resulted in *The March of Time* program, where announcers read in dramatic tones a half-hour digest of the news every Friday night on the CBS radio network.

While conservative on domestic issues and generally hostile to New Deal legislation and Franklin D. Roosevelt, Luce came to agree with the president in the late 1930s that America needed to help Britain and other countries struggling against Nazi Germany and militarist Japan. *Time* reflected this consensus, becoming a strongly prointernationalist publication by the end of the decade.

Time remains the best-selling newsweekly magazine in the United States to the present day.

See also: newspapers and magazines; radio; Luce, Henry.

Bibliography

Elson, Robert T. *Time, Inc.: The Intimate History of a Publishing Enterprise, 1923–1941.* New York: Atheneum, 1968.

Tebbel, John. *The American Magazine: A Compact History.* New York: Hawthorn Books, 1969.

TOBACCO ROAD

Among the best-selling books of the 1930s, Erskine Caldwell's *Tobacco Road*, published in 1932, told the sadly funny story of a poor Georgia tobacco farmer named Jeeter Lester, his family, and his neighbors. The desperately impoverished conditions of the protagonist's life made the title *Tobacco Road* a synonym for poverty-stricken and ignorant rural areas.

In 1934, a play based on the novel opened on Broadway. This dramatic version, penned by Jack Kirkland, became an immediate hit and remained on the stage through 1941. It has continued to be a staple of large and small theater production houses ever since. In 1941, the play was turned into a film by director John Ford.

See also: *God's Little Acre;* literature; Caldwell, Erskine.

Bibliography

Cook, Sylvia Jenkins. *Erskine Caldwell and the Fiction of Poverty: The Flesh and the Spirit.* Baton Rouge: Louisiana State University Press, 1991.

Miller, Dan B. *Erskine Caldwell: The Journey from Tobacco Road: A Biography.* New York: Knopf, 1995.

One of the best-selling novels of the Great Depression era, the 1932 *Tobacco Road* was turned into a popular 1934 Broadway play, whose cast is shown in this photo. The book and play captured the poverty of the rural South. *(Brown Brothers)*

TOWNSEND PLAN

According to legend, California physician Francis E. Townsend was standing at his window one morning in late 1933 when he noticed three elderly women rummaging through his garbage looking for food. According to Townsend, "a torrent of invectives tore out of me, the big blast of all the bitterness that had been building in me for years. . . . I let my voice bellow with wild hatred" for the state of America's elderly during the Depression. Driven by this episode, Townsend set about formulating a plan for federal assistance to the elderly. Thus, the Old Age Revolving Pensions (OARP) Plan (also known as the Townsend National Recovery Plan) was born.

In reality, Townsend would later admit, he had been working on a relief plan for at least three years before his first public expressions of what would become the Townsend Plan. Originally outlined in a series of letters to the editor of the Long Beach, California, *Telegraph* published between September and December 1933, Townsend's relief plan was the first old-age pension plan to generate significant interest during the Depression years. According to Townsend's scheme, the federal government would levy a small "transaction tax" on goods at every stage from raw material to finished product. With this income, the government would then issue $150 each month (shortly raised to $200) to everyone over the age of sixty. He would later amend the plan to require the pensioner to spend the entire sum within thirty days. According to Townsend, this pension, when combined with the spending requirement, would stimulate the economy by removing the elderly from the employment rolls, thus opening jobs for younger workers. Furthermore, Townsend believed that, for every dollar a pensioner spent on, for example, groceries, the grocer would pay a dollar or more to the wholesaler, and so on. The pension dollars would thus "revolve," stimulating the economy and pulling the country out of the Depression.

While the Townsend Plan was not the first such plan devised during the Depression years (author Bruce Barton and Seattle dentist Stuart McCord independently drafted similar, but mostly unpublicized, plans between 1931 and 1933), it was the first to come to national prominence. From an economic point of view, however, the Townsend Plan was, without question, wholly unworkable. The $20 to $24 billion necessary to provide $200 monthly to the roughly 6.6 to 7.5 million elderly Americans would have consumed about one-half of the entire national income in the early 1930s. Economic critics of the plan also noted that the "transaction tax" in any form—Townsendites rarely if ever offered a specific tax rate—needed to raise this huge sum was a regressive tax that would cause economic chaos. The economic realities of the Townsend Plan, however, were, in the eyes of its adherents, never as significant as the social and political potential it represented.

Within a matter of days after his first public letter, the *Telegraph* received thousands of letters echoing Townsend's frustration and supporting his call for action. By the end of 1933, Townsend decided to devote his energies to making his plan a national political issue. To this end, Townsend turned to a young real-estate broker, Robert Earl Clements, to help him promote the idea across the country. Together, Clements and Townsend formed Old Age Revolving Pensions, Ltd. began compiling mailing lists and distributing literature, drafted local spokespersons to promote the plan, and eventually started a newspaper, *The Townsend Weekly*.

The response OARP, Ltd., received was impressive. By January 1935, nearly 1,200 Townsend Clubs had sprouted across the country; leaders boasted of a membership nearing 500,000. While these numbers cannot be confirmed (reliable membership figures are not available before 1937), it is clear that Townsend had tapped into a significant political undercurrent in America. The social changes wrought by industrialization—a shrinking emphasis on rural America, the dispersion of families in search of work, and the greater impact of business cycles on the average worker—had left a significant portion of America's elderly feeling disenfranchised. Townsend's crusade offered both a personal and political outlet for these collective frustrations.

While the political momentum generated by the Townsendites was significant, they did not constitute a

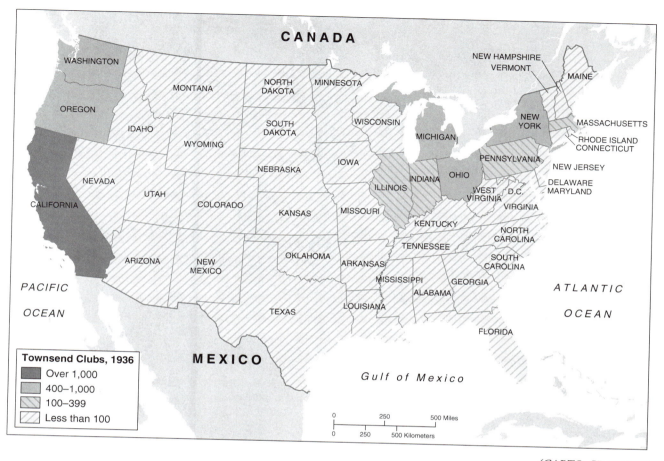

CANADA

WASHINGTON
OREGON
CALIFORNIA
NEVADA
IDAHO
MONTANA
WYOMING
UTAH
COLORADO
ARIZONA
NEW MEXICO
NORTH DAKOTA
SOUTH DAKOTA
NEBRASKA
KANSAS
OKLAHOMA
TEXAS
MINNESOTA
IOWA
MISSOURI
ARKANSAS
LOUISIANA
WISCONSIN
ILLINOIS
MICHIGAN
INDIANA
OHIO
KENTUCKY
TENNESSEE
MISSISSIPPI
ALABAMA
GEORGIA
FLORIDA
SOUTH CAROLINA
NORTH CAROLINA
VIRGINIA
WEST VIRGINIA
D.C.
PENNSYLVANIA
NEW YORK
NEW HAMPSHIRE
VERMONT
MAINE
MASSACHUSETTS
RHODE ISLAND
CONNECTICUT
NEW JERSEY
DELAWARE
MARYLAND

PACIFIC OCEAN

ATLANTIC OCEAN

MEXICO

Gulf of Mexico

Townsend Clubs, 1936
Over 1,000
400–1,000
100–399
Less than 100

0   250   500 Miles
0   250   500 Kilometers

(CARTO-GRAPHICS)

particularly large national movement (by 1936, the OARP movement's zenith, membership totaled approximately 7,000 clubs and 2.1 million members). Public and political perception of the Townsendites, however, was altogether another matter. While Townsendites regularly inflated claims of their own membership (claiming variously throughout 1935 a membership of between 3 and 4 million), national news organizations offered up even more outrageous numbers—for example, in January 1935, *Time* reported the existence of 25,000 OARP clubs across the country. In hindsight, it is easy to dismiss these inflated claims as mere political hyperbole; however, between 1933 and 1936, national politicians, clearly concerned by what appeared to be a "revolution of the elderly," *perceived* the Townsend movement to be one of the greatest potential political threats of the early New Deal.

The seemingly widespread public support for Townsend's pension plan was not lost on President Franklin D. Roosevelt. Support for the Townsend Plan was growing across the nation during 1934, a congressional election year. In an attempt to both stall the Townsendites' political momentum and address the issue of relief for the elderly, Roosevelt established the cabinet-level Committee on Economic Security in June 1934. Roosevelt noted, "Congress can't stand the pressure of the Townsend Plan unless we have a real old-age insurance system, nor can I face the country without . . . a plan which will give some assurance to old people of systematic assistance upon retirement." The end result was the Social Security Act of 1935.

The combination of the passage of the Social Security Act and Townsend's dismal defense of his plan at congressional hearings in 1936 undercut much of the political momentum behind the Townsend Plan. Townsendite representatives in Congress (particularly Representative John S. McGroarty [D-CA], who owed his election in 1934 in part to a strong OARP showing) offered various bills between 1937 and 1951 in the hopes of implementing a modified form of the Townsend Plan, but in each case the bills were defeated by wide margins.

Townsend, however, never gave up hope that some form of his Old Age Revolving Pensions Plan would be implemented. To this end, he joined, albeit reluctantly, with Gerald L. K. Smith and Father Charles Coughlin in supporting William Lemke's bid for the presidency on the Union Party ticket in 1936. In fact, Townsend continued to lecture on the merits of his plan until his death in 1960 at the age of ninety-three.

JUSTIN HOFFMAN

See also: elderly; election of 1936; Social Security Act; Union Party; Coughlin, Father Charles; Lemke, William; Long, Huey P.; Smith, Gerald L. K.; Townsend, Francis.

Bibliography

Brinkley, Alan. *Voices of Protest: Huey Long, Father Coughlin, and the Great Depression.* New York: Vintage Books, 1983.

Gaydowski, J. D. "Eight Letters to the Editor: The Genesis of the Townsend National Recovery Plan." *Southern California Quarterly* 20:10 (1985): 365–82.

Holtzman, Abraham. *The Townsend Movement: A Political Study.* New York: Bookman, 1963.

Leuchtenburg, William E. *Franklin D. Roosevelt and the New Deal 1932–1940.* New York: Harper, 1963.

McCoy, Donald R. *Angry Voices: Left-of-Center Politics in the New Deal Era.* Lawrence: University of Kansas Press, 1958.

Townsend, Dr. Francis E. *New Horizons.* Chicago: J. L. Stewart, 1943.

"Follow Me!"

The budget-busting cost of the Townsend Plan, guaranteeing $200 a month to all seniors, is ridiculed in this 1935 cartoon.

TRADE UNION UNITY LEAGUE

The Trade Union Unity League (TUUL) was created in 1929 by the Communist Party of the United States (CPUSA) as a radical alternative to the conservative and procapitalist American Federation of Labor (AFL).

The history of the TUUL, however, goes back to the immediate post–World War I era. In 1920, the CPUSA founded the Trade Union Educational League as an organization designed to infiltrate the AFL and radicalize it. In 1929, Profintern, the international labor union wing of the Soviet-led Communist International, ordered the reluctant CPUSA head, William Z. Foster, to found an independent trade union network, the TUUL.

Shortly after the stock market crash in late 1929, the TUUL established Unemployed Councils around the country, to agitate on behalf of the jobless. Major marches and demonstrations were organized over the next few years. By early 1933 and the passage of the National Industrial Recovery Act—which included tentative protections for organizing workers—the TUUL represented a significant threat to the AFL, especially in the unorganized mass industries like automobiles and steel. The Maritime Workers Industrial Union, a member of the TUUL, also played an important role in the San Francisco general strike of 1934.

Still, most of the TUUL unions remained small. With the mid-1930s rise of the Congress of Industrial Organizations (CIO), which targeted mass industries, the TUUL was increasingly eclipsed, with its constituent unions losing members to the CIO and a reinvigorated AFL. With the declaration of the Popular Front in the mid-1930s, in which Communists pledged to work with mainstream trade unions and other liberal forces, the TUUL was abandoned.

See also: American Federation of Labor; Communist Party; Congress of Industrial Organizations; Popular Front; strikes, general; Unemployed Councils; Foster, William Z.

Bibliography

Honig, Nathaniel. *The Trade Union Unity League Today: Its Structure, Policy, Program and Growth.* New York: Labor Unity Publishers, 1934.

Ottanelli, Fraser. *The Communist Party of the United States: From the Depression to World War II.* New Brunswick, NJ: Rutgers University Press, 1991.

UNEMPLOYED COUNCILS

The Unemployed Councils were established across the United States beginning in late 1929 by the district bodies of the Trade Union Unity League, the communist-led trade union federation.

The Unemployed Councils of the communist-led Trade Union Unity League helped organize numerous hunger demonstrations in the 1930s, including a national march on December 7, 1931. *(Brown Brothers)*

Responding to rising unemployment rates following the stock market crash, the organizers of the Unemployed Councils visited homeless camps, relief offices, the gates of closed-down factories, and other places where the jobless gathered. The councils organized protest marches and demonstrations—known as "hunger marches"—demanding public works programs and criticizing the failures of the capitalist system. In addition, the councils organized rent strikes and eviction resistance. Oftentimes, council offices would be raided by police, and marchers and demonstrators attacked.

In March 1932, the Detroit Unemployed Council organized a "hunger march" to the Ford Corporation's giant River Rouge plant, but were attacked by company security forces and local police, leaving four demonstrators dead and dozens wounded. The Unemployed Councils remained active through the early 1930s but were largely suspended once the Communists joined forces with liberals and trade unionists in the Popular Front period after 1935.

See also: Communist Party; Ford Motor Corporation; hunger marches; Popular Front; Trade Union Unity League.

Bibliography

Honig, Nathaniel. *The Trade Union Unity League Today: Its Structure, Policy, Program and Growth.* New York: Labor Unity Publishers, 1934.

Ottanelli, Fraser. *The Communist Party of the United States: From the Depression to World War II.* New Brunswick, NJ: Rutgers University Press, 1991.

UNION PARTY

The Union Party was formed in June 1936 by Father Charles E. Coughlin, the charismatic Roman Catholic "radio priest" who enjoyed a national listening audience during the Great Depression. The party included a disparate following of people with one

THE THREE MUSKETEERS!

The Union Party, a populist-type political organization, was headed by Gerald L. K. Smith, old-age pension plan advocate Francis Townsend, and radio preacher Father Charles Coughlin. A three-way struggle for control debilitated the party and contributed to its dismal showing in the 1936 presidential election. *(Brown Brothers)*

thing in common—dissatisfaction with the pace and direction of the New Deal.

In November 1934, Coughlin had founded the National Union for Social Justice (NUSJ), a loose-knit organization of about 1 million or so listeners who, then, supported President Franklin D. Roosevelt and the New Deal. Over the next year, Coughlin and the NUSJ grew increasingly disenchanted with the New Deal programs, charging—in a contradictory fashion—that they were both too conservative and too socialistic.

Deciding to enter the political arena as a political kingmaker, rather than a candidate himself, Coughlin formed the Union Party. The new organization soon gathered followers of Huey P. Long, whose radical Share Our Wealth movement had collapsed after Long's assassination in 1935, and Francis Townsend, a California doctor who advocated government payments to senior citizens.

Shortly after its formation in June 1936, the Union Party found its candidate for president in William Lemke, a North Dakota congressman once active in the radical Non-Partisan League. But Lemke, whose ticket garnered 2 percent of the popular vote and no electoral votes, was swamped in the landslide reelection of Roosevelt. The Union Party disappeared soon after that.

See also: National Union for Social Justice; Share Our Wealth Society; Townsend Plan; Coughlin, Father Charles; Long, Huey P.; Lemke, William.

Bibliography

Brinkley, Alan. *Voices of Protest: Huey Long, Father Coughlin, and the Great Depression.* New York: Vintage Books, 1982.

Warren, Donald I. *Radio Priest: Charles Coughlin, the Father of Hate Radio.* New York: Free Press, 1996.

UNIONS AND UNION ORGANIZING

During the years from 1929 to 1941, which we now call the Great Depression and New Deal era, many changes occurred throughout American society. One of the most significant changes of the decade was the birth and growth of industrial unionism. Born out of the exigencies of the Great Depression and nurtured during the New Deal was a sweeping American labor movement that had been rendered dormant during the 1920s. During the Great Depression, unemployment reached astronomical proportions, from 1.6 million industrial workers unemployed just after the stock market crash in 1929 to over 13 million by 1933. Unemployment in industrial cities like Akron, Cleveland, and Toledo hovered at huge percentages, reaching the 80 percent mark with little relief in sight. By 1933, unemployment peaked at 25 percent of the workforce.

NATIONAL RECOVERY AND THE WAGNER ACT

As part of the New Deal, President Franklin D. Roosevelt's administration proposed legislation seeking higher employment rates and higher wage rates while keeping prices stable. The National Recovery Act (NRA) of 1933 set up a procedure for adopting codes to regulate fair competition. The codes set a minimum wage and prescribed work hours and prices in the marketplace. The Supreme Court declared the NRA unconstitutional because it gave law-making authority to the president that rightfully belonged to Congress. In the NRA's place, after much debate among New Deal advocates, the Roosevelt administration proposed the National Labor Relations Act (NLRA). As one of its chief sponsors and architects, Senator Robert Wagner's name is attached to the NLRA. Passed in 1935, several provisions of the Wagner Act greatly aided the cause of labor. In particular, Section 7 of the act provided the following: "Employees shall have the right to self-organization, to form, join, or assist labor organizations, to bargain collectively through representatives of their own choosing, and to engage in other concerted activities for the purpose of collective bargaining or other mutual aid or protection."

For the first time in the history of the United States, the basic right of workers to form organizations of their own choosing became codified into law. A second critical aspect of the Wagner Act established the National Labor Relations Board (NLRB) with adjudicating powers. With the creation of the NLRB, workers and their unions gained the right to petition a government board for redress of their grievances. With the advent of the Wagner Act, organized labor grew in leaps, doubling and tripling in just a few years. The Committee for Industrial Organization, for example, later renamed the Congress of Industrial Organizations, grew from 800,000 members in 1936 to 3.4 million in 1937. Although not as dramatic, the World War II years 1941 to 1946 also witnessed tremendous growth in union membership.

THE BIRTH OF WORKER ACTIVISM

Although it was an important landmark law, other factors besides the passage of the Wagner Act led to labor's resurgence. Prior to the passage of the Wagner Act, workers had been under constant siege. The AFL's status as the major national labor organization began in the 1890s, but the AFL had been battered by the open shop drive in the 1920s and the loss of jobs during the Great Depression. The Wagner Act passed Congress with opposition from business because the act's mission included leveling the relationship between labor and management, which strengthened labor's ability to negotiate with management. Feeling the brunt of the day-to-day horrors of the Great Depression, working people seized upon the Wagner Act's pro-labor provisions and demonstrated a readiness to act on their own behalf.

Corporations who opposed the Wagner Act refused to accept the act's union recognition provisions and instead balked at acknowledging newly formed union organizations. Working people were ready to fight and the Great Depression marked a period of great labor unrest. Before the enactment of the Wagner Act, workers were already on the move. Spurred by the hope embodied in the NRA, which allowed cooperative action among trade groups, pockets of workers' union

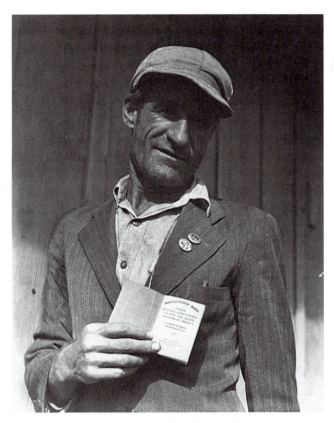

A California farmworker proudly displays his union membership book in November 1938. He wears a button that reads "Vote No on Number 1," a reference to an antipicketing law on the ballot. The law was defeated by California voters that month. *(Library of Congress)*

activity sprang up in industrial settings. Fearing that the law granting union recognition could be overturned, many workers and union activists began agitating and striking for union recognition.

THE STRIKING SEASON

During most of the 1920s and 1930s, workers engaged in work stoppages over wage cuts, horrendous working conditions, or dismissals. From 1925 to 1932, over 300,000 workers participated in strikes, but in 1933 the number of strikes and lockouts skyrocketed to involve 1,186,000 persons. In 1934 industrial actions involved nearly 1.5 million workers. The hopeless mood of workers gave way to a belief that change was in the air. It became a time for working people to redress grievances of the past decade. Some strikes evolved into confrontations with management, leading to class warfare.

After forming an AFL local, workers in Auto-Lite's Toledo, Ohio, plant struck for union recognition. After enduring several delaying tactics by both the company and the weakly constituted NRA labor board, workers once again employed militant actions and literally held the strikebreakers captive in the factory. Even though 900 National Guardsmen attempted to dislodge striking workers, the strikers proved too strong and well organized because they received support from the surrounding community.

In 1934, Teamsters Local 574 in Minneapolis, lead by radical Trotskyites, refused to wait for Roosevelt's New Deal administration to iron out problems contained in the NRA before it passed laws favorable to workers. The teamsters closed down the entire city of Minneapolis, demanding union recognition. Following a bloody, two-day battle, workers drove back the police. After a month of unbearable tension, employers eventually backed down, opening the way for the Teamsters to organize many of the trucking companies in the West.

Out on the West Coast, longshoremen in the port of San Francisco closed the city during a general strike. Other unions, including the teamsters and other seamen, honored the International Longshoremen's Association's (ILA) picket lines. During the strike, the ILA won much-needed support from other AFL unions, but more significantly, also won crucial support from the community at large. Public opinion began swinging to the side of labor. As a result of the strike, the bosses lost control of the shape-up, the daily gathering where bosses decided who would be hired. After the strike, the ILA would assign jobs to workers at the union hall.

An even more dramatic strike occurred in 1934. The largest single strike in American history affected textile mills from Maine to Alabama and involved over 400,000 textile workers. To aid the unemployed, textile workers demanded a thirty-hour workweek with no reduction in pay. The leaders of the United Textile Workers (UTW) called off the strike after a promise from the government that the UTW's grievances would be investigated. However, the strike ended in disaster when mill owners blacklisted returning workers.

As the United States reached the end of 1934, these three conflicts proved that militancy and even violence could win union recognition when workers were willing to take matters into their own hands. The labor struggles in 1934 showed the potential and possibilities that the Great Depression and New Deal changes in the law laid at the feet of industrial workers.

As the house of labor expanded, trouble brewed on the horizon. While the labor upheavals of 1933–34 demonstrated the willingness of rank-and-file workers to engage in concerted activity, these struggles also showed the dissatisfaction rank-and-file union activists felt toward their AFL leaders. A dispute arose within the AFL over the best method for organized labor to respond to changing conditions. Because of the AFL's reluctance to organize industrial workers and its refusal to confront factory owners with strikes and sit-downs, some leaders within the AFL became critical of the federation style of craft unionism. The method of organizing by trade, which the AFL had employed for decades, began showing its weakness as greater amounts of the workforce were concentrated in mass production industry.

THE BIRTH OF THE CIO

Old-guard leaders like AFL President William Green, William L. Hutcheson of the carpenters and woodworkers, Daniel J. Tobin of the teamsters, Matthew Woll of the photoengravers, and John P. Frey of the metal trades department of the AFL opposed industrial unionism. These AFL leaders believed that skilled workers were more readily organized than workers in less skilled and unskilled occupations, who lacked the necessary sophistication and understanding to become viable union members. They also feared that skilled union members would be outvoted within their own unions by a huge influx of new uneducated members.

Led by John L. Lewis, the feisty leader of the United Mine Workers, a group of renegade AFL leaders formed the Committee for Industrial Organization (CIO). Charles P. Howard of the Typographical Union, Philip Murray of the United Mine Workers, Sidney Hillman of the Amalgamated Clothing Workers, and David Dubinsky of the International Ladies' Garment Workers' Union joined with Lewis in advocating a new form of organization: industrial unionism. Its fundamental organizing rule rested on an industrial basis: a person who worked in a particular industry had a right to join that industry's union. Their proposal at the 1935 AFL convention in Atlantic City went down to defeat by a vote of 18,024 to 10,933. Symbolic of the break between the AFL and the embryonic CIO was the "punch" heard around the labor world. William L. Hutcheson of the Carpenters Union crossed the boundary of parliamentary decorum by calling Lewis a derogatory term. Lewis responded with a right uppercut to the jaw, signifying the division of labor into two hostile camps.

Not to be outdone by AFL leaders, Lewis and his allies set their plan in motion. For one last time, the CIO proposed that the AFL issue industrial charters for the steel, rubber, radio, and automobile industries. The AFL, still as suspicious of the CIO as it had been at the convention, charged the CIO with dual unionism and attempting to destroy the AFL. Lewis resigned as vice president of the AFL. At the 1936 AFL convention, the leaders representing the CIO were conspicuously absent. The AFL promptly suspended the ten unions who affiliated with the CIO. The Committee for Industrial Organization became the Congress of Industrial Organizations. Prior to the CIO declaring its official birth in May 1938, it had amassed a membership of 3.7 million, while the AFL mustered 3.4 million.

By the mid-1930s, it no longer mattered what position the AFL and the CIO took: workers were ready for industrial unionism. Company owners, conservative leaders, and the newspapers could clamor all they wanted about "outside foreign influences," "Communists," or "Trotskyites" agitating working people, but workers forced John L. Lewis and the newly formed CIO to respond to the demands of industrial shop-floor workers. Dire economic circumstances forced workers to seek an alternative method to address their needs. Also, President Roosevelt and his administration noticed the growing unrest in the nation's industrial centers and believed that the administration needed to respond. The New Deal, in the form of the Wagner Act of 1935, presented a legal tool that workers could employ to their advantage.

The worker unrest that first surfaced in 1933–34 continued as AFL and CIO leaders remained locked in their own dispute. In mid-1934, tire makers at Firestone and Goodyear plants walked out over wage cuts and speedups. The AFL under president William Green's leadership entered into an agreement with the tire companies that the striking workers perceived as a complete sellout. As a result, union membership dropped from 40,000 to 5,000 and rubber workers took matters into their own hands. By 1936, the sit-down strike became a regular tactic when workers adopted the principle that, when one worker stops, all workers sit down.

SPONTANEOUS ERUPTIONS: THE SIT-DOWN STRIKE

Few of the strikes occurring during this period were well-planned affairs. In late 1936, a spontaneous strike erupted against General Motors in Atlanta that quickly spread over the next several weeks to Kansas City,

Cleveland, and then to General Motors' plant in Flint, Michigan. The Flint sit-down was a turning point in the organization of the CIO. After military-like battles outside of one General Motors plant in Flint that injured fourteen workers, nine policemen, and two spectators, Lewis and the CIO reached a strike settlement with General Motors. The union failed to win all of its demands, but the strike held great significance for the entire labor movement. The success of the Flint sit-down led to a proliferation of sit-down strikes across the nation, and the United Auto Workers' (UAW) membership rolls expanded from 88,000 to 400,000. Another development directly linked to the victory in Flint occurred a month later when United States Steel, without a strike, signed an agreement with the CIO's Steel Workers' Organizing Committee (SWOC).

News of the victorious strikers at Flint had far-reaching repercussions for the labor movement. Even after unfavorable rulings by local courts, the successful use of the sit-down strike became legendary and affected other facets of American life. Before the CIO formally announced its formation in 1938, almost 500,000 people participated in sit-down actions. Every occupation, every work situation, witnessed sit-downs. Glassmakers, dressmakers, rubber workers, counter help at Woolworth's, stock clerks, garbage collectors, sales clerks, and laundry workers all sat down.

Nevertheless, the problems that beset labor during the Great Depression failed to subside. Many companies, which viewed the upstart CIO as troublemakers who threatened their right to free enterprise, were unwilling to recognize the CIO. In contrast to the rank-and-file workers, the AFL fully disavowed the sit-down and the CIO never openly supported the tactic. In spring 1937, many of the smaller steel companies refused to sign agreements similar to the one signed by United States Steel. Sixteen workers met their death when SWOC struck "little steel." In addition, middle-class Americans who had earlier recognized union organization in a positive light expressed concerns about the sit-down strike as a threat to private property. Often acrimonious debate among U.S. senators led to a resolution condemning sit-downs as contrary to the public good. By the end of 1939, the Supreme Court outlawed the sit-down strike, negating industrial unionism's most successful weapon.

THE SUCCESS OF THE LABOR MOVEMENT

After the official formation of the CIO in 1938 and the union successes in Flint and with United States Steel, the floodgates opened and industrial workers joined the labor movement en masse. Union field organizers employed by the CIO attained impressive achievements in bringing in new members to the CIO. Field organizers, standing at the gate of a factory during a shift change, would hold a union membership card over their head and workers leaving the plant would stand in line to sign up for the CIO union. At lunchtime, when workers were sitting outside eating, a CIO union field organizer would pass by and throw a handful of sign-up cards over the fence and workers would sign them and throw them back. By 1939–40, the CIO was on the rise.

Besides displaying a willingness to organize all industrial workers, including men and women, skilled and unskilled, and people of color, the CIO encouraged and even demanded participation in national and local politics. From its beginning, Lewis and the CIO understood the necessity of political participation as belonging in the realm of industrial unionism. The AFL philosophy frowned on governmental interference in labor management issues, while CIO leaders enacted a policy of fighting for greater governmental control over the economic life of the nation. To this end, the CIO helped establish the Labor Non-Partisan League and the American Labor Party with the intention of supporting Roosevelt and the gains labor made during the New Deal. Labor's support of Roosevelt clinched a sweeping victory in the 1936 election.

A key element in the success of Lewis and the CIO rested upon their willingness to accept support from any quarter, as long as that support helped to build the CIO. As a result, Communists, Socialists, and other radical activists were welcomed and served in leadership positions within the CIO from its inception. Even though the CIO and the AFL shared in the ascension of the labor movement, the interunion rivalry continued to fester. In the years to come, the presence of Communists within the labor movement would become one of the driving issues that finally split the house of labor. Culminating in 1950 and 1951, the CIO leadership expelled a total of eleven unions deemed Communist-controlled.

When the CIO formally announced its formation, it did so with thirty-three industrial unions under its wing. By the time the United States began making war preparations in 1941, the CIO had chartered an additional eight unions and its membership had increased to a high-water mark of over 5 million workers in forty-one affiliated unions. The national success of the CIO greatly benefited the industrial union movement and the growth and stability of the AFL as well, which expanded to include 4.5 million members in 106 affiliated unions by the beginning of 1941.

The labor movement reached an unprecedented

zenith of power and became a force in American society. Sitting on governmental boards and committees, labor leaders became national leaders in their own right. The question of the extent of the labor movement's effectiveness in reordering American society remains unanswered. With war brewing in Europe, Congress focused on protecting national security. Toward the end of 1941, Congress prepared to pass a bill that would curtail strikes in the defense industry, but the start of World War II, full employment, and high wages put off addressing any questions about the labor movement.

MICHAEL BONISLAWSKI

See also: American Federation of Labor; auto industry; American Newspaper Guild; Brotherhood of Sleeping Car Porters; Communist Party; Congress of Industrial Organizations; Ford Motor Company; General Motors; hunger marches; International Ladies' Garments Workers' Union; "little steel"; manufacturing and construction; Memorial Day massacre; mining; railroads; service sector; Southern Tenant Farmers Union; steel industry; Steel Workers Organizing Committee; strikes, general; strikes, sitdown; Trade Union Unity League; Unemployed Councils; unemployment; United Automobile Workers; United Mine Workers; United States Steel; Fair Labor Standards Act; National Industrial Recovery Act; National Labor Relations Act; *NLRB v. Jones & Laughlin;* Norris-La Guardia Anti-Injunction Act; Section 7 (National Industrial Recovery Act); Bennett, Harry; Bridges, Harry; Broun, Heywood; Dubinsky, David; Ford, Henry; Green, William; Hillman, Sidney; Lewis, John L.; Murray, Philip; Perkins, Frances; Randolph, A. Phillip; Reuther, Walter; Sloan, Alfred; Wagner, Robert; Documents: Norris-La Guardia Anti-Injunction Bill, March 20, 1932; National Industrial Recovery Act, June 16, 1933; National Labor Relations Act, July 5, 1935; Fireside Chat on the National Recovery Administration, July 24, 1933; Eleanor Roosevelt Press Conference Discussion on Crossing Picket Lines, January 17, 1939; *National Labor Relations Board v. Jones & Laughlin Steel Corporation,* 1937; *West Coast Hotel Company v. Parrish,* 1937.

Bibliography

National Labor Relations Board. *A Guide to Basic Law and Procedures Under the National Labor Relations Act.* Prepared in the Office of the General Counsel. Washington DC: Government Printing Office, 1976.

Biles, Roger. *A New Deal of the American People.* DeKalb: Northern Illinois University Press, 1991.

Brecher, Jeremy. *Strike.* 2nd ed. Boston: South End Press, 1997.

Dubofsky, Melvyn, and Foster Rhea Dulles. *Labor in America: A History.* Wheeling: Harlan Davidson, 1999.

Green, James R. *The World of the Worker: Labor in Twentieth Century America.* 2nd ed. Chicago and Urbana: University of Illinois Press, 1998.

McElvaine, Robert S. *The Great Depression: America, 1929–1941.* 2nd ed. New York: Times Books, 1993.

Zieger, Robert H. *The CIO, 1935–1955.* Chapel Hill and London: University of North Carolina Press, 1995.

UNITED AUTOMOBILE WORKERS

As an automobile industry based on mass production technology emerged in the United States after 1913, small craft unions and a handful of organizers from the Industrial Workers of the World sought to represent autoworkers. The large auto manufacturers easily blocked these initial efforts at unionization. Subdivided work and assembly-line production spread unevenly in the auto industry. Autoworkers who were alienated by the faster, enervating pace of work in the most technologically advanced auto factories tried to find jobs in auto plants with a slower work pace.

THE AUTO INDUSTRY IN THE 1920s AND 1930s

In the 1920s the industry vigorously practiced welfare capitalism and further intensified the pace of labor, as the time-study of jobs and assembly lines was used in most auto factories. When the Depression began, management adapted to the drop in consumer demand by scuttling seniority rules that had protected the jobs of older workers, intensified work speeds, reduced wages, and cut drastically expenditures on plant health and safety. The speedup in auto plants in the 1930s was the worst in the twentieth century. Many workers vomitted from the intense work pace, fainted while working, could not eat for hours after finishing their day's work on the assembly line, had insomnia accompanied by nightmares, and suffered from numerous injuries and fatigue-induced illnesses and muscular ailments.

Skilled autoworkers saw veteran workers laid off without regard to seniority, as auto companies sought to employ younger workers who could be paid less and would be able to withstand a more intense labor process. Many laid-off skilled workers could only find reemployment if they took exhausting mass production jobs. By 1934, these skilled workers realized that only industrial unions representing the entire auto labor force would have the bargaining power needed to obtain meaningful job seniority protection. Semiskilled and low-skilled workers were the main victims of the speedup in assembly-line production, both in the manufacture of parts and the assembly of cars and trucks. They too wanted unions for protection against being worked to death and cheated of the pay they had earned by management manipulation of the nefarious group bonus systems that had been introduced into the auto industry in the late 1920s and spread rapidly in the early years of the Depression.

In many American industries, pre-Depression efforts at forming industrial unions had failed because skilled workers did not want to be represented by unions that included larger numbers of semiskilled and low-skilled workers. The skilled workers, largely drawn from northern and western European nationalities, often were prejudiced against the ethnicity (southern and eastern European, or Hispanic) and race (African American) of the less skilled workers. Skilled workers also feared (correctly) that industrial unions would negotiate contracts that reduced the earnings advantage that skilled workers enjoyed. But the historically specific conditions in the auto factories during the Depression convinced skilled workers that, to protect their jobs and avoid serious bodily harm, they had to make common cause with the rest of the industry labor force. And by the 1930s, some southern and eastern European immigrants had moved into skilled labor jobs and did not harbor ethnic prejudices against less skilled workers from similar backgrounds.

THE IMPACT OF THE NATURE RECOVERY ADMINISTRATION

Section 7 of the National Industrial Recovery Act (1933) vaguely endorsed the right of workers to collective bargaining and created the impression that the Franklin D. Roosevelt administration would back union organizing. In 1933 and 1934, vigorous organizational efforts by rank-and-file workers and existing unions in the coal, steel, longshore, trucking, automobile, and clothing industries increased the number of workers covered by collective bargaining agreements. Thousands of autoworkers joined an independent union, the Mechanics Educational Society of America, and federal labor unions established by the American Federation of Labor (AFL). Established in 1886, the

AFL had long since organized workers by craft rather than industry, and, following past practice, the AFL leadership ordered workers who entered the federal unions to join the particular AFL craft unions that had jurisdiction over the workers' jobs in the automobile industry, e.g., carpenters to the United Brotherhood of Carpenters and Joiners and machinists to the International Association of Machinists. The craft unionists who dominated the AFL's Executive Council opposed incorporating new industrial unions into the federation. Industrial unions represented all crafts in a factory or industry. The AFL leaders did not want to share power with new leaders, distrusted the radicals who were playing an important role in grassroots organizing of workers into industrial unions, and had a strong distaste for the first- and second-generation immigrants from southern and eastern Europe who had moved into the industrial labor force in large numbers since 1900.

To forestall an auto strike in April 1934, President Roosevelt dictated the labor provisions of the National Recovery Administration code for the automobile industry. Roosevelt allowed multiple unions to represent workers in the same company, which ran contrary to the wishes of most autoworkers. By 1934, most autoworkers had concluded that only industrial unions would be strong enough to take on the auto manufacturers. In August 1935, the International Union, United Automobile Workers of America (UAW) was formed. But the AFL Executive Council gave the new union a charter that drastically limited its jurisdiction over auto workers; the AFL also appointed the top officers of the UAW.

THE IMPACT OF THE NATIONAL LABOR RELATIONS ACT

The passage of the National Labor Relations Act (NLRA) in May 1935 aided the UAW in two ways. First, the NLRA specified that only one union, the union selected by a plurality of voting workers in a given bargaining unit, would be selected as the collective bargaining agent for all workers in the unit. Senator Robert Wagner (D-NY) had insisted on this provision because he felt it would create stronger unions throughout the nation. Second, the NLRA stipulated that employers had to enter into negotiations with any certified collective bargaining agent (designated by a formal representation election conducted by the National Labor Relations Board.)

In April 1936, encouraged by the formation of the Committee for Industrial Organization, which soon became the Congress of Industrial Organizations (CIO), the second convention of the UAW democratically elected its officers and resolved to ignore the AFL's ban on industrial unionism. With financial aid from the CIO, the UAW launched new organizing drives at auto plants in the Midwest.

President Roosevelt's landslide reelection in November 1936, with strong financial support from the CIO, led many militant labor leaders to conclude that the Democratic president and many Democratic governors would side with industrial workers in their efforts to force management to recognize industrial unions. In the auto plants, small groups of militants (some of whom were Socialists and Communists) took the lead in starting strategic sit-down strikes in General Motors plants in Cleveland on December 28, 1936, and Flint, Michigan, on December 30. The Flint sit-down strike (several factories were occupied by autoworkers at different times during the strike) succeeded because of the tactical astuteness of the rank-and-file leaders of the groups occupying the factories and because Michigan's newly elected governor, Frank Murphy, was a pro-union New Deal liberal who was strongly influenced by reform Catholic theology.

When the local police tried to remove the autoworkers from the Flint factories, pitched battles ensued and the police were forced to withdraw. Governor Murphy then brought in the Michigan National Guard to keep order and dictated that the Guard act in a neutral manner. CIO President John L. Lewis, who came to Flint to lead the bargaining with General Motors, refused to accede to the company's demand that the autoworkers leave the Flint plants they had occupied, telling Governor Murphy that if he used the National Guard to remove strikers from GM's property, the resulting violence would be Murphy's responsibility. Behind the scenes, Secretary of Labor Frances Perkins and President Roosevelt pressured GM executives to make concessions. On February 11, 1937, GM recognized the UAW for six months as the bargaining agent for UAW members. In March, GM signed a one-year contract that gave UAW members a weak grievance system. Massive sit-downs in March 1937 in Chrysler Corporation's Detroit plants forced the company to sign a collective bargaining agreement in April.

DIVISIONS AMONG AUTOWORKERS

But the momentum of auto organizing was broken in the fall of 1937 when a group of labor leaders loyal to the AFL split off from the UAW and formed a rival union. This action meant that in 1938, 1939, and much of 1940 there were no labor contracts in the auto industry, while the two unions contended for the authority to represent autoworkers. In this environment, groups of workers who labored together on the factory floor often used physical force against foremen who followed company directives to pressure workers to work at a faster pace. Long strikes and brief work stoppages also were directed against the speedup. Fellow workers who did not want to cooperate in slowing down the pace of production were often threatened and assaulted.

UAW leaders defeated the AFL faction in representation elections held in 1939 and 1940. With the threat of dual unionism eliminated, the UAW was able to obtain significantly stronger contracts with the top auto manufacturers. The GM 1940 contract and the 1943 Chrysler and Ford contracts set the pattern for later contracts. Workers could strike whenever a contract expired. But during the term of a contract, autoworkers and union leaders were prohibited—with one important exception—from staging or supporting strikes. All disputes over management decisions about pay classifications, seniority, and worker behavior had to be pursued through a multistage grievance mechanism. A neutral umpire or arbitrator would decide all unresolved worker grievances. When there were disputes over production standards—the amount of work required from an autoworker during each day—the umpires were not involved and autoworkers were allowed to stage authorized strikes, if approved by the UAW's Executive Council. This new system of industrial democracy offered significant protections to autoworkers against unfair management discipline and against many kinds of speedups. A minority of rank-and-file workers, however, opposed this system, preferring total freedom to strike.

Ford Motor Company held out longest against unionization. Blue-collar workers at Ford were tightly controlled by a corrupt service department. Spies were placed in bathrooms to eavesdrop on workers and to pressure workers to return quickly to their work stations. Workers who complained about management practices or talked to fellow workers about the advantages of trade unionism were severely beaten by thugs employed by the service department.

Henry Ford also hired many African-American workers at his Detroit plants, controlling them by playing on black workers' strong consciousness of race, which led them to distrust whites. Ford also made large donations to African-American churches, with the expectation that black ministers would

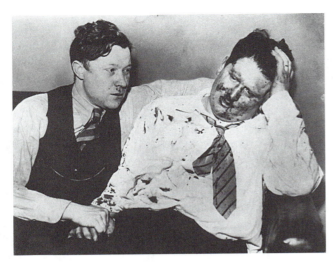

United Automobile Workers organizer Richard Frankensteen (*right*) is comforted by union president Walter Reuther, after he was attacked by Ford Motor Company security personnel in May 1937. (*Brown Brothers*)

tell their parishioners to stay clear of unions. UAW leaders were able to convince African-American ministers, elected officials, and black autoworkers in the Detroit region to back the UAW's organizing effort. UAW spokesmen promised that the UAW would combat racial discrimination by management. The UAW won the violent Ford strike in April 1941, because black workers backed the union. Now the UAW was the bargaining agent for GM, Ford, and Chrysler workers.

THE LATE DEPRESSION YEARS

Throughout the late 1930s, multiple factions, based on ideology and personal ties, struggled to control the UAW. Homer Martin, the UAW president during this period, was an ineffective leader. Walter Reuther, a former Socialist who dropped his party membership in 1938, led a group of very talented Socialists and former Socialists—especially Emil Mazey and Reuther's brothers, Victor and Roy—and centrist militants like Richard Leonard. A center-communist coalition included centrist New Deal liberal Democrats like George Addes and Richard Frankensteen and many communist leaders. In the late 1930s and during World War II, the center-communist coalition dominated the UAW. Between 1945 and 1947, as the Cold War intensified, the center-left alliance collapsed. Many centrists now joined with Walter Reuther's coalition. In 1947 Reuther captured the presidency of the UAW. Emerging from the Korean War in full control of the union, Reuther and his associates advocated a pro–Cold War foreign policy, close ties to the Democratic Party, and a liberal domestic agenda.

ROBERT ASHER

See also: American Federation of Labor; Congress of Industrial Organizations; Ford Motor Company; General Motors; National Industrial Recovery Act; Ford, Henry; Lewis, John L.; Murphy, Frank; Perkins, Frances; Reuther, Walter. Documents: National Industrial Recovery Act, June 16, 1933; National Labor Relations Act, July 5, 1935.

Bibliography

Asher, Robert, and Ronald Edsforth, eds. *Autowork*. Albany: State University of New York Press, 1995.

Halpern, Martin. *UAW Politics in the Cold War Era*. Albany: State University of New York Press, 1988.

Lichtenstein, Nelson. *The Most Dangerous Man in Detroit*. New York: Basic Books, 1995.

UNITED MINE WORKERS

First founded in Columbus, Ohio, in 1890, the United Mine Workers (UMW) successfully lobbied for federal legislation protecting workers, supported the rights of unskilled labor, and became one of the most influential unions in the United States during the New Deal. Early in its history, the UMW appealed to disgruntled mine workers who feared that laborsaving technology, as well as the arrival of poor, unskilled Europeans and African Americans to the coalfields, threatened their status as skilled workers. In 1898, under the energetic leadership of John Mitchell, the UMW won wage increases and union recognition for mine workers in the Midwest and, in 1902, it engaged in a triumphant strike against anthracite mine operators in eastern Pennsylvania. Over the next two decades, such achievements helped the UMW thrive. By 1914, the union boasted 377,688 members in twenty states. When John L. Lewis was elected union president in 1920, this number had nearly doubled, and the UMW had become the largest and most powerful member of the American Federation of Labor (AFL).

In the 1920s, the UMW faced a series of crises that threatened its prominent position within the American labor movement. By the middle of the decade, coal was an ailing industry that produced more than Americans wanted or needed. As demand for coal dropped, mine operators laid off workers and cut wages, and more and more miners struggled to find steady employment and earn a living. At the same time, many American politicians and business leaders increasingly denounced unions and championed the open shop. In 1922, in particular, corporations won a number of decisive struggles with industrial unions, including the UMW, that either led to open shops or sapped union strength. Finally, the dreadful economic depression that struck the nation in November of 1929 devastated mine workers and ravaged the already weakened UMW. As consumers, railroads, steel mills, and utility companies used less and less coal, mines closed, coal prices and wages collapsed, and thousands of mine workers lost their jobs. As a result, by the early 1930s, many miners unable to find work, pay bills, or feed their families abandoned the UMW, and union membership dropped to less than 100,000. The UMW, one of the great American unions of the early twentieth century, had become just a shadow of its former self.

Following the election of Franklin D. Roosevelt in 1932, the UMW underwent a period of revitalization that helped it regain its influential position in the American labor movement. Unlike Herbert Hoover, Roosevelt was willing to listen to the concerns of labor and encouraged workers in all industries to demand the right to unionize. Building on this wave of excitement, Lewis encouraged UMW organizers to criss-cross the nation's minefields in an effort to rebuild the struggling union. By June 1933, these efforts had brought in hundreds of thousands of new members, and total membership in the UMW approached what it had been at its height during the 1910s. The union's newfound strength encouraged Lewis to lobby for federal legislation to protect laborers. In 1933, the union ardently supported Section 7 of the National Industrial Recovery Act (NIRA), which guaranteed workers the right to organize and bargain collectively with their employers. The UMW also continued to call for special legislation to protect mine workers. In 1937, in response to this demand, Congress passed the Guffey-Vinson bill, which required collective bargaining in the coal industry, regulated prices and allocated markets among producers, and created a federal enforcement agency. As the UMW rallied membership and lobbied Congress, it also worked hard to defend the interests of unskilled industrial workers. Between 1935 and 1940, Lewis and the UMW left the AFL and helped found the Congress of Industrial Organizations (CIO), a new federation of unions dedicated to organizing unskilled workers in mass production industries like steel and automotives. By 1940, the UMW, which had seemed on the verge of collapse just a decade earlier, had rebuilt its membership, helped shape New Deal labor policy, and become one of the most vocal advocates for unskilled workers in the United States.

The year 1940, however, marked the peak of the UMW's influence in the American labor movement. That year, Lewis, who had become disillusioned with New Deal labor policy, resigned his post as head of the CIO to protest Roosevelt's reelection for a third term. Furthermore, between 1941 and 1946, Lewis exacerbated tensions between the UMW and the federal government when he led a series of strikes against the coal industry for higher wages and better benefits. Although these strikes proved successful, popular opinion quickly turned against the union for threatening an industry vital to America's war effort. By the 1950s, the UMW faced growing public criticism and had become isolated from both the AFL and CIO.

The efforts of the UMW and its leaders to fight for the rights of labor during the New Deal, in particular, left two lasting legacies. First, by supporting groundbreaking legislation that granted workers the right to organize, particularly Section 7 of the NIRA, the union and its leaders helped guarantee that labor would maintain a voice in American politics for decades to come. Second, the fateful decision of Lewis and the UMW to break with the AFL and organize unskilled workers, particularly in the steel and automotive industries, laid the groundwork for the United Steelworkers and United Automobile Workers, two of the most powerful industrial unions in the nation during the second half of the twentieth century.

ERIC J. MORSER

See also: American Federation of Labor; Congress of Industrial Organizations; mining; unions and union organizing; National Labor Relations Act; Norris-La Guardia Anti-Injunction Act; Section 7 (National Industrial Recovery Act); Lewis, John L.; Documents: Norris-La Guardia Anti-Injunction Bill, March 20, 1932; National Industrial Recovery Act, June 16, 1933; National Labor Relations Act, July 5, 1935;

Bibliography

Dubofsky, Melvyn, and Warren Van Tine. *John L. Lewis: A Biography.* New York: Quadrangle/The New York Times Book Co., 1977.

Finley, Joseph E. *The Corrupt Kingdom: The Rise and Fall of the United Mine Workers.* New York: Simon & Schuster, 1972.

Laslett, John H. M., ed. *The United Mine Workers of America: A Model of Industrial Solidarity?* University Park: Pennsylvania State University Press, 1996.

UNITED STATES STEEL CORPORATION

The United States Steel Corporation—now known as USX—was by far the largest steel company in America and the world in the 1930s. Hard hit by the Great Depression, U.S. Steel—as it was better known then—was the first steel company to recognize the Steel Workers Organizing Committee (SWOC).

U.S. Steel was organized as America's first billion-dollar corporation at the turn of the century by financier J. Pierpont Morgan. Under the leadership of businessman Elbert Gary, the company grew even larger during the World War I era and the 1920s, merging with other companies along the way and resisting government attempts to break it up as a monopoly. With collapsing demand for steel after 1929, the company began to lay off workers and cut wages for those remaining on the payroll.

Long resistant to unionization—having defeated a nationwide strike just after World War I—the executives of U.S. Steel, led by Chairman of the Board Myron Taylor, grew worried after the sit-down strikes at General Motors in the winter of 1936–37 led to that company's recognition of the United Automobile Workers. Taylor then went into secret negotiations with John Lewis, head of the Congress of Industrial Organizations. On March 1, 1937 Lewis and Taylor announced that U.S. Steel had agreed to recognize SWOC as the sole bargaining agent for its employees.

While U.S. Steel usually led the industry on such things as wages and prices, this time its lead was spurned by so-called "little steel" companies, which largely refused to accept SWOC until the eve of World War II.

See also: Congress of Industrial Organizations; General Motors Corporation; "little steel"; steel industry; Steel Workers Organizing Committee; strikes, sit-down; Lewis, John L.

Bibliography

Bertin, Amy. *Competition and Productivity in the Depression-Era Steel Industry.* Thesis. Harvard University, 1994.

Reutter, Mark. *Sparrows Point: Making Steel, the Rise and Ruin of American Industrial Might.* New York: Summit Books, 1989.

UTILITIES INDUSTRY

The history of public utilities during the New Deal is generally one of growth of service, along with increased federal regulation after a decline in the early years of the Depression.

The term "public utility" is not well defined in law or economics. There are no consistent criteria that define an entity as a public utility, but the public utilities industry in the United States generally consists of electric power, natural gas, telecommunications, and sometimes water services, although the latter are more often provided by the public rather than private section. Utilities are often seen as "natural monopolies," such that only one firm can efficiently serve a particular market, but this is not necessarily the case. Public utilities are usually regulated by federal and state government commissions and are issued "certificates of public convenience and necessity" that establish their market territory and require certain conditions of service, including "just and reasonable" rates, nondiscriminatory access, safe and adequate service, and a prohibition against discrimination. Regulated utilities are not free to end or "abandon" service without regulatory authority. Formal legal proceedings, the rulings of which are subject to court review, are established for rate and service changes. The regulatory commission combines executive, legislative, and judicial functions in a hybrid governmental entity that has withstood court challenge.

Government supervision of businesses that have a public aspect to them goes back to medieval English common law, which regulated of the conditions, including a "just" price, under which guilds and chartered businesses had to provide service to all comers. In the United States, *Munn v. Illinois* (1877) established the right of the state to regulate grain elevators that were "affected with the public interest." The interstate commerce clause and the supremacy clause of the U.S. Constitution give the federal government certain powers to regulate commerce. Common carriers (which may or may not be utilities, depending more on the history and specifics of legislation than anything else) were the first to be regulated at the federal level under the Interstate Commerce Act (ICA) of 1887, and under subsequent legislation, first rail, then oil pipelines, and finally trucking were added.

Public utility legislation and regulation during the New Deal was quite often patterned after the methodology established under the ICA. Independent regulatory commissions were established with an odd number of commissioners, no more than a simple majority of whom could be from one political party. They were appointed for a fixed term (unlike many state regulatory commissions whose commissioners were elected) and confirmed by the Senate. Professional staffs were hired to do the work. Each regulatory body established a uniform accounting system, for each regulated utility under its jurisdiction to follow.

The New Deal era was a period of great expansion in the federal regulation of public utilities. The regulatory methodologies that were established during this era still exist, although the regulatory mood at the beginning of the twenty-first century generally prescribes more competition and less regulation. The reasons for the increased federal regulation in the 1930s were advancements in technology that allowed public utilities to serve customers at greater distances, adverse court decisions limiting the regulatory authority of state commissions combined with the weaknesses of these regulatory bodies, and the financial excesses of the 1920s, particularly by electric holding companies, as well as a concern over the exercise of monopoly power and "unfair" competition.

Seamless pipeline, electricity transmission, and telephone technology developed in the 1920s such that long-distance transmission of gas, electricity, and voice became feasible, reliable, and profitable. Furthermore, gas fields, with enough gas to serve distant markets were developed in Kansas, Oklahoma, Texas, and Louisiana. This gas was of much higher Btu count than the manufactured gas used for industrial processes and street lamp lighting. The increased interstate transmission soon led to regulatory problems, particularly when states found that utility companies were selling across state lines at rates that states considered too low and were designed to eliminate competition. Rhode Island attempted to set the rates for electricity that Narragansett Electric Lighting Company sold to Attleboro Steam and Electric Company across the border in Massachusetts, charging that the rates offered were too low. In *Public Utilities Commission v. Attleboro Steam and Electric Company* (1927), the Supreme Court ruled that

Rhode Island lacked authority to regulate these inter-state rates. Likewise, in cases beginning with *Kansas State Corporation Commission v. Kansas Pipeline Company* (1919) and ending with *Kansas State Corporation Commission v. Wichita Gas Company* (1934), the Supreme Court ruled that Kansas lacked jurisdiction over interstate gas sales for resale.

In addition to these decisions, there were abuses by electric holding companies in the 1920s, leading Will Rogers to quip that "a Holding Company is a thing where you hand an accomplice the goods while the policeman searches you." Holding companies, which bought up electric operating companies, engaged in pyramiding, inflationary write-ups of company assets in the transactions, and excessive service fees due to transactions among the operating companies and holding companies that were not at all arm's-length deals (although at least one author of a major text on public utilities in the early 1930s defends these arrangements). State commissions were unable to properly regulate these holding companies. The crash of 1929 caused many to fail, including the largest, Middle Western Utilities, which was run by the Chicago tycoon Samuel Insull. Thus, the failure of regulation was a major issue in the presidential election of 1932.

PUBLIC UTILITY LEGISLATION PASSED UNDER THE NEW DEAL

Major legislation was passed during the New Deal to set public policy for utilities. The Securities Act of 1933 and the Securities and Exchange Act of 1934 were among the first pieces of legislation. These acts were not specifically directed at utilities, but affected the electric holding companies in particular as they were intended to do. The Securities and Exchange Commission (SEC) was created by the latter legislation.

On July 5, 1934, Franklin D. Roosevelt established a committee, headed by Harold Ickes at the Public Works Administration, to coordinate federal power policy. From this came the Public Utility Act of 1935 (Wheeler Rayburn Act). It included Title 1, which became known as the Public Utility Holding Company Act (PUHCA), and Title 2, which extended Federal Power Commission (FPC) jurisdiction to the interstate transmission of electricity and called for appointed independent commissioners. The FPC had originally been established in 1920 to regulate hydropower dams and was at the time made up of the secretaries of war, agriculture, and interior.

Charles F. Phillips, a noted public utilities econo-mist writing in the 1960s, called PUHCA "the most stringent law ever passed by Congress." While the bill was watered down after intensive lobbying by the electric industry, it did contain a "death sentence clause" that abolished holding companies more than twice removed from their operating subsidiaries and gave the SEC powers over holding company practices. Additionally, Title 2 gave the FPC the authority to approve mergers among electric companies and also the responsibility for approving the rate schedules of the Southeastern, Southwestern, and Bonneville Power Administrations as well as those of the Bureau of Reclamation.

Between 1910 and 1934, the Interstate Commerce Commission (ICC) regulated interstate telegraph and telephone companies, while the Commerce Department had responsibility for issuing broadcast licenses before 1927, when the Federal Radio Commission (FRC) was created. Roosevelt created a commission headed by Senator Clarence Dill and Representative Sam Rayburn in 1933 to study telecommunications and broadcasting. From recommendations of this commission came the Federal Communications Act of 1934. It established the Federal Communications Commission (FCC) to replace the FRC and consolidate the regulation of wire, broadcasting, and cable services into one agency.

In response to a resolution of Congress passed in 1936, the FCC conducted a major investigation of the telephone industry, which it completed in 1939. It found that there was no pyramiding as practiced by other utilities (i.e., electric companies), that the Bell System had systematically tried to eliminate competition in line with its creed of "One System, One Policy, Universal Service," and that competition was not possible at that point so regulation was necessary. While the Bell System was a monopoly, its corporate vision was directed toward serving all customers more than toward financial wheeling and dealing.

The final public utility legislation under the New Deal was the Natural Gas Act of 1938. Natural gas pipelines were originally to be regulated under Title 3 of the Public Utility Act, but there were objections to making pipelines, which were also the major gas producers, common carriers. Additionally, the industry did not want direct sales to industrial customers, which comprised most of the customer base at the time, regulated. As a result, the Title 3 legislation did not pass out of committee.

Three years later, the Natural Gas Act, which was based on a final Federal Trade Commission report authorized by the Seventieth Congress in 1929, and issued in 1936, gave the FPC the authority to regulate the interstate rates of gas sales for resale but not the rates charged to industrial customers. It required certificates for new pipeline construction in areas already served, but did not require authority to build in areas not served. This act created difficulties when several pipelines sought to serve new markets, particularly in terms of "wasteful" competition. In 1942, the act was amended to require certificates for all interstate pipeline construction.

Financial transactions among interstate gas companies are not subject to review by the FPC other than indirectly through its powers to establish just and reasonable rates. Also, the FPC was not given the authority to require an increase in pipeline rates. Interestingly, while the FPC seemingly was given more authority over electric rates than gas pipeline rates, subsequent history did not prove this to be the case. The FPC actively regulated gas prices and pipelines, but has historically been fairly inactive in electric utility regulation, perhaps due to the prohibitions placed on electric utility holding companies after their excessive consolidation in and anti-competitive practices of the 1920s.

GAINING REGULATORY CONTROL AND NEW DEAL COURT DECISIONS

Before the New Deal era, there was a laxness in utility accounting systems, often by design as much as anything else, since it is difficult to regulate without knowing costs. Accounting control of public utilities was gained in the 1930s with uniform systems of accounts at the federal and state level. Courts had a long history of approving accounting regulations.

The most significant court decision involving public utilities that is associated with the New Deal is *FPC v. Hope Natural Gas* (1944). The FPC, basing its methodology on original cost less depreciation, ordered Hope to lower its rates. The appeals court reversed the FPC, but the Supreme Court, with Justice William O. Douglas writing for the majority, stated that it is the end result that counts rather than the actual methodology used to determine the rates. This decision modernized the longstanding *Smyth v. Ames* (1898) "fair value" methodology. Prior to Hope, the standard practice was to base rates upon the value of a utility's assets, although the change to an original cost less depreciation standard used by the FPC was not abrupt and had been recommended by a number of professionals in the field. As noted, accounting systems had been lax before the 1930s and valuation was often a difficult process. Furthermore, the use of original cost less depreciation sometimes allowed utilities to charge higher rates, since the value of their assets may have declined during the Depression.

Other court decisions, such as *Montana Public Service Commission v. Great Northern Utilities Company* (1933), involved the ability of commissions to determine that rates were too low. The courts generally upheld commission findings of "unfair" competition.

INDUSTRY GROWTH DURING THE NEW DEAL

While telephone usage declined in the Depression from 15.7 million calls per year in 1930 to 13.9 million in 1935, the pattern of decline in other public utility industries was soon reversed and the New Deal era saw growth. Natural gas sales went from 389,000 mcf in 1906 to 1.9 million mcf in 1929. These sales, primarily for industrial use, since home heating with natural gas did not develop as a significant market until after World War II, declined to 1.8 million in 1934, but grew to 2.4 million mcf by 1939.

The number of electric utility customers was only 600,000 in 1902 and 21.8 million in 1927 and was 27.2 million by 1937, even though streetcar usage had declined since the early 1920s. Industry earnings grew from $88.7 million in 1902 to $2.48 billion in 1937.

While there was an increase in regulation of public utilities during the New Deal, these companies were not nationalized. Some competition was provided to the privately owned companies by offering low-cost government-backed loans to rural electric and telephone cooperatives, public funding of the Tennessee Valley Authority, and other activities, but this was directed primarily toward customers that were not served privately.

HENRY E. KILPATRICK

See also: Public Utilities Holding Act; Rural Electrification Administration; Tennessee Valley Authority; Wheeler-Rayburn Act; Insull, Samuel; Norris, George; Wheeler, Burton; Documents: Hoover's Veto of Muscle Shoals Bill, March 3, 1931; Tennessee Valley Act, May 18, 1933; *Ashwander v. Tennessee Valley Authority,* 1936.

Bibliography

Barnes, Irston R. *The Economics of Public Utility Regulation.* New York: F.S. Crofts, 1942.

Glaeser, Martin G. *Public Utilities in American Capitalism.* New York: Macmillan, 1957.

Nash, L. R. *The Economics of Public Utilities.* New York: McGraw-Hill, 1931.

Phillips, Charles F., Jr. *The Economics of Regulation.* Homewood, IL: R. D. Irwin, 1969.

Schlesinger, Arthur M., Jr., *The Age of Roosevelt: The Crisis of the Old Order.* Boston: Houghton Mifflin, 1956.

Troxel, Emery. *Economics of Public Utilities.* New York: Rinehart, 1947.

Welch, Francis X. *Cases on Public Utility Regulation.* Washington, DC: Public Utilities Reports, 1946.

WAR OF THE WORLDS, THE RADIO BROADCAST

The *War of the Worlds*, a radio broadcast that simulated a newscast about an invasion from Mars, was performed on October 30—Halloween eve—1938 by Orson Welles and the players from his Mercury Theatre cast.

As historians of the medium note, radio was still fresh enough in the late 1930s that audiences often took what they heard over the airwaves quite literally as the truth. Recognizing this, Welles decided on a Halloween eve broadcast that would provide a thrilling retelling of the H. G. Wells novel *The War of the Worlds*, in which technologically sophisticated invaders from Mars attack Earth.

The reality of the newscast-style broadcast—combined with the increasingly frightening pre–World War II news coming out of Europe at the time—led many listeners to panic. Local and state police along the eastern seaboard, where the fictional invasion was supposed to take place, reported thousands fleeing their homes and jobs. Even some officials were caught off-guard and reported for duty as if there was a real invasion. Welles later apologized for causing such a panic.

See also: Mercury Theatre; radio; Welles, Orson.

Bibliography

Brown, Robert J. *Manipulating the Ether: The Power of Broadcast Radio in Thirties America.* Jefferson, NC: McFarland, 1998.

Cantril, Hadley. *The Invasion From Mars: A Study in the Psychology of Panic: With the Complete Script of the Famous Orson Welles Broadcast.* Princeton: Princeton University Press, 1982.

WISCONSIN PROGRESSIVE PARTY

The Wisconsin Progressive Party was founded in 1934 as an organizational vehicle for the candidacies of the progressive Republican brothers Philip La Follette and Robert La Follette Jr., running for governor and the U.S. Senate, respectively.

Sons of Robert La Follette Sr., who had run as the Progressive Party candidate for the presidency in 1924, Philip and Robert Jr. were fearful that they would lose their races should they run on the Republican ticket in 1934, given how popular President Franklin D. Roosevelt and the Democrats were that year.

With Roosevelt's blessing and a tacit nod of approval from the national Democratic party, both the La Follettes won their respective races that year. In 1936, Philip was reelected and the Wisconsin Progressive Party gained control of both houses of the state legislature.

But a split with Roosevelt over foreign policy—Robert Jr. advocated an isolationism that ran counter to the administration's growing internationalism—led to the Wisconsin progressives' estrangement from the Democrats. In 1938, an alliance between Republicans and Democrats defeated Philip's efforts to win a third gubernatorial term, although Robert Jr. was reelected to the Senate by a narrow margin in 1940. The party was disbanded in 1946.

See also: Democratic Party; Republican Party; La Follette, Philip; La Follette, Robert, Jr.

Bibliography

Dykstra, Robert R., and David R. Reynolds. "In Search of Wisconsin Progressives, 1904–1952." In *The History of American Electoral Behavior*, ed. Joel Silbey et al. Princeton: Princeton University Press, 1978.

Johnson, Roger T. *Robert M. La Follette, Jr. and the Decline of the Progressive Party in Wisconsin*. New York: Anchor, 1970.

WIZARD OF OZ, THE

Based on the 1900 book by L. Frank Baum, *The Wizard of Oz* (1939) is one of the most enduring films from the 1930s, telling the story of a young Kansas girl named Dorothy who gets transported by a tornado to the magical land of Oz. But while *The Wizard of Oz* has become a classic, it was only moderately successful upon its release, being overshadowed at the time by the premiere of the hugely popular *Gone With the Wind*.

Produced by Metro-Goldwyn-Mayer and directed by several directors (under the overall authority of Victor Fleming), *The Wizard of Oz* starred Judy Garland (Dorothy), Ray Bolger (Scarecrow), Jack Haley (Tin Man), Bert Lahr (Cowardly Lion), Margaret Hamilton

Among the most popular movies of the '30s, *The Wizard of Oz* (1939) featured Bert Lahr as the Cowardly Lion, Judy Garland as Dorothy, Ray Bolger as the Scarecrow, and Jack Haley as the Tin Man. *(Brown Brothers)*

(Wicked Witch of the West), and Frank Morgan in the title roles.

The film was technically unusual in that the opening and closing sequences in Kansas were shot in black and white (by the renowned director King Vidor), while the scenes in Oz were photographed in the then very expensive process of Technicolor. The memorable music score features the ever-popular "Over the Rainbow" sung by Garland.

The Wizard of Oz did not turn a profit until it was bought for television by CBS in 1956. Between then and the year 2000, it has been listed seven times among the twenty-five most-watched events in TV history. No other film is listed more than once.

See also: films, feature; Metro-Goldwyn-Mayer; Vidor, King.

Bibliography

Fricke, John, Jay Scarfone, and William Stillman. *The Wizard of Oz: The Official 50th Anniversary Pictorial History.* New York: Warner Books, 1989.

Harmetz, Aljean. *The Making of "The Wizard of Oz."* New York: Delta, 1989.

WOMEN

By the end of the 1920s, the precarious yet prosperous American economy began to falter, culminating in the stock market crash of 1929. In the eleven years that followed, Americans endured varying degrees of economic deprivation. For many American women, however, the 1930s brought a setback in social opportunity in addition to the severe economic contraction. From late 1929 through the mid-1940s, American women's lives centered on the struggle to meet the needs of their families. They creatively stretched their meager resources beyond normal limits to provide food and clothing for their loved ones. Many sought out paid labor in the male-dominated work force. Battling the obstacles of scarcity and deprivation, these women also endured the scorn and condemnation of a society that persisted in the notion that women belonged in the home, not in the job market taking work away from men who had families to support. Without the benefit of a cohesive women's organization, American women during the years of the Great Depression and the New Deal struggled on a predominantly individual basis to reclaim the social advances they had made during the 1920s and to extend their influence into the world of sociopolitical policy making.

BEFORE THE CRASH

The 1920s were a liberating phase in American history for many women. The decade began with the ratification of the Nineteenth Amendment to the Constitution. For the first time in American history, women had the right to vote in federal elections. During the 1920s, women's hemlines and hairstyles were shortened, restrictive undergarment and dress designs were cast aside, and women experienced a degree of physical and social freedom unknown to earlier generations. Drinking, smoking, and sexual activity, facilitated by more reliable and widely accessible means of birth control, were more common among young women of the 1920s than before. This shift in what was considered by the American people to be acceptable behavior for women appeared to indicate an opening up of opportunity for women, a dramatic departure from the narrow domestic sphere of home and family to which so many women had been consigned. The Great Depression, however, effectively restricted those opportunities.

To understand how the seemingly endless opportunity of the 1920s dissipated so quickly for American women, one needs only to peer beneath the surface of American social attitudes. Although women in the 1920s were allowed more physical and social freedom, to participate in the frivolity of the decade, they were still, on a more fundamental level, expected to fulfill the role of nurturer and caretaker of the family. As historian William H. Chafe explains, the "shift in manners and morals did not interfere with the perpetuation of a sexual division of labor where women assumed responsibility for the home and men went out into the world to earn a livelihood." When the Great Depression hit, American acceptance of the hedonism of the 1920s eroded. The shift in manners and morals that had permitted this carefree new behavior for women swung back to a more conservative conception of woman's proper role. The survival of the American people during this period of profound economic difficulty was predicated upon conventional gender roles. Consequently, the center of most American women's lives was the welfare of their families.

MAKING DO

The same notion of gender roles that made it difficult for women to find paid employment also made it difficult for men to accept chronic unemployment and their inability to meet their assigned role as breadwinner for their families. As a consequence, many men left their homes and families or, in extreme cases, committed suicide. This placed even more of a burden on women to keep their families going, since many assumed the role of head of their households.

Unemployment took a tremendous toll, reaching as high as 80 percent in some cities. This economic turmoil impelled many Americans to return to the comforting notion of the home as a haven from the outside world. Women's duty was to make that haven as comfortable as possible. Shortages and a dramatic, overall 55 percent decrease in income coupled with a sharp decline in purchasing power made that task ever more challenging. Advertising and women's magazines fostered the image of women placing the needs of their families above all else. For many women, home production and recycling provided the means to meet those needs. Women planted gardens and preserved their produce by canning what was not immediately consumed. Meals were stretched, often by adding fillers, such as increasing the number of servings of meat loaf by adding bread or crackers. Worn out clothing was resized and sewn into garments for younger members of the family. Clothes and shoes were handed down. Many families economized by moving in with their relatives, with the extended family working cooperatively to survive. When these efforts were not enough to meet the needs of their families, however, women had to turn to other sources.

Women extended their traditional, domestic role to provide assistance to the community at large. Community and religious charity programs stepped in when families could not provide for themselves. Women furnished most of the labor in these community service projects, providing food, clothing, and comfort to people in need.

WOMEN IN THE WORKFORCE

Wages for working-class men, and for many of the middle class as well, were simply not sufficient to support their families. Furthermore, by 1933, the unemployment rate was over 25 percent. With so many male heads of household earning inadequate pay or out of work altogether, necessity drove increasing numbers of women to seek paid employment. Unfortunately, the popular mentality that insisted women be the nurturers of their families made it very difficult for women to find work outside the home. Women experienced a tremendous amount of animosity in the workplace. As historian Glenda Riley explains, there was a "general antipathy toward female laborers." Despite that hostility, prevalent throughout the Depression, the number of women in the workforce steadily rose, from 22 percent in 1930 to 25 percent by 1940. These women endured long hours, suffered abuse, and labored in often dangerous conditions. For married women, those experiences were compounded by a public opinion even more prejudiced against them.

With jobs so scarce, societal attitudes insisted that available work should be reserved for men. Male-dominated labor unions endeavored to deny women the right to work. Even though these women were looking for work to support their families, the general belief persisted that they were seeking pin money to fund their frivolous desires. This public antipathy toward women was reinforced by New Deal legislation that restricted the numbers of married women in the workplace, as well as the number of hours they could work. The Economy Act of 1933, for example, discriminated against married women by dictating that two people in the same family could not be employed by the federal government. This meant that women working in federal governmental service whose husbands also held federal jobs were fired. Before the act was repealed in 1937, 1,600 women in federal positions had been forced out. State and local governments followed suit, denying women access to those positions in many of those governments as well. Throughout the country, businesses excluded women in general and married women in particular. Despite the hostility toward them, the percentage of married women in the workforce increased by 50 percent during the 1930s, with married women comprising 35 percent of the total female laborers. Necessity drove them to surmount the twin obstacles of open discrimination and societal pressure that women's proper place was in the home.

The issue that escaped most Americans in their efforts to restrict the paid employment of women was that, in reality, these women were not in competition with men. The jobs they were taking were predominantly in areas where men did not seek employment. In fact, women were losing ground in some work areas that had been traditionally female. In teaching, nursing, social work, and library work, men increasingly displaced female workers. Women were able to hold their ground only in areas that most men found undesirable: clerical and service work. Underlying these discriminatory policies was the notion that, despite such advances as the Nineteenth Amendment, women did not deserve of treatment equal to that afforded to men, no matter what the circumstances. By 1937, women's yearly wages were little more than half those earned by men. Women without jobs, homes, or families were in an even more difficult situation. They were virtually ignored by society. Unemployable, these marginalized women had very few resources and often wandered the streets.

RURAL WOMEN

Women in rural areas did not fare much better. Women in farming communities were engaged in home production to a greater degree, canning fruits, vegetables, and meat. Materials were recycled to meet the needs of their families. Food staples, like flour and grains, were often packaged in cotton fabric bags, which women used to sew into dresses, aprons, curtains, and such. The patterns printed on the grain sacks were similar to the fabric patterns available on the ready-made clothing rural women saw in shops and catalogs like Montgomery Ward's. As the Depression wore on and conditions worsened, many farm families emphasized cash crops rather than subsistence agriculture in an effort to stay on top of their mounting debt. Yet for many more rural women, subsistence and home production were infeasible. The Depression, combined with the intense environmental catastrophe of the dust bowl, drove many farm families off their land. For women whose families were on the move looking for work, keeping food on the table and clothes on their backs was more than difficult.

MEXICAN AND MEXICAN-AMERICAN WOMEN

The ever growing numbers of white farm families that took to the road looking for work displaced the existing migrant workers. Mexican farm workers in particular suffered. The American people had little sympathy for this group, many of whom were forced to emigrate back to Mexico, even those who were American citizens. The Mexican population in the United States decreased by 50 percent from 1930 to 1940, most of them concentrated in urban centers. The employment patterns for many of those who remained changed significantly. Chicanas, who were traditionally unlikely to seek employment outside the home, increasingly entered the workforce during the Depression, taking advantage of New Deal relief programs that offered them jobs. Many young Chicanas, however, turned their wages over to their fathers, who, despite often being unemployed themselves, remained the patriarchal authority in the family.

AFRICAN-AMERICAN WOMEN

Women in general faced Depression-era unemployment with far fewer resources than men did. Black women, more so than any other group of women, had even fewer resources. Unemployment rates for black women were significantly higher than for white women. More than 50 percent of black women lost their jobs as compared to only 30 percent of white women. The manufacturing and clerical jobs that were available to women were, for the most part, closed to blacks and other women of color. These women increasingly turned to domestic service. The percentage of nonwhite women working as domestic laborers field rose dramatically from 55 percent in 1930 to 64 percent by 1940. Those black women who could not find employment often found themselves excluded from New Deal relief programs, particularly in the South.

THE NEW DEAL AND AMERICAN WOMEN

In spite of its shortcomings, the New Deal offered women not only some relief from their economic difficulties, but also a way to participate in federal policy making to an unprecedented degree. During the 1920s, women solidified a position for themselves in professions related to their traditional roles in providing for the health, education, and well-being of their families. Society generally accepted women employed as nurses, teachers, and social workers. When President Franklin D. Roosevelt took office in 1932, he began to address the needs of American women. During his administration, women had a strong voice in the shaping of American policy.

The general hostility toward women in the workforce was substantiated by numerous reports of poor working conditions, starvation wages, and homeless women wandering the streets without assistance. These reports did not go unnoticed. Originating at the state and local levels, legislation to regulate women's working conditions ultimately reached the federal level. The National Industrial Recovery Act of 1933 addressed the needs of working women by setting maximum hours and minimum wages—for women as well as for men. The position, upheld in 1938 with the Fair Labor Standards Act, guaranteed protective labor legislation for men and women.

Unlike the Economy Act of 1933, not all New Deal policies and legislation restricted opportunity for women. Although most work relief programs tended to ignore the needs of women, the Women's and Professional Division of the Works Progress Administration (WPA) focused on the needs of working women. The White House Conference on the Emergency Needs of Women, organized by Eleanor Roosevelt in November 1933, resulted in the employment of approximately 300,000 women. This conference pushed the Civil Works Administration (CWA) and the Federal Emergency Relief Administration into placing women in jobs as teachers, office workers, and nurses, as well as in positions engaged with the production and distribution of food and clothing. The Conference also encouraged the WPA and the Civilian Conservation Corps (CCC) to include more women in their programs. Women's artistic creativity was fostered through a variety of New Deal programs, including theater, writing, mural painting, and photography. Dorothea Lange was sent out by the head of the Historical Section of the Farm Security Administration (FSA) to document the lives of migrant workers in the West and to generate support for Agricultural Adjustment Act programs. The FSA put Lange's photographs before the eyes of the American middle class in magazines, newspapers, and traveling exhibits. Perhaps no single image more clearly depicts the struggle of the Great Depression than Lange's *Migrant Mother* (1936) (see page 204).

Ellen S. Woodward, who became the director of the Women's and Professional Division of the WPA in 1935, promoted the idea that many women were heads of their families, who were deserving of every degree of assistance afforded to men. Woodward's job programs trained women not only in the traditional skills of sewing and domestic work, but also in nontraditional areas like bookbinding and mattress making.

Under Woodward's influence, the WPA put nearly 400,000 women to work—almost 20 percent of the total number of WPA workers. The WPA wages of many of these women enabled them and their families to elude starvation.

NATIVE AMERICAN WOMEN AND THE NEW DEAL

Native Americans have traditionally been marginalized by white American society. During the New Deal era, however, Indian women were able to benefit from many of the education and relief programs. The Indian Reorganization Act (IRA) of 1934 reshaped governmental policy toward Native Americans. The IRA promoted respect for native culture and religion and advocated tribal autonomy and protection of tribal lands. For Native American women, this meant that the New Deal programs offered them training and jobs in agriculture, a traditionally female task among most native groups, nursing, office work, childcare, and the domestic arts of cooking, sewing, and canning. Indian women were employed as supervisors and workers in the CCC Indian Work Camps, and they held clerical positions with the CWA and the WPA.

WOMEN'S VOICES IN SHAPING POLICY

As important as the wages and training provided by New Deal programs was the opportunity for political influence enjoyed by a select group of women during the Roosevelt administration. Due in large part to his wife, Eleanor, Roosevelt placed a number of women, black and white, in positions of leadership. Roosevelt appointed Frances Perkins to the post of secretary of labor, making her the first woman cabinet member. As chairman of the Committee on Economic Security, Perkins helped secure the passage of protective labor legislation restricting the number of hours and setting a minimum wage for American workers. She also helped to pass Social Security legislation. Perkins made the health and safety of American workers her priority, drawing heavily from her past experience as a social worker, and Roosevelt's industrial commissioner during his years as governor of New York.

Female social reformers played a critical role in the development of New Deal policies. They established a network within the administration that encouraged Roosevelt to appoint many other "first" women, in addition to Perkins. Florence Allen became the first woman on the United States Circuit Court of Appeals. Ruth Bryan Owen was the first woman ambassador. Roosevelt's support of female leadership crossed race lines as well. Mary McLeod Bethune, the Negro Affairs director for the National Youth Administration, served as the unofficial leader of the "black cabinet," an elite group of African-American advisers to the president. Making the fight against racial injustice, rather than women's rights, her priority, Bethune procured the appointment of many blacks to influential administrative positions.

CONCLUSION

Throughout the 1930s, American women struggled to care for themselves and their families in the face of intense economic contraction. With very few resources, women "made do," creatively reusing, recycling, and conserving to meet their families' needs. Out of necessity, however, many women were forced out of the domestic sphere proscribed by American society and into the workplace. Enduring discrimination, abuse, and, at times, wretched working conditions, women struggled for their families' survival. With Roosevelt's election to the presidency in 1932, the situation gradually improved. Eleanor Roosevelt encouraged her husband to put strong, intelligent women into leadership positions. Working diligently, these women drew on their traditional backgrounds of social service, to dramatically improve conditions for many American citizens. Their focus, however, was more on improving the lives of all American workers, or American youth, or African Americans, rather than on pushing forward a feminist agenda. Even though women in the 1930s and early 1940s held more influential political positions than ever before, the accepted role of women in American society changed very little.

Lisa Miles

See also: African Americans; Hispanic Americans; Native Americans; Civil Works Administration; Civilian Conservation Corps; Fair Labor Standards Act; Indian Reorganization Act; National Industrial Recovery Act; Works Progress Administration; Bethune, Mary McLeod; Perkins, Frances; Roosevelt, Eleanor.

Bibliography

Chafe, William H. *The American Woman: Her Changing Social, Economic, and Political Roles, 1920–1970.* New York: Oxford University Press, 1972.

Badger, Anthony J. *The New Deal: The Depression Years, 1933–40.* New York: Hill and Wang, 1989.

Evans, Sara M. *Born for Liberty: A History of Women in America.* New York: Free Press/McMillan, 1989.

Gordon, Linda. "Black and White Visions of Welfare: Women's Activism, 1930–1945." In *Unequal Sisters: A Multicultural Reader in US Women's History.* eds. Vicki L. Ruiz and Ellen Carrol DuBois. New York: Routledge, 1994.

Kessler-Harris, Alice. "Gender Ideology in Historical Reconstruction: A Case Study from the 1930s." *Gender and History* 1 (Spring 1989): 31–44.

Riley, Glenda. *Inventing the American Woman: A Perspective on Women's History 1865 to the Present.* Arlington Heights, IL: Harlan Davidson, 1986.

Rosenberg, Rosalind. *Divided Lives: American Women in the Twentieth Century.* New York: Hill and Wang, 1992.

Scharf, Lois. *To Work and to Wed: Female Employment, Feminism, and the Great Depression.* Westport, CT: Greenwood Press, 1980.

Ware, Susan. *Beyond Suffrage: Women and the New Deal.* Cambridge, Harvard University Press, 1982.

———. *American Women in the 1930s: Holding Their Own.* Boston: Twayne, 1982.

WORLD'S FAIRS

The 1851 Crystal Palace Exhibition in London inspired a series of world's fairs in western nations that trumpeted technological progress, imperial expansion, and artistic achievement, all within festive, international settings. During the years of the Great Depression, however, world's fairs in America also reflected a growing anxiety among the country's elites. Massive unemployment and economic dislocation had prompted many Americans to question the legitimacy of their democratic, capitalist system. Socialist and communist ideologies, with their promise to remove disparities of wealth and to smooth harsh economic cycles, gained new adherents. To reassure the disillusioned, America's business and political leaders turned to the persuasive power of utopian fairs. Striking architecture, innovative consumer goods, and imagina-

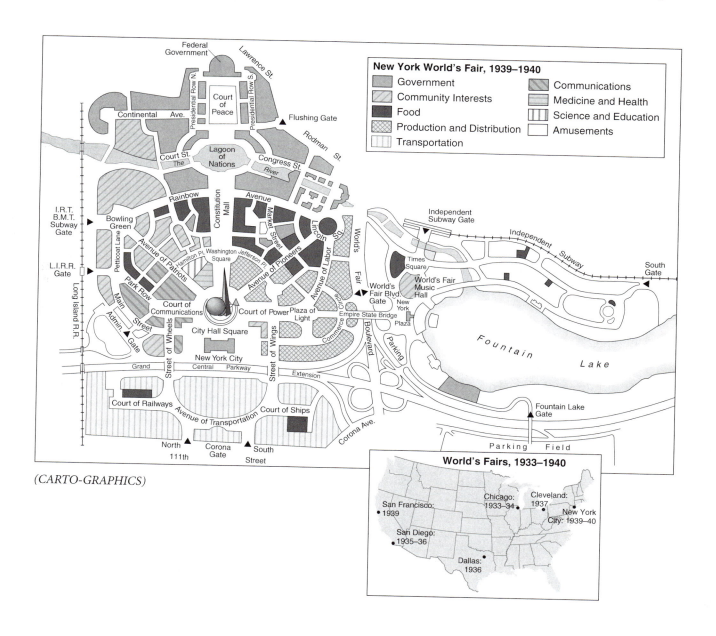

(CARTO-GRAPHICS)

tive entertainment encouraged belief in a bright future of unlimited consumption, abundance, and technological progress, all firmly anchored in existing economic, gender, and racial power relationships.

The first of the decade's three major fairs was the 1933–34 Chicago Century of Progress Exposition, which was built on a narrow, three-mile strip of land along Lake Michigan and timed to celebrate the city's centennial. The fair's futuristic theme of scientific and industrial progress was suggested in both its name and the functional, modernist design of its buildings. The most impressive of the structures, the Travel and Transport Building, had a 125-foot-high domed roof suspended from twelve exterior towers by steel cables. Although the design and layout of the fair's buildings drew criticism from a number of contemporary architects, they influenced industrial design throughout the decade as well as the architecture of the later world's fair in New York City.

Fair participants sometimes spent enormous sums to sell their products and philosophies to the public. Major corporations, like General Motors and Sears, Roebuck and Company, constructed their own pavilions to display current merchandise, and the federal government used its building to market New Deal programs. Five foreign countries also maintained exclusive pavilions, while many others shared the Hall of Nations in the Travel and Transportation Building. On the midway, visitors attended movies, animal shows, and a wide variety of exhibits, including several that reinforced racial stereotypes. African-American visitors experienced discrimination at many restaurants and concession stands, a practice that was banned only after protests forced the passage of a special act of the state legislature. And the idea of women as objects of desire was reinforced by Sally Rand's popular and controversial fan dance, which ended with Rand lifting her fans and exposing her nude body.

The success of the Chicago fair inspired the New York World's Fair of 1939–40. Adopting the motto "Building the World of Tomorrow," fair organizers chose an ash dump in Queens as the site of their temporary utopia. The focal point of the fair was the futuristic Trylon and Perisphere, a 610-foot triangular tower and a 180-foot globe connected by a curving ramp. They were linked to the federal government building by Constitution Mall and a giant statue of George Washington, a spatial arrangement that emphasized the continuity of past, present, and future political systems. Inside the Perisphere was one of the fair's principal attractions, Democracity, which portrayed the harmonious, industrious metropolis of to-

The New York World's Fair of 1939 and 1940 was the biggest and best attended of the several world's fairs of the Great Depression era. (*Library of Congress*)

morrow. Technological achievements introduced at the fair included the television, and amusements ranged from the Parachute Jump and Aerial Joy Ride to several striptease shows.

General Motors' Futurama was the most heavily attended exhibit at the New York fair. Conceived by Norman Bel Geddes, a leading industrial designer, the exhibit featured a model of the American landscape in the far-off year of 1960, when technology was expected to have solved most of society's problems. Not surprisingly, the key feature of General Motors' vision of the future was an extensive system of highways that made ownership of a car, and the availability of public infrastructure to support its use, the centerpiece of future prosperity.

New York's fair faced some competition from the San Francisco Golden Gate International Exposition, which ran during the same years. A celebration of the completion of the Golden Gate Bridge and the San

Francisco–Oakland Bay Bridge, the fair was held on a 400-acre rectangle of filled land in San Francisco Bay called Treasure Island. Fair designers emphasized a Pacific Basin theme that showcased the cultures surrounding the Pacific Ocean. Entering the fair between two large elephant towers, visitors found themselves in the Court of Honor standing before the 400-foot, art deco Tower of the Sun. An 80-foot statue of Pacifica, a symbol of peace, overlooked another court. Although less utopian than the fairs in Chicago or New York City, the San Francisco fair projected visions of the future through a diorama of what the city might look like in 1999 and a robot designed by Westinghouse. Sally Rand, well known for her performances at the Chicago fair, appeared in a Nude Ranch.

The 1930s also saw three smaller fairs: the 1935–36 California Pacific Exposition, San Diego, the 1936 Texas Centennial Exposition, Dallas, and the 1937 Great Lakes and International Exposition, Cleveland. In contrast to the poor showing at the one fair held in America during the prosperous 1920s (the financially disastrous Philadelphia Sesquicentennial Exposition), the six fairs of the Depression era collectively attracted almost 100 million visitors. The Chicago fair actually turned a profit—a rare achievement for any world's fair. Paradoxically, the economic and social difficulties of the time were responsible for the success of the fairs: anxious elites needed to point the way to a more promising future, governmental leaders wanted to create

jobs and confidence in the existing political system, and a tired public longed for distraction from the present and hope for a better tomorrow.

The advent of World War II at the end of the decade ensured that the 1940s would see few large fairs anywhere in the world (the United States would not host another fair until 1962). The utopian visions of the Depression melted into the realities of war as New York's Trylon and Perisphere were reduced to scrap metal for military use and San Francisco's Pacifica was pulled down to make way for a U.S. navy base on Treasure Island.

MICHAEL J. RAWSON

See also: General Motors; New York World's Fair.

Bibliography

Findling, John E., ed. *Historical Dictionary of World's Fairs and Expositions, 1851–1988.* Westport, CT: Greenwood Press, 1990.

Kihlstedt, Folke T. "Utopia Realized: The World's Fairs of the 1930s." In *Imagining Tomorrow: History, Technology, and the American Future,* ed. Joseph J. Corn, pp. 97–118. Cambridge: MIT Press, 1986.

Rydell, Robert W. *World of Fairs: The Century-of-Progress Expositions.* Chicago: University of Chicago Press, 1993.

Rydell, Robert W., and Nancy Gwinn, eds. *Fair Representations: World's Fairs and the Modern World.* Amsterdam: VU University Press, 1994.

YOUTH

The onset of the Great Depression at the end of the 1920s brought about profound changes in the lives of American youth. For most, the hard times of the 1930s produced a reduction in income and status, but for far too many the Depression also made the struggle to survive the focus of their lives. By 1933, as economic conditions worsened and private avenues of support became exhausted, President Franklin D. Roosevelt initiated a series of New Deal programs designed to alleviate some of the hardship. The Civilian Conservation Corps and the National Youth Administration would have the most direct impact on the lives of America's youth. These programs experienced varying degrees of success, providing opportunities for many young Americans, yet failing to meet the needs of numerous others. Despite the adversity faced by

these young people, many were able to find ways to survive, as well as to entertain and enjoy themselves.

IMPACT OF THE DEPRESSION ON YOUTH CULTURE

The experiences of young Americans during the 1930s were markedly different from those of young people just a few years earlier. Due to restrictive child-labor laws and laws enforcing school attendance, children and adolescents during the 1920s spent most of their time interacting with their peers rather than working alongside adults. Their lives revolved around school and social activities, such as athletic events, parties, dating, and movies. Mass production and a period of economic prosperity meant that new products like automobiles and radios were widely available and affordable. The automobile enabled young people to escape the watchful gaze of their parents and explore their developing sexuality by petting and necking in parked cars. Young women became more independent, adopting more revealing clothing styles, and many took up smoking and drinking. More so than ever in the past, young Americans spent significant periods of time socializing in the mixed company of their peer group. The world of the 1920s appeared to offer boundless opportunity to these young people. However, by the early 1930s, the economic austerity brought on by the Great Depression seemed to have erased the promise of a bright future for many young Americans.

The lower a family's economic level, the harder it was hit by the Depression. The youth of the middle and upper classes experienced a reduction in income that resulted in a decline in status. The money simply was no longer available to enable them to keep up with the latest clothing trends or to buy gasoline for their automobiles. These young people tightened their belts, along with the rest of their families, and managed to get by with less. Young adults delayed getting married, and many continued living with their parents for much longer than in earlier generations. Young women assumed more domestic responsibilities in the home, while many young men worked at part-time jobs to contribute to the economic survival of their families. For the most part, young people resented this deprivation, which was often accompanied by a sense of shame or embarrassment over the loss of socioeconomic status.

The economic impact, however, was felt most profoundly by the youth of the rural and urban poorer classes. It took more than frugality for the working classes to survive. By the early 1930s, a national unemployment rate of close to 25 percent made it very difficult for young people to find employment outside the home. During this period, the unemployment rate for youth ages sixteen to twenty-four was between 20 and 30 percent. Young men lucky enough to find jobs turned their checks over to help support their families. By the end of the Depression, young men's wages were less than half of what men their fathers' ages were earning. Some of the less fortunate left their homes to wander the country looking for work, thereby enabling their younger siblings living at home to have more to eat. Starvation was a very real concern for many working-class Americans. By 1933,

the Children's Bureau estimated that 20 percent of American children were not adequately fed. The New York City welfare agency reported twenty-nine deaths and more than fifty people seeking medical care due to starvation that year. In addition, malnutrition-related illnesses claimed the lives of 110 other New Yorkers in 1933, predominantly children. Poor diet and insufficient medical and dental care could easily become life-threatening challenges for American youth.

NEW DEAL PROGRAMS AND AMERICAN YOUTH

In response to the difficulties faced by the urban poor, President Roosevelt established the Civilian Conservation Corps (CCC) in 1933. The CCC was the first relief program of the New Deal and one of Roosevelt's favorite projects. The CCC laborers were eighteen to twenty-five years old, unmarried young men, and came predominantly from the cities. Over the nine-year period in which it operated, the CCC put more than 2.5 million young men to work. They implemented conservation programs by planting trees, cutting breaks to prevent forest fires, and constructing fire towers, dams, and reservoirs. They demonstrated soil conservation techniques and administered irrigation and flood control programs to farmers. The young men also cleared campgrounds and beaches, strung telephone wires, and built parks, fish ponds, and hiking trails. They earned $35 a month and received room and board at more than 2,000 CCC camps. They received useful vocational and academic training, benefited from gainful employment, and were able to make a financial contribution to their families back home. The CCC proved to be widely popular with the American public. Not only did it provide these young men with vastly improved living conditions, but it gave them the opportunity to engage in constructive physical labor, reinforcing the traditional American value of hard work.

Unfortunately, however, the benefits of working for the CCC were not equally accessible to all American youths. Of the 2.5 million young men enrolled in the Corps, only 200,000 were African Americans, in spite of the fact that the situation for young blacks during the 1930s was more extreme than that confronting most white youths. Black youths faced a significantly higher unemployment rate of about 40 percent, in addition to enduring discrimination based on racial prejudice. Yet in Mississippi during 1933, for example, though blacks made up over 50 percent of the population, only 143 of the state's 3,710 CCC enrollees were African Americans. The CCC camps themselves were segregated: There were white camps, black camps, and Indian camps. Despite the inequalities they encountered, those black and Native American young men who were able to secure positions found that the CCC offered them better living conditions, educational opportunities, and job training than they would have received without it.

One group of young Americans was excluded from the Civilian Conservation Corps altogether: young women. It would take a different program to address their needs and the needs of other young Americans who still needed assistance. In 1935, Secretary of Labor Frances Perkins explored options for providing young people with opportunities for work, recreation, and education. Congress authorized the allocation of funds through the Emergency Relief Appropriation Act to create a new program to provide jobs for 4.5 million young people. This program operated under the Works Progress Administration and later became an independent agency, the National Youth Administration (NYA). The NYA provided part-time employment to more than 2 million high school and college students. It expanded the liberal arts focus of the public school curriculum by offering vocational training. The NYA also provided assistance for more than 2.5 million young Americans who were not enrolled in schools. Besides vocational training, the NYA also instilled notions of social integration and training in citizenship responsibilities.

The NYA reached a much more diverse audience than the CCC. The NYA addressed the needs of rural youth who had been overlooked by the CCC, providing them with industrial training and education. While the young women the NYA worked with most often received instruction that emphasized their domestic roles, they were given some education concerning broader economic forces. In addition, the young women's centers were the most racially integrated. Indeed under leaders like Mary McLeod Bethune and executive director Aubrey Williams, the NYA followed a policy of racial equality that far surpassed that of the CCC. New Deal programs aimed at assisting young Americans during the 1930s vastly improved their living conditions and opened up opportunities that the Great Depression had seemed to push beyond their grasp.

LEISURE ACTIVITIES

Despite the deprivation and austerity, American youth, even those who did not directly benefit from New Deal programs, continued to devise ways to entertain and amuse themselves. Most of the young Americans who were able to remain in high school reported that they were able to get most of their assignments done at school, which left their afternoons and evenings free. Since about 90 percent of American families owned radios, many young people spent their time listening to radio programs. Movies were another popular form of entertainment. By the mid-1930s, more than 60 percent of Americans attended films weekly.

Middle-class youth took full advantage of these forms of entertainment. They also found time to collect stamps, read books and magazines, build models, and attend parties. Working-class young people, boys in particular, entertained themselves playing sports. In general, young men and women of all economic classes still preferred to spend as much time as they could manage in the company of their peer groups, though those who were less affluent did not have as much free time or the extra money for social interaction and hobbies.

Lisa Miles

See also: education; Aid to Dependent Children; Civilian Conservation Corps; Emergency Educational Program; National Youth Administration; Bethune, Mary McLeod; Williams, Aubrey.

Bibliography

Badger, Anthony J. *The New Deal: The Depression Years, 1933–1940.* New York: Hill and Wang, 1989.

Bailey, Beth L. *From Front Porch to Back Seat: Courtship in Twentieth-Century America.* Baltimore: Johns Hopkins University Press, 1988.

Bird, Caroline. "The Discovery of Poverty." In *The Way We Lived: Essays and Documents in American Social History,* ed. Frederick M. Binder and David M. Reimers, pp. 205–16. Lexington, MA: D. C. Heath, 1988.

Clausen, John A. *American Lives: Looking Back at the Children of the Great Depression.* New York: Free Press, 1993.

Elder, Glen H., Jr. *Children of the Great Depression: Social Change in Life Experience.* Chicago: University of Chicago Press, 1974.

Fraser, Steve, and Gary Gerstle. *The Rise And Fall of the New Deal Order, 1930–1940.* Princeton: Princeton University Press, 1989.

Gower, Calvin W. "The Struggle of Blacks for Leadership Positions in the Civilian Conservation Corps: 1933–1942." *Journal of Negro History* 61:2 (1976): 123–135.

Modell, John. *Into One's Own: From Youth to Adulthood in the United States, 1920–1975.* Berkeley: University of California Press, 1989.

Reiman, Richard A. *The New Deal and American Youth: Ideas and Ideals in a Depression Decade.* Athens: University of Georgia Press, 1992.

Salmond, John A. "The Civilian Conservation Corps and the Negro." *Journal of American History* 52:1 (1965): 75–88.

PART III
GOVERNMENT

INTRODUCTION TO PART III

Part III of the *Encyclopedia of the Great Depression and the New Deal* focuses on government: domestic legislation, agencies, congressional committees, and court decisions. (Legislation, agencies, and congressional committees concerning foreign affairs are in Part IV; minor legislative acts are listed in the glossary.)

More than any other decade that preceded it—and, proportionally, more than any decade to follow—the 1930s saw the greatest peacetime expansion in the size and scope of the federal government in American history. The qualifier "peacetime" is noteworthy. During his campaign for the presidency in 1932 and upon coming to office in 1933, Franklin D. Roosevelt evoked the idea of the Great Depression as a warlike emergency period, requiring a fundamental change in the role of the government in domestic affairs.

Of course, the Roosevelt administration was not the pioneer of this expansion. While both contemporary Democratic politicians and traditional pro–New Deal historians like Arthur Schlesinger Jr. played up the differences between the administrations of Roosevelt and his predecessor, Republican Herbert Hoover, more nuanced views have emerged in the past few decades. In his award-winning 1966 history of the New Deal, *The First New Deal*, the original "Brain Truster" Raymond Moley admitted that "most of the [anti-Depression] devices we used" were initiated by Hoover.

Still, for both political and ideological reasons, Hoover was unable and/or unwilling to move beyond a cautious voluntarism, whereby the federal government prodded business, industry, and financial institutions to coordinate their efforts to overcome the effects of the Great Depression. Roosevelt, in his first few years, employed Hoover's ideas of voluntary private sector cooperation, most notably in the National Recovery Administration (NRA), but expanded them immensely. Moreover, the new president did not shy away from creating regulatory agencies designed to prevent the speculative excesses of Wall Street, eliminate overproduction in agriculture, and shore up a shaky banking system—all of which, indeed, had helped set off the Depression in the first place.

Then, under political pressure from the Left in the mid-1930s, the Roosevelt administration went even farther in what is sometimes referred to as the "Second New Deal." With the Social Security Act and the National Labor Relations Act (NLRA) of 1935, government had taken on new and unprecedented roles in the economy, assuring pensions for all senior citizens (except in agricultural and domestic service occupations, where the poorest whites and African Americans predominated) and guaranteeing the right of workers to organize independent trade unions.

Yet there were limits to the flexibility of the administration's thinking and Congress's and the Supreme Court's willingness to go along with federal government expansion. Until the beginning of World War II, Roosevelt remained committed in theory—if not always in practice—to a balanced budget, even at the cost of setting off the recession of 1937 and 1938 that bears his name. Nor was Congress willing to go along with the "soak the rich" tax plan Roosevelt proposed in 1935, instead watering it down so that it had little effect on government revenues, the estates of the upper classes, and the distribution of the nation's wealth. And a conservative, largely Republican-appointed Supreme Court was even more recalcitrant, striking down several components of the First New Deal, including the Agricultural Adjustment Administration and the NRA. Later, after the president threatened to stack the Court with liberal jurists, key swing-vote justices moderated their ideological opposition to federal and state governmental economic activism and ruled the NLRA and Social Security constitutional.

Ultimately, many of the agencies created during the emergency of the Great Depression were dismantled, either because conservative justices and members of Congress opposed them on ideological grounds or because they were seen as irrelevant during the economic boom years of World War II. Some—most notably Social Security and the National Labor Relations Board—have long outlasted the 1930s. Indeed, if the Roosevelt administration had been responsible simply for the creation of Social Security—still the most popular governmental program in American history—it would have gone down as one of the most important presidencies of the twentieth century. But, of course, the Roosevelt administration did far more than that—it literally reinvented government and its relationship to the American people.

AGRICULTURAL ADJUSTMENT ACT (1933)

During the First Hundred Days of the New Deal, President Franklin D. Roosevelt introduced to Congress the Agricultural Adjustment bill to restore the purchasing power of farmers. Because overproduction was crippling the profits of farmers due to high prices and surplus yields, the federal government had to persuade farmers to produce less. The domestic allotment plan paid farmers to reduce their acreage or plow under crops already in the field. As a result of cooperation, farmers received a parity payment based on prewar prices from 1914 to 1919. Congress passed the bill in May 1933, creating the Agricultural Adjustment Administration (AAA).

The law created and authorized the Agricultural Adjustment Administration to 1) enter into voluntary agreements to pay farmers to reduce production of some basic commodities; 2) make advanced payments to farmers who stored their crops; 3) create marketing agreements between farmers and middlemen; and 4) levy processing taxes to pay for production adjustment and market development.

The act met harsh criticisms after millions of acres of cotton and wheat were plowed under and hogs were wastefully slaughtered. The public outcry was significant. Horrific living conditions, some of which were exacerbated by New Deal programs, made the public, especially the poorer classes, weary of government policy and intervention.

The act of 1933 was declared unconstitutional by *United States v. Butler* (297 U.S. Code 1, 68, 1936), which stated that it was an encroachment upon the reserved rights of the states.

THE BEGINNING OF THE AAA

President Roosevelt and Secretary of Agriculture Henry A. Wallace faced a formidable crisis in American agriculture when they came into office. Prior to 1933 there had already been outbreaks of violence on American farms. Some reporters and other observers warned that the American countryside was on the brink of revolution. In response, Wallace urged the president to call a special session of Congress, where broad emergency powers would be given to the executive branch. Congress passed the Agricultural Adjustment Act on May 12, 1933. This act authorized production adjustment programs as well as the use of marketing agreements and licenses. The Agricultural Adjustment Administration was built upon ideas set forth in Hoover's administration by the Federal Farm Board. The Farm Board supported agriculture prices by lending money to cooperatives to buy products and keep them off the market. But the allotted resources were not enough to maintain levels of effectiveness. Roosevelt was more willing than Hoover to experiment to alleviate the ravages of the Depression. The AAA was one such experiment.

Because of the situation faced by U.S. producers during the Great Depression, Congress formed several new programs, domestic and international, to assist farmers through monetary support and supply stabilization. One piece of legislation passed was Section 22. Added to the Agricultural Adjustment Act by amendment in 1935, it was the first nontariff legislation for the general regulation of agricultural imports.

The Commodity Credit Corporation (CCC) was incorporated under the laws of the state of Delaware to carry out financial activities, including making mandatory nonrecourse loans on the designated basic (storable) crops. Commodity loan programs carried out by the CCC during 1933–37 covered cotton, corn, rosin, turpentine, tobacco, peanuts, dates, figs, and prunes.

Between 1932 and 1935, farm income increased by more than 50 percent. During the same years that farmers were encouraged to take land out of production—displacing tenants and sharecroppers—a severe drought and dust storm hit the Great Plains states, significantly reducing production. Although benefit payments totaled over $1.5 billion by 1936, the increase in commodity prices was attributed to the severe drought.

AAA CAUSES TROUBLE

The first section of the AAA is the most controversial. Title I established the domestic allotment plan for basic agricultural commodities. The voluntary contracts agreed to by the producers gave the Department of Agriculture the power to set production levels. The basic idea hinged on a decrease in production that would increase demand and raise price levels to assure parity. And until the parity level was met, the government would pay the producer between current prices and parity prices.

In 1933, in the government's first call for commodity reduction, 10.4 million acres of cotton and 9 million acres of wheat were plowed under and 6 million pigs were slaughtered. Pig production was the first market to cause major trouble for the AAA. Those of the 6 million hogs too small to be processed for food consumption were rendered into tankage or liquids to be used for lard and other by-products. The processors responsible for slaughtering, packaging, and rendering could not handle the mass quantity, and carcasses were seen floating down rivers or dumped in rot piles, with meat still on them. To the public, not only was this a source of contamination, but more drastically it showed the public government methods of waste during such a profound time of starvation and deprivation all across America.

For the landowners of the South, whose millions of acres of cotton supported the southern economy, the AAA had a vastly different effect. Southern landowners quickly signed the voluntary domestic allotment contracts, which paid them to plow under the cotton. For them, the program was a great success. But landowners were not generally those who worked the land, and the sharecroppers and tenants who did the labor rarely received the cotton reduction money paid to landowners. The owners often misrepresented facts and figures to the mostly illiterate workers, cheating them of their share and leading to a mass displacement of croppers and tenants because there was no land to be worked.

As a result of limited federal assistance through the AAA to sharecroppers and tenants, the number of croppers fell drastically, thus defeating the desire to keep people on their land and stop the migration of workers from rural America. In addition to limited resources allotted for sharecroppers and tenants, there was no assistance for migratory farm workers under the AAA. Mexican American and Native American populations were essentially ignored.

DISMANTLING THE AAA

The Agricultural Adjustment Act provisions for production control and processing taxes were declared unconstitutional in *Butler v. United States* by the Hoosac Mills decision of 1936. The court decided that agricultural issues were a local problem that, according to the Tenth Amendment, were subject to state, not federal, action. With the *Butler v. United States* decision ruling the AAA unconstitutional, Congress passed the Soil Conservation and Domestic Allotment Act of 1938, the Agricultural Marketing Act of 1937, and the Agricultural Adjustment Act of 1938, whereby the government provided compensation to producers who adjusted the acreage of their soil-depleting crops, parity price adjustments to those who did not overplant, federal crop insurance, and other benefits.

KYES STEVENS

See also: agriculture; dust bowl; Farm Holiday Association; Okies; Southern Tenant Farmers Union; Commodity Credit Corporation; Farm Security Administration; Federal Surplus Relief Corporation/Commodities Corporation; Jones-Connally Farm Relief Act; New Deal, first; Resettlement Administration; Soil Conservation and Domestic Allotment Act; Soil Erosion Service/ Soil Conservation Service; *United States v. Butler et al.;* Peek, George; Wallace, Henry A.; Documents: Agricultural Adjustment Act, May 12, 1933; *United States v. Butler et al.,* 1936.

Bibliography

Kennedy, David M. *Freedom from Fear: The American People in Depression and War, 1929–1945.* New York: Oxford University Press, 1999.

Parsons, Kenneth H., Raymond J. Penn, and Philip M. Raup. *Land Tenure.* Madison: University of Wisconsin Press, 1951.

U.S. Department of State. *The United States Senate Committee on Agriculture, Nutrition, and Forestry 1825–1998,* Washington, DC: GPO, 1998.

Watkins, T. H. *The Hungry Years: A Narrative History of the Great Depression in America.* New York: Henry Holt, 1999.

AID TO DEPENDENT CHILDREN

On August 15, 1935, President Franklin D. Roosevelt signed into law the Social Security Act, a major piece of legislation dealing specifically with the country's social welfare. The act established federal old-age benefits as well as federal assistance to states, enabling "adequate provision for aged persons, blind persons, dependent and crippled children, maternal and child welfare, public health and the administration of their unemployment compensation laws." The Social Security Act was divided into categorical aid programs, promising limited amounts of matching federal to state funds. In approving these programs, the government claimed the participating individuals as federal responsibilities.

Social Security concentrated on providing federal financial assistance for the elderly, thus freeing state funds to be used, in part, for the care of dependent children. Among the various Social Security programs, Aid to Dependent Children (ADC) was formally created. The purpose of ADC was to assist mothers who could not support their dependent children on their own. The program was highly criticized because people feared that a program designed to aid single women would be perceived as governmental encouragement to destroy the traditional family structure. Therefore, in its original form, aid was given only to widowed mothers. Although ADC was intended as a liberal piece of legislation, the money allotted to it was much less than other Social Security programs got.

Interest in ADC and congressional committee recommendations largely resulted from a report to the Committee on Economic Security by the U.S. Children's Bureau. This report, focusing solely on harsh conditions faced by dependent children during the Great Depression, was aimed at insuring adequate income to all age groups.

Because of this report, experts in the area of welfare believed that the administration of the proposed grants-in-aid to states for dependent children would therefore be the responsibility of the Children's Bureau. However, in the final stage of planning, individuals within the Federal Emergency Relief Administration (FERA) took the position that aid to dependent children was a form of public assistance and therefore, it should be administered by their organization.

Opposition to FERA's jurisdiction over the proposed ADC arose, particularly from the Ways and Means Committee. It objected on the same grounds on which it had opposed the FERA's administration of old-age grants: The committee opposed handing over the administration of any part of the Social Security bill to an emergency agency. The House Ways and Means Committee then moved to vest the administration of federal grants in the Social Security Board. During its debate in the Senate, representatives of the Department of Labor suggested that administration of ADC be vested in the Children's Bureau. The Senate Finance Committee debated this briefly but offered no amendment to make this change. The Committee on Economic Security finally established FERA's responsibility for the administration of grants-in-aid to the states for ADC.

In its original form, the bill stated that the federal government would not pay more than one-third of the amounts expended by local and state governments on aid to dependent children. The Ways and Means Committee, however, proposed a maximum amount corresponding to the maximum amount granted in old-age compensation. One representative proposed that the amount should be the same as the maximum pension payable to children of servicemen who had died in World War I. This limitation would grant $18 a month for the first child and $12 for each additional child. However, one fact overlooked entirely during the debate was the $30 per month payment the widow received under the Veteran's Pension Act, which allowed for the care of the mother of the dependent children. The Senate adopted a motion on this provision and fixed federal aid for dependent children at $6 a month for the first child and $4 each for additional children.

Edwin Witte, the executive director of the Committee on Economic Security in 1935, argued that it was illogical to expect a mother with dependents to live solely on the $18 a month granted by the act, plus the $6 stipend for a first child and $4 stipend for each additional child. While his criticism was acknowledged, he claimed that little interest in removing the limitation existed on the part of Congress; thus no attempts were made to strike out the restriction. He further claimed that Congress exhibited little interest in general regarding ADC, as demonstrated by the limitation of federal compensation at one-third compared to other grants equaling one-half of the local and state expenditures.

Aid to Dependent Children is one of several programs emerging from the Social Security Act of 1935 that have remained and grown exponentially. Within the first few years of its existence, the number of recipients qualifying for ADC doubled, and the program was expanded to include children from broken homes. The program's name was changed in the 1950s to the more inclusive Aid to Families with Dependent Children.

JENNIFER FORBES

See also: women; youth; National Youth Administration.

Bibliography

Axinn, June, and Herman Levin. *Social Welfare: A History of the American Response to Need.* New York: Dodd, Mead, 1975.

McGovern, James R. *And a Time for Hope: America in the Great Depression.* Westport, CT: Praeger, 2000.

Patterson, James T. *America's Struggle Against Poverty 1900–1980.* Cambridge: Harvard University Press, 1981.

Witte, Edwin E. *The Development of the Social Security Act.* Madison: University of Wisconsin Press, 1962.

BANKING HOLIDAYS

A banking holiday occurred when a state or federal government ordered all banks to close for a given period of time to prevent panics in which mass numbers of depositors—fearful of bank failures—rushed to remove their money. These panics created liquidity crises that, in themselves, could precipitate the very failures that the depositors feared.

While bank runs and bank failures were hardly unknown in the 1920s, they escalated after the stock market crash in 1929 and especially after Britain announced it was going off the gold standard in September 1931. Whereas about 500 banks failed in an average year in the 1920s, roughly that number failed in the first month after the British gold decision. For 1931 as a whole, some 2,294 banks failed in the United States. Indeed, the United States was particularly prone to bank failures as it had a tradition of small, single-branch banking, which meant most banks did not have the financial resources to weather a run on deposits.

As the banking situation worsened in 1932 and early 1933, a number of states ordered banking holidays of varying length. During the interregnum between the Herbert Hoover and Franklin D. Roosevelt administrations—from November 1932 to March 1933—the banking situation grew drastically worse. As banks failed across the country, Hoover pleaded with the president-elect to make a reassuring statement about the safety of the banking system. But Roosevelt—wanting a fresh start when he took office—refused.

The crisis deepened. By the time Roosevelt took the oath of office on March 4, 1933, some thirty-two states had declared a banking holiday; in six others, virtually all banks were closed on the decision of their directors; and, in the remaining states, withdrawals were limited to small amounts per day.

On March 5, Roosevelt used the World War I–era Trading with the Enemy Act, which granted to the president the right to halt all transactions in gold, to announce a national banking holiday for four days—from Monday, March 6 until Thursday, March 9. Roosevelt and his advisers then sent the Emergency Banking Act to Congress. Among other things, the act gave the president broad powers over gold and foreign exchanges, expanded the Federal Reserve Board's capacity to issue currency, and authorized the opening of banks under close government control. Equally important was the psychological effect of this action, as well as the reassuring tones in which Roosevelt explained the act in his first fireside chat.

Due to technicalities, the banks could not open until Monday, March 13. And when they did, the panic had passed. Indeed, in most states, there were more deposits on opening day than withdrawals.

See also: banking; Emergency Banking Act; Federal Reserve Bank; Gold Reserve Act; Documents: Hoover's Outline of Program to Secure Cooperation of Bankers to Relieve Financial Difficulties, October 6, 1931; Fireside Chat on the Banking Crisis, March 12, 1933.

On his first full day as president in March 1933, President Franklin D. Roosevelt ordered a banking holiday—temporarily closing the nation's financial institutions—in order to revive depositor confidence. *(Brown Brothers)*

Bibliography

Kaufman, George G. *Banking Risk in Historical Perspective.* Chicago: Federal Reserve Bank of Chicago, 1986.

Wicker, Elmus. *The Banking Panics of the Great Depression.* New York: Cambridge University Press, 1996.

"BLACK CABINET"

The "black cabinet," as it was called, was a group of black intellectuals and activists who came to serve as advisers in the various government agencies of the Franklin D. Roosevelt administration. Virtually all of these "black cabinet" members advised the government on how to include Africans Americans in New Deal programs.

Until the 1930s, no African American had ever served as a government adviser, and, at first, the same was true of the Roosevelt administration. When the National Association for the Advancement of Colored People (NAACP) pressured the new administration to appoint an adviser on Negro affairs in 1933, Roosevelt and his Interior Secretary Harold Ickes chose a white civil rights activist, Clark Foreman, because Roosevelt feared alienating the white southerners in Congress whom he needed to get his New Deal legislation passed. Meanwhile, although the NAACP approved of Foreman, it did not like the idea of a white man representing black America.

Pressure on Ickes continued until a compromise was struck. Foreman would remained the adviser, while black economist Robert Weaver served as his assistant. Then, under the urging of the president's wife Eleanor, Ickes and Roosevelt established the Interdepartmental Group Concerned with the Special Problems of the Negroes, a group of blacks who met with white officials of various New Deal programs to assure that blacks were being included in these programs.

Gradually, more blacks were appointed to various junior positions within the administration, numbering forty-five by mid-1935. In 1936, these government advisers formed the Federal Council on Negro Affairs, referred to popularly as the "black brain trust" or the "black cabinet." Among its members were educator Mary McLeod Bethune, an informal adviser to Eleanor Roosevelt; NAACP head Walter White; and A. Philip Randolph, chief of the Brotherhood of Sleeping Car Porters. The group advised the administration on black issues and pushed for more black inclusion in New Deal public works and other programs. Strongly supportive of Roosevelt, they worked in the 1936 and 1940 elections to rally the northern black vote to support the administration and the Democrats.

See also: African Americans; National Association for the Advancement of Colored People; Bethune, Mary McLeod; Randolph, A. Philip.

Bibliography

Kirby, John B. *Black Americans in the Roosevelt Era: Liberalism and Race*. Knoxville: University of Tennessee Press, 1980.

Sitkoff, Harvard. *A New Deal for Blacks: The Emergence of Civil Rights as a National Issue*. Volume 1, *The Depression Years*. New York: Oxford University Press, 1978.

BONUS BILL

In 1924, Congress passed the World War Adjusted Compensation Act, which promised World War I veterans partial payment for their wartime service. This compensation, or bonus, would not be paid until 1945. With the coming of the Depression, however, many veterans lost their jobs and found themselves immersed in poverty. Desperate for assistance, they urged Congress to speed up payment of their bonuses.

In spring 1932, thousands of veterans descended on Washington, demanding a new bonus bill. While the Bonus Army, as these veterans were called, was camped in the city in June, the House of Representatives passed a bonus bill providing payment of $2.4 billion that had been promised for 1945. The Senate, however, rejected the bill. Most of the veterans then left Washington but about 2,000 remained. In July, President Herbert Hoover called for them to disperse. The veterans refused, and the government, using cavalry, infantry, and tanks, forcibly removed the remaining members of the Bonus Army.

In 1933, another attempt was made to enact a bonus bill, but President Franklin D. Roosevelt opposed the measure. Indeed, the new president—in an attempt to balance the federal budget—even cut veteran benefits by 50 percent. In 1936, Congress finally passed a new bonus bill. President Roosevelt vetoed it, but Congress overrode the veto, and the bonus promised to World War I veterans was paid.

See also: Bonus Army; Garner, John Nance; Hoover, Herbert; Wagner, Robert; Document: Veto of Amendment to World War Veterans' Bonus Act, June 26, 1930.

Bibliography

Bartlett, John Henry. *The Bonus March and The New Deal*. Chicago: M. A. Donohue, 1937.

Daniels, Roger. *The Bonus March*. Westport, CT: Greenwood, 1971.

BRAIN TRUST

Originally known as the "brains trust," a term coined by a *New York Times* political reporter, the Brain Trust referred to a number of academics who were brought into the Franklin D. Roosevelt administration to advise on measures necessary to combat the economic depression gripping the country in the 1930s.

Raymond Moley, a Columbia University criminal justice professor, was the original member of the Brain Trust. He had worked with Roosevelt on justice issues when the latter was governor of New York state from 1928 to 1932. As Roosevelt began to plan his first presidential campaign in early 1932, he asked Moley to bring in other academics to advise him on various issues.

Over the next few months, Roosevelt began to meet regularly with Columbia University economist Rexford Tugwell and Columbia Law School professor Adolf Berle Jr. Along with Roosevelt's old law partner Basil O'Connor and Hugh Johnson, a protégé of financier and Democratic Party leader Bernard Baruch, these men formed the Brain Trust.

Unifying this team were an intense loyalty to Roosevelt, a belief that the Depression was essentially a domestic—as opposed to international—economic problem, a conviction that regulatory bodies needed to be created to fix the problems of the American capitalist system, and a general support of inflationary government policies. Still, there were great differences among the members as well. Berle, for example, was a conservative former Herbert Hoover supporter, while Tugwell was quite liberal and advocated income redistribution.

The Brain Trust was important for both substantive and psychological reasons. Its ideas helped shape much New Deal policy while its presence in the administration—much touted in the national press—helped convince many Americans that the best minds were at work on the problems the nation faced.

See also: New Deal, first; election of 1932; Baruch, Bernard; Berle, Adolf, Jr.; Johnson, Hugh; Moley, Raymond; Tugwell, Rexford.

Columbia professor Rexford Tugwell was a key member of Franklin D. Roosevelt's so-called Brain Trust of economic advisers. *(Brown Brothers)*

Bibliography

Rosen, Elliot A. *Hoover, Roosevelt, and the Brains Trust: From Depression to New Deal.* New York: Columbia University Press, 1977.

Tugwell, Rexford. *The Brains Trust.* New York: Viking, 1968.

BUDGET, FEDERAL

The Great Depression drove federal budget policy in the 1930s. Federal outlays increased, government commitments expanded, and, by the end of the decade, a new economic worldview was adopted by federal policy-makers, all results of the attempt to mitigate the economic devastation of the Depression for business and the unemployed. Government taxing and spending went through a period of sustained expansion throughout the New Deal. From 1932 to 1941, federal tax receipts rose 281 percent from $3.1 billion to $8.7 billion, and spending increased 291 percent from $4.7 billion to $13.7 billion.

THE DEPRESSION AND DEFICIT SPENDING

In the 1932 presidential election, Democratic standard-bearer Franklin D. Roosevelt blasted President Herbert Hoover's management of the budget, blaming him for creating a $2.6 billion deficit. (The cause of the deficit was a Depression-sparked 29 percent falloff in tax receipts from the previous year.) Roosevelt promised to cut federal spending and close the deficit. Early in 1933, Congress passed the Roosevelt administration's Economy bill, a measure that cut war pensions and federal salaries.

Throughout his presidency, Roosevelt maintained a commitment to balancing the budget, at least in theory. Roosevelt believed that "sound budgeting" would restore business confidence, and he shared the Democratic Party's traditional distrust of federal spending and deficits as threats to individual liberty. But facing the crisis of massive unemployment, breadlines, business failure, and farm and home foreclosures, Roosevelt came to accept a more expansive view of budgeting, popular among members of his Brain Trust, that the budget should be balanced over the course of the business cycle, running deficits during economic downturns and surpluses during boom times. Such an outlook allowed Roosevelt to stake out the middle ground between the demands of southern conservatives and industrialists for frugality and the calls of liberals, labor unions, and big-city mayors for spending programs to aid the unemployed. It also allowed the administration a degree of freedom in managing budget policy that was not bound to any rigid ideological framework or faction.

In the first few years of the New Deal, Roosevelt trimmed traditional department expenditures to pacify conservatives and build business confidence, but increased emergency appropriations for work relief and public works. The president argued that additional federal spending was the best method of restoring balanced budget conditions and assured the public that the New Deal recovery program was built on "granite foundations in a period of confusion." In 1933, most of a $3.3 billion appropriation under Title II of the National Industrial Recovery Act was funneled through the Public Works Administration (PWA) to underwrite the costs of large capital construction projects. The amount of $1.7 billion was appropriated to the Federal Emergency Relief Administration to provide grants to the states for welfare relief for the unemployed, an increase of 260 percent from the previous year. When unemployment spiked in the fall of 1933, $805 million was appropriated to the Civil Works Administration (CWA) to carry out labor-intensive, light-capital projects. The administration also started a system of cash transfers and price supports for farmers under the Agricultural Adjustment Act of 1933. Appropriations for the Agricultural Adjustment program averaged $496 million a year from 1934 to 1938.

Despite the increase in emergency appropriations, the administration remained committed to balanced budget orthodoxy. With signs of recovery in the spring of 1934, Roosevelt shut down the CWA. Administration officials like PWA administrator Harold Ickes and Budget Director Lewis Douglas hoped that state and local governments would eventually repay the federal government for the emergency loans and grants made for capital projects once economic conditions improved.

Emboldened by Democratic gains in 1934, and frustrated by the slow pace of the economic recovery, Roosevelt shepherded the Emergency Relief Appropriation Act to passage in 1935. Congress appropriated $4.9 billion in emergency funding, giving Roosevelt a blank check to disperse aid as he saw fit. An additional $1.2 billion was funneled through a newly created agency, the Works Progress Administration (WPA), headed by Roosevelt's close aide, Harry Hopkins. Much like the CWA, the WPA was a job program intended to put the unemployed to work on light construction and civic enrichment projects. The WPA became the most important social welfare discretionary program for the remainder of the New Deal, with average expenditures of $1.9 billion a year from 1936 to 1941.

Much of the growth of government was also fueled by the "off-budget" expenditures of the Reconstruction Finance Corporation (RFC), which was charted by Congress to offer credit to state and local governments, businesses, and emergency relief agencies. The RFC authorized $8 billion in loans from 1933 to 1936.

Roosevelt's turn to the left in the "Second New Deal" also brought about the passage of the Social Security Act in 1935, the first major universal entitlement program aimed at providing retirement benefits for the elderly, as well as modest disability and unemployment insurance for workers and aid to dependent mothers and children. Despite the historic significance of the Social Security Act, the budgetary impact of the new social welfare programs it created was small in the 1930s. The dedicated payroll tax for Social Security collected in a trust fund, and there were no significant draws on the account until the 1940s. Federal aid to the states to administer Social Security and supplement welfare payments totaled an average expenditure of $329 million a year from 1937 to 1941. In this period, the Revenue Act of 1935 made the income tax structure more progressive, creating a top rate of 75 percent. The tax bill added $250 million in government revenue in fiscal year 1936.

Roosevelt trimmed spending at the first sustained signs of economic recovery, cutting federal government by 9.8 percent, and lowering the deficit to $89 million, for fiscal year 1938. The subsequent downturn was dubbed the "Roosevelt recession." Liberals blamed the recession on the spending cuts. Influenced by Harry Hopkins, Roosevelt reversed course for fiscal year 1939, increasing total spending by 134 percent from the previous year in order to stimulate economic growth. The budget deficit, which nearly had been zeroed out the year before, ballooned to a then historic high of $2.8 billion. Gearing up for the conflict in Europe, Roosevelt increased military expenditures in the late 1930s too. Spending on national defense increased 655 percent from 1937 to 1941, with an average expenditure of $1.2 billion from 1937 to 1941, jumping to $6 billion in 1942.

FEDERAL BUDGET POLICY AND ECONOMIC THEORY

A long-standing question surrounding federal budget policy in the 1930s concerns the impact of the economic thought of English economist John Maynard

Keynes among administration officials and the president himself. In its most distilled form, Keynesian theory argues that depressed economies enter into "liquidity traps" that no amount of monetary manipulation (that is, low interest rates) can remedy. In the depths of a severe depression, confidence is low, and business will not seek out credit to expand, produce, and hire. Government spending puts cash in the hands of consumers and stimulates production. Government deficits and work and relief programs, long viewed by traditional economists as wasteful, inefficient drags on the economy, are in the Keynesian paradigm, tools to be employed to keep the national income high and the economy at its most productive, to make sure that no resources remain idle.

Keynes met with Roosevelt on one occasion, but the economist had little direct impact on the president's thinking. Most American policy intellectuals did not absorb Keynesian thought until the late 1930s. But proto-Keynesian views—policy proscriptions without theoretical foundations—were popular among the president's advisers. There was a general sense among administration officials, such as PWA administrator Ickes, WPA director Hopkins, and Federal Reserve Board chair Marriner Eccles, that government programs were needed to revitalize the economy and that deficits were an insignificant side effect of the interventionist cure. Traditionalists like treasury secretary Henry Morgenthau remained influential within the administration, however, arguing that a balanced budget would restore business confidence, which, in turn, would power a recovery. Budget director Lewis Douglas went so far as to write the president in 1934 that the "immediate fate of western civilization" hinged on Roosevelt's "real determination to bring the budget into balance."

The president's attempt to balance the budget in fiscal year 1938 demonstrates that he was temperamentally disposed to favor budget orthodoxy over newer approaches. But after the brush with "Roosevelt's depression," the administration moved toward a classic fiscal stimulus response to an economic slowdown, suggesting that the administration was slowly learning the techniques of modern economic management.

THE FEDERAL BUDGET AND CONSTITUTIONAL ISSUES

The balance of power over budget policy shifted from Congress to the president in the 1930s. Solid Democratic majorities in Congress yielded power to their party leader in the White House because of the prevailing sense of economic crisis. Congress allocated

TABLE 1
TOTAL RECEIPTS, OUTLAYS, AND SURPLUS/DEFICIT, FEDERAL BUDGET, 1931–41 (IN MILLIONS OF DOLLARS).

Year	Receipts	Outlays	Surplus/Deficit
1931	3,116	3,577	−462
1932	1,924	4,659	−2,735
1933	1,997	4,598	−2,602
1934	2,955	6,541	−3,586
1935	3,609	6,412	−2,803
1936	3,923	8,228	−4,304
1937	5,387	7,580	−2,193
1938	6,751	6,840	−89
1939	6,295	9,141	−2,846
1940	6,548	9,468	−2,920
1941	8,721	13,653	−4,941

Source: Office of Management and Budget. *Budget of the United States Government, Fiscal Year 2000, Historical Tables.* Washington, DC: Government Printing Office, 2000.

lump-sum emergency appropriations with responsibility for disbursement, policy-making, and oversight carried out by the administrators of the "alphabet soup" agencies of the New Deal. Most famous, the 1935 Emergency Relief Act appropriations cleared Congress before the president decided on the establishment of the agency that would control most of those funds, the Works Progress Administration. In addition to congressional quiescence, the executive branch's power over the budget increased because of the growing complexity of federal commitments and administration. The 1939 Reorganization Act moved the Bureau of Budget (BoB) from the Treasury Department into the newly created Executive Office of the President. From its new perch closer to the White House, BoB became the central clearinghouse for the executive branch's spending proposals and management initiatives.

The growth in the federal budget in the 1930s also changed the relationship among federal, state, and local governments. Before the 1930s, separate, legally restricted spheres of conduct defined American federalism, with little interaction between governments. The 1930s marked a new era of cooperation. Much of the emergency expenditure of the New Deal was funneled to state and local governments through a grants-in-aid system that provided for federal matches, funding formulas, loans, and outright awards to subfederal governments to build public construction projects and provide relief. Big-city mayors worked closely with the federal government to coordinate policy, establishing a lobbying organization in Washington to maintain a presence in national politics.

Finally, in the New Deal the federal government in the 1930s adopted new commitments and responsibilities to provide for social welfare and insurance protections, agricultural market stabilization, and public works development. Perhaps most important, the president assumed responsibility for management of the macroeconomic policy, a duty that voters hold the contemporary president accountable to today.

See also: Keynesian economics; Economy Act; Federal Reserve Bank; public works; Revenue Act of 1932; Taxation; Wealth Tax Act; Eccles, Marriner; Documents: Veto of Amendment to World War Veterans' Bonus Act, June 26, 1930; Hoover's speech warning on deficit spending, February 25, 1930; Democratic Party platform, 1932; Republican Party platform, 1932; Democratic Party platform, 1936; Republican Party platform, 1936; Democratic Party platform, 1940; Republican Party platform, 1940.

RICHARD FLANAGAN

Bibliography

Amenta, Edwin. *Bold Relief: Institutional Politics and the Origins of Modern American Social Policy.* Princeton: Princeton University Press, 1996.

Bureau of the Census. *Statistical Abstract of the United States.* Washington, DC: Government Printing Office. Various editions.

Office of Management and Budget. *Budget of the United States Government, Fiscal Year 2000, Historical Tables.* Washington, DC: Government Printing Office, 2000.

Savage, John. *Balanced Budgets and American Politics.* Ithaca: Cornell University Press, 1990.

Stein, Herbert. *The Fiscal Revolution in America.* Chicago: University of Chicago Press, 1969.

CIVIL RIGHTS SECTION (DEPARTMENT OF JUSTICE)

The Civil Rights Section (now the Civil Rights Division) of the United States Department of Justice was created by Attorney General Frank Murphy in 1939 to investigate civil rights violation and racial discrimination within the federal government.

Murphy had a distinguished record supporting civil rights and workers' rights. As governor of Michigan, he had refused to call in the National Guard during the sit-down strikes at General Motors in 1936–37. He was a member of the board of directors of the National Association for the Advancement of Colored People and a personal friend of its executive secretary, Walter White.

Murphy's decision to create the Civil Rights Section was one of his first decisions at the Justice Department. Its purpose, he said, was "the aggressive protection of fundamental rights inherent in a free people." In a letter to President D. Franklin Roosevelt, Murphy explained his decision: "For the first time in our history, the full weight of the Department will be thrown behind the effort" to enforce existing civil rights laws, as well as to make inquiries "into the need for additional legislation."

African-American leaders were exhilarated. As William Hastie, one of the few relatively high-ranking black officials in the Roosevelt administration, wrote to White, "the worst fears of the unregenerate [white] south are being realized."

See also: African Americans; National Association for the Advancement of Colored People; Hastie, William; Murphy, Frank; White, Walter.

Bibliography

Kirby, John B. *Black Americans in the Roosevelt Era: Liberalism and Race.* Knoxville: University of Tennessee Press, 1980.

Sitkoff, Harvard. *A New Deal for Blacks: The Emergence of Civil Rights as a National Issue.* Vol. 1, *The Depression Years.* New York: Oxford University Press, 1978.

CIVIL WORKS ADMINISTRATION

One of the more short-lived of the New Deal agencies, the Civil Works Administration (CWA) was created on November 9, 1933, and ended on March 31, 1934. Nevertheless, during its nearly five months in operation, the CWA paid out over $800 million and put some 4.2 million unemployed men and women to work.

The CWA was the brainchild of Harry Hopkins, the former social worker who had been put in charge of the Federal Emergency Relief Administration (FERA) at the very beginning of the Franklin D. Roosevelt presidency. But Hopkins had grown disenchanted with the FERA for several reasons: it offered more relief than work; it imposed demeaning means testing; and it was administered by unsympathetic local authorities.

With another desperate winter of the Depression approaching, Hopkins convinced Roosevelt to set up the CWA, which would be open to all unemployed persons, provide work instead of relief checks, pay the prevailing minimum wage in the region, and be administered through federal agencies like the Veterans Administration and the newly created Public Works Administration.

While the CWA built few large projects—there were not enough blueprints and engineering plans available—it refurbished roads, bridges, schools, and hospitals. It even constructed over 150,000 sanitary outhouses for rural families. But Roosevelt, still worried that people would become too dependent on government relief, decided to cancel the program as soon as the weather turned warm again in spring 1934.

See also: Federal Emergency Relief Administration; New Deal, first; Public Works Administration; Hopkins, Harry; Roosevelt, Franklin D.

Bibliography

Hopkins, Harry Lloyd. *Spending to Save: The Complete Story of Relief.* New York: W. W. Norton 1936.

Hopkins, June. *Harry Hopkins: Sudden Hero, Brash Reformer.* New York: St. Martin's, 1999.

CIVILIAN CONSERVATION CORPS

The Great Depression struck hard at the U.S. economy as it did other countries, leaving roughly 14 million Americans unemployed. Upon taking office for his first term, President Franklin D. Roosevelt launched a series of measures and programs known as the New Deal, which was created to combat the Great Depression. One of the main programs was the Civilian Conservation Corps (CCC). The CCC sought to create work and stability for many young unemployed men throughout the country. By the end of the program in 1942, almost 3 million men had found gainful employment through the CCC. Created in April 1933, the agency was a significant component of Roosevelt's economic package and would become one of the most successful, popular, and well known of the New Deal programs as well as a particular point of pride for Roosevelt.

The Roosevelt administration was reluctant to provide relief without work requirements because it believed such relief would contribute to laziness and spiritual demoralization among recipients. At the same time, the federal government recognized the need to provide relief, often referred to as "priming the pump," due to the severe economic distress of the country. The creation of the CCC seemed to provide straightforward answers to these needs and concerns. The unemployed masses could be utilized to address environmental and infrastructure problems that had been worsening in the previous decades.

Control and management of the CCC was placed in the hands of the Department of War, and the units were organized along military lines. The Departments of Agriculture and Interior designated and supervised specific work projects. Enrollees were paid $30 a month, $25 of which was sent home, leaving the enrollees with $5 spending money. This system provided relief funds for families and spread the money across the economy. Although the CCC initially instituted age limitations and one-time enrollments of six months, the program grew politically popular and garnered further and increased appropriations so age limits were

expanded and enrollees were allowed to serve multiple terms.

THE CIVILIAN CONSERVATION CORPS MISSION

Popular images of the CCC depict workers building roads, planting trees, and working on erosion control projects. These images are accurate: CCC workers built hundreds of thousands of miles of trails and roads, planted billions of trees, and restored and protected millions of acres of land through rangeland restoration and erosion-control measures. Erosion control was an important element in the CCC mission. Intensive farming coupled with years of intense drought—the most vivid example being the dust bowl of the Great Plains states—had created damaging erosion on farmlands throughout the country. Under CCC auspices, new dams were built to control water flow, and soil control techniques such as terrace farming were initiated. CCC workers built many of the new terraces on agricultural land. Also, the young men cleared out ditches filled with downed trees, stabilized stream banks through shrub and tree plantings, and used numerous other strategies to control erosion. An important consequence of the erosion-control program was that many corps workers from farming communities took erosion-control methods home with them after their term of service to implement in their own farming practices, thereby spreading knowledge and practice of new, important agricultural ideas.

The CCC was not limited to tree planting, erosion control, and trail building, but engaged in a wider variety of projects than those popularly depicted. The agency also responded to emergency situations, which strengthened its widespread popularity and expanded the representation of the federal government. The corps fought floods in New York in 1937 and in Colorado in 1942, blizzards in the West during the winter of 1937–38, and even a hurricane in New England in 1938. The corps was also employed extensively to fight

The Civilian Conservation Corps put hundreds of thousands of mostly young Americans to work in rural parts of the country during the 1930s. *(Library of Congress)*

forest fires, on both private and national forest land and land throughout the country, and to build close to 100,000 miles of road improving access to fire-prone forests. Additionally, the corps built thousands of towers that were used for fire detection. Members of the agency improved habitat for wildlife, stocked fish in some areas, and embarked on many campaigns of pest control, particularly those threatening the health of national forests.

CIVILIAN CONSERVATION CORPS AND EDUCATION

While the CCC is justifiably well known for its public works projects, the corps also provided a useful function in educating young men and providing them with basic work skills. Members of the corps were provided with education in high school subjects, vocational courses, and even some college-level courses. Many high school diplomas and even a few college degrees were granted through the educational program. Teachers within the CCC particularly targeted illiteracy, and

by the end of the program roughly 40,000 illiterate members had learned to read and write. Much has been made of this educational effort, but it must be noted that many teachers suffered from inadequate classroom space and a paucity of educational materials and were often teaching outside of their fields. Consequently, the turnover rate for teachers in the CCC was high. Overall, though, the program succeeded in teaching basic skills. Similarly, the CCC's vocational training focused on skills such as truck driving, construction, and masonry, helping enrollees obtain better paying jobs after leaving the CCC.

NATIVE AMERICANS AND AFRICAN AMERICANS IN THE CIVILIAN CONSERVATION CORPS

The CCC extended its mission onto Indian reservations in an effort to provide employment for Indian men and accomplish necessary restoration projects. These units shared the same principles as the regular units but varied in significant ways. The Bureau of Indian Affairs rather than the Department of War, managed the Indian CCC. It did not set age limitations, and it demonstrated much more flexibility in camp construction. The Indian CCC set up small camps of men on the reservation; it created family camps of varying quality; and in some places, such as in Oklahoma, where Indians owned small farms and lived close together, the enrollees continued living at home and were picked up by CCC trucks for work.

The activities of the CCC on Indian reservations focused on restoring degraded landscapes. Land of marginal quality in most cases had deteriorated severely due to the pressures of overgrazing, logging, and erosion. The workers enacted erosion control measures such as check and diversion dams, planted trees, and restored grazing lands on Indian reservations throughout the country. The goals of these projects were to restore and improve Indian self-sufficiency on the reservations as well as provide necessary jobs and income.

The leadership of the Indian CCC resisted implementing educational programs for several years until increasing pressure from Washington, D.C., forced them to institute classes focusing on literacy and vocational skills. The educational efforts on the reservations improved after 1938 so significant vocational training accompanied CCC projects. Enrollees were educated in surveying skills while working on rangelands, masonry techniques while building dams for water storage and control, and in the operation of heavy equipment like trucks.

The black experience in the CCC differed in many ways from those of the Indian and white enrollees. If anything, African Americans needed relief more than white enrollees, since most African Americans suffered disproportionately from the economic impacts of the Great Depression. Young African-American men rushed to sign up for enlistments in the CCC but quickly encountered obstructions. In the South, there was a marked reluctance to allow blacks to enroll in the program, and in the West, there was little effort to publicize the program in African-American communities. Upon joining the CCC, many blacks encountered racist attitudes on the part of white fellow enrollees and white leadership. Racial slurs triggered a race riot at Camp Osborne Springs, Idaho, and there were violent incidents at CCC camps in the Cleveland National Forest and near Chico, California. In fact, local white communities protested against black CCC units throughout the country. This resistance to racially integrated camps led CCC director Robert Fechner to institute segregation between blacks and whites throughout the corps and to curb the number of African-American enrollees.

The policy of segregation came under intense attack immediately. Members of the NAACP directed their complaints not only to Fechner but also to Roosevelt. These complaints were ignored because the leadership of the CCC argued that African-American enrollees preferred segregation, a belief not supported by the opinions of the enrollees themselves. The segregated African-American CCC camps were similar to other camps in that the enrollees were provided with limited educational classes and recreational sports, working on projects during the day. Despite the racism they met, many black workers remember the experience with fondness, and the relief provided through the agency strengthened many families in dire straits.

PROBLEMS WITHIN THE CIVILIAN CONSERVATION CORPS

Although the CCC never lost its popular appeal for the mass of Americans, it did suffer from a few significant problems. Desertion of enrollees represented a major problem for the CCC throughout its existence. A number of factors contributed to this problem. The lack of a well-developed orientation program hindered the ability of the young men, many away from home for the first time, to adjust to barracks life, the military regimen, and the rural locale of their new jobs. Many left due to homesickness and an inability to cope with camp life. During later years, when the economy improved, some deserted in order to pursue newly available jobs. When World War II broke out in Europe and Asia, some enrollees were increasingly reluctant to remain in the CCC for fear that it might lead to their being drafted into military service.

In addition to the problems with desertion, there were some well-publicized mutinies by discontented workers. In fall 1937, roughly 100 enrollees in five CCC camps in Shenandoah National Park in Virginia were dismissed from the agency for refusing to work. In a camp in Virginia in 1939 there was a riot between southern enrollees and Pennsylvania enrollees, with several young men receiving serious injuries.

THE SUCCESS OF THE CIVILIAN CONSERVATION CORPS

The corps was successful in a number of respects. Most important, it provided meaningful employment and income for millions of unemployed men during a period of despair, thereby creating hope and self-confidence. Through the distribution of funds, the government ensured that this program supported families. The CCC also likely contributed to social stability during this time by keeping young men, always a potentially volatile group, busy with physical labor and meaningful work. Moreover, the CCC proved successful in improving the infrastructure and environment of American society. Beautiful Timberline Lodge on Mt. Hood in Oregon still stands as a tourist resort and a reminder of the accomplishments of this agency, as do numerous state parks, reservoirs, and hiking trails. Additionally, many members of the CCC still recall their experiences as largely positive and tranformative in their lives.

The end for the CCC came primarily for economic reasons. The shifting of the depression economy to a war economy created full employment across the country, with many well-paying jobs. The CCC had failed to achieve any status beyond that of relief agency, so, with full employment available, the justifications for continuing the program faded. Finally, in 1942, a popular program that employed 3 million men, kept families from starvation, and provided necessary infrastructure improvements came to a quiet end.

JEFF CRANE

See also: agriculture; youth; Soil Conservation and Domestic Allotment Act; Soil Erosion Service/Soil Conservation Service.

Bibliography

Cole Olen, Jr. *The African-American Experience in the Civilian Conservation Corps*. Gainesville: University Press of Florida, 1999.

Hill, Edwin G. *In the Shadow of the Mountain: The Spirit of the CCC*. Pullman: Washington State University Press, 1990.

Lacy, Leslie Alexander. *The Soil Soldiers: The Civilian Conservation Corps in the Great Depression*. Radnor, PA: Chilton Book Company, 1976.

Merrill, Perry H. *Roosevelt's Forest Army: A History of the Civilian Conservation Corps*. Barre, VT: Northlight Studio Press, 1981.

Parman, Donald L. "The Indian and the Civilian Conservation Corps." In *The American Indian*, ed. Norris Hundley. Santa Barbara: University of California Press, 1974.

Salmond, John A. *The Civilian Conservation Corps, 1933–42: A New Deal Case Study*. Durham, NC: Duke University Press, 1967.

COMMODITY CREDIT CORPORATION

The Commodity Credit Corporation was created in October 1933 to offer government loans to farmers. The collateral for those loans was provided by the farmer's crops, but the loans given were for more than the market price of those same crops.

Based on Herbert Hoover's Farm Boards—which were part of his Reconstruction Finance Corporation (RFC), an economic coordination agency—the Commodity Credit Corporation was originally funded through an RFC appropriation and intended largely for cotton farmers.

Under the Commodity Credit Corporation, farmers repaid the loans if market prices rose. If they did not, then the farmers did not have to pay the loan, but the government kept the crop. While it was initially hoped that government production controls would drive up crop prices and prevent the government being overwhelmed with crops, surpluses nevertheless grew quite large. By 1940, the corporation held over $300 million worth of cotton, as well as smaller amounts of grains.

See also: agriculture; Agricultural Adjustment Act; Farm Credit Administration; Federal Crop Insurance Program; Reconstruction Finance Corporation.

Bibliography

Saloutos, Theodore. *The American Farmer and the New Deal*. Ames: Iowa State University Press, 1982.

ECONOMY ACT (1933)

Introduced during the very first days of the Franklin D. Roosevelt administration, the Economy Act cut the federal budget by $500 million.

Roosevelt, whose campaign against Herbert Hoover included criticism of the growing federal budget, introduced the Economy Act to Congress with the remark that "for three long years the Federal Government has been on the road to bankruptcy." Like many others at the time, Roosevelt in 1933 believed that a balanced budget was essential for economic recovery.

While as much as one-third of the Democratic caucus in Congress protested the measure, it passed on the votes of Republicans and conservative Democrats. Ultimately, the act aggravated the deflationary crisis, hurting farmers in particular and leading to passage of the Agricultural Adjustment Act in May 1933.

See also: Agricultural Adjustment Act; budget, federal.

Bibliography

Moley, Raymond, and Eliot A. Rosen. *The First New Deal*. New York: Harcourt, Brace & World, 1966.

Romasco, Albert U. *The Politics of Recovery*. New York: Oxford University Press, 1983.

EMERGENCY BANKING ACT (1933)

The Emergency Banking Act was one of the very first pieces of legislation of the Franklin D. Roosevelt administration, passed by Congress on March 9, 1933. The act gave Roosevelt extraordinary powers to save the American banking system, including control over foreign exchange and gold transactions. The act also gave the Federal Reserve Board expanded powers to issue currency and allowed the government, through the Reconstruction Finance Corporation, to buy stock in banking companies. Finally, the act allowed for the reopening of banks—closed by Roosevelt on March 4—under careful government supervision.

The background for the act was the banking panic of early 1933, when most of the nation's states had declared banking holidays, closing financial institutions to prevent runs by depositors which had caused thousands of bank failures in the early years of the Depression. When Roosevelt came to office, he declared a national banking holiday under the World War I–era Trading with the Enemy Act, which gave the president extraordinary powers over the banking system.

The banking holiday had an immediate positive effect. When banks reopened on March 13, the panic had ended and there were more deposits than withdrawals. Many critics of the banking system, demanding nationalization, were disappointed that Roosevelt had chosen to rescue, rather than dismantle, the existing financial order. As one congressman said, remarking on the new president's inaugural address that was highly critical of the nation's financial leaders, "The President drove the moneychangers out of the Capitol on March fourth—and they were back on the ninth."

See also: banking holidays; Banking Act (1935); Federal Reserve Bank.

Bibliography

Freidel, Frank. *Launching the New Deal*. Boston: Little, Brown, 1973.

Moley, Raymond. *After Seven Years*. New York: Harper and Brothers, 1939.

EMERGENCY RELIEF AND CONSTRUCTION ACT

EMERGENCY EDUCATIONAL PROGRAM

The Emergency Educational Program (EEP) was a division of the Civil Works Administration (CWA) that put some 50,000 teachers to work. It also helped educate more than 1 million students in grade and high schools, colleges, and adult education programs nationwide.

The Civil Works Administration itself was passed by an executive order of President Franklin D. Roosevelt in November 1933. Under the order—advocated by relief coordinator Harry Hopkins—some $400 million was shifted from other government programs to finance job programs under the CWA.

The impetus behind the EEP was the dire financial shape of many of the nation's school districts during the Great Depression. With city and state budgets collapsing under the weight of lower tax revenues and expanded relief programs, school financing was cut drastically, leading to the firing of many teachers. Many educators, like those in Chicago, had been working for months without pay, while others, like those in New York, had seen their salaries cut by up to 33 percent. In rural areas, school finances were even worse, with some school districts closing down altogether.

Ultimately, the EEP provided but a fraction of the funds necessary to get the nation's schools back on a sound financial footing. Still, the program was the first significant acknowledgement of the federal government's role in education since the Freedmen's Bureau schools of the Reconstruction era in the 1860s and 1870s.

See also: education; Civil Works Administration; Hopkins, Harry.

Bibliography

Cremin, Lawrence. *American Education: The Metropolitan Experience.* New York: Harper & Row, 1988.

Moreo, Dominic W. *Schools in the Great Depression.* New York: Garland, 1996.

EMERGENCY RELIEF AND CONSTRUCTION ACT

The Emergency Relief and Construction Act was passed by Congress in the early summer of 1932 and signed into law by President Herbert Hoover on July 21. The act provided $322.2 million in federal money for public works programs. The legislation also authorized another $300 million in Reconstruction Finance Corporation loans to states that could demonstrate extraordinary need.

Hoover was reluctant to sign the bill, as it went against his philosophical belief that relief was a local and state matter and that balancing the budget was the federal government's main duty in fighting the economic depression gripping the nation. Indeed, Hoover had vetoed a much larger public works bill of some $2.2 billion the previous February. Deemed "neither an adequate nor an impressive piece of legislation" by *Fortune* magazine, the act is viewed by most historians as providing too little, too late, to alleviate the employment crisis facing the country in 1932.

See also: Reconstruction Finance Corporation; Hoover, Herbert.

Bibliography

Smith, Gene. *The Shattered Dream: Herbert Hoover and the Great Depression.* New York: William Morrow, 1970.

Smith, Richard Norton. *An Uncommon Man: The Triumph of Herbert Hoover.* New York: Simon & Schuster, 1984.

EMERGENCY RELIEF APPROPRIATIONS ACT (1935)

The largest peacetime appropriations bill in American history up to its time, the Emergency Relief Appropriations Act of 1935 authorized nearly $5 billion to be spent on public works programs, including nearly $1 billion shifted from other government programs. The act provided additional funds for existing public works programs—including the Public Works Administration and the Civilian Conservation Corps—and financed entirely new ones, most notably, the Works Progress Administration.

Calling it the "big bill," President Franklin D. Roosevelt, who introduced it into Congress in early spring, did not see it as emergency legislation, despite its name. Instead, Roosevelt viewed the bill as a means to create permanent full-time employment by permitting the government to hire surplus unskilled and uneducated labor.

Roosevelt insisted that the act would fund labor-intensive projects that would enhance the nation's infrastructure, rather than temporary make-work projects. And, indeed, the Works Progress Adminstration eventually built thousands of schools, bridges, public buildings, highways, airports, and other major infrastructure projects.

See also: public works; Civilian Conservation Corps; Public Works Administration; Works Progress Administration; Roosevelt, Franklin D.

Bibliography

Howard, Donald S. *The WPA and Federal Relief Policy*. New York: Russell Sage Foundation, 1943.

Rose, Nancy E. *Put to Work: Relief Programs in the Great Depression*. New York: Monthly Review Press, 1994.

FAIR EMPLOYMENT PRACTICES COMMITTEE

The Fair Employment Practices Committee was established by President Franklin D. Roosevelt's Executive Order 8802, issued in June 1941. The committee was created to prevent racial discrimination in hiring and promotions at defense plants. Under the order, the committee had the power both to investigate complaints and to require remedies.

The impetus for the order came from the March on Washington Movement. Organized by Brotherhood of Sleeping Car Porters head A. Philip Randolph, the march was supposed to bring thousands of African Americans to Washington to demand equal hiring practices at defense plants, the integration of the military, and other racial justice measures.

To avoid a potentially explosive racial reaction by conservatives in Congress and elsewhere, Roosevelt agreed to issue the order if Randolph called off the march. Ironically, while desegregation of the military was Randolph's main concern, the order included no mention of it. Ultimately, the FEPC did very little to alleviate discrimination at defense plants. Underfunded and understaffed, the committee could investigate in timely fashion only a fraction of the complaints brought before it, and the FEPC offering very few remedial actions.

See also: March on Washington Movement; Randolph, A. Philip.

Bibliography

Garfinkel, Herbert. *When Negroes March: The March on Washington Movement in the Organizational Politics for FEPC*. New York: Atheneum, 1959.

Pfeffer, Paula. *A. Philip Randolph: Pioneer of the Civil Rights Movement*. Baton Rouge: Louisiana State University Press, 1990.

FAIR LABOR STANDARDS ACT

The Fair Labor Standards Act of 1938 (FLSA) was one of the last great pieces of New Deal legislation. Coming after the Social Security Act and the National Labor Relations Act, it is all too often overlooked, yet its impact was widespread. Although greatly amended, major sections of it are still in force today. The FLSA outlawed child labor and established a national minimum wage, maximum workweek, and mandatory time-and-a-half for overtime for workers in industry. (Workers in agriculture and domestic service were not covered.) Like other New Deal acts, the FLSA had a long and complicated history. And, like all social legislation, it was far from perfect.

EARLY REFORM EFFORTS

The roots of the FLSA date to the early twentieth century social reform movement. Progressive Era reformers organized to end the more oppressive working conditions in industrial America and to deal with the contradictions of modern industrial life. The minimum wage movement, like many reform efforts of the era, sought a legislative remedy. It took as its model the 1909 British Trades Board Act, which permitted the government the right to intervene in industrial affairs. The British law argued that sweatshops were parasitic, forcing labor costs onto other businesses and charities, and that sweating created a catch-22, which could not be broken but by a powerful external force.

In the United States, reformers converted this economic argument into a gendered argument. The reason for this shift was the level of opposition they faced. Business, unions, and the courts stood firmly opposed to all inclusive minimum wage efforts. Yet, when the movement focused on women workers only, the opposition was less of a problem. "A minimum wage for women was politically convenient," according to scholar Vivien Hart, "easing and speeding passage of the laws." American reformers, led by the National Consumers' League (NCL), also shifted the focus from economics to health. Women, as the "weaker sex," needed to be protected. Massachusetts passed the first gender-specific minimum wage law in 1915. By 1919, sixteen states and the District of Columbia had similar laws, most modeled on the NCL's efforts. This "half-loaf option" was made more palatable by a 1908 Supreme Court decision, that upheld gender-specific reforms.

Then, in 1923, the Court reversed itself. In *Adkins v. Children's Hospital of Washington D.C.*, it declared such gender-specific laws unconstitutional. *Adkins* left the minimum-wage movement without a direction. The movement did not revive until 1933. Part of the reason for the revival was the Great Depression, which made talk of minimum wages seem logical. Also, there was a changing of the guard in the movement. Older leaders died and a new corps of leaders such as Frances Perkins arrived. When Franklin D. Roosevelt won his 1932 election, and with his 1936 landslide, social reform seemed not only possible, but practical.

Adkins, while a setback, offered a new method to achieve minimum wages. The decision hinted that while arguments based on health and a "living wage" would no longer work, laws based on a doctrine of fairness might. What was needed, therefore, was a legal definition of fair wages. The movement, however, held onto its gender-specific approach until 1936, when the court called such laws discriminatory.

THE PUBLIC CONTRACTS ACT

"President Roosevelt," wrote Frances Perkins, secretary of labor, "had come to Washington in 1933 prepared to devise a method of placing limitations upon hours of labor and a floor under wages." In fact, Perkins tells us that this commitment was given to her when she accepted Roosevelt's offer to lead the Labor Department. It was her one and only requirement. Early on in her tenure, she had drafted wage and hour legislation that she kept "locked" in her desk drawer, waiting for the right political moment to push for it.

In 1933, wages and hours legislation was covered under the National Industrial Recovery Act. Roosevelt issued a "Re-employment Agreement" that acted like a blanket wage and hour provision for employers who signed onto the National Recovery Administration (NRA). Employers were required to pay workers a minimum of $15 per week for a maximum of forty hours per week. This "agreement" would be in effect until the industrial codes were established. Under the

NRA, which dropped the nation's antitrust provisions, each industry was to develop a standard, which included wages, hours, and conditions. While the NRA was mainly aimed at stabilizing industry, the codes did aid workers by improving conditions. Then, on May 27, 1935, in *A. L. A. Schechter Poultry Corporation v. United States*, the Supreme Court overturned the National Industrial Recovery Act, the legislation that created the (NIRA).

During this crisis, Perkins told Roosevelt, that "I have something up my sleeve," referring to the two wage and hours bills locked in her desk. The Public Contracts Act of 1936 was the first to see the light of day. Perkins was appalled at how many government contractors paid below NRA codes. This act sought to make the federal government a model employer, with the hope that private industry would follow. It mandated the eight-hour day and forty-hour week. It allowed the secretary of labor to set a prevailing minimum wage. Then Perkins got to work on the second bill, the FLSA.

DRAFTING THE FLSA

The path the FLSA took was a torturous one. In 1935, the Roosevelt administration was cautious about socioeconomic legislation. Roosevelt wanted the constitutional issues worked out first. Many in the administration wanted to see what the Supreme Court did about the Guffey Act, or "mini-NRA" for the coal industry. When the Court invalidated the Guffey Act, it essentially voided the government's ability to regulate the economy through the commerce clause. In 1936, the Court dealt the wage and hour movement another setback. In *Moorehead v. New York ex rel. Tipaldo*, the Court invalidated a state's right to limit the working hours of women. In early 1936, with the NRA dead, the New Deal was drifting and wage and hour legislation was in a quagmire.

President Roosevelt made his 1936 reelection effort a mandate for New Deal social legislation. After his landslide win, Roosevelt ordered Perkins to redouble her efforts on what by then was called Fair Labor Standards (FLS). Like most of Roosevelt's programs, FLS was being worked on in more than one department. The Department of Commerce had been working on similar proposals for over a year. It submitted a draft of its bill to Congress in 1935, but, without Roosevelt's endorsement, it died in committee. It called for the licensing of businesses. Businesses that did not abide by FLS were to lose their licenses. After the 1936 elec-

tion, Perkins and her solicitors, Charles Gregory and Gerard D. Reilly, ruled out the Commerce Department's idea of licensing as impractical. Also, they wanted enforcement to be within the Labor Department.

Perkins's FLS endorsed set wages and hours and authorized "labor-management councils." If the secretary of labor found conditions in an industry nonconducive for commerce, the official could order the formation of a council—a tripartite board of business, labor, and government. This council would create "articles of labor standards," which, if the president signed them, would have the force of law. There would be a National Advisory Board to aid the secretary in devising uniform industrial codes. The bill banned child labor and recognized the right to collectively bargain. The big issue, as always in these matters, was whether the Supreme Court would accept the bill. The Court, after all, had voided laws when Congress ceded its legislative authority to private groups (e.g., the NRA). Perkins hoped that the quasi-governmental function of her bill would get around that obstacle.

As Perkins was working on her bill, the Commerce Department was reworking its own bill. This bill placed FLS enforcement with the Federal Trade Commission (FTC). Here the FTC could regulate hours and wages as part of what was considered fair competition through trade practice agreements. This bill was opposed by the Labor Department, which favored its own bill, and by labor unions. Also, because this bill had the feel of the NRA, its constitutionality was unclear.

To work out these differences, Roosevelt enlisted Solicitor General Stanley Reed in the fight for the bill. Reed and his staff quickly agreed that the Commerce Department's proposal was both impractical and probably unconstitutional. Reed became most concerned with passing a law that the Supreme Court would accept, since he believed that no social legislation would be approved by the Court. Reed suggested that Roosevelt confront the Court. Shortly after, the president put forth his court-packing scheme. His proposal was that, for every justice who refused to retire after seventy years of age, the president could appoint another Associate Justice, up to six. In short, all Roosevelt needed was one appointee to break the deadlock. In the end, Justice Owen Roberts shifted to Roosevelt's side and, in 1937, the Supreme Court issued two decisions that signaled a change. First was the reversal of *Adkins*, upholding a minimum wage for women. Second was the Court's upholding the Wagner Act.

At the time, Reed, Roosevelt political adviser Thomas G. Corcoran, and legal adviser Benjamin V.

Cohen were divided on what approach to take with the bill. Corcoran and Cohen wanted a larger omnibus bill, including a ban on child labor. Reed, still fearful of the Supreme Court, wanted a much more scaled-down bill. Deadlocked, they met with Roosevelt in August 1937. The president sided with Corcoran and Cohen. There was some compromise. Though national in scope, rather than set a national standard, the bill allowed hours, wages, and conditions to be set by either Congress or a governmental agency. The final bill allowed for a workweek of no more than thirty-five hours and a wage not less than $1,500 per year. Perkins and others initially opposed it as a watered-down version of what they had hoped for, but because the president supported it and because they thought that something was better than nothing, it finally got their support.

GETTING THE FLSA THROUGH CONGRESS

On May 24, 1937, the FSLA was presented to Congress. Roosevelt's message of support was clear: "A self-supporting and self-respecting democracy can plead no justification for the existence of child labor, no economic reason for chiseling workers' wages or stretching workers' hours."

The bill met unexpected opposition from within the Democratic Party that hinted at the party's shift in coming decades. The South was opposed and labor was divided. It passed the Senate (fifty-six to twenty-eight) and might have narrowly passed the House, but a coalition of southern Democrats and Republicans bottled it up in the House Rules Committee, killing the bill.

On October 12, 1937, Roosevelt called for a special congressional session to deal with a wave of new legislation, including the FLSA. Representative Mary Norton (D-NJ), chair of the House Labor Committee and a strong supporter of the measure, was instrumental in breaking the deadlock. She offered an amendment, that changed the five-member National Advisory Board to an administrator in the Labor Department and got 218 signatures on a petition to get the bill out of the Rules Committee. Once it was out of the Rules Committee, Roosevelt was dealt a severe blow when the House voted 218 to 198 to send it back to the Labor Committee. This was the first time a major New Deal bill was defeated on the floor of the House.

On January 3, 1938, Roosevelt demanded "legislation to end starvation wages and intolerable hours" in his annual address to Congress. He ordered Perkins and company back to work. And, because it was thought that part of the problem was the bill's complexity and lack of clarity, Roosevelt asked Perkins, "Can't it be boiled down to two pages?" Perkins submitted a ten-page revision to Roosevelt in late January.

Once it was resubmitted to Congress, Representative Norton created a special subcommittee on the new bill, which, in an effort to gain its passage, replaced it with a compromise bill. This compromise included the forty-cent per hour and forty-hour maximum and removed the administrator and restored the five-member board, though with much less power. When the Labor Committee voted down this compromise bill, a bare-bones version made it out. To avoid the bill's being "pickled" or held up, in the House, as Roosevelt observed, the president worked hard behind the scenes for passage.

In 1938, several key southern elections weakened the southern delegation in Congress. In addition, opinion polls suggested that 67 percent of Americans supported some form of FLS. In the end, southerners and key industries got exemptions and compromises to gain their support. On June 13, the bill passed the House and won Senate approval quickly. On June 25, Roosevelt signed it and on November 15 it became law.

The FLSA of 1938 was not the law that FLS reformers had hoped for. In 1938, because of its exceptions, it covered barely 20 percent of American workers. Almost all transportation workers were exempt, as were agricultural and domestic workers. In 1938, the minimum wage was set at only twenty-five cents per hour, going to thirty in 1938 and forty by 1945. Regardless of these shortcomings, the FSLA was a success. "The FLSA also established a principle, that the state has an interest in and the right to guarantee basic labor standards for workers," writes Vivien Hart. "In addition, the act declared that the sex of workers was irrelevant to their right to such standards, resolving a paralyzing debate about gender-based protective legislation."

RICHARD GREENWALD

See also: National Industrial Recovery Act; *Schechter Poultry Corporation v. United States*; Corcoran, Thomas G.; Perkins, Frances; Reed, Stanley; Roberts, Owen; Documents: National Industrial Recovery Act, June 16, 1933; National Labor Relations Act, July 5, 1935; *Schechter Poultry Corporation v. United States*, 1935; *West Coast Hotel Company v. Oregon*, 1937.

Bibliography

Grossman, Jonathan. "Fair Labor Standards of 1938: Maximum Struggle of a Minimum Wage." *Monthly Labor Review* 101:6 (1978): 22–30.

Hart, Vivien. "Minimum-Wage Policy and Constitutional Inequality: The Paradox on the Fair Labor Standards Act of 1938." *Journal of Policy History* 1:3 (1999): 319–43.

Martin, George. *Madam Secretary: Frances Perkins.* Boston: Houghton Mifflin, 1976.

Mettler, Suzanne. *Dividing Citizens: Gender and Federalism in New Deal Public Policy.* Ithaca, NY: Cornell University Press, 1998.

Paulsen, George. *A Living Wage for the Forgotten Man: The Quest for Fair Labor Standards, 1933–1941.* Selinsgrove, PA: Susquehanna University Press, 1996.

———. "Ghost of the NRA: Drafting National Wage and Hour Legislation in 1937." *Social Science Quarterly* 67:2 (June 1986): 241–54.

Perkins, Frances. *The Roosevelt I Knew.* New York: Viking, 1946.

Storrs, Landon R. Y. *Civilizing Capitalism.* Chapel Hill: University of North Carolina Press, 2000.

FARM SECURITY ADMINISTRATION

Although now remembered primarily for the photographic record that it compiled, the Farm Security Administration (FSA) was one of the most important and controversial agencies of President Franklin D. Roosevelt's New Deal. The Great Depression affected all sectors of the nation's economy, but farmers were hit especially hard for a number of reasons. Most farmers did not share in the prosperity of the 1920s, making the Depression even more damaging to their livelihood. Through much of the 1930s, the farming industry was one of the most seriously depressed sectors of the economy, with net farm income dropping from $6.1 billion in 1929 to $2 billion in 1933. The significance of this decrease is magnified by the fact that farmers accounted for 30 percent of the nation's work force in 1933. Indeed, in 1933, virtually every farmer in the nation faced significant economic difficulty. The problems of farmers were compounded by a long-term drought that gripped large portions of the nation's agricultural regions from 1929 to 1936. Even with the end of the drought in 1937, agriculture remained depressed, and in 1939, the per capita farm income was still 40 percent less than nonfarm income. Throughout his presidency, Roosevelt was dedicated to addressing the plight of the nation's farmers.

The FSA was established in 1937 by the Bankhead-Jones Farm Tenant Act as the successor to the Resettlement Administration (RA), which had been formed in 1935 when Roosevelt consolidated several small administrative units into a single federal agency. The first administrator of the RA was Rexford Tugwell, an outspoken advocate of agricultural reform and a member of the Brain Trust assembled in 1932 to advise Roosevelt on national policy issues. The Brain Trust helped shape the ideas and issues at the heart of the New Deal. However, by 1936, Tugwell's outspokenness became a political liability and he left his position at the end of the year, when the RA was transferred to the Department of Agriculture. Tugwell was succeeded by Will Alexander, who served as administrator of the RA/FSA until 1940, when he was replaced by C. B. Baldwin, who served until 1943, when Congress slashed the FSA's appropriations and halted some of its programs. After a brief interim with Robert Hudgens as acting administrator, Franklin W. Hancock was named administrator. Hancock served until 1945 and was succeeded by Dillard P. Lasseter, who was administrator of the FSA when it was abolished in 1946 and replaced by the Farmers Home Administration (FHA).

While many of the New Deal initiatives that addressed the problems of agriculture focused on efforts to boost the prices of farm commodities, the FSA sought to alleviate the immediate hardships of some of the country's worst-off farmers. Because of its mandate to address the effects of rural poverty, the FSA was referred to as "the poor man's Department of Agriculture." The Bankhead-Jones Farm Tenant Act contained numerous provisions for aiding the rural poor. Through the Rural Rehabilitation Program, the FSA provided farm loans, grants, and technical assistance to needy families. The Tenant-Purchase Program provided loans to help tenant farmers become land owners, an important step toward self-sufficiency. The Resettlement Program provided leases or purchase contracts for over 10,000 families. The FSA promoted cooperative associations, such as cooperative grain elevators, and purchased cooperatives for medical and dental services, veterinary services, seed, utilities, and other goods. In one of the most ambitious cooperative programs, the FSA leased large tracts of land, then subleased sections of the land to individual farm families. By 1943, this program had established fifty-two such cooperative associations, holding a total of 136,368 acres, primarily in Arkansas and Louisiana. The FSA also created four large-scale cooperative farms that involved around 450 families. Such programs prompted some members of Congress to view the FSA as too "socialistic," a criticism that limited congressional support for FSA programs.

Because the clientele of the FSA tended to be poor and unorganized, it was without the political clout to persuade Congress to provide sufficient appropriations to fund the FSA programs. With the needs so much greater than the resources, only about 5 percent of applicants could hope to receive financial assistance. The FSA became the center of some of the most intense domestic policy debates after the United States entered World War II, resulting in further cuts to an already underfunded agency. In 1942, the FSA had 19,045 full-time employees. By 1945, that number had dwindled to 8,742, a decline of 54 percent. Nineteen forty-three was the pivotal year in the decline of the FSA. After a bitter fight in Congress, funds for rural rehabilitation were cut by 43 percent from the previous year, the Tenant-Purchase Program was cut by 8 percent, and cooperative activities and the purchasing and leasing of land were prohibited. By 1945, the year before the FSA was abolished, only 1,853 Tenant-Purchase loans were made, down from 7,844 in 1942. Similarly, funds for rural rehabilitation in 1945 were $91,843,816, down from $179,539,399 in 1942.

As beneficial as the FSA programs were to the rural poor, they could not turn back countervailing forces of modernization. With the increasing mechanization of agriculture, many of the nation's small family farms would not be economically viable even if there had been no Depression. Nevertheless, one of the successes of the FSA was to slow the flight of displaced farmers to urban areas. Although many such farmers would become members of the urban working class, particularly after 1940, there was not enough industry through most of the 1930s to absorb the displaced rural population. The FSA helped slow the pace of this urbanization, while providing very real opportunities that allowed some tenant farmers to become farm owners and other small farm owners to hold onto their land.

MARK RICE

See also: Agriculture; dust bowl; Resettlement Administration; Alexander, Will; Tugwell, Rexford.

Bibliography

Badger, Anthony. *The New Deal: The Depression Years.* New York: Noonday Press, 1989.

Bellows, Sidney. *Poverty and Politics: The Rise and Decline of the Farm Security Administration.* Chapel Hill: University of North Carolina Press, 1968.

Gilbert, Jess, and Carolyn Howe. "Beyond 'State vs. Society': Theories of the State and New Deal Agricultural Policies." *American Sociological Review* 56 (1991): 204–20.

Kirkendall, Richard S. "The New Deal and Agriculture." In *The New Deal,* ed. John Braeman, Robert H. Bremner, and David Brody, pp. 83–109. Columbus: Ohio State University Press, 1975.

McConnell, Grant. *The Decline of Agrarian Democracy.* New York: Atheneum, 1969.

FEDERAL ART PROJECT

Part of Federal One—an agency within the Works Progress Administration (WPA) created to give employment to writers, scholars, and visual and performing artists—the Federal Art Project (FAP) employed impoverished visual artists to create projects that would enhance public buildings throughout the country.

Although funding for the Federal Art Project was just a tiny part of the overall funding for the Works Progress Administration, and although it hired but a fraction of the people that the larger program did, the FAP had a major impact on the artistic and architectural achievements of the Great Depression.

Under Project Director Holger Cahill, FAP artists painted thousands of murals in post offices and other buildings, such as Coit Tower in San Francisco, between 1935, when the WPA was authorized, and 1943, the year it was disbanded. Many of the murals were heavily influenced by the works of Mexican artists Diego Rivera and

The Federal Art Project of the Works Progress Administration put thousands of artists to work on murals, posters, and other public art project in the late 1930s. (*Library of Congress*)

Clemente Orozco, whose stylized, social realism seemed well suited to capture the everyday heroics of American life as popularized by the FAP. The FAP also produced many posters promoting New Deal programs and conducted numerous art education programs.

Among the artists put to work by the FAP were such important figures of American art as Ben Shahn, Jackson Pollack, and Willem De Kooning. Altogether, some 4,000 artists and 2,000 art teachers and researchers were hired by the FAP.

Summing up the value of the art created by the program, President Franklin D. Roosevelt declared "some of it good, some of it not so good, but all of it native, human, eager and alive—all of it painted by their own kind in their own country, and painted about things that they know and look at often and have touched and loved." But critics of the program complained that many of the murals were little more than New Deal propaganda.

See also: arts, fine; Federal Music Project; Federal Writers' Project; Federal Theater Project; Works Progress Adminstration.

Bibliography

Bustard, Bruce I. *A New Deal for the Arts*. Seattle: University of Washington Press, 1997.

DeNoon, Christopher. *Posters of the WPA*. Los Angeles: Wheatley Press, 1987.

FEDERAL BUREAU OF INVESTIGATION

Until the 1930s, law enforcement was considered to be (generally) a state concern. Until the New Deal, there were few laws giving the federal government jurisdiction over crimes not related directly to the Treasury Department (counterfeiting, bounty violations, tax crimes, etc.). However, the role of the Bureau of Investigation, the forerunner to the modern Federal Bureau of Investigation (FBI), slowly grew as Congress enacted legislation granting federal jurisdiction over a variety of interstate crimes, including the transportation of women across state lines for "immoral purposes," mainly prostitution (the Mann Act, 1910), and interstate transportation of stolen automobiles (the Dyer Act, 1919). Furthermore, with the onset of World War I, increasing concerns over internal security led to the expansion of the bureau's duties to include investigating potential saboteurs and spies. As the United States became directly involved in the conflict, Congress enacted a series of laws (the Espionage Act, 1917; the Sedition Act, 1918; the Immigration Act,

1918) covering the investigation and arrest of a variety of potential "threats." Finally, both the continuing arrival of immigrants and the Bolshevik Revolution (1917) greatly enhanced fears of internal political agitation and possible revolution.

However, by 1924, the bureau, now famous for its questionable methods (such as using blank "telegraphic" warrants to round up immigrants and Communists in the Palmer Raids of 1920; the regular use of wiretaps; and the political surveillance of critics of the Harding administration) was mired in scandal, and bureau director William Burns was forced out. In 1924, Attorney General Harlan Stone banned the use of wiretaps during investigations and rewrote the bureau's guidelines in an effort to prevent similar abuses in the future. As Burns's successor, Stone appointed the former head of the bureau's General Intelligence Division (its "radical squad") and chief architect of the Palmer Raids, J. Edgar Hoover, the man who would come to define the image of the bureau for the next five decades.

THE BIRTH OF THE "G-MAN"

The early 1930s, however, saw the dramatic expansion of federal law enforcement responsibilities as well as a significant rise in both the prestige and power of the Justice Department's investigative arm. The agency would also see three name changes, becoming the United States Bureau of Investigation in 1932, the Division of Investigation in 1933, and, finally, the Federal Bureau of Investigation (FBI) in 1935.

The early 1930s saw a string of kidnappings and bank robberies across the country that the local authorities seemed powerless to stop. The initial catalyst behind the expansion of the bureau's role was the March 1, 1932, kidnapping of Charles A. Lindbergh Jr., the infant son of the famed aviator. The sensational nature of the case, combined with the New Jersey State Police's failure to recover the child or apprehend the abductor, caused Congress to enact legislation on June 22, 1932, despite President Herbert Hoover's reluctance to intrude on state police powers, making kidnapping a federal offense if the victim was transported across state lines—the so-called "Lindbergh Law." The law was amended on May 18, 1934, as part of President Franklin D. Roosevelt's Twelve Point Crime Program, to establish federal jurisdiction in any kidnapping case if the victim was not located within seven days. This,

in effect, made nearly every kidnapping case a federal offense and the bureau the lead investigative agency.

Furthermore, throughout the early Depression years, criminals of all stripes were taking advantage of the lack of federal criminal statutes to commit crimes in one state and race across state borders in order to escape arrest. The national media regularly reported on the myriad exploits of such figures as George "Machine Gun" Kelly (who is credited with coining the bureau's most famous nickname when he shouted "Don't shoot, G-Men!" at the agents who arrived to arrest him for the 1933 kidnapping of wealthy oilman Charles Urschel), Alvin "Creepy" Karpis, and John Dillinger. President Roosevelt and Attorney General Homer Cummings sought to use the highly publicized "crime wave" as the springboard for the dramatic enlargement of the federal role (the Twelve Point Crime Program) in investigation and law enforcement. While not all of the Twelve Points were enacted, by June 1934 federal jurisdiction was extended to cover kidnapping, bank robbery, extortion, transporting stolen goods across state lines, and interstate racketeering. Furthermore, during this same time, bureau agents were given the power to execute warrants and make arrests.

Bureau director Hoover, well versed in the arts of opinion molding and public relations, used these expanded powers to great effect. The high-profile arrests or slayings of many of the leading gangsters of the 1930s (including Hoover's personal arrests of Karpis in 1936 and gangster Louis Buchalter in 1939) pushed the bureau into the national spotlight, where it was generally portrayed as the paragon of efficient, professional investigation and law enforcement. The bureau's aggressive operations to curb criminal activities were met with great success and much public fanfare, and the image of the coolly professional "G-Man" was one Hoover actively cultivated. However, the Roosevelt administration also opened the door for Hoover to engage again in the abusive practices that had marked the bureau's methods in the early 1920s.

DOMESTIC SURVEILLANCE

After the Nazis' rise to power in Germany in 1933, the Roosevelt administration became increasingly concerned about possible fascist agitation within the United States. In May 1934, Roosevelt ordered the bureau to investigate quietly various American profascist groups to determine if they had any direct connection to Hitler's government. This intelligence-gathering mis-

The Federal Bureau of Investigation promoted the incorruptibility and vigor of its "G-Men" agents through publicity photos like this one. *(Brown Brothers)*

pursue intelligence operations throughout South America and to "take charge of [investigating] . . . espionage, sabotage, and violations of the neutrality regulations." As with the "war on crime" of the 1930s, the bureau's campaign against spies and saboteurs during the war years was, for the most part, a rousing success—dozens of spies and potential saboteurs were arrested under the bureau's expanded powers. Furthermore, the bureau's new status as the nation's top domestic security agency also brought exceptional institutional growth: from 896 agents and an $8.8 million budget in 1940 to 4,886 agents and a 42.8 million budget in 1944.

The downside, however, of Hoover's domestic security operations was the bureau's enthusiastic use of wiretaps and break-ins for gathering information. This, combined with Roosevelt's apparent belief that the 1934 federal ban on the use of wiretaps (part of the Communications Act of 1934) did not apply in the case of national security investigations, gave Hoover great latitude over civil rights concerns in conducting steady domestic surveillance operations against any individual or organization he deemed to be a potential security threat. In fact, Hoover would continue these activities, in one form or another, under every administration from Roosevelt to Nixon.

JUSTIN HOFFMAN

See also: Communist Party; crime; fascism, domestic; German-American Bund; Prohibition; Silver Shirts; Socialist Party; House Un-American Activities Committee; Smith Act; Dillinger, John; Floyd, "Pretty Boy"; Hoover, J. Edgar; Nelson, "Baby Face."

sion was further expanded in August 1936 when Roosevelt ordered Hoover to pursue investigations of all "subversive activities in the United States, particularly Fascism and Communism." Hoover used this directive (combined with an obscure 1916 law that gave the bureau, at the request of the State Department, broad powers to investigate any domestic ties to foreign governments) to implement a broad surveillance program in order "to obtain from all possible sources information concerning subversive activities conducted . . . by Communists, Fascists, and representatives . . . [of] groups advocating the overthrow" of the U.S. government. Using this program as his foundation, Hoover would successfully expand the bureau's domestic surveillance activities throughout the war years.

As had been the case during World War I, the outbreak of war in Europe in 1939 brought significant administration pressure on the bureau to monitor possible subversive activity, both at home and abroad. In 1940, for example, Roosevelt authorized Hoover to

Bibliography

O'Reilly, Kenneth. "A New Deal for the FBI: The Roosevelt Administration, Crime Control, and National Security." *Journal of American History* 69 (December 1982): 683–58.

Powers, Richard Gid. *G-Men: Hoover's FBI in American Popular Culture.* Carbondale: Southern Illinois University Press, 1983.

Preston, William. *Aliens and Dissenters: Federal Suppression of Radicals, 1903–1933.* Cambridge: Harvard University Press, 1963.

Theoharis, Athan, et al. *The FBI: A Comprehensive Reference Guide.* New York: Checkmark Books, 2000.

Theoharis, Athan, and John Stuart Cox. *The Boss: J. Edgar Hoover and the Great American Inquisition.* New York: Bantam Books, 1990.

FEDERAL COMMUNICATIONS COMMISSION

The Federal Communications Commission (FCC) was created by the Communications Act of 1934, succeeding the Federal Radio Commission (FRC) and taking on the additional task of regulating the telecommunications industry.

When President Franklin D. Roosevelt appointed the seven-member FCC, there were 593 AM radio stations broadcasting regularly. The commission was faced with regulating an industry developing new technologies such as television, short-wave, and fax broadcasting (722 experimental licenses were in force in 1935). The advertising industry had begun to master the art of radio, and some people were concerned about the captive audience radio provided for those commercials. Isolated stations were gaining programming by affiliating with one of three networks: two set up by David Sarnoff's Radio Corporation of America (RCA), the other by a Columbia Records executive, William Paley. The economic and political power these networks developed instigated another serious debate facing the commission as war approached.

THE FAILURE OF BROADCAST REFORM

When the crash of 1929 came, the radio industry was in the midst of a restructuring process. The Radio Act of 1927 had put the FRC in charge of arbitrating various disputes among stations sharing frequencies. The act said that the FRC should issue new licenses to broadcasters who served the "public interest, convenience and necessity." It touched off an intermittent, if intense, battle between commercial and educational broadcasters (and other broadcast reformers) that would not fully ebb until 1935. This centered first on the issue of advertising and later on reserving some portion of the broadcast spectrum for nonprofit stations.

Grievances against the "radio setup" were numerous: Then as now, no one liked commercials except those who benefited from them. For some reformers, the great prospect of educating masses of adults in a "University of the Air" was being wasted on cheap, lowbrow entertainment. Those without the money to invest in radio equipment—farmers, workers, and other have-nots—were unable to use the public air-waves. These were the issues that the motley band of broadcast reformers was focused on. Some wanted public ownership of all radio broadcasting, based on the British system. Most simply wanted a portion of the public airwaves to be used for public purposes.

The reform movement, which took several forms and engaged these issues with varying degrees of enthusiasm, reached its peak when Senators Robert F. Wagner (D-NY) and Henry Hatfield (R-WV) sponsored an amendment to the Communications bill of 1934 mandating that 25 percent of all licenses be reserved for nonprofit institutions. The amendment, strongly backed by a coalition of Catholic broadcasters, trade unionists, and universities, was defeated, though the FCC was ordered to study the problem.

The FRC fully adopted the "American Plan" of commercial advertising in a 1932 report. Among the first things the newly created FCC did in 1934 was hold hearings on the question of reserving a portion of the airwaves for nonprofits. The networks used the hearings to parade a series of celebrity witnesses testifying to the educational and cultural benefits of network programming. The commission then issued a report defending the commercial stations and opposing nonprofit use. That policy did not change until educational institutions were handed the FM band in 1940.

NEW TECHNOLOGIES: FM AND TELEVISION

On June 9, 1934, Edwin H. Armstrong first broadcast "static-less" radio using a technique called frequency modulation (FM). The system would require new radio sets, but offered enormous bandwidth, higher fidelity for music, and no annoying static. When Armstrong offered the technology to his friend David Sarnoff at RCA, the reaction was surprisingly quiet. In the wake of the Depression, Sarnoff believed that the public would not buy more expensive radios just to get rid of the static. Instead, RCA was pouring all its research dollars into radio-with-pictures: television. As the largest company in the radio industry, RCA had tremendous clout with the commission. The discovery of FM became widely known in technical circles in 1935, but in the FCC's annual report that year, FM was not even mentioned. Television was competing for the same area of the radio spectrum.

The FCC's new take on FM angered Sarnoff and RCA fought Armstrong at every turn. Shortly after the commission's chief engineer testified against Armstrong's 1936 permit for an experimental FM station in New York, he was hired as RCA's chief engineer. Armstrong eventually got his permit, and by the fall of 1939 there were 150 applications on file for FM broadcast licenses. Meanwhile, Sarnoff presented television—invented in the 1920s—to a wide audience at the 1939 New York World's Fair. Shortly thereafter, the FCC authorized limited commercial television broadcasting.

In May 1940, the FCC settled the war between FM and TV. The commission gave Channel One to the FM band. Television sound would be FM sound, and commercials would be allowed on both FM and television. The war put further development of these technologies on hold.

THE NEW DEAL COMES TO BROADCASTING: THE STUDY OF "CHAIN BROADCASTING"

In 1938, the commission had begun a study into the antitrust implications of network broadcasting. RCA controlled two networks, National Broadcasting Corporation (NBC) Red and the smaller NBC Blue. Columbia Broadcasting Systems (CBS) had begun making inroads into NBC's territory, and the Mutual Broadcasting System was trying to get off the ground.

The study was not completed until the summer of 1941, but its publication made FCC chair James L. Fly a lightning rod for the broadcast industry. The report, adopted by a five to two vote, demanded the breakup of the two NBC networks. It called for an end to CBS's "network option" clause in its affiliation contracts, which forced local stations to cede time whenever the network demanded it. The report also pledged to investigate further into the networks' practice of creating "artist bureaus," which were supposed to function as talent agencies, but instead bound radio actors to their networks.

The networks quickly sold their talent agencies, but the other battles would go on for some time. Congressional friends of the broadcast industry launched investigations into the FCC and Chairman Fly, alleging communist infiltration and other scandals. Fly survived the investigations, and the Supreme Court sided with the commission on the other primary issues. In 1943, RCA sold NBC Blue, which became the American Broadcasting Company (ABC).

MICHAEL MCCALLISTER

See also: radio.

Bibliography

Barnouw, Erik. *The Golden Web*. New York: Oxford University Press, 1968.

Flannery, Gerald V., ed. *Commissioners of the FCC, 1927–1994*. Lanham, MD: University Press of America, 1995.

Lewis, Tom. *Empire of the Air: The Men Who Made Radio*. New York: Edward Burlingame Books, 1991.

McChesney, Robert W. *Telecommunications, Mass Media, and Democracy: The Battle for the Control of U.S. Broadcasting, 1928–1935*. New York: Oxford University Press, 1993.

FEDERAL DEPOSIT INSURANCE CORPORATION

The Federal Deposit Insurance Corporation was created in 1933 as a response to the banking crisis that beset the United States between 1929 and 1933. During this period, over 4,000 banks failed or became insolvent. The initial response to the wave of failures was the Emergency Banking Act of 1933. However, this was only a stopgap measure to sort out which banks could eventually survive.

The Banking Act of 1933, the legislation that put in place the bulk of Depression era law regarding banking, was designed to address structural defects in the banking industry. As such, it authorized the creation of the Federal Deposit Insurance Corporation. The idea of deposit insurance was not completely alien to the American banking system. In fact, several states already had bank deposit insurance schemes in place prior to the banking crisis. However, they had been unsuccessful in staving off the wave of failures.

On March 6, 1933, President Franklin D. Roosevelt, in one of his first official acts, declared a national banking "holiday." Banks were closed for business and customers could not withdraw funds. The purpose of the holiday was to allow banks that were solvent to steady themselves against the onslaught of customers who were demanding their money in response to the general climate of fear. The problem with customers demanding their funds en masse is that banks do not keep all deposits locked in a vault awaiting customer withdrawal demands. Bankers lend the bulk of customer deposits to others and only keep a fraction on hand to meet withdrawal requests. This system of "fractional reserves" is necessary if banks are to make a profit and fulfill their lending function.

In talking to the American people about the state of banking in his March 12, 1933, "fireside chat," President Roosevelt discussed how banks operated, particularly the fractional reserve system. He emphasized that, going forward, they would need to trust the system and break the cycle of fear. His last words to the public were "Together we cannot fail."

When the banking "holiday" ended, the government needed some way to assure the public, aside from President Roosevelt's words, that the reopened banks would be financially stable and that customers would be able to obtain their funds as needed. The psychology was as follows: if customers believed that they could get their money on demand, they would not rush to the bank to withdraw it. When customers do not make runs on banks, the fractional reserve system works quite well. Federal deposit insurance served as a mechanism for alleviating fears. If the bank did not have the funds to pay customers, then the federal government would step in and make up the difference.

The public overwhelmingly supported the idea of federal insurance for deposits. However, the views of policy-makers were, to say the least, mixed, and it was by far the most controversial banking reform proposal. President Roosevelt, for all of his public admonitions, was actually against federal insurance for bank deposits, since insurance had not worked on the state level, and threatened to veto the proposed banking legislation if it contained such provisions. Nevertheless, most Democrats in Congress, who enjoyed a majority in both houses, favored a guarantee. Senator Carter Glass, a principal sponsor of the bill, initially disfavored deposit insurance but recognized that public sentiment was so much in favor of the measure that he eventually acquiesced.

The banking community generally opposed deposit insurance, which would be partially funded by levying an assessment on banks. In particular, the bigger, predominantly East Coast banks did not support deposit insurance because it would mean that larger and more competently managed banks would inevitably have to subsidize weaker institutions. They argued that the guarantee would be an incentive for smaller banks to take even more risks. However, there was some sentiment for insurance among smaller banks.

In the end, President Roosevelt, being an astute politician, agreed to a compromise that would lead to a partial insurance system—despite the sentiment in the banking community. There was simply too much popular support for the provision. Deposits up to $10,000 would be fully guaranteed. Deposits between $10,000 and $50,000 were 75 percent guaranteed, with deposits above $50,000 only 50 percent guaranteed. This compromise allowed for sufficient assurances that the "little people" would feel safe leaving their money with banks as opposed to stuffing it in mattresses.

In signing the Banking Act of 1933, President Roosevelt took full credit for all of its provisions. However, if it were not for the threat of even more radical proposals fully guaranteeing bank deposits, he might not have acquiesced to the partial insurance scheme and the entire banking reform plan might have failed. In the end, it became one of the hallmarks of American banking law.

JAMES HACKNEY

See also: banking; banking holidays; Emergency Banking Act; Glass-Steagall Act; Roosevelt, Franklin D.; Document: Fireside Chat on the Banking Crisis, March 12, 1933.

Bibliography

Burns, Helen. *The American Banking Community and New Deal Banking Reforms: 1933–1935.* Westport, CT: Greenwood Press, 1974.

Kennedy, Susan. *The Banking Crisis of 1933.* Lexington: University Press of Kentucky, 1973.

Klebaner, Benjamin. *American Commercial Banking.* Boston: Twayne, 1990.

"President Roosevelt's March 12, 1933 'Fireside Chat.'" In *Documentary History of Banking and Currency in the United States,* ed. Herman Krooss. New York: Chelsea House, 1969.

FEDERAL EMERGENCY RELIEF ADMINISTRATION

The first major federal effort in the nation's history to provide financial relief directly to unemployed and impoverished Americans, the Federal Emergency Relief Administration (FERA) was a makeshift agency created in the first months of the Franklin D. Roosevelt administration's New Deal. Headed by a former New York social worker named Harry Hopkins, the FERA provided some $500 million in aid over a five month period between May and October 1933.

BACKGROUND TO FERA

Throughout American history, government relief for the poor had come rarely and grudgingly, especially at the federal level. Washington offered no help to the nation's poor and unemployed during the large-scale industrial depressions of the late nineteenth century. When, for example, an army of unemployed descended on the nation's capital during the depression of the 1890s—a protest movement known as Coxey's army, after its leader, Jacob Coxey—the only response of the government was to disperse the marchers and arrest their leaders.

Republican president Herbert Hoover, who presided over the nation during the first few years of the Great Depression in the 1930s, was no different. Hoover felt that direct government handouts would only lengthen the hard times by sapping the spirit and encouraging indolence. The Hoover administration believed that relief was a local affair and that private charity should and could handle the needs of the poor and unemployed.

But as the Depression deepened through the early 1930s, it became increasingly apparent that local and private efforts to ward off hunger, homelessness, and want were insufficient. By the time Roosevelt was inaugurated president in early March 1933, the economic situation facing millions of Americans was dire. Nationally, some 25 percent of the workforce was unemployed; in many industrial areas, where the Depression hit hardest, the jobless rate stood at 50 percent and higher. Collapsing farm incomes, due to depressed agricultural prices, spread the misery to the countryside.

While not an eager advocate of direct relief himself, Roosevelt recognized that the nation faced an economic catastrophe of unprecedented urgency. As governor of New York, he had established the Temporary Emergency Relief Administration (TERA), which offered $20 million in relief to the state's unemployed and impoverished. The TERA dispensed the aid in the form of matching funds. For every $6 spent by a city or locality on direct relief, the state would add another $4. While these funds represented but a fraction of the money needed to meet the emergency, they established Roosevelt as a politician willing to break with precedent and provide direct government aid to the poor.

LAUNCHING FERA

Shortly after his election to the presidency in November 1932, Roosevelt assembled a team of experts to plan for federal government poverty relief. The group included future labor secretary Frances Perkins, several liberal senators—including Robert Wagner (D-NY) and Robert M. La Follette Jr. (Progressive-WI)—and TERA chief Hopkins. The team sought out ideas from such welfare groups as the American Association of Social Workers. By the time Roosevelt came to office in March 1933, the team had put together a plan that resembled the TERA, but on a bigger, national scale. There was also consensus on who should lead the effort—Hopkins himself.

On March 21, 1933, just over two weeks after coming to Washington, Roosevelt presented legislation to Congress calling for the establishment of the FERA. On May 9, Congress passed the legislation, authorizing $500 million for direct relief, all of it to come from the Reconstruction Finance Corporation, the Hoover-era agency established to make emergency loans to businesses on the verge of bankruptcy. The $500 million was to be distributed in two parts. Half would be dispersed to the states on a matching grant basis, with one federal dollar being provided for every three state dollars spent on direct relief. The other $250 million went into a discretionary fund, under Hopkins's control; he would then disperse the money where he felt it was most needed. The liberal and energetic Hopkins made a point of spending money immediately, proudly boasting that he gave out $5 million in the first two hours as head of the FERA. But, as some contemporary critics of the New Deal noted, Hopkins had other, more political, criteria than mere need. Indeed, a disproportionate amount of FERA funds was given to electoral swing states.

Like the TERA, the FERA gave control over much of the funds to local and state officials. There were several reasons for this decision. First, the federal government of 1933 was relatively small, lacking the bureaucracy and outreach necessary to run a nationwide relief effort. Moreover, the administration believed that there would be less resistance to direct federal government relief if authority over how those funds were spent was shared with local and state officials. Indeed, many states were reluctant to take the funds, seeing direct relief as something that should be handled by localities and private charities. Finally, as in the geographic pattern of funding, there were political motives. Roosevelt hoped to strengthen the pro–New Deal constituency by turning over control of the funds to local officials, including mayors, sheriffs, and others who held sway over blocs of voters.

But this decision to allow for local decision-making often came at a price, and that price was paid in a variety of ways by the recipients of the aid. First, many local authorities refused to create work relief or give out cash, preferring instead to make the funds available in the form of food and clothing. Although Hopkins considered this demeaning—giving the aid recipients little control over what they received—he could do little to prevent the practice. Moreover, as his chief investigator Lorena Hickok pointed out, most FERA money was handed out reluctantly, with recipients forced to wait for hours to receive paltry sums or food and to undergo humiliating means testing that often included intrusive visits by local officials to people's homes and batteries of questions that pried into their personal lives. In some areas, officials refused to give out funds or even food and clothing to those they deemed unworthy of it, including many immigrant families in northern cities and much of the African-American population of the South.

THE DEMISE OF FERA

By October 1933, Hopkins was growing tired of the FERA. He was frustrated by the inefficient, understaffed bureaucracy of the agency and angry at the way local officials dispersed the federal money. Moreover, he had spent virtually all of the $500 million originally allotted by Congress. Believing that a better way to provide aid to the poor and unemployed was through work relief, Hopkins asked Roosevelt to establish an agency that would put people to work. The president agreed and appointed Hopkins to run the Civil Works Administration, which, by March 1934, spent some $800 million and put 4.2 million men and women on the government payroll in work relief programs.

Still, for all of its limitations, the FERA established the precedent of direct federal government relief to the poor. The creation of the FERA, says historian David Kennedy, "began, however modestly, to chart the path toward the modern American welfare state."

See also: charity and philanthropy; New Deal, first; Civil Works Administration; Reconstruction Finance Corporation; Temporary Emergency Relief Administration; Hopkins, Harry; Hoover, Herbert; La Follette brothers; Perkins, Frances; Roosevelt, Franklin D.

Bibliography

Freidel, Frank. *Franklin D. Roosevelt: Launching the New Deal.* Boston: Little, Brown, 1973.

Hickok, Lorena A. *One-Third of a Nation: Lorena Hickok Reports on the Great Depression.* Urbana: University of Illinois Press, 1981.

Hopkins, Harry Lloyd. *Spending to Save: The Complete Story of Relief.* New York: W. W. Norton 1936.

Schlesinger, Arthur M., Jr. *The Coming of the New Deal.* Boston: Houghton Mifflin, 1958.

FEDERAL HOUSING ADMINISTRATION

The Federal Housing Administration (FHA) was created by the National Housing Act (48 Stat. 1246) on June 27, 1934. It attempted to address the Great Depression's effects on home ownership and mortgage financing.

BACKGROUND TO THE FHA

On the eve of the Great Depression, most home mortgages were financed by savings and loan associations. These institutions usually wrote mortgages for terms of ten to twelve years, with down payment requirements of at least 25 percent. Since first mortgages and down payments did not always cover the full purchase price, second mortgages, charging 12 to 18 percent interest, were written for the balance. Though national home ownership rates increased during the 1920s, purchasing a home remained beyond the financial reach of most Americans (no more than 40 percent of nonfarm housing was owner occupied). The Great Depression made home ownership even more precarious. Between 1929 and 1933, there were no fewer than 9,760 commercial bank suspensions. Savings and loan associations were adversely affected since they relied on short-term loans from commercial banks to meet their withdrawal demands (they had borrowed more than $400 million from commercial fiduciaries prior to the worst wave of bank failures). In turn, the closure of savings and loan associations had a deleterious effect on the residential mortgage market (89.6 percent of all savings and loan assets were held as mortgages, which amounted to $7.8 billion in 1929). By 1933, mortgage foreclosures were averaging 1,000 per day nationwide.

The Hoover administration sought to ameliorate the plight of home owners by supporting passage of the Federal Home Loan Bank bill on July 27, 1932, which created twelve Federal Home Loan Banks (47 Stat. 725). These banks would supply credit to their member institutions (mostly savings and loan associations) either by making loans against the security of the saving and loan associations' first mortgages or by reducing the saving and loan associations' liquidity requirements (the percentage of deposited funds that had to be kept in cash or government bonds). Although this measure provided some help to struggling savings

and loan associations, it did little to aid large numbers of home owners. Thus, the Roosevelt administration lobbied for additional legislation, including the Home Owners Loan Corporation (HOLC), which was enacted on June 13, 1933 (48 Stat. 128). The HOLC's function was not to loan money (actual "home owners" did not receive "loans"), but to purchase and refinance mortgages that were either in default or foreclosure. The HOLC did reduce foreclosure rates by liberalizing financing requirements, though its emphasis on impaired mortgages did little to increase the funds available for new mortgages or home repairs.

ENACTMENT AND CONSEQUENCES OF THE FHA

To stimulate additional mortgage lending, construction of new housing, and rehabilitation of existing dwellings, the Seventy-third Congress passed the most important housing legislation to date, the National Housing Act of 1934. Supported by a broad coalition of business and financial leaders, the 1934 housing act established four new programs: federally backed loans for housing repairs, the creation of national mortgage associations, deposit insurance for savings and loan associations, and insurance for private mortgage lenders. This last program was to be administered by a new agency, the FHA. The FHA attempted to stimulate mortgage financing by means of a novel mechanism: it guaranteed mortgages that adhered to certain guidelines against the risk of default (fiduciaries were permitted to exchange FHA mortgages for government bonds if borrowers failed to meet their payments). Home buyers benefited as well. The FHA's guidelines stipulated that the mortgages it backed were to be fully amortized, financed over a twenty-year period (subsequently extended to thirty years), and were to cover 80 percent of a dwelling's appraisal value. Furthermore, only institutions approved by the FHA as financially sound could offer such mortgages. Ultimately, FHA-insured mortgages made it easier for average citizens to become home owners.

In addition to administering the mortgage insurance program, the FHA aggressively promoted home

This Depression-era advertisement touts the opportunities for home ownership offered by the Federal Housing Administration, a New Deal agency. *(Brown Brothers)*

ownership as a cultural ideal. By early 1935, the FHA was using 6,174 "Better Housing Committees" to instruct citizens how they could use government programs to purchase their own homes. FHA pamphlets, including *Selling Better Housing* (1935) and *How to Have the Home You Want* (1936), described the virtues associated with buying and selling single family dwellings. The FHA, in concert with the U.S. Chamber of Commerce, also circulated posters and millions of pieces of literature extolling home ownership; loaned models of houses to real estate developers; conducted radio programs featuring nationally known speakers discussing the importance of their homes; and even promoted specific subdivisions in tandem with local banks. Some housing reformers, such as Charles

Abrams, criticized these efforts as not going far enough to meet housing demands, but the general public remained supportive of the FHA's activities, including its stance on racial segregation. In its *Underwriting Manual* (1938), the FHA recommended high valuation ratings only for properties in neighborhoods that were racially homogeneous. It even provided an example of a legal device, a restrictive covenant, that homeowners could use to prevent their property from being sold to certain racial groups. This policy, though officially dropped in 1950, helped create residential segregation patterns that persist today.

Within a few years of its inception, supporters of the FHA argued that it had already dramatically increased home ownership rates. Indeed, by capping interest at 5 percent (eventually lowered to 4.5 percent), extending the length of financing terms, and eliminating widespread use of second mortgages, the FHA's policies opened up home ownership to millions of additional Americans. The FHA's critics, while not denying these benefits, contended that too many costs were shifted onto borrowers. For example, in addition to interest, borrowers also had to pay a 1 percent (subsequently reduced to .25 to .50 percent) insurance premium that exclusively benefited mortgage lenders. Critics also pointed out that lower down payment requirements did not necessarily translate into lower monthly mortgage premiums. Today, scholars and commentators generally agree that the FHA successfully promoted home ownership, though they disagree over how successful it was in achieving its initial macroeconomic goal of blunting certain aspects of the Great Depression.

A. SCOTT HENDERSON

See also: Walter-Steagall Housing Act.

Bibliography

Henderson, A. Scott. *Housing and the Democratic Ideal: The Life and Thought of Charles Abrams.* New York: Columbia University Press, 2000.

Jackson, Kenneth T. *Crabgrass Frontier: The Suburbanization of the United States.* New York: Oxford University Press, 1985.

Radford, Gail. *Modern Housing for America: Policy Struggles in the New Deal Era.* Chicago: University of Chicago Press, 1996.

FEDERAL MUSIC PROJECT

Part of Federal One, an agency within the Works Progress Administration (WPA) created to give employment to writers, scholars, and visual and performing artists, the Federal Music Project (FMP) employed impoverished musicians, singers, conductors, composers, and music teachers to write, perform, and teach music throughout the country.

The least controversial of the various arts programs, the FMP promoted both classical and indigenous American music. Under director Nikolai Sokoloff, former conductor of the Cleveland Symphony Orchestra, the FMP established thirty-four symphony orchestras in small and medium-sized cities, effectively quadrupling the number of such ensembles. The program also sponsored chamber orchestras, choral groups, and string quartets, which often traveled into areas previously unfamiliar with classical music concerts. Altogether, over 30 million people attended more than 36,000 concerts during the life of the program, from 1935 to 1943. In addition, over 6,000 music teachers offered 1 million classes in music to nearly 14 million students, young and old.

But while Sokoloff had little patience for popular or modern music, the program nevertheless sponsored all kinds of indigenous American forms of music, including jazz, swing, bluegrass, cowboy, gospel, and marching band. Indeed, the FMP sponsored music by writers and performers of all races and ethnic backgrounds. Many of these popular musicians performed at FMP-sponsored festivals like the annual three-day American Music Festival held around Washington's birthday in February.

See also: music; Federal Art Project; Federal Theater Project; Federal Writers' Project; Works Progress Administration.

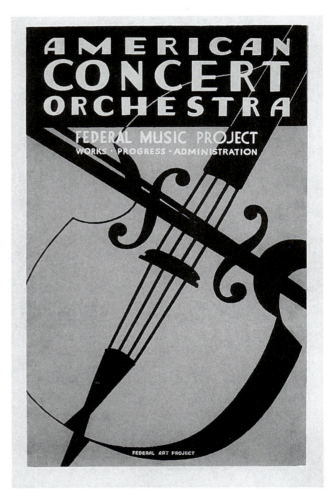

The Federal Music Project hired musicians, composers, and conductors to put on free or low-cost concerts throughout the country in the late 1930s. *(Library of Congress)*

Bibliography

Bindas, Kenneth J. *All of This Music Belongs to the Nation: The WPA's Federal Music Project and American Society.* Knoxville: University of Tennessee Press, 1995.

Stowe, David W. *Swing Changes: Big Band Jazz in New Deal America.* Cambridge: Harvard University Press, 1994.

FEDERAL RESERVE SYSTEM

Although the United States had fleeting experiences with national banking in the past, it was not until 1913, when the Owen-Glass Federal Reserve Act was passed, that a formal, centralized banking institution was established. As the central bank of the United States, the Federal Reserve System (often nicknamed "the Fed") consists of not one bank, but twelve regional banks that are coordinated by a central board located in Washington, D.C. Acting as a bank for banks, the system as a whole holds deposits for member banks, makes loans to them, and creates its own credit through additional legal reserves. All of this allows the Federal Reserve System to affect economic conditions through the control of the country's flow of credit.

During the first decade of the Federal Reserve System's existence, the institution struggled to gain the confidence of the banking community. Indeed, it was not until the 1920s that the Federal Reserve System contained nearly 80 percent of the nation's banking resources and began using its powers to control the country's money supply. Even then, many critics complained that the system, led by Benjamin Strong, the head of the New York regional bank, was hesitant in curtailing the speculative boom of the late 1920s.

With the stock market crash of October 1929, the country's entire banking system was placed in peril. Between 1930 and 1932, more than 5,000 banks failed, and in the following year an additional 4,000 banks collapsed. Whether the Federal Reserve would have been able to stop this collapse by lowering interest rates and easing credit remains a debatable issue among scholars.

Regardless, after 1933, the administrations of both Hoover and Roosevelt attempted to overhaul the Federal Reserve System. Even before that, in January 1932, Congress, at the urging of President Herbert Hoover, established the Reconstruction Finance Corporation (RFC). When the RFC failed to provide sufficient credit to stop the banking crisis, Congress tried to spur the Federal Reserve System's lending by easing the security requirements for loans to member banks with the first Glass-Steagall Act. When this too failed to halt the banking collapse, Congress passed the Emergency Relief and Construction Act in July 1932. President

Franklin D. Roosevelt signed the Emergency Banking Act in March 1933 as one of his first acts as president. Among other provisions, the law allowed Roosevelt to declare a banking "holiday," closing the nation's banks and temporarily halting the drain on bank reserves.

The Banking Act of 1933 established the Federal Deposit Insurance Corporation, the federal agency that insures the deposits of the country's banks. This meant depositors' savings would not be lost if their bank failed. The act's main goal was to inhibit the speculative frenzy that many policy makers at the time believed was the cause of the Great Depression. Accordingly, the new law separated commercial banking from investment banking and gave the Federal Reserve System additional power to supervise the loans and investments of member banks; it also granted statutory recognition of the system's Open Market Committee, the body that oversees the sale and purchase of government securities by the Fed.

The Open Market Committee had informally existed since the 1920s, operating under the control of private bankers who represented the Fed's member institutions. This ad hoc private control continued right through the Banking Act of 1933. It was not until the Banking Act of 1935 that the Open Market Committee was brought under the direct and exclusive control of the Federal Reserve's Board of Governors. With this new law, the Federal Reserve System took on the form of a true central bank. The system's powerful influence on the money supply and the availability of credit was nearly complete.

In addition to stewarding these legislative initiatives, the Roosevelt administration also increased the powers of the Federal Reserve System indirectly by severing monetary policy from the gold standard. Historically, the gold standard served as a check on inflation by acting as a monetary base. Intent on reviving the economy by any means necessary, Roosevelt abandoned the gold standard in the summer of 1933 and incidentally paved the way for the Federal Reserve System to have greater control of the money supply and economic conditions in general.

The Fed did not always use its newfound influence over monetary policy wisely during the late 1930s. While the new Keynesian theories of macroeconomics suggested that the Fed keep interest rates low, in 1936–37 the board chose to double reserve requirements. With the growing threat of war in Europe and the United States as a relative haven for capital, member banks began accumulating large excess reserves. As these reserves increased, member banks became less dependent upon Federal Reserve policy-making. With less control over member banks, the Fed was unable to prevent—and may have even exacerbated—the 1937 recession. With the onset of World War II, board chairman Marriner Eccles was ultimately able to restore a low interest rate standard that promoted investment, increased employment, and generally supported the war mobilization effort.

In the end, the New Deal invigorated the authority of the Federal Reserve System, ushering in a new era of centralized banking. Faced with a banking crisis reaching astronomical proportions, Roosevelt's early policies provided stability and confidence in the nation's banking system. The creation of the Federal Deposit Insurance Corporation gave new meaning to the government's control over the banking sector. The New Deal's later policies similarly enhanced support for the Federal Reserve System. The codification of the Open Market Committee's control over the money supply provided the Fed with powers that to this day allow it enormous influence over the flow of credit and the overall well-being of the nation's economy.

AJAY K. MEHROTRA

See also: banking; Keynesian economics; banking holidays; Emergency Banking Act; Federal Deposit Insurance Corporation; Glass-Steagall Act; Reconstruction Finance Corporation; Documents: Hoover's Outline of Program to Secure Cooperation of Bankers to Relieve Financial Difficulties, October 6, 1931; Fireside Chat on the Banking Crisis, March 12, 1933.

Bibliography

Patrick, Sue Carol. *Reform of the Federal Reserve System in the Early 1930s: The Politics of Money and Banking.* New York: Garland, 1993.

Timberlake, Richard H. *Monetary Policy in the United States: An Intellectual and Institutional History.* Chicago: University of Chicago Press, 1993.

FEDERAL SECURITIES ACT

The Federal Securities Act was an early piece of New Deal legislation designed to assure the purchasers of stocks and other securities that they were receiving truthful financial information.

The law, passed in May 1933, made publicly held corporations that were floating stock provide full and accurate information to the buying public about the condition and value of the company. It also set up a mechanism whereby investors could sue for civil damages if they could prove that the stock-offering corporation had provided misleading information.

The act was bolstered by the establishment of the Securities and Exchange Commission in the following year, which also demanded full disclosure and independent auditing of financial information by publicly traded corporations.

See also: stock market; Securities and Exchange Commission.

Bibliography

DeDedts, Ralph F. *The New Deal's SEC: The Formative Years.* New York: Columbia University Press, 1964.

Phillips, Susan M., and J. Richard Zecher. *The SEC and the Public Interest.* Cambridge: MIT Press, 1981.

FEDERAL SURPLUS RELIEF CORPORATION/FEDERAL SURPLUS COMMODITIES CORPORATION

The Federal Surplus Relief Corporation (FSRC) was established by President Franklin D. Roosevelt in September 1933 to buy up surplus agricultural produce for distribution in food relief programs.

The impetus for the program was the embarrassment caused the administration by the purposeful destruction of crops and livestock under the Agricultural Adjustment Act, including the killing of some 6 million hogs and piglets in the spring and summer of 1933.

This destruction was part of a program of reducing the agricultural surplus in order to raise the price of crops and livestock. But to many Americans, the juxtaposition of crop and livestock destruction with hungry people was too much to bear. Thus, when Roosevelt adviser Rexford Tugwell and Federal Emergency Relief Administration head Harry Hopkins came to Roosevelt with a plan to buy up crops and livestock to distribute as relief, the president eagerly approved, earmarking $75 million for the task and establishing the Federal Surplus

Relief Corporation under the Federal Emergency Relief Administration. In 1935, the FSRC was shifted to the Department of Agriculture and renamed the Federal Surplus Commodities Corporation.

Ultimately, the agency would be turned into the food stamp program in 1938 and become one of the few New Deal programs to survive to this day. Some scholars argue that it endured because all three programs were primarily created to aid politically potent farmers, rather than the disenfranchised poor and hungry.

See also: agriculture; Agricultural Adjustment Act; Federal Emergency Relief Administration; Hopkins, Harry; Tugwell, Rexford.

Bibliography

Hopkins, Harry. *Spending to Save: The Complete Story of Relief.* New York: Norton, 1936.

Saloutos, Theodore. *The American Farmer and the New Deal.* Ames: Iowa State University Press, 1982.

FEDERAL THEATER PROJECT

The Federal Theater Project (FTP) was one of four Federal Art Projects created by the Works Progress Administration (WPA) and easily the most controversial. Upon passage of the Emergency Relief Appropriations Act of 1935, President Franklin D. Roosevelt commanded the WPA into existence on May 6, 1935. The Federal Theater Project was launched later that summer with former Vassar professor Hallie Flanagan at its helm as project director.

THEATER'S PECULIAR PLIGHT

With unemployment still high in 1935, those belonging to theatrical professions suffered from a unique

set of dire circumstances. The prevalence of the cinema had already mushroomed when the Depression began thinning people's wallets. The theater—pricier and less ubiquitous than the movies—was in danger of losing its audience altogether. Hollywood starlets outshone stage actors, technical crews were outmoded by the demands of new technology, and theater after theater went dark, abandoned by patrons for twenty-five-cent movie house seats. Hollywood and the Depression had together stranded the country's show people.

WPA administrator Harry Hopkins addressed the plight of show people around the country by including theater in the plans for the new Federal Art Projects.

As a collective branch of the WPA, the arts programs were required to recruit 90 percent of their employees from the public relief rolls. The Federal Theater faced especially challenging hiring decisions, as the theater world was mired in a complex web of unions. Some unions had forbidden their members to accept relief, while others objected to the use of amateur and non-union personnel in FTP productions. Weighing the myriad complaints, Flanagan determined that hiring would be restricted to theater people who had once been gainfully employed in the field and were likely to be so employed in the future. Flanagan also insisted on an audition process, which preserved the integrity of the project's productions but drew criticism for delaying its output. Despite the challenges, the theater project remained essentially true to the mandated quota of relief personnel.

RELIEF FOR THE THEATER

In *Arena*, her personal account of the Federal Theater's short history, Flanagan defines the project as a "federation of theaters" inspired by a growing interest in regionalism that she herself shared. The project was divided into five regions—East, South, Midwest, West, and New York City—and assigned to regional directors. Each region operated under the Federal Theater umbrella as a fairly independent company. Flanagan's guiding intent, as paraphrased by Midwest regional director E. C. Mabie, was "to set up theaters which have possibilities of growing into social institutions in the communities in which they are located and thus to provide possible future employment for at least some of those who now present an immediate and acute problem to the government." While her desire to rescue theater professionals agreed with the overall WPA mission, this bold plan to create something substantial and enduring antagonized politicians and officials who had no interest in funding a permanent national theater.

A variety of specialized theatrical "units" formed within each region. The scope of the project was highly inclusive; units ranged from Shakespearean and social drama to children's theater, vaudeville, the circus, marionette troupes, and pageant productions. The greatest number and diversity of units existed in New York City. Among these were the popular price theater, intended to revive and expand the audience of the theater; experimental theater, which focused less on public reception than on collaboration with the playwright; and the try-out theater, established to introduce audiences to new, innovative productions. John Houseman directed the Negro Theater unit in Harlem, which was the largest of sixteen black theaters in the country and received high praise for its adaptation of *Macbeth*.

The Federal Theater built its credentials slowly, based on the merit of its productions rather than on celebrity involvement. Most of its personnel were essentially unknown, though a few celebrated individuals did appear on its employment rolls, among them Houseman, Orson Welles, Arthur Miller, John Huston, Dale Wasserman, Sidney Lumet, and Elia Kazan. While FTP-employed playwrights could not retain copyright or collect royalties on plays written for the project, the FTP did pay for the rights to produce works by independent playwrights such as George Bernard Shaw, Eugene O'Neill, and Sinclair Lewis. The simultaneous seventeen-city premiere of Lewis's *It Can't Happen Here* in 1936 was the project's biggest public relations coup.

LIVING NEWSPAPERS

Probably the best remembered unit was the living newspaper. Organized by playwright Elmer Rice, the living newspaper was a collaborative effort of journalists and theater people to dramatize current affairs. These were lively, low-cost productions capable of involving large casts. They also heightened public awareness and debate of controversial issues. Rice resigned his FTP post as New York City regional director when the first living newspaper, *Ethiopia*, was canceled by the federal government on the grounds that it threatened national security. However, other living newspapers such as *Triple-A Plowed Under*, a leftist commentary about U.S. agriculture, went on to achieve critical acclaim and anger conservatives in Washington.

CONGRESSIONAL INVESTIGATION

Flanagan maintained that only 10 percent of Federal Theater productions fell into the category of social drama, but insisted that the project should choose socially relevant scripts. In July 1938, the House Un-American Activities Committee (HUAC) accused the project of being not just "socially relevant," but socialist. Headed by Representative Martin Dies (D-TX), this committee lambasted all of the Federal Art Projects for spreading "un-American" propaganda and for keeping Socialists and Communists on their payrolls. Of all the

The Federal Theater Project sponsored numerous productions such as this performance of *Dance of Death*, a poetic drama by W. H. Auden. *(Brown Brothers)*

arts programs, none drew more fire during these proceedings than the Federal Theater Project. When the committee had concluded its inquiries, Representative Clifford Woodrum (D-VA) organized a second one to continue the investigation. Ironically, both of these committees succeeded in undermining support for the arts projects largely because the project directors had followed the law in not hiring or firing personnel on the basis of political views or affiliations.

DEMISE OF THE FEDERAL THEATER PROJECT

When the smoke in Congress finally cleared, Federal Theater was finished. The Senate seconded the House's vote to abolish it, and while the other arts programs were permitted to continue in diminished capacities under local or private sponsorship, the theater project was slated for complete termination in accordance with the Federal Emergency Relief Act of 1939. Roosevelt, upon reluctantly signing the bill, remarked that the singular treatment of the theater project was "discrimination of the worst type." However, even if the House committees had not managed to dissolve all the Federal Art Projects, the changing political climate of the day would have likely effected the same result. With the threat of a second world war looming, concerns about national defense had supplanted Roosevelt's strong support of the relief employment programs. Dissolution of the Federal Theater Project was in fact just one stark consequence of the 1939 Relief Act; at the same time, the WPA itself was shrunk and absorbed into the Federal Works Administration.

CATHERINE WHITTENBURG DOLINSKI

See also: House Un-American Activities Committee; Works Progress Administration; Dies, Martin; Hopkins, Harry; Lewis, Sinclair; Welles, Orson.

Bibliography

Bentley, Joanne. *Hallie Flanagan: A Life in the American Theatre.* New York: Knopf, 1988.

Brown, Lorraine, and John O'Connor, eds. *Free, Adult, Uncensored: The Living History of the Federal Theatre Project.* Washington, DC: New Republic Books, 1978.

Flanagan, Hallie. *Arena.* New York: Duell, Sloan, and Pearce, 1940.

Kazacoff, George. *Dangerous Theatre: The Federal Theatre Project as a Forum for New Plays.* New York: Peter Lang Publishing, 1989.

FEDERAL WRITERS' PROJECT

Within the Emergency Relief Appropriations Act of 1935, which authorized the creation of the Works Progress Administration (WPA) employment programs, there existed a simple proviso for a government-funded arts project. By issuing an executive order, President Franklin D. Roosevelt signed the Works Progress Administration into existence on May 6, 1935; two months later, the Federal Writers' Project (FWP) was launched under its auspices. The writers' project was one of several projects belonging to the arts branch of the WPA, collectively known as Federal One.

WRITERS IN NEED

"For the first time in the history of the United States writers are working for the government as writers," FWP director Henry Alsberg announced in a letter to the *Saturday Review of Literature* in January 1936. The mission of the project, he explained, was "to care for the large number of destitute writers who were fighting off starvation" during the Depression. This goal of providing relief unified all of the WPA projects, including Federal One. WPA regulations mandated that 90 percent of the writers' project staff be hired from public relief rolls—a stipulation that drew immediate attack from various writers' groups, but was nonetheless left virtually unaltered for the duration of the project.

Defining what constituted the status of "writer" was more difficult than deciding what constituted a pauper. With relief provision as its primary goal, the project directors were in no position to set elitist guidelines for hiring writers. On the other hand, if standards of editorial competency were not enforced, the output of the project would disappoint public expectation and undermine support for the project's continuation. Alsberg addressed this issue by approving a national FWP focus capable of including (and withstanding) contributions from the least as well as the most qualified writers: the American Guide Series.

THE AMERICAN GUIDE SERIES

Inspired by Karl Baedeker's international guidebook series, the American guide incorporated reports about each U.S. state on a myriad of subjects, a state tour being a central component of each. Originally envisioned as a single volume about the United States supplemented by several regional guides, it evolved instead as a series comprising a separate volume for each state and territory, as well as Manhattan and the District of Columbia. To realize this giant undertaking, the project employed professors and recent college graduates; newspaper reporters and seasoned editors; established literary authors and occasional freelancers; librarians, lawyers, and numerous other white-collar workers who could be classified as "writers." Those who did not qualify for editorial positions might still find employment as clerks or typists. Richard Wright, Ralph Ellison, Conrad Aiken, Zora Neale Hurston, Margaret Walker, Katherine Dunham, and John Cheever are among the best-known names appearing on the FWP employment rosters.

THE STATE OFFICES

The writers' project established its headquarters in Washington, D.C., and authorized local offices in each state and territory. Headquarters appointed state and regional directors and instructed them to hire staffs of local writers, the collective qualifications of which varied drastically. This discrepancy was a major stumbling block for the project, for while certain regions fairly teemed with literary talent, many state directors were hard-pressed to find sufficient staff with even minimal qualifications. An extreme example of this situation emerged in Idaho, where the state director ultimately wrote 374 of the 405 pages of the state guide himself. This director, a historical novelist named Vardis Fisher, declared it impossible to hire the standard quota of editorial personnel on the grounds that "Idaho, of course, is not a state of unemployed writers."

A far cry from Idaho, the writers' project in New York City benefited and suffered from a more typically urban set of circumstances. Overrun with unemployed literary talents, Manhattan was granted a separate writers' project "state" office of its own. It soon emerged as the office most embroiled in conflict. While layoffs and budget cuts plagued every state office, the resulting backlash was most dramatic in Manhattan, where warring political factions exacerbated fears and hostilities. Demonstrations and protests over the Depression, sometimes violent, occurred repeatedly. This turmoil counts among the reasons that, despite its rich reserves of talented writers, the Manhattan office was slow to produce its guidebook. Noted too for its particular concentration of feuding communist factions and sympathizers, it became the prime target of a Congressional investigation.

BEYOND THE GUIDE SERIES

Building on the prior efforts of the Federal Emergency Relief Administration (FERA), the project adopted folklore research and ethnic studies as important secondary aims. Southern writers' projects produced vibrant collections of folk tales, among them *Gumbo Ya-Ya: A Collection of Louisiana Folktales*. The ex-slave narratives project expanded to involve eighteen states, and some states assigned writers to record the history and experiences of their African-American populations. In Manhattan, twenty-seven writers formed a "Living Lore Unit" to compile the stories, experiences, and traditions of the ethnic populations living in the city.

The FWP produced little in the way of purely literary work; it did, however, sponsor several short-lived literary magazines. Project writers in San Francisco launched *Material Gathered* in 1936 during the same month in which their Nebraska colleagues were publishing a lighter-hearted periodical, titled *Shucks*. A year later, D.C. headquarters published the first issue of *American Stuff*, an anthology representing the after-

hours literary work of project employees around the country.

CONGRESSIONAL INVESTIGATION

Early on, the Federal Writers' Project came under attack for political reasons. The Republican National Committee accused the FWP staff of communist activity in 1936, and two years later the House Un-American Activities Committee (HUAC) condemned the project fiercely. Headed by Representative Martin Dies (D-TX), this committee lambasted all of the Federal One projects for spreading communist and other "un-American" propaganda. After this committee concluded its proceedings, Representative Clifton Woodrum (D-VA) organized a second to continue the inquiries. Ironically, the Dies and the Woodrum committees were able to undermine public support and government sponsorship of Federal One largely because the directors of the projects had complied with the law in not hiring or firing employees based on their political affiliations.

DEMISE OF THE FEDERAL WRITERS' PROJECT

Even if the committees had not managed to hasten the collective demise of the federal art projects, the changing political climate would likely have led to the same result eventually. The possibility of a second world war was looming large in 1939, and President Roosevelt, no longer at liberty to focus so much of the nation's resources on relief and employment programs, had turned to issues of national defense. In accordance with the Federal Emergency Relief Act passed in 1939, the Works Progress Administration was shrunk and absorbed into the Federal Works Administration. Federal One was terminated altogether.

The writers' project survived in a diminished capacity for several more years under individual state sponsorship. The last installment in the American Guide Series, *Oklahoma: A Guide to the Sooner State*, was published in 1941. It took the project six years to publish the fifty-one guidebooks. The exact number of pamphlets and books published under FWP auspices has not been conclusively documented, though in 1942 the National Archives reported holdings of approximately 1,000 titles. Many of the project's works received considerable critical acclaim at the time of their publication, especially the American Guide Series. All of the titles in the series have since been reprinted, some as revised editions. Other FWP publications, such as the collected narratives of ex-slaves, have received renewed attention from scholars in recent years.

CATHERINE WHITTENBURG DOLINSKI

See also: American Guide Series; literature; House Un-American Activities Committee; Dies, Martin; Hurston, Zora Neale; Wright, Richard.

Bibliography

Bold, Christine. *The WPA Guides: Mapping America.* Jackson: University Press of Mississippi, 1999.

Hobson, Archie, ed. *Remembering America: A Sampler of the WPA American Guide Series.* New York: Columbia University Press, 1985.

Mangione, Jerre G. *The Dream and the Deal: The Federal Writer's Project, 1935–1943.* Philadelphia: University of Pennsylvania Press, 1983.

Weisenberger, Bernard A., ed. *The WPA Guides to America: The Best of 1930s America As Seen by the Federal Writers Project.* New York: Pantheon Books, 1985.

GLASS-STEAGALL ACT

The Banking Act of 1933, popularly known as the Glass-Steagall Act, was passed in order to stave off any future bank crises. The congressional focus was on the causes of bank failures, including intermingled investment and commercial banking activities. The Glass-Steagall Act was passed, in no small part, to separate the two.

Historically, commercial banks had stayed out of the investment banking business as a matter of custom—as opposed to any legal restriction. Commercial banks primarily provided short-term loans to individuals or businesses on a contractual basis. This is in contrast with investment banking, in which financial institutions "underwrite" securities offered by businesses. In underwriting securities, banks issue stock of businesses to the public in exchange for a fee from the company.

Despite their commitment to short-term lending, commercial banks had always deviated from the course at their discretion and as a matter of market necessity: the need to provide long-term financing for a growing commercial sector. Initially, the comptroller of the currency had legally prohibited commercial banks from directly underwriting corporate securities due to a narrow interpretation of the National Banking Act of 1863. However, beginning in the 1900s, the comptroller began to loosen the regulatory grip due to market pressures and in the face of widespread bank circumvention.

National banks began to set up different types of corporate structures that effectively let them engage in corporate securities underwriting. This development was capstoned in 1924 when the comptroller of the currency promulgated a ruling that provided even more leeway for commercial banks to engage in investment banking. Following this bit of regulatory fiat, the 1927 McFadden Act explicitly allowed commercial banks to engage in securities underwriting, setting the stage for the wholesale speculation in securities that would mark the pending banking crisis. It is no small coincidence that by 1929, the eve of the banking crisis, commercial banks were underwriting over half of the securities being issued by business enterprises. The linkage between commercial and investment banking was viewed, at the time, as responsible for the 1929 stock market crash.

Banks had gotten involved in speculation by accepting risky securities as collateral for loans. Basically, investors were borrowing from commercial banks and stock brokerage houses to purchase securities on credit. When the stock market crashed, these investors had to withdraw funds they held in banks in order to pay off the credit owed on their securities balances. This inevitably meant that there was less money to lend out for standard loans or cover demands for deposit withdrawals. The money crunch, along with a myriad of other economic factors, contributed to the Depression. Given the sordid role that commercial banking played in the stock market crisis and economic downturn, it is little wonder that lawmakers quickly turned their attention to guarding against any such future occurrence.

The stars were perfectly aligned for a reform push. Bankers, who up until 1933 had vigorously attacked any attempt to disallow their securities operations, now favored disassociation with the securities industry. A pivotal turning point came with the "Pecora hearings."

From 1932–33, the Senate Banking and Currency Committee held hearings regarding the intermingling of banking and securities operations. The testimony was, to say the least, embarrassing to the banking community. Banker after banker testified to unethical and nefarious practices, including making loans to securities purchasers to prop up artificially inflated prices and other insider transactions.

The Pecora findings caused some bankers to voluntarily terminate securities activities. For example, Winthrop Aldrich, chairman of the powerful Chase National Bank, announced that the bank would voluntarily sever all ties with its securities affiliates. Aldrich went so far as to lobby President Franklin D. Roosevelt and Senator Carter Glass, the chief architect of the 1933 act, to include a universal bar against bank involvement in the securities industry. Roosevelt and Glass favored the policy, and with a Democratic Congress also in agreement the move was relatively uncontroversial.

Democrats had staked out a position on the issue in their 1932 party platform, calling for the "severance of affiliated security companies from, and the divorce of the investment banking business from, commercial banks." Even the Republican Party platform of the same year raised concerns regarding commercial bank affiliation with securities firms. With such widespread support, the separation became a cornerstone of banking reform.

The Glass-Steagall Act prevented banks from engaging, except to a very limited extent, in corporate securities underwriting. It also prohibited securities firms from undertaking commercial banking activities. The effect on the banking industry was almost immediate. For example, J. P. Morgan and Company (later to be renamed Morgan Guaranty Trust) spun off its securities operation to the Morgan, Stanley and Company investment banking partnership. Indeed, the law required all commercial banks to divest themselves of securities affiliations within a year. Glass-Steagall had truly reshaped the landscape of American finance.

JAMES HACKNEY

See also: banking; insurance; stock market; Federal Deposit Insurance Corporation; Pecora investigation; Securities and Exchange Commission; Federal Securities Act; Glass, Carter.

Bibliography

Burns, Helen. *The American Banking Community and New Deal Banking Reforms: 1933–1935*. Westport, CT: Greenwood, 1974.

Eccles, George. *The Politics of Banking*. Salt Lake City: University of Utah Press, 1982.

Kennedy, Susan. *The Banking Crisis of 1933*. Lexington: University Press of Kentucky, 1973.

Klebaner, Benjamin. *American Commercial Banking*. Boston: Twayne, 1990.

"1932 Democratic Platform." In *Documentary History of Banking and Currency in the United States*, ed. Herman Krooss. New York: Chelsea House, 1969.

GOLD STANDARD

The gold standard was the monetary system of the United States from the late nineteenth century through April 19, 1933, when President Franklin D. Roosevelt took the country off it by executive order. Under the gold standard, the dollar's value was set at a fixed quantity of gold, and all dollars were freely convertible into that fixed quantity of gold both at home and internationally.

Throughout the late nineteenth and early twentieth centuries, the gold standard was a pillar of American finance, supported by Republicans and conservative Democrats alike. While it maintained financial stability, the gold standard had its drawbacks. For one thing, it kept the dollar at a relatively high value. Indeed, a highly valued dollar kept inflation at bay and, for a time in the late nineteenth century, created a deflationary economy because world gold supplies were limited. To debtors, this was a bane because it meant that their loans had to be repaid in ever more valuable dollars.

During the 1890s, the Populist Party arose to challenge the gold standard, insisting that the dollar be convertible to more plentiful silver as well, which would have created inflation and lowered the burden of debtors. But bankers and other creditors, who disliked the idea, essentially prevailed upon Washington to maintain the gold standard. Discoveries of new gold deposits in South Africa and the Yukon at the end of the nineteenth century alleviated the deflationary crisis for debtors.

But the worldwide crisis of the Great Depression lowered demand for products around the world, creating a new deflationary cycle. To combat this, the British decided to abandon the gold standard in September 1931. Although the conservative Herbert Hoover administration resisted making a similar move, the British decision sent panic through American banks, as depositors, fearing that the United States might do likewise, withdrew their deposits while they were still backed by gold.

Upon coming to office in March 1933, Roosevelt declared a banking holiday under legislation that gave the president the right to control gold exchanges. In other words, Roosevelt prevented depositors from taking their gold-backed money out of the nation's banks for a period of about ten days, in order to restore stability and prevent continuing depositor runs.

On April 19, just weeks after ending the banking holiday, Roosevelt declared the United States to be off the gold standard. Then, in October 1933, he announced that the Reconstruction Finance Corporation—the Depression-fighting agency established by the Hoover administration—would purchase gold at "prices to be determined from time to time after consultation with the Secretary of the Treasury and the President." Thus, every morning, he and Secretary Henry Morgenthau would decide the price of gold over breakfast, generally raising the price of gold by small amounts, sometimes quite capriciously. One morning Roosevelt decided to raise it by twenty-one cents because he said it was a lucky number.

The method behind this madness was simple. By gradually inflating the price of gold, they were deflating the price of the dollar and creating more inflation. By doing so, they were raising prices and hopefully profits and employment, as outstanding debt values were lowered.

The tactic, however, was largely a failure and was widely criticized by economists, including John Maynard Keynes, who called the policy the "gold standard on booze." Indeed, while it did raise the price of gold somewhat, it did nothing to halt the deflationary cycle in prices. Indeed, between October 1933 and January 1934, when the gold-buying scheme was abandoned, prices continued to fall. Finally, in January, Congress passed the Gold Reserve Act, fixing the price of gold in the United States at $35 per ounce, where it remained until 1971.

See also: banking; banking holidays; Emergency Banking Act; Reconstruction Finance Corporation; Great Britain; Morgenthau, Henry.

Bibliography

Eichengreen, Barry. *Golden Fetters: The Gold Standard and the Great Depression, 1919–1939.* New York: Oxford University Press, 1992.

Keynes, John Maynard. "Open Letter to the President." in *New York Times*, December 31, 1933, sec. 8, p. 2.

HATCH ACT

The Hatch Act was a 1939 piece of legislation that effectively created a firewall between federal employees, federal funding, and electioneering. It prohibited federal employees from engaging in electioneering and it prohibited the use of federal money for campaign purposes.

The act prohibited the use of either public works or relief money for electioneering purposes. In addition, it prevented federal officials from using job offers, promotions, contracts, or any other benefit to coerce campaign contributions or any other form of political support.

On one hand, the Hatch Act was a straightforward attempt at election reform. On the other, it was a partisan move by Republicans and conservative Democrats to head off the use of public works moneys and personnel in pro-Roosevelt and pro–New Deal electioneering. Indeed, the creation of mass public works projects and mass federal hiring created a real threat that these would be used to coerce campaign support from those benefiting from the programs. And, in fact, there was evidence that this had occurred, especially in connection with the Tennessee Valley Authority.

An amendment added in 1940 extended the Hatch Act restrictions to state and local employees.

See also: election of 1936; election of 1940; public works; Tennessee Valley Authority.

Bibliography

Creese, Walter L. *TVA's Public Planning: The Vision and the Reality.* Knoxville: University of Tennessee Press, 1990.

Leuchtenburg, William E. *Franklin D. Roosevelt and the New Deal, 1932–1940.* New York: Harper & Row, 1963.

The Hatch Act of 1939 prevented federal workers from participating in politics. The half-man, half-chicken depicted in this 1939 cartoon is Republican senator Carl Hatch; the man leaning on the coop is Attorney General Frank Murphy. (*Library of Congress*)

HOME OWNERS LOAN CORPORATION

Among the first agencies created by the incoming Franklin D. Roosevelt administration in spring 1933, the Home Owners Loan Corporation (HOLC) had two missions: to protect homeowners from foreclosures on their mortgages and to shore up failing home lending institutions burdened with unpaid mortgages on their ledgers.

Between 1933 and 1936, the HOLC prevented 4 million foreclosures. More than that, it limited much of the risk previously involved in home buying, by creating nationwide standards for home mortgages and lending, prompting the development of standardized methods of appraisal and construction, and facilitating the development of the mortgage insurance system.

See also: banking; Federal Housing Administration.

Bibliography

Jackson, Kenneth. *Crabgrass Frontier: The Suburbanization of the United States.* New York: Oxford University Press, 1985.

HOUSE UN-AMERICAN ACTIVITIES COMMITTEE (DIES COMMITTEE)

The House Un-American Activities Committee (HUAC) was charged with conducting congressional investigations into subversive activities in the United States. The House committee—along with its Senate counterpart—would eventually become synonymous with American anticommunist hysteria during the Cold War. While its Cold War activities are perhaps best known, HUAC (and its predecessors) were actively pursuing alleged subversives well before the start of World War II.

In January 1934, the House passed a resolution calling for the creation of a temporary committee to investigate subversive activities. The Special Committee on Un-American Activity (more popularly known as the McCormack-Dickstein Committee, after its chair, Representative John McCormack [D-MA], and its most outspoken member, Representative Samuel Dickstein [D-NY]), investigated possible ties between Hitler's government and American fascists, anti-Semites, isolationists, and extreme conservatives. McCormack-Dickstein hearings were often marked by Dickstein, over the objections of his chairman, inserting unverified secret testimony into the *Congressional Record*, leveling unsubstantiated espionage charges at witnesses, and lecturing witnesses about the immorality of their political views.

Two years after his committee published its findings, Dickstein, concerned that Nazi propaganda efforts continued to be quite active, asked the House to renew and expand its investigations into subversive activities. Rather than establish a committee chaired by Dickstein, who, as an ardent New Dealer, had fallen out of favor with increasingly conservative Democratic congressional leadership, the House instead considered a similar motion, this one sponsored by the more popular Representative Martin Dies (D-TX). Dies, originally a New Dealer, had soured on the Franklin D. Roosevelt administration and hoped to use this committee to investigate communist influence in the New Deal programs he hated. In contrast, Dickstein and many remaining New Dealers supported Dies's motion because the new committee would resume investigations of anti-Semites and American fascists. Dies's motion was approved with broad bipartisan support on May 26, 1938, establishing the House Un-American Activities Committee. It would, in short order, come to be known as the "Dies Committee." Its initial members were Arthur D. Healey (D-MA), John J. Dempsey (D-NM), Joe Starnes (D-AL), Harold G. Mosier (D-OH), Noah M. Mason (R-IL), and J. Parnell Thomas (R-NJ).

The foci of HUAC's investigative energies were divided roughly into three broad categories: communist influence in the public and industrial realms; communist influence in New Deal programs; and, to a much smaller extent, the extreme right. To this end, Dies would assemble a staff of investigators and cultivate contacts within state law enforcement agencies and the Federal Bureau of Investigation (FBI). Perhaps the most important member of HUAC's staff was its chief investigator, J. B. Matthews, the author of *Odyssey of a Fellow Traveler* and a famous ex-Communist-turned-anticommunist-crusader. Under Matthews's direction, HUAC's investigators spent countless hours compiling endless lists of names clipped from communist publications such as the *Daily Worker*. It does not appear that Matthews placed great weight on actually verifying whether or not those named were actually Communists—that they were named in a red paper or pamphlet was enough. Also, HUAC investigators, usually with the cooperation of local police "red squads," would charge into a communist organization's (or front group's) offices and simply seize publications, files, and records and cart them off to be copied for HUAC's files.

In HUAC's first few weeks, Dies publicly identified approximately 640 organizations, 480 newspapers, and 280 labor unions as communistic in one form or another. And, like Dickstein before him, Dies opened his committee to ridicule by allowing unsubstantiated allegations and fantastic tales into the record. For example, in an effort to demonstrate communist influence in Hollywood, Matthews presented a 1939 letter to French communist paper *Ce Soir* signed by Hollywood stars Clark Gable, Robert Taylor, James Cagney, and Shirley Temple, leading Roosevelt aide and Public Works Administration chief Harold Ickes to quip that

House Un-American Activities Committee investigator John Metcalfe displays a Nazi-style salute to chairman Martin Dies. The committee, however, spent more time examining the activities of Communists rather than of Nazis. *(Brown Brothers)*

Dies would next be "leading a *posse comitatus* in a raid upon the ten-year-old Shirley Temple's nursery to collect her dolls as evidence of her implication in a Red Plot." One witness, Walter Steele of the patriotic umbrella organization, the American Coalition, even went so far as to question the loyalty of the Camp Fire Girls.

While HUAC hearings could often degenerate into anticommunist political theater, it must be noted that the committee could also wield significant political power. Shortly before the 1938 elections, HUAC witnesses testified that a variety of liberal candidates around the country were tainted by communism. In one case, a HUAC witness testified that Michigan governor Frank Murphy had worked with communist elements of the Congress of Industrial Organizations and was guilty of "treasonable action" for not using force to end a sit-down strike at General Motors in 1937. Outraged at the committee's maneuvers, President Roosevelt issued a statement condemning HUAC for "an unfair and un-American attempt to influence an election." Despite the president's support, Murphy could not escape the charge that he was "soft" on communism and was defeated.

HUAC also managed to inflict damage on the New Deal programs Dies so despised. The most notable example was HUAC's assault on the Works Progress Administration, particularly the Federal Theater Project.

J. Parnell Thomas, echoing the sentiments of most members of the Dies committee, stated that "practically every play" presented by the project was "sheer propaganda for Communism or the New Deal." Because of HUAC's aggressive attacks on the project (combined with the strong anti-New Deal sentiments in the House at large), Roosevelt killed the program in 1939.

During the war, the Dies Committee continued to aggressively pursue alleged Communists on the government payroll. Dies would later claim that HUAC had compiled a list of 5,000 federal employees who had "questionable backgrounds." Pressure on the administration from both HUAC and the House in general (particularly provisions in the Hatch Act [1939], which prohibited federal employees from membership in any organization dedicated to the overthrow of the U.S. government) would lead Roosevelt to institute a loyalty program for government employees. However, the business of conducting the war, the wartime alliance with the USSR, and the often hysterical tone of HUAC hearings slowly drained the committee of its political relevance. The Dies Committee simply expired in December 1944. The spirit of the committee, however, would be rekindled in January 1945 when Representative John Rankin (D-MS) forced a roll-call vote to establish a permanent House Un-American Activities Committee (HUAC), later succeeded by the House Internal Security Committee (HISC).

JUSTIN HOFFMAN

See also: Communist Party; fascism, domestic; fascism, Italy; Federal Bureau of Investigation; Federal Theater Project; Hatch Act (1939); Smith Act; Nazi Germany; Soviet Union; Barkley, Alben; Dies, Martin; Hoover, J. Edgar.

Bibliography

Donner, Frank J. *The Un-Americans*. New York: Ballantine Books, 1961.

Leuchtenburg, William E. *Franklin D. Roosevelt and the New Deal 1932–1940*. New York: Harper, 1963.

O'Reilly, Kenneth. *Hoover and the Un-Americans: The FBI, HUAC, and the Red Menace*. Philadelphia: Temple University Press, 1983.

Powers, Richard Gid. *Not Without Honor*. New York: Free Press, 1995.

Sirgiovanni, George. *An Undercurrent of Suspicion: Anti-Communism in America During World War II*. New Brunswick, NJ, and London: Transaction Publishers, 1990.

INDIAN REORGANIZATION ACT

The Indian Reorganization Act (IRA) of 1934 represented a significant shift in U.S. federal Indian policy. In the decades following the Civil War, federal policy had emphasized the rapid assimilation of Native Americans into white culture. One of the key measures of this so-called Assimilationist Era was the 1887 General Allotment Act, also known as the Dawes Act. This legislation initiated the breakup of tribally owned lands in favor of land ownership by individual Indians. The goal was to transform Indians into small farmers. Later amendments to the act authorized the sale or lease of allotted lands. As a consequence of the allotment process, Indians lost perhaps 80 percent of their most valuable lands and an estimated two-thirds of their total land base.

Allotment was paired with the creation of off-reservation boarding schools. The first such school, Pennsylvania's Carlisle Indian Industrial School, exemplified the mission of boarding schools. In the infamous words of the school's founder, Richard Henry Pratt, the goal was to "kill the Indian and save the man." Boarding school students found themselves immersed in an alien culture, forbidden to speak their own language, and instructed in vocational skills. For many students, like Lakota Sioux Luther Standing Bear, who later wrote in *Land of the Spotted Eagle* of his experiences at Carlisle, the experience was traumatic and ill prepared them for life after they returned to their reservations.

In 1928, a congressionally appointed committee investigating conditions on the nation's reservations made disturbing findings. Its report, unofficially titled the Meriam Report, detailed the poverty, despair, and disease rampant among reservation communities. The report also called for extensive overhauling of federal polices regarding Indians. For white reformers the findings were troubling and pointed out that failed federal policy indeed needed to be revamped. Once such reformer was John Collier. When Secretary of the Interior Harold Ickes chose Collier as his new commissioner of Indian affairs in 1933, Collier embarked on a mission to dramatically change the direction of federal policy.

At Collier's urging, senators Burton Wheeler (D-MT) and Edgar Howard (D-NE) introduced far-reaching legislation in 1934. Organized into four different sections, the Wheeler-Howard Act proposed a variety of significant changes in Indian policy. Title I of the act, "Indian Self-Government," called for the renewal of tribal governments and the strengthening of their role in the affairs of their respective communities. Title II, "Special Education for Indians," promoted the study of Indian cultures and traditions through such forums as classrooms at reservation schools. Title III called for an end to the allotment process and a return of lands to tribal control. Title IV authorized the creation of a federal court to deal solely with Indian matters.

Not surprisingly, the Wheeler-Howard bill met with opposition in Congress. Several legislators believed that the provisions of the act would retard the process of assimilation. Others, with less than noble agendas, feared that it would shut off valuable agricultural lands from white farmers and ranchers. Less anticipated, however, was opposition to the bill within Indian communities themselves. Some Indian opposition leaders felt that it would take away their privately owned lands. Others were concerned that the bill vested too much authority in tribal governments or feared that it would destroy rights guaranteed by treaty.

Determined to push the measure through Congress and shore up Indian support, Collier arranged a series of "Indian congresses" to meet with Indian delegates and hear their concerns about the bill. In the end, the majority of those Collier met with supported the legislation. As a result of the meetings and congressional hearings, a significantly modified bill was reintroduced into Congress and signed into law by President Franklin D. Roosevelt in June 1934. The amended act, titled the Indian Reorganization Act (IRA), was a watered-down version of the Wheeler-Howard Act. The IRA weakened the power of tribal governments authorized in the original bill and did not provide for the creation of a federal Indian court.

Nonetheless, the IRA represented a significant change in federal policy and initiated a renewal of tribal identity. It ended the allotment process, authorized the creation of tribal governments, and launched a series of cultural programs. Some 181 tribes later approved the IRA, and 93 drafted tribal constitutions. Of those tribes that rejected the IRA, the most notable were

The Indian Reorganization Act of 1934 granted Native Americans more self-government. Here, Secretary of the Interior Harold Ickes hands the first constitution issued under the act to representatives of the Confederated Tribes of the Flathead Indian Reservation. *(Library of Congress)*

the Navajos, who voted down the act in 1935. Navajos incorrectly associated the IRA with the stock reduction program instituted earlier under Collier. Stock reduction was an effort to stem soil erosion due to overgrazing by sheep. As a result, thousands of sheep were slaughtered. To Navajos, especially those with small sheep holdings, this program was not only economically destructive but a callous abuse of power by federal bureaucrats. Collier became a symbol of Navajo discontent over the program, and thus anything associated with Collier carried the stigma of stock reduction.

Collier had the most success with the IRA among New Mexico's Pueblo communities, most of which adopted the provisions of the act. Collier had always had a good relationship with the Pueblos, beginning with his activism on their behalf in the 1920s. In fact,

some critics who opposed the IRA felt that Collier had based it on his understanding of Pueblo communities and that it had far less applicability to other tribes around the nation.

It is fair to say that the IRA was not the great success that Collier had envisioned. It was accepted by some communities and rejected by others. The IRA had also been considerably diluted from its original form. Even so, the IRA represented a significant change in federal policy and in the life of reservation communities. The overall philosophy held that tribes should assume a greater role in governance and that tribalism and Indian identity should be strengthened and encouraged.

By the mid-1940s, federal policy would again change direction. Policy-makers returned to the older assimilationist goals. The 1950s witnessed programs to terminate reservations and to relocate Indians to cities such as Los Angeles, Chicago, and Minneapolis. Yet the IRA's belief in strengthening Indian communities and tribal self-government had laid the groundwork for opposition to a renewed assimilationist assault. By the 1960s, the assimilationist movement ebbed and the call for self-determination rose once again. Tribal councils, most of them created as a result of the IRA, led the way in exerting Indian control over reservation affairs and resources.

SCOTT C. ZEMAN

See also: Native Americans; Ickes, Harold; Wheeler, Burton.

Bibliography

Hoxie, Frederick, and Peter Iverson. *Indians in American History*. Arlington Heights, IL: Harlan Davidson, 1988.

Iverson, Peter. *The Navajo Nation*. Albuquerque: University of New Mexico Press, 1981.

Philp, Kenneth. *John Collier's Crusade for Indian Reform, 1920–1954*. Tucson: University of Arizona Press, 1981.

JONES-CONNALLY FARM RELIEF ACT

Adopted April 7, 1934, the Jones-Connally Farm Relief Act authorized the Department of Agriculture to purchase cattle in order to drive up the price of livestock and beef. The law also included $200 million in drought relief for the Midwest.

Unlike the Agricultural Adjustment Act of May 1933, which included a highly publicized hog destruction program that proved embarrassing to the administration, the Jones-Connally Act was simply a purchase program. Cattle owners did not have to destroy cattle or even prevent their breeding; instead, the government agreed to buy enough cattle to maintain a price that would allow cattlemen to stay in business. At the same time, cattle owners agreed to establish a "Committee of Twenty-Five" that would control further cattle production. The act also came to cover goat and sheep production.

During the program's life, up to 600,000 head of cattle were being purchased weekly by the federal government. By the time the program ended in January 1935, when even the cattlemen deemed it no longer necessary since cattle had climbed above the $20 per head last-resort price paid by the Agricultural Adjustment Administration, the government had purchased and quietly destroyed 9 million cattle, to avoid the negative publicity like that connected with the hog killing.

See also: agriculture; Agricultural Adjustment Act; Federal Surplus Relief Corporation/Federal Surplus Commodities Corporation.

Bibliography

Lambert, C. Roger. "The Drought Cattle Purchase 1934–1935: Problems and Complaints." *Agriculture History* 145:2 (1971): 85–93.

Saloutos, Theodore. *The American Farmer and the New Deal*. Ames: Iowa State University Press, 1982.

NATIONAL CREDIT CORPORATION

Also known as the National Credit Association, the National Credit Corporation (NCC) was a private corporation established by the nation's largest banks in October 1931 to provide $500 million in credit to troubled financial institutions.

The NCC was created under the urging of President Herbert Hoover and fit with his vision that government-led voluntary action was a more appro- priate way to fight the Depression than federal programs. But the bankers were reluctant participants and proved parsimonious in doling out the $500 million. Ultimately, only $153 million was dispersed to 575 banks in 1931 and 1932, at a time when thousands more were failing.

Many historians argue that the NCC was a classic example of the failures of Hoover's voluntaristic approach to depression fighting. However, the failure did spur the creation of the far larger and somewhat more effective Reconstruction Finance Corporation.

See also: banking; Reconstruction Finance Corporation; Hoover, Herbert.

Bibliography

Hoover, Herbert. *The Memoirs of the Great Depression, 1929–1941.* New York: Macmillan, 1952.

Romasco, Albert U. *The Poverty of Abundance: Hoover, the Nation, the Depression.* New York: Oxford University Press, 1965.

NATIONAL INDUSTRIAL RECOVERY ACT

The National Industrial Recovery Act (NIRA) was the cornerstone of President Franklin D. Roosevelt's early New Deal efforts, what historians call the First New Deal (1933–1935). Scholars tend to view the New Deal as evolving in roughly two stages. The first stage, concerned with economic recovery, was centered around the NIRA. The Second New Deal, after the Supreme Court invalidated the National Recovery Administration (NRA), focused on acts such as the National Labor Relations Act (Wagner Act) and the Social Security Act, laws aimed at increasing consumer purchasing and spending power.

When Roosevelt, elected in 1932, was sworn in 1933, the nation was in the throes of the worst economic disaster in its history. Begun after the stock market crash of October 1929, the Great Depression became *the* central issue for the decade. In fact, the New Deal and the Great Depression are so connected that to discuss one without the other is an oddity. Roosevelt's prime effort was coming up with an economic recovery plan. Roosevelt, at least in 1933, was a fiscal conservative leery of grand economic planning. However, he surrounded himself with some of the nation's leading economic and policy experts—often referred to as the "Brain Trust" because the number of Ph.Ds they had made them a rival of any college faculty. Although his advisers were deeply divided on most issues, there was strong support for what would eventually become the NIRA.

EARLY EFFORTS TO CONTROL THE ECONOMY

Many business leaders recognized that the intense competition of the American economy, falling rates of consumption, and industrial unrest all required a new approach to business practice. Since the late nineteenth century, businesses had witnessed waves of instability. Industrial leaders, seeking stability, first turned to monopoly control of industry. During the late 1800s, reformers aggressively pursued monopolies under the Sherman Antitrust Act and the Clayton Antitrust Act. Having had that approach taken from them, business leaders sought stability next through mergers. The early twentieth century witnessed an unprecedented merger mania, which peaked in the 1920s. Mergers, however, had a limited effect and failed to solve the problem of destructive competition. At the start of the 1920s, far-sighted business leaders sought a new method to stabilize the economy and encourage economic growth. Key industries realized that cooperation rather than cutthroat competition might point the way. Many businesses turned to trade associations, groups of businesses organized by industry. "Trade Associations," writes historian Colin Gordon, "focused on standards of competition within an industry and sought to replicate the advantages of merger or monopoly by taking an active, even coercive, interest in the behavior of members."

Historians such as Gordon and Robert Himmelberg suggest that at the heart of the NIRA movement stood these trade associationists, along with economic planners, liberal business leaders, and certain trade unionists. Since the 1920s, these groups had coalesced around Herbert Hoover, then secretary of commerce. With his reputation as a man of efficiency, Hoover turned the Commerce Department of the 1920s into the center of business planning. Industrialists quickly recognized that they needed governmental support for their project. They lobbied hard for liberalization of antitrust laws. Hoover, a supporter of industrial planning, offered them assistance. Through his office, he could oversee trade association agreements, helping the associationists get as close to the anti-trustline as possible without stepping over it.

Associationists encountered another problem—enforcement. As voluntary groups, they had a difficult time enforcing their own codes. In short, what would stop a member, when the economic mood suited it, from simply breaking away? If enough businesses did this, the industry would return to anarchy. In this, the trade associations were caught in a bind. As Colin Gordon states, "trade associationists wanted both free competition and protection from its excesses." In 1933, suffering from four years of depression, many in the business community began to look toward the federal government to solve their problems. They wanted a vehicle that could enforce industrial codes and yet protect business from their excesses. Historian Jordan Schwarz argues that, by 1933, businesses "craved federal assistance regardless of the price on their souls." Industrialists watched as their party, the Republican Party, seemed to collapse as quickly and thoroughly as the economy. They recognized the risks: in order to achieve the gains of government regulation, they would have to pay the costs. They could not back out as they could from voluntary agreements. Still, many put their faith in the New Deal, as long as they could have a hand in shaping its policies.

DRAFTING THE NIRA

It is clear, however, that Roosevelt did not have a plan for something like the NIRA when he was campaigning nor when he took office. It was not until after April 1933 that such a plan developed, after he surrounded himself with advisers who in various degrees were inclined to support something such as the NIRA. According to Himmelberg, there were five groups influencing the president on what would become the NIRA: trade associationists, national planners, public works supporters, labor-standards reformers, and business leaders. Each group had some influence in drafting the bill.

Efforts to design an administration recovery measure did not begin in earnest until the Senate passed the Black bill on April 6, 1933. Senator Hugo Black (D-AL) had presented a bill that called for a thirty-hour national workweek, with no reduction in wages. The president believed the Black bill was dangerous because of its inflexibility, and this sparked him to design his own recovery measure as a substitute. In the five weeks between the introduction of the Black bill and the passage of the NIRA on May 17, in a frenzy of activity, the first industrial recovery act of the New Deal emerged.

On April 11, as a reaction to the Black bill, Roosevelt ordered his adviser, Raymond Moley, to review legislative alternatives to the Black bill. He also ruled out antitrust revision, a favorite of the business community, and encouraged Secretary of Labor Frances Perkins to draft an alternative to the Black bill. Perkins, a long-standing supporter of labor standards, included provisions in her substitute measure calling for a national board to grant exemptions to the thirty-hour week, with industrial boards to set wages. Under her plan, the secretary of labor could limit a company's production if it controlled too much of the industrial market.

Roosevelt supported Perkins's bill and wanted to include some form of public works spending, a priority among New Dealers. Historians have argued that the New Deal was guided by three Rs: relief, reform, and recovery. Public works spending was the central weapon to achieve relief. With unemployment reaching an all-time high, Roosevelt had to stem the tide of misery—quickly.

At the same time Roosevelt encouraged Perkins to move forward on her bill, he also encouraged others to find substitutes. Moley, by April 18, was working with Senator Robert Wagner (D-NY) on what was called a start-up plan, a plan to jump-start industry. When word leaked to the press that Wagner was working on an alternative to the Perkins measure, Roosevelt said and did nothing. This silence encouraged Wagner and his circle of advisers. During mid- to late April, Wagner and key presidential advisers began drafting a recovery measure. Roosevelt slowly moved away from the Perkins plan toward the Wagner plan. This was typical of Roosevelt. In the frenzy of the First Hundred Days (the first three months of his administration), he often had competing teams of people working on the same legislation.

On April 26, Roosevelt ordered Secretary of the Interior Harold Ickes to start drafting a measure for a public works program that Ickes would head. This measure was not to become part of Perkins's plan. Himmelberg suggests that Roosevelt moved away from Perkins's plan in part because it included a very large public works component—over $5.5 billion. Members of the business community as well as the secretary of the treasury warned of the dangers of excess spending. Therefore, Roosevelt wanted a much smaller public works plan, which, coupled with the narrowness of Perkins's plan, explains why he quickly abandoned it.

Another reason that Roosevelt abandoned the Perkins effort was business opposition. Business leaders opposed to the Black bill were equally opposed to the Perkins wage and hour bill. Labor unions were cautious of Perkins's plan because it vested too much authority, as they saw it, in governmental bodies. Businesses opposed almost all government regulation. Labor, however, feared that the minimum wages would become the maximum and argued that unions—not the government—should increase wages. Roosevelt could not realistically support a bill that was opposed by these two powerful groups if he hoped to instill economic confidence in the country.

Business groups, however, supported the emerging Wagner plan. Slowly, Wagner became convinced that a system of industry-wide agreements that ended cut-throat competition, improvements in hours and wages, and a small public spending plan could provide recovery. Meanwhile, former army general and Roosevelt adviser Hugh Johnson and his assistant Donald Richberg were working on their own plan. Johnson, a longtime Washington insider, was close to Bernard Baruch, a key administration adviser. Business leaders feared that the Johnson plan, while containing none of the industrial self-government provisions of the Wagner plan, would be pro-labor, because Richberg had a reputation of supporting unions.

Wagner and Johnson both sent drafts of their bills to the president on May 10. To deal with the myriad of proposals, Roosevelt created a new committee to draft the recovery plan: Wagner, Johnson, Richberg, and Lewis W. Douglas. The NIRA finally emerged in Congress on May 17, eleven weeks after Roosevelt's inauguration. This omnibus bill, according to scholar Bernard Bellush, "sought to satisfy advocates of social reform, public works, trust-busting, organized labor, self-regulation, state capitalism, and economic planning."

THE NIRA BECOMES LAW

The bill that emerged in Congress contained three parts. Title I declared a national economic emergency, gave enormous powers to the president, and partially suspended antitrust laws for two years. It also allowed members of an industry, working with the National Recovery Administration (NRA), the body created to administer the act, to draw up industrial code for their entire industry. The president could approve the codes, amend them, set them aside, or impose his own. Title I also contained Section 7, the labor section. Section 7(a) gave American workers the right to organize and collectively bargain. Section 7(b) gave workers the freedom to join a labor organization without fear of employer reprisal. Section 7(c) required business compliance with hours, wages, and conditions as written

in the codes and approved by the president. Title II created the Public Works Administration (PWA) and provided $3.3 billion for public works projects. Title III dealt with changes in tax code to pay for Title II.

The NIRA became law on June 16, 1933. That day Roosevelt appointed Johnson to head the NRA, the organization empowered to enforce Title I. He also appointed Harold Ickes to head the PWA, which was in charge of Title II. On July 9, Roosevelt issued a blanket code: the President's Reemployment Agreement (PRA). While voluntary, it called for a thirty-five-hour workweek and a forty-cents-per-hour minimum wage. Johnson exhorted the nation to adhere to the PRA and by August opened a drive to push businesses to adopt the "Blue Eagle," the symbol of the NRA. Thousands of posters and postcards with the symbol were sent out, and soon the Blue Eagle was everywhere. NRA chief Johnson used rallies, parades, and speakers to convince employers to "do their part" for recovery. In many ways, this drive was reminiscent of the Liberty Loan drives of World War I. It is hard to measure the effects of the drive, but it is clear that it speeded submission of industrial codes.

"The NRA," Colin Gordon has written, "was an ad hoc synthesis of disparate industrial or trade association recovery plans." Scholars have argued that the NRA had an impossible task. In "writing its own rules and implementing them simultaneously," according to Gordon, it proved a bureaucratic nightmare. Industries learned early that while they needed the NRA, the NRA needed them just as much. One problem was that in their rush to sign on industries in a short time, businesses dominated the code-writing authorities. In some cases, aggressive trade associations hijacked their industry codes. Also, Johnson proved an early problem. He was "so fearful of a test case [in the courts] that might strike down the NRA and cost him his job that he caved in repeatedly to business demands." Johnson was quickly removed and replaced by Richberg, industrialist Averell Harriman, and Donald Nelson, president of Sears.

Another problem with the NIRA was that industries soon realized that, if they did not like the code in their industry, they could easily declare themselves part of another industry. Rather than having one uniform code for an industry, industries like ladies' garment manufacturing saw a multiplicity of codes. With this fluidity, enforcement of codes was difficult at best.

Not all businesses supported the NIRA. Small businesses accused it of favoring large businesses and engaging in price-fixing, that is, of allowing large firms to act like monopolies. Senators William Borah (D-ID)

The National Recovery Administration, symbolized by the blue eagle, created a host of industrial codes designed to limit cutthroat competition and bolster prices and wages. *(Brown Brothers)*

and Gerald Nye (D-ND), two longtime progressives, argued the case of small business in Congress, demanding investigation into these charges. Roosevelt eventually conceded to certain irregularities, and he created the National Recovery Review Board (NRRB) to look into the matter. Noted lawyer Clarence Darrow headed the NRRB. Darrow's board issued two reports detailing the abuses and problems of the NRA. By the time the second report was issued in summer 1934, public support for the NRA was waning.

THE NIRA IS DECLARED UNCONSTITUTIONAL

In 1935, a lawsuit filed by Schechter Brothers, a small New York poultry company, worked its way to the Supreme Court. In May 1935, the Court declared that the NIRA was unconstitutional, (which voided the NRA) because it delegated too much legislative authority to an executive branch agency. For a brief period, the New Deal was without a recovery plan. In response, it drafted what became known as "mini-NIRAs" for key industries. But it was obvious that many of these would not pass the legal litmus test the Court had constructed. At best, these attempts would be temporary. Although American business had opposed all forms of labor law and labor unions for years, now some leading businesses encouraged labor legislation.

One of the central concerns of the NIRA had been

to stabilize production costs, especially the cost of labor. One of the successes of the NIRA had been Section 7, which, by giving labor the right to organize, had the effect of stabilizing wages for industry. Heralded as labor's Magna Carta by labor leaders, Section 7 unleashed an unprecedented rise in union membership and coincided with the rise of a new form of unionism: industrial unions. For years, industrial unions had chafed under the rule of craft unionism. Within the American Federation of Labor (AFL), workers were organized by skill and job. Yet certain industries such as garment manufacturing and mining organized on a larger industrial scale: all the workers of a shop or mine were in the same union regardless of skill level. Section 7 gave a boost to industrial unions. In 1934, John L. Lewis of the miners' union and leaders of the garment workers created a Committee for Industrial Organization (CIO) within the AFL to organize the unorganized along industrial lines. By 1935, the CIO changed its name to the Congress of Industrial Organizations and withdrew from the AFL. Whether planned or not, the NIRA aided the CIO in organizing millions of workers.

Many within the Roosevelt administration were supportive of the CIO's efforts. Some saw the new union as a vehicle to stabilize industry. An aide to Senator Wagner saw "two ways in which code enforcement can be secured: one is by the techniques written into the codes themselves, and the other is through the policing of industry by organized labor." Where the codes worked, enforcement came from organized labor. Unions singled out uncooperative firms and through strikes brought them back into line. The labor section of the NIRA suggested what would come: increasing consumer purchasing power via support of labor unions. The NIRA also fit with the move towards Keynesian economics that the Second New Deal would take.

When the NIRA was pronounced dead, businesses were ready to accept another form of labor code as long as it had an economically stabilizing effect. Immediately after the *Schechter* decision, New Dealers got to work on labor and industrial codes. The result was the National Labor Relations Act (known more widely as the Wagner Act) and the Fair Labor Standards Act. Together, these laws brought industrial regulation to new heights and increased consumer purchasing power. These two laws became the centerpiece of what became known as the Second New Deal.

RICHARD GREENWALD

See also: unions and union organizing; Brain Trust; National Labor Relations Act; New Deal, first; *Schechter Poultry Corpora-*

tion v. United States; Section 7 (National Industrial Recovery Act); Black, Hugo; Ickes, Harold; Johnson, Hugh; Moley, Raymond; Perkins, Frances; Roosevelt, Franklin D.; Wagner, Robert; Documents: National Industrial Recovery Act, June 16, 1933; Fireside Chat on the National Recovery Administration, July 24, 1933; *Schechter Poultry Corporation v. United States*, 1935.

Bibliography

Bellush, Bernard. *The Failure of the NRA.* New York: W. W. Norton, 1975.

Bernstein, Irving. *The New Deal Collective Bargaining Policy.* Berkeley: University of California Press, 1950.

Cohen, Lizbeth. *Making a New Deal: Industrial Workers in Chicago, 1919–1939.* New York: Cambridge University Press, 1990.

Dubofsky, Melvyn. *The State and Labor in Modern America.* Chapel Hill: University of North Carolina Press, 1994.

Gordon, Colin. *New Deals: Business, Labor and Politics in America, 1920–1935.* New York: Cambridge University Press, 1994.

Himmelberg, Robert. *The Origins of the National Recovery Administration: Business, Government, and the Trade Association Issue, 1921–1933.* New York: Fordham University Press, 1976.

NATIONAL LABOR RELATIONS ACT (WAGNER ACT)

The National Labor Relations Act (1935), also known as the Wagner Act, is among the most far-reaching and monumental of all New Deal legislation. It redefined the American worker's relationship with employers and the federal government, arguably gave employees much more power over shop floor issues, and, in the words of its major architect, Senator Robert F. Wagner (D-NY), helped to "solve the thorniest problem" of its day by becoming "one of the chief bulwarks" of "future economic prosperity and social justice." It reversed a trend that began in the middle of the nineteenth century and reached a pinnacle in the 1920s, when the idea and reality of industrial democracy all but disappeared. From the late nineteenth century to 1931, over 500 federal courts and 1,300 state courts issued injunctions against unions. At the same time, courts typically enforced yellow-dog contracts and utilized the Sherman and Clayton Anti-Trust acts against labor organizations. With the advent of welfare capitalism in the 1920s, employers created thousands of company unions and employee representation plans (ERPs) that ostensibly represented worker interests. The National Labor Relations Act changed that situation by making the federal government the guarantor of labor rights in America.

BACKGROUND: SUPPORTERS AND OPPONENTS

The Wagner Act was the product of two intertwined events: the spectacular rise in labor activism in the early years of the Great Depression and the inability of the Roosevelt administration to stabilize labor relations. With the passage of the National Industrial Recovery Act (NIRA) in 1933, industrial relations changed permanently. The NIRA's Section 7 provided workers with the rights to organize unions and bargain collectively. Union organizers told workers that "the president wants you to join the union," and workers did so by the hundreds of thousands. Employers and their organizations, such as the National Association of Manufacturers (NAM), vigorously opposed not only the growth of unions but also their recognition. In general, employers did not see the benefits of unions, which, according to New Dealers, were wage and benefit stabilization. In part, Section 7 was designed to mitigate the cutthroat competition among businesses who continually sought to reduce costs and hire cheap labor. To foster industrial peace and thus enforce Section 7, President Franklin D. Roosevelt created the National Labor Board (NLB), whose chair, Senator Wagner, had no powers other than persuasion to make employers work with democratically elected unions. In fact, employers tried to evade the NLB by establishing industry-specific labor boards, such as the Automobile Labor Board, in order to diminish the impact of Section 7. The plan worked. To shore up the authority of the NLB, in 1934, Roosevelt re-created it by executive order, renaming the new committee the National Labor Relations Board (NLRB). The NLRB had the same fundamental problem as its predecessor: Neither agency had implementation powers; compliance was voluntary. Few employers sought to earn their Blue

Eagle—a symbol of New Deal support—by cooperating with independently formed unions. More often, they either recalcitrantly refused to submit to Section 7 or they used it to expand company unions, the numbers of which actually rose during the first year of the New Deal.

With the Supreme Court's ruling against the NIRA and the growing frustrations of the NLRB members, Senator Wagner began to push his own plan to reshape employer-employee relations. Legally based on the precedents of domestic wartime changes in federal labor policy during World War I, the 1926 Railway Labor Act, the 1932 Norris-La Guardia Act, and the ability of the federal government to regulate interstate commerce, the National Labor Relations Act rested on the same four concepts as Section 7. First, the act assumed that worker unrest and strikes, low wages, low purchasing power, and fluctuations in employment were obstructions to commerce and remedied by collective bargaining of union representatives. Second, the act assumed that corporate or other forms of ownership associations of workers by themselves did nothing to eliminate the inequality of bargaining power between employers and employees. Third, the act expressed the belief that democratically elected unions that bargained collectively would increase the economic power of labor and mitigate the conditions and causes of the Depression. Fourth, the act posited the notion that the most effective means to facilitate the bargaining process was to give legal authority to the National Labor Relations Board.

While there was a need for such legislation, Wagner's labor bill faced tremendous opposition from predictable and somewhat unpredictable sources. The NAM, the United States Chamber of Commerce, and other employer associations lobbied stridently against the bill. Their basic arguments were that the proposed legislation was not only unconstitutional but also decidedly pro-labor, thus encouraging class conflict. These opponents drew attention to what they saw as the growth in industrial peace brought by welfare capitalism and ERPs. Joining ranks behind employers were two groups on the Left, the Communist Party (CP) and the American Civil Liberties Union (ACLU). Both feared that the intervention of the federal government in labor matters would result in the destruction of independent unions, creating a kind of fascist state. In addition to crushing workers' liberties, the CP and the ACLU believed that a reinvigorated NLRB would cause problems for left-wing labor organizations. The NRB had set several operating procedures under the so-called Reading Formula, by which the federal government sought to enforce, among other things, secret balloting in union elections and majority rule. This last issue meant that, after the election, the union with the most votes would bargain for the entire group, leaving the minority who might want to belong to another union (a Communist-led union, for instance) represented by the majority. On principle, the ACLU opposed such a policy, which appeared to attack the rights of the less powerful. The Communists feared the practical impact that foreshadowed the possible decline of their influence in organized labor. The union that stood to gain from such losses was the American Federation of Labor (AFL), whose unflagging support for the National Labor Relations Act was a marked change in policy. Until the New Deal, the AFL had been for pure-and-simple unionism, a stance that excluded state intervention. Along with the nation's largest labor organization stood a large number of labor relations experts, government officials, and the Socialist Party, which supported plans to expand the scope of the New Deal.

PASSAGE

Despite its opposition, the Wagner Act passed Congress, and President Roosevelt signed it into law on July 5, 1935. The effects were immediate. During its first year in operation, the new NLRB docketed 575 cases involving 141,209 workers. Nearly two-fifths of the cases concerned discrimination because of union membership. In 166 cases, the main complaint was failure of employers to bargain with the union. In ninety-five cases, the board was petitioned to hold an election for representation. Although the board was quite active and successful in its first year, employers failed to take the Wagner Act and its enforcement seriously. In general, business leaders and their associations believed that the law was unconstitutional. Indeed, they had reason to think that the Supreme Court might rule in their favor. In the 1918 *Hammer v. Dagenhart* ruling striking down an anti–child labor law, the Court made a distinction between manufacturing and interstate commerce, arguing that Congress could not regulate industry. Employers hedged their bets that the Court would again serve capitalists and thus refused to concede to workers' demands. Yet, by 1937, the Court had changed significantly, largely as a result of political pressure applied by President Roosevelt. Thus, in 1937, the Supreme Court ruled that the Wagner Act was constitutional. In *NLRB v. Jones & Laughlin Steel Corporation*, Chief Justice Charles Evans Hughes, writing for the majority, asserted that "employees have as clear a right to organize and select their representatives for lawful purposes as [employers have] to organize [their] business and select [their] own officers and agents." Moreover, "discrimination and coercion to prevent the free exercise of the right of employees to self-organization and representation is a proper subject for condemnation by competent legislative authority."

After the Supreme Court's ruling, the number of NLRB cases skyrocketed. From 1937 to 1938, there were 10,430 cases docketed. In the next three years, over 22,000 cases would be taken up by the board. In more practical terms, the presence of the Wagner Act gave many unions, such as the rayon and paper workers, who for years languished and suffered at the hands of employers, their spies, and local police, the opportunity to secure their membership and work toward permanent organizational and wage advancements. Furthermore, the successes of the National Labor Relations Act prompted states to pass similar "little" Wagner Acts whose "baby" NLRB's helped workers not covered by the federal legislation. Not all state labor relations laws were as supportive of unions as the Wagner Act, and jurisdictional ambiguities meant that particular cases could become complicated quickly. Nevertheless, the groundbreaking nature of the National Labor Relations Act transformed the American legal and business culture at all levels of employment.

Historians and other scholars tend to disagree sharply on the importance, meaning, and legacy of the Wagner Act. Especially since the 1960s, when the gains that workers and unions made since the Great Depression began to fade, critics of the New Deal attacked the National Labor Relations Act and its enforcement agency for failing to alter the economic power structure in America. They maintain that the law did not bring about justice but instead secured the position of capital. It stabilized wages, benefits, and unions so that employers could more rationally predict production costs, avoid strikes, and compete with rivals. Moreover, radical scholars insist that the NLRB provided union bureaucrats and not workers with the benefits of the law. It led to the creation of large union organizational structures that limited shop floor militancy and squashed the fundamental rights of strikes and protest.

Local autonomy was circumscribed because union leaders were often given the power to call strikes and bargain with employers. Finally, some maintain that the Wagner Act linked working people politically to the federal government, which meant that little activism could take place without state sanction. In another way, unionists became politically tied to Washington while the party of Roosevelt became the party of workers. Although this meant that Democratic presidents from Harry S. Truman to Bill Clinton could rely on these voters, it also meant that, at times, workers' support was taken for granted and their needs went unaddressed.

Criticism notwithstanding, the Wagner Act remains the centerpiece of American labor law, setting the playing field for employees and employers. Although hostile amendments to the National Labor Relations Act, such as the Taft-Hartley Act of 1947, have made it more difficult for unions to fight for rights and benefits, the Wagner Act has improved the life of the average worker and remains central to the future of the labor movement.

ANDREW E. KERSTEN

See also: American Federation of Labor; Communist Party; Congress of Industrial Organizations; Charles Evans Hughes; New Deal, second; Section 7 (National Industrial Recovery Act); Socialist Party; strikes, general; strikes, sit-down; unions and union organizing; Wagner, Robert F.

Bibliography

Auerbach, Jerold S. "New Deal, Old Deal, or Raw Deal: Some Thoughts on New Left Historiography." *Journal of Southern History* 35:1 (February 1969): 18–30.

Daniel, Cletus E. *The ACLU and the Wagner Act: An Inquiry into the Depression-Era Crisis of American Liberalism.* Ithaca: Cornell University Press, 1980.

Doan, Mason C. "State Labor Relations Acts." *Quarterly Journal of Economics* 56:4 (August 1942): 507–59.

Gordon, Colin. *New Deals: Business, Labor, and Politics in America, 1920–1935.* Cambridge: Cambridge University Press, 1994.

MacDonald, Lois. "The National Labor Relations Act." *American Economic Review* 26:3 (September 1936): 412–27.

NATIONAL YOUTH ADMINISTRATION

The National Youth Administration (NYA) was part of a pantheon of New Deal relief programs that included the Civil Works Administration, the Civilian Conservation Corps, and the Public Works Administration. The NYA was brought into being by Executive Order 7086, signed by President Franklin D. Roosevelt on June 26, 1935. The NYA, technically a subdivision of the Works Progress Administration (WPA), was designed to provide aid to young men and women whose families were on relief.

Young people were very much on the minds of social and political leaders during the Depression. Surveys revealed that, during the early to mid-1930s, between 3 and 5 million eighteen to thirty year-olds were both out of school and unemployed. Many feared that this pool of rootless youth could grow disaffected with a capitalist society that could not provide for their welfare and coalesce into a force advocating radical changes in the system. The NYA was designed to mute this group's potential for revolutionary action by providing jobs and citizenship training.

Working with an initial budget of $50 million and headed by Aubrey Williams, one of WPA head Harry Hopkins's principal assistants, the NYA worked to keep more young people in school by procuring part-time jobs for them. Over half of the people who came to the NYA had never before held a job. Wages were low for NYA-employed youth—high school students earned, on average, $6 per month, while college students averaged $15. These were certainly below-average wages, but this small subsidy often meant the difference for families that wanted their kids to stay in school but could not afford to support them entirely. The NYA also assisted unemployed youth who were not in school. Not unlike the Civilian Conservation Corps, the NYA established a series of resident training centers in rural areas, each one operating with a great deal of independence. These centers—by 1940, there were 595 of them across the United States—took young men from both cities and the countryside and gave them jobs. From 1935 to 1937, the NYA also ran camps for women. Initially, the NYA focused on public works projects, building schools, playgrounds, and parks. Responding to proddings from Eleanor Roosevelt and Brain Truster Charles Taussig, however,

President Roosevelt eventually redirected the NYA more into vocational training and job placement. NYA participants were primarily prepared for clerical and factory careers, but some received instruction in the professions. Some history students, for example, were given jobs in state historical societies. This new approach was not without its problems, however, as many who completed NYA programs discovered that there were simply no jobs available in their new field. In 1939, with war fast approaching, the NYA again shifted its emphasis, this time to preparing the youth to work in defense industries. During its eight-year tenure, the NYA gave part-time employment to over 600,000 college students and 1.5 million high schoolers and aided 2.6 million unemployed youths who were not in school.

Although it was a relatively small agency, the NYA was subject to attacks throughout its brief existence. The NYA's efforts to guide students into careers and its attempts to instill faith in democracy through the espousal of self-government in training camps brought charges from educators that the NYA was merely the first step toward the federalization of the school system. The NYA's liberal attitude on race incited other detractors. The NYA initiated the first federal affirmative action program, an aid program for black graduate students, and its Division of Negro Affairs, headed by educator Mary McLeod Bethune, was the first intragency bureaucracy in the federal government devoted to the problems of blacks. Fortunately for the NYA, some of its most potentially inflammatory activities, like its program to resettle refugees from Nazi Germany, remained unnoticed by critics.

Congress rewarded the NYA's success in providing work for youths with increased appropriations, which peaked at $119 million in 1941. Moreover, in 1939, the NYA was detached from the WPA and given administrative autonomy. Once the war began, however, the need for the NYA to provide jobs and democratic training for young people evaporated. Its funding was slashed in 1942 and the program was terminated in 1943.

DAVID WELKY

The National Youth Administration offered jobs and vocational education to thousands of young people in the Great Depression era, including these apprentice mechanics in Illinois. *(Library of Congress)*

See also: education; youth; Civilian Conservation Corps; Bethune, Mary McLeod; Williams, Aubrey

Bibliography

Davis, Kingsley. *Youth in the Depression.* Chicago: University of Chicago Press, 1935.

Lindley, Betty, and Ernest K. Lindley. *A New Deal for Youth: The Story of the National Youth Administration.* New York: Viking, 1938.

Reiman, Richard A. *The New Deal & American Youth: Ideas and Ideals in a Depression Decade.* Athens: University of Georgia Press, 1992.

NLRB V. JONES & LAUGHLIN

One of the most important United States Supreme Court cases of the Great Depression era, the 1937 *NLRB v. Jones & Laughlin* decision upheld the National Labor Relations Act (NLRA) of 1935 and the key agency created by that legislation, the National Labor Relations Board (NLRB).

The case arose when ten workers were fired from the Jones & Laughlin steel corporation's plant in Aliquippa, Pennsylvania, known to workers as "little Siberia," because they had joined a union. Jones & Laughlin was one of the so-called "little steel" companies that, even as the case was being heard in April 1937, refused to accept the Steel Workers Organizing Committee (SWOC) as the collective bargaining agent for its employees, something that United States Steel ("big steel") had done in March.

The workers had then filed a complaint with the NLRB that the company had violated the NLRA's prohibition of unfair labor practices. Jones & Laughlin insisted that the NLRB had no right to receive or remedy workers' complaints and that the NLRA was therefore unconstitutional.

Many legal experts expected the Supreme Court to rule against the workers and the NLRB. It had already ruled against a broad interpretation of the commerce clause in the *Schechter Poultry Corporation v. United States* decision of 1935, ruling the National Recovery Administration unconstitutional. The commerce clause of the Constitution gave the federal government the right to regulate interstate business.

But while the conservative core of the Court remained conservative, its chief justice, Charles Evans Hughes, had shifted somewhat to a broader interpretative position. Writing the majority decision, Hughes ignored the *Schechter* precedent and said that the NLRA fell within the parameters of the commerce clause. Some historians have said that Hughes changed his position under the threat of Franklin D. Roosevelt's so-called court-packing plan of January 1937, whereby the president asked for the right to add one new justice for every sitting justice over the age of seventy, in order to liberalize the Court.

Over the next few months, the Court would prove that the *NLRB* decision was no fluke, as it ruled various provisions of the Social Security Act constitutional as well.

See also: court-packing plan; "little steel"; steel industry; Steel Workers Organizing Committee; unions and union organizing; United States Steel; National Labor Relations Act; *Schechter v. United States*; Supreme Court; Hughes, Charles Evans.

Bibliography

Leuchtenburg, William E. *The Supreme Court Reborn: The Constitutional Revolution in the Age of Roosevelt.* New York: Oxford University Press, 1995.

Pusey, Merlo John. *Charles Evans Hughes.* New York: Macmillan, 1951.

NEW DEAL, FIRST

During the First New Deal, President Franklin D. Roosevelt and Congress enacted legislation that attempted to alleviate the social and economic problems associated with the Great Depression, accommodating the interests of both workers and employers and incorporating several racial-ethnic groups in their decision making. The period can be characterized by government reforms and relief efforts, and limited recovery—mainly through government planning in industry and agriculture.

The concept of a New Deal began in late June 1932, when Roosevelt accepted the Democratic presidential nomination by pledging himself "to a new deal for the American people." Roosevelt won the election and was inaugurated on March 4, 1933. The United States, in the midst of a Depression that had begun in late fall 1929, needed the assistance of the federal government to reverse the downturn. In his inauguration speech, President Roosevelt signaled the beginning of a new era, declaring, "the only thing we have to fear is fear itself." Roosevelt, believing that the United States was in the middle of a national emergency, expressed his desire to use "broad executive power to wage a war against the emergency." The First New Deal began with the first of the Hundred Days legislation and ended with the rise of conservative business opposition in spring 1934.

This period of reform legislation began with a special congressional session that marked the beginning of the First Hundred Days. President Roosevelt's first priority was to fix the banking system; in early March 1933, he called a special session of Congress to that end, and Congress swiftly approved his proposed declaration of a banking holiday. One week later, Roosevelt called for national planning in agriculture. These were the first of a series of proposals designed gradually to reform the American economy. When Roosevelt called for federal regulation of agriculture, he introduced a new planning philosophy and demonstrated that he was prepared to take over a vital sector of the economy. Two months later, Roosevelt called for organization of industry and commerce under federal authority. His decision to seek central management of agriculture and industry determined the shape of the First New Deal.

THE NEW DEALERS AND THE FIRST HUNDRED DAYS

Roosevelt derived his planning experiments from a diverse multitude of ideas and interests, and he called on legal and academic intellectuals to assist the federal government. This group of New Dealers included intelligent young persons of all classes, but they were predominantly middle-class—most of them lawyers, professors, labor leaders, economists, politicians, social workers, and other professionals, both white and black. From urban and rural areas throughout the country, they were university educated and skilled in the analysis of ideas. Roosevelt appointed a cabinet that included fiscal conservatives, progressive agrarians, and social welfare liberals, Democrats, Republicans, and independents. Roosevelt formed his policies from the ideas of various New Dealers, sometimes defying political philosophy and logic. He thought of governmental policy as a flexible system including elements of coordination and decentralization, nationalism and internationalism, and he prevented any planning from moving to extremes. The New Dealers and Roosevelt converged on Washington determined to solve the deepening economic crisis. Roosevelt recruited men and women who were committed to reform, and his administration was one of the most colorful groups

ever assembled. These individuals included Secretary of Labor Frances Perkins, Secretary of the Interior Harold L. Ickes, Secretary of the Treasury Henry Morgenthau, and Secretary of State Cordell Hull. Roosevelt coordinated this group of individuals with mastery, bringing their suggestions to Congress.

Roosevelt and his administration of New Dealers found a Congress willing to listen to their suggestions because the situation of many Americans, after several years of depressed economic conditions, was desperate, and the conservative approach of former president Herbert Hoover had been unsuccessful in solving the problems. In early 1933, over 13 million Americans were unemployed. Farmers in the Midwest went on strike as banks foreclosed on thousands of farms. During the First Hundred Days, Roosevelt and his administration grasped the opportunity to take unprecedented administrative action, initiating more legislation than in any other similar period. Roosevelt listened to varied American interests, including the unemployed, farmers, laborers, small business owners, and industry. He responded to their comments with experimental programs in governmental management and planning of the economy, one program coming from the president himself. The First Hundred Days legislation was mainly a swift response to pressing problems, although some had long-lasting impact.

REFORM LEGISLATION

On March 9, 1933, Roosevelt implemented a four-day banking holiday, since Congress needed time to pass legislation that would provide relief to the banking system. The banking holiday also gave Roosevelt and his administration time to propose a plan to Congress. Roosevelt wanted to save the banking system rather than change it entirely, since he needed to restore confidence and obtain the support of bankers themselves. The banking holiday was a symbolic pause in the depressed economic conditions. Roosevelt had thought of sending Congress home after the emergency banking legislation, but he realized that he had some momentum in Congress and decided to move for more reforms. Initial reform legislation from Congress came in the form of the emergency Glass-Steagall Banking Act of 1933, that both reorganized the banking system and provided psychological uplift to millions of Americans mired in the Depression. In 1932 alone, almost 1,500 banks had failed and $715 million in deposits were lost. During the first two months of 1933, approximately 4,000 banks closed and $3.6 billion was lost. On March 9, the banking act was introduced, and by March 13, banks began to reopen, with around 75 percent run by Roosevelt personnel. Roosevelt demonstrated that he was a fiscal conservative who consistently called for a balanced budget and wanted to refine the capitalist system. Closing banks and the banking act were a successful effort to stabilize the banking system through its reorganization.

The banking act authorized the secretary of treasury to take over gold bullion and currency in exchange for paper and to undertake the review of closed banks and their reopening through a licensing system.

These reforms aimed at providing temporary relief and public employment for the unemployed. Roosevelt chose Harry L. Hopkins, a former relief administrator in New York City, to head federal relief programs. Congress, agreeing with the administration that federal unemployment assistance was necessary, passed the Federal Emergency Relief Act (FERA) in May 1933. Through that act, the Reconstruction Finance Corporation provided $500 million in the form of outright and matching grants to states. Roosevelt and Congress immediately granted $5 million to several states as states raised money through taxes, bond issues, borrowing, and other means, including limited work-relief programs.

Ultimately, the Hundred Days legislation included the Emergency Banking Act; the Economy Act; the establishment of the Civilian Conservation Corps (CCC); abandonment of the gold standard; the Federal Emergency Relief Act (FERA); the Agricultural Adjustment Act (AAA); the Thomas Amendment, an inflationary measure aimed at reducing the gold content of the dollar; the Tennessee Valley Authority (TVA) Act;

TABLE 1
MAJOR PIECES OF NEW DEAL LEGISLATION DURING ROOSEVELT'S FIRST HUNDRED DAYS

March 9	Emergency Banking Relief Act
March 20	Economy Act
March 31	Civilian Conservation Corps
April 19	Abandonment of the gold standard
May 12	Federal Emergency Relief Act
May 12	Agricultural Adjustment Act
May 12	Emergency Farm Mortgage Act
May 18	Tennessee Valley Authority Act
May 27	Federal Securities Act
June 5	Gold Repeal Joint Resolution
June 13	Home Owners Loan Act
June 16	National Industrial Recovery Act
June 16	Glass-Steagall Emergency Banking Act
June 16	Farm Credit Act

the Federal Securities Act; abrogation of the gold clause in public and private contracts; the Home Owner's Loan Act; the National Industrial Recovery Act; the Glass-Steagall Banking Act; the Farm Credit Act; and the Railroad Coordination Act. During his first three months as president, Roosevelt presented fifteen major laws and fifteen messages to Congress, gave ten speeches, and held press conferences and cabinet meetings twice a week.

RECOVERY PROGRAMS

The two most important recovery programs, the Agricultural Adjustment Act and the National Industrial Recovery Act, restricted output and controlled competition in order to raise prices, in accordance with the administration's call for better distribution and planned production.

On May 15, 1933, Congress passed the National Industrial Recovery Act (NIRA) in two parts: Title I created the National Recovery Administration (NRA), designed to control prices and wages, and Title II created the Public Works Administration (PWA). Congress also suspended federal antitrust legislation for two years. The NRA included industry-wide plans to develop price and wage codes and establish working hours and conditions; businesses within a given industry would agree to operate under the codes, which would end sharp practices, unfair treatment of labor, and unjust price-cutting by some firms. Section 7 of the NIRA, awarded labor the right to organize and bargain collectively: it also set up a National Labor Relations Board to negotiate disputes. This provided the greatest government control of industry since the War Industries Board of World War I. General Hugh Johnson was chosen to administer the NRA. The bureaucracy and NRA regulations never functioned well, however, and business leaders resisted the controls and opposed the government's favorable relationship with industrial labor. The agency was later dismantled, but its legacy was the establishment of a new relationship between government and business and between government and labor.

Interior secretary Harold Ickes headed the PWA and its $3.3 billion budget. Beginning in June 1933, it was responsible for funding 34,508 projects at more than $6 billion over six years. These were more public works projects than ever before, but many people criticized the administration of the program because it was slow to complete many of the projects. PWA money was used to harness water and power resources in the

West: irrigation and electrical projects transformed the region, encouraging population growth and bringing a water supply to the desert. The PWA provided $50 million for the Tennessee Valley Authority (TVA) to develop power in the Tennessee River Valley, one of most impressive public works projects in history. It brought cheap power and fertilizer, flood control, soil and forest conservation, improvement of inland waterways, and new recreational areas to the valley. Fertilizer factories produced 100,000 tons of phosphate fertilizers a year, but the greatest impact was in the supply of electrical power.

In late October, 1933, Hopkins announced a plan for a major work program to employ 4 million people during the winter, and within two weeks, 800,000 people were employed, with a total payroll of around $7.8 million. By mid-January, 1934, over 4 million people were employed, with a total payroll of around $62 million. The employees worked on thousands of projects, including highway and road construction and repair, bridges, schools, parks and playgrounds, hospitals, airports, flood control, privies, and other public works. In spring 1934, Congress appropriated another $950 million to the PWA and $450 million to the CWA.

Farmers, mainly in the Midwest, continued to have financial difficulties, and agriculture secretary Henry A. Wallace and Roosevelt wanted to end the decline of farm sizes and income. On May 12, 1933, Congress passed the Farm Relief Act, which created the Farm Credit Administration for mortgage relief and the Agricultural Adjustment Administration (AAA), authorizing the president to adjust the value of the dollar to implement inflation. Farmers had long supported this measure, although conservative economists objected. The AAA was designed to control production and raise farm prices by paying farmers to take land out of cultivation or reduce their livestock production. Payments were financed by taxes on industries that processed agricultural products. Approximately 3 million farmers participated in the program plowing under 10 million acres of cotton and killing 200,000 sows and 6 million piglets. Although the program had some positive effects, the public was outraged at the waste, and, in response, the Federal Surplus Relief Corporation was created to purchase surplus crops and livestock and distribute them to the public. As a result, millions of pounds of produce and meat were distributed.

The Farm Relief Act provided for use of inflation and other measures toward economic recovery, but more farm legislation was enacted in 1934. Senator Elmer Thomas of Oklahoma helped pass the Thomas Amendment, which gave the president power to inflate the currency, and Roosevelt abandoned the gold standard for the dollar and sanctioned measures to support the price of silver, stabilizing the currency at 60 percent of its former value. In 1934, Congress and New Dealers passed the Federal Farm Bankruptcy Act, the Commodity Credit Corporation, and the Jones-Connally Farm Relief Act. These acts expanded the federal government's role in the farm industry and increased overall prices of farm products. The federal government and the farm industry continued to work together to solve the problems in the agricultural economy.

Roosevelt, federal administrators, and the unemployed themselves were opposed to direct relief believing that it was demeaning. Roosevelt believed that the government should provide some form of employment in exchange for relief. Under his direction, Congress created the Civilian Conservation Corps (CCC), whose officials enlisted an army of workers in the national forests, national parks, and other federal programs, mainly in reforestation and conservation projects. On April 5, 1933, the CCC began enlisting 250,000 workers, U.S. citizens between the ages of sixteen and twenty-seven, in 1,468 camps, with $500 million provided for their employment. Approximately 2,500 members of the Bonus Army, a group of military veterans in search of military bonuses promised earlier, enlisted in the CCC. In summer 1934, Roosevelt increased CCC enlistment to 350,000 members and, by 1935, to 500,000, ultimately employing 3 million "soil soldiers." The TVA supervised eighteen camps.

ADMINISTRATION OF THE NEW DEAL

New Deal relief programs were less than perfect, since federal officials could not fully control them at the local level. The CCC was laden with discrimination and bigotry, and many New Deal work-relief programs were temporary and inadequate. The bureaucracy moved slowly, industry objected to high wages, and 5 million unemployed people were left to rely on state relief programs. Programs like FERA and CWA did, however, permanently change the lives of the majority of Americans who relied on them for relief. Americans and the federal government worked with each other to develop solutions to their mutual problems. And the Roosevelt administration, committed to solving those problems, transformed the public and private landscape through social and economic programs.

The Roosevelt administration passed legislation that introduced cooperative planning in an effort to control the fluctuations and inconsistencies of the free market and laissez-faire economics. In its view, a federal public works program was necessary to repair and improve the nation's existing physical infrastructure, create thousands of long-term jobs, stimulate local economies, develop hydropower and irrigation projects to enhance the growth and economic health of entire regions, and generate general industrial recovery by creating markets for iron, steel, concrete, and other products. Recovery of the economy was the major goal, but the federal government lacked a policy backed by consistent economic theory.

The AAA and the NIRA formed a political-economic pattern that implied that reorganization of American economic institutions would solve the causes of the Depression. According to this pattern and in light of global economic decline, the United States should isolate its economy and solve its own problems first, protecting national recovery programs from exports of other nations. The world was moving toward economic nationalism and the United States needed to follow. The nationalism inherent in the AAA and NIRA legislation aimed to free the national economy from international monetary institutions that prevented domestic planning. Roosevelt and Congress had little interest in permanently increasing tariff barriers, believing that, in the short run, the government should adopt a high tariff and low imports but not in the long run. Roosevelt never committed to a completely nationalist philosophy, but conservatives and liberals agreed that a policy of economic nationalism was necessary.

MINORITIES AND THE NEW DEAL

New Dealers attempted to redefine the role of government and politics in modern life for groups traditionally on the margin of national politics. These groups included industrial workers, sharecroppers, African Americans, Native Americans, and Hispanic Americans, whom New Dealers assisted with relief and reform. The Depression also forced Americans to deal with the poverty in the South and its associated race problem, especially the sharecropping system that had spread after the end of the Civil War.

Many southerners requested federal intervention and supported the First New Deal, as long as they controlled the administration of New Deal legislation. New Deal programs stirred the stagnant economic and political relationships that had persisted in the South. They provided federal work relief and credit, but leg-

islation promoting labor unions threatened the culture of dependency based on the supply of cheap labor.

Following World War I, the number of potential African-American wage earners increased significantly, but they were excluded from labor unions that could improve their working conditions. Thousands of African Americans migrated to the North, but conditions did not improve for those that remained: the problems of poverty, unemployment, and land exploitation were pervasive throughout the South.

The federal government realized that millions of Americans were incapable of self-support through employment during the Depression: By 1934, 17 percent of whites and 38 percent of blacks were unemployed. In numerous large cities, between 25 and 40 percent of African Americans were on relief, which was mainly administered on a discriminatory basis.

African Americans viewed relief and recovery programs as especially beneficial to them initially, since black advisers were involved in decision-making, although later some would criticize the administration of relief. Franklin and Eleanor Roosevelt quickly earned a large African-American following since they were proactive in improving blacks' living conditions. Eleanor Roosevelt, especially, was friendly to African Americans, working with influential blacks, black schools, federal projects, and organizations. African Americans increased their political action, running successfully in state and local elections. The "black cabinet" was one of most important factors in the achievement of political respectability on the part of blacks as specialists and advisers in various governmental positions. Roosevelt differed from earlier presidents in placing a fairly large number of blacks in positions of importance in the government. Harold Ickes, Secretary of the Interior, and Clark Foreman, a liberal Georgia politician, hired their own racial advisers who sought to increase opportunities for employment of African Americans in government and industry. New Deal reformers encouraged protests against discrimination, political action, and the organization of traditionally disfranchised groups.

African Americans benefited from the establishment of agencies to ameliorate the conditions of the Depression. Officials, however, often discriminated against African Americans in administering the programs. NRA codes led to discrimination against African Americans. The AAA crop reduction program negatively affected American farmers, as cash benefits totaling billions of dollars were misappropriated and landowners kept the checks intended for sharecroppers and tenants. Some blacks did benefit from the programs and others were allowed to vote on AAA referenda. Blacks benefited from the TVA, the Rural Electrification Administration, the Federal Land Bank, and local production credit associations. The CCC, although maintaining a policy of strict segregation, employed 200,000 African-American young men in conservation, reforestation, soil erosion prevention, and educational programs under supervision of black advisers.

The PWA and similar agencies constructed black hospitals and other public buildings, employing African Americans in the process. PWA officials, however, sometimes ignored provisions to employ African Americans in projects, and the program still could not employ a sufficient number of people. The FERA and the WPA provided relief in food, clothing, commodities, and employment, and there was greater fairness toward African Americans in material relief although there were inconsistencies in employment regionally. Although outright discrimination against African Americans remained in local administration of New Deal programs in the South, substantial progress was made toward breaking down the traditional pattern of discrimination. The New Deal programs relieved suffering for both whites and blacks and forced equality in administration of benefits. White southern leaders resented power in Washington, however, and they maintained some control in congressional committees.

Eleanor Roosevelt was also instrumental in improving living conditions for women. Interested in women's role in politics and the workplace, she assisted women in obtaining influential appointments to courts and the Roosevelt administration. In August 1933, she persuaded Hopkins to create a women's division in FERA, and Ellin Woodward was hired to run it. On November 20, 1933, the White House Conference on the Emergency Needs of Women convened to discuss women's issues during the Depression. By February 1934, more than 300,000 women were working for the CWA, and over half were eligible for relief. They worked in varied occupations, including sewing, furniture repair, nursing, dentistry, public records, surveys, highway and park beautification, secretarial work, and home economics. The successful CWA ended on March 31, 1934, but it influenced FERA and other programs to include many more female workers.

New Dealers broke with tradition in dealing with American Indians, attempting to reverse discriminatory policies aimed at assimilation of Native Americans at the expense of Indian culture. Interior secretary Harold Ickes appointed John Collier as commissioner of Indian affairs, and Collier quickly made certain that Native Americans were included in the relief and work-relief programs of the FERA and the CWA. The CCC contained an Indian Emergency Conservation Work program, otherwise known as the CCC Indian Division. This program displayed the effort of the federal government to adhere to the cultural needs of the Indians. Officials encouraged participation of the Indians in the actual management of the programs. The most enduring accomplishment was in Collier's influence in reversing the fifty-year insistence on assimilation, a result of the Dawes Severalty Act of 1887. Collier wanted to establish a system that would allow Indians to maintain cultural pluralism while surviving in American society. He pushed the Indian Reorganization Act of 1934 through Congress, which repealed the Dawes Act and attempted to rationalize and equalize the unworkable land-allotment scheme that it had established. The new legislation organized the reservation tribes into self-governing bodies and allowed them to police themselves and act as legal entities in their relationship with federal, state, and local governments. While not all tribes agreed with Collier's method, his determination to preserve the cultural traditions and tribal character of Native Americans remained one of the most important contributions of the First New Deal.

During the 1930s, when the crisis in agriculture included droughts, hurricanes, and floods, white farmers began to compete with and displace Mexican farmers. In the main, New Deal programs intended to help agriculture negatively affected Mexican workers. Some New Deal programs hastened the demise of small and middle-sized farms. Crop-reduction programs on land farmed by Mexican tenants forced them out of production. Displacement of former landowners and sharecroppers increased the supply of rural labor, and the gap between urban and rural wages widened. This led to a series of strikes across the country. The AAA provided little help for tenant farmers and agricultural laborers. Many farmers saved money by calling immigration authorities to deport Mexican laborers before they got paid. The poorly organized relief efforts of the FERA, the CWA, and the WPA required citizenship or first papers for employment. It was widely publicized that undocumented workers were ineligible for employment, and native-born whites demanded that federal jobs be limited to them. In addition, fixed wage policies during the Depression, mainly in the AAA and NRA, excluded farmworkers from minimum-wage provisions. The AAA mainly helped owners of large farms and the NRA allowed stabilization of prices and production, but Section 7 excluded farmworkers, although some farmworkers did organize anyway.

THE CONSERVATIVE OPPOSITION

During the first months of the New Deal, there was general agreement between New Dealers, business leaders, small business owners, industrial laborers, farmers, and the unemployed. Most officials, business leaders, and workers accepted New Deal planning due to the depressed economic conditions. They welcomed the reopening of banks, cuts in government spending, and the end of Prohibition. Business leaders were not really affected by the AAA, and they had typically supported the NRA because it depended on close business/government collaboration. The NRA was the first stronghold of government/business cooperation along with the Reconstruction Finance Corporation. And popular sentiment in spring 1933 was that business had caused the Depression and needed reform.

A basic tenet of the First New Deal was that the technological revolution had rendered large corporations inevitable and that a laissez-faire approach to business competition could no longer be relied on to protect social interests. Several of Roosevelt's advisers believed that the solution to business planning and stability was in combination and cooperation of business with an enlarged federal government. The New Dealers called for creation of new institutions, public and private, that would alter the pattern of economic decision, especially on investment, production, and price. They saw the problem of institutional reorganization in the context not of economic growth but of "economic maturity." The First New Deal was the natural reaction to stagnant industrial and agricultural production and declining prices. Many people believed that America's capacity to produce had surpassed its capacity to consume, and population growth seemed to be at a standstill. Business stagnation and the slowed rate of economic growth would continue unless governmental policies reformed the situation. America needed reorganization of its resources and economy, and intelligent national management was necessary for continued growth.

As the Depression worsened in early 1933, many Americans viewed big business as unethical. Congress launched an investigation of Wall Street that lasted from spring 1933 into 1934. The Senate Finance Committee collected information on what was wrong with stock exchanges and soon thereafter passed the Federal Securities Act of March 27, 1933. The Federal Deposit Insurance Corporation was a successful accomplishment of the First Hundred Days. Regulation of finance implied

that the concept of business was erratic and irresponsible and required strict social discipline. Americans were suspicious of bigness and of industrial self-government. Instead of laissez-faire government, they proposed the use of federal power to revitalize and police the competitive economy. During fall and winter 1933–34, the Senate investigation of shipping and airplane subsidies, headed by Hugo Black of Alabama, provided evidence of sharp business practices and led to cuts in federal subsidies, straining the relationship between government and business. Business and government leaders increasingly opposed Roosevelt and heightened the pace and intensity of criticism of his administration.

A major point of contention between business leaders and the Roosevelt administration was a bill to regulate stock exchanges that accompanied the Federal Securities Act of 1933. The act had three objectives: to protect investors from insiders' manipulations of securities market, to protect investors from misrepresentation by requiring the registration of new securities and of all securities traded on exchanges, and to reduce speculation by controlling the amount of borrowed money in the market through the regulation of margin requirements. By encouraging investment rather than speculation, the bill would protect investors and economic stability, but business leaders condemned the bill, arguing that it would deter investment. On June 6, 1934, the Securities and Exchange Commission was set up to license stock exchanges, regulate trade, and prohibit price manipulation. Business leaders helped develop the banking and securities acts but not all of them supported the new regulations. In addition, business leaders expressed disenchantment with the NRA and the Roosevelt administration's favorable relationship with labor. Private utility companies objected to the TVA, a public corporation. Moreover, business leaders objected to temporary public employment and work-relief programs because they feared the creation of a limited welfare state. In March 1934, relations between the administration and the business community worsened, blocking Roosevelt's momentum and effectively ending the First New Deal.

Historians have largely considered the policies of the First New Deal conservative—that is, they did not go far enough to bring about full recovery. The National Industrial Recovery Act, which established the NRA and the AAA, was the greatest achievement of the Hundred Days legislation. Congress considered both traditional constituent interests of industry and large farmers. Many Americans, however, did not support federal government involvement in free enterprise price supports and wages, but there was a change in the relationship between government and business.

Americans were mired in the effects of the Depression, and the election of Roosevelt stirred the expectations of people and constituencies who had never completely secured representation in the national political arena. The First New Deal did not solve the problems of the Great Depression, but its legacy was the development of the present day infrastructure of politics and government.

JEFFERY GLENN STRICKLAND

See also: agriculture; banking; Commonwealth Club speech; election of 1932; election of 1934; fireside chats; insurance; Jackson Day speech (FDR); manufacturing and construction; mining; Prohibition; service sector; stock market; unemployment; utilities; Agricultural Adjustment Act (1933); banking holidays; Brain Trust; budget, federal; Civil Works Administration; Civilian Conservation Corps; Commodity Credit Corporation; dams; Economy Act; Emergency Banking Act; Emergency Educational Program; Federal Deposit Insurance Corporation; Federal Emergency Relief Administration; Federal Housing Administration; Federal Surplus Relief Corporation/ Commodities Corporation; Glass-Steagall Act; gold standard; Home Owners Loan Corporation; Indian Reorganization Act; Jones-Connally Farm Relief Act; National Industrial Recovery Act; New Deal, second; public works; Public Works Administration; Public Works of Art Program; *Schechter Poultry Corporation v. United States;* Section 7 (National Industrial Recovery Act); Securities and Exchange Commission; Silver Purchase Act; Soil Erosion Service/Soil Conservation Service; Supreme Court; Tennessee Valley Authority; Federal Securities Act; *United States v. Butler et al.;* London Economic Conference (1933); Baruch, Bernard; Berle, Adolph A. Jr.; Black, Hugo; Brandeis, Louis; Butler, Pierce; Byrnes, James F.; Cohen, Benjamin V.; Corcoran, Thomas G.; Eccles, Marriner; Farley, James; Frankfurter, Felix; Garner, John Nance; Glass, Carter; Hickok, Lorena; Hopkins, Harry; Howe, Louis; Hughes, Charles Evans; Ickes, Harold; Johnson, Hugh; Kennedy, Joseph P.; Moley, Raymond; Morgenthau, Henry Jr.; Norris, George; Peek, George; Perkins, Frances; Rankin, John; Rayburn, Sam; Roberts, Owen; Robinson, Joseph; Roosevelt, Franklin D.; Smith, Ellison D.; Stone, Harlan; Sutherland, George; Tugwell, Rexford; Van Devanter, Will; Wallace, Henry A.; Wheeler, Burton; Documents: Agricultural Adjustment Act, May 12, 1933; Tennessee Valley Act, May 18, 1933; Abandonment of the Gold Standard, June 5, 1933; National Industrial Recovery Act, June 16, 1933; Democratic Party platform, 1932; Roosevelt's New Deal Speech to Democratic Convention, July 2, 1932; Roosevelt's First Inaugural Address, March 4, 1933; Fireside Chat on the Banking Crisis, March 12, 1933; Fireside Chat on the National Recovery Administration, July 24, 1933; *Schechter Poultry Corporation v. United States*, 1935; *United States v. Butler et al.*, 1936; *Ashwander v. Tennessee Valley Authority*, 1936.

Bibliography

Acuna, Rodolfo. *Occupied America: A History of Chicanos.* (4th ed). New York: Longman, 2000.

Badger, Anthony J. *The New Deal: The Depression Years, 1933–40.* London: Macmillan Education Ltd., 1989.

Blackford, Mansel G., and K. Austin Kerr. *Business Enterprise in American History.* 3rd ed. Boston: Houghton Mifflin, 1994.

Franklin, John Hope, and Alfred A. Moss Jr. *From Slavery to Freedom: A History of African Americans.* 7th ed. New York: McGraw-Hill, 1994.

Schlesinger, Arthur M., Jr. *The Coming of the New Deal.* Boston: Houghton Mifflin, 1958.

Sullivan, Patricia. *Days of Hope: Race and Democracy in the New Deal Era.* Chapel Hill: University of North Carolina Press, 1996.

Watkins, T. H. *The Great Depression: America in the 1930s.* New York: Back Bay Books, 1993.

NORRIS–LA GUARDIA ANTI-INJUNCTION ACT

The 1932 Norris–La Guardia Anti-Injunction act forbade federal courts from issuing injunctions to enforce so-called yellow-dog contracts. A yellow-dog contract was the negative slang name workers gave to contracts often demanded by anti-union employers in which the potential worker agreed—as a condition of employment—never to join an independent union. In effect, the contract made it impossible to organize unions without employers' consent, and it was bitterly resented by workers and union leaders. A common contract in the late nineteenth century, the "yellow dog" had been upheld as constitutional in the 1917 *Hitchman Coal and Coke Company v. Mitchell* Supreme Court decision. The Norris–La Guardia was introduced into Congress by progressive Republican senator George Norris of Nebraska and Republican representative Fiorello La Guardia of New York. President Herbert Hoover, who reluctantly signed the bill, questioned its constitutionality. Later legislation—particularly the National Labor Relations Act—provided a legal structure on top of the Norris–La Guardia Act that rendered the federal government essentially neutral in employer/employee disputes.

See also: unions and union organizing; Section 7 (National Industrial Recovery Act); National Labor Relations Act; La Guardia, Fiorello; Norris, George; Document: Norris-La Guardia Anti-Injunction Bill, March 20, 1932.

Bibliography

Bernstein, Irving. *The Lean Years: A History of the American Worker, 1920–1933*. Boston: Houghton Mifflin, 1960.

Levine, Rhonda F. *Class Struggle and the New Deal: Industrial Labor, Industrial Capital, and the State*. Lawrence: University of Kansas Press, 1988.

OFFICE OF PRODUCTION MANAGEMENT

The Office of Production Management (OPM) was established through an executive order issued by President Franklin D. Roosevelt in January 1941. The mission of the OPM was to mobilize the nation's industries for defense production.

While modeled after the War Industries Board (WIB) of World War I, the OPM was unique in one important feature: it was headed by two chairmen, General Motors chief William Knudsen and Amalgamated Clothing Workers Union president Sidney Hillman, representing the interests of management and labor, respectively.

But the OPM was relatively weak and not particularly effective in organizing the nation's industries for defense. Not only did the two chairmen differ on most issues, but the president gave them very little room to act. The OPM worked essentially on a voluntary basis, with business executives and union officials being asked to cooperate with the agency's agenda. The inadequacy of this arrangement would become plain enough when the United States went to war in late 1941, when new and more coercive rules and agencies were adopted to reorganize the nation's economy and put it on a war footing.

See also: World War II, early history of; Hillman, Sidney.

Bibliography

Brinkley, David. *Washington Goes to War*. New York: Knopf, 1988.

Polenberg, Richard. *War and Society: The United States, 1941–1945*. Philadelphia: Lippincott, 1972.

PECORA INVESTIGATION

Officially known as the Senate Banking and Currency Committee, but better known by the name of its chief counsel, Ferdinand Pecora, the Pecora committee began its investigation of irregularities in banking and securities trading in January 1933.

Pecora was an Italian immigrant, educated at the City College of New York and the New York University Law School, who had made a name for himself investigating unethical and illegal activities in the securities business.

As chief counsel of the Senate committee, he went even further, revealing how major financial players on Wall Street had manipulated the market and created elaborate holding companies to hide their earnings. To conduct his research, Pecora hired over 100 investigators to dig up evidence of malfeasance and then brought dozens of the nation's wealthiest and most powerful financiers to testify before the committee.

The first such witness was Charles E. Mitchell of the National City Bank (later Citibank, now part of the Citigroup), who admitted illegally shifting $2.8 million to his wife in order to hide it from income tax. The cross-examination of Mitchell set the tone for the testimony of other witnesses.

Ultimately, the Pecora investigation led to the formation of the Securities and Exchange Commission, which was created in 1934 to regulate the activities of Wall Street.

See also: banking; stock market; Securities and Exchange Commission; Mitchell, Charles E.

Bibliography

Pecora, Ferdinand. *Wall Street Under Oath: The Story of Our Modern Money Changers.* New York: Simon & Schuster, 1939.

Wicker, Elmus. *The Banking Panics of the Great Depression.* New York: Cambridge University Press, 1996.

PRESIDENT'S ORGANIZATION OF UNEMPLOYMENT RELIEF

The President's Organization of Unemployment Relief (POUR) was established by Herbert Hoover in August 1931 as a voluntary group of businesspersons, scholars, and others whose task it was to investigate the growing problem of unemployment and help convince businesses to hire more workers.

Replacing the President's Emergency Committee for Employment, which had been established in July 1930 as a purely investigative group, POUR was given more money than the earlier group and spent much of it on an advertising campaign designed to lift the spirits of American workers.

The organization jibed with Hoover's voluntaristic—as opposed to federal public works—approach to fighting the Depression and was headed by American Telephone and Telegraph president Walter Gifford, whose grasp of the problem was questioned by many when he offered simplistic solutions to the unemployment problem to a congressional committee. "I think that what we need," he told the legislators, "is that everybody go back to work and have full pay for all jobs."

See also: unemployment; Hoover, Herbert.

Bibliography

Smith, Gene. *The Shattered Dream: Herbert Hoover and the Great Depression.* New York: William Morrow, 1970.

Warren, Harris Gaylord. *Herbert Hoover and the Great Depression.* New York: Oxford University Press, 1959.

PUBLIC UTILITY HOLDING COMPANY ACT (1935)

The Public Utility Holding Company Act (PUHCA) of 1935 governs companies formed to own stock in privately owned companies that operate gas or electric utility businesses. The purpose of the law is to protect investors and customers of public utility companies by simplifying the corporate structure of utility holding companies and by requiring that utility holding company systems are integrated rationally.

PUHCA specifically authorized the Securities and Exchange Commission (SEC) to regulate and supervise the reorganization of a number of holding companies. According to the law these were corporations which held at least 10 percent of the stock of a company that operated the electric or gas utility distribution business. In the 1930s, there were many utility holding companies that combined holdings in a number of geographically separate utilities with no contiguous service areas or any other features that made their combination logical in order to better serve customers. There was concern among Roosevelt administration officials and legislators that these corporations were organized to make money and provide economic clout for a limited number of investors without regard to the needs of utility customers or smaller investors. The complex structure of many of these holding companies in the 1930s enabled utilities to escape supervision by the state public utilities commissions, which were supposed to ensure the adequate, fairly priced supply of gas and electricity.

Historically, corporations had been chartered to

operate a specific business and were not permitted to hold stock of other companies, except in very limited cases, until the development of the holding company as a legal entity in the late nineteenth century. A parent company could use holding companies to maintain separate operations in different states, to keep different portions of its operations legally distinct, or to incorporate operating subsidiaries to take advantage of state corporation laws that favored corporations incorporated in-state. Holding companies became particularly important in the utilities field for a variety of reasons. Holding companies permitted large enterprises like Edison, Bell, and General Electric to maintain far-flung operations. Since many state regulatory agencies prohibited utility companies from diversifying, a parent entity could diversify by holding stock in entities with divergent businesses, each of which was subject to regulation and prohibited from diversification. Another purpose for which holding companies were used was to construct an elaborate structure in which a small investment would enable an investor to control a number of enterprises. For example, Electric Bond and Share Company had invested $212 million in a variety of securities that permitted it to control holding and operating companies worth a total of $2,458 billion. Some corporate structures employed intermediate holding companies between the parent entity and the operating companies. In some cases, interlocking control of various holdings companies and operating companies made it unclear who was actually in charge of the structure or effectively diluted the interest of investors. In one example of particular complexity, parent entity Associated Gas and Electric controlled 264 corporate entities, including 40 holding companies.

In 1928, the United States Federal Trade Commission (FTC) began an investigation of public utilities that produced a 101-volume study that was critical of the holding company systems, arguing that they were driven more by an interest in profits of investors than by any concern over the provision of service to the public dependent on the utility companies. President Franklin D. Roosevelt, who had struggled in dealing with power companies while governor of New York, was particularly determined to secure legislation permitting the regulation or abolition of utility holding companies. To organize the administration's proposals to Congress, Roosevelt appointed the National Power Policy Committee under the chairmanship of Secretary of the Interior Harold Ickes. Tommy Corcoran and Benjamin Cohen, two young lawyers and protégés of Supreme Court Justice Felix Frankfurter, were the chief drafters of the bill, which was presented to Congress by progressive Senator Burton K. Wheeler (D-MT) and

Representative (and later House Speaker) Sam Rayburn (D-TX). The Texas delegation in Congress, led by Rayburn and staunch New Deal supporter Maury Maverick, was among the most vocal supporters of the bill. Other supporters included Wheeler's fellow Western progressives, rural southerners such as John Rankin of Mississippi, and radical Vito Marcantonio of New York City. Many supporters of PUHCA also favored the Tennessee Valley Authority and other measures designed to increase the federal government's role in ensuring the provision of reliable, affordable utility service, especially to rural areas. The utility industry lobbied intensely against the passage of any such bill, arguing that the people who would be hurt by any move against utility holding companies were not company executives but the small investors who held shares in utility holding companies. The utility holding lobbying effort failed to win over Congress, especially when an investigation by Senator Hugo Black, later a Supreme Court Justice, discovered the expenditure of $1.5 million to generate a flood of mail to Capitol Hill, including telegrams purportedly from constituents who had not sent them.

The House and Senate passed different versions of the bill, differing over the so-called "death penalty" that would have authorized the SEC to dissolve utility holding companies that failed to produce "a geographically and economically integrated system." The final bill gave the SEC authority over utility holding companies owning at least 10 percent of the stock of an electric utility or gas distribution business or otherwise exercising control over the business. The law limited each holding company system to one integrated public utility system, meaning that the operating companies in any utility holding company systems to was forced to conduct operations in one narrowly defined geographic area. PUHCA also encouraged simplification through the elimination of intermediate holding companies and redistribution of voting power among security holders of affected entities. As part of the operation of PUHCA, many holders of securities in holding companies were issued new securities of the underlying operating companies.

After passage of PUHCA, many of the utility holding companies argued that federal government regulation of the holding companies was unconstitutional. An important test in establishing the constitutionality of the PUHCA was *Electric Bond and Share Co. v. Securities and Exchange Commission*, decided in favor of the SEC in March 1938. The Supreme Court found the PUHCA constitutional and approved the SEC's scheme for regulating the public utility holding companies. The utility holding companies then proceeded to comply with SEC's requirements under the act, which still today governs public utility holding companies.

JOHN A. SOARES JR.

See also: stock market; utilities; Wheeler-Rayburn Act; Insull, Samuel; Wheeler, Burton

Bibliography

Hawes, Douglas W. *Utility Holding Companies.* New York: Clark, Boardman, 1987.

Loss, Louis. *Fundamentals of Securities Regulation*, 2d ed. Boston: Little, Brown, 1988.

Skousen, K. Fred. *An Introduction to the SEC.* Cincinnati: South-Western, 1976.

PUBLIC WORKS ADMINISTRATION

The Public Works Administration (PWA) was a federal agency established under the 1933 National Industrial Recovery Act (NIRA). Its purpose was to create public works projects that would provide jobs for millions of unemployed workers.

Funded with some $3.3 billion, the PWA was employing approximately 500,000 workers per year by 1935. Between 1933 and 1939—when the agency was folded into the Federal Works Agency, along with the competing Works Progress Administration (WPA)—the PWA built projects in all but three of America's 3,073 counties. These projects included 583 municipal water systems, 622 sewage systems, 368 road projects, 522 schools, and 263 hospitals. Among the major projects was the reconstruction of Long Beach, California, after the 1933 earthquake; the Queens-Midtown and Lincoln tunnels in New York City; and the San Francisco–Oakland Bay Bridge. In addition, moneys were given to cities and states for public works projects, and some $200 million was loaned to railroads for various improvements.

According to scholars, the mission of the PWA was to complement other aspects of the NIRA. While the National Recovery Administration attempted to raise prices and wages by reducing hours and controlling competition, the PWA was supposed to increase demand by putting money directly in the pockets of working-class consumers.

Yet despite this massive outpouring of money and projects, many in the administration and without complained that director Harold Ickes was too reticent in okaying projects, which thereby undermined the overall effectiveness of the NIRA. Among the critics was Federal Emergency Relief Administration head Harry Hopkins, who, in late 1933, was put in charge of the Civil Works Administration. Later Hopkins headed the WPA, which competed with the PWA for federal money.

In 1937, federal spending cutbacks forced the PWA to reduce its employment by some 140,000 jobs, which, say scholars, played a part in setting off the "Roosevelt recession" of that year. In 1939, the PWA and the WPA—renamed the Works Projects Administration—were combined into the Federal Works Agency, which itself was discontinued in 1943, due to full wartime employement.

See also: public works; Civil Works Administration; Works Progress Administration; Hopkins, Harry; Ickes, Harold.

Bibliography

Ickes, Harold. *Back to Work: The Story of the PWA.* New York: Macmillan, 1935.

Rose, Nancy E. *Put to Work: Relief Programs in the Great Depression.* New York: Monthly Review Press, 1994.

The first of the major public works programs of the New Deal, the Public Works Administration helped reconstruct the Philadelphia Navy Yard pictured here. *(Brown Brothers)*

PUBLIC WORKS

Throughout the Great Depression and the New Deal, public works were an important instrument of government policy, used by both the Hoover and Roosevelt administrations as part of their efforts to end the economic downturn, reduce unemployment, and develop the nation's infrastructure. In turning to public works to produce these outcomes, both administrations relied on a policy tool with a long history.

PUBLIC WORKS BEFORE THE NEW DEAL

The idea of using publicly funded construction to counter the effects of unemployment dates as far back as the economic slumps of the 1830s, the 1850s, and the 1870s. It was not until the financial panic of 1893, though, that cities began to use public works extensively in this fashion. Over the next forty years, a growing number of progressive intellectuals, journalists, and politicians began to consider seriously the use of widespread public works to combat unemployment and swings in the business cycle. The American Association for Labor Legislation (AALL), founded in 1906, became a clearinghouse for translating concerns over unemployment into concrete policy measures. With funding from such men as John D. Rockefeller and Elbert H. Gary, the AALL attracted a wide range of progressives, including Richard T. Ely, Henry Rogers Seager, Henry Farmer, John R. Commons, John B. Andrews, Irene Osgood, Jane Addams, and Charles Henderson. In 1914, the AALL published *A Practical Program for the Prevention of Unemployment in America*, proposing such measures as the creation of unemployment insurance and the planning of public works projects in order to stabilize the economy.

While this plan was reprinted several times, public works advocates achieved only occasional state-level legislative success before the 1930s. The debate over the merits of using publicly funded construction to ease mass unemployment, however, continued. At the close of World War I, Congress created a new division of the Department of Labor, the Division of Public Work and Construction Development, intended to prod states and cities into conducting public works projects. AALL member Otto T. Mallery headed the division, but his efforts were mostly limited to uplifting bulletins sent to the mayors of various cities. While some members of Congress, led by Senator William S. Kenyon of Iowa, pushed for the formation of a federal board to supervise public works construction, little was accomplished at the federal level.

President Warren G. Harding's 1921 conference on unemployment, organized by commerce secretary Herbert Hoover, provided a new forum for public works advocates. The conference, after hearing from Mallery, recommended that the nation plan for "future cyclical periods of depression and unemployment by a system of public works," even advocating that federal loans be advanced to municipalities during periods of depression. While this recommendation led in the short run only to several bills in the House that failed to pass, it did help to shape the boundaries of the debate over the uses of the federal government. In 1928, Washington senator Wesley L. Jones proposed the initiation of a "prosperity reserve" of federal public works plans, to be used during periods of depression to restore balance to the economy. Other students of government policy took notice of this activity, linking the concept of the business cycle with public works programs and arguing that government construction contained the potential to minimize the cycle's depths. A genera-

tion of businessmen and politicians soon came to associate public works spending with economic stabilization and economic growth. Wilsonians such as Hoover, William Gibbs McAdoo, and Bernard Baruch combine a southern prodevelopment heritage with a western desire for infrastructure and growth, laying the groundwork for southern and western progressive Republicans to unite with Democrats to quench a shared thirst for public works projects. While politicians, businessmen, and civic boosters advocated permanent improvements to public infrastructure, reform-minded organizations such as the National Unemployment League and the AALL pressed for nationally planned public works, making the case for their effectiveness as relief measures.

This pressure took on fresh urgency with the stock market crash of 1929. President Herbert Hoover moved in early 1930 to increase public road building by $75 million in order to counter the growing Depression, using planned public works to minimize this oscillation in the business cycle. When this effort seemed to have little effect, Hoover asked Congress to appropriate $150 million for emergency construction projects, and he created the President's Emergency Committee for Employment, (PECE) naming Colonel Arthur Woods, former New York City police commissioner, chairman. The increases in federal construction, however, were not sufficient, given the enormous decline in state and local construction due to the collapse of such revenue sources as the property tax. Woods soon overstepped his role as PECE chair, advocating more spending on construction than Hoover wanted and finally resigning in April 1931 to voice his dissatisfaction with the administration.

Progressive senators, most notably New York's Robert Wagner, Wisconsin's Robert La Follette Jr., and Colorado's Edward P. Costigan, along with publishing magnate William Randolph Hearst, led renewed demands for increased spending on public works. In the states, governors such as Franklin Roosevelt in New York enacted relief programs of their own, using public works to address the crisis of the Depression. La Follette and Wagner were in the forefront of Senate debates over these issues, championing public works measures, employment stabilization, and increased funding for the gathering of labor statistics. Within the federal government, the Employment Stabilization Act of 1931 brought together members of the Agriculture, Commerce, Labor, and Treasury Departments to develop a six-year plan for public works projects.

With the creation of the Reconstruction Finance Corporation (RFC) and the signing of the Emergency

Relief and Construction Act (ERCA) in 1932, Hoover again seemed to be taking significant steps to counter the Depression. Modeled after the War Finance Corporation of World War I, the RFC provided loans to banks and railroads. Although the ERCA was not a rousing success, it did provide the legislative blueprint for Roosevelt's Public Works Administration (PWA). The ERCA broadened the powers of the RFC, with the act's first title providing for $300 million to be loaned to the states for direct and work relief at 3 percent interest, with the federal government to be repaid out of future federal allotments for highways. Title II allowed for $1.5 billion to be loaned to the states for self-liquidating public works projects, such as dams, bridges, and roads, with the potential to make back the costs of their construction. The third title appropriated $322 million for national public works projects such as Hoover Dam, hospitals, military airports and bases, and other public buildings, bridges, and utilities, to stimulate the heavy construction industry. Although the $300 million from Title I was distributed to the states for relief, the second title's strict self-liquidating requirement and higher interest rates resulted in only $147 million in projects approved (and of that, only $15.7 million spent) by the end of December 1932. Title III was even less of a success, with scarcely $6 million spent on public works. Despite these financial shortcomings, however, the ERCA established an important precedent. The RFC had created a new division to supervise the construction of self-liquidating public works, forging direct financial relationships between the federal government and state and local levels of government. The New Deal would soon expand and nourish these relationships.

THE NEW DEAL AND PUBLIC WORKS

During the weeks following President Roosevelt's inauguration, many New Dealers supported public works programs, but often with different justifications. The head of the Federal Emergency Relief Administration,(FERA) Harry Hopkins, thought that public works could quickly put people back to work. This philosophy shaped Hopkins's subsequent leadership of the Civil Works Administration (CWA) and the Works Progress Administration (WPA). Interior secretary and head of the PWA Harold Ickes envisioned public works more as an opportunity to improve the nation's infrastructure and stimulate employment in fields related to the construction industry. Hugh Johnson, in charge of the National Recovery Administration (NRA), departed

from both of these rationales. Johnson thought that the proper role of public works spending was to complement the NRA's industrial codes, providing a two-pronged effort to revitalize the nation's industrial firms. While these New Dealers approved of public works, the fiscally conservative director of the Bureau of the Budget, Lewis Douglas, who was deeply skeptical of large government expenditures, pushed for reductions in public works spending. While Roosevelt was sympathetic to Douglas's belief in fiscal orthodoxy, public works captured his imagination and interest. Before his inauguration, he toured Muscle Shoals, Alabama, with Senator George Norris, and after taking office he championed the creation of the Tennessee Valley Authority (TVA). The president delivered speeches at project dedications and personally approved PWA allotments, regularly conferring with Ickes over the details of projects. The Civilian Conservation Corps was one of Roosevelt's favorite New Deal measures, confirming his belief that fresh air and hard work on various forestry projects would rebuild the morale of unemployed young men.

The PWA, created in 1933 by the National Industrial Recovery Act, concentrated on heavy construction and large-scale building. Armed with an initial appropriation of $3.3 billion, the PWA gradually deployed its funds in the form of loans and grants in 3,068 of the nation's 3,071 counties. The PWA helped to pay for projects such as the TVA and Hoover Dam. The PWA's emphasis on the capacity of public works to provide necessary municipal improvements, employment on work sites, and indirect employment in related industries drew on a generation of thinking articulated by such engineers and economists as Otto T. Mallery, Leo Wolman, Arthur D. Gayer, and John Kenneth Galbraith. The PWA was also committed to national planning, superseding the planning board created by the 1931 Employment Stabilization Act with the National Resources Planning Board (NRPB). Frederick Delano, Charles Merriam, and Wesley Clair Mitchell composed the NRPB's advisory committee, and Mallery soon found a position on the planning board's public works committee.

Outside of the government, a number of groups were interested in the PWA's public works projects. In the construction industry, professional building contractors welcomed a chance to go back to work on government contracts, while organized labor, especially the American Federation of Labor building trades, similarly looked forward to a return to employment. Organizations such as the National Unemployment League, the United Relief Program, the National Conference of Catholic Charities, and the Joint Committee on Unemployment thought that public works would provide broad-based relief of unemployment.

By 1939, the PWA had authorized the construction of 34,508 projects costing about $6 billion, completing 34,448 of them. Ickes's agency funded 17,831 projects costing $1.9 billion built by federal agencies, and 16,677 projects costing $4.2 billion sponsored by nonfederal bodies. Streets and highways were the most common PWA project, with 33 percent of all PWA projects accounting for over 15 percent of total PWA spending. Educational buildings were the next most common undertaking (22 percent of all PWA projects), comprising about 14 percent of PWA spending. By July 1936, one or more PWA school projects had been placed in 47 percent of all counties. The PWA explicitly targeted some of its school and several of its hospital projects for African Americans, building in twenty-four states but concentrating its efforts in North Carolina, Alabama, Georgia, Florida, Missouri, and Tennessee. Flood control and reclamation projects, while comprising only 1.4 percent of PWA projects, accounted for 10.4 percent of all PWA spending. Public buildings, along with sewer and water projects, were also favored targets of PWA funds, taken together comprising 25.3 percent of PWA projects and 20.3 percent of PWA spending. During the period 1933–40, the PWA made possible about 80 percent of all sewer construction in the nation, allotting funds for more than 1,500 projects. While the PWA did sponsor a housing program, it was small. The PWA's seven limited-dividend federal housing projects accounted for 0.02 percent of all PWA projects and 0.2 percent of total PWA spending, while the fifty-one federal low-cost housing projects sponsored by the PWA made up 0.15 percent of all projects and 3.2 percent of all PWA spending. PWA funds also were used to build vessels for the Navy (0.75 percent of all projects receiving 6.4 percent of PWA funds), including the *Yorktown* and the *Enterprise*, and to modernize the nation's railroads (0.09 percent of all projects, using 4.7 percent of PWA funds). Overall, the projects most favored by the PWA were streets, highways, roads, and bridges; schools; and public buildings such as court houses, post offices, auditoriums, armories, city halls, prisons, community centers, and government office buildings.

Although the PWA and Ickes gained a reputation for moving too slowly against the Depression, with *Business Week* criticizing Ickes for cautiously running an emergency agency as if it were a fiscally sound bond house, the stock of Hopkins and his approach to public works rose. With the creation of the Works Progress Administration (WPA) in 1935, the New Deal put $4.8 billion toward using public works in the fight to remove people from the unemployment rolls. The WPA avoided private contractors; it also generally avoided heavier construction projects in order to put the maximum possible number of people to work. Its original charter was to assemble a program of "small useful projects," and the WPA nominally handled small projects costing under $25,000 while the PWA undertook more expensive and substantial projects. Hopkins, however, skirted this rule by treating larger projects—such as the airport that the WPA built at La Guardia Field in New York—as a series of smaller endeavors, often to Ickes's annoyance. Although 75 percent of the WPA's funds went to traditional public works construction such as roads and buildings, the remainder went to a series of "white collar" or professional projects such as the Federal Writers' Project.

Between 1933 and 1938, the PWA generated 535,000 jobs on site and 641,000 off the project site, for a total of 1,176,000 employed. During the same period, the FERA, CWA, and WPA had a higher average on-site employment of 1,422,000 but only employed 220,000 off-project sites, for a total average of 1,642,000 employed. The greater ability of the PWA to generate off-site employment was due to the many different materials required for the projects it built.

PUBLIC WORKS IN RECESSION AND WAR

The advent of the "Roosevelt recession" of 1937–38 again brought public works programs to the center of government debates. New Dealers such as Hopkins and Ickes, economists Lauchlin Currie and Leon Henderson, Chairman of the Federal Reserve Board Marriner Eccles, joined by advisers Thomas Corcoran and Benjamin Cohen, urged Roosevelt to propose increases in federal spending, particularly on public works. By April 1938, they had overcome Roosevelt's allegiance to the more fiscally cautious course urged by such advisers as treasury secretary Henry Morgenthau, commerce secretary Daniel Roper, and RFC head Jesse Jones. Among other steps, Roosevelt called for more than $2 billion to be spent by various governmental bodies, including the WPA, the U.S. Housing Authority, the Farm Security Administration, and the PWA, on public works such as roads, housing, reclamation projects, and various buildings.

The reorganization of the executive branch of government in 1939 consolidated federal public construction functions in a new organization, the Federal Works Agency (FWA). The FWA contained the WPA (now renamed the Works Projects Administration), the PWA, the Public Buildings Administration (formerly in the Treasury Department), the Public Roads Administration (transferred from the Agriculture Department), and the U.S. Housing Authority. Roosevelt selected John Michael Carmody to run the new agency. Carmody, formerly head of the Rural Electrification Administration, and before that an engineering administrator in the CWA, had a strong background in engineering and advocated the adoption of scientific management principles. Before and during World War II, the FWA sponsored construction of child care centers, community centers, and housing for defense workers under the Lanham Act; improved and modernized military buildings; improved access roads to military bases; trained workers for jobs in defense industries; built airports; and made plans for public works projects to ease the conversion back to a peacetime economy. General Philip B. Fleming, an Army Corps of Engineers officer who had worked for Ickes in the PWA and subsequently ran the Labor Department's Wages and Hours Division, took over as FWA head in 1941. Fleming ran the FWA until 1949, when Jesse Larson took over the agency and supervised its conversion into the General Services Administration. While public works did not manage to bring an end to the Great Depression, they did succeed in employing a great number of people and built a wealth of projects across the nation.

JASON SCOTT SMITH

See also: Civil Works Administration; Civilian Conservation Corps; dams; Federal Art Project; Federal Music Project; Federal Theater Project; Federal Writers' Project; New Deal, first; New Deal, second; Public Works Administration; Public Works of Art Project; Rural Electrification Administration; Tennessee Valley Authority; Works Progress Administration; Hopkins, Harry; Norris, George; Roosevelt, Franklin D.; Documents: Hoover's Veto of Muscle Shoals Bill, March 3, 1931; Tennessee Valley Act, May 18, 1933; Roosevelt's Fireside Chat on Work Relief Programs, April 28, 1935; *Ashwander v. Tennessee Valley Authority,* 1936.

Bibliography

Amenta, Edwin. *Bold Relief: Institutional Politics and the Origins of Modern American Social Policy.* Princeton: Princeton University Press, 1998.

Brinkley, Alan. *The End of Reform: New Deal Liberalism in Recession and War.* New York: Knopf, 1995.

Daniels, Roger. "Public Works in the 1930s: A Preliminary Reconnaissance." In *The Relevancy of Public Works History: The 1930s—A Case Study.* Washington, DC: Public Works Historical Society, 1975.

Federal Works Agency. *Final Report on the WPA Program, 1935–1943.* Washington, DC: Government Printing Office, 1946.

Galbraith, John Kenneth, assisted by G. G. Johnson Jr. *The Economic Effects of the Federal Public Works Expenditures, 1933–1938.* Washington, DC: Government Printing Office, 1940.

Gayer, Arthur D. *Public Works in Prosperity and Depression.* New York: National Bureau of Economic Research, 1935.

Howard, Donald S. *The WPA and Federal Relief Policy.* New York: Russell Sage Foundation, 1943.

Isakoff, Jack F. *The Public Works Administration.* Urbana: University of Illinois Press, 1938.

MacMahon, Arthur W., John D. Millett, and Gladys Ogden. *The Administration of Federal Work Relief.* Chicago: Public Administration Service, 1941.

Mallery, Otto T. "Prosperity Reserves." *Survey* 62:1 (April 1, 1929).

Mund, Vernon Arthur. "Prosperity Reserves of Public Works." *Annals of the American Academy of Political and Social Science* 149, Part II (May 1930): 1–47.

Public Works Administration. *America Builds: The Record of PWA.* Washington, DC: Government Printing Office, 1939.

Reeves, William D. "PWA and Competitive Administration in the New Deal" *Journal of American History* 60 (September 1973): 357–72.

Sautter, Udo. *Three Cheers for the Unemployed: Government and Unemployment before the New Deal.* Cambridge: Cambridge University Press, 1991.

Schlesinger, Arthur M., Jr. *The Coming of the New Deal.* Boston: Houghton Mifflin, 1958.

Schwarz, Jordan A. *The New Dealers: Power Politics in the Age of Roosevelt.* New York: Knopf, 1993.

Williams, J. Kerwin. *Grants-in-Aid under the Public Works Administration: A Study in Federal-State-Local Relations.* New York: Columbia University Press, 1939.

PUBLIC WORKS OF ART PROJECT

The Public Works of Art Project (PWAP) was created by President Franklin D. Roosevelt in December 1933 to hire artists to create murals and public works of art for nonfederal public buildings throughout the country. It was funded by the Civil Works Administration, an experimental program in federal work relief, providing the unemployed with secure jobs.

Less well known, smaller in size, and shorter-lived than the Federal Art Project (FAP) under the 1935 Works Progress Administration, PWAP nevertheless hired some 3,700 artists between its inception at the end of 1933 and its demise—along with the Civil Works Administration—in April 1934. It was soon revived as the Section of Fine Arts within the Treasury Department.

More elitist in spirit than FAP, the PWAP was seen by its directors less as a way of hiring unemployed artists than as a way of raising the cultural standards of the American people. Among the artists PWAP commissioned were Grant Wood, John Sloan, and Thomas Hart Benton.

See also: Civil Works Administration; Federal Art Project; Works Progress Administration; Benton, Thomas Hart; Sloan, John; Wood, Grant.

Bibliography

Marling, Karal Ann. *Wall-to-Wall America: A Cultural History of Post-Office Murals in the Great Depression.* Minneapolis: University of Minnesota Press, 1982.

McDonald, William F. *Federal Relief Administration and the Arts: The Origins and Administrative History of the Arts Projects of the Works Progress Administration.* Columbus: Ohio State University Press, 1969.

RECONSTRUCTION FINANCE CORPORATION

The Reconstruction Finance Corporation (RFC) attempted to restore business confidence by increasing the credit available in the financial marketplace. A centerpiece of President Herbert Hoover's recovery program, the RFC took on greater importance during President Franklin D. Roosevelt's administration. Under Roosevelt, the RFC, led by Houston banker Jesse Jones, made low-interest loans and bought and sold securities during the Great Depression and World War II, serving, in effect, as the New Deal's bank.

Created when Hoover signed the Reconstruction Finance Corporation Act on January 22, 1932, the RFC was explicitly modeled on the War Finance Corporation (WFC) of World War I. The War Finance Corporation was run by Eugene Meyer under the auspices of treasury secretary William Gibbs McAdoo, loaning money to banks, public utilities, and building and loan associations. By 1930, bankers such as Meyer—who was by this point head of the Federal Reserve—were advising Hoover that he ought to revive the WFC to fight the Depression. Following the failure of the National Credit Corporation, a volunteerist effort organized at Hoover's urging by a collection of bankers, Hoover overcame his longtime opposition to the idea and hesitantly agreed with Meyer. He urged Congress to enact the RFC, declaring it a temporary measure necessary for the economic emergency. Following the template of the WFC, the RFC had thirty-three regional offices throughout the country to examine loan applications. Similarly, the RFC adopted an eight-part structure, consisting of secretarial, treasury, legal, auditing, agency, statistical, railroad, and examining divisions. In its haste to assemble qualified bureaucrats, especially legal and financial personnel who could review loan applications, the RFC also employed many who had worked for the WFC. Drawing on about $2 billion in capital with which to make loans, the RFC placed loan repayments into a revolving fund. The RFC could draw on this fund to make more loans instead of asking Congress for further appropriations.

Hoover named four Republicans and three Democrats to the RFC's board. Eugene Meyer was the RFC's first chair; Charles Dawes, the former U.S. vice president, was RFC president. Treasury secretary Ogden Mills and Federal Farm Loan board head H. Paul Bestor were the other two Republicans; the three Democrats were Arkansas railroad expert Harvey Couch, Texas banker Jesse Jones, and Utah banker Wilson McCarthy. The RFC had to issue reports each month and quarter, but it did not have to disclose who received its loans. By July 1932, the RFC had loaned $1 billion to banks, railroads, and other financial institutions, but to little effect.

In the summer of 1932, in response to its growing unpopularity—Representative Fiorello La Guardia (R-NY) termed the RFC a "millionaire's dole"—Hoover reshuffled the RFC's board, giving the Democrats a majority and agreeing with Congress that the RFC could make relief loans to states and would make public the recipients of its loans. Under the Emergency Relief and Construction Act of 1932, the RFC was authorized to make $1.5 billion in loans for self-liquidating public works and $300 million in relief loans to the states. The RFC's new chair, Atlee Pomerene, a former Democratic senator from Ohio, established self-liquidation and emergency relief divisions within the agency to attend to these functions. These public works projects, such as bridges, dams, sewer systems, and toll roads, were slow to plan and execute, however. By the time Hoover left office, the RFC had approved only ninety-two projects worth $197 million and had paid out only $20 million of this amount. Harold Ickes's Public Works Administration would eventually take over many of these projects. The new emergency relief division, however, quickly ran through its allotted $300 million to loan to states for unemployment relief, with five states requesting $200 million in one day. The RFC's early ineffectiveness in fighting the Great Depression solidified Hoover's image as a man willing to lend billions to banks and big institutions, but unwilling to give adequate assistance to the unemployed.

During Roosevelt's presidency, Jesse Jones became the head of the RFC and, with the advent of the New Deal, drastically expanded its power and scope. The 1933 Emergency Banking Act allowed the RFC to buy stock in banks, somewhat easing financial pressures on them. The RFC became the funding source for agencies such as the Home Owners Loan Corporation, the Export-Import Bank of Washington, the Regional Agricultural Credit Corporation, the Farm Credit Corporation, the Federal Home Loan Banks, the Federal Farm Mortgage Corporation, the Federal Housing Administration, the Rural Electrification Administration, and the Resettlement Administration. The RFC purchased the bonds bought by the Public Works Administration from local governments; when the Works Progress Administration was created in 1935, the RFC quickly provided it with $1 billion. In 1937, Congress authorized the RFC to establish a Disaster Loan Corporation, to provide loans to areas hit by earthquakes, floods, and other natural calamities. In 1938, the RFC created the Federal National Mortgage Association, or "Fannie Mae."

A conservative Democrat from the South with ties to the business community, Jones himself served as an important political asset to Roosevelt. He continued to oversee the RFC after joining the cabinet as administrator of the Federal Loan Agency, following the 1939 reorganization of the executive branch, and eventually became commerce secretary. During World War II, Jones and the RFC remained active, funding a number of agencies such as the Defense Plant Corporation, the Defense Supplies Corporation, and the Defense Homes Corporation. By the close of World War II, the RFC had lent over $50 billion in pursuing its goals.

JASON SCOTT SMITH

See also: Emergency Banking Act; Federal Housing Administration; Home Owners Loan Corporation; Public Works Administration; Resettlement Administration; Rural Electrification Administration; Works Progress Administration; Hoover, Herbert.

Bibliography

Jones, Jesse H., with Edward Angly. *Fifty Billion Dollars: My Thirteen Years with the RFC (1932–1945)*. New York: Macmillan, 1951.

Olson, James S. *Herbert Hoover and the Reconstruction Finance Corporation, 1931–1933*. Ames: Iowa State University Press, 1977.

Olson, James S. *Saving Capitalism: The Reconstruction Finance Corporation and the New Deal, 1933–1940*. Princeton: Princeton University Press, 1988.

Schwarz, Jordan A. *The New Dealers: Power Politics in the Age of Roosevelt*. New York: Knopf, 1993.

RESETTLEMENT ADMINISTRATION

In 1929, the stock market crash reverberated throughout the American economy. Banks closed, businesses failed, and the unemployment rate reached record levels. Farmers especially felt the onset of economic disruption. Overproduction coupled with decreasing farm prices and rising international trade barriers resulted in a drastic decline in farmers' income and a rash of foreclosures. For example, between 1929 and 1932, farm prices had dropped by 60 percent but with only a 6 percent corresponding reduction in agricultural production. Hoping to offset lower prices, many farmers continued to overproduce, thereby further depressing their own profits. Drought, infestations of grasshoppers, insatiable dust storms, and the loss of personal savings accounts added to the desperate plight of American farmers.

ROOSEVELT AND THE FARMERS

After defeating Herbert Hoover in 1932, President Franklin D. Roosevelt spent his First Hundred Days in office passing through Congress a variety of legislation intended to ease the severity of the Depression. To control the plummeting decline in farm commodities, Congress passed the Agricultural Adjustment Act (AAA), in 1933 which offered farmers subsidies to take land out of production with the goal of eliminating excess. Although farmers complied with the act, many simply retired their least profitable lands from production, collected the governmental subsidies, and then used improved mechanization, seeds, and fertilizers to produce more on fewer acres.

Meanwhile, the reduction in farming acreage led to the dislocation of tenant farmers and sharecroppers who were forced off lands retired by farm owners. To deal with the growing numbers of unemployed and homeless rural poor, the Federal Emergency Relief Administration (FERA), created in 1933, provided limited funds for resettlement and job training, while the National Industrial Recovery Act (NIRA) allocated $25 million dollars for the construction of subsistence homesteads. Neither program, however, had enough funds nor sustained effort to effectively provide widespread relief.

REXFORD TUGWELL AND THE RESETTLEMENT ADMINISTRATION

While serving as undersecretary of agriculture, Rexford Tugwell became more and more disgruntled over the lack of organized federal support to aid the rural poor. At his urging, President Roosevelt diverted nearly $4.9 billion from the recently passed Emergency Relief Appropriation Act and established the Resettlement Administration (RA) by executive order on May 1, 1935. Roosevelt appointed Tugwell as director of the RA, and the new agency assumed the rural relief programs of the FERA and the subsistence homestead communities of the NIRA. The RA, furthermore, adopted a broad array of new programs dedicated to aiding both the rural and urban poor.

A primary goal of the RA focused on relocating farmers from substandard agricultural regions to areas providing more fertile soil. In these new communities, the RA would provide new housing, cooperative services, and training in the latest innovations in farming techniques. Tugwell's goals for the RA, however, extended beyond simply creating governmentally funded cooperative communities. He wanted the RA personnel to educate farmers in areas of conservation and irrigation management. Tugwell hoped that better farming practices would stave off the corrosive effects of soil erosion, especially in the Appalachian regions and the southern cotton belt. Along with educational and housing benefits, the RA also offered credit and loans to small farmers, tenant farmers, and sharecroppers. The RA, however, continually hampered by under-funding, helped less than 1 percent of the roughly 500,000 families in need and constructed only a few dozen rural communities.

Despite limited funding, Rexford Tugwell also sought to aid the urban poor by establishing "greenbelt" communities outside major cities. He wanted to relocate urban working families from crowded inner cities to planned suburban environments where they would actively participate in their own self-government. Limited funds, again, limited development, and the RA built only three of the nine planned greenbelts outside Washington, D.C., Milwaukee, and Cincinnati.

CONSERVATIVE OPPOSITION

In conjunction with funding shortages, conservative opposition, prompted by the underlying socialist tone of federally planned and centralized greenbelt and farm communities, also limited RA programs. Moreover, southern politicians denounced the agency's equal treatment of African Americans, and southerners feared they would lose their cheap labor source. Tugwell, himself, also drew heated criticism for his liberal views and finally resigned as director.

Before his resignation, however, Tugwell launched a massive public relations campaign to counteract conservative opposition. Within the RA, he developed the Information Division Department and appointed Roy Stryker, Tugwell's former teaching assistant at Columbia University, as director. The Information Division focused on highlighting to the general public the desperate plight of America's poor, especially the rural poor. Stryker distributed information describing the benefits of the RA's programs, and he hired the nation's leading photographers to document the plight of rural America. These pictures emerged as the RA's most important contribution to the American people.

Despite such efforts, Congress, under the Bankhead-Jones Farm Tenancy Act, replaced the RA with the Farm Security Administration (FSA) in 1937.

The FSA continued the photographic work and the nondiscriminatory policies of the RA. It also supervised established resettlement communities, but the new agency capitulated to conservative critics and deemphasized resettlement by focusing upon improving existing farms and helping individual farm owners. Like the RA, the FSA never received nearly enough money to help the thousands of rural and urban poor devastated by the Depression.

PATTIE DILLON

See also: agriculture; dust bowl; Okies; Farm Security Administration; Federal Emergency Relief Administration; National Industrial Recovery Act; Tugwell, Rexford.

Bibliography

Badger, Anthony J. *The New Deal: The Depression Years, 1933–40.* New York: Farrar, Straus and Giroux, 1989.

Biles, Roger. *A New Deal for the American People.* DeKalb: Northern Illinois University Press, 1991.

———. *The South and the New Deal.* Lexington: University Press of Kentucky, 1994.

Conkin, Paul. *The New Deal.* Arlington Heights, IL: Harlan Davidson, 1975.

McElvaine, Robert S. *The Great Depression: America, 1929–1941.* New York: Times Books, 1984.

REVENUE ACT

The Revenue act of 1932—initiated by President Herbert Hoover and passed by a Republican-controlled Congress—put into place the largest peacetime tax hike in American history, raising, among other things, the tax rate on incomes of over $1 million to 63 percent.

While many economic historians consider the act one of the worst blunders of the Hoover administration, arguing that it dampened both consumer spending and capital investment, the tax hikes it imposed were quite modest by later standards, as it raised corporate taxes to just 1.75 percent and left 85 percent of American families paying no federal income tax whatsoever. And even for incomes of $20,000—which put a family into the very upper reaches of the middle class in the 1930s—the tax rate was just 8.1 percent.

Still, the act did impose a number of excise taxes on manufactured goods that acted like sales taxes and may have cut into demand somewhat. The act was superseded by new revenue acts in 1935 and 1936 that raised the rates on top incomes marginally, although nothing close to the amount asked for by President Franklin D. Roosevelt in his much-criticized "soak the rich" tax plan of 1935.

See also: taxation; Wealth Tax Act; Hoover, Herbert.

Bibliography

Brownlee, W. Elliot. *Federal Taxation in America: A Short History.* New York: Cambridge University Press, 1996.

Leff, Mark H. *The Limits of Symbolic Reform: The New Deal and Taxation.* New York: Cambridge University Press, 1984.

RURAL ELECTRIFICATION ADMINISTRATION

The Rural Electrification Administration was an agency created by the Franklin D. Roosevelt administration in 1935 to bring electrical power to rural areas and thereby rectify the long-standing imbalance in access to power between rural and urban areas.

RURAL AREAS LEFT OUT OF THE ELECTRICAL AGE

After Thomas Edison installed the world's first commercial power station in Manhattan in 1882, excitement about the possibilities of the new electrical age spread to all corners of the nation. By the turn of the century, electricity was powering industrial machinery and lighting streets, homes, offices, and stores. Engineers created new uses for electricity each year as they designed new electric stoves, fans, irons, radios, refrigerators, water pumps, and smaller gadgets such as curling irons and electric toys.

Electricity was available in the early 1900s mainly in urban areas, where a density of population and industrial, commercial, and domestic customers meant that utility companies could operate profitably in the industry's early days. Utilities chose not to build power lines to reach farms and small towns even as the industry matured during the 1920s, however, because they believed that farmers, an unprofitable market, had little use for electrical power in growing crops and tending livestock. Farmers, disagreeing, formed committees and worked through local chapters of the Grange and other farm groups to pressure utilities to build lines to their homes and farms. Social and political reformers joined farmers' efforts to bring this modern source of power to the countryside. The desires of rural residents for rural electrification were for the most part ignored by Congress during the 1920s, but the 1932 elections brought to power men who were more sympathetic to the hardships of rural life. Although 85 percent of urban residents had electricity in 1930, only 10 percent of rural residents did, and New Dealers saw this disparity as a social and economic problem. They supported the idea of a government agency to help rural residents gain the benefits of electricity for their homes, farms, small towns, and rural institutions.

THE CREATION AND OPERATION OF THE REA

The plan for a Rural Electrification Administration was written by Morris Cooke, an electrical engineer who had worked for utility companies early in his career, then for the state of New York's Power Authority during Roosevelt's term as governor. Cooke was also a member of the Mississippi Valley Committee, a group that studied the river valley region's economic and social problems after the 1927 flood. In the 1920s, he wrote several articles advocating, low-price electrification and urging utility companies to provide power to rural areas. Cooke wrote a report indicating that the lack of electricity in the countryside contributed to rural poverty and hardship. He proposed a plan for an electrical grid system that would distribute power to cities and rural areas alike, and, with the support of several members of Congress and of Roosevelt's cabinet, he circulated this plan among members of Congress in 1934.

Cooke's plan became the outline for the Rural Electrification Administration (REA), which Roosevelt inaugurated as a temporary work-relief agency by executive order on May 11, 1935. Representative Sam Rayburn of Texas and Senator George Norris of Nebraska wrote the REA Act that made the REA a permanent agency, and Roosevelt signed the act into law on May 20, 1936. Cooke was named chairman of the REA, with the goal of bringing electricity to as many farms as quickly as possible. He believed at first that the best way to do this was for the government to provide financial incentives for utility companies to build rural lines, because these companies already had expertise and experience in this work. After meeting with the heads of several utility companies, though, Cooke realized that this approach would have limited results. Utility companies put many conditions on their participation in such a program, and they were more interested in making profits than in making promises to serve all residents of the rural areas surrounding their core urban markets. Cooke had to find a new way to implement his program, and farmers themselves provided the answer.

Many farmers belonged to producer and marketing cooperatives, which are essentially member-owned companies that provide services and goods to members. Cooperatives provided grain elevator and marketing services, group buying of seed, fertilizer, and farm equipment; and creameries and mills to turn raw farm products into processed goods. The Tennessee Valley Authority, created in 1933 in part for the purpose of bringing inexpensive electricity to the Tennessee River valley region, had used electrical cooperatives to spread the costs and benefits of building rural electric lines. Cooke borrowed this idea for the REA.

By working with farmers' cooperatives, the REA, a federal agency based in Washington, D.C., enjoyed the advantages of its own engineering, legal, and business experts as well as a network of local residents to plan, organize, and implement the building of electrical lines in a given county. The REA operated by supplying legal, engineering, and managerial expertise to local co-ops and by extending low-cost loans to co-ops to buy the poles, wire, transformers, and other equipment needed to build rural lines. Cooperative members convinced their neighbors to join the co-op, mapped out rural distribution lines, and hired workers to erect the poles and string the wires. The REA also encouraged co-op members to use electricity abundantly and to buy electrical farm tools and home appliances. A typical cooperative during the 1930s served between 1,200 and 2,000 members with 500 to 800 miles of distribution lines. Not only farms and homes, but rural schools, churches, and towns were served by REA systems. In addition to member-owned cooperatives, which received about 90 percent of REA loans over the life of the program, municipally owned and private utilities also received REA loans for building rural line extentions.

THE IMPACT OF THE REA

To nearly all rural residents, electricity was a welcome sign of modernity, and their new electric water pumps, irons, washing machines, and radios provided new comforts and conveniences. Electricity made the lives of farm wives easier as they processed raw milk, canned garden produce, sewed, cooked, cleaned, and cared for farm animals. Electricity replaced muscle power in the work of grinding feed for livestock, sharpening tools, milking cows, and many other farm tasks. To most farmers, the monthly electric bill represented a cost worth paying because it made possible greater productivity, product diversification, and a more comfortable life.

In a 1943 speech to the National Rural Electric Cooperative Association, President Roosevelt praised the REA in glowing terms. "Year by year . . . I have followed the advance of the rural pole lines, like a peaceful army, to the conquest of a better life for those who produce the nation's basic agricultural products." Roosevelt emphasized that electrified farms better served the nation's wartime needs: "Production and preservation of food have become of critical importance to the defense of democracy. Thus the extension of electrical service to a million farms was an important step in preparedness." The REA had the full support of the president, who saw a healthy rural economic sector as important to the well-being of the industrial sector. As the "peaceful army" of electric poles marched across the countryside, more people were able to buy the refrigerators, water pumps, and light fixtures manufactured in towns and cities, and so industry was able to hire more workers. During the 1930s, the average electric co-op member bought $180 worth of appliances. The REA's supporters saw rural electrification as a means of improving the overall economy, as well as a way to slow down the rural-to-urban migration that packed the cities with homeless, restless, unemployed people.

Rural electrification improved rural schools, churches, hospitals, and town life, making possible well-lit classrooms, modern sanitation and refrigeration, and home economics and manual training courses. Electricity made it possible for small rural towns to offer some of the attractions of city life, such as movie theaters and ice cream parlors.

Other government agencies supported the work of rural electrification. The Department of Agriculture's Extension Bureau offered short courses to teach farmers how to get the most out of new electrical farm tools, such as feed grinders, soil warmers, hatcheries, and automatic milking machines. Farm wives were offered training in the best use of cream separators, refrigeration, electric stoves, and smaller kitchen implements such as roasters and mixers. The Home Extension Bureau, in fact, carried on a great deal of outreach work through rural women's clubs, the 4-H, farm radio programs, and home economics classes. Cooks and housewives were offered new recipes that took advantage of the precise temperature controls and timers that electric ovens made possible as well as recipes for making ice cream in the refrigerator, advice about food storage, and even kitchen-planning guides that showed how to arrange appliances and cabinetry for utmost efficiency. In all of these programs, experts advised farmers about how to use modern tools and how to live a modern lifestyle.

Because electricity made possible modern refrigeration and sanitary systems, it contributed to improvements in the health of rural people. Running water and toilets eliminated diseases associated with outhouses, such as cholera. Meat and dairy products could be stored safely for longer periods in all seasons in refrigerators and freezers. Not only did refrigeration have health benefits, but it cut down on spoilage that lowered profits, as well.

The REA was a success, but its policies limited its overall effectiveness. Farmers in poorer rural areas could not afford to repay even low-cost line-building loans. Tenant farmers and sharecroppers, especially those in the South, were usually unable to pay the cost of wiring their homes or buying electrical equipment. But it made no provision to help the poorest farmers whose lives were most destitute of modern comforts.

The REA achieved modest success in spreading electricity to the countryside by the time World War II broke out in Europe in 1939, for by then 22 percent of all farms in the United States were electrified, compared to only 10 percent in 1930. World War II slowed the progress of rural electrification because materials were needed for wartime production, but by 1944, 42 percent of farms were electrified. After 1945, the REA increased its activities, and by 1964, 98 percent of all farms in the nation received electricity. The REA extended over $5 billion in loans for generating stations and the construction of more than 1.5 million miles of electric lines between 1935 and 1964. By the 1960s, 54 percent of the nation's farms were serviced by entities that received REA loans for rural line distribution, including member-owned cooperatives, privately owned utilities, and municipally owned utility companies. Rural electrification deserves a great deal of credit for the large increases in agricultural productivity that occurred in midcentury. Electricity made possible automation, mass production, and diversification.

During the 1950s, the REA also applied its expertise to supplying rural areas with telephone service. Rural telephone cooperatives, which operated as the electrical cooperatives had done, applied for REA loans to build telephone lines along country roads, linking the country to the city in yet another way. As more urban residents moved beyond the suburbs to rural areas during the 1970s and 1980s, REA loans were used increasingly to build generating plants and transmission facilities to serve the larger rural population.

An anonymous poet expressed the value of the REA program in the *Rural Electrification News*, the REA newsletter:

> Leave your plow, lad, a moment. Press your ear
> In wonder to this post. You hear the hum?
> It is the song of heartstrings, the faint cry
> Of generations.
> Out of the darkness, light. Out of despair,
> The new fulfillment of equality.

The REA continued to exist until Reagan-era budget cuts eliminated the program.

TAMARA KING

See also: agriculture; utilities; public works; Tennessee Valley Authority; Norris, George; Rayburn, Sam; Documents: Hoover's Veto of Muscle Shoals Bill, March 3, 1931; Tennessee Valley Act, May 18, 1933

Bibliography

Childs, Marquis. *The Farmer Takes a Hand.* New York: Doubleday, 1952.

Cooke, Morris Llewellyn. "National Plan for the Advancement of Rural Electrification Under Federal Leadership and Control With State and Local Cooperation and As A Wholly Public Enterprise." February 1934. Box 230, Morris Cooke Papers, Franklin and Eleanor Roosevelt Library, Hyde Park, New York.

Papers of the Rural Electrification Administration, Record Group 221, National Archives and Records Administration, College Park, Maryland.

Wise, Rebecca, ed. *Rural Electric Fact Book.* Washington, DC: National Rural Electric Cooperative Association, 1964.

SCHECHTER POULTRY CORPORATION V. UNITED STATES

Among the most important Supreme Court decisions of the 1930s, *Schechter Poultry Corporation v. United States* (1935) ruled that the National Recovery Administration (NRA) and its parent act, the National Industrial Recovery Act (NIRA), represented an unconstitutional delegation of legislative power to the executive branch of the government.

The NRA had been established by the NIRA as an anti-Depression measure to regulate prices, wages, and marketing of products in order to bolster demand. But the Court, dominated by conservative justices, said that Congress had no right to create an executive agency with such sweeping powers over the economy. At the same time, the decision left untouched other provisions of the NIRA, including the public works component.

The Schechter Poultry Corporation was a Brooklyn kosher chicken supplier that sued the federal government over the latter's right to regulate hours, wages, and product inspection.

While President Franklin D. Roosevelt attempted to dismiss the decision by saying that he was ready to abandon the largely ineffectual NRA anyway, the decision nevertheless threatened other New Deal institutions, which could also be viewed as excessive delegations of legislative power to the executive. Indeed, Schechter threatened to overturn the very idea of independent rule-making agencies.

Along with the *United States v. Butler et al.* and other anti–New Deal decisions, Schechter was one of the main reasons Roosevelt would try to liberalize the Supreme Court in his politically disastrous court-packing plan of 1937.

See also: court-packing plan; Supreme Court; *United States v. Butler et al.*; Documents: National Industrial Recovery Act, June 16, 1933; Fireside Chat on the National Recovery Adminstration, July 24, 1933; *Schechter Poultry Corporation v. United States*, 1935.

Bibliography

Freedman, Max, ed. *Roosevelt and Frankfurter: Their Correspondence, 1928–1945.* Boston: Little, Brown, 1967.

Leuchtenburg, William E. *The Supreme Court Reborn: The Constitutional Revolution in the Age of Roosevelt.* New York: Oxford University Press, 1995.

SECTION 7 (NATIONAL INDUSTRIAL RECOVERY ACT)

Section 7 of Title I of the National Industrial Recovery Act (NIRA) attempted to regulate work conditions in American industry. The section created a Labor Advisory Board for this purpose while declaring that employees had "the right to organize and bargain collectively through representatives of their own choosing."

Viewed by many in the labor movement and among pro-labor New Dealers in the Franklin D. Roosevelt administration as a kind of "emancipation proclamation" for American labor, the section ostensibly recognized labor's right to be a partner—with business—in getting the country out of the Depression.

But Section 7 along with the rest of Title I was deemed to be an unconstitutional delegation of legislative powers to the executive branch by the 1935 *Schechter Poultry Corporation v. United States* Supreme Court decision. Even before that decision, however, the effective power of the section was limited in two ways. First, like the rest of the NIRA, it was essentially voluntarist: Companies could not be coerced to obey the decisions of the Labor Advisory Board. And second, the section failed to outlaw company unions, or employee representation plans, as they were called, which effectively adhered to the letter of Section 7 but not its spirit, since companies could threaten workers who refused to join the Employee Representation Plan with termination of their employment. In other words, Section 7's declaration of employees' rights to "bargain collectively through representatives of their own choosing" was a hollow promise.

Ultimately, the failures of Section 7 would lead to passage of the National Labor Relations Act, which established a National Labor Relations Board with far more enforcement powers, thereby helping to set off a wave of union organizing within American mass industries like automobiles, rubber, and steel.

See also: unions and union organizing; National Industrial Recovery Act; National Labor Relations Act; *Schechter Poultry Corporation v. United States*; Documents: National Industrial Recovery Act, June 16, 1933; Fireside Chat on the National Recovery Administration, July 24, 1933; *Schechter Poultry Corporation v. United States*, 1935.

Bibliography

Bernstein, Irving. *The Turbulent Years: A History of the American Worker, 1933–1940*. Boston: Houghton Mifflin, 1970.

Gross, James. *The Making of the National Labor Relations Board*. Albany: State University of New York Press, 1974.

SECURITIES AND EXCHANGE COMMISSION

The Securities and Exchange Commission (SEC) was established in 1934 when President Franklin D. Roosevelt signed into law the Securities Exchange Act of 1934. The SEC is the federal government agency that regulates both corporate securities and the trading of these securities. Securities are the instruments by which corporations raise money from investors, including equity securities, such as shares of stock, in which an investor purchases a share of ownership in a company; and debt securities, such as bonds, debentures, and other instruments, by which a company receives money from investors in return for a promise to repay the investment plus interest according to offered terms. Companies whose securities are traded publicly are required to make periodic filings with the SEC to ensure that information is made available to investors to permit knowledgeable evaluation of investment opportunities. Filings must be made quarterly, annually, and upon the occurrence of certain specified events. Publicly traded securities include those listed on specific exchanges, such as the New York Stock Exchange (NYSE), and those traded over-the-counter. The SEC does not purport to pass judgment on the merit of securities, only to ensure that investors have access to the information needed to make knowledgeable investment decisions.

ORIGIN OF THE SECURITIES EXCHANGE COMMISSION

Regulation of securities and trading seemed essential to restore public confidence in capital markets and to ensure that money would be available for legitimate corporate purposes after the damage done to public confidence by the Great Depression. During the eco-nomic boom of the 1920s, many investors purchased securities, with 20 million people purchasing stock. While many strong companies issued legitimate securities, many worthless securities were issued and bought by investors. It was common for stock to be purchased on margin, or with money loaned with the stock as collateral. Banks loaned money for the purchase of stocks with the expectation that stock prices would continue to increase. When stock prices began falling in October 1929, investors were forced to sell stocks to meet their margin calls, or demand for payment of the money due for their stock purchases. Panic selling ensued as declining stock prices meant investors would not be able to make enough money from the sale of their stock to cover their margin debts. Banks that had loaned money for stock purchases found that they could not recoup their investments, triggering concern among bank depositors that their savings would not be available when they wanted to withdraw them. Panicking investors triggered runs on the banks, whose reserves could not accommodate this increasing demand, and thus a number of banks failed. To stabilize the economy and prevent such a situation from recurring, the U.S. government during the New Deal undertook regulation of securities and securities trading, banks, insurance of deposits, and the separation of deposit and investment banking.

Interest in federal regulation of the securities markets was fueled by a 1932 Senate investigation that revealed the abuses by investment bankers to enrich themselves at the expense of investors. One of the key figures in this investigation was the counsel to the investigating committee, former New York prosecutor Ferdinand Pecora. During Roosevelt's First Hundred Days, Congress passed the Federal Securities Act of 1933, which required corporations to file prospectuses with the Federal Trade Commission (FTC) twenty days before any new securities issues. The law required that these filings contain complete and accurate information about the offering; corporate officers and directors were liable for the accuracy of the disclosure statements. This reform, however, was soon deemed inaccurate, leading to passage of the Securities Exchange Act, which Roosevelt signed into law on June 6, 1934. The Securities Exchange Act established the SEC and required publicly traded corporations to make periodic, detailed filings. This covered all publicly traded securities, not just the new issues covered by the 1933 Securities Act.

The powers of the SEC were enhanced by subsequent legislation. The Public Utilities Holding Company Act of 1935 gave the SEC power to supervise the reorganization of companies formed to hold stock in certain utilities. The Trust Indenture Act of 1939 strengthened the provisions of the Securities Act of 1933 for dealing with debt securities by requiring the filing of a trust indenture and imposing conditions on the trustee. The Investment Company Act and the Investment Advisers Act, both passed in 1940, gave the SEC authority to regulate companies that generated investment in capital markets and to regulate the practices of those persons and companies that provide advice to investors.

A leading historian of the New Deal calculates that, by 1941, the SEC had 1,678 staff members, ten regional offices, and a budget that had increased from $1.5 million in 1934 to $5.3 million. By that time, the SEC supervised twenty stock exchanges, led by the New York and American Stock Exchanges; it also supervised 7,000 brokers and dealers and the trading of 93,000 securities.

THE COMMISSIONERS

The first chairmen and commissioners established the credibility of the SEC and set the framework for its future performance. The first SEC chairman was Joseph P. Kennedy, who later served as ambassador to the United Kingdom and is perhaps most famous as the father of President John F. Kennedy. The elder Kennedy had been an important financial contributor to Roosevelt's 1932 presidential campaign; he was a successful financier thought by some of the most ardent New Deal reformers to be too conservative or too closely tied to business leaders for the position. Roosevelt privately explained his selection of Kennedy as SEC head by saying, "Set a thief to catch a thief." Some observers thought that Kennedy's purpose was to

serve as a link between the administration and Wall Street and to reassure the financial community of the administration's benevolent intent. Others worried that Kennedy's presence meant the administration was not serious about addressing problems with securities markets. Yet Kennedy believed his wealth brought social obligations and thought businessmen foolish who exalted profits above all else. During the height of the Depression, he reportedly said that he would trade half his wealth if he could keep the other half safe. Most observers, even the most vociferous critics of Kennedy's appointment, ended up crediting Kennedy for helpful service during his fifteen-month tenure as SEC chairman; he was recognized for assembling an able staff and for his efforts to encourage steps by the exchanges, companies, and traders that would minimize the need for government intervention while simultaneously improving the markets and restoring public confidence in them.

Joining Kennedy among the initial commissioners were Ferdinand Pecora, George C. Mathews, Robert E. Healey, and James M. Landis. Pecora was the counsel behind the Senate investigation of investment bankers that was the precursor of New Deal regulation of capital markets. Matthews was one of two Republicans on the bipartisan commission; he had prior experience on the Railroad Commission of Wisconsin, as a professor of public utilities at Northwestern University, and as director of the securities division of the Wisconsin Public Service Commission. His success in dealing with securities regulation at the state level won him strong support from progressive Sen. Robert M. La Follette Jr. and made him the sort of Republican with whom New Dealers in the Roosevelt administration were comfortable. Judge Robert Healy, the other Republican initially appointed to the SEC, had been an associate justice of the Vermont state supreme court and counsel to the FTC. In 1928 President Coolidge had appointed Healy to direct an inquiry into public utilities; reportedly, Coolidge was hoping for a superficial investigation, but instead Healy took four years to do a thorough investigation that revealed a number of questionable practices and earned him the wrath of investment bankers.

James Landis, one of the original commissioners, was just thirty-six years old when he succeeded Kennedy as chairman after the latter resigned in September 1935. Landis had been a law professor at Harvard, where he had built a reputation as an authority on legislation that led to his involvement in the drafting of securities legislation at the start of the New Deal. Landis believed in the importance of the administrative agency in the modern economy, and he concluded that the overwhelming reelection of President Roosevelt in

1936 proved public support for this view. During his tenure as SEC chairman, the commission established many of its practices and procedures. Landis also began work on a number of studies and reports mandated by early securities legislation concerning the proper role for the SEC. The leadership of Kennedy and Landis was essential in restoring public confidence in the securities markets and in convincing executives of the regulated companies that the restoration of public confidence worked to their benefit.

Many of the studies begun under Landis were completed under his successor as SEC head, William O. Douglas. Best known for his service as a U.S. Supreme Court justice from 1939 to 1975, Douglas was a Yale law professor and noted expert on bankruptcy law who had been appointed to the commission to fill the opening created when Kennedy resigned as chairman. Douglas assumed the chairmanship at a time when the NYSE was resisting suggestions that it reform itself to become more democratic in its operation and less a preserve of well-connected businessmen who looked out primarily for each other's interests. Reforms adopted in 1935 had accomplished little substantively and kept the traditional financial powers in place. With the recession of 1937 and the consequent drop in stock prices, many of the traditional leadership in the NYSE chose to ignore other factors contributing to the drop in prices and to argue that plummeting securities values were the logical result of overregulation and that a retreat from reform and regulation was in order. In November 1937, Douglas delivered a barely concealed ultimatum that the NYSE would have to produce a plan for genuine reform or the SEC would use powers granted to it by Congress to impose its own solution on the NYSE. Under this pressure, the NYSE established a committee under the direction of Continental Can chairman C. C. Conway. The so-called Conway Committee produced a report recommending a number of reforms, including a simplified system for governing the NYSE, a salaried management that would be independent of pressures from NYSE companies, and an advisory committee that would represent listed companies and the public. These reforms were approved in January 1938.

The SEC preferred to work with participants in the financial industry to arrange for self-regulation, but participated in several important cases in the New Deal years that established its authority. In one case, a nationally known broker named Michael J. Meehan was expelled from the NYSE on grounds of his role in manipulating the stock of Bellanca Aircraft; this admin-

istrative judgment was not appealed to the courts. In the case of *Electric Bond and Share Co. v. Securities and Exchange Commission*, the SEC won an important victory in receiving Court recognition of the validity of the Public Utilities Holding Company Act, under which the SEC would regulate companies holding stock in utility operating companies.

In the years since the New Deal, the SEC has continued to play a role in ensuring investor confidence in U.S. capital markets. In recent years, several well-publicized events have involved the SEC. During the 1980s, the SEC drew headlines for its actions to prevent insider trading, the purchase or sale of securities based on information not available to the public, which can fuel speculation or otherwise undermine the integrity of financial markets. Also during the 1980s, the SEC began developing its Electronic Data Gathering Analysis and Retrieval (EDGAR) system, which was put into use between 1993 and 1996. Publicly traded companies now make required filings electronically using the EDGAR system, and these filings are then available almost immediately to investors through the SEC's Internet Web site. In this way, the SEC continues to fulfill its historic mission of providing the tools investors need to make informed investment decisions.

JOHN A. SOARES JR.

See also: banking; stock market; Glass-Steagall Act; Pecora investigation; Federal Securities Act; Douglas, William O.; Kennedy, Joseph P.

Bibliography

Allen, James, ed. *Democracy and Finance: The Addresses and Public Statements of William O. Douglas As Member and Chairman of the Securities and Exchange Commission.* Port Washington, NY: Kennikat Press, 1969.

DeDedts, Ralph F. *The New Deal's SEC: The Formative Years.* New York: Columbia University Press, 1964.

Khademian, Anne M. *SEC and Capital Market Regulation: The Politics of Expertise.* Pittsburgh: University of Pittsburgh Press, 1992.

Loss, Louis. *Fundamentals of Securities Regulation,* 2nd ed. Boston: Little, Brown, 1988.

Phillips, Susan M., and J. Richard Zecher. *The SEC and the Public Interest.* Cambridge: MIT Press, 1981.

Seligman, Joel. *The SEC and the Future of Finance.* New York: Praeger, 1985.

Skousen, K. Fred. *An Introduction to the SEC.* Cincinnati: South-Western, 1976.

SILVER PURCHASE ACT

The Silver Purchase Act of 1934 committed the government to buying silver at higher-than-market prices until the amount of silver possessed by the federal government equaled one-third of the government's gold stock by value.

Since the late nineteenth century, farmers and other debtors had advocated the monetization of silver, that is, the use of silver to back U.S. currency. Because it was more plentiful than gold, silver would make dollars cheaper and lower the costs of paying back debts. The Great Depression renewed the call for this inflationary move, as prices and wages declined precipitously. In fact, the government only monetized a small portion of its new, enlarged silver supply, largely in the form of coins and "silver certificates," both of which continued until 1964.

Ultimately, the Silver Purchase Act did little to spur inflation and had little effect on the economy, other than to put a few thousand silver miners to work in the West and to make their employers rich.

See also: gold standard; Document: Abandonment of the Gold Standard, June 5, 1933.

Bibliography

Eichengreen, Barry. *Golden Fetters: The Gold Standard and the Great Depression, 1919–1939.* New York: Oxford University Press, 1992.

Keynes, John Maynard. "Open Letter to the President." *New York Times*, December 31, 1933, sec. 8, p. 2.

SMITH ACT

The Smith Act of 1940 was a product of Depression-era concern over internal subversion; it became an instrument of political repression in the Cold War. The Smith Act traces its legislative lineage at least as far back as 1917. With American entry into World War I and the government's own successful propaganda effort to mobilize support for that war, growing concern over the problem of antigovernment propaganda during wartime led to the passage of the Espionage Act of 1917 and the Sedition Act the following year. The Russian Revolution of 1917 and the domestic Red Scare of 1919 further intensified efforts by some lawmakers, seeking to protect American institutions from what they saw as menacing foreign influences, to squelch radical, anarchist, and other antigovernment voices by enacting legislative and administrative controls on radical publications. These efforts drove the fledgling Communist Party of the United States (CPUSA) underground in an attempt to evade legal actions against it. Such secretiveness, the fact that the party was home to many immigrant members, and the close ties the party maintained to the Soviet Union led many Americans to regard the

CPUSA as an alien organization. Various measures to limit radical activity were enacted throughout the 1920s, but these had limited effect by continually running afoul of the free speech protections of the First Amendment.

The Depression made Franklin D. Roosevelt's New Deal popular, but economic difficulty also increased the chorus of voices protesting against mainstream American capitalism. The CPUSA, gaining in popularity and political power throughout the decade, continued to look to Joseph Stalin's Soviet Union as a model for a new kind of society. The success of the CPUSA, which increased its membership to nearly 100,000 by 1939, confirmed the fears of conservatives and anti-Communists that radical elements in the United States constituted a clear and present danger to the operations and stability of the government. On the Right, a smaller group of extremists looked to Germany and the new regime of Adolf Hitler as the exemplar of the future. For many Americans of both mainstream political parties, foreign developments thus came to represent an increased threat to traditional American political practices, a threat intensified as Europe inched closer to war. The Roosevelt administration's apparent willingness to cooperate with communist-influenced organizations deepened those fears and increased pressure in Congress to proscribe antigovernment propaganda. The last straw came in the form of the Spanish Civil War (1936–38), which introduced the concept of the so-called fifth column, a metaphor for the threat of internal sabotage and subversive propaganda in the service of a foreign power. The combination of nontraditional discontent at home and foreign unrest abroad produced a deepening of traditional American isolationism. From this urge to remain aloof of the troubles in Europe came the Smith Act and the attempt to purge the United States of alien influences.

The Nazi-Soviet Pact of 1939 confirmed for many in Congress the reality of the foreign danger by linking the two principal totalitarian regimes in what appeared to be a belligerent posture toward the democratic West. In response, Congress proposed a flurry of antisubversive bills in late 1939 and into 1940, most of which the civil liberties–minded president was able to deflect. But the pressure increased through the spring of 1940 as the Nazi armies poured through Western Europe. The Smith Act, named for Representative Howard Smith (D-VA), who proposed the bill, was adopted on June 28, 1940, as Title I of the Alien Registration Act. Title I outlawed undermining morale in the armed services by radical infiltrators, or publishing material advocating the overthrow of the government. Titles II and III of the Alien Registration Act, amendments to earlier legislation, demonstrated the anti-immigration bias of domestic anticommunism by granting the attorney general power to deport an alien who advocated overthrowing the government or for other criminal offenses and by requiring aliens to register with the Department of Justice. The Smith Act lowered the burden for successful prosecutions by making *advocacy* of revolution, rather than any actual terrorist activity, punishable by fines and imprisonment. Consequently, Smith Act prosecutions focused on a defendant's language and political associations, as prosecutors sought to prove that typical communist rhetoric was actually a kind of code for revolution and that the CPUSA was in fact a Soviet auxiliary.

The first prosecutions occurred in 1941, directed against the Socialist Worker's Party in Minneapolis, a Trotskyist splinter group. The Stalinist CPUSA, long at odds with American Trotskyists, supported the government's prosecutions. Yet few radicals were actually threatened during the war, because the administration sought homefront cooperation from the American Communists, whose support of the Soviet Union made them staunch allies of the Roosevelt administration. After the war, however, as the Cold War drove a wedge between American liberals and their former communist allies, the CPUSA's support of the earlier Smith Act prosecutions came back to haunt the party. In 1947, under mounting political pressure from the Right, the Truman administration stepped up its attack on Communists. The so-called Smith Act trials of 1947 are widely regarded as political show trials in which the Truman administration warded off charges that it was soft on communism by proving its mettle in going after American Communists. Radicals and some liberals condemned the Smith Act as an assault on the Constitutionally protected rights of free speech and association. Other anticommunist liberals and the conservative Right, backed by a Supreme Court receptive to prosecutions against Communists, saw the Smith Act as a vital tool in the worldwide battle against communism. Between 1947 and 1961, 141 Communists were indicted under the Smith Act, with 29 serving prison time. These prosecutions significantly damaged the operations of the CPUSA; alongside important international developments, the Smith Act helped ensure the near-total demise of the CPUSA by 1956.

The era of détente later in the Eisenhower era and a softened Supreme Court posture in relation to domestic radicalism gradually undermined support for Smith Act prosecutions. In late 1962, the last Smith Act defendant, Junius Scales, was released from prison.

JONATHAN SNYDER

See also: Communist Party; German-American Bund; Nazi-Soviet Pact; Spanish Civil War; Joseph Stalin.

Bibliography

Belknap, Michael R. *Cold War Political Justice: The Smith Act, the Communist Party, and American Civil Liberties.* Westport, CT: Greenwood Press, 1977.

Caute, David. *The Great Fear: The Anti-Communist Purge Under Truman and Eisenhower.* New York: Simon & Schuster, 1978.

Draper, Theodore. *The Roots of American Communism.* New York: Viking, 1957.

Heale, M. J. *American Anticommunism: Combating the Enemy Within, 1830–1970.* Baltimore: Johns Hopkins University Press, 1990.

Powers, Richard Gid. *Not Without Honor: The History of American Anticommunism.* New York: Free Press, 1995.

SOCIAL SECURITY ACT

Periods of economic depression, characterized by high unemployment and fiscal uncertainty, proliferate throughout the annals of American history. While the federal government often took steps to mitigate economic downturns to ensure the continuation of American economic and industrial growth, few federal officials concerned themselves with how the economy impacted the lives of individual Americans. The onset of the Great Depression, however, marked a new departure. Steeped in the progressive movement of the turn of the century, social reformers, politicians, and economists increasingly looked to the federal government to provide solutions to the nation's economic problems. While not all Americans approved of the government's expanding interventionist role, the ensuing New Deal legislation, specifically the Social Security Act, irrevocably positioned the federal government as the nation's leading welfare agency.

The federal government's assumption of this new role, however, occurred several years after the onset of the Depression. Following his election as president in 1932, Franklin D. Roosevelt focused the First Hundred Days in office on recovering the economy and providing basic unemployment relief. While these efforts successfully stabilized the banking industry and offered a modicum of employment to select Americans, they failed to fully halt the economic collapse. By 1935, as Roosevelt campaigned for reelection, a number of charismatic figures, including Huey P. Long, Father Charles E. Coughlin, and Dr. Francis E. Townsend, garnered large numbers of followers by challenging Roosevelt to introduce more far-reaching programs to end the Depression. Despite their political supporters, Long's plan for redistribution of wealth and Coughlin's call for silver inflation appeared too radical for most politicians, and their ideas failed to translate into federal legislation. However, Townsend's proposal of governmental support for the elderly eventually formed the basis of the Social Security Act.

DR. FRANCIS TOWNSEND AND THE TOWNSEND PLAN

Townsend's call for old-age assistance partially stemmed from his own economic circumstances. At sixty-seven years old and with only $100 in savings, Townsend lost his job as a public health officer in Long Beach, California. Townsend's plight reflected the conditions of many aged Americans at that time. By 1930, only about one-half of all women and one-third of all men over 65 still enjoyed gainful employment. Townsend saw these numbers reflected in his daily walks through his neighborhood streets where he came across many of the unemployed and homeless elderly. Although he empathized with their condition, it was the sight of three old women scavenging through garbage cans for scraps of food that propelled him into action.

In September 1933, Townsend submitted a letter to a Long Beach newspaper in which he contended that old-age relief offered the key to end the Depression. Readers enthusiastically responded to his suggestion, and within weeks the newspaper dedicated an entire page to letters discussing elderly assistance. Energized by this response, Townsend and his supporters organized Townsend Clubs throughout the nation to publicize his ideas. The Townsend Plan proposed that the federal government pay every American sixty years and older a monthly stipend of $200 on the condition that they leave the work force and spend the money within thirty days. Based on these figures, a married couple, both sixty years old, would receive $4,800 a year at a time when 87 percent of American families barely earned an annual income of $2,500. Townsend claimed, however, that his plan would equally benefit both the young and old. Younger workers would no longer compete with their elders for scarce jobs, and the elderly would help to rejuvenate the economy by spending their monthly stipend. Funding for the stipend, Townsend proposed, would come from the passage of a 2 percent transaction tax that would be equally shared by all Americans.

Although Townsend perceived his plan as universally beneficial, most economists denounced it as too expensive, claiming that funding would exceed 50 percent more than the combined budgets of all local, state, and federal governments. Moreover, the passage of a transaction tax would result in an 80 or 90 percent increase in the price of consumer goods, which would further reduce Americans' buying power. Despite these numerous obstacles, however, many Americans, particularly middle-class Americans, called for some form of old-age assistance, and by 1936 Townsend Club leaders reported to have enrolled 3.5 million members. Drawing from these membership rolls, Townsend's supporters amassed over 200 million signatures on an old-age assistance petition, which represented one-fifth of all American adults. Notwithstanding the economic quagmire created by Townsend's plan, politicians, especially those facing reelection, could not afford to ignore these numbers.

FRANKLIN D. ROOSEVELT AND OLD-AGE ASSISTANCE

While President Roosevelt, examining his own reelection options, also found it pertinent to address the issue of elderly assistance, his support for the aged was more than just an expedient campaign strategy. As early as 1928, after his election as New York's governor, Roosevelt pushed for passage of legislation designed to aid the elderly along with governmentally funded unemployment insurance. In June 1934, to gain passage of similar legislation on the national level, President Roosevelt created the cabinet-level Committee on Economic Security to draft a social security bill. To head the committee, which included the secretaries of agriculture and the treasury, the attorney general, and Harry Hopkins of the Federal Emergency Relief Administration, Roosevelt appointed Secretary of Labor Frances Perkins, the first female cabinet member.

FRANCES PERKINS AND THE COMMITTEE ON ECONOMIC SECURITY

Frances Perkins's long and distinguished career as a labor advocate prepared her for this role. After graduation from Mount Holyoke College in 1902, Perkins worked at Hull House and Chicago Commons, two Chicago settlement houses. Eight years later, while studying for her master's degree in economics and sociology at Columbia University, she received a fellowship from the Russell Sage Foundation to research working conditions in New York's notorious Hell's Kitchen neighborhood. After joining the Consumers' League, she campaigned for the regulation of women's work hours and served as an investigator for the 1911 Triangle Shirtwaist Company factory fire in which over 100 young female garment workers died. Based on her activist résumé, New York Governor Al Smith appointed Perkins to the State Industrial Commission, and his successor, Governor Roosevelt, hired her as

Industrial Commissioner of New York. Later, as president, Roosevelt named her secretary of labor in 1933.

Drawing on her notable experience, Perkins readily assumed leadership of the Committee on Economic Security. After months of extensive research, Perkins invited the committee members to her home to agree on a final report. Within six hours, they had developed a draft that Perkins presented to the president on the following day. On January 17, 1935, Senator Robert Wagner of New York and Representative David Lewis of Maryland introduced the Wagner-Lewis bill in Congress, which closely replicated the committee's draft. After months of further research, debate, and revision, both houses passed the bill, which President Roosevelt signed as the Social Security Act on August 14, 1935. To coordinate the various provisions of the act, Roosevelt also created the Social Security Administration.

PROVISIONS OF THE SOCIAL SECURITY ACT

One key component of the Social Security Act was the enactment of an old-age pension. Under this provision, Americans sixty-five and older would receive a monthly payment, starting on January 1, 1942, initially ranging from $10 to $85. A payroll tax, equally shared by employers and employees, would provide the funding and determine the amount received by each recipient; the more a worker had paid into the system, the larger his or her monthly payment. In 1937, the new tax, or Federal Insurance Contribution Act (FICA), first appeared on workers' paychecks. President Roosevelt strongly supported this program for funding Social Security. He argued that payroll contributions provided the beneficiaries with a moral and legal right to receive their benefits, removing the stigma of accepting governmental funds because the workers had themselves contributed to their payment.

Not all workers, however, benefited from Social Security. In a move to appease southern politicians, who feared that Social Security payments would hinder their ability to control their labor supply, the act exempted domestic and agricultural workers. Although Frances Perkins wanted all workers covered under Social Security, she acquiesced in the exclusion of agricultural laborers and domestics, believing that they could be easily included once the bill passed. However, these workers remained excluded from the social security system until August 1950.

Another component of the Social Security Act provided for unemployment insurance. Traditionally, the unemployed sought help from religious, charitable, or

President Franklin D. Roosevelt signs the 1935 Social Security Act. The woman standing behind him is Secretary of Labor Frances Perkins, the main author of the act. *(Brown Brothers)*

voluntary organizations to ease their transition between jobs. However, by 1931, in the wake of massive layoffs and business failures, less than 116,000 workers received some form of assistance. To fund unemployment insurance, the government levied a federal tax on payrolls of employers with eight or more workers. Within several years of the act's passage, over 28 million people weekly received between $15 and $18 in unemployment compensation. Nevertheless, as under Social Security, some of the unemployed failed to receive any benefits because certain employers were exempt from paying the tax, specifically those who hired agricultural workers.

The third portion of the Social Security Act allocated federal funds to be used by individual states to aid the disabled and families with dependent children.

Although at that time twenty-four states provided some form of assistance to the blind and forty-five offered help to female-headed households, these amounts proved minuscule in comparison to the need. The Social Security Act also established maternity and infant care programs, job training, and social services for delinquent children.

OPPOSITION TO THE SOCIAL SECURITY ACT

While most Americans supported the idea of assistance for the unemployed, elderly, disabled, and dependent children, the Social Security Act nevertheless drew heated criticism. Many economists predicted that the

THE AMERICAN PEOPLE—

HOW THEY ARE AFFECTED
BY THE FEDERAL-STATE
PROGRAM FOR SOCIAL SECURITY

WAGE-EARNERS (Includes those normally employed but at present unemployed) 38 million men 11 million women	ADULTS, OTHER THAN WAGE-EARNERS 5 million men 31 million women	CHILDREN (UNDER 16 YEARS) 19 million boys 19 million girls
May be eligible for: *	**May be eligible for:** *	**May be eligible for:** *
1. Federal Old-Age Retirement Benefits. †	1. Aid to the Needy Aged.	1. Aid to Dependent Children
2. Unemployment Compensation.	2. Aid to the Needy Blind.	2. Maternal and Child Health Services
3. Maternal and Child Health Services.	3. Maternal and Child Health Services	3. Services to Crippled Children
4. Public Health Services.	4. Public Health Services.	4. Child Welfare Services
5. Vocational Rehabilitation.	5. Vocational Rehabilitation	5. Public Health Services
6. Aid to Needy Aged		
7. Aid to Needy Blind		

SOURCE: 1930 CENSUS

PREPARED BY INFORMATIONAL SERVICE
SOCIAL SECURITY BOARD WASHINGTON D C

* WITH SOME EXCEPTIONS
† ONLY BENEFIT FEDERALLY
ADMINISTERED

This early government advertisement helped explain the benefits of the newly created Social Security Administration. *(Brown Brothers)*

payroll tax, enacted to fund Social Security, would deepen the Depression because the tax withdrew money from the marketplace at a time when increased consumer spending was viewed as the primary factor needed to restimulate the economy. The other problem with the tax stemmed from its regressive nature: a uniform payroll tax resulted in lower-income workers paying a higher percentage of their wages in taxes than those who received higher salaries.

Not all critics, however, denounced the Social Security Act based on its cost. Several vocal opponents lambasted the conservative nature of the act, claiming that the legislation excluded too many workers and that the paltry payments received by its beneficiaries failed

to significantly help the poor and underprivileged. Furthermore, in order to gain support from the politically powerful American Medical Association lobbyists, the final form of the act eliminated the provision to enact a national health insurance system. In contrast to its liberal critics who denounced the Social Security Act for being too shortsighted, conservative opponents deemed the act too liberal. Many contended that passage of the legislation marked the first step toward the enactment of a socialist government and the eventual erosion of state and local governmental autonomy.

LASTING IMPACT OF THE SOCIAL SECURITY ACT

Despite criticism from both sides of the political spectrum, the Social Security Act provided the bedrock for the nation's new welfare state. In 1937, the Supreme Court upheld the constitutionality of the act, ending speculation that the legislation illegally expanded the role of the federal government. In fact, the Social Security Act permanently sanctioned the government's expansionist role by ensuring Americans that it would provide them with a "safety net," a modicum of financial aid and support in times of economic and personal crisis.

PATTIE DILLON

See also: Share Our Wealth Society; Townsend Plan; New Deal, second; Coughlin, Father Charles; Hopkins, Harry; Long, Huey P.; Perkins, Frances; Roosevelt, Franklin D.; Smith, Al; Townsend, Francis; Wagner; Robert; Documents: Social Security Acts, August 15, 1935; Fireside Chat on Social Security Acts, January 17, 1935.

Bibliography

Badger, Anthony J. *The New Deal: The Depression Years, 1933–40.* New York: Farrar, Straus and Giroux, 1989.

Biles, Roger. *A New Deal for the American People.* DeKalb: Northern Illinois University Press, 1991.

Conkin, Paul. *The New Deal.* Arlington Heights, IL: Harlan Davidson, 1975.

Lubove, Roy. *The Struggle for Social Security, 1900–1935.* Cambridge: Harvard University Press, 1968.

McElvaine, Robert S. *The Great Depression: America, 1929–1941.* New York: Times Books, 1984.

Ware, Susan. *Beyond Suffrage: Women in the New Deal.* Cambridge: Harvard University Press, 1981.

SOIL CONSERVATION AND DOMESTIC ALLOTMENT ACT

The Soil Conservation and Domestic Allotment Act was a 1936 piece of legislation that created a cooperative system whereby farmers received payments to reduce their crops and thereby bolster agricultural prices. The payments were made from money collected through a processing fee on crops.

The act was passed in reaction to the Supreme Court's *United States v. Butler et al.* decision of the same year, in which the justices ruled the Agricultural Adjustment Act—and its more coercive crop reduction mechanisms—unconstitutional. In the end, too few farmers joined the cooperative to make it effective in bolstering agricultural prices. As crop surpluses continued to pile up, Congress and the administration passed a new law—the Agricultural Adjustment Act of 1938—that established quotas on farm production.

See also: agriculture; Agricultural Adjustment Act (1933); Agricultural Adjustment Act (1938); *United States v. Butler et al.* Document: *United States v. Butler et al.*

Bibliography

Saloutos, Theodore. *The American Farmer and the New Deal.* Ames: Iowa State University Press, 1982.

SOIL EROSION SERVICE/ SOIL CONSERVATION SERVICE

The Soil Erosion Service was created in 1933 as a Department of the Interior agency with a mandate to restore agricultural lands damaged by drought and poor farming practices. It was later moved to the Department of Agriculture and given the more positive-sounding name, the Soil Conservation Service.

As the Soil Erosion Service, the agency established some forty erosion control demonstration projects, involving more than 4 million acres in over thirty states. Later, as the Soil Conservation Service, it worked with the Civilian Conservation Corps to create over 500 "soil camps" that restored millions of acres of damaged farmland. Still, the agency had no power to limit production on the restored land and thus could not prevent the same overly intensive farm practices that had led to the destruction of the land in the first place.

See also: agriculture; dust bowl; Civilian Conservation Corps.

Bibliography

Saloutos, Theodore. *The American Farmer and the New Deal.* Ames: Iowa State University Press, 1982.

Worster, Donald. *Dust Bowl: The Southern Plains in the 1930s.* New York: Oxford University Press, 1979.

SUPREME COURT

The Constitution of the United States vests "the judicial power of the United States" in "one Supreme Court, and in such inferior courts as the Congress may from time to time ordain and establish." The Supreme Court has original jurisdiction in certain cases and appellate jurisdiction in all other federal cases and controversies, according to rules set by Congress. Further, the supremacy clause, in Article VI, provides that the U.S. Constitution and federal law are "the supreme law of the land" binding states regardless of conflicting state law.

THE COURT BEFORE THE DEPRESSION

Following Chief Justice John Marshall's 1803 opinion in *Marbury v. Madison*, the Supreme Court has been recognized to have the power to declare void acts of Congress that the Court considers to conflict with the Constitution. This federal court power to rule a law unconstitutional—and hence to overturn and nullify it—has been recognized to extend over the states since 1816, with the opinion by Justice Joseph Story in *Martin v. Hunter's Lessee*. These powers were very rarely used for the first seventy-five years of the Court's history, although they were very controversial in the few cases when they were, such as in the Court's 1857 *Dred Scott* decision, which struck down the Missouri Compromise of 1820 and ruled that Congress had no power to outlaw slavery.

The late 1800s saw an increase in the Court's willingness to overturn federal and state statutes. These decisions were seen by many to promote the interests of corporations and rich individuals. Although there was considerable inconsistency among opinions, between 1880 and 1920 the Court overturned federal and state regulations of businesses to limit the effects of some of the progressive legislation passed by both Congress and the state legislatures. The Court acted on a variety of constitutional grounds, notably according to the due process clauses of the Fifth and Fourteenth Amendments and to the contracts clause of Article I. Under the Fourteenth Amendment, the Court both limited state obligations to prevent discrimination and barred states from regulating corporations' profits and workers' wages. Applying the Fifth Amendment, the Court struck down the income tax and limited or overturned a variety of labor protections. A constitutional amendment, ratified in 1913, was necessary to enable Congress to pass an income tax.

The high-water mark for these cases is often said to be *Lochner v. New York* (1905), in which a majority of the Court overturned a New York state law limiting bakers' working hours to eight hours a day, as a matter of health and safety, finding that the statute interfered with the freedom of contract and the Fourteenth Amendment.

The opinion was widely divided. Justice Oliver Wendell Holmes Jr., in dissent, branded the opinion as a reflection of laissez-faire philosophy used to interpret the Constitution, and Justices John M. Harlan, Edward D. White, and William R. Day argued that the majority had contradicted the Court's other state powers opinions. The broadest effects of *Lochner*'s ruling were short-lived; in 1908, the Court held in *Muller v. Oregon* that a state could limit the maximum hours in a woman's workday. Still, cases continued for the first quarter of the century pitting the will of the courts against popular legislative reforms, with the Court overturning price regulation of theater tickets, employment agencies, and gas stations, as well as other laws.

The Court even thwarted the most morally tinged pro-labor argument of the day. In *Hammer v. Dagenhart* (1918) and *Bailey v. Drexel Furniture* (1922), the Court overturned federal laws and taxes limiting the use of child labor because the laws and taxes violated states' rights under the Tenth Amendment.

THE JUSTICES BEFORE THE NEW DEAL

The character of the Court by the 1920s was well known throughout the nation, particularly through the fame of the chief justices. William Howard Taft, chief justice from 1921 to 1930, had been a progressive Republican president, and although as chief justice he was generally conservative, he supported the president's control over lower federal officials, promoted the construction and decoration of an imposing new building for the Court, and lobbied for the Judge's Act (1925), which removed much of the Court's mandatory jurisdiction and gave the Court increased discretionary power to use the writ of certiorari to determine what types of disputes it would hear. Charles Evans Hughes succeeded Taft and served as chief justice for eleven years. Hughes was also famous, having already served as associate justice from 1910 to 1916, as governor of New York, as Republican nominee for president in 1916, and as secretary of state from 1921 to 1925. Although he was opposed by liberal senators during his confirmation, Hughes was a moderate, voting for some New Deal plans and against others.

The Court had developed an essential split between four conservative justices and three fairly liberal justices who favored removing legal impediments to legislation. The majority during the 1920s and early 1930s were widely seen as conservative in their politics and social philosophy. Willis Van Devanter, a lawyer for the western railroads, was appointed to the Court in 1910. James McReynolds, a former law professor at Vanderbilt University in Nashville, Tennessee, was appointed in 1914 by President Woodrow Wilson, for whom McReynolds had been an assistant attorney general. George Sutherland, a former senator from Utah, was appointed by President Warren G. Harding in 1922. Pierce Butler, also a lawyer for the railroads, was from Minnesota and had a high-profile law practice before being appointed to the Court by Harding on Chief Justice Taft's recommendation in 1922. These four justices differed from one another on a variety of issues but were so often allied against statutes regulating business that they became known as the "four horsemen," a reference to the agents of the apocalypse made current in the 1920s by Grantland Rice in a widely read football essay and applied to the conservative judges in the 1930s. Despite their conservative image, other than the New Deal cases the four supported a variety of progressive views, including women's suffrage, limited suits to interfere with federal spending, and the protection of aliens from state discrimination.

The most famous judge on the Court, however, was the aged Oliver Wendell Holmes Jr., the Union army veteran, Harvard law professor, and Massachusetts judge appointed to the Court by President Theodore Roosevelt in 1902. Holmes served until 1932 and was an outspoken proponent of judicial restraint from interference with the statutory results of the legislative process, although he also argued for some limits on governmental restraints on individual liberty, particularly arguing in dissent in *Abrams v. United States* (1919) and *Gitlow v. New York* (1925) against the Court majority's allowance of statutes limiting the freedom of speech.

Holmes's greatest ally was liberal attorney Louis

Brandeis, appointed by President Woodrow Wilson in 1916 in a nomination marked by strong opposition from probusiness and anti-Semitic members of the U.S. Senate. Brandeis employed his great industry and formidable intellect to support progressive legislation and protect civil liberties.

In 1925, President Calvin Coolidge appointed his attorney general, Harlan Fiske Stone Jr., to replace retiring justice Joseph McKenna. Stone, a former dean of Columbia Law School, had been effective in investigating the Teapot Dome Scandal. Although Stone was an ally of corporations, he often sided with Holmes and Brandeis against the majority, both in arguing to uphold progressive legislation and in protecting civil rights.

In 1932, Holmes retired at the age of 91, and President Herbert Hoover appointed New York chief judge Benjamin Nathan Cardozo to replace him. Cardozo had been active in law reform movements and was a leader in the sociological criticism of law.

Not all justices enjoyed such renown. Edward T. Sanford, a Tennessee federal judge appointed to the Court by President Harding in 1923, generally voted along with Chief Justice Taft. A bankruptcy expert, Sanford attracted very little notice throughout his career, which ended with his death in 1930. In that year, President Hoover, having failed to succeed to appoint a more well-known conservative, named Owen Roberts, another prosecutor of Teapot Dome defendants. While less well known than many on the Court, Roberts soon appeared as a slightly liberal but unpredictable vote. Moving, as did Chief Justice Hughes, between the liberal and conservative blocs in high-profile cases, Roberts became known early as a swing vote, a role that would be crucial to the Court in its conflict with President Franklin D. Roosevelt in the 1930s.

THE MODERATION OF RESTRICTIONS ON THE STATES IN THE 1930

With the appointments of Chief Justice Hughes and Justice Roberts in 1930, the Court falteringly distanced itself from the excesses of laissez-faire constitutional limits on state and federal statutes. In *O'Gorman & Young, Inc. v. Hartford Fire Ins. Co.* (1931), the Court upheld a state law that barred companies from paying unfair commissions to fire insurance agents. Brandeis's majority opinion was based on a presumption in favor of constitutionality, an approach that was opposed by Van Devanter, McReynolds, Sutherland, and Butler, who argued the regulation could be supported only if it was proven necessary. Despite similar results in up-

The so-called "nine old men" of the Supreme Court of the early 1930s ruled much New Deal legislation unconstitutional. Pictured: (*standing, from left*) justices Owen Roberts, Pierce Butler, Harlan Stone, Benjamin Cardozo; (*seated, from left*) Louis Brandeis, Willis Van Devanter, Charles Evans Hughes (chief justice), James McReynolds, George Sutherland. (*Brown Brothers*)

holding a chain-store tax in 1930, in 1932 Hughes and Roberts sided with the conservatives to overturn a law limiting competition in ice delivery, finding that the business was not "charged with a public use." Brandeis's lengthy dissent argued for judicial restraint to allow the states to serve as regulatory laboratories.

By 1934, Hughes and Roberts were arguing to uphold progressive statutes against the attacks of the conservatives. The *Blaisdell* case (1934) brought a challenge of Minnesota's emergency statute extending mortgage redemption periods for two years, which would allow borrowers to reclaim foreclosed properties once the Depression eased. In a strong opinion, Chief Justice Hughes repudiated an original intent construction of the contracts clause and upheld the statute as only altering a remedy and not a contract. A few months later,

in *Nebbia v. New York* (1934), Roberts implicitly adopted Brandeis's 1932 approach, writing for a majority, including Chief Justice Hughes, that the Court would leave intact regulations that were a "reasonable exertion of governmental authority" and only overturn those that were "arbitrary or discriminatory."

THE COURT AND THE CONGRESS

Initially, the Hughes Court read broadly the powers of Congress to regulate interstate commerce. In 1930, the Court upheld the Railway Labor Act provision giving rail workers the right to choose representatives, because "Congress may facilitate the amicable settlement of disputes which threaten the service of the necessary agencies of interstate transportation." In *Crowell v. Benson* (1932), Hughes wrote a groundbreaking opinion to uphold the Longshoremen's and Harbor Workers' Compensation Act of 1927, a national workers' compensation scheme, even though it required a commission with the power to make final rulings on matters of fact that would bind the courts.

Despite such increases in the Court's willingness to accept novel congressional and administrative action, there were exceptions, and the Court overturned both the railroad pension, in *Railroad Retirement Board v. Alton R.R.* (1935) (with Roberts writing for the majority and Hughes in the four-justice dissent), and the president's power to remove presidential appointees, in *Humphrey's Executor v. United States* (1935).

Neither of these cases was as far-reaching as the Court's response when confronted with the centerpiece of Roosevelt's first recovery program, the National Industrial Recovery Act (NIRA). Under the NIRA, Congress gave the president the power to prohibit interstate and foreign commerce in excess of state quotas on petroleum production and refining. In *Panama Refining v. Ryan* (1935) the Court, with only Cardozo dissenting, held that Congress had delegated too much of its authority to the president without any limits on how he would exercise his discretion. The NIRA also gave the president the authority to develop codes of fair competition for various industries, including the poultry business. In *Schechter Poultry Corporation v. United States* (1935), the Court overturned the conviction of the Schechter brothers for violating the wage and hour provisions of the code and for selling sick chickens. Chief Justice Hughes wrote for a unanimous Court that Congress's delegation to the president of the legislative power to create laws of this type was both an overbroad delegation of legislative power and a violation of states' rights. Even Cardozo balked, writing in a concurrence joined by Stone that, under the NIRA, "anything that Congress may do within the limits of the commerce clause for the betterment of business may be done by the President . . . by calling it a code. This is delegation running riot."

Roosevelt provided a suave response to the media, calling Hughes's idea of commerce a "horse-and-buggy" definition, and it seemed as if the damage done to his New Deal package of regulations might be limited to the NIRA. But the following year saw the fall of more New Deal legislation in eleven different opinions, chiefly the Bituminous Coal Conservation Act, in *Carter v. Carter Coal Co.* (1936), and the Agricultural Adjustment Act, in a six to three split in *United States v. Butler*. The year 1936 even saw an ap-

parent reversal of the *Nebbia* opinion, when the Court by five to four overturned a New York minimum wage law in *Morehead v. New York ex rel. Tipaldo*.

ROOSEVELT'S COURT-PACKING PLAN

Roosevelt's tolerance had reached its limit, and on February 5, 1937, the president announced his court-packing proposal, a plan to enlarge the nine-member Court to fifteen. Although he spoke of the inefficiency of aging justices, no one missed the point that the additional judges would all be his appointees and so likely to favor New Deal statutes. The bill, S.1392, provided for the appointment of one new judge for each member of the Court who had reached the age of seventy, had sat for ten years, and had neither resigned nor retired within six months thereafter. In 1937, these criteria were met by six of the nine justices. Roosevelt argued for his bill in a national address in March, claiming that the "Court has been assuming the power to pass on the wisdom of . . . acts of the Congress. . . . [W]e must take action to save the Constitution from the Court."

Through February and March 1937, Roosevelt and the Senate majority leader, Joseph Robinson (D-AR), lobbied heavily for the bill, which met stiff and increasing opposition from many corners of the political landscape. Most critics believed that the bill's success would irrevocably weaken the Court, while giving Roosevelt nearly unstoppable authority. Popular opinion, usually with Roosevelt, was split and leaning away from him.

Chief Justice Hughes responded on two fronts. In an unusual step, he sent a letter to Burton Wheeler, a liberal Montana senator, which refuted Roosevelt's stated argument for efficiency, and Wheeler read the letter to the Senate Judiciary Committee. Hughes's greater move, however, was in the careful release of opinions.

On December 19, 1936, Justice Roberts had swung his vote away from the conservatives and back to the liberals during the private conference to vote to uphold a Washington State minimum wage law by overruling *Hammer*, the 1918 precedent that had supported *Morehead*, the 1936 case in which Roberts had just agreed to strike down New York's similar wage law. Roberts's new opinion had not been released, because of a delay to allow Justice Stone to recover from illness to vote, and Hughes saw to it that the five to four decision, *West Coast Hotel v. Parrish* (1937), was released on March 27, making it appear that the Court had changed its position in the face of Roosevelt's plan. It was a grand act, often called in the press the "switch in time that saved nine."

Despite opinions in April and later upholding the Wagner Act and the Social Security Act, Roosevelt continued to promote the court-packing plan, even announcing that he would nominate the loyal (but very conservative) Senator Robinson to the Court when it passed. Robinson died from a heart attack on July 14, and the bill died on July 22, by a vote of twenty to seventy.

RESOLUTION

The true shift on the Court to support the New Deal, and to tame the practice of judicial sniping at state and congressional statutes, came in April, with the opinions in three labor cases brought on appeal against the National Labor Relations Board (NLRB). That agency, created under the National Labor Relations Act to protect labor organization, had found that three companies—the nation's largest steel-maker, its largest trailer producer, and also a small clothing producer—were each companies in which a work stoppage from labor unrest would affect interstate commerce. The Court's opinion in *NLRB v. Jones & Laughlin* (1937), written by Hughes and joined by Roberts and the liberals, was important not just because it stated the agency's findings, but because it found that Congress had the power to regulate such activity and to delegate such investigations to an agency, and the Court would uphold any reasonable conclusions reached by the agency.

Other opinions followed in quick succession, upholding more of the New Deal and congressional authority. *Helvering v. Davis* (1937) upheld seven to two the old-age benefits provided through Social Security. *Steward Machine Co. v. Davis* (1937) upheld five to four a federal tax meant to coerce states to provide unemployment insurance. *Sonzinsky* (1937) unanimously upheld a federal firearms tax.

Such gains, made largely through the resolution of Hughes and Roberts, were made more secure by personnel changes on the Court. The year 1937 saw the retirement of Van Devanter and his replacement by Alabama liberal Hugo Black. Sutherland resigned in 1938, to be replaced by Stanley Reed, and Pierce Butler was succeeded by the archliberal William O. Douglas in 1939. Even the loss in the same year of the stalwart Louis Brandeis led to the appointment of Harvard's Felix Frankfurter.

These new appointees and the sense of irrevoca-bility that followed the opinions of 1937 led to resolution along new lines. A new test was evolved for the evaluation of economic regulations by Congress, in *United States v. Carolene Products Co.* (1938), by which statutes were presumed constitutional and would only be reversed if they had no rational basis at all. This pattern continued until, finally, in *United States v. Darby* (1941), the Court overruled *Hammer v. Dagenhart* to uphold a federal minimum wage for employees engaged in production. Similar license was given to the states, and, in *Olsen v. Nebraska* (1941), the court characterized arguments against a state limit on employment agency fees as "notions of public policy embedded in earlier decisions of this Court but which, as Mr. Justice Holmes long admonished, should not be read into the Constitution."

Steve Sheppard

See also: Agricultural Adjustment Act; National Industrial Recovery Act; National Labor Relations Act; *NLRB v. Jones & Laughlin*; *Schechter Poultry Corporation v. United States*; Social Security Act; *United States v. Butler et al.*; *West Coast Hotel v. Parrish*; Black, Hugo; Brandies, Louis; Butler, Pierce; Cardozo, Benjamin; Douglas, William O.; Frankfurter, Felix; Hughes, Charles Evans; Robert, Owen; Reed, Stanley; Robinson, Joseph; Stone, Harlan; Sutherland, George; Van Devanter, Will; Documents: Agricultural Adjustment Act, May 12, 1933; National Industrial Recovery Act, June 16, 1933; National Labor Relations Act, July 5, 1935; Social Security Acts, August 15, 1935; Reform of the Federal Judiciary, 1937; Adverse Report on Reform of the Federal Judiciary from the Senate Committee on the Judiciary, June 7, 1937; *Schechter Poultry Corporation v. United States*, 1935; *United States v. Butler et al.*, 1936; *National Labor Relations Board v. Jones & Laughlin Steel Corporation*, 1937; *West Coast Hotel Company v. Oregon*, 1937.

Bibliography

Ackerman, Bruce. *We the People: Transformations.* Cambridge: Harvard University Press, 1998.

Arkes, Hadley. *The Return of George Sutherland: Restoring a Jurisprudence of Natural Rights.* Princeton: Princeton University Press, 1994.

Bickel, Alexander M. *The Least Dangerous Branch: The Supreme Court at the Bar of Politics.* New Haven: Yale University Press, 1986.

Currie, David P. "Constitution in the Supreme Court: The New Deal, 1931–1940." *University of Chicago Law Review* 40 (1987): 504.

Cushman, Barry. *Rethinking the New Deal Court: The Structure of a Constitutional Revolution.* New York: Oxford University Press, 1998.

Hughes, Charles Evans. *The Autobiographical Notes of Charles Evans Hughes.* Cambridge: Harvard University Press, 1973.

———. *The Supreme Court of the United States: Its Foundation, Methods and Achievements: An Interpretation.* New York: Columbia University Press, 1928.

Konefsky, S. J. *The Legacy of Holmes and Brandeis: A Study in the Influence of Ideas.* New York: Macmillan, 1956.

Leuchtenberg, William E. *Franklin D. Roosevelt and the New Deal.* New York: Harper & Row, 1963.

———. *The Supreme Court Reborn: Constitutional Revolution in the Age of Roosevelt.* New York: Oxford University Press, 1995. JFE 95–10757

Mason, Alpheus Thomas. *Harlan Fiske Stone: Pillar of the Law.* New York: Viking Press, 1956.

Schlesinger, Arthur M. *The Politics of Upheaval.* Cambridge, MA: Houghton Mifflin, 1960.

TAXATION

Throughout the nation's history, taxation has remained a flexible instrument of state control, responding to the social needs and the historical contexts of the times. Such flexibility, however, has come under extreme strain during moments of national crisis, such as wartime and economic depression.

In the 1930s, the American system of taxation underwent significant change. Specifically, tax policy focused on short-run efforts to stimulate the economy, as it increased the power of the federal government to raise revenue. During the Great Depression and the New Deal, federal tax collections more than doubled, from a figure of nearly $3 billion in 1929 to approximately $7.5 billion in 1941.

Expansionist fiscal policy—the notion of decreasing taxes and increasing government spending—began with the Republican presidential administration of Herbert Hoover. In response to the stock market crash of 1929, Hoover initially pursued a vigorous program of cutting taxes and increasing spending on such large-scale infrastructure projects as Boulder Dam. This expansionist policy was short-lived, however. By 1931, the growing federal deficit, which reached approximately $902 million, and tight monetary policy caused officials within the Hoover administration to fear that higher interest rates would inhibit private investment. Accordingly, Hoover reversed his fiscal policies, and, in an attempt to balance the budget, his administration requested that Congress increase taxes and lower exemptions. The Revenue Act of 1932, the last tax legislation enacted by Congress before the New Deal, imposed the largest peacetime tax increases in the nation's history, while at the same time allocating tax burdens in a more progressive manner than in previous years.

With the election of Franklin D. Roosevelt in 1932 and the large Democratic majorities in both houses of Congress, a flurry of legislation aimed at economic recovery was enacted. Many of these early New Deal laws provided for increased taxes. The Agricultural Adjustment Act included taxes on food processing, for example, while the National Industrial Recovery Act levied a 5 percent tax on dividends and revived the excess profits tax at a modest level. Congress also restored the earned-income tax credit, made income tax rates slightly more progressive, and increased capital-gains taxes.

Despite these minor enhancements, federal tax policy remained relatively unchanged from the Hoover administration to the early years of the New Deal. Although Roosevelt had campaigned as an advocate of both balanced budgets and redistributional taxation, the early phase of the New Deal brought no progressive fiscal innovations. From his election to 1935, Roosevelt followed a path of fiscal conservatism—adopting only modest increases in income taxes and proposing a tightening of loopholes, rather than any radical structural change.

In 1935, Roosevelt changed the course of federal tax policy. His words, if not his actions, were aimed at attacking the concentrated wealth of big business and distributing, across class lines, the burdens of financing a modern, regulatory state. Treasury secretary Henry Morgenthau worked with the Democratic leadership in Congress to enact a "soak the rich" tax law in 1935 that included a graduated corporation tax ranging from 12.5 to 15 percent; a tax on dividends received by holding companies; an increased estate and gift tax; and a surtax on incomes over $50,000 that raised the income tax to 75 percent on all incomes over $500,000. Ultimately, the 1935 law did not reach many taxpayers, but the symbolism was significant, especially considering that Roosevelt and the New Deal were coming under increased attack from the political Left by such figures as Senator Huey P. Long (D-LA) and his radical "Share the Wealth" tax program.

Much of the progressiveness of the 1935 Revenue Act was eventually counterbalanced by the regressive nature of the payroll taxes enacted as part of the 1935 Social Security Act. Although the dissonance of the two laws may suggest that New Deal tax policy was merely symbolic rather than substantive or reformist, it is more likely that Roosevelt saw Social Security as an old-age insurance program separate from his "soak the rich" tax policy.

Roosevelt's attack on wealth during the second half of the 1930s was not limited to legislation. With Roosevelt's approval, treasury secretary Morgenthau also set out to prosecute wealthy alleged tax evaders, including Alfred P. Sloan, the president of General Motors, and even former treasury secretary Andrew Mellon. With this twofold policy of tightening the tax code and prosecuting tax evaders, New Deal officials believed that the federal deficit would be restrained as the economy attempted a recovery. But this was not to be. When the Supreme Court in 1936 struck down the processing tax of the Agricultural Adjustment Administration and Congress overrode Roosevelt's veto of a bonus bill for World War I veterans, increased federal deficits loomed.

Emboldened by the achievements of the 1935 Revenue Act and early signs of an economic recovery, the Roosevelt administration set out to enact an even more vigorous tax increase. The Revenue Act of 1937 contained many provisions aimed at increasing federal revenues, including increased tax rates on personal holding companies, decreased deductions on corporate benefits, and limited privileges for nonresident taxpayers. This measure would be Roosevelt's last gasp at tax reform, for the coming year brought with it not only a reversal in the economic recovery, but also a political setback with the failure of Roosevelt's court-packing plan.

The last years of New Deal tax policy were marked by a conservative backlash. In 1938 and 1939, conservative members of Congress passed tax laws—on occasion without Roosevelt's signature—that eviscerated the taxes on concentrated wealth put in place by Roosevelt. By 1940, the tax on the retained earnings of corporations, also known as the "undistributed profits tax," and the graduated corporate income tax had been eliminated.

Ultimately, New Deal fiscal policies did not radically transform the American tax system. Rates became slightly more progressive, and concentrated pockets of wealth were warned to pay their fair share of the burden. But most important, the New Deal ushered in a tax regime that underscored the state's ability to use the powers of taxation, a regime that at the very least increased the capacity of the federal government to generate increased revenues.

AJAY K. MEHROTRA

See also: Share Our Wealth Society; Agricultural Adjustment Act; National Industrial Recovery Act; Revenue Act (1932); Social Security Act; Wealth Tax Act; Hoover, Herbert; Long, Huey P.; Mellon, Andrew; Morgenthau, Henry Jr.; Roosevelt, Franklin D.; Sloan, Alfred; Documents: Agricultural Adjustment Act, May 12, 1933; National Industrial Recovery Act, June 16, 1933; Social Security acts, August 15, 1935.

Bibliography

Brownlee, W. Elliot. *Federal Taxation in America: A Short History.* New York: Cambridge University Press, 1996.

———, ed. *Funding the Modern American State, 1941–1995: The Rise and Fall of the Era of Easy Finance.* New York: Woodrow Wilson Center Press and the Press Syndicate of the University of Cambridge, 1996.

Leff, Mark H. *The Limits of Symbolic Reform: The New Deal and Taxation.* Cambridge: Cambridge University Press, 1984.

TEMPORARY EMERGENCY RELIEF ADMINISTRATION

Established by New York state governor Franklin D. Roosevelt in August 1931, the Temporary Emergency Relief Administration (TERA) was a statewide public relief and jobs program that served as a model for later New Deal agencies created by Roosevelt after he became president in 1933.

The idea for TERA was first prompted by reports made to Roosevelt by state industrial commissioner (and, later, secretary of labor) Frances Perkins in January 1930 that unemployment was rising in the wake of the stock market crash of late 1929. By 1931, unemployment in the state was rising precipitously, overwhelming local public and private relief agencies.

In an address to the state legislature that accompanied the TERA bill, Roosevelt said that aid to unemployed workers "must be extended by Government, not as a matter of charity, but as a matter of social duty." Once the bill was passed, Roosevelt appointed former social worker and adviser Harry Hopkins (later, head of the Federal Emergency Relief Administration and the Works Progress Administration) to run the program.

Reflecting his own and Roosevelt's interest in conservation, Hopkins set up work camps around the state and put tens of thousands of unemployed persons to work in land reclamation and tree planting, as well as other public works projects.

As the first governor to initiate a public relief and works program, Roosevelt attracted national attention, and it has been argued that the formation of TERA helped win the Democratic nomination in 1932 for the New York governor.

See also: public works; unemployment; Federal Emergency Relief Administration; Works Progress Administration; Hopkins, Harry; Perkins, Frances; Roosevelt, Franklin D.

Bibliography

Davis, Kenneth S. *FDR: The New York Years, 1928–1933.* New York: Random House, 1985.

Schlesinger, Arthur A. Jr. *The Age of Roosevelt: The Crisis of the Old Order, 1919–1933.* Boston: Houghton Mifflin, 1957.

TENNESSEE VALLEY AUTHORITY

One of the most successful New Deal acts created the Tennessee Valley Authority (TVA). Sponsored by progressive Republican senator George W. Norris of Nebraska and Representative Lister Hill (D-AL) and signed by President Franklin D. Roosevelt on May 18, 1933, it was designed to transform the Tennessee River so that people affected by it could have a more abundant life. The TVA had a direct effect on the lives of millions of people, achieving an economic miracle in the South, but its indirect impact went far beyond the region.

The Tennessee River and its tributaries touch seven states (Alabama, Tennessee, Kentucky, Mississippi, Georgia, North Carolina, and Virginia). The river's valley was one of the nation's poorest and most underdeveloped areas. Valley families were trapped in an agricultural system that fostered poverty, tenancy, and sharecropping. Few industries other than lumbering and mining furnished employment in the valley, and they gave work to a small group at extremely low wages. Per capita income was less than half the national average. The river should have been the farmer's friend, but annual floods devastated large portions of the valley, damaging the soil and forests. Commercial navigation was difficult even when the waters were stable, for shipping channels were too small for large ships to ply portions of the Tennessee. The most difficult navigational problem was in northwest Alabama near the

The Tennessee Valley Authority, established in 1933, built several hydroelectric dams across the South, providing power to industry and residences in the region, like this newly electrified home. *(Brown Brothers)*

community of Muscle Shoals, where the river began a precipitous drop of 140 feet over a thirty-mile stretch. This problem also created opportunity, for the energy produced by the falling river could be converted into electric power.

ROOTS OF THE TVA

Unlike most New Deal legislation, the TVA was an idea that had been germinating since World War I. In 1916, Congress passed a National Defense Act giving President Woodrow Wilson authority to choose a suitable place to produce nitrates for explosives. He decided to build a dam at Muscle Shoals to provide electricity for a nitrate factory; when the military no longer needed nitrates, the plant would be used to make fertilizer. Wilson Dam was not completed until after the war in 1919, but Senator George W. Norris was already calling for more dams to produce fertilizers for farmers and cheap electric power to develop the whole valley. In the 1920s, Congress considered ways to use Muscle Shoals,

but faced the dilemma of whether the government should control future development or turn the property over to private business.

Norris believed that only a government-chartered corporation would serve the common good. Public awareness of the corrupt and monopolistic practices of the nation's electric utilities had grown, and Norris wanted a government facility on the Tennessee River to provide a yardstick by which the nation could judge utility performance. Congress rejected bids by multi-millionaire businessman Henry Ford, the Alabama Power Company, and a fertilizer company named American Cyanamid to take over the Shoals project.

Eight times between 1921 to 1933, Norris introduced legislation to create a public corporation at the Shoals. In 1928 and again in 1931, Congress passed his bills, but Republicans Calvin Coolidge and Herbert Hoover vetoed them. Only with the election of liberal Democrat Franklin Roosevelt as president did Norris, the maverick Republican, gain White House support. As governor of New York, Roosevelt had grown suspicious of the tactics of electric utility companies and sought ways to defuse their power. In January 1933, before his inauguration, he publicly endorsed the Norris proposal. Ten weeks after he took office, the TVA became law.

ADMINISTRATION

The vision of Norris and Roosevelt led to a public agency with authority that included but went far beyond the mere production of fertilizer and electricity. Roosevelt wanted the agency to improve river navigation, control floods, stop soil erosion, protect forests, eliminate marginal lands from agricultural use, and bring industries to the region. The law encompassed all of these, as well as vague injunctions giving the TVA unprecedented power to alter the valley's environment and improve the public welfare.

Agency control went to three directors appointed by the president. Each had equal voting power, but distinct administrative responsibilities. Roosevelt named Arthur E. Morgan, president of Ohio's Antioch College and a self-taught hydraulic engineer, as the TVA's first chairman. An admirer of the writings of the utopian Edward Bellamy, Morgan had grandiose ideas about the kind of society the agency could create in the valley. Morgan was also chief engineer with the immediate task of building a series of dams on the river. Associate directors were David Lilienthal, a Harvard-trained lawyer and expert on electric utilities, and Harcourt A. Morgan, etymologist and president of the University of Tennessee. Lilienthal oversaw the disbursement and marketing of TVA electric power, and H. A. Morgan ran the farm and fertilizer programs. More realistic than their chairman about the society and political atmosphere in which they operated, they soon clashed with the visionary Arthur E. Morgan.

By the end of 1933, the TVA had already begun construction of Norris Dam, near Knoxville, Tennessee, and Wheeler Dam, a few miles east of Muscle Shoals. By 1936, three more dams were under way. At a time of high unemployment, the construction of the dams gave work to 40,000 people. By 1945, sixteen dams had been built on the river, and each one was an engineering and architectural marvel. The river was completely under control and flooding was virtually eliminated. Navigation from Knoxville to Paducah, Kentucky, was eased when the TVA built a larger shipping channel.

David Lilienthal aggressively marketed and sold electricity to municipal systems and rural cooperatives, leading to intense competition with other electric util-

ities. The TVA demonstrated that it could sell at a much cheaper rate than the privately owned companies, but Lilienthal worried that demand for electricity in the underdeveloped valley would subside. Infuriated utility executives watched as he enlisted other New Deal agencies to increase demand and expand the TVA's market. The Public Works Administration made loans to municipalities that allowed them to create their own utility companies and buy from the TVA. A little known agency, the Electric Farm and Home Authority, made loans to people to buy appliances. Private utility companies reaped huge profits from the appliance sales at the same time that they challenged the legality of the TVA.

Two major lawsuits attacked the TVA because of its massive amounts of time, energy, and money. One, filed by preferred stockholders of the Alabama Power Company, challenged the federal government's right to sell electricity from Wilson Dam. It resulted in a 1936 decision of the U.S. Supreme Court upholding the sales, but only those from Wilson. Only a few weeks after this decision, nineteen utility companies filed a suit that sought to have the entire TVA power program declared unconstitutional. Leading this fight for the utilities was the Commonwealth and Southern Corporation (C&S), headed by future Republican presidential candidate Wendell Willkie. Commonwealth and Southern sold electricity in various southern states, but its largest market was in Tennessee. When the Supreme Court decided against the utilities in 1939, Commonwealth and Southern sold its affiliate, the Tennessee Electric Power Company, to the TVA. At a public ceremony, Willkie turned over the company to Lilienthal in return for $78,600,000.

By the end of the 1930s, people all over the valley were turning light switches on in their businesses and homes. In 1933, fewer than 10 percent of valley farms had electricity, but a decade later nearly three-quarters of them had the service. As the TVA's territory expanded, farms all over the South gained electric power, and private utility rates for electricity came down all over the region. New electric cooperatives, serviced by the TVA, moved into rural areas and brought light and power to people who marveled at the change. The electricity led to the growth of manufacturing plants in the area, eventually making the Tennessee Valley one of the most industrialized parts of the South.

As Lilienthal sold electricity, Harcourt Morgan worked with the agricultural experimental stations at the South's land-grant universities to teach farmers new methods of growing crops and even set up test-demonstration farms. Morgan, careful to work through local farm agents and the Farm Bureau Federation, was accused of perpetuating the agricultural establishment in the area. Critics charged that the TVA did little to help tenant farmers and small landowners, but Morgan's experiments weaned farmers away from reliance on corn and cotton, increased crop rotation, and led farmers to use their land more efficiently. The agency also built lakes and parks, increased recreation in the valley, and developed rural libraries that were turned over to local communities. The control of the water levels by the TVA dams led to the eradication of malaria, which had been at epidemic levels in areas near the river.

The TVA's board attempted to give the agency a progressive image by encouraging all who worked for it to join unions and engage in collective bargaining, but where black workers in the South were concerned the board failed. Much needed employment was given to hundreds of blacks, but they were placed in the lowest level jobs at the lowest wages and were strictly segregated from whites in eating and recreational areas. At no time did any of the TVA's programs deviate from southern traditions in the area of race. Criticism also came from those who were appalled at the way certain property owners were treated by the agency. The building of TVA lakes and the necessary flooding of certain areas led to the forced removal of hundreds of people from their land. Many families had to leave land that had been in their families for several generations. The TVA paid the people for the land and even attempted to move family cemeteries, but many residents deeply resented this upheaval.

Despite all of its good work, an internal squabble at the agency nearly destroyed it. Arthur E. Morgan strongly disagreed with the methods of the other two directors and was increasingly frustrated when they voted against him on a number of proposals. Distressed at the rapidity with which the TVA was moving the valley away from its rural culture toward industrial development and opposed to the manner in which Lilienthal expanded the power program, the chairman accused the other two directors of dishonesty and malfeasance. President Roosevelt demanded that he prove his charges, and when he was unable to do so the president removed him from office in 1938. A. E. Morgan's criticism led to a lengthy congressional investigation of the TVA that eventually exonerated both Lilienthal and Harcourt Morgan.

With the outbreak of World War II, the TVA shifted its emphasis to national defense. The agency furnished electricity to plants making the aluminum necessary in American warplanes and eventually played a major role in providing power to the nuclear facility at Oak Ridge, Tennessee. The fertilizer plants at Muscle Shoals began to produce ammonium nitrate for American munitions. Two more dams were built during the war to assist in these tasks, and by 1945 the TVA was producing more electricity than any other American utility.

Although the TVA continued to furnish cheap electricity to its customers through the 1950s, in the '60s and '70s the huge costs of the operation led to rate increases that angered those dependent upon it. By the 1980s, the TVA's wholesale electric rates were little different from those of other southern utilities. Many critics also charged that the company had abandoned its traditional role of protecting the welfare of the people in the valley. In its rush to provide increasing amounts of power, the TVA ran afoul of state and federal environmental regulations. Many of its contractual obligations led to cozy relationships with southern coal companies that were despoiling the environment, and it had a questionable safety record in the operation of a number of its nuclear power generating facilities. It seemed to some that the Tennessee Valley Authority, like other bureaucratic agencies, was more concerned with its survival than with serving the people. Such an outcome would have deeply disappointed Senator George W. Norris.

SAMUEL WEBB

See also: utilities; dams; Public Utilities Holding Act; public works; Public Works Administration; Rural Electrification Administration; Wheeler-Rayburn Act; Norris, George; Willkie, Wendell; Documents: Hoover's Veto of Muscle Shoals Bill, March 3, 1931; Tennessee Valley Act, May 18, 1933; *Ashwander v. Tennessee Valley Authority*, 1936.

Bibliography

Hargrove, Erwin, and Paul Conkin, eds. *TVA: Fifty Years of Grassroots Bureaucracy*. Urbana: University of Illinois Press, 1983.

Droze, Wilmon H. *High Dams and Slack Waters: TVA Rebuilds a River*. Baton Rouge: Louisiana University Press, 1965.

Schwarz, Jordan A. *The New Dealers: Power Politics in the Age of FDR*. New York: Knopf, 1993.

Tindall, George Brown. *The Emergence of the New South 1913–1945*. Baton Rouge: Louisiana University Press, 1967.

UNITED STATES V. BUTLER ET AL.

United States v. Butler et al. was a decision by the Supreme Court in January 1936 that declared the Agricultural Adjustment Act (AAA) of 1933—the central farm program of the New Deal—unconstitutional.

Among other things, the AAA placed a tax on grain elevators and other processors of crops and livestock that would be used to pay farmers not to grow crops. The thinking behind this program was that, by limiting production, crop prices and farm incomes would rise. But the Court decided that the tax and the AAA program were a violation of the Tenth Amendment, which reserved all powers that were not explicitly given to the federal government in the Constitution to the states.

Liberal justice Harlan Stone, in writing the dissent, called the majority's opinion "a tortured construction of the Constitution" that implied that the courts were "the only agency of government that must be assumed to have capacity to govern."

The demise of the AAA led to a predictable collapse of prices that prompted yet more New Deal programs, including the Soil Conservation and Domestic Allotment Act of 1936 and a new Agricultural Adjustment Act in 1938.

See also: agriculture; Agricultural Adjustment Act (1933); Agricultural Adjustment Act (1938); Soil Conservation and Domestic Allotment Act; Supreme Court; Stone, Harlan. Documents: Agricultral Adjustment Act, May 12, 1933; *United States v. Butler et al.*, 1936.

Bibliography

Leuchtenburg, William E. *The Supreme Court Reborn: The Constitutional Revolution in the Age of Roosevelt.* New York: Oxford University Press, 1995.

Saloutos, Theodore. *The American Farmer and the New Deal.* Ames: Iowa State University Press, 1982.

WAGNER-STEAGALL HOUSING ACT

The Wagner-Steagall Housing Act, passed in 1937, was designed to encourage the creation of public and other forms of low-cost housing. It established the United States Housing Authority to carry out this mandate.

The act called for direct investment of the federal government in public housing construction and in providing loans for the construction of low-cost housing. However, conservatives in Congress watered down the legislation until the act provided only the most modest sums for housing. At the time, many contemporaries—and, subsequently, many historians—saw the limitations of the bill as a sign that both President Franklin D. Roosevelt and the New Deal were losing steam by the early years of the second term.

See also: New Deal, second; Roosevelt, Franklin D.; Wagner, Robert.

Bibliography

Brinkley, Alan. *The End of Reform: New Deal Liberalism in Recession and War.* New York: Knopf, 1995.

WEALTH TAX ACT

The Wealth Tax Act was a piece of legislation passed by Congress in 1935 that raised taxes modestly on corporations and inheritances. Also known as the Revenue Act of 1935, it left the basic income tax rate at 4 percent for the small percentage of Americans that made over $4,000 a year. Ultimately, the act raised federal revenues by a minuscule $250 million annually.

While modest, the act was the outcome of the tumultuous politics of the mid-1930s. By 1935, President Franklin D. Roosevelt and the New Deal faced several major challenges from the Left. The most threatening politically came from Louisiana senator Huey P. Long's Share Our Wealth movement, whose platform insisted on a major redistribution of the nation's wealth.

With the Depression lingering, Long and other radicals were gaining political momentum. In 1935, Roosevelt introduced a number of measures to counter that threat. He offered the Works Progress Administration to put the unemployed to work, the Social Security Act to protect seniors, and the National Labor Relations Act to aid organized labor. In addition, the president offered a highly redistributive tax plan that critics and the media called the "soak the rich" tax.

Intending to rob Long of his main political message, Roosevelt was, in fact, somewhat lackluster in his support of the tax plan. Ultimately, conservatives in Congress were able to eviscerate it. The result of that legislative process was the Wealth Tax Act of 1935. While it placed a top tax rate of 79 percent on incomes over $5 million, this only applied to one American— John D. Rockefeller.

Below that, it left income taxes at the relatively low rates that existed in the 1920s. For example, the top 1 percent of households—making $12,000 a year— paid but $600 in federal taxes, or about 5 percent of their income.

See also: Share Our Wealth Society; taxation; National Labor Relations Act; Social Security Act; Works Progress Administration; Long, Huey; Roosevelt, Franklin D.

Bibliography

Leff, Mark H. *The Limits of Symbolic Reform: The New Deal and Taxation.* Cambridge: Cambridge University Press, 1984.

Schlesinger, Arthur, Jr. *The Politics of Upheaval.* Boston: Houghton Mifflin, 1959.

WEST COAST HOTEL V. PARRISH

Although it did not directly involve any New Deal legislation, the March 1937 *West Coast Hotel v. Parrish* Supreme Court case remains a key legal decision of the 1930s, as it was the first time the Depression-era Court chose to interpret broadly the government's right to regulate business affairs, specifically the conditions of employment.

The case involved a chambermaid named Elsie Parrish, who worked at the Cascadian Hotel in Wenatchie, Washington, which was owned by the West Coast Hotel Corporation. Laid off in 1935, she sued the West Coast Hotel Corporation for $216.19 in pay owed to her under Washington state's minimum-wage law. The hotel refused to pay the full amount, arguing that the law was unconstitutional.

Most experts expected the Court to rule against Parrish, as it had ruled a New York state minimum wage law unconstitutional in the *Tipaldo* decision just one year earlier. And while the Court's four most conservative justices held that minimum-wage laws were an unconstitutional intrusion on the rights of individuals and corporations to establish contracts free of government intrusion, Chief Justice Charles Evans Hughes—who wrote the *Parrish* decision—changed his mind, ignoring the precedent set in *Tipaldo*.

In a major reverse from over a half century of American jurisprudence, Hughes argued that judicial activism—that is, courts deciding to overturn regulations and laws passed by legally elected legislatures— should be reined in. The *Parrish* decision signaled to legal experts that the Court was now more likely to allow the constitutionality of New Deal legislation, as proved to be the case in the April 1937 *NLRB v. Jones & Laughlin* decision, upholding the National Labor Relations Act of 1935.

Some historians say that Hughes's change of heart may have come about because of Franklin D. Roosevelt's efforts to pass legislation permitting the president to appoint one justice for every sitting justice over the age of seventy. Since the majority of justices were of advanced age, the so-called court-packing plan would have liberalized the Court and made it more amenable to New Deal legislation. While the plan never made it through Congress, it nevertheless had an effect, argue historians, on the Court's position regarding governmental activism in the economy.

See also: court-packing plan; National Labor Relations Act; *NLRB v. Jones & Laughlin*; Supreme Court; Hughes, Charles Evans.

Bibliography

Leuchtenburg, William E. *The Supreme Court Reborn: The Constitutional Revolution in the Age of Roosevelt.* New York: Oxford University Press, 1995.

Pusey, Merlo John. *Charles Evans Hughes.* New York: Macmillan, 1951.

WHEELER-RAYBURN ACT

The Wheeler-Rayburn act of 1935 limited the size of public utility holding companies. Under this legislation, these companies could have only two levels of ownership—the holding company itself and the operating utility. Previous to passage of the bill, many utility holding companies owned other holding companies that owned other holding companies that owned the actual operating utilities. These elaborate corporate constructs were widely viewed as oligopolistic business entities that constrained trade and kept utility rates higher than they needed to be.

In his January 1935 State of the Union address, President Franklin D. Roosevelt called for the elimination of all public utility holding companies. This so-called death sentence for utilities was seen by many contemporaries as a kind of declaration of war on business by the president. Roosevelt's request was then adopted by Democratic senator Burton Wheeler of Montana and Democratic representative Sam Rayburn of Texas.

Utilities and the business community at large immediately attacked the plan as dangerously socialistic. Indeed, the utilities generated a false grassroots campaign against the bill, inundating Congress with 250,000 telegrams and over 5 million letters. The campaign had its effect. The "death sentence" was removed from the act, though utility holding companies were limited to just one level of ownership above the operating utility.

Many historians have since dated the new radicalism of the Roosevelt administration—and the heightened levels of business hostility directed against the administration—to the introduction and passage of this bill.

See also: New Deal, second; utilities; Roosevelt, Franklin D.; Wheeler, Burton.

Bibliography

Barnes, Irston. *The Economics of Public Utility Regulation.* New York: F. S. Crofts, 1942.

Schlesinger, Arthur M., Jr. *The Age of Roosevelt: The Crisis of the Old Order.* Boston: Houghton Mifflin, 1956.

WORKS PROGRESS ADMINISTRATION

The Works Progress Administration (WPA) (1935–1943) was the central program in the New Deal's effort to combat unemployment. During its eight-year existence, the WPA spent almost $11 billion constructing public works projects, such as roads, sewers, buildings, and airports. At its high point in 1938, the WPA employed around 3 million people; over its life span, the WPA estimated that it employed about one-third of all unemployed workers, providing wages to 8.5 million families. While three-quarters of its funds went to pay for traditional public works construction, providing between 75 and 80 percent of all WPA jobs, the WPA spent 25 percent of its resources on service, or white-collar, projects, such as sewing programs, research and records projects, and arts projects. These included the Federal Writers' Project, which produced the American Guide Series, and the federal art, theater, and music projects.

The establishment of the WPA by Executive Order 7034 on May 6, 1935, grew out of the Roosevelt administration's experience with unemployment. In 1933, President Franklin D. Roosevelt put Harry Hopkins in charge of the Federal Emergency Relief Administration (FERA) and, when it looked like special measures were needed during the brutal winter of 1933–34, gave him the task of running the Civil Works Administration (CWA). Both organizations tried to ease the burdens of unemployment by putting people to work on public works projects. Hopkins, a social worker from Iowa who had administered relief in New York state when Roosevelt was governor, possessed both idealistic fervor and a keen sense of political realism. As Joseph E. Davies famously put it, Hopkins "had the purity of St. Francis of Assisi combined with the sharp shrewdness of a race track tout."

Following large electoral victories for the Democrats in 1934, Hopkins and other New Dealers made the case to Roosevelt for strengthening the federal government's commitment to work relief in place of a simple dole. In response to Roosevelt's January 4, 1935, message to Congress, the House and Senate passed the 1935 Emergency Relief Appropriation (ERA) Act, totaling $4.8 billion. Hopkins and the head of the Public Works Administration, Secretary of the Interior Harold Ickes, immediately set to work lobbying Roosevelt, each seeking to be put in charge of this new works program. By April, Roosevelt accommodated their rivalry by creating a new layer of bureaucracy. Frank C. Walker, a Democratic lawyer with a talent for soothing egos, was placed in charge of a new Division of Application and Information (DAI). Walker's DAI screened project applications and sent them to an Advisory Committee on Allotments (ACA), chaired by Ickes, which reviewed them and passed its recommendation along to Roosevelt. Hopkins's WPA was then to be in charge of expediting selected projects and running smaller public works projects directly. Roosevelt's desire to reduce unemployment through public works, however, led him to favor Hopkins's WPA and to slight Ickes, who envisioned public works as an efficient way for government to expand the nation's infrastructure. A September 1935 conference at Roosevelt's Hyde Park residence, attended by the president, Walker, Ickes, Hopkins, acting budget director Daniel Bell, economist Rexford Tugwell, and others, resolved the confusing situation by giving clear preference to the WPA and rendering the ACA and DAI irrelevant. In 1939, the WPA was renamed the Work Projects Administration—the acronym stayed the same—and made part of the Federal Works Agency.

ORGANIZATION AND PERSONNEL

The WPA built on the organization of the FERA and the CWA, drawing on much of the same administrative personnel. The WPA was federally administered and organized by region and state, with a separate organization for New York City. The Senate confirmed WPA staffers—generally state administrators—who made more than $5,000 a year. The WPA contained engineering and construction, service projects, finance, employment, management, statistics, research, investigation, information, and legal divisions. In 1941, the WPA established a division of training and reemployment after the program was authorized to train workers for defense industry work. Hopkins's key aides included Aubrey Williams, who also ran the National Youth Administration, Ellen S. Woodward, Florence Kerr, Corrington Gill, Jacob Baker, Lawrence Westbrook, Howard O. Hunter, Alan Johnstone, and David K. Niles.

(CARTO-GRAPHICS)

Hopkins also drew on engineering expertise, particularly relying on Army Corps of Engineers Colonel Francis C. Harrington, who replaced Hopkins as the head of the WPA at the end of 1938. Although hesitant initially, Hopkins embraced the notion of using army engineers in the WPA. They had the technical know-how to speed the execution of public works projects, and their air of military and scientific authority helped quiet charges of political favoritism in the WPA. The WPA in New York City and Los Angeles was run by officers from the Army Corps of Engineers.

WORKING ON THE WPA

In order to receive a work assignment on a WPA project, a person applied to a local public welfare agency and was certified through a means test as eligible for public relief. Employment was limited to one member from a family, usually the head of the household. In 1941, the average age of white workers on WPA projects was 43.2 years while the average for black workers was 41.1 years. Workers had to be physically able to

perform the labor required by their assignment. People serving prison sentences were prohibited from working for the WPA, a requirement adopted to prevent convict labor. Workers had to register with the United States Employment Service, be at least sixteen years old (the minimum age was raised to eighteen in 1938), and generally could not collect Social Security or unemployment benefits while working on WPA projects. The 1937 ERA Act granted an employment preference to veterans, while the 1939 ERA Act prohibited the employment of aliens, Communists, and members of Nazi-Bund organizations. The 1939 ERA Act further mandated that all WPA workers with at least eighteen consecutive months' employment be laid off, in order to spread work over a larger pool of recipients. Workers were paid a security wage based on their occupation and location, generally making around $55 a month for doing between 120 and 140 hours of work. In response to pressure from organized labor, however, the WPA allowed skilled workers to make their monthly security wage in fewer hours of work by paying them at prevailing hourly rates of pay. In order to employ

The main goal of the Works Progress Administration was to put Americans back to work. Formerly unemployed men are shown here laboring on an urban construction project. *(Brown Brothers)*

enough skilled labor on projects, 10 percent of project workers were exempt from the WPA's requirements. After 1937, this exemption was lowered to 5 percent.

While the WPA primarily employed white men, it did provide work to women and to African Americans. Through June 1940, women comprised between 12 and 18 percent of WPA employment rolls, working on sewing projects or doing clerical tasks. With the coming of war, however, men left WPA employment at higher rates than women. By June 1942, women accounted for 27 percent of WPA workers; by December 1942, this figure stood around 41 percent. African-American workers made up just over 14 percent of the WPA workforce in February 1939; this figure rose to nearly 20 percent in late 1942 as white men returned to work in defense-related occupations.

SERVICE AND WHITE-COLLAR PROJECTS

The WPA service projects can be divided into three groups: public activities (writing, arts, theater, and music projects; adult education; and recreational and library staffing); research and records (historical records surveys; economic and social surveys; and research assistance at state universities); and welfare projects (school lunch programs; gardening and canning; and public health work). Music, theater, art, writing, and historical records survey projects were administered under the WPA's Federal Project Number One, or "Federal One" as it was called. The writers' project, headed by Henry Alsberg, produced fifty-one volumes in the American Guide Series of travel guidebooks, em-

The Works Progress Administration financed and supervised numerous artistic projects, including the painting of this mural at a school in Wilton, Connecticut. *(Brown Brothers)*

ploying such writers as Ralph Ellison, Richard Wright, and Saul Bellow. The writers' project generated many other studies as well, recording regional folklore, compiling indexes and encyclopedias, and interviewing ex-slaves. Russian-born violinist Nikolai Sokoloff ran the WPA's music project, employing out-of-work musicians in ensembles or as music teachers. WPA orchestras in Buffalo, Oklahoma, and Utah remained successful organizations after the WPA was liquidated in 1943. The WPA art project, directed by Holger Cahill, produced such artifacts as oil paintings, murals, sculptures, mosaics, stained glass windows, tapestries, rugs, ceramics, posters, and pottery. In all, over 2,500 murals were placed in public buildings, such as schools and post offices, and more than 18,000 sculptures and 108,000 easel works were created by WPA artists. The WPA theater project, led by Hallie Flanagan, concentrated on the areas with the highest unemployment in the theatrical professions: New York City, Chicago, and Los Angeles. It mounted such socially inspired productions as *The Cradle Will Rock, Power, One-Third of a Nation, Triple-A Plowed Under,* and *It Can't Happen Here.* The theater projects were shut down in 1939

after charges of communist influence were aired in Congress before the House Un-American Activities Committee (HUAC), or Dies Committee, and Representative Clifton Woodrum's (D-VA) Subcommittee on Appropriations.

PUBLIC WORKS PROJECTS

While the WPA's cultural activities attracted a lot of attention, the vast majority of the WPA's efforts were devoted to constructing public works projects. Unlike the Public Works Administration (PWA), which privately contracted its public works, the WPA built its projects by force account, directly paying for labor and materials. In theory, the WPA was supposed to handle smaller projects that cost less than $25,000, while the PWA took on the larger, more expensive projects. Hopkins got around this obstacle, however, by dividing bigger projects into several discrete segments. Municipal and state government sponsors of WPA projects contributed around 22 percent of the total project cost, when measured over the life span of the WPA.

The WPA performed work on a variety of projects, including municipal and engineering projects, airports and airways, public buildings, highways and roads, conservation projects, and engineering surveys. While the WPA built around 24,000 miles of sidewalks and paths and improved 7,000 miles more, it built or improved around 28,000 miles of curb. It created or improved about 500 water-treatment plants, 1,800 pumping stations, and 19,700 miles of water mains and distribution lines. It constructed over 350 new airport landing fields and improved or expanded almost 700 old ones. The WPA built more than 100,000 new public buildings, such as schools, hospitals, dormitories, and government office buildings. Building roads and highways was the most common WPA project, because these were easy to plan and could employ large numbers of unskilled workers. The WPA built or improved around 650,000 miles of roads, 75,000 bridges, and over 1,000 tunnels.

"BOONDOGGLING" AND POLITICS

Despite this productivity, the WPA was a controversial agency. In a 1939 poll, the WPA was simultaneously ranked as Roosevelt's "greatest accomplishment" and as the "worst thing" he had done. The WPA's emphasis on employment, which favored using manual labor over heavy machinery, coupled with the discrepancy in the hours worked by skilled and unskilled workers, meant that unskilled workers were often seen standing around the project site. This lent some support to the popular image of WPA employees as shiftless workers leaning on their shovels. Critics created derisive nicknames for the program, such as "We Piddle Around." This stereotype, coupled with the impression that some WPA projects were needless "boondoggles," led to

charges that the organization was wasteful, merely providing political patronage to Roosevelt's allies. Concerns over the political use of the WPA spurred hostile investigations by the House and Senate and led to the 1939 Hatch Act, restricting the political activities of federal employees. During World War II, the WPA emphasized the production of public works that aided the war effort and trained workers for defense industry work, but decreasing unemployment and a conservative Congress helped convince Roosevelt to give the agency an "honorable discharge" in 1943.

JASON SCOTT SMITH

See also: American Guide Series; Emergency Relief Act; Federal Art Project; Federal Emergency Relief Administration; Federal Theater Project; Federal Writers' Project; Harry Hopkins; House Un-American Activities Committee; Harold Ickes; New Deal, second; Public Works; Public Works Administration.

Bibliography

Adams, Grace. *Workers on Relief.* New Haven: Yale University Press, 1939.

Amenta, Edwin. *Bold Relief: Institutional Politics and the Origins of Modern American Social Policy.* Princeton: Princeton University Press, 1998.

Federal Works Agency. *Final Report on the WPA Program, 1935–1943.* Washington, DC: Government Printing Office, 1946.

Hopkins, Harry. *Spending to Save: The Complete Story of Relief.* New York: W. W. Norton, 1936.

Howard, Donald S. *The WPA and Federal Relief Policy.* New York: Russell Sage Foundation, 1943.

MacMahon, Arthur W., John D. Millett, and Gladys Ogden. *The Administration of Federal Work Relief.* Chicago: Public Administration Service, 1941.

McDonald, William F. *Federal Relief Administration and the Arts.* Columbus: Ohio State University Press, 1969.

PART IV
INTERNATIONAL AFFAIRS

INTRODUCTION TO PART IV

The Great Depression era—particularly its latter years—was a critical transitional period in the history of American foreign policy. For obvious reasons, much of the 1930s saw the country preoccupied with domestic concerns. The economic disaster that is the hallmark event of the period absorbed virtually all of the time and energy of government and was the central issue of the era's politics. The 1930s also saw a continuation of the isolationist attitudes and policies of the previous decade. If anything, the so-called lesson of World War I—that an ocean-protected America had no reason to become involved in the dangerous follies of Europe (and Asia)—was recited with even more intensity as its applicability to the increasingly worrisome international situation lessened with the rise of Benito Mussolini in Italy, the militarist cabal in Japan, and, finally and most threateningly, Adolf Hitler in Germany.

At the same time, however, the decade saw the emergence of America—if still only latently—as the dominant power in world affairs. While isolationist forces within the country railed against American involvement in the affairs of Europe (sometimes, stepping over the line of excusing German and Italian behavior), the administration of Franklin D. Roosevelt was developing the idea of America as "the arsenal of democracy" and preparing the public for such a role. The final years of the Depression saw the country begin its dramatic shift from domestic scarcity to defense-related prosperity, even as New Deal hostility toward business gave way to wartime cooperation.

The Great Depression era also saw an equally significant change in U.S. relations with two other critical areas of the globe: East Asia and Latin America. In the former, the United States adopted the role of regional strongman, attempting to control the hegemonic power in the region, Japan. In Latin America, America adopted a less interventionist approach with Roosevelt's Good Neighbor policy. While the United States maintained its forceful role in Asia, the noninterventionist credo for Latin America did not last, giving way instead to the exigencies of the Cold War after 1945.

The entries in this section reflect both the tension of international affairs in this period and the transitional nature of American foreign policy during the 1930s and early 1940s. They are divided into several types. Some entries outline the history of foreign countries: Canada, China, France, Germany, Great Britain, Japan, Mexico, the Soviet Union, and Spain. Other entries describe the various international events that precipitated World War II, including Italy's war against Ethiopia, the Munich Conference, and the Spanish Civil War. Third, there are entries on domestic events, organizations, and legislation that affected U.S. foreign policy. Finally, entries describe a few miscellaneous events that fit into none of these categories, but are nevertheless of critical importance to the period. These include the Atlantic Charter, the League of Nations, the London Economic Conference of 1933, and the Berlin Olympics of 1936.

ABRAHAM LINCOLN BRIGADE

The Abraham Lincoln Brigade was a contingent of Americans who volunteered to fight on the side of the republican government of Spain, during that country's civil war, from 1936 to 1939. Several thousand persons—mostly Communists or Communist Party sympathizers—were involved in the brigade.

In July 1936, a group of rightist military officers led by General Francisco Franco tried to seize power in a coup. While failing to topple the government, they were able to seize about half the country—and were backed by the Catholic Church and much of the middle and upper classes. Their efforts to seize the rest of the country led to the Spanish Civil War.

In the tense international political climate of the 1930s, the war quickly drew in outsiders. Both Fascist Italy and Nazi Germany sent men and matériel to support the nationalist rebels while the Soviet Union aided the republican Loyalists. To leftists around the world, the war represented a struggle against fascism and Nazism.

While the U.S. government—as well as Great Britain and France—remained neutral, many left-wing Americans were determined to join the fight against fascism. With the Washington ban on travel to Spain, most of the volunteers headed to France, making their way secretly across the Pyrenees to Spain.

In February 1937, some 450 members of the brigade fought in the battle of Jarama Valley, near the Spanish capital of Madrid, which was still in republican hands. Ill-equipped and poorly trained, they were decimated by the superior nationalist forces; some 120 Americans were killed in the battle and another 175 wounded.

In the end, the republicans lost the war and the Nationalists took power, with Franco ruling Spain until his death in 1975. The war left a bitter feeling in the hearts of many Abraham Lincoln Brigade members. Disappointed with their own government's lack of support for the antifascist struggle, many also felt that they had been cynically used by the Soviet Communists in Spain for propaganda purposes. Both the idealism and the disappointment of the Abraham Lincoln Brigade were captured in the best-selling novel by Ernest Hemingway—himself a volunteer—*For Whom the Bell Tolls.*

See also: Communist Party; Soviet Union; Spanish Civil War; Hemingway, Ernest.

Bibliography

Landis, Arthur H. *Death in the Olive Groves: American Volunteers in the Spanish Civil War, 1936–1939.* New York: Paragon House, 1989.

Lawson, Don. *The Abraham Lincoln Brigade: Americans Fighting Fascism in the Spanish Civil War.* New York: T.Y. Crowell, 1989.

AMERICA FIRST COMMITTEE

The America First Committee (AFC) was the most influential political group opposing United States aid to Britain in the early 1940s. It was formed in the summer of 1940, just after Nazi Germany had overrun France and much of Western Europe and was attacking Britain from the air, in what many believed was preparation for a sea-borne invasion.

President Franklin D. Roosevelt issued an executive order in 1940 releasing surplus military supplies to Britain and giving Britain fifty World War I destroyers in exchange for American rights to British military bases in the Western Hemisphere. In response, the America First Committee was formed in July 1940 by General Robert E. Wood, aviator Charles A. Lindbergh, and Republican senator Gerald Nye of North Dakota, who had chaired an influential mid-1930s Senate committee that had investigated the munitions industry and its role in pushing the United States into World War I.

At its peak, the AFC claimed some 800,000 members, who issued petitions, marched in demonstrations, and wrote letters to Congress in opposition to every

Famed aviator Charles A. Lindbergh was a founder of the America First Committee, an organization dedicated to keeping the United States out of the European war in the late 1930s and early 1940s. Here, he speaks at a committee rally in Chicago in April 1941. *(Brown Brothers)*

effort by the Roosevelt administration to help the Allies fight Nazi Germany and militarist Japan, including the Lend-Lease Act of early 1941, American naval escorts of convoys carrying aid to Britain, and repeal of the neutrality acts.

The AFC was disbanded immediately after the Japanese attack on Pearl Harbor in December 1941, when the leaders of the committee asked its members to support the war effort.

See also: Great Britain; neutrality acts; Nye Committee; World War II, early history of; Lindbergh, Charles A.

Bibliography

Cole, Wayne S. *America First: The Battle Against Intervention, 1940–1941.* New York: Octagon Books, 1971.

Doenecke, Justus D., ed. *In Danger Undaunted: The Anti-interventionist Movement of 1940–1941 as Revealed in the Papers of the America First Committee.* Stanford, CA: Hoover Institution Press, 1990.

ATLANTIC CHARTER

An agreement reached between President Franklin D. Roosevelt and British Prime Minister Winston Churchill in August 1941, the Atlantic Charter pledged the two countries to seek a post–World War II order that guaranteed the principles of self-determination, free trade, freedom of the seas, and non-aggression. It also contained a vague mention of a postwar organization that would guarantee global security.

The charter was reached in a meeting held between the two leaders aboard the British warship HMS *Prince of Wales* off the coast of Newfoundland. Churchill had initiated the meeting in the hopes of an anti-Nazi alliance between the United States and Britain. The principles enunciated in the charter were meant to assure Americans that democratic ideals would unite the Allies, despite the fact that communist Russia was now fighting the Nazis as well.

At the same time, Roosevelt agreed that the U.S. Navy would provide armed escorts for supply ships as far as Iceland and the mid-Atlantic. However, there was no formal declaration of the alliance Churchill sought.

See also: Great Britain; Soviet Union; World War II, early history of; Churchill, Winston; Document: Atlantic Charter, August 14, 1941.

Bibliography

Brinkley, Douglas, and David R. Facey-Crowther, eds. *The Atlantic Charter*. New York: St. Martin's, 1994.

Commission to Study the Organization of Peace. *Comment on the Eight-Point Declaration of President Roosevelt and Prime Minister Churchill, August 14, 1941. With Study Questions and Suggested References*. New York: Commission to Study the Organization of Peace, 1941.

CANADA

Canada was severely affected by the worldwide Depression of the 1930s. Between 1929 and 1933, gross national expenditure declined by 42 percent. By 1933, 30 percent of the labor force was unemployed, and one in five Canadians depended upon the government for relief. Canada, in sharp contrast to the United States, was reliant on foreign trade. Nearly 33 percent of Canada's gross national income was derived from exports, and the Canadian economy was damaged by the international trend toward tariff hikes that became popular by the end of the 1920s. Canada's four western provinces depended almost exclusively on the export of primary products. They were, for all practical purposes, bankrupt by 1932. The economies of Ontario and Quebec were more diversified but still experienced heavy unemployment. The Maritime Provinces had begun to decline economically in the 1920s and were already in difficult straits. Canadian newspapers carried news of collapsing wheat prices, shrinking pulp and paper markets, bankrupt businesses, closed factories, and building projects that were never finished. The collapse in price levels was the same in the United States and Canada. There is little doubt that overproduction and over-capacity helped bring down prices, especially once demand started to fall in Canada's major export markets—the United States, Great Britain, and the rest of the British empire. Canada did not fully recover from the Great Depression until World War II.

INDUSTRY AND AGRICULTURE

Heavy industry was hard hit by the Depression. The number of railway cars manufactured fell to thirty-one in 1933–34, and Canada, one of the world's great railway nations, produced no locomotives. Car production in Ontario, the industry's hub, dropped from 128,496 units in 1929 to 30,606 in 1933, and truck and bus production fell from 25,762 to 6,062. Automobile production rebounded in the mid-1930s, however, and by 1937, it exceeded even the levels of the late 1920s.

Canadian agriculture was devastated by the Depression. Western Canada, hardest hit by drought, dust, and insects, faced an agricultural crisis. The dust bowl conditions in Alberta, Saskatchewan, and Manitoba forced farmers to watch as their topsoil blew away. The prairie wheat pools collapsed as wheat prices dropped to record lows and wheat crop productivity dropped simultaneously. Because of low prices and crop failures, the agricultural population suffered great deprivation. The Canadian Wheat Board was created in 1935 by the federal government to establish a base price for wheat. Other marketing boards were created in British Columbia and other provinces to market everything from fruit to dairy products.

RELIEF

Although unemployment was a national problem, federal administrations led by the Conservative prime minister R. B. Bennett (1930–35) and the Liberal prime minister William Lyon Mackenzie King (1935–48) mostly refused to provide work for the jobless and insisted that their care was primarily a local and provincial responsibility. The result was fiscal collapse for the four western provinces and hundreds of municipalities, makeshift relief projects, and horrible standards of living for many of the unemployed. Government at any level was ill equipped to cope with the influx of unemployed from the farms to the cities and towns.

It was difficult to be declared eligible for relief. Single young men were shipped out of the cities from 1932 to 1936 to Unemployment Relief Camps run by the Department of National Defence. These camps became a national scandal as the conditions deteriorated. The camps paid the men twenty cents a day for construction work in remote areas of the bush. The "On to Ottawa Trek" was organized to protest pay and conditions in the relief camps. The Trekkers planned to ride the freight trains from Vancouver to Ottawa to confront R. B. Bennett's government in Ottawa. The Trek culminated in the Regina Riot of July 1, 1935, brought on by the attempted arrest of the Trek leaders by the Royal Canadian Mounted Police. One policeman was killed, dozens of men were injured, and 130 were arrested.

POLITICS AND THE NEW DEAL

At the beginning of 1930, prime minister King, leader of the Liberal Party, called an election. King's opponent, Conservative R. B. Bennett, a millionaire lawyer, successfully attacked King's relief policy (King had promised to give not a "five-cent piece" to a Conservative provincial government) to pull off an upset victory at the polls. There was a sharp contrast between the two politicians: Bennett was the explosive man of action, while King was the experienced politician and insider. Bennett promised Canadians to use tariffs to "blast a way into the markets that have been closed to you." Fundamentally, both Bennett and King believed in the policies of a balanced budget, a sound dollar, and manipulation of the tariff to allow the private marketplace to bring about recovery. Once elected, Bennett raised the tariff to unprecedented heights and made several efforts to revive trade, including the Ottawa Agreements of 1932, which set up a system of imperial preferential trade.

The Bennett "New Deal" was a Canadian version of the New Deal that Franklin D. Roosevelt presented to the American people so successfully. In January 1935, Bennett took to the airwaves, giving five stirring radio addresses declaring himself for reform and against the capitalist system and its inequities. He wanted to mobilize the power of the state in the war against the Depression. The "New Deal" was the creation of Bennett's closest advisers, William D. Herridge, his brother-in-law and Canada's diplomatic representative in Washington, and his personal secretary, Rod Finlayson. The announcement of the Bennett "New Deal" helped Bennett regain the initiative for a while, but he remained deeply unpopular and was defeated in the 1935 election by King. The courts later declared most of Bennett's "New Deal" legislation unconstitutional. The "New Deal" took attention away from Bennett's minister of commerce H. H. Stevens, the

Chairman of the Royal Commission on Price Spreads, which had taken on Canada's retail giant Eaton's because of its unfair business practices. Bennett had failed to implement Stevens' recommendations and Stevens had quit the Conservative Party over it.

The Depression led to attempts at political reform. Reformers operated primarily at the provincial level, and some were able to achieve power. In Alberta, the inflationary theory of "Social Credit" was spread by William "Bible Bill" Aberhart (premier of Alberta 1935–43). The Union Nationale of Maurice Duplessis came to power in Quebec on a reform platform, and T. Dufferin Pattulo, the Conservative premier in British Columbia, promised "work and wages."

At the federal level, J. S. Woodsworth gave moral leadership to the Co-operative Commonwealth Federation's (CCF) form of social democracy. H. H. Stevens formed his own Reconstruction Party to combat the banks and big interests. By the late 1930s, W. D. Herridge was leading the New Democracy Movement, an effort to unite all of the reform movements under one banner. The Communist Party of Canada, while active during the 1930s, was forced underground when nine of its leaders were arrested and convicted of being members of an "unlawful association" in 1931. Related political groups and unions were responsible for organizing the unemployed in protest marches and demonstrations in Canadian cities, including the "On to Ottawa Trek."

EFFECTS OF THE DEPRESSION

Throughout the Great Depression, the federal government remained a stable force and its power steadily grew. As the provincial governments faced severe difficulties, the Dominion government was forced to prop up the shaky finances of the provinces with loan guarantees to protect the country's own credit rating. The National Employment Commission report (1938) and the report of the Royal Commission on Dominion-Provincial Relations (1940) were major influences on the future of government in Canada. The latter was important in generating the idea of equalization payments, a method of promoting a level standard of living across the nation. The Depression ultimately resulted in an expansion of state responsibility for the economy and for social welfare. In 1934, Bennett's government enacted legislation to establish the Bank of Canada to regulate monetary policy, and in 1940 the federal government introduced a national unemployment insurance scheme and employment service which began to operate in the summer of 1941.

STEPHEN A. HOOGENRAAD

See also: Bennett, Richard Bedford; King, William Lyon MacKenzie

Bibliography

Bothwell, Robert, Ian Drummond, and John English. *Canada, 1900–1945*. Toronto: University of Toronto Press, 1987.

Glassford, Larry A. *Reaction and Reform: The Politics of the Conservative Party Under R. B. Bennett, 1927–1938*. Toronto: University of Toronto Press, 1992.

Hillmer, Norman, and J. L. Granatstein. *For Better or For Worse*. Toronto: Copp Clark Pitman, 1991.

Neatby, H. Blair. *The Politics of Chaos: Canada in the Thirties*. Toronto: Copp Clark Pitman, 1986.

Stacey, C. P. *Canada in the Age of Conflict: A History of Canadian External Policies, Volume 2: 1921–1948: The Mackenzie King Era*. Toronto: University of Toronto Press, 1981.

CASH-AND-CARRY POLICY

Cash-and-carry was a policy developed during congressional debate over the extension of the Neutrality Act in 1937. While trading in military goods to countries engaged in warfare was banned under the existing Neutrality Act, the cash-and-carry policy stipulated that all nonmilitary goods being sold to a country at war—regardless of whether it was the aggressor or not—had to be paid for in advance and carried from American ports in that country's ships or in the ships of a third-party country.

The "carry" part of the policy was new, but the "cash" element was redundant, since the earlier Johnson Act already banned loans or credit to countries that had failed to pay back their World War I debts to America, a list that included every American ally from that war except Finland. But in the late 1930s, isolationist sentiment was at a peak, and no effort to keep America out of European war was considered excessive. The isolationists who controlled Congress—both Democrats and Republicans—were applying, with cash-and-carry, the lessons they had learned in World War I. Then, the sinking of American ships trading with France and England had led—these isolationists argued—to U.S. involvement in the fighting against Germany.

Indeed, cash-and-carry had a more deleterious effect in the struggle against military aggression in Asia than it did in Europe. Though Japan had the ships and money to buy American goods, financially strapped China did not, while Europe, France and England—with ships and capital of their own—were able to take advantage of American production.

While it remained on the books through America's entry into the war in December 1941, cash-and-carry was eviscerated by the policy of "lend-lease," passed in early 1941, which traded British bases in the Caribbean for American military ships.

See also: Great Britain; Johnson Act; Lend-Lease Act; neutrality acts; World War II, early history of.

Bibliography

Cole, Wayne S. *Roosevelt and the Isolationists*. Lincoln: University of Nebraska Press, 1983.

Jonas, Manfred. *Isolationism in America*. Ithaca, NY: Cornell University Press, 1966.

CHINA

The history of China during the 1930s is a history of revolution, invasion, political turmoil, and warfare. Once a powerful empire, most of imperial China had gradually succumbed to western control during the course of the nineteenth century. While the country had largely avoided outright colonization, it was nevertheless divided up into so-called spheres of control where various European powers—including Britain, France, Germany, and Russia—and Japan held economic and political sway.

Following the failed anti-foreigner Boxer Rebellion of 1900, the country underwent a nationalist revolution in 1911, leading to the formation of the Republic of China under Sun Yat-sen in 1912. But this achievement did little to loosen the grip of Japan and the West over the country's economy.

The continuing political humiliation of China and the dire poverty of its people led to an upsurge in revolutionary activity by the newly formed Communist Party of China in the early 1920s. In 1923, Sun Yat-sen reorganized the ruling Nationalist Party, or Kuomintang, army on advice from the Cominterm, or Communist International, a Moscow-led organization of the world's communist parties.

But Sun Yat-sen died suddenly in 1925, leaving a power vacuum at the top that was seized by Chiang Kai-shek, the general in command of the Kuomintang army. In 1926, Chiang led the army on an offensive against the warlords of the northern part of the country and against the Communists. The latter were forced out of the cities and retreated into remote mountain areas, notably around Jui-chin in the southeast, where they established the Kiangsi soviet, or worker/peasant council government, from 1929 to 1934.

By the end of the decade, the Kuomintang loosely controlled most of the country, but many provinces enjoyed a great deal of autonomy. Only in the populous center of the country, around the lower Yangtze River and the cities of Nanjing and Shanghai, did the central government hold full sway.

In 1931, a militarist Japan invaded the northern province of Manchuria and, two years later, turned it into the puppet state of Manchukuo. Shortly afterward, Japan annexed neighboring Jehol province and, in 1935, attempted unsuccessfully to establish another puppet regime over most of northern China. Meanwhile, in Manchukuo, the Japanese built a strong industrial base, laid a network of railroads, and established military bases and settler colonies.

In 1934, Chiang attacked the Kiangsi soviet, forcing the Communists, under the leadership of Mao Zedong, to retreat on their famous "long march" to the Yenan area in northwest China. Chiang's attack on Kiangsi, even as the Japanese threatened the rest of the country, reflected the Kuomintang leader's conviction that the Communists—as opposed to the Japanese—represented the main threat to the Nationalist government.

But in 1936, Chiang was forced, under threat of deportation and even assassination by leaders within his own army, to form a united front against the Japanese. In response, the Japanese launched a massive invasion of China, forcing the Nationalist government out of its capital at Nanjing, where the Japanese engaged in a brutal massacre of the civilian population. By 1938, the Japanese controlled most of northern and central China, and the Nationalists were forced to retreat into the mountains of western and southwestern China.

Back in the United States, there were loud protests over the Japanese invasion, just as there had been over the annexation of Manchuria in 1931. But Washington was unwilling to do more than express outrage, even after the Japanese accidentally sank an American gunboat on the Yangtze River, killing two sailors. (Japan issued an official apology to the United States and paid $2 million in reparations.)

By the decade's end, most of the populous eastern half of the country lay under Japanese control, although it was far from complete. The invaders largely controlled the cities and lines of communication; the countryside included large pockets of resistance, much of it led by Communist Party cadres.

Beginning in 1940, America became more involved in the anti-Japanese struggle in China. The Franklin D. Roosevelt administration began to provide a little credit to the Kuomintang to purchase military supplies, and allowed American military pilots to resign their positions and join the so-called Flying Tigers to deliver aid over the Himalayan Mountains from India and Burma.

With America's entry into World War II, the supplies increased dramatically. And while the Chinese were unable to dislodge the Japanese from China or Manchukuo during World War II, they did tie down over 1 million Japanese soldiers. With the defeat of Japan in August 1945, the civil war between the Nationalists and the Communists that had been suspended since the 1936 united front decision of Chiang resumed. In 1949, the Communists were victorious and established the People's Republic of China under the leadership of Mao Zedong. Chiang Nationalists fled to the island of Taiwan, where they created the Republic of China.

See also: Japan; Manchuria, invasion of; World War II, early history of; Chiang Kai-shek; Mao Zedong.

Bibliography

Borg, Dorothy. *The United States and the Far Eastern Crisis of 1933–1938.* Cambridge: Harvard University Press, 1964.

Eastman, Lloyd E. *The Abortive Revolution: China Under Nationalist Rule, 1927–1937.* Cambridge: Harvard University Press, 1974.

———. *Seeds of Destruction: Nationalist China in War and Revolution, 1937–1949.* Stanford, CA: Stanford University Press, 1984.

Schaller, Michael. *The U.S. Crusade in China, 1938–1945.* New York: Columbia University Press, 1979.

Schwartz, Benjamin I. *Chinese Communism and the Rise of Mao.* Cambridge: Harvard University Press, 1951.

Sheridan, James E. *China in Disintegration: The Republican Era in Chinese History, 1912–1949.* New York: Free Press, 1975.

ETHIOPIAN WAR

On October 3, 1935, Italian forces under the leadership of Fascist dictator Benito Mussolini attacked Ethiopia from bases in the Italian colony of Somalia. Employing bombers and modern arms, the Italian forces decimated Ethiopian defenders, thereby conquering the last of two independent states on the continent of Africa, the other being Liberia.

The invasion produced immediate and widespread condemnation from around the world. A week after the initial attack, the League of Nations voted to take collective action against Italy, including an embargo on oil sales. But when the league approached nonmember America to join the embargo—the United States produced roughly half the world's oil in the 1930s—it was rebuffed.

While sympathetic to the plight of the Ethiopian emperor, Haile Selassie, and his people, President Franklin D. Roosevelt knew that including America in the embargo would be difficult to achieve. The Neutrality Act, which banned the sale of military goods to belligerents, did not include oil. Having just signed the act, Roosevelt did not feel he could now ask for exemptions that applied to a single country. Without America's participation, the oil embargo largely failed. Many internationalists at the time—and many historians since—said that the failure of the League of Nations in Ethiopia was yet another sign that Western democracies were unwilling or unable to punish or stop military aggression by dictators like Mussolini and Adolf Hitler, thereby encouraging them.

See also: fascism, Italy; League of Nations; neutrality acts.

Bibliography

Coffey, Thomas M. *Lion by the Tail: The Story of the Italian-Ethiopian War.* New York: Viking, 1974.

Harris, Brice. *The United States and the Italo-Ethiopian Crisis.* Stanford, CA: Stanford University Press, 1964.

FASCISM, ITALY

Shortly after World War I, Italian veterans created the Nationalist Fascist Party (PNF). The militant Blackshirts were led by Benito Mussolini, son of a blacksmith, who had already been a Socialist. In November 1914, Mussolini had turned his newly founded newspaper *Il Popolo d'Italia* into a pro-war organ.

The informal *fascio* or leadership cadre of the PNF, in 1919 demanded annexation of the Yugoslavian city of Fiume as a reward for Italian support of the Allies. Britain, France, and the United States refused, and many Italians became profoundly disillusioned with socialism and liberalism. The Fascists demanded that Italy mount an imperial challenge to French and British dominance in the Mediterranean.

From 1919 to 1922, Italy was suffering from unemployment and teetering on the verge of social revolution led by Italian Maximal Socialists. King Victor Emmanuel III, backed by conservative and reactionary parties, appointed Mussolini as premier in 1922, after the Fascists had marched on Rome. Italy's elite classes imagined that they had thereby forestalled a dreaded revolution such as that of Lenin's Bolsheviks. Mussolini, taking the party title of "duce," or leader, gradually changed himself, his party, and the state administration into a total dictatorship. He presented himself to Europe as a new type of revolutionary, delighting in the term "totalitarian" invented by a Fascist propagandist in 1932. Mussolini claimed that fascism was the answer to revolutionary Leninism and the wave of the future.

As early as 1922, Italian fascism demonstrated eight major characteristics. First, it was a single-party dictatorship. Second, it emphasized militarism. Third, it involved counterrevolution, or reaction. This third characteristic was shared with other European fascist movements. The ideal of the ancient Roman empire was Mussolini's inspiration, whereas Hitler glorified the Aryan "race," supposedly dominant before Christianity. Both Hitler and Mussolini were raised in the authoritarian Catholic Church, although Hitler became a pantheist and Mussolini an atheist. But appealing to traditional conservatism among the people, the leaders of the two fascist parties tapped into clerical anticommunism and authoritarianism to help destroy Liberal, Socialist, and Communist Parties.

Fourth, imperialism: The duce adopted symbols from the Roman empire: an arm band bearing the double ax, bound to bundled shafts, or fasces, and the Roman salute. He officially proclaimed Italy an empire in May 1936 after his conquest of Ethiopia. Later, fascist armies fought in Spain, Albania, Greece, Yugoslavia, Tunisia, southern France, and Egypt. On November 1, 1936, Mussolini dubbed his entente with Hitler, which eventually solidified into an alliance, the "Axis."

The fifth characteristic of fascism was populism and street radicalism promoted by propaganda. Mussolini's Blackshirts stemmed from the lower and middle classes, and he romantically claimed to be the radical leader of the people. He opened a classbound society to jobs for all classes. In partial imitation of the duce, strong fascist movements sprang up in Germany, Austria, Hungary, Romania, Croatia, and Spain, yet they were also independently motivated by their own countries' social, economic, and national problems. Weak fascist movements also appeared in the democratic, liberal states of France, Britain, and the United States. What was called fascism in the 1930s would be called the radical right today.

The Communists, liberals, conservatives, and democratic socialists, while rejecting some of fascism's characteristics, still thought they could ally with other fascist ideals. Liberal nationalism respected international law and the Law of Nations reflected in the U.S. Constitution. To dupe these democratic governments, fascist nationalists or chauvinists hid their imperial claims against other people's territory, capital, labor, and culture. The socialist left feared the reactionary rhetoric of Mussolini, while the conservative right feared the street brawls of the Blackshirts. Both persuaded themselves that Mussolini could be their ally against communism. For these reasons, some disillusioned Liberals, Socialists, and Communists drifted into fascism.

Sixth: Already by 1922, Mussolini had a fanatic Manichaean ideology of a global struggle between good and evil. He preached anticommunist, antiliberal, antisocialist, anti-Masonic and anti-Semitic doctrines. What the Fascists opposed was often clearer than what they favored. Mussolini's anti-Semitism was mild compared to that of his fellow fascist, Adolf Hitler, and only became obsessive after 1938.

Italian dictator Benito Mussolini reviews a mass demonstration of young Fascists at the Mussolini stadium in Rome in 1934. (*Brown Brothers*)

The seventh element of fascism was the ideal of a quasi-mystical state, greater than the individual and even the duce. The fundamental positive tenet of fascism was glorification of the state. Among the National Socialists (Nazis), Hitler presented the ideal of the German nation, which in his mind was identical with the Aryan race.

The eighth characteristic of fascism promoted self-sufficient autarky, a national economy that might be regarded as neomercantilist. Fascism rejected the laissez-faire principle of an international market.

Hitler shared with Mussolini all eight characteristics of fascism, and he implemented the fascist, National Socialist programs far more efficiently in Germany then Mussolini could ever have hoped to do in Italy. Mussolini was more intellectual and original than Hitler, and National Socialism only differed in certain technical details from Italian fascism. Both movements were spawned by the same crisis—World War I—and both feared that the Bolshevik revolution and communism would spread to their countries.

Some Americans, like the ambassador to Rome, Richard Child, saw Mussolini as an answer to Lenin and the Soviet experiment. Governor Huey P. Long of Louisiana, the Ku Klux Klan, J. Edgar Hoover, the director of the FBI, and General Douglas MacArthur demonstrated certain fascist tendencies, but did not embrace all eight fascist characteristics. Some Manichaean and authoritarian Christians admired fascism. Some American racists allied themselves with Hitler and Mussolini before 1941. Such sympathies led to appeasement from 1933 to 1941 in the democracies, appeasement which Stalin himself tried from 1939 to 1941.

President Franklin D. Roosevelt opposed fascism, although he believed from 1936 to 1940 that Mussolini could be cajoled away from commitment to Hitler and National Socialism. On the other hand, some extreme laissez-faire liberals thought that Roosevelt himself, and his New Deal agencies, were fascist-inspired.

In May 1936, Mussolini, as compared to Hitler, was the major fascist leader in Europe. During their intervention in the Spanish Civil War, in 1937, the Axis balance turned in favor of Hitler. To aid him, Mussolini found it opportune to attack France in June 1940, declare war on Britain, and invade the Balkans. Later he sent an expeditionary unit to the Soviet Union to assist Germany.

After Pearl Harbor, Italy declared war on the United States. In July 1943, the American and British armies invaded southern Italy. Most Italians quickly concluded that Mussolini and fascism had lost the war. Hitler's SS and army rescued Mussolini and other major PNF leaders. The German army with eight divisions resisted the advance of Anglo-American armies in Italy for almost two years. Italian partisans, or antifascist guerrillas, executed the discredited Mussolini on April 28, 1945, two days before Hitler committed suicide in his Berlin bunker.

ROBERT WHEALEY

See also: fascism, domestic; Ethiopian war; neutrality acts; Spanish Civil War; World War II, early history of; Mussolini, Benito; Documents: Roosevelt's "Quarantine" of Aggressor Nations Speech, October 5, 1937; Roosevelt's Fireside Chat on European War, September 3, 1939

Bibliography

Bosworth, R. J. B. *The Italian Dictatorship: Problems and Perspectives in the Interpretation of Mussolini and Fascism.* London: Arnold, 1998.

Cannistraro, Philip V. *Historical Dictionary of Fascist Italy.* Westport, CT: Greenwood Press, 1982.

Cassels, Alan. *Fascism.* New York: Thomas Y. Crowell, 1975.

————. "Fascism for Export: Italy and the United States in the Twenties." *American Historical Review* 69 (April 1964): 707–12.

Deakin, F. W. *The Brutal Friendship: Mussolini, Hitler, and the Fall of Italian Fascism.* London: Weidenfeld and Nicolson, 1962.

De Grand, Alexander J. *Italian Fascism: Its Origins and Development.* Lincoln: University of Nebraska Press, 1982.

Diggins, John P. "Flirtation with Fascism: American Pragmatic Liberals and Mussolini's Italy." *American Historical Review* 71 (January 1966): 487–506.

————. "Mussolini and America: Hero Worship, Charisma, and the 'Vulgar Talent.' " *The Historian* 28 (August 1966): 559–85.

————. "American Catholics and Italian Fascism." *Journal of Contemporary History* 2 (October 1967): 51–68.

————. "The Italo-American Anti-Fascist Opposition." *Journal of American History* 54 (June 1967): 579–98.

Hamilton, Alastair. *The Appeal of Fascism: A Study of Intellectuals and Fascism.* New York: Macmillan, 1971.

Hughes, H. Stuart. *The United States and Italy.* Cambridge: Harvard University Press, 1965.

Mack Smith, Denis. *Mussolini.* New York: Knopf, 1982.

Michaelis, Meir. *Mussolini and the Jews: German-Italian Relations and the Jewish Question in Italy, 1922–1945.* New York: Oxford University Press, 1978.

Payne, Stanley G. *A History of Fascism, 1914–1945.* Madison: University of Wisconsin Press, 1995.

Pitigliani, Fausto. *The Italian Corporative State.* New York: Macmillan, 1934.

Salvemini, Gaetano. "Economic Conditions in Italy, 1919–1922." *Journal of Modern History* 23 (March 1951): 29–37.

————. *Prelude to World War II.* London: Gollancz, 1953.

Sarti, Roland. *Fascism and the Industrial Leadership in Italy, 1919–1940: A Study in the Expansion of Private Power under Fascism.* Berkeley: University of California Press, 1971.

Schmidt, Carl T. *The Corporate State in Action: Italy under Fascism.* New York: Oxford University Press, 1939.

Tasca Rossi, Angelo. *The Rise of Italian Fascism, 1918–1922.* New York: H. Fertig, 1966.

Whealey, Robert H. "Mussolini's Ideological Diplomacy: An Unpublished Document." *Journal of Modern History* 39 (December 1967): 432–37.

————. *Hitler and Spain: The Nazi Role in the Spanish Civil War 1936–1939.* Lexington: University Press of Kentucky, 1989.

FRANCE

The Wall Street crash of October 1929 unleashed the worldwide Depression, but initially its impact was little felt in France. This was largely due to the nature of the French economy, which was relatively less industrialized, based largely on peasant farmers, artisan labor, and small shopkeepers. But the arrival of the Depression in France was only delayed, and, when it came in 1932, its effects persisted until 1938, despite the upswing in the world economy in 1935.

The Depression hit the peasantry first. From 1930 to 1935, agricultural prices fell by half, and many could not sell their produce without a loss. Agricultural incomes declined by 16 percent between 1930 and 1932, and by a further 17 percent between 1932 and 1934. Many peasants joined the Communist or Socialist Party, peasant defense committees, or the protofascist organization called the Green Shirts.

Unemployment became a major problem in the Depression peaking in 1935 at 16.6 percent of the French workforce. However, many industries cut wages and hours. Indeed, wages may have fallen by an average of 15 percent between 1930 and 1935. Self-employed businessmen saw their incomes decline by 23 percent, and bankruptcies rose from 6,500 in 1929 to 13,370 in 1935.

The Depression persisted longer in France than elsewhere; it was the only country not to recover, in terms of production, from the Depression by 1937. French overseas trade dropped and domestic demand declined, thus lowering production and output. By 1932, production had fallen 27 percent from its 1930 level. Even in 1938, industrial production was 15 percent below the 1928 level. Between 1929 and 1935, output dropped by one-fifth. French goods were overpriced in the world market, and consequently exports fell by 50 percent between 1929 and 1936.

A main cause of economic problems was the franc. Governments refused to consider devaluation, mainly for political reasons. Also, while other nations abandoned the gold standard and allowed currencies to float free, the franc remained overvalued. As a consequence, French goods became less competitive.

The political and economic establishment failed to combat the Depression. French governments displayed a lack of innovation, pursuing deflationary economic policy, balanced budgets, and expenditure cuts, including cuts in pensions and the salaries of civil servants. Successive governments aimed at balancing the budget and maintaining the franc, although neither of these goals was achieved. After 1931, France suffered from budget deficits and a rising debt that limited the government's freedom of maneuver.

This seemingly endless series of ineffectual governments, incapable of dealing with the country's deepening financial crisis, fueled much resentment, particularly among the radical right and left. Frustrations mounted in the Stavisky scandal, which broke at the end of 1933. This concerned the questionable dealings of a shady financier, Serge Stavisky, who had swindled municipal bonds. When the police finally tracked him down in January 1934, Stavisky committed suicide. Right-wing circles were quick to claim that the government had Stavisky "suicided" in order to cover up its own wrongdoing, since Stavisky had connections with many politicians. The Stavisky scandal was an ideal target for the radical right to attack the entire parliamentary system as corrupt.

Tensions exploded on the night of February 6, 1934, when over 100,000 demonstrators from fascist and quasi-fascist groups such as the *Croix de Feu* and the *Action Française* massed in the Paris Place de la Concorde with the apparent intention of invading the Chamber of Deputies. Police fired into ranks of demonstrators, killing fourteen and wounding 236.

In response to a perceived fascist threat to the Republic, workers organized a general strike on February 12. Action at the grass-roots level was soon followed by a "unity of action" pact between Socialists and Communists in the summer of 1934. Ultimately, this resulted in the creation of the Popular Front, which was soon joined by the Radical Party.

Radicals, Socialists, and Communists fought the 1936 elections on a common program of defense of democracy, economic recovery, and antifascism. The Popular Front coalition emerged victorious, winning 5.5 million votes as opposed to 4.5 million for the Right. Socialist Leon Blum assumed the premiership on June 5, 1936. He hoped to install in France a program similar to Franklin D. Roosevelt's New Deal in the United States.

Once in power, Blum faced a crisis in the form of sit-in strikes by workers. Assembling representatives from labor and management, Blum negotiated the Matignon Agreements, which conceded the right of collective bargaining and granted a general wage increase of 12 to 15 percent. Parliament soon passed other reforms, including a two-week paid vacation, a forty-hour workweek, and compulsory arbitration. The Popular Front began public works, restructured the Bank of France, and nationalized the armaments industry. In addition, the government raised the salaries of civil servants and increased pensions for veterans. It also began a program of loans and subsidies to farmers and small businessmen. To aid an ailing agricultural sector, the government established a National Wheat Board to oversee grain production and sales. Although Blum had promised to avoid devaluation, by the fall of 1936, he was forced to devalue because of continued pressure against the franc. A second devaluation followed in the spring of 1937 and a third in 1938.

The Popular Front earned many enemies among banking and business interests. A hostile and apprehensive business community withdrew funds and investments from France. Because of its pressure, Blum was forced to call for a "pause" in his reforms in March 1937—a "pause" that proved to be permanent. Denied decree powers by the Senate to deal with the financial crisis, Blum resigned in June 1937. The Popular Front held on until the spring of 1938, when it was replaced by Edouard Daladier and the Radicals.

Daladier began a conservative economic program. The finance minister, Paul Reynaud, issued decrees that limited the workweek to forty hours, increased taxes, and cut government expenditure. The Daladier government also dismantled much of the recently enacted social legislation. Rearmament, already well advanced under the Popular Front, sped up. By 1938, national defense claimed one-third of the budget and absorbed the bulk of tax revenues. After 1938, the economy began to improve, unemployment shrank, and industrial production rose. It was not until 1939 that French industrial production reached the 1929 level. As elsewhere, only war and mobilization solved France's economic problem.

KAREN LEWIS

See also: Munich Conference; neutrality acts, Rhineland, reoccupation of, World War II, early history of; Blum, Léon; Daladier, Edouard; Document: Roosevelt's Fireside Chat on European War, September 3, 1939.

Bibliography

Jackson, Julian. *The Politics of Depression in France, 1932–1936.* New York: Cambridge University Press, 1985.

———. *The Popular Front in France: Defending Democracy 1934–1938.* New York: Cambridge University Press, 1988.

Kemp, Tom. *The French Economy, 1913–1939: The History of a Decline.* London: Longman, 1972.

Sauvy, Alfred. *Histoire économique de la France entre les deux guerres.* 3 vols. Paris: Fayardy 1965–75.

GOOD NEIGHBOR POLICY

The Good Neighbor policy was the name used to describe President Franklin D. Roosevelt's approach to foreign relations with the Latin American republics from 1933 to 1945. Determined to improve relations between the United States and its southern neighbors, Roosevelt announced in his inaugural address that his administration was dedicated to the "policy of the good neighbor." Under the Good Neighbor program, Roosevelt expanded former President Herbert Hoover's largely negative policy of nonintervention in Latin American affairs to include a program of positively directed noninterference and the extension of economic improvement and cultural exchange. As a result of efforts by numerous Roosevelt administration officials, the United States initiated over twenty inter-American treaties, ended all American military occupations in Central and South America and the Caribbean, assisted in creating a united hemispheric response to the wars in Europe and Asia, improved inter-American social and cultural understanding, and provided a blueprint for global peace and organization in the postwar world.

THE IMPLEMENTATION OF THE GOOD NEIGHBOR POLICY

The Good Neighbor policy extended to all areas of the relationship between the United States and Latin America, but was especially evident in three specific cases: the Cuban crisis, the enhancement of United States participation in inter-American conferences, and United States reaction to the Bolivian and Mexican expropriation crises.

Cuban president Gerardo Mercado's mildly dictatorial government lost popular approval after 1929 when the Depression caused the collapse of international sugar prices and plunged Cuba into economic crisis. As Mercado turned increasingly to the Cuban military to support his regime, democracy in Cuba disappeared. In 1933, Roosevelt dispatched Sumner Welles as the new American ambassador to Cuba with instructions to call for popular elections. Mercado resigned and fled the country when a general strike broke out and the military withdrew its support of the dictator. Dr. Carlos Manuel de Cespedas assumed office as interim president, but, despite Welles's personal support, was soon ousted by a military coup. Welles immediately requested military intervention. Unlike many of his predecessors in similar situations, Roosevelt refused to land troops. Instead, he sanctioned a policy of nonrecognition of the military regime and worked through the new ambassador, Jefferson Caffrey, to reestablish constitutional order and reinstitute democratic elections. In spite of criticism that Roosevelt's nonintervention remained highly intrusive into Cuban domestic politics, stability was restored in 1934 with the election and official United States recognition of President Carlos Mendieta.

Roosevelt's commitment to the Good Neighbor policy was also evident in 1933 when the United States expanded its participation in the inter-American conference system. Cordell Hull's attendance at the Montevideo conference was the first ever by an American secretary of state. Hull used the opportunity to support a resolution condemning unilateral military intervention by any hemispheric state and also called for increased inter-American economic cooperation. Montevideo was followed by six additional inter-American meetings over the next twelve years, including four specifically called to gather the foreign ministers of the American republics.

Four of the six meetings predated American entry into World War II and helped create unity among the American republics that lasted throughout that conflict. At the Buenos Aires conference in 1936, both Roosevelt, who attended personally, and Hull, who led the U.S. delegation, gained personal recognition for their support of pan-American goodwill. The delegates agreed to establish a convention for the maintenance of peace in the face of growing hostilities in Europe and Asia, rapid consultation in the event of hemispheric crisis, increased cultural exchange, and liberal trade policies. The Lima conference of 1938 reaffirmed hemispheric agreement regarding noninterference and expanded the Buenos Aires rapid consultation policy, allowing a single nation to call for a meeting of the American states. At Panama in 1939, delegates created a neutrality zone encircling the United States and Latin America to keep war from American shores. The Havana conference of 1940 produced a nontransfer declaration to keep occupied countries' possessions in the Western Hemisphere from falling into Axis hands. The delegates also agreed to treat an attack upon one American state as an attack upon all. In each case, the United States sought and received the approval, cooperation, and respect of the other American republics.

The Bolivian and Mexican expropriation crises also proved tests of American commitment to the Good Neighbor policy. Long-standing grievances between the Latin American states and American oil companies exploded in 1938 and 1939 when Bolivia and Mexico expropriated corporate properties and canceled foreign concessions on their natural resources. After refusing the oil companies' requests for military intervention and investigating the Bolivian and Mexican complaints, Roosevelt decided that the right to expropriation was appropriate so long as the countries provided reasonable compensation for company losses. Extensive legal battles in both Bolivia and Mexico ended in 1941 only after Roosevelt's representatives made it clear that they expected cooperation from the oil companies and settlement on the host nations' terms. Favorable solution of these disputes made it possible for the United States not only to enter World War II free of serious disagreement with the other American states, but also to avoid further expropriations in countries with extensive oil reserves during the war.

THE GOOD NEIGHBOR POLICY AS MODEL RELATIONSHIP

During World War II, Roosevelt frequently held up the Good Neighbor relationship to his allied partners as a model of peace and mutual respect to be emulated by the rest of the world in the postwar period. Following the Japanese attack on Pearl Harbor and the subsequent German and Italian declarations of war, the American states had risen almost as one to break diplomatic relations with, and resist actions of, the Axis powers. During the war, inter-American trade, cultural exchange, and military cooperation flourished. These successes led the president to expect both the United

States and Latin America to emerge from the war enjoying better relations than ever before in their history.

Despite wartime advances, the Good Neighbor policy was overshadowed as the conflict drew to a close. The international commitments undertaken by the United States meant that global, not regional, relationships would dominate the postwar world. The creation of the United Nations and the outbreak of the Cold War in Europe and Asia caused United States foreign policy decisions to be made within a global framework that increasingly ignored the Good Neighbor and reduced the Latin American states to a position of diminished importance.

MARK ROEHRS

See also: Mexico; Cárdenas, Lázaro; Documents: Roosevelt on Good Neighbor Policy, December 1, 1936; Act of Havana on Hemispheric Defense, July 29, 1940.

Bibliography

Gellman, Irwin. *Good Neighbor Diplomacy*. Baltimore: Johns Hopkins University Press, 1979.

Guerrant, Edward O. *Roosevelt's Good Neighbor Policy*. Albuquerque: University of New Mexico Press, 1950.

Haines, Gerald K. "Under the Eagle's Wing: The Franklin Roosevelt Administration Forges an American Hemisphere." *Diplomatic History* 1 (Fall 1977): 380–87.

Kimball, Warren. " 'Baffled Virtue . . . Injured Innocence': The Western Hemisphere as Regional Role Model." In Warren Kimball, *The Juggler*. Princeton: Princeton University Press, 1991.

Pike, Frederick. *FDR's Good Neighbor Policy: Sixty Years of Generally Gentle Chaos*. Austin: University of Texas Press, 1995.

Wood, Bryce. *The Making of the Good Neighbor Policy*. New York: Columbia University Press, 1961.

GREAT BRITAIN

Between the wars, Britain's circumstances were sadly reduced. Except for three years immediately after the end of World War I, the British economy was depressed throughout the 1920s. The 1920s also witnessed a high rate of unemployment, averaging 12 percent annually; the number out of work never fell below 1 million.

From mid-1929, the British economy entered a severe and protracted depression. The volume of British exports fell sharply, thus raising unemployment in export industries. Britain's export trade was hurt by the loss of markets, the general contraction of demand, and the widespread use of protection and exchange controls. By the mid-1930s, invisible earnings were insufficient to cover the large trade deficit. Decline was permanent; the British export trade did not recover in volume or value to the 1929 level.

The most serious problem facing Britain during the Depression was unemployment, which reached 1.7 million by 1930 and over 3 million, or 25 percent of the labor force, by 1932. From 1930 to 1935, unemployment averaged roughly 18 percent, with between 6 and 7 million people dependent on the dole, or government relief. Unemployment figures showed a marked regional pattern. From 1929 to 1937, the low point of the Depression in Britain, the registered unemployment rate was twice as high in Wales and the industrial North as in the Midlands and Southeast. In 1937, the proportion of "long-term unemployed" (twelve months and over) ranged from 9.6 percent in the Southeast to 40.3 percent in the North. The export industries of the North and Northwest were the hardest hit: in 1932, almost one-half of the workers in iron and steel were unemployed, and the figures were one-third in coal and nearly two-thirds in shipbuilding. Such distress propelled the famous "hunger marches," which involved thousands of workers. While the North and Northwest were renamed the "depressed areas," the South and Southeast witnessed the growth of "new" industries, such as automobiles, chemicals, and electricity.

The British government took a number of steps to combat unemployment, none of which was entirely successful. Unemployment relief was extended to cover most workers. Poor relief expenditure increased between 1935 and 1936 from £12 million to £51 million. The government also attempted to remedy structural defects in the economy. This included efforts to modernize older industries and retrain and move surplus labor from these industries to expanding ones through the Industrial Transference Board. The Special Areas Act of 1935 provided for a limited number of public works to improve the infrastructure of depressed areas, as well as incentives for firms to move into the Special

Areas, including loans, low-rent buildings, and tax inducements. Public works on a large scale were not attempted since the government aimed at a balanced budget and maintenance of the gold standard.

Many politicians devised schemes to reduce unemployment. For example, Harold Macmillan's *Peace and Reconstruction* (1935) advocated government spending on public works such as electrification and housing. The socialist Ernest Bevin and liberal David Lloyd George had similar ideas. In 1936, the economist John Maynard Keynes published his *General Theory of Employment, Interest, and Money*, which argued that public works schemes and deficit spending were the roads out of the Depression. The National Government, however, rejected all such ideas because they cost too much money to implement. Orthodox economic policy demanded cuts in government expenditure and a balanced budget. It was assumed that market mechanisms would eventually restore prosperity.

The 1929 election had returned a Labour government, under James Ramsay MacDonald, that could not find a remedy for the Depression. A special commission in 1931 warned that unemployment benefits would create a huge budget deficit and endanger the pound; it advised drastic economies, particularly cuts in unemployment relief, which Labour found unacceptable. The cabinet divided over the issue, and it was widely expected that the government would resign. Instead, MacDonald announced the formation of a National Government that would include members of all three political parties. Although MacDonald was expelled from the Labour Party, the 1931 elections returned the National Government with a substantial majority. MacDonald remained prime minister until 1935, but the Conservatives, in particular Stanley Baldwin, held the real power.

The National Government initiated several changes in economic policy. On September 21, 1931, Britain went off the gold standard and allowed the pound to float; the pound depreciated rapidly and by the end of 1931 was 30 percent below par. To balance the budget, the government raised taxes and cut unemployment benefits and government salaries. In 1932, Parliament passed the Import Duties Bill, which placed a 10 percent tariff on all imports, except those from the empire. The Ottawa Imperial Conference of 1932 further extended imperial preference. In the context of previous British economic policy, these steps were a dramatic break with the past. Within a year, Britain had abandoned the gold standard and free trade—the two premises of British commercial policy for almost a century.

The policies of the National Government produced significant recovery. By 1934, industrial production had expanded a bit above the 1929 level, thus making Britain the first country to achieve restoration of that level of production. By 1937, total production was about 20 percent higher than in 1929. The government's encouragement of lower interest rates helped usher in the largest private housing boom in British history. This housing boom boosted the domestically based recovery and spurred further growth in related industries. Those people who remained employed generally saw their standard of living improve due to a rise in real incomes. Despite these improvements, a substantial level of unemployment remained; in 1937, the number of jobless had fallen to just below 1.5 million.

MacDonald resigned as prime minister in June 1935 because of ill health and was succeeded by the Conservatives Stanley Baldwin (1935–37) and Neville Chamberlain (1937–40). Ultimately, armament production and mobilization for the war pulled Britain out of the Depression and ended the unemployment problem.

KAREN LEWIS

See also: America First Committee; Atlantic Charter; cash-and-carry policy; Johnson Act; Lend-Lease Act; London Economic Conference (1933); Munich Conference; neutrality acts; Nye Committee; World War II, early history of; Baldwin, Stanley; Churchill, Winston, MacDonald, Ramsay; Documents: Roosevelt's Fireside Chat on European War, September 3, 1939; Lend Lease Act, March 11, 1941; Atlantic Charter, August 14, 1941

Bibliography

Kindleberger, Charles. *The World in Depression, 1929–1939*. Berkeley: University of California Press, 1986.

Skidelsky, Robert. *Politicians and the Slump: The Labour Government of 1929–1931*. London: Macmillan, 1967.

Youngson, A. J. *The British Economy, 1920–1957*. Cambridge: Harvard University Press, 1960.

JAPAN

The Depression that struck most of the world in 1929 and 1930 actually began significantly earlier in Japan. While the United States experienced unprecedented prosperity in the late 1920s, a series of bank failures shook Japan between 1926 and 1929. By the time of the American stock market crash, over a third of Japan's banks had closed their doors. A deep economic recession followed as textile and other industries cut back production in the face of declining demand.

More serious still was the reaction of Western nations to the economic conditions in their own countries. Japan's economy had long been reliant on foreign trade, and the increase in tariffs worldwide dealt a devastating blow to the nation's exports. By 1931, the price of raw silk—one of Japan's most important exports—had fallen by more than two thirds from its 1926 level. Overall industrial production declined by 25 percent, and while complete and accurate statistics on unemployment are not available, it is estimated that as many as 3 million Japanese were out of work.

THE MILITARY CRITIQUE OF CIVILIAN GOVERNMENT

The economic crisis encouraged social and moral decay. Historically, crime in Japan had been extremely low, but between 1926 and 1933 the crime rate doubled. Vagrancy, infanticide, suicide, prostitution, and theft all became significant features in a society previously known for its industriousness and respect for the law. Even more ominous was the prevailing attitude among a rising generation of bright young men from the countryside. Unable to afford college, they instead entered the military and naval academies and gradually filled the lower ranks of the officer corps. Having themselves experienced poverty, they blamed Japan's plight on politicians and on the *zaibatsu*, the great industrial combinations that dominated the Japanese economy. They denounced the liberalism and materialism that they believed had taken hold of Japan in the post–World War I era and called for a renewal of traditional values.

These young officers combined their critique of ci-

vilian government and business with hostility toward Japan's foreign policy since World War I. Instead of pursuing military glory in the samurai tradition, this critique declared, the cowardly government pursued cooperation with China and the West. The officers also criticized agreements limiting the size of the country's armed forces, most recently the London Naval Treaty of 1930. Japan, the young officers insisted, had to abandon internationalism in favor of an aggressive imperialist policy in Asia.

The result of this dispute was an alliance between young army and navy officers and right-wing civilian extremists who sought to overthrow the government in favor of a military regime that would act in the name of the emperor. This new government would embark on a new policy of overseas expansion, which would solve all of Japan's problems in the process. Manchuria and other parts of China would serve as sources of unlimited raw materials required for Japanese industry. At the same time, expansion would require vast military expenditures that would also reinvigorate the economy. Further, military glory would encourage a renewal of traditional values and a renunciation of materialism among the people. Finally, conquests in Asia could also serve as an outlet for Japan's "surplus population" and as markets for Japanese goods.

Initially these radicals were limited in their influence. Japan continued to be ruled by a civilian government, and even the upper ranks of the army and navy remained skeptical of their goals. As a result, the young army officers and their right-wing civilian allies increasingly turned to violence. On two occasions in 1931, they conspired to overthrow the government, but both plots were uncovered before any action could be taken. However, the radicals enjoyed their first success in 1932 with the assassination of the prime minister, Inukai Tsuyoshi. In each case those involved received only light punishments, as no civilian politician wanted to risk problems with the army.

THE CONQUEST OF MANCHURIA

It was not only at home that the young radicals began to use violent tactics. In Manchuria, officers of the Kwantung Army planned to stage an incident that might be used as a pretext for a Japanese conquest of the region. On the night of September 18, 1931, a small group of soldiers blew up a section of the Japanese-owned South Manchurian Railroad near the Manchurian capital of Mukden. The officers promptly announced that it was the work of Chinese "bandits," and by the morning the entire city was in Japanese hands. When the government in Tokyo sent orders to cease and desist, the Kwantung Army ignored them, and Japanese troops soon fanned out to occupy the entire province. The government continued to protest, but it became clear that the conquest of Manchuria had widespread support among the press and public opinion.

The Chinese government called on the League of Nations to take action, but the European powers were unwilling to risk a war against Japan. The league passed a resolution calling for withdrawal of troops from Manchuria, but took no other steps to back up this statement. In March 1932, the Kwantung Army set up the state of Manchukuo, under the nominal leadership of the former emperor of China, P'u-i. When the league declared Japan's actions illegal and Manchukuo illegitimate, the Japanese delegation responded by walking out of the proceedings. Soon afterward, Japan withdrew from the League of Nations altogether, formally marking the country's abandonment of its internationalist foreign policy.

THE FEBRUARY 26 INCIDENT

By the mid-1930s, the radicals had attracted a number of high-ranking supporters in the military and perhaps even in the imperial family. They were also becoming more daring in their terrorism, brazenly murdering the prominent conservative general, Nagata Tetsuzan, in November 1934. This time the assassin turned his trial into an opportunity to expound his political philosophy and was widely regarded as a sincere, selfless patriot.

This public relations victory encouraged the radicals to make another attempt at overthrowing the civilian government. On the morning of February 26, 1936, more than 1,400 soldiers took to the streets of Tokyo, occupying key government buildings. After killing three prominent officials, they issued a manifesto defending their actions and calling on the minister of war to set up a military government. But although they claimed to be acting on behalf of Emperor Hirohito, the emperor intervened personally to demand that the rebels be subdued. When he issued a direct order that

the troops return to their barracks, the uprising began to unravel. Army and navy units loyal to the government entered Tokyo, forcing the final holdouts to surrender on March 1.

Unlike in previous coup attempts, the government took a far harsher line in punishing the plotters. Thirteen of the insurgency's leaders were executed, and hundreds more were purged from the army. Further, to ensure that no radical could ever rise to a position of power, an old rule was revived stipulating that only active admirals and generals could serve in the cabinet as ministers of war and the navy. However, this had the effect of strengthening military control over the government, since the rule gave the army and navy effective veto power over the formation of any cabinet.

ECONOMIC RECOVERY AND THE WAR WITH CHINA

Even as the military expanded its role in the government at the expense of the civilian leadership, the country was bouncing back from the Depression more rapidly than most other industrial nations. Increased arms expenditures were the principal reason for this recovery: spending on the army and navy increased 250 percent between 1931 and 1935. This spending revitalized the country's heavy industry and, ironically, benefited the very *zaibatsu* that so many army officers had been denouncing. Although average real wages remained low—by 1937 they were only about 76 percent what they had been in 1931—unemployment declined sharply, and it appeared that the country was well on its way to a full economic recovery.

Yet the arms spending that fueled the recovery also encouraged the military to seek new opportunities for overseas expansion. Japanese troops continued their depredations in China, adding chunks of territory to Manchukuo and issuing demands that the Chinese government recognize the new country. Finally, during the night of July 7, 1937, a skirmish broke out between Japanese and Chinese troops at Marco Polo Bridge, just outside Peking. Both sides sent reinforcements to the area, and the fighting spread to other parts of the country. By the end of the summer the two countries were at war.

Initially the war went well for Japan. Shanghai soon fell, followed by the Chinese capital of Nanking, where a six-week massacre left over 200,000 civilians and prisoners of war dead. But while the Japanese managed to seize and hold most of China's largest cities and industrial areas, the sheer vastness of the country even-

In 1937, Japan launched a massive invasion of China. Here, troops, under the "rising sun" flag of the Japanese military, attack nationalist Chinese defenders in Shanghai. *(Brown Brothers)*

tually proved an insurmountable obstacle. By late 1938, the offensive had bogged down, as there were simply not enough troops available both to sustain the advance and to garrison the parts of China that were already held. Nevertheless the prime minister, Prince Konoe Fumimaro, announced that Japan's goal was the establishment of a "New Order" in East Asia, including not only China but much of Southeast Asia as well.

The war in China had serious repercussions in Japan itself. In 1938, the government enacted the National Mobilization Law, which provided for full state control and utilization of all the nation's manpower and resources for national defense. More ominously, the authorities cracked down on socialism, pacifism, and liberalism as "un-Japanese" ideas. There was a wave of firings within the universities, and the list of prohibited books grew longer and longer. Newspapers and magazines were subjected to increasingly stringent censorship, so that virtually no criticism of the war effort found its way into print. A rising current of anti-Western sentiment led to condemnation of American and European clothing and music as frivolous and decadent. At the same time, school textbooks were revised to encourage a more militaristic and nationalistic outlook among children.

THE ROAD TO WAR, 1940–41

In 1940, events in Europe were coming to take on great significance for the war in China. The German conquest of France and the Low Countries in May and June made those countries' possessions in Asia appear ripe for the picking. Particularly tempting were French Indochina and the Dutch East Indies, the former for its strategic position along China's southern border, the latter for its vast oil deposits. In September, the Japanese government signed the Tripartite Pact with Germany and Italy in an attempt to dissuade the United States from involving itself in Asian affairs. Later, Japanese troops occupied Indochina in an effort to end Japan's need for Western trade, by accessing new sources of raw materials.

All these moves put Japan on a collision course with the United States, where public opinion lay overwhelmingly on the side of China. President Franklin D. Roosevelt responded with an escalating series of economic sanctions, culminating in a near-complete embargo on trade with Japan in July 1941. This last move was particularly devastating to Japan, as 80 percent of the country's oil supply came from the United States.

Since oil was an absolute necessity if the war in China was to continue, the government in Tokyo was faced with a terrible choice—either end the war in China or obtain an alternate supply of oil by seizing the Dutch East Indies by force. Since the military flatly refused to consider the former course, plans were immediately begun for a widening of the war.

Yet this course had even larger consequences. The Japanese leadership assumed that any attack on the Dutch East Indies would lead to war with the United States and Great Britain. The British, fully engaged against Germany in Europe, were not expected to pose a serious problem, but the U.S. Pacific Fleet based at Pearl Harbor could interfere with Japanese designs on Southeast Asia. Therefore the Imperial Navy devised a plan to launch a surprise attack on the American fleet in port using carrier-based aircraft. When last-minute negotiations in the autumn of 1941 failed, the attack took place on December 7. Japan and the United States were now at war—a war that would both revive the American economy and destroy the Japanese empire.

JOHN MOSER

See also: League of Nations; Manchuria, invasion of; Documents: State Department Report on Imperial Japan, December 27, 1934; Roosevelt's "Quarantine" of Aggressor Nations Speech, October 5, 1937, Roosevelt's War Message to Congress, December 8, 1941

Bibliography

Barnhart, Michael. *Japan Prepares for Total War: The Search for Economic Security, 1919–1941.* Ithaca, NY: Cornell University Press, 1987.

Butow, Robert J. C. *Tojo and the Coming of the War.* Stanford, CA: Stanford University Press, 1961.

Crowley, James B. *Japan's Quest for Autonomy: National Security and Foreign Policy, 1930–1938.* Princeton: Princeton University Press, 1966.

Fletcher, William Miles. *The Search for a New Order: Intellectuals and Fascism in Prewar Japan.* Chapel Hill: University of North Carolina Press, 1982.

Mitchell, Richard H. *Thought Control in Prewar Japan.* Ithaca, NY: Cornell University Press, 1976.

Shillony, Ben-Ami. *Revolt in Japan: The Young Officers and the February 26, 1936, Incident.* Princeton: Princeton University Press, 1973.

Titus, David Anson. *Palace and Politics in Prewar Japan.* New York: Columbia University Press, 1974.

Yoshihake Takehiko. *Conspiracy in Manchuria: The Rise of the Japanese Military.* New Haven: Yale University Press, 1963.

JOHNSON ACT

The 1934 Johnson Act, sponsored by Republican senator Hiram Johnson of California, prohibited American loans to governments that were in default on previous loans to the United States. The act largely applied to those European countries that had borrowed money from the United States during World War I to pay for their war effort.

Due to the continuing Depression, the crushing debt, and high U.S. tariffs that prevented them from selling their goods in the United States and thereby gaining the dollars to pay back the loans, all of the European debtor countries defaulted on their loans in June 1934, thereby cutting themselves off from future loans.

As Nazi Germany grew in power and threatened the Western democracies in the middle and late 1930s, the Johnson Act—along with the various neutrality acts of the United States—prevented countries like France and Britain from buying U.S. weapons and supplies on credit, weakening these countries' ability to defend themselves against the Nazi regime.

See also: cash-and-carry policy; France; Great Britain; Lend-Lease Act; neutrality acts.

Bibliography

Cole, Wayne S. *Roosevelt and the Isolationists*. Lincoln: University of Nebraska Press, 1983.

Jonas, Manfred. *Isolationism in America*. Ithaca, NY: Cornell University Press, 1966.

LEAGUE OF NATIONS

Predecessor to the United Nations, the League of Nations, headquartered in Geneva, Switzerland, was founded after World War I as an organization of international cooperation. Although President Woodrow Wilson was one of the original architects of the organization, he was unable to win Senate approval to make the United States a member.

Because the United States was a major power at the end of World War I and the biggest creditor nation in the world, its absence from the organization greatly weakened the League of Nations' abilities to fulfill its mandate to provide collective security, arbitrate international disputes, reduce armaments, and prevent secret treaties.

A Peculiar Breed

Created after World War I, the League of Nations proved itself increasingly unable and unwilling to confront military aggression in the 1930s, as this 1931 *Chicago Tribune* cartoon illustrates. (*Brown Brothers*)

By the time the Great Depression hit in the early 1930s, the league was a greatly weakened organization. When the League of Nations condemned Japan for its aggression in Manchuria, Japan notified the organization in March 1933 that it intended to pull out by the end of 1935, which it did. In October 1933, Adolf Hitler—intending to rearm Germany in violation of the same post–World War I Versailles treaty that created the league—pulled his country out of the organization. The league's attempt to impose an oil embargo against Italy after that country's invasion of Ethiopia was undermined by America's unwillingness to participate.

By the late 1930s, the league was moribund, and it ceased virtually all of its activities during World War II. It was officially superseded by the United Nations in 1946.

See also: Ethiopian war; Japan; Manchuria, invasion of; Nazi Germany.

Bibliography

Kuehl, Warren F. *Keeping the Covenant: American Internationalists and the League of Nations, 1920–1939.* Kent, OH: Kent State University Press, 1997.

Walters, F. P. *A History of the League of Nations.* Westport, CT: Greenwood Press, 1986.

LEND-LEASE ACT

The Lend-Lease Act was a 1941 piece of legislation that authorized the sale of military and other supplies to those nations whose defense was deemed vital to American national security by the president. The act also allowed those nations to pay for the supplies "in kind or property, or any other direct or indirect benefit which the President deems satisfactory." While the act was initially designed to help Britain, it was later extended to China, the Soviet Union, and other countries fighting the Axis powers of Germany, Italy, and Japan.

The history behind lend-lease reflects part of the Roosevelt administration's struggle against the strong current of isolationism in Congress and among the public at large as well as the increasingly dire war situation in Europe. By June 1940, all of Western Europe save Britain had succumbed to the Nazi onslaught. That summer, President Franklin D. Roosevelt issued an executive order providing "surplus" material supplies to the English, followed in September by another executive order that exchanged loaned-out U.S. destroyers for American leases on British bases in the Western Hemisphere.

But lend-lease required direct expenditures and thus needed congressional approval. It proved to be one of the most difficult political fights of Roosevelt's presidency, requiring him to use all of his powers—including radio talks to the American people and legislative favors to members of Congress—to push it through against strong isolationist sentiment.

In March 1941, Congress passed the act. By the end of World War II in 1945, nearly $50 billion in lend-lease aid would go to America's allies. The bulk of it—some 63 percent—went to Britain and British Commonwealth countries. The Soviet Union received 22 percent, and the rest was sent to some forty other nations.

See also: Battle of Britain; fireside chats; Great Britain; neutrality acts; World War II, early history of; Churchill, Winston; McCormick, Robert; Roosevelt, Franklin D.

Bibliography

Cole, Wayne S. *Roosevelt and the Isolationists.* Lincoln: University of Nebraska Press, 1983.

Langer, William L., and S. Everett Gleason. *The Undeclared War: 1940–1941.* New York: Harper, 1953.

LONDON ECONOMIC CONFERENCE (1933)

The London Economic Conference was convened to stabilize international exchange rates and reestablish the international gold standard in the wake of the collapse of the world economy in the Great Depression. Some fifty-four countries, including the United States, were expected to attend.

The conference, called for the summer of 1933, was hailed at first by President Franklin D. Roosevelt, who went on record in favor of currency stabilization. But on July 3, Roosevelt issued a stunning announcement: the United States would not be a party to the stabilization efforts nor would it attempt to return to the gold standard itself. Without the participation of the United States—then the biggest economy and creditor nation in the world—there was little for the attendees to do.

Roosevelt's decision to abstain from the stabilization efforts grew out of his conviction that retaining the gold standard would continue the deflationary trend that had gripped the world economy since the beginning of the Depression. As prices and wages dropped, so did spending power and, hence, the need for production. While most of the world's leaders, as well as leading bankers and economists, denounced Roosevelt's move, others saw its logic. John Maynard Keynes, the British economist whose template for recovery included inflationary deficit spending, praised the president.

See also: banking; gold standard; Keynesian economics; Keynes, John Maynard; Roosevelt, Franklin D.

Bibliography

Freidel, Frank. *Launching the New Deal.* Boston: Little, Brown, 1973.

Moley, Raymond. *After Seven Years.* New York: Harper and Brothers, 1939.

MANCHURIA, INVASION OF

In September 1931, the Imperial Japanese Army launched a massive invasion of Manchuria, a northern province of China that was its most industrialized, coal-rich region.

Technically, the invasion was triggered by an act of sabotage, the blowing up, allegedly by Chinese partisans, of a section of a Japanese-owned railway in the province. But Japan's extremely swift and overwhelming response led many at the time to believe that the act had been staged. By February, the Japanese felt so confident in their control of Manchuria that they installed their own puppet government and renamed the new, nominally independent state Manchukuo. Ultimately, the Japanese hoped to exploit the province's natural resources and industries, as well as use it for the settlement of Japanese colonists.

The League of Nations immediately called for a boycott of Japan following the invasion, but President Herbert Hoover refused to participate. This undermined the league's efforts and ultimately led the Japanese to leave the organization in 1935. But Hoover's move was popular with a country that—remembering the debacle of World War I—was caught up in its own economic troubles and unwilling to get involved in international problems. At the same time, the United States refused to recognize the new state.

Japan would not vacate the province until the very end of World War II, when the Soviet Union sent in the Red Army and Japan had been hit by two American atomic bombs.

See also: China; Japan; League of Nations; World War II, early history of.

Bibliography

Nish, Ian Hill. *Japan's Struggle with Internationalism: Japan, China, and the League of Nations, 1931–33.* New York: K. Paul International, 1993.

Young, Louise. *Japan's Total Empire: Manchuria and the Culture of Wartime Imperialism.* Berkeley: University of California Press, 1998.

MEXICO

A barely industrialized country, with much of its population consisting of small land-holding peasants, tenant farmers, and agricultural laborers, Mexico was not hit particularly hard by the worldwide Depression of the 1930s. Yet the world economic downturn did slow the land reforms set in motion by the recent Mexican Revolution, until General Lázaro Cárdenas, president from 1934 to 1940, instituted a new round of reformist politics.

The Mexican Revolution from 1910 to 1917 produced the modern Mexican Constitution and, after 1920, a relatively stable government, first under General Álvaro Obregón from 1920 to 1924 and then under northern politician Plutarco Elías Calles from 1924 to 1928. At the end of his term, Calles established the predecessor to the Institutional Revolutionary Party, better known by its Spanish acronym PRI, which ruled until 2000.

While the PRI and its antecedants remained committed to the principles of the revolution, notably land reform and anticlericalism, it slowed the distribution of land to the peasants, citing the need to maintain economic continuity in the face of the global economic downturn, which undermined the price of Mexico's main export earner, oil.

In the election of 1934, the PRI leaders gave their nod to a lesser general of the revolution named Lázaro Cárdenas. Not well known, but expected to toe the party line, Cárdenas proved to be his own man, more radical than the PRI leaders had wanted. He soon instituted a number of reforms, including a strengthening of the labor movement and a reorganization of the PRI. He also sped up the land reform process, so that by the end of his term in 1940, approximately 40 percent of the peasantry was working land that belonged to them, in the form of cooperatives, or *ejidos*, more than doubling the total. Even more controversial were his efforts to rein in the power of the Catholic Church.

But Cárdenas's most important reform—the one that affected the United States most directly—was his expropriation of foreign-owned oil companies, following labor union demands for wage increases and a say in the running of the companies. When the companies refused to comply and went to court to defend their interests, Cárdenas issued a nationalization decree on March 18, 1938, and created Petróleos Mexicanos, better known as Pemex, which runs the oil industry in Mexico to this day.

The move was wildly popular with the Mexican population, which ranks March 18 alongside May 5—Mexico's national day—as a day of national celebration, marking the country's economic independence from foreign powers, most notably the United States.

In 1940, Cárdenas stepped down, as per the Constitution's one-term rule, and was replaced by General Manuel Ávila Camacho, a supporter of Cárdenas. Camacho was more reconciliatory than Cárdenas and made an effort to heal the breach Cárdenas had created with the Catholic Church.

See also: Cárdenas, Lázaro.

Bibliography

Ashby, Joe C. *Organized Labor and the Mexican Revolution Under Lázaro Cárdenas.* Chapel Hill: University of North Carolina Press, 1967.

Hodges, Donald, and Ross Gandy. *Mexico, 1910–1982: Reform or Revolution?* 2nd ed. Westport, CT: Zed Press, 1983.

MUNICH CONFERENCE

The Munich Conference—which produced the Munich agreement—was the last in a series of 1938 meetings between British prime minister Neville Chamberlain, and the German dictator, Adolf Hitler, to decide the fate of Sudetenland, an area of Czechoslovakia in which a majority of the people were of German ethnic origin.

Having absorbed Austria in March 1938, Hitler made it clear that he was interested in annexing the Sudetenland. Czechoslovakia, which had defense agreements with France and the Soviet Union, looked to outside help to protect its territory.

The Soviet Union, however, indicated that it was not willing to defend Czechoslovakia unless France agreed, and France wanted British help. But neither of the Western democracies felt ready to confront the growing military might of Germany. In September 1938, Chamberlain flew twice to Germany to discuss the Sudetenland with Hitler, once at the dictator's retreat in Berchtesgaden, once at the German resort of Bad Godesburg.

Hitler cynically insisted that the Versailles peace treaty of 1919—which he had condemned, but which called for the self-determination of European peoples—be applied. But Chamberlain's request for a gradual absorption of the Sudetenland was brushed aside by Hitler. As Britain and France prepared for war, Chamberlain flew to Munich, where he agreed to all of Hitler's demands. Returning to London, the prime minister declared he had achieved "peace in our time." German troops then marched into the Sudetenland.

In Washington, President Franklin D. Roosevelt felt that the British and the French, who went along with the agreement, had betrayed Czechoslovakia. Secretly, he condemned Chamberlain's policy of appeasement, whereby the prime minister hoped to prevent a European war by giving in to Hitler's demands. But faced with an isolationist Congress and public, Roosevelt could do little. Six months after Munich, the Germans invaded the rest of Czechoslovakia, ending the policy of appeasement and leading to the onset of World War II in September 1939, when Hitler invaded Poland.

See also: Nazi Germany; neutrality acts; World War II, early history of; Chamberlain, Neville; Hitler, Adolf.

Bibliography

Cole, Wayne S. *Roosevelt and the Isolationists.* Lincoln: University of Nebraska Press, 1983.

Leibovitz, Clement. *In Our Time: The Chamberlain-Hitler Collusion.* New York: Monthly Review Press, 1998.

NAZI GERMANY

Most historians trace the immediate causes for the rise of Nazism in Germany to World War I and the events that immediately followed that conflict. Germany, along with the Austro-Hungarian Empire and Ottoman Empire, were, of course, defeated by the Allies—including France, Great Britain, and the United States in November 1918. (Another ally, Russia, dropped out of the war after its Bolshevik Revolution in 1917.). In 1919, the victorious nations—notwithstanding a dissent from President Woodrow Wilson—imposed what has widely been regarded by historians as an extremely punitive peace accord, known as the Versailles Treaty. Not only was Germany blamed for the conflict, but was forced to pay $33 billion in reparations. The latter left the country's economy crippled, resulting in a bout of hyper-inflation that wiped out the savings of many middle-class Germans in the mid-1920s. This economic crisis helped undermine the stability of Germany's new and fragile democratic regime, known as the Weimar Republic.

In 1923, Adolf Hitler, a former corporal in the German army, led a group of Storm Troopers from the newly formed National Socialist, or Nazi Party, in a failed putsch, or coup, and was briefly imprisoned. During his nine-month stint in jail, he wrote *Mein Kampf* (My Struggle), which outlined his plans for a resurgent German empire in the heart of Europe. Upon emerging from prison, Hitler and the Nazis began to organize politically. With the stock market crash of 1929, Germany's economy—highly dependent on heavy industry and trade—went into a tailspin. Rising unemployment, labor unrest, and a powerful communist movement led many German citizens to embrace the extreme nationalist doctrines of the Nazi Party. In January 1933, Hitler was elected Chancellor of Germany. Claiming the title of führer, or supreme leader, Hitler established what he called the Third Reich and consolidated his position by assuming dictatorial powers and destroying the communist movement.

Overseas, he soon made manifest the plans for German world domination that he had outlined in *Mein Kampf*. He pulled his country out of the League of Nations (the international peacekeeping organization established after World War I) and began rearming, a violation of the Versailles Treaty. In 1936, he reoccupied the industrial Rhineland district and began sending arms and troops to support fascist Nationalists in the Spanish Civil War. In 1938, Hitler annexed Austria and demanded that the Sudetenland, a German-speaking region of neighboring Czechoslovakia, be folded into the German empire. Despite these aggressive actions, the former Allies—that is, Britain, France, and the isolationist United States—did little to stop him.

Meanwhile at home, Hitler was bringing to fruition the domestic agenda laid out in *Mein Kampf*. While this entailed a number of actions—including the destruction of the communists, the subordination of all independent institutions, most notably trade unions, and remilitarization of the German state—the most notorious action was the systematic attack on the nation's Jews. Blaming them for Germany's defeat in World War I and seeing them as a threat to Germany's racial identity, the Nazis issued the punitive 1935 Nuremburg laws which stripped German Jews of their citizenship. Then, on the night of November 11, 1938, the twentieth anniversary of the end of World War I, the Nazis and their supporters went on the attack, murdering Jews and destroying Jewish synagogues, homes, and businesses. This event, known as Kristallnacht, or night of broken glass, shocked the world, but prompted no retaliation against the Nazis.

Indeed, just two months earlier, Hitler had torn up the agreement on the Sudetenland that he had signed with England and France, and annexed all of Czechoslovakia. Throughout this period the rest of the world did nothing to stop Hitler. Only when the Nazis launched their blitzkrieg, or lightning war, against

Poland on September 1, 1939, did the Allies declare war. But by this time, Hitler's war machine had grown to immense proportions. Meanwhile, across the Atlantic, a highly isolationist United States watched the events in Germany with dismay, but did little beyond filing protests.

During the 1920s, the United States had helped reintegrate Germany into the Western political and economic community. The rise of Hitler, however, had led to a heightened fear of fascism and dictatorship as Americans heard of the increasing brutality of the Nazi government. This fear of dictatorship and totalitarianism led to negative public sentiment against assistance to Germany. Most Americans had adopted an isolationist stance toward international affairs and favored a nationalist economic policy that emphasized domestic improvements. At the same time, opposition to the New Deal domestic economic policies increased as conservatives used the example of Nazi Germany to strengthen their argument against economic planning and other liberal policies—even progressive business leaders sympathetic to the New Deal joined in the criticism.

In 1933, the establishment of the Third Reich introduced an ideological element into the relationship between Germany and the United States. It soon became clear that the friendly relationship that had existed throughout the previous decade would end. The economic depression had rendered American financial assistance toward the restoration of Germany impossible, and Germany's rearmament and autocratic government were ideologically opposed to America's disarmament and democratic government. Immediately following the establishment of the Third Reich and the fall of the Weimar Republic, the American embassy in Berlin began reporting to Washington on acts of discrimination, persecution, and violence against Jews. Hitler and Nazi government officials had broken up the Socialist trade unions and arrested political opponents—many of whom were former leaders of the Weimar Republic—and imprisoned them in concentration camps. In May 1933, President Franklin D. Roosevelt warned Hjalmar Schacht, the president of the Reichsbank, who was visiting Washington on a diplomatic mission, of the threat to diplomatic relations between Germany and the United States.

Between January and March 1933, Secretary of State Cordell Hull and the State Department had hesitated to condemn persecution of Jews in Germany. The American Jewish Committee, American Jewish Congress, and B'nai B'rith scheduled a demonstration rally that took place at New York's Madison Square

Over 160,000 Nazi storm troopers listen to German dictator Adolf Hitler address a rally in Nuremberg to celebrate the founding of the Nazi Party. *(Brown Brothers)*

Garden on March 27, 1933. It was attended by many people who weren't Jewish including Mayor John P. O'Brien, Senator Robert F. Wagner, William Green of the American Federation of Labor, and Bishops William T. Manning and Francis J. McConnell. As German persecution of Jews increased in April, Jewish leaders organized a boycott of German goods in retaliation for the German government's boycott of Jewish firms. By the end of the year, they had formed two boycott organizations: the Non-Sectarian Anti-Nazi League to Champion Human Rights and the Boycott Committee of the American Jewish Congress. The movement was minimally successful in New York because of more adequate funding and staffing but it was unsuccessful and disorganized elsewhere.

In March 1933, President Roosevelt appointed Cordell Hull as the new secretary of state. Hull's first concern was the World Disarmament Conference that had opened in February 1932. The United States had proposed a nine-point plan, and former President Herbert Hoover had suggested that all nations reduce armaments by a third. No significant progress was made and France, Britain, Germany, and Italy could not reach an agreement after thirteen months. Germany wanted equality of strength and the German delegation led by Rudolf Nadolny considered the American delegation more sympathetic than the French who wanted a guarantee of security, since the British and Americans only wanted limitations on offensive armaments. Germany threatened to pull out of the talks because France, Britain, and Italy wanted a unilateral treaty. The United States wanted to avoid such a treaty because it would limit American neutrality, and Hull was sent to Geneva to assist with the armament discussions. In March 1933, Hans Luther replaced Friedrich W. von Prittwitz und Gaffron as German ambassador to the United States when Prittwitz resigned his post under the German foreign minister Konstantin von Neurath in response to the political changes in Germany. Most Americans did not believe the rise of Hitler would affect the positive relationship between Germany and America, and long-term objectives of the Hitler government did not appear to be an immediate concern.

Although more committed to national economic policies than international ones, President Roosevelt hoped to stimulate favorable sentiment toward the World Economic Conference. On April 5, 1933, Roosevelt and British Prime Minister Ramsay MacDonald met in Washington and began calling for leaders of France, Italy, Germany, Japan, China, Argentina, Brazil, Chile, Mexico, and Canada to meet them there. Currency stabilization was a major point of contention. Initially, Roosevelt refused to commit the United States to currency inflation, but domestic and foreign pressures quickly forced him to do so. It became clear to Roosevelt in April that agricultural and industrial measures would not raise domestic prices fast enough. On April 19, Roosevelt took the United States off the international gold standard and embraced the Thomas Amendment to the Agricultural Adjustment Act that authorized the president to inflate the dollar, bringing the United States into disagreement with nations seeking currency stabilization. In response, Hitler sent Hjalmar Schacht to Washington.

During the talks in Washington, Prime Minister MacDonald discussed his plan to reduce production of offensive weapons but Germany insisted on rearmament. Roosevelt viewed Germany as the only obstacle to reaching a disarmament treaty, and he was aware that world economic recovery and international political stability depended on the economic discussions in Washington. He declared a willingness to work with France and Britain toward currency stabilization and cancelled the interest payment on the upcoming debt installments. On May 16, Roosevelt addressed Hitler and other world leaders with a four-step peace and disarmament program but Hitler emphasized his intent to rearm Germany on equal par with Western nations.

In June 1933, representatives from sixty-six nations attended the World Economic Conference in London. That same month, Roosevelt chose William E. Dodd as American ambassador to Germany. The World Economic Conference opened formally on June 12. Mac-

Donald wanted to discuss war debts but British and French delegates were mainly interested in international stabilization of the gold exchange rate of the dollar, pound, and franc. Although Roosevelt entertained the idea, he changed American policy in a message delivered at the conference on July 2. In this message, Roosevelt adopted a nationalist approach to relief rather than an internationalist approach that called for revival of trade and world economies through gold stabilization. The United States continued to support disarmament. On October 15, however, Hitler, determined to rebuild the military, withdrew Germany from both the Disarmament Conference and the League of Nations.

Throughout 1934, relations between Germany and the United States worsened, as American diplomats Dodd and Hull failed to moderate the policies of Hitler. In late 1933, the German government announced a policy of discriminatory interest payments on long-term debts and threatened to reduce payments on bonds while paying the Swiss and Dutch. In response, Senator Millard E. Tydings (D-MD) introduced a resolution calling for the restoration of civil and political rights to Germany's Jews, and Representative Samuel Dickstein (D-NY) proposed an investigation into the nature and extent of Nazi propaganda in the United States in January 1934. The Dickstein Resolution was approved on March 20, and the House Un-American Activities Committee began its investigation. The United States became more isolated in response to the domestic economic crisis at home and to increasing foreign political turmoil. Roosevelt failed to achieve an international agreement on disarmament and congressional authorization to halt a selective embargo on arms exports. In an effort to protect itself from future military conflict, the United States formally enacted neutrality legislation in 1935, 1936, and 1937.

On April 12, 1934, Congress passed the Johnson Act that prohibited loans to countries in default and set up the Nye Committee to investigate the munitions industry. Both were actions to keep the United States out of a future war. Public sentiment was changing, however, toward Congress abandoning old-style neutrality, but no agreement existed on what should take its place. Isolationists urged an impartial law that would embargo arms, bar loans, and limit trade to all belligerents. Collective-security advocates and pacifists who wanted to assure peace through international cooperation urged neutrality legislation that would contain discretionary powers for the president. Roosevelt asked the Nye Committee to prepare a neutrality law that combined both views. He was more concerned with domestic economic conditions and adopted a more isolationist stance, as the United States sought to distance itself from the threats posed by the establishment of the Third Reich and its rearmament.

Trade warfare was inevitable as both Germany and the United States instituted policies that discriminated against the other. First, Congress enacted the Reciprocal Trade Agreements Act on June 12, 1934, that provided for the mutual lowering of tariffs on selected items through bilateral agreements and extended the unconditional most-favored-nation principle to these arrangements. Of course, Germany would be left out of these arrangements. On September 1, 1934, Germany began to balance its commerce in its "New Plan" to trade with Latin American and Balkan countries and to decrease trade with the United States and Western Europe. Germany's New Plan imposed quota limits on imports, bilateral trade and payment balances, import limitation and planning in accordance with national priorities, and on the encouragement of exports on a barter basis. The United States had protested the quota system as a violation of the trade treaty of 1923, and refused to enter into reciprocal trade arrangements since they would negatively affect American balance of payments. On October 13, 1934, Germany announced its intention to terminate the unconditional most-favored nation provisions of its trade treaty with the United States.

The period between January 1935 and March 1936 was critical for diplomatic relations between the United States and Germany. On January 13, the people of the Saar voted to reunite with Germany. On January 29, the Senate voted that the United States should not join the Permanent Court of International Justice at The Hague or The World Court. On May 9, 1935, Germany announced the existence of an air force and reintroduced conscription one week later. Britain, France, and Italy protested and called a conference at Stresa that condemned the acts as a violation of the Versailles Treaty. The United States remained isolationist and did not protest even though it did not approve of Germany's actions. Trade between Germany and the United States had been greatly reduced by the onset of the Depression, and as the American economy improved in the course of the decade, Germany did not share in the revival of U.S. foreign trade. By 1935, exports to Germany amounted to less than 20 percent of 1927 and 1928 levels and imports were a third. On June 30, 1935, Secretary of the Treasury Henry Morgenthau invoked the 1930 Smoot-Hawley Tariff Act that required application of countervailing duties or higher tariffs to subsidized German exports.

By the beginning of 1936, Roosevelt recognized that German political and military aggression were escalating. German forces reentered the Rhineland on March 7, 1936, and the United States rejected a request from the French foreign minister, Pierre-Etienne Flandin, that the action be condemned. The President and the State Department agreed that the act did not affect American rights or interests because the United States was not party to the Locarno Pact of 1925 and the Rhineland provisions of the Versailles Treaty. Following reoccupation, Hitler proposed a twenty-five-year Western nonaggression pact that Roosevelt saw as an opportunity for peace. And when Hitler moved on July 25 to provide aircraft, supplies, and eventually troops to the forces of General Francisco Franco, the United States did not embargo arms sales to either Germany or Italy. Instead, the United States merely placed a moral embargo on such sales since domestic public sentiment was opposed to further action.

On August 4, 1937, Ambassador Dodd returned to the United States and proclaimed that Hitler's objective was to destroy democracy. Hugh R. Wilson then replaced Dodd as ambassador to Germany, and on October 5, 1937, Roosevelt delivered his Quarantine Speech in Chicago. In this speech, Roosevelt denounced the Nazi reign of terror and rearmament of aggressive weapons. He also warned that American isolation would last only so long as England was not threatened and that the United States would side with Great Britain. On November 11, Roosevelt called upon all ambassadors accredited to the United States for a world peace conference to deal with Germany's increasing aggression.

In September 1938, British Prime Minister Neville Chamberlain, French Premier Edouard Daladier, Italian dictator Benito Mussolini, and Hitler met at the Munich Conference. Hitler indicated to Chamberlain his desire that Britain and Germany should never go to war. Hitler agreed not to move on Czechoslovakia but otherwise the situation in Germany remained tense. In the fall of 1938, Roosevelt felt powerless to aid Germany's 500,000 persecuted Jews. Since 1933, 30 percent of this group had become refugees and the National Origins Act of 1924 restricted immigration to the United States except for a token amount. American officials feared adding to the nation's unemployment and only three-fourths of the quota was actually filled.

In 1938, Hitler invited the United States government to send a diplomatic representative to the Nuremberg Congress of the Nazi Party. The State Department accepted the invitation, outraging some Americans, including Dieckhoff who blamed the passivity of the American public and called on a stricter American policy toward Germany. When Germany annexed Austria on March 12, 1938, the United States responded two months later by stripping Austria of most-favored nation status. On September 1, Congress passed the Helium Act which barred the sale of helium to Germany for military purposes. The previous May, Congress had passed the important Vinson Naval Expansion Act which authorized the expenditure of $1 billion over the next ten years, indicating that the United States might be prepared to use force to stop further German expansion. Following the annexation of Austria, and Nazi efforts to expel Austria's 190,000 Jews, the United States made its most serious effort to assist Jewish refugees. Roosevelt invited thirty-two nations to join the United States in setting up a committee to facilitate the emigration of refugees from Nazism.

The absence of relations between Germany and the United States by the summer of 1938 sharply limited American options in dealing with German aggression. Trade and investment were negligible so economic pressure would not work, and the only option was the threat of force in union with European nations. Roosevelt and Chamberlain discussed American support if war broke out but U.S. policy remained cautious and noncommittal. The following fall brought Kristallnacht and the destruction of Jewish homes and neighborhoods. Jews were barred from trade, one of the few occupations still open to them, and fined collectively 1 billion marks. Americans were outraged and Roosevelt ordered the recall of American ambassador Wilson in Berlin. Dieckhoff returned to report on events in Germany. It was not a formal declaration of a break in diplomatic relations but the two ambassadors never returned to their positions.

In his State of the Union Address on January 4, 1939, Roosevelt emphasized military preparedness and the revision of restrictive neutrality legislation. He emphasized German attacks on religion, democracy, and international relations and warned that the United States would defend itself against acts of aggression. Roosevelt requested the military budget be increased by 30 percent to $1.3 billion and an additional $500 million for the purchase of aircraft. On March 14, Hitler violated his promise at Munich and annexed Czechoslovakia, and he followed with demands for Memel in Lithuania and the return of Danzig and the Polish Corridor. Chamberlain abandoned appeasement and pledged aid to Poland in case of war. On March 17, the Roosevelt administration condemned the action and the State Department pressed Pittman

into introducing a revised Neutrality bill which became the Peace Act of 1939. It eliminated the mandatory arms embargo and placed all trade on a cash-and-carry basis. The law assured that Britain and France would have free access on the Atlantic Ocean to receive arms and supplies in times of war. American public opinion was in favor of selling war materials to England and France if they were fighting Germany and Italy. On April 14, Roosevelt sent a message to the European dictators, asking for formal pledges that thirty-one particular countries in Europe and the Middle East not be attacked for at least ten years but Hitler refused.

As relations grew tenser, trade between Germany and the United States diminished to $100 million—only 1.8 percent of America's total. During late spring and summer of 1939, the world was heading for war and American concern increased. Henry L. Stimson and others called for American intervention in economic terms but some Americans were concerned about trade, jobs, and living standards. The main issues remained ideological and military, and Roosevelt pleaded with Hitler and President Ignaz Moscicki of Poland to solve their differences. Germany invaded Poland on September 1, 1939, and Britain and France declared war on Germany on September 3. The United States and Germany did not interact significantly between September and December 1941, as each country followed separate courses in attempts to deal with the other. The United States steadily increased its commitment to the Allied war effort and the defeat of Germany. On December 11, 1941—four days after Japan bombed Pearl Harbor and three days after the United States declared war on Japan—Germany declared war on the United States. American participation in World War II would help cause the surrender and collapse of Nazi Germany in 1945.

Jeffery Glenn Strickland

See also: fascism, domestic; German-American Bund; Silver Shirts; League of Nations; Munich Conference; Nazi-Soviet non-aggression pact; neutrality acts; Olympics (Berlin, 1936); Rhineland, reoccupation of, World War II, early history of; Hitler, Adolf; Documents: State Department Report on Nazi Germany, April 17, 1934; Roosevelt's "Quarantine" of Aggressor Nations Speech, October 5, 1937, Roosevelt's Fireside Chat on European War, September 3, 1939

Bibliography

Brinkley, Alan. *The End of Reform: New Deal Liberalism In Recession and War.* New York: Vintage Books, 1996.

Cole, Wayne S. *Roosevelt and the Isolationists*. Lincoln: University of Nebraska Press, 1983.

Dallek, Robert. *Franklin D. Roosevelt and American Foreign Policy, 1932–1945*. Oxford: Oxford University Press, 1995, 1979.

Jonas, Manfred. *The United States and Germany: A Diplomatic History*. Ithaca, NY: Cornell University Press, 1984.

NAZI-SOVIET NONAGGRESSION PACT

Also known as the Molotov-Ribbentrop Pact—after Vyacheslav Molotov and Joachim von Ribbentrop, the respective foreign ministers of the Soviet Union and Nazi Germany—the Nazi-Soviet nonaggression pact was an agreement that pledged both countries to refrain from attacking each other. The pact also contained a secret clause, in which they agreed to divide up Poland between them once Germany had invaded that country.

Each side had its reasons for signing. Soviet leader Joseph Stalin, fearing the growing might of the Nazi military, hoped to gain time to build up his country's defenses. Germany's Adolf Hitler wanted to neutralize the Soviet Union while he invaded Western Europe.

In Washington, the agreement was seen as a prelude to war, which indeed it was. Signed on August 23, 1939, it was followed less than ten days later by the Nazis' *blitzkrieg*—or "lightning war"—invasion of Poland on September 1. Sixteen days later, the Soviet Red Army moved in to occupy the eastern half of the country.

While the Nazi-Soviet pact was supposed to last for ten years, it was torn up by Hitler less than two years later, when he launched the German army on a massive invasion of the Soviet Union in June 1941.

See also: Nazi Germany; Soviet Union; World War II, early history of; Hitler, Adolf; Stalin, Joseph.

Bibliography

Shirer, William. *The Rise and Fall of the Third Reich*. New York: Harper & Row, 1962.

Watt, Donald Cameron. *How War Came: The Immediate Origins of the Second World War, 1938–1939*. New York: Pantheon Books, 1989.

NEUTRALITY ACTS

The neutrality acts were a series of laws passed annually between 1935 and 1939 pledging the United States to remain neutral in all international conflicts. The acts reflected the strong isolationist sentiment that had gripped Congress and the country since the end of World War I.

Indeed, the failure of the Versailles Peace Treaty after World War I to bring a just and lasting peace to Europe had soured many Americans on the idea of becoming involved in global—and especially European—affairs. And with the rise to power of the Nazis in Germany in 1933—and the increased tensions they brought to the continent in the years thereafter—isolationist sentiment in America grew and hardened.

The first neutrality act, signed reluctantly by President Franklin D. Roosevelt in October 1935, required the president to impose an embargo on all arms shipments to countries at war. Roosevelt insisted on and received the power to impose embargoes selectively, against aggressor nations only. The act as signed also empowered the president to warn Americans that if they traveled on the ships of belligerents, it would be at their own risk. To many isolationists, it was American arms shipments—and the lost lives of Americans on board ships transporting those arms—that had drawn the country into World War I.

Ironically, the first Neutrality Act worked against itself the very first time it was tested. Following Italian dictator Benito Mussolini's invasion of Ethiopia within days of the act's passage, the League of Nations called on the United States to halt oil shipments to Italy. But the act did not include oil in its list of embargoed goods, and so the United States kept trading with the aggressor.

The Neutrality Act of 1935 was renewed for fourteen months in February 1936 and renewed again in 1937. In the latter year, Congress strengthened the provision concerning Americans traveling aboard belligerents' ships by making such action illegal. In addition, the new act added a cash-and-carry clause whereby belligerents purchasing nonmilitary supplies had to pay for them in cash and carry them away from American ports in their own ships.

Though renewed yet again in 1939, the Neutrality Act was soon superseded by an executive order in 1940 allowing for the purchase of "surplus" American military supplies by the embattled British and by 1941's Lend-Lease Act, which allowed for the direct exchange of American war supplies for a variety of nonmonetary forms of compensation.

See also: cash-and-carry policy; Johnson Act; Nye Committee; World War II, early history of.

Bibliography

Cole, Wayne S. *Roosevelt and the Isolationists.* Lincoln: University of Nebraska Press, 1983.

Jonas, Manfred. *Isolationism in America.* Ithaca, NY: Cornell University Press, 1966.

NYE COMMITTEE

Chaired by progressive Republican and isolationist senator Gerald Nye of North Dakota, the committee that bore his name occupied itself from 1934 to 1936 investigating how arms manufacturers and the bankers who funded the arms trade had helped draw the United States into World War I.

The committee was an outgrowth of the growing peace and isolationist movement in the United States, which was determined to prevent the same thing happening again—a prospect that the committee considered a distinct possibility as Europe once again descended to belligerence and potential war in the mid-1930s.

At first, President Franklin D. Roosevelt supported the committee's work as it exposed the "crimes" of those big-business political adversaries, such as Du Pont and big Wall Street bankers, who opposed his New Deal programs. But the Nye Committee intensified isolationist sentiment in Congress and among the public at large. As Roosevelt sought more flexibility in dealing with the Nazi and Japanese threats in the late 1930s, he came to regret the opposition to U.S. international involvement that the committee had stirred up.

See also: cash-and-carry policy; Johnson Act; neutrality acts; World War II, early history of.

Bibliography

Cole, Wayne S. *Roosevelt and the Isolationists.* Lincoln: University of Nebraska Press, 1983.

Cole, Wayne. *Senator Gerald P. Nye and American Foreign Relations.* Minneapolis: University of Minnesota Press, 1962.

OLYMPIC GAMES (BERLIN 1936)

The 1936 Olympic Games were hosted by Germany in Berlin and designed to showcase the accomplishments of the Nazi regime. Hitler aimed to use them as a propaganda instrument for the alleged physical superiority of the so-called Aryan race, a fictional racial category that supposedly encompassed Germans and other northern Europeans.

The games were controversial even before they opened, since dictator Adolf Hitler refused to allow German Jewish athletes to participate. For over a year, American sporting organizations—including the Amateur Athletic Union (AAU) and the American Olym-

pics Committee—debated a possible boycott. Avery Brundage, head of the committee, encouraged Americans to participate, while the AAU voted narrowly to reject a boycott. Meanwhile, at the games themselves, America's track and field coach prevented the only Jewish track athletes—Sam Stoller and Marty Glickman—from competing for fear their presence on the team would upset the Nazi hosts.

While many American Jews were disappointed by these events, they got some comfort in the accomplishments of the African-American track athlete Jesse Owens, whose four gold medals mocked the idea of

American track phenomenon Jesse Owens won four gold medals at the 1936 Berlin Olympics, upsetting Nazi dictator Adolf Hitler's belief in German racial superiority. Among the competitors Owens beat in the race were German (*center*) and Canadian runners. (*Brown Brothers*)

Aryan athletic superiority. Three other black American athletes—Archie Williams, John Woodruff, and Cornelius Johnson—won gold medals as well.

See also: sports; Nazi Germany; Hitler, Adolf.

Bibliography

Glickman, Marty. *The Fastest Kid on the Block.* Syracuse, NY: Syracuse University Press, 1996.

Mandell, Richard D. *The Nazi Olympics.* New York: Macmillan, 1971.

REFUGEES

During the 1930s, a growing number of refugees from Nazism—largely persecuted Jews—sought refuge in the United States and other Western democracies. While a few were accepted in the United States, most were turned away, because the government was unwilling to make large-scale exceptions to the limited quotas established under the Immigration Act of 1924.

Even before taking power in 1933, Adolf Hitler and the Nazi party made it clear that Jews were unwelcome in Germany. Immediately upon taking power, they organized boycotts of Jewish businesses, while Nazi paramilitaries attacked Jews on the streets. In 1935, the regime passed the infamous Nuremburg laws, banning Jews from virtually all professions, as well as government employment. In March 1938, these laws were applied to Austria, when that country was absorbed into Germany.

In November 1938—following the assassination of a German diplomat in Paris by a Jew—Hitler unleashed brutal reprisals against the Jewish community. Dozens of Jews were killed, over 20,000 arrested, and their businesses, homes, and synagogues destroyed. It was known as *Kristallnacht* ("crystal night") because of all the broken glass.

AMERICA HESITATES TO HELP REFUGEES

Long before *Kristallnacht*, however, the American public had become quite aware of the persecution of the Jews in Germany through numerous newspaper and magazine accounts, including a series by journalist Dorothy Thompson. While many private Americans and the government expressed outrage against Nazi brutality, a variety of factors conspired to limit the number of Jewish refugees permitted into the United States. Indeed, by 1938, the American consulate in Stuttgart, Germany, alone had a backlog of some 110,000 visa applications.

There were a variety of reasons for this reticence.

First, of course, Americans could not predict that the persecution—wrong as it was—would lead to the supreme evil of the Holocaust. Facing the highest unemployment rates in their history, the American people were generally unwilling to accept new potential job-seekers into the country. And since Germany allowed Jews to leave with no more than about five dollars to their name, the acceptance of refugees meant the acceptance of paupers who would need government assistance, already stretched to the limit by the Depression.

Another problem concerned divisions within the Jewish community. On one side were the more recent Eastern European Jewish immigrants. Led by Rabbi Stephen Wise and the American Jewish Congress, they organized boycotts of German goods and staged mock trials of Hitler. But American Jews of German-speaking background, many of whom had been in the United States for generations, were reluctant to protest. Well assimilated, they feared bringing attention to themselves and worried that too much agitation on the Jewish issue would stir anti-Semitic feelings in the United States.

Still, the main reason that refugees from the Nazis were allowed into the United States so grudgingly was the law. American immigration laws were so inflexible that they did not allow the government to increase the allocation for one country by taking from the allocation for another. That is to say, the quota on Germans was fixed and could not be increased by lowering the quota from, say, France. The law made no exceptions for political or religious refugees of any kind.

CONGRESS REFUSES TO AID REFUGEES

Congress could have acted to change the law, but it did not. Largely isolationist and unconcerned with international affairs, it was fearful that accepting refugees might be the first step toward involvement in European

Fifty-one Jewish refugee children from Europe arrive in New York aboard the S.S. *Serap Pinto* in 1938. President Franklin D. Roosevelt ordered expedited visas for 50,000 refugees in 1938. *(Brown Brothers)*

politics. There was also a significant anti-Semitic undercurrent to American politics in the 1930s, with some isolationists and economic populists clinging to the idea that Jewish bankers were somehow responsible for the Depression.

Indeed, Congress refused to even make minor adjustments. When Jewish congressman Samuel Dickstein (D-NY) introduced legislation that would have "mortgaged" the quotas for 1940 and 1941—that is, borrowed from the quotas for those years and applied them to 1938 and 1939—it was voted down, as was a bill to allow 20,000 Jewish children to enter the country under a special exception to the 1924 immigration law.

Meanwhile, President Franklin D. Roosevelt did little to push Congress to change the law. Struggling to overcome the strict neutrality laws that tied his hands

on war preparation and aid to potential allies like England and France, the president was in no mood to antagonize needed votes in Congress on an issue that concerned so few Americans directly.

Still, Roosevelt did what he could in his capacity as head of the executive branch of government. After Germany's takeover of Austria, in 1938, he insisted on the expediting of Jewish visa applications, a move that permitted more than 50,000 Jews to enter the United States. But that did not help the 950 refugees aboard the SS *St. Louis*, who, when refused the right to disembark in the United States in 1939, were forced to sail back to Europe.

See also: Nazi Germany; Wise, Stephen.

Bibliography

Feingold, Henry L. *The Politics of Rescue: The Roosevelt Administration and the Holocaust, 1938–1945.* New York: Holocaust Library, 1970.

Lipstadt, Deborah E. *Beyond Belief: The American Press and the Coming of the Holocaust, 1933–1945.* New York: Free Press, 1986.

Morse, Arthur D. *While Six Million Died: A Chronicle of American Apathy.* New York: Random House, 1968.

RHINELAND, REOCCUPATION OF

In March 1936, some 30,000 German troops marched into the Rhineland, a region along Germany's western border with France. This action was in violation of the Versailles Treaty, signed in 1919 after World War I, that established a demilitarized buffer zone along the Rhine River between Germany and France.

According to many historians, the reoccupation of the Rhineland by the military was a calculated attempt by German dictator Adolf Hitler to test the resolve of France and England. Their unwillingness to challenge the Nazi move has been viewed since as a failure to exploit an opportunity to stop Hitler early. Like the other Western democracies, the United States protested the move, but did nothing to reverse it.

Soon after the reoccupation, Hitler signed the anti-Comintern pact uniting Germany, Italy, and Japan in a military alliance that came to be called the Axis. Also, within months, Germany and Italy would send arms to support the Fascists of Spain in their efforts to take over that country.

See also: Nazi Germany; Spanish Civil War.

Bibliography

Shirer, William. *The Rise and Fall of the Third Reich.* New York: Simon & Schuster, 1960.

SMOOT-HAWLEY TARIFF

The Smoot-Hawley tariff of 1930 raised import duties on a wide variety of goods to their highest level in American history. The tariff increased the value-added rates from an already high 33 percent—established by the Fordney McCumber tariff of 1922—to 40 percent.

A call for higher tariffs had been part of the Republican platform in 1928. President Herbert Hoover supported the idea, especially for agricultural goods, as that sector of the economy had been in depressed conditions nearly since the end of World War I. Hoover hoped that a tariff would eliminate cheap imports and raise farm prices. He also wanted the creation of a tariff commission, under executive control, in order to curtail the age-old practice of tariff logrolling in Congress, whereby legislators added tariffs to please local business interests.

With the coming of the Great Depression, the Republican-controlled Congress quickly decided to raise tariffs in order to bolster prices, but they dispensed with Hoover's tariff commission idea. Economists warned that the 1930 tariff would create havoc both abroad and at home. First, Europeans—heavily indebted to the United States since World War I—would not be able to pay back their debts by selling their products in the United States. In addition, it was argued, foreign countries would retaliate against American products by raising high tariffs of their own. Indeed, 1,000 economists signed a petition pleading with Hoover to veto the bill, an opinion with which Secretary of the Treasury Andrew W. Mellon agreed. But the president—although opposed to the tariff himself—feared alienating Congress and so signed the bill.

Ultimately, the effects of the tariff may not have been as disastrous as the economists predicted. Earlier tariffs were already high and only a tiny proportion of the American economy was devoted to trade. Still, the passage of the Smoot-Hawley tariff was part of an international beggar-thy-neighbor strategy that contributed to economic nationalism and international tensions in the 1930s.

See also: taxation; World War II, early history of; Hoover, Herbert.

Bibliography

Hoover, Herbert. *The Memoirs of Herbert Hoover: The Cabinet and the Presidency, 1920–1933.* New York: Macmillan, 1952.

Warren, Harris G. *Herbert Hoover and the Great Depression.* New York: Oxford University Press, 1959.

SOVIET UNION

On March 3, 1918, the new Bolshevik government of Russia, led by Vladimir Ilich Ulyanov, better known as Lenin, signed the Treaty of Brest-Litovsk, ending the fighting between Russia and Germany during World War I. The Allied powers, including the United States, felt that the new Soviet government had betrayed the Allies through this separate peace, allowing Germany to shift its forces against the Western Front in France. Thus, the relations between the United States and the newly born Soviet Union began with feelings of distrust and disillusionment. These would be constant factors affecting American foreign policy with the Soviet Union throughout the period of the Great Depression.

Before the Depression and the election of President Franklin D. Roosevelt in 1932, American policy centered on the issue of granting formal recognition to the Soviet government. Following the 1917 Bolshevik revolution, the United States refused to recognize the new state of the Soviet Union, primarily because of the Soviet government's insistence that it was not liable for debts and other obligations incurred by the former czarist Russian government. The Soviets, on the other hand, were angered by U.S. intervention in Russia, which included the introduction of American troops in the port cities of Archangel and Vladivostok between 1918 and 1920.

While no official recognition was granted, there were U.S.-Soviet contacts before the Great Depression. During the presidency of Warren G. Harding, the American Relief Administration, headed by Herbert Hoover, was active in the western Soviet Union from 1921 to 1923. This effort, utilizing American agricultural surpluses, helped prevent starvation in the western Soviet Union. Also, there were some nongovernmental contacts between American businessmen and the Soviet government. For example, businessman Armand Hammer won the first American concession in the Soviet Union in 1921 to operate an asbestos mine. Others, like financier W. Averell Harriman and Henry Ford, also established business contacts in the Soviet Union in the 1920s. However, mutual distrust was the general theme regarding U.S.-Soviet relations up to the election of President Roosevelt in 1932.

RECOGNITION, 1933

The economic depression of 1929 opened new opportunities for U.S.-Soviet relations. Domestically, the crash gave support to those American business interests that wished to expand trade between the United States and Soviet Union. U.S. exports to Russia grew from $68 million in 1925 to $114 million in 1930. The Soviets also wished for increased contact with the United States. In 1928, Joseph Stalin, successor to Lenin as leader of the Soviet Union, launched the first five-year plan, an effort to industrialize the country and make it self-sufficient agriculturally. Therefore, the Soviets sought technical help, and, by 1931, over a thousand American engineers were working in the Soviet Union. By the time of Roosevelt's election in 1932, both sides saw benefits in increased cooperation.

The U.S. desire to further relations was also enhanced by the growing threat of Germany and Japan. In 1931, the Japanese soldiers of the Kwangtung Army were involved in the Mukden incident, which resulted in the Japanese occupation of Manchuria by 1932. In Europe the next year, Adolf Hitler became chancellor of Germany. Both the United States and the Soviets saw these events as threats to their own national security and sought some kind of agreement to counter these aggressive states. In October 1933, Roosevelt contacted the Soviet president Mikhail Kalinin and offered to initiate talks aimed at opening official diplomatic relations. The Soviets sent their commissar for foreign relations, Maxim Litvinov, to begin formal negotiations.

The issue of debt settlement still plagued future relations. However, since the 1917 revolution, two new issues had also appeared. One was the Moscow-based Comintern, established in March 1919 to disseminate communist propaganda throughout the world. Many Americans saw this as a direct attack against domestic tranquillity. Second, there was the issue of religious freedom for foreign nationals living in the officially atheist Soviet Union. The possibility of mutual benefits, however, outweighed these disputes, and a compromise was achieved.

After two months of negotiations, the Roosevelt-Litvinov Agreements were signed in December 1933, resulting in the recognition of the Soviet Union by the United States and the creation of formal diplomatic ties between the two countries. The right to freedom of religion was easily granted to Americans working in the Soviet Union. The questions of debt and the Comintern required a bit more work. Eventually, the Soviets agreed not to present propaganda designed to produce civic unrest in the United States. Regarding the debt, the two sides could not agree on an appropriate sum to be paid by the Soviet Union so they made a vague promise to clarify this issue in the future. Both sides were pleased with the agreements, and Roosevelt hoped that recognition would lead to trade expansion and that the Soviets might help keep the peace in Europe and the Pacific.

FROM RECOGNITION TO WORLD WAR II

Roosevelt's hopes for tangible benefits from Soviet recognition were unrealized. The first American ambassador to the Soviet Union, William Bullitt, arrived in Moscow early in 1934 and from March 1934 to January 1935 found himself deadlocked in negotiations over the specifics of debt repayment. Communist propaganda through the Comintern also remained a serious problem.

The American Communist Party grew from approximately 12,000 in 1932 to 100,000 in 1939. Besides actual members of the Communist Party, many Americans were disenchanted with capitalism. Some critics felt that capitalism and international economic competition were the causes of World War I. With the coming of the Great Depression, many of these same people questioned whether a capitalist, democratic nation was capable of instituting policies that would help the poor. Marxist-Leninist ideology predicted the collapse of capitalism from within as the rich and poor would fight over the distribution of wealth. The Depression seemed to be the fulfillment of this prophecy.

Therefore, in the eyes of a number of U.S. citizens, the actions of the Comintern and its host, the Soviet Union, appeared to be promoting the overthrow of the American government. Leading American Communists, like Earl Browder and Thomas Green, were elected to the executive committee of the Comintern. American Communist Party cells, such as the Harold Ware group, attempted to infiltrate the U.S. government during its time of expansion in Roosevelt's New Deal. This led to an official note of protest on August 27, 1935, to the Soviet government, claiming that the Soviets were interfering in American domestic matters. Ambassador Bullitt even felt there existed enough reasons for the United States to suspend diplomatic relations with the Soviet Union. Finally, contact and trade with the United States declined substantially when Stalin unleashed his purge of the Communist Party and the Soviet military in the mid-1930s.

It was, however, Soviet foreign policy that greatly strained U.S.-Soviet relations. As Hitler began to expand into the Rhineland, Austria, and Czechoslovakia, the United States continued its policy of isolation from European affairs. Stalin, fearing Germany, attempted to form a collective front with Great Britain and France to oppose German expansion but failed. This failure prompted the Soviets to switch tracks and, in May 1939, replaced Commissar Litvinov with Vyacheslav Molotov, who was more acceptable to Germany. The fruits of this change soon became apparent with the signing on August 23, 1939, of the Nazi-Soviet nonaggression pact, which allowed Hitler to invade Poland in September without fear of fighting both the Western allies and the Soviets. Through secret contacts between the new U.S. ambassador to the Soviets, Charles Bohlen, and Hans-Heinrich von Bittenfeld, a member of the German embassy in Moscow, the United States was aware of secret protocols within the nonaggression pact. These agreements between the Nazis and the Soviets gave the Soviets a free hand in the Baltic countries of Estonia, Latvia, and Lithuania. All three were absorbed into the Soviet Union in July 1940, much to the dismay of the United States. Refusing to recognize the disintegration of the Baltic states, the United States continued to recognize the previous governments and froze their American assets, preventing the Soviets from using them.

Most distressing to U.S.-Soviet relations, however, was the Soviet-Finnish winter war of 1939–40. The Soviets demanded in October 1939 that Finland give some of its territory to the Soviets for reasons of Soviet national security. When Finland refused, the Soviets invaded Finland on November 30, 1939. American public opinion overwhelmingly supported Finland, and, on December 2, 1939, the United States declared a moral embargo, asking American aircraft manufacturers not to negotiate contracts with countries that used terror bombing. Also, the United States gave $100 million in nonmilitary aid to Finland and allowed it to purchase forty-six War Department surplus airplanes. Finally, the United States cooperated with other nations to expel the Soviet Union from the League of Nations in December 1939. Finland eventually succumbed to the Soviet Union in March 1940.

While the United States was angry and bitter over Soviet foreign policy, Roosevelt did not seriously consider a clear break with the Soviet Union. U.S. intelligence predicted that the Nazis and Soviets were unnatural allies who soon would be fighting each other. Following the fall of France in the spring of 1940, Roosevelt was determined to aid Great Britain as much as possible, and he believed that the Soviets would soon be drawn into the war against Germany. Therefore, in January 1941, Roosevelt lifted the moral embargo against the Soviets, and, when the Lend-Lease Act passed in March 1941, Roosevelt ensured that there would be no congressional opposition to possible lend-lease aid to the Soviets. This strategy proved to be important because on June 22, 1941, Germany invaded the Soviet Union. Despite some pressure from American leaders who urged the United States to stand back and allow the Nazis and Soviets to destroy each other, Roosevelt began shipments of supplies to the Soviets. Also, in July 1941, he sent Averell Harriman and Harry Hopkins to Moscow to assure Stalin that the

United States would support his war effort. The Soviets responded in November 1941 with the appointment of pro-Western Maxim Litvinov as Soviet ambassador to the United States. Within weeks, the Japanese launched their attack against the United States naval base at Pearl Harbor, Hawaii, on December 7. Hitler declared war against the United States four days later. The Soviets and the United States were now allies in World War II.

PAUL WANKE

See also: Communist Party; Depression and World War II; Manchuria, invasion of; Nazi-Soviet nonaggression pact; Nazi Germany; Joseph Stalin.

Bibliography

Bennett, Edward M. *Franklin D. Roosevelt and the Search for Security: American-Soviet Relations, 1933–1939.* Wilmington, DE: Scholarly Resources, 1985.

Boyle, Peter G. *American-Soviet Relations: From the Russian Revolution to the Fall of Communism.* London: Routledge, 1993.

Dunn, Dennis J. *Caught Between Roosevelt and Stalin: America's Ambassadors to Moscow.* Lexington: University Press of Kentucky, 1998.

Gaddis, John Lewis. *Russia, the Soviet Union and the United States: An Interpretive History.* New York: John Wiley, 1978.

SPANISH CIVIL WAR

The Spanish Civil War (1936–39) can be seen as a climactic event of the tumultuous 1930s, forming a bridge between the economic struggles and political activism of the Depression years and the looming of World War II. In nearly three years of war, which devastated Spain and left some 500,000 people dead, the rightist Nationalist rebels defeated the leftist supporters of the elected government of the Spanish Republic. Far from being a purely Spanish issue, however, the Spanish Civil War served as a prelude to the coming World War, as Fascist Italy and Nazi Germany, the Soviet "Popular Front" antifascist strategy, and the Western democracies each played a crucial part in the war.

The immediate cause of the Spanish Civil War was the incomplete success of a July 17, 1936, military coup led by a cabal of rightist military officers, among whom General Francisco Franco eventually emerged as supreme leader. The rebel officers' attempt to seize control of the entire country in one swift blow failed due

to unexpectedly fierce resistance from a broad spectrum of liberal and radical supporters of the democratically elected moderate leftist government of the five-year-old Second Spanish Republic. On the other hand, a large portion of the Spanish population, including most of the middle and upper classes, religious Catholics, monarchists, and members of Spain's small protofascist organizations, supported the rebel officers' goal of crushing the leftist forces in the country and restoring the conservative economic and social structure to power. With each party left in control of about half of the country after the coup attempt, the bitter rivalry between the Loyalist or Republican supporters of the leftist government and the Nationalist rebels and the broad support enjoyed by both sides ensured that the ensuing struggle would be protracted and bloody. While the roots and immediate causes of the civil war in Spain rested in long-running internal rivalries, however, the character of the conflict would be fundamentally shaped by the intense worldwide reaction that it elicited.

The intersection of Spain's internal struggle with the growing tensions in international relations in the mid-1930s ensured that the war would become a focus of international attention. The opposing forces of Soviet communism and German-Italian fascism, already girding for future conflict, perceived the Spanish war as an important precursor to the coming struggle. Accordingly, Germany and Italy intervened in the first days of the war to assist the Nationalists, while the Soviet Union soon countered by aiding the Republic. While the governments of Britain, France, and the United States sought to prevent the spread of hostilities and were more reluctant to take sides in the confusing Spanish struggle, the success of the Soviet push for a Popular Front against fascism aroused some Westerners to passionate support for the Republic.

German and Italian motives for participation in the Spanish Civil War centered on strategic preparations for approaching general war. Hitler felt that the war in Spain would distract the Western powers while Germany finalized its preparations for war and offered the possibility of a resource-rich fascist ally poised at the entrance to the Mediterranean. From the Italian perspective, the Nationalists' appeal for help flattered Mussolini and offered an opportunity to challenge British control of the Western Mediterranean. In accordance with their strategic interests and sympathy for the rebel cause, both Italy and Germany provided the Nationalists with vast quantities of armaments and outright military intervention on a large scale. Nazi Germany sent the 5,000-man "Condor Legion," a multipurpose force including over a hundred aircraft, armored forces and antitank units, and supporting elements. For its part, Fascist Italy provided over 50,000 troops, including infantry, armored units, and air forces, plus ninety-one surface ships and submarines of the Italian navy.

Although the left-leaning French government sympathized with the Republic and wanted to send weapons and aircraft, British distaste for the conflict prevailed. Still weak from World War I and alarmed by increasing German power, France relied on collective action with Britain to maintain its security and felt compelled to secure British support for any foreign policy initiatives. The British were reluctant to act in Spain because they were as worried by the prospect of a Soviet-led surge of communism across Europe as they were by German and Italian aggression. To preserve unity of action with Britain, the French proposed a policy of "nonintervention" in which no arms sales or other help would be provided to either side in Spain. In practice, the nonintervention agreement was a farce. The only intervention it prevented was potential French aid to the Republic, while war material and military personnel from Germany, Italy, and, to a lesser extent, the Soviet Union streamed into Spain.

The Soviet Union felt compelled to support the Spanish Republic, as the war, in effect, presented a trial by fire of Soviet diplomatic strategy. Worried by the rise of fascism in Germany and Italy in the mid-1930s, the Soviet Union had attempted to strengthen its position by fashioning a strategy of collective security with France and Britain against the fascist nations. This policy, which encompassed both diplomatic rapprochement and instructions to the foreign elements of the Communist International to tone down their rhetoric and begin cooperating with noncommunist progressives and even liberals, was known as the Popular Front. The Soviets feared that the 1935 nonintervention agreement of cooperation with France, one of the few successes of the collective security strategy, might be rendered useless if France was threatened on three sides by fascist nations after a Nationalist victory in Spain. At the same time, however, the war in Spain also presented some positive opportunities to the Soviets, as it offered tangible proof of the fascist threat that could entice France and Britain into closer cooperation with the USSR. Stalin therefore chose to follow a very cautious policy toward the Spanish Republic. Throughout the war, the USSR provided the vast majority of the Republic's arms, but the Soviets refused to risk intervening sufficiently to make a decisive impact on the course of the war. In part, Soviet hesitation stemmed from a desire to avoid alarming the democracies with the specter of onrushing communist influence. Stalin also had more Machiavellian underlying motives, however: the continuation of the conflict preserved Soviet freedom of action while producing an international situation that would increasingly threaten Britain and France's Mediterranean interests.

Fearful of alarming the democracies or provoking open hostility from Germany, Stalin nonetheless came to believe that Soviet interests in the preservation of the Republic required intervention by the USSR in violation of the nonintervention agreement. The political and logistical problems behind large-scale commitment of Red Army ground troops led the Soviets to focus on more discreet intervention, primarily sending war matériel and military "advisers." Nonetheless, the scale of Soviet assistance to Loyalist Spain was substantial, including hundreds of tanks and combat aircraft, 1,200 to 1,500 artillery pieces, 500,000 rifles, millions of rounds of artillery and small arms ammunition, and a variety of miscellaneous military equipment. Accompanying the Soviet war matériel were hundreds of Soviet officials and military advisers, some of whom took direct command of Republican forces in the heat of battle. In addition, there were two Soviet combat units directly involved in the fighting. A Soviet tank brigade comprised the bulk of the Republic's armored forces throughout the war, and Soviet pilots under the command of a Red Air Force general operated most of the Republic's Soviet-made aircraft. A Soviet secret police unit also traveled to Spain, ostensibly to help organize the Republican political police force—in truth, however, its primary purpose was to aid the small Spanish Communist party as it rose to dominate the Republican government.

A more unusual form of foreign intervention in the Spanish Civil War was the enlistment of thousands of international volunteers on the Republican side. While small numbers of foreign progressives and radicals rallied to the Republican cause independently, the bulk of the 40,000 foreign volunteers served in the "International Brigades," units covertly organized by the USSR in fall 1936 as a means of shoring up the Republic's precarious military situation without risking more Soviet forces or further trampling the fiction of nonintervention. The Soviets had employed foreign units in their own civil war and, through the Communist International and the Communist parties of the European nations, had a ready-made recruiting apparatus in place. Usually working through thinly veiled front groups, the Comintern was able to rapidly man battalions of volunteers and transport them through France to fight in Spain. The arrival of the first International Brigades at the height of the fighting around Madrid in November 1936 buoyed the Republican cause both militarily and morally, helping to stem the Nationalist advance and allowing the Republic to regroup. While the largest number of volunteers were recruited among exiled German, Italian, and Eastern European leftists, fifty-three nations were represented in the International Brigades, among them three battalions of Americans. Despite myths of the presence of large numbers of liberals, students, and middle-class idealists in the ranks of the International Brigades (myths often spread by communist recruiters and organizers seeking to emphasize the Popular Front character of the war), the volunteers were predominantly working-class in origin, and the vast majority were Communists or close party sympathizers. In the context of the turbulent labor relations and economic struggles of the 1930s, however, the decision to enlist

in the Spanish war seemed to many working-class activists to be a logical means of halting fascist aggression before it reached their homelands. The International Brigades continued to serve as elite units of the Republican Popular Army until their high casualties and the declining fortunes of the Spanish Republic caused their numbers to dwindle in the last months of the war.

While the war in Spain affected the United States to a lesser extent than Europe, among interested groups the reaction was nonetheless intense. The policy of the U.S. government was to steadfastly support the nonintervention agreement—as with France and Britain, nonintervention on the part of the United States was essentially a means by which to justify avoiding entanglement in the messy conflict. Though most Americans remained relatively unconcerned with events in Spain throughout the war, substantial minorities developed strong feelings on the Spanish situation. While a small number of Americans—among them Catholics, far right groups, and corporations with economic interests in Spain—supported the Nationalist cause, American public opinion tended to offer tepid moral support to the Republic. For some liberals and progressives, however, the war in Spain became a virtual (and in some cases, actual) call to arms.

In the context of the 1930s, the identification of American leftists with the cause of the Republic is understandable. During the so-called Red Decade of the 1930s, many American liberals and progressives had moved significantly leftward in response to the nation's economic crisis. Nonetheless, the Communist Party of the United States of America (CPUSA) had made little progress in gaining acceptance as a legitimate part of the American political scene, even after the institution of less inflammatory Popular Front–oriented tactics and rhetoric. With the outbreak of the Spanish Civil War, however, the CPUSA's vocal antifascism and active support for the Republican cause attracted the admiration of large numbers of noncommunist liberals who sympathized with the Republic. The CPUSA's membership nearly doubled during the war. Even as its membership increased, the CPUSA worked secretly through a variety of front organizations to muster support for the Republic. Through its control of the North American Committee to Aid Spanish Democracy, the Party was able to raise money, campaign against U.S. nonintervention policy, and administer a galaxy of smaller organizations organized on local, ethnic, and workplace lines. The many prominent liberals who contributed to and were active in the North American Committee and its subsidiaries were unaware of the Party's role in their efforts—while many respected the

Party's antifascist stance and pro-Republic activism, they would have been surprised to learn the true extent of communist control of the entire pro-Republican movement. Less likely than their liberal sympathizers to harbor illusions about the extent of communist influence were the 3,000 or so Americans who enlisted in the International Brigades, of whom around 1,000 died in Spain. Though the three American battalions performed fairly well in combat, the Republican armies were eventually overwhelmed by the weight of the Nationalists' German and Italian–supplied firepower.

By spring 1939, the Nationalists crushed the remaining Republican forces in Spain and installed the Franco dictatorship that would rule the country into the 1970s. The Soviet Union, observing the failure in Spain of its efforts to build collective security (further undermined by British and French acquiescence to German aggression in Czechoslovakia in 1938), jettisoned the Popular Front strategy that had fueled Western enthusiasm for the Republican cause. In August 1939, the Nazi-Soviet nonaggression pact would be signed instead, setting the stage for the outbreak of World War II. For the many American and European liberals and progressives who had worked to aid the Republican cause, the outcome of the war and its aftermath were profoundly disillusioning. The cause itself, however, remained for many "The Good Fight," the last gasp of 1930s idealism before the grim years of World War II.

ERIK BLAINE COLEMAN

See also: Abraham Lincoln Brigade; fascism, Italy; League of Nations; Nazi Germany; refugees; Soviet Union; Franco, Francisco.

Bibliography

Guttmann, Allen. *The Wound in the Heart: America and the Spanish Civil War*. New York: The Free Press of Glencoe, 1962.

Preston, Paul. *The Coming of the Spanish Civil War: Reform, Reaction and Revolution in the Second Republic*. 2nd ed. New York: Routledge, 1994.

Richardson, R. Dan. *Comintern Army: The International Brigades and the Spanish Civil War*. Lexington: University Press of Kentucky, 1982.

Rosenstone, Robert A. *Crusade of the Left: The Lincoln Battalion in the Spanish Civil War*. New York: Pegasus, 1969.

Thomas, Hugh. *The Spanish Civil War*. 3rd ed. London: Hamish Hamilton, 1977.

WORLD WAR II, EARLY HISTORY OF

In 1929, sixty-four nations signed the Kellogg-Briand Treaty, "outlawing war as an instrument of foreign policy." In less than a decade, the optimistic belief that international treaties and collective security might prevent future wars had faded. Actual hostilities related to World War II began in 1931, when Japan, eager to tap into the rich industrial base of northern China, invaded Manchuria. Bent on exercising control over the Far East, Japan also occupied key coastal cities in China, including Nanking. Japan's goal for hemispheric supremacy challenged the Western-backed Open Door Policy in China and eventually led to a rupture in its relations with the United States.

Europe had its own share of problems during the interwar years, witnessing the rise of fascism in Mussolini's Italy in the 1920s and then in Hitler's Germany. By the mid-1930s, Hitler had broken free of most of the restraints the Treaty of Versailles had imposed on Germany at the end of World War I. Germany rearmed itself, remilitarized the Rhineland, and began to implement its plan for hegemony in Europe. France and England, exhausted from their last war with Germany and hoping to avoid a showdown with Hitler, pursued a policy of appeasement. The partition of the Czechoslovakian Republic at Munich, in 1938, showed how much the West was willing to accommodate Hitler in an effort to preserve the peace. Hitler's failure to honor the territorial integrity of the existing rump Czech state, in the spring of 1939, demonstrated the fragility of appeasement. When Nazi forces invaded Poland in September 1939, France and England declared war on Germany.

During the Depression decade, the United States had turned its attentions to economic recovery rather than foreign policy. In the 1930s, growing disillusionment about America's role in World War I led Congress to pass a series of neutrality laws that limited trade with belligerent nations and restricted Americans' ability to travel into war zones. Franklin D. Roosevelt hoped to reverse this isolationist trend in 1937 when he spoke

War in Europe: 1939–1941

- Axis territory, September 1939
- Axis occupied
- Axis satellites
- Allies
- Soviet occupied territory
- Neutral
- ← Axis offensives
- ← Allied offensives   ◄--- Allied retreat

(CARTO-GRAPHICS)

out against the dangers of "outlaw nations" in his famous "Quarantine Speech." Most Americans, however, were not yet ready to stand up to the threats of militarism in Europe or Asia.

Even after World War II began, American public opinion remained sharply divided over how much and what kind of aid the United States should extend to nations in Europe. Just before his reelection in 1940, Roosevelt shrewdly courted bipartisan support for national defense. He named two prominent Republicans, Henry L. Stimson and Frank B. Knox, to serve, respectively, as his secretary of war and of the navy. His efforts paid off when Congress passed the Selective Service Act, the nation's first peacetime draft, by one vote.

Most historians agree that the December 7, 1941, Japanese attack on the United States naval base at Pearl Harbor, Hawaii, marked the end of the Great Depression era. *(Brown Brothers)*

Roosevelt gradually expanded America's commitment to the Allies, declaring in a fireside chat in December 1940 that the United States would become "the arsenal of democracy." By supplying matériel and financial aid to Great Britain, Roosevelt argued, the United States could stay on the sidelines. While officially neutral, Roosevelt did his best to further the Allies' cause. In March 1941, he was able to win passage of the Lend-Lease Act. Within a matter of months, vital war matériel flowed to Great Britain and the Soviet Union, following Germany's invasion of that country in June 1941.

Despite the Roosevelt administration's preoccupation with a Hitler-dominated Europe, the United States became directly involved in the war because of its deteriorating relations with Japan. Tensions escalated in July 1941 when Imperial Japanese forces invaded

French Indochina. Roosevelt responded by freezing Japanese assets, cutting off trade between the two nations. Japanese envoys in Washington conducted protracted negotiations with Secretary of State Cordell Hull, but they yielded few results. As talks continued, the Imperial Japanese Navy finalized its plans to attack American positions in the Pacific.

American military intelligence experts had broken Japan's diplomatic code. Roosevelt and his advisers knew that an attack was imminent, but the exact location remained unknown. On Sunday morning, December 7, 1941, radiomen frantically typed out the message: "Air Raid, Pearl Harbor. This is not [a] drill!" In two waves of attack, Japanese planes inflicted profound losses. Eight battleships, three light cruisers, three destroyers, and other small craft were damaged, capsized, or sunk. Moreover, 2,403 military personnel

War in Asia, 1933-1941

- Japan, 1928
- Japanese expansion, 1933
- Japanese expansion, 1941
- Under Japanese influence
- ★ Japanese conflicts with the Soviet Union
- ← Japanese offensives
- ■ Allied bases

died and almost 1,200 more were injured in the attack. The following day, President Roosevelt addressed a joint session of Congress, asking it to declare war on Japan. Three days later, Hitler declared war on the United States.

The attack on Pearl Harbor galvanized public opinion in support of the war. Isolationism ceased to exist. Only one member of Congress, Representative Jeanette Rankin (D-MT), a devoted pacifist, voted against the war resolution. For the next six months, however, Americans had little cause for optimism. In the Atlantic, German U-boats sank supply ships with impunity just off U.S. shores. At the same time, Hitler's forces pushed further eastward into the Soviet Union, and Japan consolidated its gains in the Far East. Finally, in June 1942, at the Battle of Midway, the United States handed Japan its first defeat. Within a matter of months, Allied counteroffensives in North Africa and in the Soviet Union turned back Hitler's forces with dramatic victories.

Increasingly, Roosevelt, Great Britain's prime minister Winston Churchill, and Soviet premier Joseph Stalin discovered that effective military cooperation was difficult to coordinate. Nevertheless, an important step toward strengthening the alliance was taken at the Casablanca conference in January 1943. Long before an Allied victory appeared certain, Roosevelt and Churchill agreed upon the "unconditional surrender" of Germany and Japan as a joint war aim.

Robert Miller

See also: China; fascism, Italy; Great Britain; Japan; Munich Conference; Nazi Germany; Manchuria, invasion of; Churchill, Winston; Hitler, Adolf; Hull, Cordell; Knox, Frank; Roosevelt, Franklin D.; Stalin, Joseph; Stimson, Henry.

Bibliography

Dalleck, Robert. *Franklin D. Roosevelt and American Foreign Policy, 1932–45.* New York: Oxford University Press, 1981.

Goodwin, Doris Kearns. *No Ordinary Time: Franklin and Eleanor Roosevelt: The Home Front in World War II.* New York: Simon & Schuster, 1994.

Irye, Akira. *Pearl Harbor and the Coming of the Pacific War: A Brief History with Documents and Essays.* Boston: Bedford/St. Martin's, 1999.

Kennedy, David M. *Freedom From Fear: The American People in Depression and War, 1929–1945.* New York: Oxford University Press, 1999.

Lyons, Robert. *World War II: A Short History.* Englewood Cliffs, NJ: Prentice Hall, 1999.

Prange, Gordon. *At Dawn We Slept: The Untold Story of Pearl Harbor.* New York: McGraw Hill, 1981.

Weinberg, Gerhard L. *A World at Arms: A Global History of World War II.* Cambridge: Cambridge University Press, 1994.